The
Dictionary
of
WEDGWOOD

Robin Reilly and George Savage

Antique Collectors' Club Ltd.

ISBN 0 902028 85 5

British Library CIP Data
Reilly, Robin
    The Dictionary of Wedgwood.
      1. Wedgwood ware — Dictionaries
    I. Title II. Savage, George
    III. Antique Collectors' Club Ltd.
    738'.0942   NK4335

Published for the Antique Collectors' Club
by the Antique Collectors' Club Ltd.

Printed in England by
Baron Publishing, Woodbridge, Suffolk

Frontispiece

'Britannia Triumphant'. One of Wedgwood's most imposing jasper groups, modelled c.1800 by Henry Webber to celebrate British naval victories in the war with France. The portraits of Admirals Duncan, Howe, Nelson and St. Vincent, which ornament the plinth, were modelled by John De Vaere in 1798. Height of group with plinth 32ins. The group, which appears to be the only surviving example, is in a private collection. The plinth is one of two in the Wedgwood Museum.
Photograph: Wedgwood.

End Papers

The unveiling of the statue of Josiah Wedgwood, 'The Father of the Potteries', at Stoke-on-Trent, 1863.

Why not join —

The Antique Collectors' Club

The Antique Collectors' Club was formed in 1966 and now has a five figure membership spread throughout the world. It publishes the only independently run monthly antiques magazine *Antique Collecting* which caters for those collectors who are interested in increasing their knowledge of antiques, both by increasing the members' knowledge of quality as well as in discussing the factors which influence the price that is likely to be asked. The Antique Collectors' Club pioneered the provision of information on prices for collectors and still leads in the provision of detailed articles on a variety of subjects.

It was in response to the enormous demand for information on "what to pay" that the price guide series was introduced in 1968 with the first edition of *The Price Guide to Antique Furniture* (completely revised, 1978), a book which broke new ground by illustrating the more common types of antique furniture, the sort that collectors could buy in shops and at auctions, rather than the rare museum pieces which had previously been used (and still to a large extent are used) to make up the limited amount of illustrations in books published by commercial publishers. Many other price guides have followed, all copiously illustrated, and greatly appreciated by collectors for the valuable information they contain, quite apart from prices. The Antique Collectors' Club also publishes other books on antiques, including horology and art reference works, and a full book list is available.

Club membership, which is open to all collectors, costs £7.95 per annum. Members receive free of charge *Antique Collecting,* the Club's magazine (published every month except August), which contains well-illustrated articles dealing with the practical aspects of collecting not normally dealt with by magazines. Prices, features of value, investment potential, fakes and forgeries are all given prominence in the magazine.

Among other facilities available to members are private buying and selling facilities, the longest list of "For Sales" of any antiques magazine, an annual ceramics conference and the opportunity to meet other collectors at their local antique collectors' club. There are nearly eighty in Britain and so far a dozen overseas. Members may also buy the Club's publications at special pre-publication prices.

As its motto implies, the Club is an amateur organisation designed to help collectors to get the most out of their hobby: it is informal and friendly and gives enormous enjoyment to all concerned.

For Collectors   —   By Collectors   —   About Collecting

The Antique Collectors' Club, 5 Church Street, Woodbridge, Suffolk

BY THE SAME AUTHORS

by Robin Reilly
The Rest to Fortune: The Life of Major-General James Wolfe
The Sixth Floor
The British at the Gates
William Pitt The Younger
British Watercolours
Wedgwood Jasper
Wedgwood: The Portrait Medallions (with George Savage)
Wedgwood Portrait Medallions: An Introduction

by George Savage
Dictionary of Antiques
Dictionary of 19th Century Antiques
18th Century English Porcelain
Porcelain Through the Ages
18th Century German Porcelain
17th and 18th Century French Porcelain
A Concise History of Interior Decoration
The American Birds of Dorothy Doughty (with Dorothy Doughty)
The British Birds of Dorothy Doughty
A Concise History of Bronzes
Forgeries, Fakes and Reproductions
French Decorative Art
The Art and Antique Restorers' Handbook
Glass and Glassware
Selected Letters of Josiah Wedgwood (with Ann Finer)
Wedgwood: The Portrait Medallions (with Robin Reilly)
&c.

Contents

Colour Plates

Introduction

The wares of Josiah Wedgwood are collected on both sides of the Atlantic. Societies have been formed to study them, museums have been founded to exhibit nothing else, and the name is synonymous everywhere with pottery and porcelain of the finest quality. Many books have been written about Wedgwood: biographies of the great potter, who founded a dynasty of potters, and studies of the factory's products. Inevitably, as the years have passed, errors and misapprehensions have accumulated, and it has become increasingly evident that the subject needs to be reassessed in the light of modern research. No comprehensive work of reference exists. This *Dictionary,* setting out the salient facts and correcting some time-worn errors which have been handed down from one generation of writers to the next, is intended to lay the foundation for a detailed examination of the entire history and work of the Wedgwood firm.

It would be impossible, given the ordinary limits of space, time and finance, to produce a work to answer every conceivable question that might be asked about so vast a subject, and for this reason the authors' guiding principle has been to provide information of the kind most likely to prove helpful to collectors of 18th and 19th century wares, both useful and ornamental. The more important 20th century wares and their designers have also been included, in the sure knowledge that if they are not already collected, they will be in the future.

The information has been presented in such a way as to enable readers faced with problems of attribution to make their own assessment of authenticity, date, nature and source of subject, artist or designer and, wherever possible, relative scarcity of specimens. We have offered critical opinions, and some attributions based on knowledge of styles and techniques, but unqualified statements are founded upon documentary evidence, especially the numerous surviving letters of Josiah Wedgwood. In many instances we have found good reason for correcting previously accepted opinions and attributions.

The work contains biographical material relating to many people connected with the firm, particularly during the 18th century, and information has also been provided on more recent personalities, such as Harry Barnard, Tom Lyth, and Daisy Makeig-Jones. A comprehensive bibliography is appended for those who may wish to pursue the subject. All the works named have been consulted by the authors of this *Dictionary,* but consultation may not be assumed to imply agreement.

Although this book is in the form of a dictionary, it has been our constant endeavour to make it attractive to the general reader, and any subject may be followed through with the aid of the numerous cross-references. An asterisk in the text indicates that an entry relating to the preceding word or words may be found under that heading. Major cross-references are placed at the end of an entry, or, if more appropriate, bracketed in the entry itself. Italics are used for Wedgwood pattern names, and for the titles by which the subjects of relief ornament are recorded. They are also used to denote works of fictional or mythological characters; all others are either living or historical personalities or people who may be presumed to have existed (i.e. part legendary figures from ancient history).

Quotations from Josiah Wedgwood's letters retain the original orthography and punctuation unless alteration has been necessary for reasons of clarity.

We owe a special debt of gratitude to Sir Arthur Bryan, Chairman of the Wedgwood Group of Companies, for his help and continuing interest in this work. We are also grateful to those others who have provided photographs, research material, and information. Some are named in the formal acknowledgements, and the source of all photographs is credited under each illustration.

RR
GS

December 1979

Acknowledgements

In the preparation of this *Dictionary* the authors have received encouragement and particularly generous assistance from Sir Arthur Bryan (Chairman, Josiah Wedgwood & Sons Ltd.), Mr. Fred de Costobadie (Group Sales Director), Mr. Derek Halfpenny (Public Relations Executive) and Mrs. Lynn Miller (Assistant Curator, Wedgwood Museum) at Barlaston; and from Mr. Ray Smyth (President), and Mr. John Thomas and Miss Claudia Coleman (Vice-Presidents), of Josiah Wedgwood & Sons Inc., New York. The majority of the illustrations are reproduced by permission of the Trustees of the Wedgwood Museum, and many were photographed specially for this book.

Important illustrations were also obtained through the co-operation of many private collectors, the authorities of museums, and the directors and staff of auction houses. These sources are acknowledged in the text, but the authors wish to record their special thanks to Mr. and Mrs. Dwight L. Beeson, Mr. David Buten (Director, The Buten Museum of Wedgwood) and Mrs. Nettie Buten, Mr. and Mrs. S. Laver, and Mr. and Mrs. David Zeitlin, whose generous assistance in the provision of photographs was accompanied by equally generous hospitality in the United States of America; to Mr. Hugo Morley-Fletcher and Mr. Anton Gabszewicz (Christie's); Miss Caroline Fisher (Sotheby's) and Mr. David Battie (Sotheby's Belgravia); Mrs. Constance Chiswell; Mr. Alan Drake; and Miss Yvonne Willsmore.

Mr. John des Fontaines kindly wrote the entry for the Wedgwood Society, London; and Mrs. Una des Fontaines not only provided essential illustrations, but also made available to the authors her expert advice on the subject of lustre wares and the work of Daisy Makeig-Jones.

No work of this nature can be undertaken without unsparing help from many sources. To all those whose generosity is acknowledged here or in the text, the authors offer their grateful thanks.

Absolon, William (1751-1815)

An independent decorator working from about 1790 on wares bought from a variety of sources, including creamware from Wedgwood. His painting was naïve, and largely directed to the souvenir trade. A Wedgwood egg-cup stand* bears the words 'A present from Yarmouth' and is also painted with trophies, and a bird bearing a banner inscribed 'Peace and Plenty'. Absolon's orders for creamware include feeding cups, tooth-powder boxes, paint boxes, inkstands, and oyster trays. Some of his work is signed: 'Absolon Yarm'. His signature is also found on Chinese porcelain and glass. Absolon's daughter is believed to have assisted her father.

Acanthus

A plant, mainly of southern Europe, also known as bear's breech. The leaf has been used as a decorative motif from very early times. As ceramic ornament it is used in painted and moulded forms, either stylised or naturalistically rendered. It also occurs in a profile form which is known as an acanthus scroll. It is very common in classical art of all kinds, and was frequently used by Wedgwood to decorate objects in the neo-classical* style.

Acanthus. *Vase of variegated creamware with applied ornament of acanthus foliage, alternating with plain leaves on the foot, and a border of interlacing circles enclosing rosettes. c.1775.* Wedgwood.

Achilles

The hero of Homer's *Iliad*. The son of Peleus, King of the Myrmidones, and the Nereid, Thetis, he was educated by Phoenix in eloquence and the arts of war, and by Chiron, the centaur, in the healing arts. According to legend, Thetis sought to make him immortal by dipping him in the river Styx but failed to immerse the heel by which she held him, which remained vulnerable to human assault. Later, to preserve him from the Trojan war, she sent him to live among the daughters of Lycomedes, King of Scyros. There, dressed as a woman, Achilles was discovered by Ulysses, but not before he had taken advantage of his disguise to impregnate Deidamia, daughter of Lycomedes, who bore him a son, Pyrrhus. Offered the choice between a short but heroic life and a long and inglorious one, Achilles chose the former and set out for the war, where he was, at first, in the forefront of the battle. After a quarrel with Agamemnon, however, he retired to sulk in his tent. His friend, Patroclus, persuaded him to allow his men, horses and armour to be used, and when Patroclus was slain, Achilles, stricken with grief and remorse, rejoined the battle. Wearing new armour, he killed numerous Trojans, including King Priam's son, Hector, whose body he tied to his chariot and dragged round the walls of Troy before yielding it to Priam, who came in person to beg for it. Achilles fell in battle before Troy was taken, slain, it is said, by an arrow shot by Paris* which struck him in the heel.

Achilles, and the legends associated with him, are subjects of many Wedgwood cameos, plaques, and tablets. These include an important series of reliefs depicting scenes from the life of Achilles. Modelled by Pacetti* c.1790-92, these are all adapted from the Luna marble disc (c.800-400 B.C.) now in the Capitoline Museum, Rome. The series comprises six groups which were used singly or in sequence, according to the size of the plaque or tablet:

1. *Birth of Achilles,* and 2. *Dipping of Achilles.*
3. *Thetis delivering Achilles to Centaur,* and 4. *Centaur with Achilles on his back, hunting the Lion.*
5. *Achilles in Scyros among the Daughters of Lycomedes.*
6. *Achilles dragging the body of Hector around the walls of Troy.*

Pacetti modelled a second version of *Achilles in Scyros,* taken from a relief on the erroneously named sarcophagus of Alexander Severus, also in the Capitoline Museum. This is frequently mis-described as *Sacrifice of Iphigenia.* From the same source, and also attributed to Pacetti, are *Priam begging for the body of Hector from Achilles, Two Warriors and a Horse* (adapted from *Achilles takening leave of Lycomedes),* and *Three Wariors and a Horse.* Several of Pacetti's reliefs were used also on vases. A third version of *Achilles in Scyros,* also known as *The Discovery of Achilles* and *Achilles and the daughters of Lycomedes* was probably modelled by De Vaere* c.1790. A second, smaller, version of *Achilles dragging the body of Hector around the walls of Troy* (with the subject reversed and a figure of Achilles that dwarfs the horses) was probably copied from a cast by Tassie* from a gem by Pichler*.

Centaur teaching Achilles the Lyre, one of the Herculaneum* roundels intended for "the Decoration of Large Halls and Stair Cases" dates from 1770-71, and Wedgwood's immediate source was the set of moulds taken from bas-relief copies in the possession of the Marquess of Lansdowne.

Acid-Etched Gold (Acid Gold)

A form of decoration, first introduced in Britain by Minton in 1863, by which patterns are etched into the surface of the ware by the use of hydrofluoric acid. An acid-resistant transfer-print is applied to the glazed ware and rubbed firmly to produce perfect adhesion of the print before the paper is removed. The

Achilles. *Original drawing by Pacetti for the tablet,* Achilles on the back of a Centaur hunting the Lion. *The relief on the original Luna marble disc in the Capitoline Museum shows a female centaur. Pacetti's centaur appears to be hermaphrodite.* Wedgwood.

rest of the piece, back and front, is then 'stopped out' by coating it with acid-resistant material, before immersing it in hydrofluoric acid. The acid 'bites' away the exposed parts of the glaze, etching the required pattern. The pattern is then given a first coat of 22-carat liquid gold, which is fired into the glaze. A second coating of gold is applied and fired again, and the pattern is then burnished to produce a polished relief design against a matt gold background. Patterns produced by this method are normally narrow border designs and are among the most expensive to produce. The Wedgwood range of bone china tableware still includes a number of patterns of this type.

Acorn Finial
Finials* in the form of an acorn were commonly employed on wares, particularly silver and ceramics, in the neo-classical* style. They are still sometimes used today.

Adam, Robert (1728-1792)
Architect and designer in the neo-classical* style. In 1752 Adam travelled to Italy, and thence to Dalmatia (now Yugoslavia). In Dalmatia his drawings of Diocletian's palace influenced his early work as a designer. When, in 1762, he returned to Britain he was appointed architect to the King, and his work, and that of his brother, James, with whom he was in partnership, did much to promote neo-classicism in England. In 1773 the brothers began to publish their chief designs in a series of engravings collected together under the general title of *Works in Architecture*. These designs considerably influenced such manufacturers as Wedgwood and Boulton, and the colours chosen by Wedgwood for his jasper grounds are closely related to those used by Adam in interior decoration.

In 1771 Wedgwood referred in a letter to the practice of Mr. Adams (*sic*), who was keeping modellers in Rome employed in making bas-reliefs, something Wedgwood did himself in 1787, when John Flaxman* was there to supervise the work. Despite its popularity Adam's style was by no means universally admired. Two of his sternest critics were Horace Walpole and Sir William Chambers*.

See: Chimney Pieces.

Acorn Finial. *Engine-turned black basaltes vase, ornamented with ribbon ties and swags, satyr-mask handles, and acorn finial. 7½ ins. high. c.1775.* Wedgwood.

14

Adam Style

The English version of the neo-classical* style introduced soon after 1760 by Robert Adam* and his brothers, and strongly influenced by such men as James 'Athenian' Stuart*. It replaced the earlier rococo* style in the decorative arts, and tended to supersede the Palladian style in architecture. Adam's repertory of ornament is classical, and similar in many ways to the current French version of neo-classicism, although it was plainer and less luxurious. Festoons*, swags, medallions*, and urns* were commonly employed for ornamental purposes. In contrast with the asymmetry of the preceding rococo style, there is a return to strict classical symmetry. The Adam style had very little effect on the porcelain of the period, but the products of Wedgwood, especially the cream-coloured* ware, basaltes*, and jasper*, were strongly influenced by it. The prevailing Adam colour-schemes were repeated in the colouring of Wedgwood's jasper, and jasper tablets* and medallions were used architecturally in some Adam houses.

See: Chimney Pieces; Patera.

Adams, William (1746-1805)

Often erroneously described as a pupil of Josiah Wedgwood's, Adams was in business at Burslem from 1769, and opened a factory at Greengates, Tunstall, in 1779. Adams manufactured creamware and basaltes, and began the production of jasper in the 1780s, including pale and dark blue, pale and dark green, lilac, pink, and plum-colour. The quality of his jasper is very close to that of Wedgwood, but the colours are stronger, and the blue more violet. Some of these wares were mounted in Sheffield. Adams also made caneware with reliefs in blue or olive-green. The mark was 'ADAMS', 'ADAMS & CO.', or 'W. ADAMS & CO.' impressed. The firm declined after William Adams's death in 1805. It is not to be confused with that of William Adams (1772-1829) of Fenton Hall who made large quantities of blue and white earthenware.

Adelphi, The

A Greek word meaning 'brothers', and the name given to the 18th century development in the neighbourhood of Charing Cross, between The Strand and the Thames, by the four brothers Adam. A great deal of this development was demolished just before World War II to make way for new building. The Adelphi Terrace, which no longer exists, has had many notable occupants, including Robert and James Adam, David Garrick and Bernard Shaw. The Royal Society of Arts* occupies a building in John Adam Street, the exterior of which is almost intact. For Wedgwood's connection with The Adelphi, see: Showrooms. It is possible that Wedgwood plaques were incorporated into some Adelphi houses, see: Chimney pieces. The scheme was never entirely completed as planned, principally because the Adam brothers were better as designers than as civil engineers.

See: Samuel More.

Adonis

A youth, beloved by Aphrodite, who died of wounds inflicted by a boar. The goddess was grief stricken by his death, and the gods allowed him to return from the underworld for six months of every year, which he spent with Aphrodite. The anemone sprang from his blood. His death and resurrection were celebrated at the Spring festivals.

Wedgwood subject:
Venus (Aphrodite) and Adonis,* 1775. Supplied by Hoskins & Grant*.

Adelphi. *Façade of the premises of the Royal Society for the Encouragement of Arts, Manufactures and Commerce in John Street, Adelphi.* Photo: Wedgwood.

Aeneas

The son of Anchises and Aphrodite, Aeneas is one of the two great Trojan heroes, the other being Hector. Aeneas survived the fall of Troy because he was under the protection of Aphrodite and Poseidon. A favourite subject with later artists is Aeneas bearing his father, Anchises, on his back from the flames of Troy. Aeneas took with him The Palladium* and, crossing into Europe, he eventually found his way to Latium in Italy and settled there, becoming the ancestral hero of the Romans. The *Aeneid* of Virgil is concerned with the wanderings of Aeneas before he reached Latium. He was driven by a storm on to the coast of North Africa, where he found Dido who fell in love with him. In Italy Aeneas founded the city of Lavinium, named after Lavinia (daughter of Latinus, King of the Aborigines), whom he married. After the death of Latinus, Aeneas became King of the Aborigines and the surviving Trojans, and fell in battle against the Etruscans. His body was not found and it was assumed that he had been translated into Heaven.

Wedgwood subject:
Aeneas bearing Anchises from the flames of Troy, cameo, attributed to John Bacon*, c.1769.

Aerograph

An apparatus invented in 1890 for applying coloured grounds and glazes to the surface of pottery and porcelain, utilising compressed air to produce a fine spray. Extensively used by Wedgwood, particularly in the 1950s for the production of bone china tea and coffee sets (e.g. *April* colours).

Aesculapius

Josiah Wedgwood referred to Dr. Erasmus Darwin* as his "favourite Aesculapius." The latter was the Greek god of medicine, although Homer refers to him only as a "blameless physician" (rare enough in any period). The son of Apollo*, Aesculapius was believed to cure the sick and restore the dead to life. Fearing that men might thus become immortal, Zeus slew him with a thunderbolt and placed him among the stars. Serpents, symbols of regeneration, were sacred to Aesculapius, and the cock was sacrificed to him. He is usually represented with a staff and serpent.

Wedgwood subjects:

Aesculapius, cameo, copied (probably from a cameo by Tassie*) from a Renaissance gem by Valerio Vicentino. This cameo figure usually appears alone, but it is occasionally found with the accompanying figure of Hygeia as it appears on the original gem.

Aesculapius and Hygeia, tablet 8¼ins. by 6⅞ins. modelled by Pacetti* in 1788 from a marble now in the Capitoline Museum.

Aesculapius. *Medallion,* Sacrifice to Aesculapius. Wedgwood.

Aesop's Fables

A series of Queen's ware* plates transfer-printed* in red with subjects from *Aesop's Fables* is in the Schreiber* Collection, Victoria and Albert Museum, London. Each print has a square rococo* border suspended from a tied ribbon by festoons* of husk pattern enamelled in green. Two of the eleven prints correspond with illustrations by Francis Barlow* to *Aesop's Fables,* London, 1687, and five correspond with printed tiles in the same collection.

Aesthetic Movement

Movement starting in the late 1860s which developed from the Arts and Crafts Movement of Morris and his associates, with which it was to some extent in disagreement. It took for its guiding principle 'Art for art's sake', adapted by Whistler from Victor Cousin, which was widely quoted. It gave place about 1890 to art nouveau*. The Aesthetic Movement was popularised in America by Oscar Wilde during his lecture tours. The Sunflower* and the Peacock were popular decorative motifs.

Agate Ware

Pottery made in imitation of polished agate, either by wedging coloured clays in the body (solid agate) or by blending coloured slips* on the surface. The colours blended together are brown, red, yellow and white. Examples are known from ancient Rome, but more notably from the T'ang dynasty of 8th century China. Agate wares thrown on the potter's wheel display a spiral swirl on the outside, caused by the circular motion of the wheel, and a smeared effect on interior surfaces resulting from the pressures of the thrower's wet hand. This technique appears to have been used in Staffordshire c.1730-40, prior to the introduction of moulds for these wares. Solid (moulded) agate may be easily distinguished from surface agate: the former shows a clear break in the veining where the two halves of the moulded piece have been joined (generally under the handles), and the colour and veining are visible in the interior of the vessel; surface agate shows the same matching striations over the whole body, and the interior is cream coloured. Wedgwood wrote in his *Experiment Book** early in 1759: "I had already made an imitation of Agate which was esteemed beautiful, and made a considerable improvement, but people were surfeited with wares of these various colours." He nevertheless continued to make surface agate, and added many other colours in imitation of semi-precious stones. Agate ware was imitated on the Continent, particularly at Apt, in the Vaucluse.

See also: Crystalline Ware; Marbling; Variegated Ware.

Agrippina (d. A.D.33)

Wife of Germanicus*, by whom she had nine children, including the Agrippina who married Nero. One of her children became the Emperor Caligula*. She shared many of her husband's campaigns, but after his death in A.D.17 her popularity caused the Emperor Tiberius to banish her.

Wedgwood subject:

Agrippina (Agrepina), bust. Supplied by Oliver & Hoskins, 1774.

Ajax

Greek warrior, son of Telamon, present at the siege of Troy, and second in bravery and prowess only to Achilles*. After the death of Achilles his armour was claimed by Ajax and Ulysses*, who contended for its possession. Ulysses was the victor, and Ajax put an end to his own life. A jasper plaque is erroneously entitled *Achilles (sic) fighting Ulysses.*

Agate Ware. *Vase with satyr mask handles, the horns extending from shoulder to rim. Surface agate decoration with traces of oil-gilding. Wedgwood & Bentley period. Wedgwood.*

Alders, Thomas (fl.mid-18th century)
Manufacturer of buttons and knife handles in agate and tortoiseshell earthenware, black wares, 'scratch blue', and salt-glazed stoneware, whose factory was at Cliff Bank, Stoke-on-Trent. In 1752-54 he was in partnership with John Harrison* the elder and Josiah Wedgwood.

Alexander the Great (356-323 B.C.)
Son of Philip II of Macedonia and Olympias. Educated by Aristotle*, and succeeded to the throne at the age of twenty. After putting down an insurrection in his own country, he led his forces into Greece, where he at once displayed military genius. Turning on the Persians, he defeated Darius at Issus. By 331 he had conquered Asia, and two years later he entered India, where he was once again uniformly successful. In 326, however, his troops, exhausted and homesick, forced him to return to Macedonia. He died three years later. He founded the city of Alexandria at the beginning of 331.

Wedgwood subjects:
Alexander, bust supplied by Hoskins & Grant*, 1779.
Alexander the Great, portrait medallion, c.1779.
Alexander with Horn, probably copied from a model supplied by Tassie*. Also called *Lysimachus,* King of Macedonia.
Masque of Alexander, bas-relief modelled by Webber*, 1786.

All Draughtsmen's Assistant
or *Drawing Made Easy* by R. Sayers* and J. Bennet, published in 1771, was a book compiled as a source of inspiration for decorators, fan painters, etc., drawings from which sometimes

appear on pottery or porcelain in transfer-printed form. A river scene with figures after Vernet from this source occurs transfer printed on Wedgwood creamware.

Allen & Hordley (fl.1830-1840)
Engravers; responsible for the engraving in 1830 of an English country house in a landscape which was blue printed with a wide rose border about 1840, as well as a landscape pattern of 1832.

Allen, G. (fl.1820-1850)
Engraver, in 1845, of the *Eastern Flowers** pattern, a tableware design in the *famille rose** style. No other Wedgwood pattern has been traced to Allen, but the quality and success of *Eastern Flowers* make it probable that he was responsible for others of a similar type.

Allen, Thomas (1831-1915)
Painter and designer; studied at the Stoke-on-Trent School of Design. Allen began to work at Minton* (perhaps, as an apprentice, as early as 1845) as a painter of figure subjects. A vase painted by him in the Sèvres manner in 1849 was included by Minton at the Great Exhibition of 1851. In 1852 Allen was awarded a national scholarship to the newly-established South Kensington School of Design, and there he remained until 1854 when he returned to Minton. He was employed there as a figure painter until 1876 when, frustrated by low wages and the domination of the art department by Leon Arnoux and M.L. Solon, he transferred to Wedgwood, where he soon became supervisor of the Fine Art Studio, chief designer, and art director (1880). He designed a number of tableware patterns for Wedgwood, but his principal work continued to be figure subjects for vases, including the decorously posed and

Allen, Thomas. *Circular wall plaque painted with a portrait of Jessica from* The Merchant of Venice *against an elaborate gold ground. One of a series of such plaques painted by Thomas Allen, 1881.* Wedgwood.

Allen, Thomas. *A fine example of Allen's figure painting on a creamware plaque, signed and dated 1891.* Wedgwood.

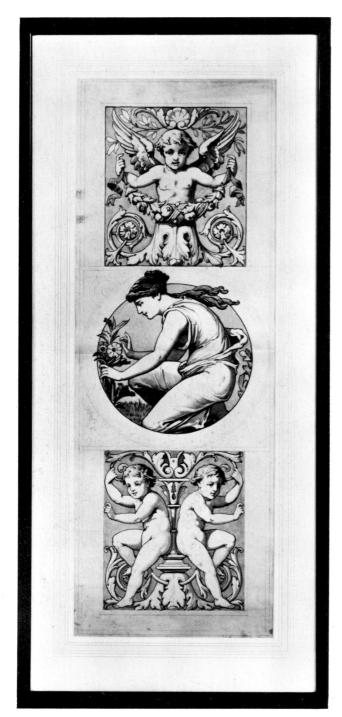

Allen, Thomas. *Original design for tile panel by Thomas Allen. The design at the top is a Renaissance type grotesque, the figure terminating in acanthus foliage. The figures at the base belong to the same type.* Wedgwood.

chastely draped semi-nudes popular among Victorian art-lovers. His technique was undeniably superb, and he is widely regarded as the leading Staffordshire figure painter of the 19th century. A large pair of vases painted with nymphs and *amorini* was shown in the Paris Exposition of 1878, where Wedgwood gained a Gold Medal.

Allen's work for Wedgwood (unlike his work for Minton) was usually signed: 'Tho Allen', or with his monogram, and often dated. In addition to vases, he painted some excellent earthenware chargers or plaques with portraits of characters from Shakespeare on gold grounds (1881), and his *Columbia* pattern is still in production after a century of almost continuous popularity. He retired in 1905.

The following are among his more important works:

Vases, ranging in height from about 15ins. to more than 30ins., richly decorated with figure subjects (generally of a somewhat sentimental character) in reserves on a coloured and gilt ground.

Plaques, 15ins. in diameter, decorated with enamel portraits of characters from Shakespeare on a gold ground, signed and dated 1881.

Tiles printed in a single colour, or print and enamel, with scenes from Scott's *Ivanhoe*.

    Banquet pattern.

    Columbia pattern (1880).

    Swallow pattern.

Colour Plate I

Left: One of the six First Day's Vases thrown by Josiah I on 13th June, 1769 with Bentley turning the wheel. Right: One of the fifty replicas made in 1930 to mark the bicentenary of the birth of Josiah I. Wedgwood.

Alpine Pink
Bone china* coloured body* introduced in 1936, and reintroduced for a short period in 1955. It was made in traditional shapes*, shell shapes (including Nautilus*) and coupe*/Savoy shapes.

Alumina
Aluminium oxide, a refractory white powder with a melting point of about 2,200°C. which is used in a variety of ways where it is desired to keep two surfaces from sticking to each other, e.g. the support of figures during firing.
See: Repairers.

American Bicentennial Editions
To celebrate the American Bicentennial Wedgwood issued limited editions of the following specially designed pieces:
Pair of Bicentennial Plates, fluted blue and white jasper with inner border of thirteen applied stars. One plate has a centre ornament of the American eagle, surrounded by applied white jasper seals of the thirteen orginal colonies; the other is ornamented with portrait medallions of the thirteen signatories of the Declaration of Independence. (Edition 5,000.)
Five-colour Trophy Plate, centre ornament of portrait medallion of George Washington surrounded by rams' heads and floral swags, classical bas-reliefs, and a formal applied border in pale blue, white, cane, lilac, and sage-green jasper. (Edition 300.)
Three-colour Goblet, 5ins. high, in pale blue, white and sage-green jasper, ornamented with portrait medallions of George Washington and Thomas Jefferson, floral swags, laurel border and three-colour diced pattern. (Edition 200.)
Two-handled Mug, black and white jasper with gold design featuring the American eagle, designed by Richard Guyatt*. (Edition 500.)
Queen's Ware Mug, the American eagle and flag within borders of thirteen stars and fifty stars, designed by Richard Guyatt. (Edition 5,000.)

Andromache. *Jasper medallion modelled by John Bacon, c.1777.* Wedgwood.

American Independence Series. *Cornwallis surrendering to the American forces at Yorktown, 1781. Jasper plate, issued to commemorate the Bicentennial in 1976. The stars represent the thirteen original colonies.* Wedgwood.

American Independence Series, 1976
A series of six pale blue and white jasper plates with centre applied ornament depicting scenes from American history, moulded inscription, and outer applied border of thirteen stars. The historical scenes are as follows: Boston Tea Party; Paul Revere's Ride; Battle of Concord; George Washington crossing the Delaware; Victory at Yorktown; and The Declaration Signed.

America's Heritage Series
A series of six blue and white jasper plates, diameter 8ins., with centre applied bas-relief ornament, moulded inscription, applied inner border of thirteen stars, and outer moulded border of fifty smaller stars. Introduced in a limited edition of 15,000 sets, the centre bas-relief scenes and moulded inscriptions are as follows: *The West by Land; The West by Sea; The Heartland by Rail; The Heartland by River; The World by Road* and *The World by Air.* Issued 1978-79.

Andromache
The wife of Hector*. On the capture of Troy her son Scamandrius was hurled from the walls of the city. She fell to the share of Neoptolemus, son of Achilles*. Later, she lived with Hector's brother, Helenus.
Wedgwood subject:
Andromache, circular medallion, diameter 8½ins., modelled by John Bacon*, 1777.

Andromeda
The daughter of Cepheus, King of Ethiopia. Her mother, Cassiopaea, boasted that Andromeda was more beautiful than the Nereids*, which angered Poseidon so much that he sent a sea monster to ravage the country. The oracle of Ammon promised that the people would be saved if Andromeda were sacrificed to the monster. She was chained to a rock, where Perseus* found her. He slew the monster and made her his

20

wife. She had been promised to her uncle, Phineus, who attacked Perseus at the wedding. Perseus turned him to stone by confronting him with the Medusa's* head. After Andromeda's death the gods placed her among the stars.

There are three Wedgwood bas-reliefs which relate to Andromeda:

Andromeda, medallion head 4¾ins. by 4ins., c.1775.

Perseus and Andromeda, cameo, and medallion 2ins. by 5ins., probably remodelled by Flaxman* after a copy (supplied by Tassie*) of a Roman gem now in the Capitoline Museum, c.1775.

The Marriage Supper of Perseus and Andromeda, plaque 6ins. by 9ins., c.1769.

Angelini, Giuseppe (1742-1811)

Angelini came to England from Rome about 1770 and joined the Royal Academy Schools in 1772. For a time he was employed by the sculptor, Nollekens, but in 1777 was in financial difficulties, and was granted assistance by the Academy. By 1787 he was back in Rome modelling for Wedgwood, and working with Flaxman*, Pacetti*, Dalmazzoni*, and Webber*.

Wedgwood bas-reliefs attributed to Angelini include:

Apollo and the Muse Erato.
Apotheosis of a Young Prince.
Bacchantes (two).
Fable of Meleager.
Fauns (two).
Pleasures of the Elysian Fields.
Pluto carrying off Proserpine, preceded by Hercules.
Silenus.
Victory and Mercury.
Rape of Proserpine (Persephone).

Anthemion

See: Honeysuckle Border.

Antinous

An extraordinarily handsome youth, born at Claudiopolis in Bithynia. He became the favourite of the Emperor Hadrian, accompanying him on all his journeys. He was drowned in the Nile in A.D.121.

Wedgwood subjects:

Antinous, bust. Supplied by Oliver & Hoskins, 1774, and refinished by Hackwood.

Antinous, figure, height 12ins., c.1910.

Antique

Correctly, appertaining to ancient Greece and Rome. In this sense the word was used throughout the 18th century and well into the 19th, and it is so employed in this *Dictionary*. The use of 'antique' to describe something as old as a century or so is comparatively new. What are now called antique shops were previously known as 'curiosity shops', and sold 'curios'. Shops dealing in genuine antiques — classical pottery, statuary, and similar objects — were always rarities.

Antiquities of Herculaneum

Work descriptive of the antiquities of Herculaneum, Volume I, Part 1, of which was published in 1773. The text was translated from the Italian by J. Martin and T. Lettice, and it was edited by O.A. Bayard. Wedgwood was a subscriber to the first volume. No succeeding volumes appear to have been published.

Antoninus Pius (A.D.86-161)

Roman Emperor, A.D.128-161. Before his death he adopted Marcus Aurelius, as he himself had been adopted by Hadrian.

A bust of Antoninus Pius was supplied by Hoskins & Grant* in 1774 and re-finished by Hackwood*. It was reproduced, 22ins. high, in basaltes.

Aphrodite

Greek goddess of love; the daughter of Zeus and Dione, but, according to later poets, she sprang from the foam of the sea. The wife of Hephaestos (Vulcan*) and mistress of Ares (Mars*), she is often depicted with her son, Eros (Cupid*). Best known among her lovers is Adonis*. A Queen's ware figure of *Aphrodite* was modelled by Arnold Machin, c.1944.

For all other Wedgwood subjects see: Venus.

Apollo

One of the principal deities of the Greeks, the son of Zeus and Leto, and twin brother of Diana. Apollo was the god of prophecy, with numerous oracles. In this guise he is called the Pythian Apollo. As the god of music he is connected with the Muses* and is called Apollo Musagetes (leader of the Muses). He was later identified with Helios, and thus became god of the sun, often being depicted driving the Chariot of the Sun across the heavens. He was also the god of rewards and punishments, and of towns and colonies. The Romans became

Apollo. *Jasper urn, 1316 shape, ornamented with foliate swags and a reduced version of the Apollo medallion, the square base with formal acanthus leaves.* Wedgwood.

acquainted with him by way of the Greeks, probably during the third century B.C.

Wedgwood subjects:

Apollo (flanked by a tripod and his lyre on a pillar), cameo* by Flaxman*, 1775, probably from a Tassie* gem (source: Montfaucon* I,i, pl.XLII.3).

Apollo, figure, 11ins., by Flaxman, 1777.

Apollo chasing Daphne, subject painted on an 'Etruscan' vase* (source: d'Hancarville* I, pl.84).

Apollo and Four Muses, bas-relief* figures supplied as casts by Flaxman Senior.*

Apollo and Nine Muses, bas-relief figures by Flaxman.

History of Apollo, set of three medallions supplied by Mrs. Mary Landré*, 1769, each 3ins. by 6ins., comprising: *Apollo and Daphne, Apollo and Marsyas,* and *Apollo and Python.*

Apollo Vase, designed for the bicentenary in 1930 by Goodwin*.

Apollo Vase

Pale blue jasper dip lidded vase 9½ ins. high designed by John Goodwin* in 1930 to celebrate the bicentenary of Josiah Wedgwood's birth. The lid is surmounted by the figure of Apollo, and the vase bears the Latin inscription: 'CC POSTNATUM CONDITOREM ANNO VIGET ARS ETRURIAE REDINTEGRATA' (which may be freely translated as: Two hundred years after the birth of the founder, the thriving art of Etruria is renewed). The vase was made in a limited edition of 50, each being numbered.

Apothecary Jars

Storage jars in three sizes decorated with geometric patterns designed by Peter Wall* and Robert Minkin* for the *Design '63* range, first exhibited at the London Showrooms* in February 1963.

Apotheosis. *Large circular jasper plaque,* The Apotheosis of Virgil. *Presented to Henry Brownsword on the occasion of his retirement.* Wedgwood.

Apotheosis

Deification, canonisation of a saint, or the exaltation of a person, ideal, or principle; also loosely used to convey the meaning of resurrection or ascension to glory. A fairly familiar subject in classical art, it was used by Wedgwood for a number of important bas-reliefs* for tablets*, at least two of which were successfully adapted for the ornamenting of vases. The most notable are *The Apotheosis of Homer** and *The Apotheosis of Virgil* by Flaxman*. Also recorded are: *The Apotheosis of a Young Prince,* attributed to Angelini*, and *The Apotheosis of Faustina,* attributed to Pacetti*.

See also: Hesiod.

Apotheosis of Homer

Known also as *A Victorious Citharist* and *The Crowning of a Citharist,* this design was copied faithfully by Flaxman* from the decoration on a calyx krater* bought by the British Museum from Sir William Hamilton* in 1772. Wedgwood refers to this relief in a letter to Bentley dated 19th August, 1778, when he writes of tablets* made for showing during the coming winter. Bentley interpreted the scene as "some honour paid to the genius of Homer*", and Hamilton confirmed this, establishing the name by which it is now known. This conformed admirably with contemporary admiration for Homer.

Some seven years later Flaxman designed the Pegasus* vase, and the *Apotheosis of Homer* relief was adapted as ornament for it. One of the first, in pale blue and white jasper, was presented by Wedgwood to the British Museum. He considered it to be one of the finest vases he had ever made, and the bas-relief* is generally considered to be the most important commission executed by Flaxman for Wedgwood. A magnificent example of the vase, in greenish-buff jasper dip with the Pegasus finial in white on solid pale blue clouds, is in the Nottingham Castle Museum. Since the destruction by bombing of a similar example in the Hull Museum, the Nottingham vase appears to be unique.

See: Homeric Vase

Apotheosis of Virgil

See: Homeric Vase; Virgil.

Apple Teapot

A teapot in the form of an apple with crabstock* handle and spout, and with applied leaves on the body and cover. It was made in biscuit* earthenware by William Greatbatch* for Wedgwood, c.1760, and finished at the Ivy House Works* with a mottled coloured glaze.

Applied Reliefs

See: Ornamenting.

Arabesque

This term, from the Italian *arabeschi,* cannot be closely defined. It consists of interlaced lines, bands, and strapwork, sometimes largely abstract, sometimes floral and foliate. Originally it was adapted by Islamic craftsmen from Roman sources, and it is related to the grotesques* with which it is sometimes confused. The principal difference is that arabesques, arising from Islamic sources, lack representations of living creatures, although these have sometimes been added by Christian designers. In the period covered by this *Dictionary* arabesques are a 19th century form of decoration, when they were frequently referred to as Moresques. Properly so-called, Moresques are arabesques with sources in Spain and Sicily, both of which were at one time under Saracen domination.

Apollo. *Jasper medallion of Apollo Musagetes with his lyre. Letter 'B' impressed on obverse. Probably a trial piece.* Wedgwood.

Apollo. *Apollo Musagetes. Jasper medallion. c.1778.* Wedgwood.

Apollo Vase. *Blue and white jasper vase, designed by Goodwin for the bicentenary of Josiah Wedgwood's birth in 1730. The Apollo Vase was made in a limited edition of 50, of which No. 1 was presented to Queen Mary.* Sotheby's Belgravia.

Architectural Details

From the existence of a few extremely rare examples, it is evident that Wedgwood experimented with the production of small creamware architectural details moulded in relief. These may have been intended to be set in above the jambs of chimney pieces*, but there is no evidence that they were ever produced in quantity and it seems probable that the idea was abandoned after the invention of jasper*.

Ares

See: Mars.

Argand Lamp

Type of oil lamp invented c.1782 by a Swiss, Aimé Argand, and made in England by Boulton*. The wick is fed from a central reservoir, and air is supplied to the flame by a glass tube. It has the usual glass chimney. From about 1810 the wick was adjustable.

See also: J. Hinks & Son.

Argyll. *Argyll or gravy-warmer with a separate compartment for hot water. Silver pattern. c.1780-90.* Buten Museum.

Argyll

A gravy-warmer with a handle and spout, somewhat similar in shape to a covered coffee pot. It has a central tube, or a separate compartment, to contain hot water, and it was made in these forms in the 18th century in cream-coloured ware by both Wedgwood and Leeds. It is said to have been invented by the third Duke of Argyll, c.1750, and was first made in silver.

Ariadne

The daughter of Minos and Pasiphaë of Crete. She fell in love with Theseus and gave him the reel of thread with which he found his way out of the labyrinth of the Minotaur. Theseus promised to marry Ariadne, and she fled with him from Crete, but he deserted her and she was found by Dionysus (see Bacchus), who made her his wife.

Wedgwood subjects:

Ariadne, bust supplied by Hoskins & Grant*, 1779.
Ariadne, medallion head modelled by Flaxman*, 1775. Listed in the 1779 catalogue in two sizes, 8ins. by 6ins., and 2ins. by 1¾ins.
Ariadne drawn by Panthers with Pan etc., tablet* modelled by

Flaxman. Listed in the 1779 catalogue, 10½ins. by 14¼ins.
Ariadne Reading, figure, height 9ins.
Ariadne Reclining, figure. Listed in the 1787 catalogue.

Aristophanes (c.444-380 B.C.)

Celebrated Greek poet and dramatist, believed to have been born in Athens about 444 B.C. He is known particularly for satirical comedies, of which eleven have survived, directed against a variety of abuses of his time. A basaltes* bust, attributed to William Keeling*, was produced c.1775, probably from a model obtained from Hoskins & Grant* or John Cheere*. A miniature jasper version is illustrated.

Aristotle (384-322 B.C.)

Philosopher, born at Stagira in Macedonia. After the death of Alexander in 322, Aristotle, regarded as a friend of Macedonia, thought it prudent to leave Athens, and he escaped to Chalcis in Euboea, where he died. A bust of Aristotle, supplied by John Cheere*, was reproduced in basaltes in 1774.

Armorial Ware

Ware decorated with the coat of arms or crest of the owner. The fashion developed from armorial engraving on silver, and the enamelled Chinese export porcelain. Wedgwood was always reluctant to accept orders of this nature. As he explained to Bentley in 1766: "Crests are very bad things for us to meddle with...Plain ware, if it should not happen to be firsts [faultless], you will take off my hands as seconds [substandard], which, if Crested, would be as useless as most other Crests, and Crest wearers are..." Ten years later, he was complaining that Guy Green*, in Liverpool, could print arms in outline and have them filled in by enamellers at one-sixth of the price that Wedgwood must charge for the same arms painted free-hand. "The painting of Arms," he wrote, "is now become a serious business, and I must either lose or gain a great deal of business by it. However, I must, at all events, come into it." Armorial ware became, as the crest books preserved in the Museum at Barlaston testify, an essential part of Wedgwood's Queen's ware business. After 1780 the arms and crests were generally transfer-printed and enamelled. Modern coats of arms are usually reproduced by lithography*.

Armstrong, Samuel (fl.1769-1774)

Painter at the Chelsea Decorating Studio* who enamelled edging and borders on the Frog* service.

Art Nouveau

An English style in the decorative arts which grew out of the Arts and Crafts Movement in the 1880s, and achieved its greatest popularity on the Continent. Ornament tends to be profuse, and most of it is floral, with sinuous, winding stems. It played a very small part in the production of most pottery and porcelain factories, but tended rather to influence the work of studio potters. Perhaps its greatest influence at Wedgwood is to be found in some of the designs of Daisy Makeig-Jones*.

Art Pottery

Decorative pottery in the style of the Aesthetic Movement, current from the late 1870s onwards. Art pottery may be factory made or studio pottery, and it was more profusely decorated than pottery intended for mere utility. Some of Wedgwood's more highly decorated wares of this period fall under this heading, but for the most part 'art' wares were made by smaller factories. The term, 'art', was widely used, and applied to 'art' furniture, 'art' metalwork, etc.

Artemis

See: Diana.

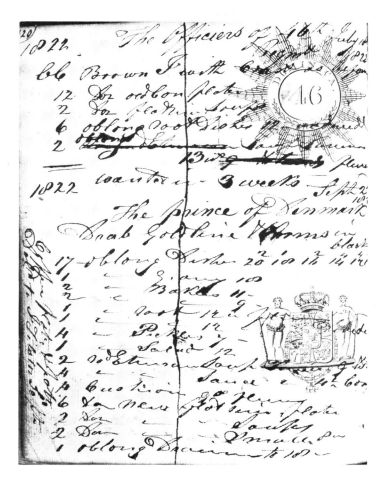

Aristophanes. *A rare miniature bust of Aristophanes in white jasper on a black basaltes socle, 4ins. high. Impressed mark 'Wedgwood & Bentley.' c.1778.* Christie's.

Armorial Ware. *Extract from Wedgwood's Crest Book, 1822.* Wedgwood.

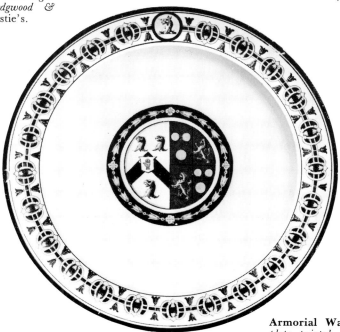

Armorial Ware. *Queen's ware plate painted with the arms of Honeywood, 1796.* Wedgwood.

Asparagus Pan

A footed dish, open at one end and rising to a tapered prow shape at the other, intended for the service of asparagus. It was made by Wedgwood in creamware and is No.20 in the first creamware Shape Book*, published in 1774.

Asparagus Shell

A flat receptacle, open at both ends, with low vertical sides, wider at one end than at the other, and about three inches long. These, often erroneously called knife rests, are asparagus shells in the *Leeds Pattern Book*. They were made of cream-coloured ware at several factories, including Wedgwood's.

Astle, Thomas (1735-1803)

Antiquary and palaeographer; elected Fellow of the Royal Society, 1766. His collection of manuscripts (Stowe Collection) is now in the British Library, London. He supplied Wedgwood with portraits (probably from medals and engravings) for the series of thirty-six Kings of England, many of which were modelled by John Flaxman.

Athene

Pallas Athene, goddess of wisdom.

See: Minerva.

Atlas (Atlantes)

One of the Titans, brother of Prometheus*. He and his brothers made war on Zeus, but they were defeated, and Atlas was condemned to bear the Heavens on his shoulders. Atlantes are male statues used in place of columns in the support of buildings, and occur in classical ornamental designs as supporters. Male versions of caryatids*, Atlantes appear as supporters of the so-called Michelangelo* vase.

Wedgwood subject:

Atlas supporting the world, cameo after an engraved gem by Giovanni Antonio de' Rossi.

Attributes

By tradition mythological figures were provided with a variety of attributes which served to identify them, and these are briefly discussed below as an aid to identification. These attributes come originally from Greek sources and have descended through the centuries with certain modifications.

In general, the face was oval. Angularity was regarded as ugly, so the forehead was rounded. The style of the hair helps to identify the personage depicted — Jupiter (Zeus) has curling hair and beard, with two locks on his forehead, brushed upwards in a form somewhat resembling rams' horns; Neptune's hair often has the appearance of being saturated with water; Pluto has long straight hair; Apollo has long hair, tied on top and hanging down at the back; Venus and Diana either have hair knotted on the nape of the neck or tied on top. Hercules has hair best described as woolly.

The eyes were large and in the case of virgin goddesses and vestals, modestly lowered. The eyebrows were fairly prominent. The mouth had a full lower lip above a round chin. In the case of divine beings the lips were sometimes open; in mortals they were closed. Teeth were only shown in the case of satyrs, Sileni, and fauns. The pectoral muscles of men were large and prominent, especially in figures of Hercules. The breasts in women tended to be small, almost virginal, and pointed. The belly was flat in men, or soft and rounded in women. The hands and feet were always carefully carved or modelled.

While these remarks apply principally to ancient sculpture, most later sculpture in the classical and neo-classical styles conformed to these principles closely, since it was directly inspired by surviving Greek and Roman sculpture and vase painting. Attributes, such as Jupiter's thunderbolt, which accompany later representations of mythological figures are described under the appropriate headings.

Often allied to figures of this kind are the allegorical subjects popular throughout the 18th century, and to be found among Wedgwood figures and reliefs. Objects allegorical of the gods, which may even stand by themselves without an accompanying figure, are the laurel of Apollo (often in the form of a wreath), the vine of Bacchus, the eagle and thunderbolt of Jupiter, the crescent moon of Diana, the lion-skin and club of Hercules, and the caduceus of Mercury.

There were also figures symbolising such concepts as the Seasons, the Continents, the Elements (Earth, Fire, Air and Water), the Five Senses (Sight, Hearing, Smell, Taste and Touch), and many other subjects. In the case of figures representing the Seasons, flowers are carried by Spring, a sheaf of corn by Summer, bunches of grapes by Autumn, and Winter is represented by a brazier. Everyone in the 18th century was expected to be able to interpret symbolism of this sort, and it became a kind of parlour-game to do so.

The *Four Seasons* were popular with Wedgwood, and *The Elements* were provided by Hoskins & Grant*, but the *Continents* and the *Senses* seem only to have been made by the porcelain factories. Subjects like *Friendship consoling Affliction* after a design by Lady Templetown* may be regarded as allegorical.

See: Trophies.

Auckland, Sir William Eden, 1st Baron.
Jasper portrait medallion of Sir William Eden, 1st Baron Auckland, modelled by Eley George Mountstephen. c.1789. Brooklyn Museum: Emily Winthrop Miles Collection.

Auckland, Sir William Eden, 1st Baron (1744-1814)

English statesman, diplomat and 'man of business'; third son of Sir Robert Eden of West Auckland, Durham. As a convinced Whig, who deserted the Opposition to serve the government under the Younger Pitt, Eden was one of Wedgwood's most influential patrons. He was minister plenipotentiary to France in 1786 and negotiated the Commercial Treaty. Wedgwood wrote him a long letter at that time on the subject of duties as they affected the import and export trade with France. Eden was created Baron Auckland in 1789. Two years later, while ambassador extraordinary at The Hague, he entertained Josiah II* and Tom Byerley* and arranged for them to show a copy of the Portland* vase to the Prince and Princess of Orange. Auckland wrote Wedgwood a letter of enthusiastic praise not only for the vase but also for the behaviour of Josiah junior, but he hinted that he was not convinced by Josiah's explanation of the relief figures. His doubts will not surprise anyone who has studied the conflicting theories that have been put forward in the past two hundred years.

Portrait medallions of Lord and Lady Auckland were modelled about 1789 by Eley George Mountstephen* and first produced in jasper in 1790. Mountstephen's original pink wax model of Auckland's portrait (Reilly Collection) was shown in the exhibition at the National Portrait Gallery, London in 1973.

Auction Sale, 1781

After the death of Thomas Bentley in 1780 it became necessary to wind up the affairs of the Wedgwood and Bentley partnership for the production of ornamental wares, and the principal asset was the stock. The decision was taken to dispose of this in a series of sales lasting from 3rd to 15th December, 1781, at the Great Rooms of Messrs. Christie* & Ansell in Pall Mall, where the Royal Academy had formerly held their exhibitions. The catalogue explicitly states that the sale was being held at the wish of Mrs. Bentley, the widow, who evidently desired to realise this part of her husband's estate more quickly than if it had been disposed of through the usual channels. There were 1,200 lots to be sold, and many contained several items (in some cases as many as ten). The catalogue of this sale is preserved in the archives of Messrs. Christie, Manson & Woods. The names of the buyers are, for the most part, identifiable, and prices are given, so that records of the sale are now a useful guide to the market of the time, as well as to the decorative wares which Wedgwood & Bentley were offering for sale, not all of which appear in the trade catalogues.

Prices at the sale seem to have been uneven. In some cases, perhaps in most, they were similar to, or slightly lower than, the prevailing showroom prices (so far as we know them) at the time of Bentley's death, and in a few cases they were actually higher. Examples include a set of five Etruscan vases*, £1 10s. 6d.; a set of three bas-relief jasper plaques for chimney pieces* £4 4s.; three tall painted Etruscan vases, £6 6s.; a chimney piece set of plaques of a *Sacrifice to Flora** and a pair of *Muses**, £9 9s.; and a chimney piece set of three encaustic* paintings, £15 4s. 6d. These prices help to put into perspective

the £35 which Wedgwood charged ten years later for copies of the first edition of the Portland* vase. They are, of course, in gold sovereigns, and would need to be multiplied by at least fifty to bring them to a notional equivalent of today's paper money (1978).

Auerbach

Russian faience factory, founded in the village of Domkino (Korchova district of the Tver province) in 1809 by Friedrich Christian Brinner. From 1810 the factory was owned by Andrei Auerbach, and rapidly achieved distinction, becoming the leading pottery in Russia. Much of the cream-coloured earthenware, particularly the services with simple hand-painted borders of vines or foliage, closely resemble Wedgwood's, and appear to be in conscious imitation of them.

The factory was sold in 1870 to the monopolist of the Russian ceramic industry, M.S. Kuznetsov.

Augustus Caesar (63 B.C.-A.D.14)

First Roman Emperor, adopted by his uncle, Julius Caesar*. His name was originally Octavian, and Augustus was a title conferred on him by the Senate and the people in 27 B.C. He was succeeded by Tiberius.

A portrait medallion*, 3ins. by 2½ins., appears in the 1777 Catalogue* among the list of Illustrious Romans, and a bust, 22ins. high, was supplied by Oliver & Hoskins* in 1774. It was re-finished by Hackwood* and reproduced in basaltes.

Aurora

The Greek Eos, goddess of the Dawn. At the end of the night she rose from the bed of her husband, Tithonus, and in a chariot drawn by swift horses she ascended from Oceanus to the heavens to announce the coming of the Sun.

Wedgwood subjects:

Aurora, goddess of the Dawn, cameo. Modelled by William Hackwood from a cast supplied by Hoskins & Grant 1779.

Aurora, black transfer print* from an engraving by W. Greatbatch* enamelled in colours on Queen's ware teapots, c.1775.

Austin, Arnold (fl.1904-1947)

Modeller at Etruria and Barlaston. He modelled a bust of Josiah Wedgwood taken from the monument in Stoke-on-Trent Church.

Austin, J.A. (fl.1904-1927)

Modeller at Etruria*; son of Arnold Austin*..

Aventurine Glaze

A glaze so called from its resemblance to the natural stone. The glaze usually has copper particles suspended in it which imitate gold. The Venetians, among others, made glass of this kind. Wedgwood's aventurine glaze was developed by Norman Wilson* in the 1950s for the decoration of ornamental pieces produced in small quantities under the general description of unique* ware. The glaze is of a distinctive deep reddish brown with flecks of metal which reflect light as dull gold. The glaze was used principally for the interior of Queen's ware bowls, the exterior being glazed black enamel. Examples are rare.

Baby Feeder

Small teapot-shaped vessel with a long curved nipple spout, made c.1810. Unmarked specimens in cream-coloured ware and stoneware occur, c.1777.

See: Bubby pot.

Bacchae or Bacchantes (Maenads)

Female companions of Bacchus, represented as crowned with vine leaves, and clothed in the skins of fawns. They were priestesses who, with the aid of wine, became frenzied during the Dionysiac festivals.

See: Bacchus.

Bacchus

The Roman name associated with Dionysus, the son of Zeus and Semele. Usually portrayed as youthful and physically effeminate, Bacchus was the god of wine. He wandered through Egypt, Syria, and much of Asia teaching mankind the cultivation of the vine and the arts of civilization. The celebration of Bacchic festivals were particularly frenzied and lascivious. Women taking part in them were known as Bacchantes, and Bacchus was also accompanied by fauns*, satyrs* and centaurs*, who pursued the women. Small boys, the dolphin*, panther and ass were all associated with Bacchus, as were the vine, laurel and ivy. A large number of Wedgwood bas-reliefs* portray Bacchus and his attendants, and the list has been complicated by the alternative names for them, some of which appear to have been used in the Catalogues* and others added by later writers.

The following have been identified:

Bacchus, bas-relief head, 2¾ins. by 1¾ins. by Flaxman*, 1777.

Baby Feeder. *Small coffee pot-shaped baby feeder or bubby pot, with long curved spout ending in a perforated nipple, printed in underglaze blue with the Hibiscus pattern. c.1810. 5½ ins. high. Buten Museum.*

Bacchus, large bas-relief head, 8ins. by 6ins., supplied by Hoskins & Grant*, 1775.

Bacchus, figure after Sansovino, height 11ins., prior to 1773.

Bacchus, large bust supplied by Hoskins & Grant, 1779.

Bacchus and Apollo, probably a bas-relief, supplied by Bacon*, 1777.

Bacchus and Faun, figure, height 17ins.

Bacchus and Panther, tablet, 6ins. by 11ins., produced prior to 1773, but new models in 1776. After the bas-relief on the monument of Lysicrates at Athens, and probably taken from an engraving published by Stuart* and Revett (*Die Althümer zu Athen);* Robert Adam* reproduced the entire frieze at Stowe in 1771.

Bacchus. Triumph of Bacchus, *blue and white jasper tablet similar to that on the facing page, but with two figures added. This and the* Triumph of Bacchus *tablet shown opposite, illustrate Wedgwood's practice of making up plaques and tablets from figures originally modelled for different subjects.* Wedgwood.

Bacchus. Triumph of Bacchus, *tablet 7⅛ ins. by 9¾ ins. in blue and white jasper. No.53 in the 1779 Catalogue. Scratched mark in script 'WEDGWOOD & BENTLEY.' Bacchus, seated in a car beneath a canopy of vine leaves and grapes, accompanied by Silenus. Modelled by Hackwood, 1778.* Dwight and Lucille Beeson Collection.

Bacchus. Bacchus and Panther. *Blue and white jasper oval tablet, 6ins. by 11ins., after the bas-relief on the tomb of Lysicrates at Athens, but probably copied from an engraving published by James 'Athenian' Stuart.* Dwight and Lucille Beeson Collection.

Bacchus. *Jasper medallion showing an elderly Bacchus, identifiable from the vine leaves and grapes.* Wedgwood.

Bacchus with urn and grapes, medallion, 3⅜ ins. by 2½ ins., prior to 1779. Attributed to Hackwood*.

Birth of Bacchus, tablet by Hackwood, 1776 (pair to *Triumph*), after a marble vase by the Athenian sculptor, Salpion*, now in the Naples Museum, and adapted from an engraving in Montfaucon*.

Birth of Bacchus, tablet copied and restored by Flaxman from a carnelian from the so-called *Cachet of Michelangelo,* 11ins. by 23ins., 1782.

Education of Bacchus, tablet, after a bas-relief on a sarcophagus in the Capitoline Museum.

Indian Bacchus, medallion, 4ins. by 5ins., by Flaxman, 1776.

Indian Bacchus, medallion, 6ins. by 4½ ins. by Hackwood, 1776 (pair to head of an old Satyr).

Sacrifice to Bacchus (also *Sacrifice to Pan*), tablet, 8¼ ins. by 19ins. and 9½ ins. by 22ins., 1778.

Triumph of Bacchus, tablet, 6½ ins. by 14ins. and 7¼ ins. by 10ins. by Hackwood. Pair to *Birth,* 1776.

Triumph of Bacchus and Ariadne, tablet, 9½ ins. by 23ins. and 10¾ ins. by 26ins., produced prior to 1773.

Bacchus. *Buff terracotta tablet, 21¼ ins. by 9¼ ins., known as* Bacchanalian Triumph *or* Bacchanalian Procession, *attributed to Voyez, c.1768-69. This subject occurs also in black basaltes. The tablet illustrated weighs 54lbs.* Dwight and Lucille Beeson Collection.

Bacchanalian Boys (at various pursuits), set of six bas-reliefs after Duquesnoy* (see also: Mrs. Mary Landré).

Bacchanalian Boys, three medallions and a large composite tablet (see: Lady Diana Beauclerk).

Bacchanalian Dance, see below: *Bacchanalian Triumph.*

Bacchanalian Figures, five separate figures ''from an antique vase'' (perhaps the Borghese* vase) by Landré*, 1769.

Bacchanalian Sacrifice, 'long square tablet', 9ins. by 21ins. (pair to *Bacchanalian Triumph* or *Procession:* see below), attributed to Voyez*, c.1768-69, after Clodion*.

Bacchanalian Triumph (Bacchanalian Procession), 'long square tablet', 9ins. by 21ins. (pair to *Bacchanalian Sacrifice*), attributed to Voyez, c.1768-69, after Clodion.

Bacchanalian Triumph (Bacchanalian Dance), tablet, 8ins. by 19½ins., ornamented with ten figures from the Borghese Vase*, now in the Louvre, Paris. Five of these may have been re-modelled from the casts supplied by Landré (see above: *Bacchanalian Figures*), but there is more reason to suppose that they were modelled afresh by De Vaere*, c.1788. Single figures from either group were used for medallions, and the entire composition appears on Wedgwood's jasper Borghese vase.

Bacchante Running, figure after Clodion.

Bacchantes, Two, bas-relief by Angelini*.

Bacchante and Children, one of the set of six bas-reliefs by Landré (see above: *Bacchanalian Boys*).

Panther and Bacchanalian Boys (erroneously *Romulus and Remus*), tablet 7½ins. by 10ins., first catalogued 1777.

Triumph of Bacchanalian Boys, cameo, 1½ins. by 2ins., c.1775.

Bacon, John, Senior, RA (1740-1799)

English sculptor, born in Southwark, London. Bacon is believed to have been apprenticed, at the age of fourteen, at a porcelain factory in Bow Churchyard, East London, and one or two Bow porcelain models of exceptional quality have been attributed to him, though without supporting evidence. About 1769 he went to work for Coade* at Lambeth, at the same time studying at the Royal Academy Schools, and early in that year he modelled two reliefs, *Day* and *Night,* for Wedgwood, to whom he had already submitted a model of *Apollo and Daphne.* A receipt preserved in the Wedgwood archives, dated 28th July, 1769, shows that he was paid £9 15s. for modelling work. In the same year he won the first Gold Medal for sculpture ever awarded by the Academy for his bas-relief* *Aeneas escaping from Troy,* and nine years later he was awarded the Gold Medal of the Society of Arts for his statues of Mars* and Venus*. He later executed a large number of statues, groups and monuments.

None of Bacon's work for Wedgwood has been identified with certainty, though the list of work attributed to him without supporting evidence is a long one. The most convincing attribution (Alison Kelly, *Decorative Wedgwood,* p.25) is that of the six plaques, 16ins. diameter, among the Herculaneum* Subjects: *Centaur* (with Bacchante on his back), *Centaur* (with child on her back), *Centaur* (teaching Achilles), *Polyphemus,* and *Marsyas and Young Olympus.* Elsewhere (see: Figures) it is suggested that figures modelled by Bacon in London may have been cast by Hoskins & Grant*.

Baddeley, Edward Gerrard (fl.1834-1889)

Engraver of Hanley; worked for Wedgwood 1852-1877.

Baddeley, William (fl.c.1795-1825)

Potter of Eastwood, Hanley, manufacturing creamware*, cane* ware and Black Egyptian*. His use of the impressed mark, 'Eastwood', generally on the lower edge of the front of his wares (not on the base), has led to the charge that he intended to mislead purchasers into believing that they were buying Wedgwood. There appears, however, to be no evidence that Baddeley was guilty of any intent to deceive. The finial in the shape of a swan with the head bent towards the tail seems to be peculiar to Baddeley.

Bail Handle

An overarching ceramic handle found on teapots and kettles. In the case of teapots, it replaces the handle on the side opposite to the spout. Wedgwood's bail handles were fixed, but some factories also made them to swivel downwards to one side. The bail handle first appears on some late 17th century Chinese porcelain spouted wine pots exported to Europe for use as teapots. It was employed in the 18th century by Wedgwood principally for basaltes* teapots, and more rarely for other bodies. Wedgwood continued to make occasional use of it in the 19th century, and porcelain teapots were made with this type of handle, which is more convenient if more vulnerable. It was also employed by Coalport* around 1820, and a specimen from this factory is in the Victoria and Albert Museum.

Bain Marie

A French term for a covered basin heated, or kept warm, by hot water. Part of a food warmer*. Made by Wedgwood in cream-coloured ware.

Bakewell, James (fl.1750-1775)

Painter at Burslem and London, 1769-73. He was evidently employed at first in the painting of Etruscan Vases*, but in May 1770, Josiah wrote to Bentley: "Bakewell has set his mind to be a good enamel Painter and really improves much both in flowers and in Copying figures". In the same year Wedgwood sent him to Liverpool to engage "half a dozen or half a score of the blue and white [delft] painters who are much better adapted to our business than the China painters [enamellers]." In April 1771, he was employed to draw flowers for Sadler & Green to engrave. Dessert plates and dishes, often with a feather edge*, painted in an attractively free style with naturalistic sprays of flowers in crimson or purple, or black and yellow, are thought to be Bakewell's work, and he was among the artists employed on landscapes for the Frog* service.

Bakewell, James. *Compôtier painted in puce with a central flower and Husk border in the style of James Bakewell. c.1765.* Wedgwood.

Ball Clay

Dark-coloured clay, which becomes paler in firing, quarried in Devon and Dorset but found elsewhere in the world. It is used in earthenware and stoneware to give strength and plasticity to the body.

Bamboo Ware

Wares such as teapots, root pots, vases, etc. made in imitation of short lengths of bamboo. The use of bamboo forms for this purpose was undoubtedly suggested by small Chinese porcelain wine pots and vases similarly moulded, which were popular during the early years of the 18th century. Wedgwood first made objects in this form about 1770 in cane* ware, and a dark coloured cane ware, approaching the colour of the bamboo, was reserved for the purpose. Bamboo objects were usually decorated with encaustic* or glossy enamels. They included flower holders (groups of graduated bamboo canes on a simulated earth base), bough pots and teaware. Similar models, occur, somewhat oddly, in jasper and basaltes, but are rare.

Bamboo shapes in primrose jasper decorated with terracotta coloured leaves, a colour scheme echoing the cane and *rosso antico* of the 18th century, were produced in 1977. Objects include a teapot, creamer and sugar box.

Banks, Sir Joseph (1743-1820)

English naturalist and friend of Josiah Wedgwood's. Educated at Harrow, Eton and Christ Church, Oxford, he accompanied Captain Cook to the southern hemisphere in 1768 and was largely responsible for introducing the sugar-cane and the bread-fruit tree into the West Indies. He was elected Fellow of the Royal Society, and was President from 1778 until his death. Created baronet in 1781, he received the Order of the Bath in 1795, becoming a Privy Councillor in 1797. Sir Joseph was an Associate of the National Institute of France, and a member of the Board of Trade. In his latter capacity he helped William Billingsley to establish his porcelain manufacture in 1814.

In 1789 Sir Joseph supplied Wedgwood with samples of clay from New South Wales, sent to him by Vice-Admiral Arthur Phillip, first governor. Phillip was responsible for the naming of Sydney (after Thomas Townshend, 1st Viscount Sydney). From this sample Hackwood modelled the jasper bas-relief* entitled *Hope addressing Peace, Art and Labour,* better known as the Sydney Cove medallion*.

A jasper portrait medallion of Sir Joseph was modelled by Flaxman* in 1775, and a large portrait (diameter of long axis 10·9ins.) was produced from another Flaxman model in 1779. A third portrait, a pair to one of Lady Banks, appears in the 1788 catalogue and was not issued before 1781.

Banks, Thomas, RA (1735-1805)

English sculptor; apprenticed to W. Barlow in 1750 and, at the same time, studied in the studio of Peter Scheemakers. He was also employed by William Kent. Banks received a premium from the Society of Arts in 1763, and in 1770 he gained a Gold Medal from the Royal Academy for a bas-relief of *The Rape of Proserpine.* In 1772 the Academy gave him a travelling student-ship, and he went to Rome where he stayed for seven years. He returned to London in 1779, and then travelled to St. Petersburg in 1781. There he executed a number of works for Catherine II* (the Great) and members of her court, returning to England in 1783. The remainder of his life was principally devoted to commissions for monuments and chimney pieces*. No definite attribution of Wedgwood models can be made to Thomas Banks at present, but in a letter of 16th June, 1787, to Sir William Hamilton, Wedgwood writes: "...Mr. Banks, a very able statuary in London, whom you must have known in Italy, and another artist in town, have promised to employ all the time they can spare for me." At that period, Banks was engaged in carving chimney pieces, including one for Beckford's Fonthill, several for Richard Cosway's house, and

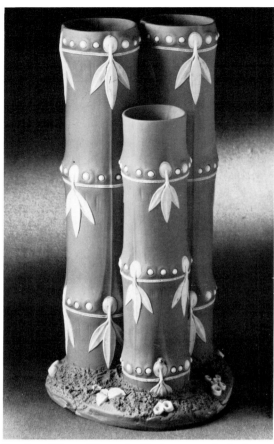

Bamboo Ware. *Cane ware part teaset, enamelled in blue, ornamented with* Bacchanalian Boys *after Duquesnoy, and moulded to simulate bamboo. The teapot and jug have unusual split bamboo handles, and the covered jug and sugar box bamboo knops to the lids. Mark 'Wedgwood' impressed. c.1785-1790.* Christie's.

Bamboo Ware. *Blue and white jasper vase in the form of three tubes of bamboo. Vases of this type were made also in cane and black basaltes.* Wedgwood.

the famous chimney piece at Warren Hastings's Daylesford House. It is possible, therefore, that Banks designed and carved chimney pieces specifically to include Wedgwood tablets*.

Barium Sulphate

An essential ingredient of jasper* ware, which consists of about 50 per cent clay, Cornish stone, and flint, and 50 per cent of barytes (heavy spar, Derbyshire Spar, or Cawk) which is composed of barium sulphate with a small quantity of barium carbonate. Jasper is the only ceramic body which contains sulphate as a major ingredient. Unless a colour is added jasper is virtually white and, if thin enough, is translucent. Ordinary porcelain, of course, is not translucent if its thickness is greater than (on the average) 5mm. Cawk (barium sulphate) is number 74 or 'Radix Jasperini' in Wedgwood's code.

See: Codes and Formulae; Spath.

Barlaston

The 382-acre estate, near the village of Barlaston, bought by Wedgwood in 1937 as the site of the new factory, the foundation stone of which was laid on 10th September, 1938. Architects for the factory were Keith Murray* and his partner, Charles White. Louis de Soissons, architect of Welwyn Garden City, was responsible for the garden village of one hundred houses for employees. The earthenware factory was moved from Etruria* shortly before the 1939-45 war, and the bone china* factory was completed in 1949, when the produc-

tion of jasper*, discontinued during the war, was resumed.

In the new factory firing is by six electric tunnel-ovens, the first to be used in Great Britain, and all mechanical processes are powered by electricity. Since the original purchase and building programme the estate has been increased to five hundred acres, and the factory, planned for seven hundred workers with a possible extension to accommodate one thousand, has been expanded to employ more than 2,500. Further expansion, costing £4½ million, will be completed at the Barlaston factory by the end of 1980.

Visitors to the factory now number more than 100,000 a year, and a large demonstration area, where they may see many of the most interesting manufacturing processes, a lecture theatre and cinema, and a new Wedgwood Museum*, were completed in 1969.

Barlaston Hall

1.   A large 18th century bow-fronted house standing on a rise overlooking the Barlaston estate. Neglected for many years by succeeding owners, it became the subject of public controversy in the 1970s when the dangerous state of the building and the enormous cost of restoration persuaded the Wedgwood directors to apply for a government grant towards its restoration, and, when adequate funds were not made available, for its demolition.

2.   A design created by Alfred Powell* in 1942, and painted in purple lustre (see lustre decoration) on a circular Queen's ware plaque, 24ins. in diameter.

Barlaston Mug

Mug designed in 1940 to mark the opening of the new factory. The designs were the work of Eric Ravilious*, who signed the mug. Drawings for prints were done by Victor Skellern*, and Paul Hulme* was responsible for the engraving.

Barlaston Shape

A full range of tableware shapes designed in 1955 by Norman Wilson* and modelled by Eric Owen* to supersede the plain coloured bodies* in traditional shapes*, the popularity of which was beginning to decline. Two-colour clay* patterns

(produced by using the techniques of inlaying and slip-decorating) included *Summer Sky* (lavender* and cream colour), *Barlaston Green* (celadon* and cream colour), *Havana* (chocolate and cream colour), *Moonlight* (grey and cream colour) and *Harvest Moon* (cane and cream colour). Among the most successful lithographed and enamelled patterns were *Brecon, Mayfield, Penshurst* and *Woodbury*.

Barlow, Francis (1626?-1704)
Painter and engraver, often described as the first English painter of sporting subjects whose name is known. His drawings for *Hunting, Hawking, and Fishing* were engraved by Wenceslaus Hollar in 1671. His best known work is his 110 illustrations to the 1687 edition of *Aesop's Fables**, a number of which were copied for the decoration of early Queen's ware transfer-printed* plates.

Barnard, Harry (1862-1933)
Artist, author, potter, designer and modeller; born in Canonbury, London. Barnard left school at fifteen to work in the modelling shop of the family business of silversmiths in St. Martin's-le-Grand, but shortly afterwards enrolled at the Royal School (now Royal College) of Art to study drawing and modelling. He later attended evening classes at the Kennington Road City and Guilds School. During this period he was already employed by Doulton, whom he had joined in 1880. At the Doulton Lambeth studios he worked under Mark Marshall, making ornamental vases, commemorative jugs ornamented with portrait medallions, and unique exhibition pieces in collaboration with Marshall, Hannah Barlow, Eliza Simmance and others. By the age of twenty-two he had become under-manager of the studios, which then employed 325 women and 45 men and boys. During his fifteen years' service he invented and perfected many processes in production and decoration.

In 1895 he resigned and joined James Mackintyre of Cobridge, where he introduced a new form of decoration, a form of *pâte-sur-pâte,* which he called 'gesso'. Two years later he joined Wedgwood at Etruria, where he applied his decorating techniques to bone china*, jasper*, majolica*, and tiles*, becoming manager of the tile department in 1899.

In 1902 he moved to London in the key sales position of London Manager, returning to Etruria in 1919. He was given the special task of expanding the Museum, then in the charge of John Cook, but in the same year he was requested by Major Frank Wedgwood to produce a new edition of the Portland* vase, the trials for which occupied him for four years (as did the first Josiah's for the issue of 1790), and he produced his first good vase in 1923. During the following twelve months he made thirteen vases, of which only seven were good, but by the end of 1930 (the bicentenary year of Josiah Wedgwood's birth) he had produced 195, of which only 13 were rejected. Most of these were mounted on a reflecting mirror stand and sold for twenty guineas. Others were set on a special stand, designed by Barnard, incorporating jasper replicas of the four panels of the original sarcophagus in miniature.

In 1927 Barnard made the largest piece of Wedgwood ware ever produced. This was a basaltes* panel 53ins. square and 5ins. thick for Beeshy's English China Store* at Ridgway, Ontario. The relief shows a Georgian potter at work on the kick-wheel, with the words: 'Within the Potter's House...surrounded by the Shapes of Clay' *(Omar Khayyam)* on the panel above. Barnard solved the problem of firing such a large panel without warping by cutting it into forty-two pieces of irregular shape, like the pieces of a stained glass window, and jointing them together in a previously-prepared screen when they came out of the oven.

Four years later Harry Barnard fell victim to the retrenchment made necessary at Wedgwood after years of trade depression. He was in his seventieth year, and a less active man might have expected to retire somewhat earlier. He

Barnard, Harry. *Spill vase. Trial piece, twice-dipped jasper — dark blue over crimson over white — with sgraffito and trailed slip ornaments, the inscription, 'H.B. trial 5.2.98' applied in pale blue. 3ins. high.* Buten Museum.

Barnard, Harry. *Pale blue and white jasper mug, 6ins. high, with floral decoration typical of Barnard's work. Signed.* Buten Museum.

Barnard, Harry. *Creamware vase designed and made by Harry Barnard. c.1920.* Zeitlin Collection.

Basaltes, Bronzed and Gilt. *Black basaltes vase with bronze and gilt ornament, 12ins. high. c.1880. Zeitlin Collection.*

Basaltes, Bronzed and Gilt. *Pair of basaltes vases with reliefs in bronze and gold. The technique and appearance of the vase decoration is to some extent influenced by contemporary interest in Japanese bronzes. 7¼ ins. high including plinth. Sotheby's Belgravia.*

accepted, with reluctance, a cut of 75 per cent in his salary, but continued to lecture on Wedgwood all round the country, and to make unique pieces of his own design which were fired at Etruria. He died in January 1933 at Newcastle-under-Lyme.

Harry Barnard's work for Wedgwood, of which no full record survives, included extensive repairs to the bust of Sir Walter Raleigh (See: Hoskins & Grant), a bust of George Bernard Shaw (1931), fifty-four portrait medallions and six busts for the Cameograph Company*, 195 Portland vases, the Beeshy basaltes panel, and some original pieces of Queen's ware and jasper (particularly the rare crimson jasper*) using traditional trailed slip and *sgraffito** techniques. Much of his work remains to be identified. In 1924 he published *Chats on Wedgwood Ware,* an admirable short study of the subject.

Barnsley, Grace (fl.1920-1950)
English pottery decorator who, with her husband Oscar Davies*, opened the Roeginga Pottery at Rainham, Kent, where she decorated matt glaze* pottery with enamel colours. She worked for Wedgwood during the 1920s and 1930s.

Barret, George, the Elder, RA (1728-1784)
A proficient landscape painter, born in Dublin, who was a founder-member of the Royal Academy and succeeded, in spite of earning 2,000 guineas a year, in becoming bankrupt. He is regarded as one of the founders of the English school of watercolour painters. His two sons and a daughter earned their living as artists, the most celebrated being George (1767-1842). Wedgwood obtained landscapes from George Barret, Senior, which were copied for the Frog* service, but no evidence has been found to support previous statements that Barret was employed at the Chelsea Decorating Studio*.

Barrett, Joseph
A painter who worked on the Frog* service at the Chelsea Decorating Studio*.

Bartolozzi, Francesco (1727-1816)
Italian engraver who arrived in England in 1764. He made many engravings after Angelica Kauffmann and Giovanni Cipriani*. He popularised the stipple engraving: one in which the picture is made up of many small dots variably spaced rather than lines, with an effect somewhat resembling an ordinary modern half-tone block. The stipple technique was first employed for the decoration of pottery and porcelain towards the end of the 18th century when it was transferred to the glaze by a process known as bat printing*.

Wedgwood copied engravings by Bartolozzi as follows:
The Children of Flora (Spring).
The Marriage of Cupid and Psyche.
The Four Seasons, Cipriani design.
Summer, Cipriani design.
Winter, Cipriani design.

Barton, Glenys (b.1944)
Glenys Barton, born in the Potteries, gained a place in the Ceramics School of the Royal College of Art, and then became a lecturer in Ceramics at the Camberwell College of Art. She was invited to become 'artist in residence' at Barlaston* in 1976, which gave her the use of facilities at the factory to develop her designs for ceramic sculpture. Subsequently, on the 14th June, 1977, the Craft Advisory Committee put on an Exhibition at their Waterloo Place Gallery, London, S.W. called *Man and Space: Glenys Barton at Wedgwood.* About thirty of her works were included. They were in bone china*, and mainly featured the nude male figure, the torso, and the head, in geometric and architectural settings. An illustrated catalogue on the exhibition was published containing an appreciation by art-critic, Edward Lucie-Smith, and a discussion of Glenys Barton's work in its historical context by John V. Mallet, Keeper of the Department of Ceramics, Victoria and Albert Museum. The majority of the pieces were produced in editions limited to four copies. A few were produced in editions ranging from ten to fifty copies. Glenys Barton's work is represented in the collections of the Victoria and Albert Museum, the Stockholm Museum, and the Pennsylvania State University Museum of Modern Art. She was the British prize winner at the International Ceramics Exhibition, 1972.

Basalt

Name of a very hard stone, black in colour, employed by the Egyptians and others for sculpture, and mainly worked with abrasive substances such as emery (carborundum). Basaltes is the name given by Josiah Wedgwood to his black stoneware from its resemblance in appearance to the stone, and, like basalt, it is extremely hard.

See: Black Basaltes.

Basaltes, Bronzed and Gilt

Basaltes vases and urns with the relief ornament decorated with bronze and gold were made for a short period from c.1880. Production seems to have been small, and fine examples are now rare.

See: Bronze and Gold; Bronzed Basaltes.

Basket Work

See: Osier.

Bas-relief

Term normally used in sculpture for decoration in low relief; i.e. ornament which projects only slightly above the level of the surface, as distinct from high relief (alto rilievo) in which perhaps as much as a half or two-thirds projects from the surface. Most jasper decoration is in bas-relief, although there are a few rare examples of high relief.

Bas-relief Ware

The name given by Wedgwood in 1800 to a white vitreous stoneware body with jasper dip* and bas-relief ornament. The range of pieces produced included teaware, jugs and flower pots. Bas-relief stoneware is rougher and more granular in texture than jasper, and is easily distinguished from it.

Bastille Medallions

The storming of the Bastille on 14th July, 1789, was announced in London by the *Morning Post* in terms of glowing approval. Charles James Fox hailed it as "...the greatest event...that ever happened in the world!" Josiah Wedgwood, Joseph Priestley*, and William Blake* were among those radicals who shared this sympathy for the Revolution. Josiah wrote to Erasmus Darwin*: "I know you will rejoice with me in the glorious revolution which has taken place in France. The politicians tell me that as a manufacturer I shall be ruined if France has her liberty, but I am willing to take my chance in that respect..." Later, with others, he was to modify this enthusiasm, but meanwhile he was not slow to take advantage of powerful Whig support for the revolutionaries. He issued a number of 'French' medallions, the most important of which were the pair commemorating the storming and fall of the Bastille. Measuring 2⅞ins. in diameter the medallions bear the inscriptions: 'LE TRIOMPHE DE LA VALEUR FRANCOISE' and: 'LE DESPOTISME ABATTU' above the bas-relief scenes illustrating the event. They were in production within fifteen weeks of the first announcement in London.

Bat

1. A thin disc of clay used in making plates on the jolley.
2. A slab of soft glue or gelatine employed in certain kinds of transfer printing (see: Bat printing).
3. A thin slab of fireclay used in placing ware in the kiln.

See: Processes of Manufacture.

Bat Printing

Towards the end of the 18th century 'bats' of soft glue or gelatine were used instead of paper for taking impressions from stipple engravings — the latter a technique popularised by Bartolozzi* in which the picture is made up of a series of dots

Bateman, S. *Plaque,* On the Mersey. *20ins. by 14⅛ins., signed and dated 1886.* Sotheby's Belgravia.

which vary in number and spacing according to the depth of tone necessary to make up the design. The impression was taken from the engraved plate on to the 'bat' *in oil,* and the surface of the 'bat' was then dusted with ceramic colour in powder form.

In modern times Wedgwood use an automatic transfer printing machine which takes an imprint from an inked copper plate on an appropriately shaped gelatine pad, which is then lowered on to the article to print the design.

See: Transfer Printing.

Batavian Ware

See: Rockingham.

Bateman, Josiah (fl.1800-1842)

Travelling salesman for Wedgwood. His orders have been preserved almost intact in the archives, as well as notes on the current public demand, and news of wares being introduced by competitors. He travelled mainly in the north and west with a horse and gig, putting up for the night at inns.

Bateman, S. (fl.1880-1890)

Artist, whose signature appears upon three Wedgwood Queen's ware plaques painted in an *impasto* technique in coloured slip*. Two of these plaques, 20ins. by 14⅛ins., are dated 1886, one showing fishing smacks at sunset on the Mersey, and the other a scene of cows in a country stream. Nothing appears to be known of Bateman, and no record of his work had been discovered among the Wedgwood archives. The presence of his monogram incised in the clay before firing indicates, however, that these plaques were not supplied by Wedgwood for decorating outside the factory.

Batteries, Electric

The Shape Book for 1880 (page 43, nos. 2041 and 2032) illustrates clylindrical pots for electric batteries, and a round porous cell. These were for the construction of Leclanché cells, a type of electric battery in which the positive pole was a zinc rod, and the negative pole a carbon rod placed inside a porous cell filled with manganese oxide and carbon, the whole being immersed in the pot, which was filled with sal ammoniac solution. This produced an electric current by chemical reaction when the circuit was closed between the positive and negative poles. Although the voltage was small, the current relatively weak, and the cell soon exhausted, nevertheless it recovered fairly quickly, and it was therefore employed in the home in the 1880s for that novelty, the electric bell, for which Wedgwood also made bell pushes. Leclanché cells were usually made of glass, and the employment of pottery for the purpose was unusual.

In the same Shape Book, no. 2040 represents a Voltaic trough, a vessel of rectangular section employed for another type of cell which nevertheless worked on the same basic principle, i.e. the production of electricity by bringing together two dissimilar metals immersed in a suitable liquid. It operated similarly to the Leclanché cells, already mentioned.

Bawden, Edward, CBE, RA (b.1903)

Painter in watercolour and book-illustrator. Born at Braintree, Essex. Studied at the Cambridge School of Art and the Royal College of Art, London, Assistant Professor, School of Design,

Beane's Patent Tea Infuser. *An urn-shaped vessel of Queen's ware with a pewter spigot, holding up to six cups of tea. The interior holds a pewter container for tea leaves. c.1890.* Buten Museum.

Beattie, William. *Carrara group,* The Sacrifice *(Abraham offering up his son, Isaac), 24ins. by 14ins. c.1857.* Buten Museum.

Royal College of Art. Freelance designer for Wedgwood from 1930. War artist during World War II. He was elected Member of the Royal Academy in 1956. The *Heartsease* pattern was designed by him in 1952 for the Orient Shipping Line.

Beane's Patent Tea Infuser

An urn-shaped vessel in Queen's ware on a high foot, with a domed cover and a pewter spigot. Inside, a pewter container holds tea leaves at varying levels according to the number of cups of tea required, from two to six. The impressed mark reads 'WEDGWOOD BEANES PATENT TEA INFUSER'. Made about 1890.

Beattie, William (fl.1829-1867)

Neo-classical* sculptor and modeller who exhibited at the Royal Academy from 1829 to 1864, and at the Great Exhibition in 1851, when he displayed a large silver vase with a statuette of the Prince Consort. He was employed as a modeller by Wedgwood, Minton*, Copeland, and Adams*, and Parian* figures by him inscribed 'A U of G' on the base were probably made for the Art Union of Glasgow. He was at Etruria from 1856 to 1864, and his works for Wedgwood include the following:

Abraham offering up his son, Isaac, majolica* group, also made in Carrara* ware.

America, Carrara ware figure. Design of 1867. *England, Ireland,* and *Scotland,* figures.

Joseph before Pharaoh, c.1856, majolica group, also made in Carrara ware.

Joseph interpreting Pharaoh's Dream, model after Benjamin E. Spence, 1867.

According to Gunnis, *Dictionary of British Sculptors,* Beattie also modelled *The Finding of Moses* and *The Flute Player* for Wedgwood.

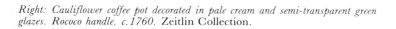

Above: A melon-shape teapot decorated in green and yellow glazes, with rococo spout and handle, and flower knop. c.1762. Zeitlin Collection.

Right: Cauliflower coffee pot decorated in pale cream and semi-transparent green glazes. Rococo handle. c.1760. Zeitlin Collection.

Left: Wedgwood & Bentley period creamware variegated vase, ornamented with an applied figure of Apollo with his lyre, the handles with mask terminals, on a black basaltes base. c.1772. Zeitlin Collection.

Below: One of a pair of crystalline bulb pots of D-shape, length 9⅝ ins., decorated in mottled green colour known as Serpentine. Some traces of original oil gilding on the relief floral swags and acanthus border. c.1785. Zeitlin Collection.

Beauclerk, Lady Diana. *Bowl on foot and a covered box, the bowl inspired by metal and decorated with a relief of* Bacchanalian Boys, *designed by Lady Diana Beauclerk in 1783, with rich festoons. The interior is lapidary polished. Diameter 8⅞ ins., height 5ins. The box is less richly ornamented with boys at play after a Beauclerk design.* Wedgwood.

Below left: **Beehive Shape.** *Cup and saucer, the cup moulded with beehive relief.* Wedgwood.

Below: **Beehive Shape.** *Queen's ware honey pot in the form of a beehive.* Wedgwood.

Beauclerk, Lady Diana (1724-1808)

Amateur artist who supplied designs to Bartolozzi* for engraving, and to Wedgwood for reproduction as bas-reliefs*. The daughter of the second Duke of Marlborough, she married Lord Bolingbroke in 1757, and, when this union was dissolved, the witty but insanitary Topham Beauclerk. Horace Walpole was her devoted friend, praising her designs and collecting Wedgwood jasper decorated with ornaments modelled from them. Her work is sometimes confused with that of Miss Crewe* and Lady Templetown*. All three designed in the sentimental manner that was part of the neo-classical* style in the last quarter of the 18th century. Diana Beauclerk ('Lady Di') supplied designs to Wedgwood from 1785 to 1789, the first being sent to Josiah by Charles James Fox. They were principally *Bacchanalian Boys,* although most of them seem singularly innocent to be companions of Bacchus. Three medallions and one tablet ornamented with her designs appear in the 1787 Catalogue*:

Group of three Boys (two carrying the third), adapted from the right-hand group of Clodion's* *Bacchanalian Sacrifice* (see: Bacchus), 5½ ins. by 4½ ins.

Group of two Boys, 5½ ins by 4½ ins. and 3½ ins. by 2¾ ins.

Four Boys, single. 4½ ins. x 3¾ ins.

Bacchanalian tablet of six boys (from the two preceding medallions) "under arbours, with panthers' skins in festoons". 5½ ins. by 26ins. A variant on this theme, with five boys, measures 5¼ ins. by 12½ ins.

Many other designs are attributed to Lady Diana, but none with certainty.

Bedford Vase

The name given to a vase of black basaltes* ware, made late in 1768 or early in 1769, and decorated with a medallion* in low relief. It was one of the first vases to be decorated with a medallion, but it cannot now be identified with certainty. It must have been extremely popular at the time, and no doubt specimens still exist, but are unrecognised. Wedgwood wrote in February, 1769: "We have about a dozen of them ordered...Mr. Cox* has been running about to several Noblemen this evening and says I must order 1000. He says the Medallion alone would sell it."

Bedson, William (fl.1773-1777)

Modeller at Etruria*. In 1777 he was sent to take casts from Sir Robert Newdigate's collection of antique marbles and plaster casts at Arbury Hall, Warwickshire. Twenty-nine of these, reproduced in jasper (some with extensive remodelling by Hackwood* and others) are listed in the 1779 Catalogue.

Beehive Shape

A shape imitating bound reeds or straw, which first appears in the form of a honey pot in the 1817 catalogue of Queen's ware shapes engraved by William Blake*. Honey pots in this shape have been produced in Queen's ware with a yellow glaze or Dysart glaze*, and in the lavender body*. The shape was also used from c.1810 for teaware and coffee ware in black jasper* and black basaltes*.

Beer-pump Handle

Jasper handles for public house beer pumps were made around 1900 and ornamented with a variety of decorative subjects.

See: Spirit barrel.

Beeshy's English China Store (Ridgway, Ontario)
In 1923 this firm constructed an Old English front to their store and commissioned Wedgwood to supply a decorative panel to be installed above the entrance. The basaltes plaque supplied, measuring about 53 inches square and weighing 800lbs., is the largest object of its kind to be produced to date. Modelled by Harry Barnard*, it depicts a potter at work using the old kick-wheel, and a quotation, in relief, from *Omar Khayyam*.

Beeson Collection, Dwight and Lucille
Notable collection of some 1,400 pieces of Wedgwood, of which more than 450 are of the Wedgwood and Bentley period.

The collection is presently displayed in rooms specially designed for it in the Birmingham Museum of Art, Alabama, where it has been on loan for some years. Since 1976 annual gifts have been made to the Museum from the collection, and it is the Beesons' intention to continue in this manner to present their collection to Birmingham.

The Beeson Collection is particularly celebrated for its two first edition Portland* vases: the Darwin copy (Number 12) and a rare slate blue version. It contains also two pieces of the Frog* service, one a full-colour trial, and a superb frieze of pale blue and white jasper tablets, some fifty in number, displayed in an Adam*-style gallery.

Beeson Collection. *Dwight and Lucille Beeson with their slate blue copy of the Portland vase.* Photo: Birmingham (Alabama) News.

Belanger, François-Joseph (1744-1818)

French neo-classical architect and landscape gardener. Belanger studied at the Paris Academy of Architecture, and enjoyed the encouragement of the Comte de Caylus*. His first work of importance was a pavilion for the Comte de Lauragais, the Hôtel de Brancas, in 1769. Missing the Prix de Rome in 1765 he travelled in England, where he made some designs for Viscount Shelbourne. In 1770 he became Dessinateur au Cabinet to the Comte de Provence (later Louis XVIII) and, in 1777, Premier Architect to the Comte d'Artois (later Charles X). Whether or not he visited Wedgwood at Etruria* is uncertain, but it is not improbable. Writing to Sir William Hamilton* seventeen years later, in June, 1787, Wedgwood refers to: "Mr. Belanger, a celebrated architect in Paris, who has sent me some excellent bas reliefs in wax, and employs some of the best artists for me there. He very kindly makes a point of recommending my medallions and employs them in his own works. He is now fitting up a superb room for the Comte d'Artois in which he introduces many of these ornaments."

Bell Pull

Bell pulls were attached to one end of a long cord or sash which hung down from the wall. The other end was connected by a wire to a bell in the servants' quarters. They were made by the porcelain factories, especially Worcester, and in jasper by Wedgwood, but they are rare from any source. The Wedgwood version is ovoid in shape, about 2¾ ins. in height, and pierced to allow the cord to pass through it. The jasper bell pull looks like a miniature water jar in shape, and the same mould was employed to make a scent bottle, which was hollowed out a little and sealed at the bottom.

Bell Pull. *Jasper bell pull, c.1790, showing method of attachment. The same mould was also employed to make perfume bottles.* Wedgwood.

Bellerophon

Son of the King of Corinth, Bellerophon was given the task of slaying the Chimaera* by the King of Lydia, who sought his destruction. Bellerophon succeeded with the aid of his horse, Pegasus*, and eventually married the King's daughter, thus becoming heir to the throne. However, he incurred the wrath of the gods by attempting to ride to Heaven on Pegasus, and ended both blind and lame.

Wedgwood subject:

Bellerophon watering Pegasus below Parnassus, cameo, produced in several sizes, modelled by Hackwood (from an engraving after Sostratos or from a Tassie* gem of the same subject) in 1773.

Bentley, A.H. 'Bert' (fl.1891-1936)

Craftsman of exceptional skill, who worked as a modeller at Etruria, and who was at one time engaged on the production of crimson jasper* in association with Harry Barnard*. He also worked on an edition of the Portland vase in 1919. Portrait medallions* with wreath borders, slotted for hanging, and bearing the initials 'BB' and an elongated 'O' impressed, belong to the Barnard and Bentley series begun in 1920, and catalogued by Barnard in 1922. Portraits of Inigo Jones mispelled 'Indigo' Jones are the work of Bentley. The elongated 'O' is his personal mark. Medallions in this series *do not* have 'Made in England' impressed.

Bentley, Thomas (1730-1780)

Josiah Wedgwood's partner in the production of ornamental wares 1769-80, and his closest friend. Bentley was born in the village of Scropton, some twelve miles south-west of Derby, the son of a well-to-do country gentleman, and educated at the Presbyterian Academy at Findern. At the age of fifteen or sixteen he was apprenticed to a Manchester firm of warehousemen in the linen trade, and later travelled on the Continent, acquiring fluency in French and Italian and a taste for antique art. In 1754, soon after his return to England, he married Hannah Oates, and three years later he was settled in Liverpool, where he opened a business as warehouseman in King Street. Shortly afterwards he founded, with Samuel Boardman, the firm of Bentley & Boardman*. Hannah Bentley died in childbirth in 1759.

At thirty Bentley was already a figure of some importance in Liverpool. In 1757 he had taken a leading part, as one of the Trustees, in the founding of the Warrington Academy, for many years the centre of intellectual activity in Lancashire and the home of liberal non-conformism. In 1761 Joseph Priestley* became Tutor of Languages and Polite Literature at the Academy, and it was probably through Bentley that Josiah Wedgwood made his acquaintance.

Bentley was introduced to Josiah by the surgeon and scholar, Matthew Turner, in 1762, when Wedgwood was confined to bed in Liverpool after an accident to his already damaged right knee. The two men quickly became firm friends and, when Wedgwood returned to Burslem, there began the correspondence between them that ended only with Bentley's death. By the middle of July 1765, Bentley was providing useful orders for Wedgwood creamware destined for export, and these increased steadily in volume until, in March 1767, Josiah was describing his friend as "a Pot mercht." Three months earlier, Wedgwood had suggested a formal partnership, and before the end of the year it was clear that Bentley was ready to accept the proposal. The partnership deeds were signed on 10th August, 1769.

Meanwhile, Wedgwood had purchased the Ridgehouse Estate and was busy building his Etruria* factory for the

Bentley, Thomas. *Portrait of Thomas Bentley, Josiah Wedgwood's partner in the manufacture of Ornamental wares, 1769-80, attributed to Joseph Wright of Derby, 1778.* Wedgwood.

manufacture of ornamental ware. On 13th June Bentley attended the official opening of the factory and provided the motive power while Josiah threw the celebrated First Day's Vases*. The partnership concerned the manufacture of ornamental wares only, for Josiah's cousin, Thomas Wedgwood*, was already his partner in the production of 'useful' wares. This division was later the cause of a minor dispute which Wedgwood settled with his customary good sense, defining useful wares as generally those which would commonly be used at meals.

Bentley settled in Burslem, but it was soon clear that his particular qualities would be of far greater value to the firm in London. In the autumn of 1769, therefore, he moved to Chelsea to take charge of the newly-acquired painting studios.

For nearly eleven years Bentley acted as Wedgwood's London Manager, a position that remained for nearly two centuries the key managerial appointment in the Wedgwood organisation. In this capacity he exerted considerable influence upon Wedgwood's production, particularly of ornamental wares. Bentley's education, good taste, social accomplishments and wide circle of friends were invaluable to Wedgwood in the acquisition of powerful patrons and the creation of a style that was at once distinctive and fashionable. Sadly he did not live to see the introduction of vases in jasper, which owed so much to his guidance.

Bentley married for the second time in 1772. After his death, eight years later, it became necessary to wind up the partnership and allot to his widow (formerly Mary Stamford of Derby) her share. The entire stock of ornamental wares was therefore sold by Christie* at auction in 1781.

Four portrait medallions* of Bentley were produced in jasper. The first, modelled by Joachim Smith in 1773, shows him in court dress and is a pair to one of Josiah Wedgwood by the same artist. The other three are in the classical style (in Josiah's words "Al antique") and are attributed to Hackwood*, 1778-80.

The memorial tablet to Bentley, placed by Wedgwood in Chiswick church, was principally the work of James 'Athenian' Stuart*. Part of the inscription reads:
"Blessed with an elevated and comprehensive understanding
Informed in a variety of science
He posessed
A warm and brilliant imagination
A pure and elegant taste."
As friend, partner and guide, Bentley was irreplaceable. The full extent of his contribution to Wedgwood's pre-eminence in the pottery industry has yet to be explored.

Bentley & Boardman
Merchants of Liverpool. Thomas Bentley* was in partnership with Samuel Boardman at the Manchester Stocking Warehouse, King Street, Liverpool, from 1764 until his death in 1780.

Bernini, Giovanni Lorenzo (1598-1680)
Major Italian baroque sculptor, whose principal work is the *baldacchino* in Saint Peter's, Rome. A Wedgwood *Triton* is modelled after a similar figure by Bernini.

Bevan, Silvanus (1691-1765)
The son of Silvanus and Jane Bevan of Swansea, Silvanus practised as an apothecary in London, founding the firm later to be known as Allen & Hanbury. His first marriage, in 1715, to Elizabeth, daughter of the celebrated master clockmaker, Daniel Quare, was attended by a number of eminent contemporaries including Sarah, Duchess of Marlborough and William Penn. Elizabeth died in childbirth, and Silvanus

married Martha Heathcote of Calthorpe. In 1724 he was elected Fellow of the Royal Society. In the following year he took as his apprentice William Cookworthy*, later founder of the Plymouth porcelain factory. Bevan was a competent ivory carver, and a number of his relief portraits were sent to Josiah I by Samuel More* in 1778.

Bevan's style, crude but lively, is easily recognisable, and the following Wedgwood reproductions of his portraits have been identified: Sir Edward Hulse, Richard Mead, Sir Hans Sloane, Henry Pemberton, and John Woodward (all physicians); William Penn; and two double portraits, of Silvanus and his second wife, and of his brother, Timothy, and his wife, Hannah. These last two portraits were evidently produced for the Bevan family, and, writing of them to Bentley* in October 1779, Wedgwood agrees to make copies in biscuit, as requested, but adds "...there is so little difference in the expence to us...& so evident a great difference in the value, & consquently in the complim[t] that I should prefer jasper to give away."

Bewick, Thomas (1753-1828)
The greatest of English wood engravers of the eighteenth century, Bewick was born a few miles from Newcastle-on-Tyne. He was apprenticed to the engraver, Ralph Beilby, with whom, after a brief visit to London in 1776, he entered into partnership, never again leaving the Tyneside district. Among his most celebrated publications are *Select Fables,* 1784, *History*

Bevan, Silvanus. *Double portrait medallion in jasper of Silvanus Bevan and his wife, Martha, taken from a cast of the ivory carving by Silvanus Bevan, sent to Etruria, with others, by Samuel More in 1778.* Wedgwood.

Bewick, Thomas. *Soup tureen, No.24 in the first Queen's ware Catalogue, printed with a landscape by Bewick, c.1777.* Wedgwood.

Below: **Biancini, Angelo.** *Black basaltes candlesticks, 17ins. high, modelled by Angelo Biancini in 1962.* Wedgwood.

of Quadrupeds, 1790 and *History of British Birds,* 1797-1804. Less famous, perhaps, but miniature masterpieces of observation, humour, and technical skill, are his landscape vignettes, which he often used as tailpieces in his books. Some of these were used by Wedgwood as decoration on Queen's ware table services as early as 1775, and the 'Bewick' pattern was reintroduced, printed in black and red, and in green, on Queen's shape in the 1950s. There is no evidence to support the statement that Bewick polished seals for Wedgwood.
See: Robert Pollard.

Biancini, Angelo (b.1911)
Italian sculptor, educated at the Academia di Santa Luca; Professor and Artistic Director, Instituto d'Arte, Faenza; regular exhibitor at Venice Biennali and Rome Quadriennali, 1934-58. In 1962, Professor Biancini visited Barlaston* and modelled a small number of busts and a double candlestick which were reproduced in terracotta* and black basaltes*. The quantities were very limited and these pieces are now rarely seen.

Bidet
Small, shallow bath on a narrow stand for female use introduced into France during the latter part of the 18th century. Arthur Young, in *Travels in France,* wrote that it was rare in England in 1790, and it remained so during the 19th century, when the word was regarded as extremely indelicate. Nevertheless, bidets were made by Wedgwood.

Billington, John (fl.1789)
Modeller at Etruria, 1789. Richard Billington (perhaps a relative, who died in 1811) was a carter who rented thirty-eight acres of the Etruria estate to graze his horses.

Black Basaltes. *Pair of silver-mounted cider mugs, impressed mark 'WEDGWOOD & BENTLEY'. The floral and foliate decoration on a dimpled ground is exceptionally sharp. The mug (left) has its original handle; the mug (right) has a contemporary carved wood silver-pattern handle of excellent quality attached by silver mounts. 5¾ ins. high. c.1775. Dwight and Lucille Beeson Collection.*

Below: **Black Basaltes.** *Urn of the First Day's Vase shape with encaustic painting in the red figure style with a meander or Greek key fret below. c.1790. Dwight and Lucille Beeson Collection.*

Bin Labels

Tablets of cream-coloured ware or pearl* ware, rectangular (6ins. by 3½ins.), circular, or triangular, made to be suspended by string through a pierced hole from a wine bin. They were painted or stencilled with the name of the contents — Port, Sherry, Hock, Claret, Wine, or Brandy — or were left blank, with a matt surface for writing on. Made by Wedgwood, Leeds Pottery*, and Minton*.

Birks, Joseph (fl.1867-1875)

Modeller at Etruria.

Birks, Simon (fl.1867-1875)

Modeller at Etruria.

Birth of Bacchus, The

Tablet modelled by John Flaxman* in 1782 as a pair to *The Dancing Hours* (also with fewer figures as an oval medallion) depicting a Bacchic scene. In Hackwood's* medallion of 1776, a pair to his *Triumph of Bacchus,* Mercury* presents the infant to a nymph flanked by classical figures.

Biscuit

French term for unglazed earthenware or porcelain which has been fired only once, despite the name. The use of unglazed porcelain for modelling figures and groups was first introduced at Sèvres* by the art director, C.C. Bachelier, early in the 1750s, and by 1770 the practice had been adopted at Derby*. The fashion was revived in the 1840s with the introduction of Parian* ware (Carrara* ware) which was at first used unglazed. Other decorative wares, such as vases, are sometimes left in a biscuit state. The Wedgwood dry bodies, including basaltes and jasper, are biscuit stonewares.

Black

Colour produced by mixing cobalt oxide, iron oxide, and manganese oxide. It formed the basis of black glazes, such as those of Jackfield, and, mixed with the body, of such wares as basaltes*. 'Black porcelain' was a term sometimes applied by Josiah Wedgwood to his black basaltes stoneware*.

See also: 'Black Egyptian'; Car.

Black Basaltes

Black basaltes ware was produced as the result of experiments addressed to the manufacture of an improved 'black Egyptian'* body towards the end of the Burslem period. 'Black Egyptian' teapots had been made by the Whieldon-Wedgwood* partnership. The first specimens of what Josiah Wedgwood later termed 'black basaltes' or 'black porcelaine' were produced about the middle of 1768. The date is often given as 1767, but those letters written referring to this body at the time all suggest that it was in the experimental stages, and only in August 1768, do we find a letter to Liverpool referring to "a basket containing two Etruscan bronze vases full of my best compliments to Miss Tarleton, and beg her acceptance of them as an offering of *first fruits*". 'Bronze' vases in this context meant polished basaltes, not merely glossy. Miss Tarleton was the daughter of the Member of Parliament for Liverpool. It is evident that, at this time, the new ware was not very tolerant of fluctuations in kiln temperature, because Wedgwood closes his letter with the words: "Every vase in the last kiln was spoil'd, and that only by such a degree of variation in the fire as scarcely affected our cream colour bisket at all." The next day similar vases were dispatched to William Cox* at the London Rooms, and Cox was cautioned to be careful in showing them. In the accompanying letter Wedgwood complains about the pirating of his designs by other Staffordshire potters. He concludes: "Show but a pair or two of the Bronze [Etruscan] vases at a time, if the price is found fault with, they cannot be lower; I am really and truly a loser by them as I have not one in 6 good, the nature of the Bronze clay to take a polish is so very delicate. NB. The Polish is natural to the composition and is given in burning. They are never oiled &c."

At this time 'Etruscan' was the term Wedgwood used to describe the new ware, and it was only later that this term was limited to vases with encaustic* painting in the manner of ancient red-figure vases. The patent for the encaustic colours was taken out in 1769; the first record of the term 'basaltes' occurs in the Ornamental Catalogue of 1773.

The catalogue by d'Hancarville* of Sir William Hamilton's* collection, which included illustrations of his vases, was in Josiah Wedgwood's library from the date of publication, if the correct interpretation has been put on a letter of February 16th, 1767, sending a book which he refers to as *Antiquitys* to Bentley in Liverpool, telling him that more volumes were at his disposal when he was ready for them. He refers to the "Earthen Vases" and continues: "Who knows what you may hit upon, or what we might strike out betwixt us." To mark the beginning of their partnership and the opening of the new Etruria factory Wedgwood threw six basaltes vases (known as the First Day's Vases*) while Bentley supplied the motive power on June 13th, 1769, and these vases were sent to London where they were decorated with encaustic painting in red of figures from the frieze, *Hercules in the Garden of the Hesperides,* taken from a hydria signed by the Meidias Painter and illustrated in d'Hancarville's catalogue Vol.1, pl.129.

Earlier, in February, 1769, Wedgwood paid a visit to London and spent a day as warehouseman, meeting Lord Bessborough, who bought two Etruscan vases at a guinea apiece, and promised to do Wedgwood every service in his power. It is difficult to be sure whether or not he was responsible, but within a very short time the demand for basaltes vases had risen to a point where urgent appeals had to be sent to Staffordshire for more. Wedgwood wrote from London: "Large ones, very large ones, are all the cry." The demand grew so great that John Coward*, the woodcarver,

was pressed into service and set to 'docter' or 'tinker' imperfect vases to make them fit for sale, adding carved wood covers and bases to those which lacked them. Wedgwood wrote: "I could sell 50 or £100 worth a day if I had them." It is in February 1769, that we find the first reference to basaltes figures: "I am collecting some figures to be made in Etruscan Earth. Mr Chambers [later Sir William Chambers*] and many others have a high opinion of them to mix with the Vases, by both these articles I hope we shall make a revolution in the chimney pieces* and strip them of their present Gaudy furniture of patch'd and painted figures."

There were three kinds of basaltes ware in demand when the 1770s opened — vases and similar objects with engine-turned decoration*, objects decorated with bas-reliefs*, and those in encaustic painting in imitation of red-figure* vases. The latter were immediately popular for libraries and galleries, and they distinguished the man of taste. Sir William Hamilton's collection of vases was bought by the British Museum in 1772, and their public exhibition no doubt helped Wedgwood's sales, but, although they continued in demand throughout the decade, sales tended to diminish as popular taste gradually turned in other directions. No doubt, also, Wedgwood's painting shop, which never really succeeded in capturing the spirit of the originals (many of which were, in any case, degenerate copies of late Greek vases) had more than sufficient to do without the Etruscan vases. The enormous Imperial Russian (Frog*) Service, for instance, must have left little time for anything else.

The black body was a superb medium for relief decoration as well as engine-turned fluting and reeding. It could be highly polished or left with a natural dull gloss. It could be treated with gold (see Bronzed Basaltes), when it closely imitated the appearance of *cire perdue* castings at a fraction of the cost. The popularity of excavated classical portrait busts among wealthy collectors, and the revival of Roman customs at the time, created a demand for basaltes busts* which Wedgwood was not slow to meet, buying casts and moulds initially from Hoskins & Oliver*, and later making moulds at Etruria from busts lent by the owners. Very soon they were replacing the plaster of Paris busts hitherto sold for interior decoration, basaltes being cheaper and much less easily damaged. The making of figures* is discussed under that heading. Although Wedgwood was considering the making of figures in 1769 it was several years before manufacture was put on anything like a substantial scale, and, here too, the initial assistance of Hoskins & Oliver was sought.

The most authoritative source of information about basaltes during the 18th century is Josiah Wedgwood himself, and a great deal of relevant information is to be culled from the Ornamental Catalogue of 1779, the last to be issued before Bentley's death in 1780, and for the preparation of which we must suppose Josiah Wedgwood to have been largely responsible.

To begin with his description, he says that black basaltes is "a fine *Black Porcelaine,* having nearly the same properties as the *Basaltes* [ie. the stone], resisting the Attacks of Acid;. being a Touchstone to Copper, Silver, and Gold [ie. it could be used by goldsmiths for testing the nature and quality of these metals in conjunction with acids]; admitting of a good Polish (if desired, by lapidary techniques); and capable of bearing to be made red hot in a furnace frequently without Damage."

"*Cameos and Intaglios:* The Intaglios in artificial Basaltes are most excellent Seals, being exact Impressions from the finest Gems, and therefore much truer than any engraved copies can be, with the singular advantage of being little inferior in

Above: **Black Basaltes.** *The Warwick Vase, adapted from the large Roman marble vase formerly at Warwick Castle. This shape was specially popular during the early years of the 19th century, and may be found in Worcester porcelain and a silver copy by Paul Storr.* Zeitlin Collection.

Right: **Black Basaltes.** *Vase-candlestick (the cover reversible) in the form of a tripod incense-burner. 11ins. high. c.1790; and a tea kettle with bail handle and 'widow' or 'sibyl' finial. c.1782.* Woburn Abbey Collection. Photo: Wedgwood.

Black Basaltes. *Covered vase with swan handles and artichoke finial, resting on the backs of two winged sphinxes, the pedestal with a meander in the form of a Greek key fret. 13⅞ ins. high. Copy, c.1930, of a Wedgwood & Bentley period model, shape no.140.* Buten Museum.

Hardness to the Gems themselves.'' The hardness is about 6 on Mohs' scale, against 7 in the case of most gems. Basaltes is about equivalent to glass and hard porcelain in this respect.

"*Busts, Small Statues, Boys, Animals, &c.* The black Composition having the appearance of antique bronze, and so nearly agreeing in properties with the Basaltes of the Ægyptians, no Substance can be better than this for Busts, Sphinxes, small Statues, &c. and it seems to us to be a great Consequence to preserve as many fine Works of Antiquity and of the present Age as we can in this composition, for when all pictures are faded and rotten, when Bronzes are rusted away, and all the excellent works in Marble dissolved, then these copies like the antique* Etruscan vases, will probably remain, and transmit the Works of Genius, and the Portraits of illustrious Men, to the most distant Times.

"*Antique vases of Black Porcelain in Artificial Basaltes (highly finished with bas-relief ornaments).* Of this Species of Vase we have a great variety of Forms, the sizes from three or four inches high to more than two Feet. The prices from seven shillings and six-pence a piece to Three or Four Guineas; excluding the very large ones, and those pieces which consist of many parts, and are very highly finished. The Sets of *five pieces* for chimney pieces* [ie. the *garniture de cheminée*] sell from about two guineas to Six or Eight Guineas a Set. From all the specimens we have seen, and the observations of others, we have reason to conclude that there are not any vases of Porcelain, Marble, or Bronze, either ancient or modern, so *highly finished* and *sharp in their Ornaments* as these Black vases...

"*Painted Etruscan Vases.* The Vases of this class are copied from the Antique with the utmost exactness, as they are to be found in Dempster, Gorius, Count Caylus*, Passerius, but more especially in the most choice and comprehensive collection of Sir William Hamilton* which, to the Honour of the Collector, and of this Nation, and for the advantage of our Artist, is now placed in the British Museum. The Art of Painting Vases in the Manner of the Etruscans has been lost for Ages, and was supposed by the ingenious Author of the Dissertation on Sir William Hamilton's Museum to have been lost in Pliny's time [d.A.D.79]. The Proprietors of this Manufactory have been so happy as to rediscover and revive this lost Art so as to give satisfaction to the most careful Judges both in their Nature and Effects.

"*Tablets and pictures for cabinets and inlaying upon plates of artificial basaltes, and upon a new kind of enamelled plate.* These paintings may be applied, and have already been employed to great Advantage in Chimney pieces* and Cabinets, and when the Effects are observed and the durable nature of the Work considered we hope the Application of them will be greatly extended. Since the First Edition of this Catalogue we have had the good Fortune to execute many large tablets in a great Variety of colours, with success, and as the Colours...are smooth, durable, and without any vitreous glare this is acknowledged...to be a higher and more perfect species of Painting than was known to the World before the Date of this Invention...These Tablets may be made from Bracelet size to pieces of Eighteen or Twenty inches Diameter, and from One guinea to Fifteen or Twenty guineas a piece...[the price] varies according to the size of the Plates, the Number of Figures, the Merit of the Hands employed, and the Degree of *finishing.*''

The earliest decoration to be employed on basaltes ware was lathe* turning, engine-turning, and, in suitable cases, moulded ornament, the latter sharpened and generally improved after moulding. Since at this time press-moulding* was in general use for this kind of work no very elaborate reliefs were attempted. Flat plaques with moulded relief decoration in one piece were first produced in 1769. The application of reliefs by sprigging* to flat surfaces came a little later, and it was not possible to overcome the difficulties of applying this kind of ornament to the curved surfaces of vases (which were, of course, thrown on the wheel) until 1776. Large tablets with applied reliefs are probably not earlier than 1775. The work needed to overcome these difficulties was of the utmost value a little later on when the problem of attaching white reliefs to the curved surfaces of coloured jasper had to be overcome. The problem in both cases is one of unequal contraction due to varying thicknesses during cooling which sets up stresses leading to firecracks and similar defects, and it was overcome in a variety of ways. An examination of Wedgwood & Bentley portrait medallions will reveal holes passing through the background as far as the applied relief, or 'thumb scoops' over the thickest part of the relief. These are to ensure a reasonably similar rate of cooling throughout the whole, and in this way the stresses which would otherwise have been set up were dispersed. They are very clear evidence of the nature of the difficulties being experienced.

The black basaltes body continued to be popular throughout the 18th century, not only for such ornamental wares as vases, but also for teapots and tea wares and a miscellany of root pots, bough pots, and flower pots, including the well known bulb holder in the form of a hedgehog. Manufacture has never entirely ceased at any time, although basaltes has always varied in its popularity. It underwent a notable revival in the 1840s and 1850s when Wyon* modelled a new series of portrait busts for this body.

Black basaltes ware enamelled with flowers in the Chinese *famille rose* style belongs to early years of the 19th century. Enamelling of this kind also occurs on a red terracotta body and on *rosso antico*.

Among the most important basaltes pieces produced in the 20th century are Arnold Machin's* *Taurus the Bull,* bowls design by Keith Murray*, the coffee set designed by Walter Robert Minkin*, and the cigarette box and lighter sets (fitted with Ronson lighters) by Peter Wall*.

Of his basaltes, Wedgwood wrote: "The Black is Sterling and Will last forever.''

Black Egyptian

The name by which Staffordshire unglazed black wares were known before the appearance of Wedgwood's black basaltes*. Although, according to Simeon Shaw, it seems to have been made fairly extensively, specimens are rare. The City of Stoke-on-Trent Museum has two teapots dating from about 1730 which are said to have been made by Joshua Twyford of Shelton. Shaw says also that the clay was coloured with a waste product found in drainage water from coal mines, which was known as car*. This contained a high proportion of iron oxide, and, being fairly heavy, it sank to the bottom of the liquid of suspension. The drainage channels were diverted from time to time, and the accumulations cleared out and sold to the potters for a guinea a cart load. Car was certainly employed by Josiah Wedgwood in the manufacture of black basaltes, but in a more carefully refined form than was customary elsewhere, and the brown-black yielded by iron oxide was converted to complete blackness by the addition of manganese. The reason for the name black Egyptian, is obscure, but, in naming his new ware black basaltes, Wedgwood was undoubtedly influenced by the fact that the Egyptians of antiquity employed basalt, a very hard stone, for sculpture, carving it with abrasives.

Blake, John Bradby (1745-1773)

English naturalist, educated at Westminster School, who became a supercargo for the English East India Company which, in the 18th century, was usually a very profitable occupation. Blake went to Canton in 1766. There he obtained seeds and plants for propagation, and he also obtained specimens of Chinese kaolin (white china clay) and fusible feldspathic rock (*pai-tun tzǔ*) for Wedgwood with which the latter made some trials of porcelain manufacture. Blake's early death put an end to the experiments. His portrait medallion, included in the 1779 Catalogue, was modelled by Joachim Smith*. It was incorrectly identified by Eliza Meteyard* as Lord Gower.

Blake, John Bradby. *Portrait medallion in jasper of John Bradby Blake, modelled by Joachim Smith and first listed in the 1779 Catalogue.* City Museum and Art Gallery, Stoke-on-Trent.

Blake, William (1757-1827)

Painter, engraver and poet; apprenticed to James Basire in 1771; studied at the Royal Academy Schools. Blake first exhibited at the Academy in 1780, but during his lifetime he enjoyed little success, his work being incomprehensible to his contemporaries. He has since been recognised as one of the few truly creative artists of his period, and the greatest visionary artist of the British School. He supported himself mainly by book illustration, and engraved plates 1-18 for Wedgwood's Queen's ware Catalogue* of 1817. He was introduced to Wedgwood by John Flaxman*. Blake also made four engravings of the Portland* vase for Erasmus Darwin's* *Botanic Garden*, 1791.

According to a surviving account with John Flaxman, the ceiling painting for the drawing-room of Etruria Hall* was designed by Flaxman and executed by William Blake, who was paid £3 17s. This ceiling was examined in recent times by Bruce Tattersall, then Curator of the Wedgwood Museum*, who was unable to find any trace of the paintings, which may, of course, have been removable.

Blancmange Mould

A deep *intaglio* mould made in a variety of shapes and used to make blancmange. Made in cream-coloured ware by Wedgwood.

See also: Jelly Mould

Blue John

See: Radix Amethyst.

Blue Pebble

A type of vase with variegated bluish-green glaze and unfired gilding on the handles and mouldings. This type almost certainly belongs to the period just after 1769, when the ornamental works had been removed to Etruria*, and they were probably made to compete with Boulton's much more expensive vases of Blue John* mounted in ormolu. A pair of vases of this kind with the mark of Wedgwood & Bentley is at Saltram*.

See also: Variegated Ware.

Boden & Smith

'Toy' makers, 8, Temple Street, Birmingham. Seal setters, who ordered a gross of seals (i.e. 144) in May, 1773. In November, 1773, Wedgwood noted in a letter to Bentley that they had bought some seals made by Voyez*. The word 'toy' did not have its modern meaning in the 18th century but referred to small decorative items like patch boxes, snuff boxes, scent bottles, etc.

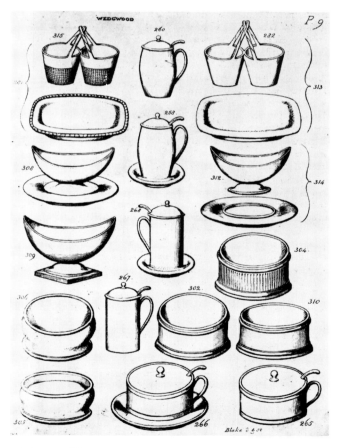

Blake, William. *A page from Wedgwood's 1817 Catalogue of Shapes, engraved and signed by William Blake.* Wedgwood.

Bone China. *Bone china part tea and coffee service decorated with landscapes by John Cutts, c.1815. At this period the service still comprised twelve saucers, twelve tea cups and twelve coffee cups.* Wedgwood.

Bone China. *Chinese decoration of 'Dogs of Fo' (the Lion of Buddha) known, oddly as Chinese Tigers pattern. Originally produced on bone china c.1815 and reproduced in 1977.* Wedgwood.

Body

Term used to denote the composite material from which earthenware, stoneware or porcelain (fired or unfired) is made. Porcelain body is more specifically known as 'paste'.

Boizot, Simon-Louis (1743-1809)

French sculptor, and head of the modelling department at Sèvres, 1774-1802. The son of the painter, Antoine Boizot, he carved marble busts of Jean Racine and the Emperor Joseph II of Austria among others, and also the vase of the Medicis in the Louvre. Wedgwood's portrait medallion* of Jean Sylvain Bailly was taken either from a medal by Duvivier or from the engraving by Cook after Boizot.

Bone China

Usually termed 'china' in England, this is a porcelain of clay and feldspathic rock with the addition of about fifty percent of calcined cattle bones (bone ash). It is fired at a lower temperature than the feldspathic porcelain of the Continent of Europe and the Orient. Although the introduction of bone china is attributed to Josiah Spode II about 1799, bone ash had been employed in the manufacture of artificial (i.e. frit or 'soft') porcelain since 1749, and Josiah Wedgwood was certainly acquainted with the substance and its properties, as witness a letter to Bentley of January 1776, discussing porcelain manufacture generally. Spode's discovery was the fact that bone ash has a completely different effect when added in massive quantities from its effect in the smaller proportions employed until that time. Bone china was introduced at Etruria by Josiah Wedgwood II* in 1812, and manufacture was discontinued about 1822, though orders were being accepted as late as 1829. The reason for the decision to give up such a promising product is clarified by a report from London in July 1813: ''The public taste has been led to expect such a dazzling mixture of color with gold in broad shades covering the whole area that their eyes are spoilt for delicate & elegant borders, which are not dazzling & do not produce a striking

Bone China. *Rare bone china teaset painted with Oriental figures in reserves against a yellow ground. c.1815.* Christie's.

effect.'' The landscapes of John Cutts*, the chaste designs of flowers and birds painted by Aaron Steele*, and the monochrome prints in Oriental styles, were too restrained for the Regency taste for opulent display. The necessary experiment had failed. Manufacture of bone china was resumed in 1878, and has been continued ever since. It has important advantages over feldspathic porcelain — it is lighter in weight, whiter in colour, and less brittle. It also allows a wider range of colours to be employed in decoration. It has not, so far, been produced to any great extent outside England, except for a few factories in the United States and Scandinavia, but Japanese factories have been experimenting with the manufacture of bone china for many years.

Boot, Thomas (fl.1769-1773)
Boot was originally employed at Burslem. In 1769 he was brought to Etruria to model ''Sphynxes, Lyons, and Tritons''. Wedgwood felt at first that he modelled ''some sad figures, but will make a useful hand.'' He became a good figure-maker at Etruria and brought up others in the craft. His work includes a lion, sphinx figure, sphinx candlestick, a triton figure, a triton candlestick, and figures for the covers of vases.
See: Figures.

Borghese Family
A celebrated Italian family which originated in Sienna in the 13th century, one member of which settled in Rome in the 16th century. His son became Pope Paul V and this greatly increased the family influence and fortunes. The later Prince Camillo Borghese married Napoleon's sister, Pauline, whose semi-nude statue by Canova* is widely known. The family possessed the Borghese Palace, one of the finest buildings in Rome, and a summer residence outside the Porta del Popolo, the Villa Borghese. The Villa's remarkable art collection was sold by Prince Borghese to Napoleon in 1806. Some of these works were returned to the Villa after Waterloo, and others were placed in the Louvre. Both the Villa and the Palace are now State property.

See also: Borghese Vase; The Dancing Hours.

Borghese Vase. *A krater-shaped covered vase of 1850 decorated with the Borghese reliefs, the pedestal with rich festoons of vine leaves and grapes. The design dates from c.1790.* Lady Lever Art Gallery.

Borghese Vase

Blue and white jasper vase and cover in the form of a Greek calyx krater, copied from an antique marble vase once in the possession of the Borghese family* of Rome and now in the Louvre. The subject of the figures in bas-relief is the *Bacchanalian Triumph*. Made about 1790, a Wedgwood specimen of this very rare vase is in the Lady Lever Art Gallery, Liverpool.

Botanical Flowers

Term used in pottery and porcelain for floral decoration consisting of more or less exactly delineated flowers and foliage, generally copied from contemporary illustrations, and often named on the reverse of plates and dishes. The style was introduced at the Chelsea factory* in the 1750s with the so-called 'Hans Sloane' flowers, and it can be traced to Meissen*, where illustrated treatises on horticulture were used as a source of inspiration for porcelain decoration in the 1730s and 1740s.

Unmarked creamware dessert services painted in this style, often with a chocolate brown edge and belonging to the period 1790-1810, are frequently attributed to Wedgwood, but the first documented Wedgwood design of this type is the *Water Lily** pattern, No.19. Wedgwood's *Botanical Flowers* pattern was produced in 1808-9 in two versions — printed and enamelled in colours, and printed underglaze in blue (see: Underglaze Blue Prints). A few years later, a third version was printed on-glaze in red. The *Botanists's Repository* by Henry C. Andrews, 1804, already used for *Water Lily,* was also copied for this pattern.

Wedgwood's introduction of this type of decoration was undoubtedly influenced by John Wedgwood's* deep interest in horticulture. He was one of the founders of the Royal Horticultural Society.

Botanical Flowers. *Bone china dessert plate painted with Botanical Flowers, c.1815.* Sotheby's Belgravia.

Bouillon, Duc de (1728-1799)
Marie de la Tour d'Auvergne

French soldier, present at the battle of Fontenoy (1744); made Governor of the Auvergne in 1776. Favouring reform, he was elected to command the National Guard at Evreux at the beginning of the Revolution. He was notorious for his erotic adventures. Flaxman* visited the Duke in 1787, when he was living in the Château of Navarre. On the 29th September, 1787, Flaxman wrote to Byerley*: "...the Duke of Bouillon made kind enquiries after you and desired me to tell you that he desires to see you at the castle of Navarre on matters of business". A "Mould of Duc de Bouillion [*sic*] for 10 portraits" is mentioned in January 1784. This portrait, which is listed in the 1787 Catalogue, has not been located, but may exist in France. The mould is also missing, the mould at Barlaston marked 'Duc de Bouillon' being that of the portrait of Dr. Thomas Bowdler.

Boulton, Matthew (1728-1809)

There were few manufacturers of decorative metalwork on a large scale in 18th century England, and chief among them was Matthew Boulton. The son of an inconsiderable button and buckle manufacturer, whose business he inherited in 1759, Boulton began to build his Soho, Birmingham, factory in 1763. In that year he entered into a partnership with John Fothergill which lasted until 1781. In 1767 the factory was enlarged and Boulton was granted royal patronage. In the following year he met James Watt*, and the two men were associated in the development of the steam engine which was later to provide the motive power for a number of 18th century factories, including Etruria. With Erasmus Darwin*, Joseph Priestley*, and others of Wedgwood's friends, Boulton and Watt were members of the Lunar Society*.

It was at Boulton's factory that Wedgwood first saw the improved engine-turning lathe* operated by a rosette*, which he wanted to buy, and he visited the Soho works on another occasion to examine the Argand lamp*. Boulton made many small decorative objects such as shoe buckles, brooches, buttons, chatelaines, bracelets and the frames for lockets in both silver and cut steel, and these were greatly enhanced by the additon of jasper cameos*. Wedgwood also supplied Boulton, at his request, with white cameos, the backgrounds of which could be painted in watercolour for setting under glass in the lids of small boxes.

While Wedgwood was concluding his partnership with Bentley* for the manufacture of ornamental ware, Boulton was striving to "supplant the French in the gilt business" and was making ormolu clock cases and vases in the French style. He discussed with Wedgwood the possibility of mounting earthenware and basaltes vases in ormolu but nothing came of it. Later, however, jasper drums* were supplied for incorporation into Boulton's ormolu mounts for glass candlesticks* and candelabra. Boulton even considered opening his own pottery. Wedgwood wrote to Bentley in September 1769: "It doubles my courage to have the first manufacturer in England to incounter [*sic*] with...I like the man — I like his spirit — He will not be a mere drivelling copyist like the antagonists I have hitherto had." Boulton abandoned his plan, and the two great men remained in friendly rivalry, Wedgwood supplying Boulton with cameos for mounting, and each providing the other with inspiration for designs.

By 1770 Boulton was employing seven hundred hands in his factory, obtaining glass smelling bottles, scent bottles, and inkstands for mounting from James Keir, also a member of the Lunar Society. He was associated with Wedgwood, Sir Richard Arkwright and others in a variety of undertakings, notably the Cornish Metal Company. Like Wedgwood, he was one of the major contributors to the Industrial Revolution in England.

Bouquetière. *White biscuit bouquetière decorated in matt black with glazed interior, pierced cover and rococo handles. 8¼ ins. high. c.1790. Dwight and Lucille Beeson Collection.*

Bouquetière

Flower pot, generally of circular or oval form, and with a pierced cover to hold the stems of flowers or small branches of flowering shrubs. It was made in many forms during the 18th and early 19th centuries in the jasper*, basaltes*, cane ware*, and white stoneware* bodies.

See: Root Pot.

Bourdalou

Small oval chamber pot for female use, made c.1710 to 1850, produced by leading Continental porcelain factories, in China for export, in England by Bow and Derby, and in cream-coloured ware by Wedgwood and Leeds. Bourdalous are supposed to derive their name from a preacher of the same name at the Court of Louis XIV, whose sermons were so long that the ladies found them indispensable. Wedgwood referred to them as coach pots, which indicates another use for them, and a name current in the 19th century was 'crinoline slipper'.

Bourn, James (fl.c.1760-1780)

Turner at Burslem, transferred to Etruria, November, 1769. Bourn was especially skilled in turning vases, particularly those of basaltes ware, which caused certain difficulties among the operatives owing to the colour. In 1774 there is a record of Bourn turning patterns for others to work to.

See: Engine-turned Decoration.

Bourdalou, *or coach pot, length 10½ ins., printed in underglaze blue with three scenes of figures in landscapes, and an inside border of roses which is repeated on the handle. c.1830. Alan Drake Collection.*

Bourne, Edward (fl.1770s)

Known as 'Old Bourne', he was a bricklayer who seems to have maintained the kilns and buildings at Etruria, and was the subject of a remarkably fine jasper portrait medallion, modelled by Hackwood* and signed on the truncation. In November, 1778, Wedgwood wrote to Bentley: "Old Bourne is the man himself, with every wrinkle, crink and cranny in the whole visage." The portrait exists with the bricklayer's trowel in different positions on the field. Two moulds survive. One is marked 'Mr Byrne [sic] Bricklayer' and is signed 'Wm Hackwood 1779'. The other is marked 'Mr Bourne Bricklayer by Hackwood 1779'.

Bourne, Edward. *Jasper portrait medallion of Edward Bourne, 'Old Bourne', a bricklayer at Etruria. Modelled by Hackwood in 1778.* Wedgwood.

Bourne, Semei (Simeon)

Engraver of Shelton, who produced engravings for Wedgwood c.1805-15. He is recorded as the supplier of at least one engraving for the *Water Lily** pattern in November 1806, and the engravings for the *Japan* pattern in November and December 1808.

Bourne, W. (fl.1770s)

Painter at the Chelsea Decorating Studio* from 1770.

Bow Porcelain Factory

A factory in Bow, East London (properly Stratford-le-Bow) producing soft-paste porcelain mainly between 1750 and 1760. The history of the factory is lacunary, but two patents registered in 1744 and 1748 both refer to Cherokee clay* under the Indian name of *unaker,* although it is not known whether this clay was eventually used. The factory was the first to employ bone ash (see: Bone china) in the manufacture of porcelain, and also the first to use transfer printing* in the decoration. Robert Hancock*, the engraver, probably learned the art of transfer-printing from John Brooks at Battersea before he worked at Bow. The process appears to have been abandoned when Hancock left for the Worcester Porcelain Factory* in 1756. Mr. Tebo*, the repairer and modeller, first made his appearance at Bow. About 1760 the factory suffered serious financial reverses, and it was probably financed for a time by William Duesbury* of Derby*, who appears to have gained control about 1762. It may still have been working after 1770, but this is uncertain.

Bowcher, Frank (1864-1938)

Sculptor and medallist; son of etcher and cartoonist, William Henry Boucher. Studied at the National Art Training College, South Kensington, 1885; exhibited at the Royal Academy; founder member of the Royal Society of British Sculptors; gained a Silver Medal at the Brussels Exposition of 1910. He modelled the portrait of Sir Joseph Hooker* which was translated into jasper for the memorial in Kew Church.

Boydell, John (1719-1804)

Prominent publisher and engraver, studied at the St. Martin's Lane Academy, and painted a series of watercolour topographical views along the Thames, which he subsequently engraved. He set up as a printseller in 1751 and rapidly achieved considerable success. He became Sheriff of London in 1785 and Lord Mayor in 1790. Boydell is frequently quoted as having been employed on the Frog* service. There is no evidence for this statement, but it is probable that he supplied Wedgwood with prints or watercolour views to be copied by artists employed at Chelsea.

Boyle, John (d.1845)

Son of Zachariah Boyle (Z. Boyle & Son of Stoke-on-Trent); manufacturer of earthenware on his own account from 1826; partner with Herbert Minton*, 1836-41. Following a disagreement with Minton, Boyle formed a business with his brothers. In 1843 he joined Francis Wedgwood* at Etruria* as partner with a half share in the firm. He died two years later.

Bramah, Joseph (1748-1814)

Inventor and cabinet maker; patented Bramah locks and the Bramah hydraulic press, 1795. Joseph Bramah supplied Wedgwood with drawings and designs for sanitary ware, including wash basins. In 1804 he wrote to Byerley* suggesting that Wedgwood should manufacture "artificial *Teeth* of such of your composition as is best suited for that purpose, and which would undoubtedly become an object of the very first Importance to human happiness." He wrote, "feelingly, because from Sundry Accidents I have for some time lost all my *Teeth in the upper Jaw.*" Nothing seems to have come of this proposal.

See: Dentures.

Brandoin, Michel-Vincent (1735-1807)

A Swiss *emigré* painter working in England. Brandoin designed the Gessner* Monument in Zürich which shows the Muses of Poetry and Painting mourning over a portrait of the poet. This was copied on a jasper medallion to which Josiah refers in a letter dated 23rd January, 1790.

See: Pretty Mantua Maker.

Brewster Teapot

A circular or oval teapot with vertical sides and a narrow gallery surrounding the opening into which the lid is recessed. Made by Wedgwood in the 1780s in jasper, and subsequently in other bodies, the shape was inspired by contemporary silver.

Colour Plate III

Top left: Creamware teapot painted with the figure of a man with a riding whip, standing in a landscape with buildings. A typical example of the work of David Rhodes, c.1774. The teapot has a cauliflower or cabbage spout, scroll handle, and characteristic pierced ball knop. Zeitlin Collection.

Top right: Rare creamware tankard enamelled by David Rhodes, c.1770. Height 5ins. Zeitlin Collection.

Centre left: Creamware teapot enamelled with a diaper or chintz pattern in pink, red, green and yellow, with rose-pink enamelling on the spout, handle and knop. c.1775. Zeitlin Collection.

Left: Reverse of creamware teapot enamelled in black and iron-red with the inscription: 'Long may we Live / Happy may we be / Blest with content / from misfortunes free.' The obverse is painted with a landscape in the style of Rhodes. Chelsea Decorating Studios, c.1774. Zeitlin Collection.

Brick House, 'Bell Works,' Burslem (1764-1769)

The Brick House works, which became known as the Bell Works from the means employed to summon the workmen, were much larger than the Ivy House* premises. Although Wedgwood concentrated on cream-coloured ware which became known as Queen's ware in 1765, he continued to experiment with other bodies, especially black basaltes*, which was first produced in 1768. The so-called 'useful'* wares continued to be made there until 1772, after which production was transferred to Etruria*, where 'ornamental'* wares had been made since 1769. Josiah's cousin, Thomas Wedgwood, became a partner in the manufacture of useful wares in 1766. They included the popular cauliflower* ware and pineapple* ware, dessert plates of leaf form, and other dessert ware covered with a green glaze as well as most tablewares.

Bridgewater, 3rd Duke of (1736-1803)
Francis Egerton

Francis Egerton, Duke of Bridgewater, devoted himself to the development of coal mines at Worsley (Lancashire) and, starting in 1759, he constructed, with the help of James Brindley*, a canal from Worsley to Manchester (Bridgewater canal). Subsequently (1762-72) he was involved, again with Brindley, in the cutting of a canal from Manchester to Liverpool. He has since come to be known as the founder of British inland navigation. He became acquainted with Josiah Wedgwood through their mutual interest in canals, and, as early as 1765, the Duke gave Wedgwood an order for "the completest Table service of Cream colour" that he could make. He became one of Wedgwood's most friendly patrons, advising him, in 1767, against applying for a patent for the exclusive use of Cherokee clay*, introducing him to Lancelot 'Capability' Brown*, and confiding to him his plans for the improvement of transport and communications by the use of inland waterways.

The portrait medallion for many years illustrated as the Duke of Bridgewater (the mould at the factory is inscribed 'D. of Bridgewater 2nd of April 1797') was correctly identified in 1965 by Vivian Scheidemantel as a portrait of Frederick William Charles I, King of Württemberg.

Brindley, James (1716-1772)

Engineer who, in 1742, was a repairer of old machinery at Leek (Staffs.). He introduced some important improvements to the design of contemporary machines. He designed a canal for the Duke of Bridgewater* to run from the Worsley coal field to Manchester, and subsequently constructed the Manchester and Liverpool (Bridgewater) canal, and the Trent & Mersey (Grand Trunk) canal. Illiterate, and unable to draw, he was nevertheless responsible for the construction of more than three hundred and fifty miles of canals in England.

A jasper portrait medallion of Brindley was probably adapted from a painting by Francis Parsons exhibited at the Society of Artists in 1771. No example of this medallion is known to exist, and the mould has been lost. There is a portrait engraving in Meteyard's* Life of Wedgwood.

See: Canal, Trent & Mersey.

Britannia Triumphant

One of Wedgwood's most important groups, it was modelled by Henry Webber* to celebrate British naval victories in the wars against France. The tall cylindrical plinth is ornamented with the portrait medallions of four great admirals: Lords Nelson and Duncan, and Howe and St. Vincent. Set in pairs, they are divided by arched niches, apparently intended for figures which are now missing. The plinth is surmounted by a splendid seated figure of Britannia, holding in her hand a portrait medallion of George III*. By her side is a rather playful-looking lion, and her right foot rests upon a fallen figure carrying a torch, evidently representing France. A shield ornamented with the British flag, a cannon, and an overturned cornucopia, complete the composition. The whole stands 32ins. high.

The Britannia figure is adapted by Webber from his Minerva* candelabrum; the portraits of the admirals were all modelled by De Vaere in 1798; and the portrait of George III is the same as that copied from the Academy Prize medal entry by Edward Burch, 1785, and reissued, with suitable scroll and inscription, to celebrate the restoration of the King's health in 1789. This large group was probably produced between 1798 and 1802. The Ackermann engraving of the York Street showrooms*, 1809, shows, in the centre of the display, a temple* within which is a figure probably intended to represent *Britannia Triumphant.*

Broadwood, John (1732-1812)

Maker of pianofortes. Until 1769 he was in partnership with Burckhardt Tschudi, a Swiss maker of harpsichords, who retired in his favour. Broadwood patented a 'new constructed pianoforte' in 1783. He achieved an international reputation, and the cases of instruments by him were sometimes decorated with inset jasper cameos and medallions. Several examples have survived, the most important being that designed by Thomas Sheraton for Manuel de Godoy in 1796 (now preserved at the Heritage Foundation, Deerfield, Massachusetts).

Brindley, James. *Engraved portrait of James Brindley (1716-72), probably adapted from a portrait exhibited at the Society of Arts in 1771. Although a jasper medallion was produced, no example appears to have survived.* Photo: Wedgwood.

Broken-column Vase

A blue jasper vase representing the time-worn base of a column and the shaft, which is broken about a third of the way up. Made in the 1790s, it is No. 1566 in the first of the ornamental Shape Books*, and it was also made in twin and triple forms. At the time there was a fashion for ruins which was part of the romantic aspect of the neo-classical style. Piranesi depicted ruins; Hubert Robert was so fond of the subject that he became known as Robert les Ruines; and relatively large-scale classical and Gothic ruins had been in vogue since before the middle of the 18th century as a kind of garden ornament. These came to be known as 'follies'.

See: Ruins.

Bronze and Gold

A deep chocolate-brown stoneware body, almost identical in composition with basaltes but containing a smaller quantity of manganese, introduced c.1880 for the manufacture of vases with richly gilt relief ornament. Limited production lasted for only a few years and fine examples are now rare.

See: Basaltes, Bronzed and Gilt; Bronzed Basaltes.

Bronzed Basaltes (Bronze Etruscan)

Also known as 'bronz'd' ware. Black basaltes* vases were bronzed by covering them with a small quantity of lightly fired metallic gold. About 1769 Boulton was able to treat vases to make them resemble antique bronze. Wedgwood probably bought the information from Boulton and in 1769 took out a patent for "the purpose of ornamenting earthen and porcelain ware with an Encaustic Gold Bronze, together with a peculiar Species of Encaustic Painting in various Colours, in imitation of the Ancient Etruscan and Roman Earthenware." The bronzing powder was prepared by dissolving pure gold in aqua regia (a mixture of hydrochloric and nitric acids), precipitating it in a minutely divided form by adding bronze filings. This powdered gold was then applied to the surface with a little flux, using oil of turpentine as a medium. For an antique* effect the gold powder was mixed with a little lamp black and caused to adhere with japanner's gold size and a light firing. Both processes were only semi-permanent.

See also: Basaltes, Bronzed and Gilt; Bronze and Gold.

Broken-column Vase. *Twin-column vase, the pedestal decorated with embossed reliefs. Simulated signs of age. c.1790.* Zeitlin Collection.

Brookes, William (fl.1805-1839)

Independent engraver of Hanley, who supplied Wedgwood with engravings for the *Ferrara** pattern, 1832, and probably *Corinth,* 1811. He was also responsible for the engraving of certain items of *Blue Palisade,* and, with Mollart* and William Hales*, for part of the *Blue Bamboo* pattern.

See: Underglaze Blue Prints.

Brooklyn Bridge

A commemorative* plate decorated with a blue-printed view of Brooklyn Bridge made to celebrate the Tercentenary of Long Island (1636-1936). The central picture of the bridge is taken from a lithograph by John Pennell; the border vignettes illustrate important Long Island Views.

Brownsword, Henry. *Pair of quiver vases painted by Henry Brownsword. Signed with monogram. 6¼ ins. high.* Sotheby's Belgravia.

Brown, Mr. (fl.1800-1812)
Resident engraver at Etruria* c.1805-12.

Brown China
Rockingham* glazed earthenware, made by Wedgwood in the 19th century.

Brown, Lancelot 'Capability' (1715-1803)
Architect of country houses, and landscape gardener in the Romantic or picturesque style. Born at Harle-Kirk, Northumberland, he laid out the grounds at Kew and Blenheim. He gained his sobriquet from the habit, when being shown a new site, of saying that it had 'capabilities'. Brown was appointed High Sheriff of Huntingdon in 1770.

Wedgwood first met Brown in London in May, 1767, and in his letter to Bentley in Liverpool he refers to "the famous Brown" who "may be of much service to me." On September 11th, 1774, he records a visit from Lord Gower, the Duke of Bedford, Lord Trentham and "the great Mr. [Capability] Brown. The latter paid me many compliments, said he would make room for our Heads, speaking of himself as an Architect...He invited me to come and see him at Hampton Court, which I shall certainly do when I come to town. He seems very much disposed to serve us." Five years later he renewed his offers of help and advice. Wedgwood showed him some of his jasper* tablets, but both Brown and Lord Gower objected to the blue ground, unless it could be made to imitate lapis lazuli. "I showed them", Wedgwood wrote sadly, "a sea green and some other colours to which Mr. Brown said they were pretty colours and he should not object to those for the ground of a room, but they did not come up to his idea of the ground of a tablet, nor would any other colour, unless it was a copy of some natural and valuable stone."

Brown advised Wedgwood to make the tablets in plain white, to imitate statuary marble, and many of the finest tablets for chimney pieces were left uncoloured. As a result of this advice, also, Wedgwood considered the production of fired relief figures with flat backs so that architects could fix them to natural stone grounds of their own choice.

Brownsword, Henry (fl.1849-1903)
Modeller and painter at Etruria for fifty-four years. He decorated Queen's ware* pieces, including ornamental plates and Quiver vases* in a style easily mistaken for Lessore's*. A self-portrait in blue and white jasper is in the Wedgwood Museum* at Barlaston*.

Brownsword, John (fl.1812-1825)
Decorator of bone china of the first period c.1812-22.

Brutus, Lucius Junius
Son of M. Junius and Tarquinia, sister of Tarquinius Superbus, King of Rome. With Tarquinius Collatinus, he was elected one of the first two Roman Consuls after the founding of the Republic in 510B.C. He should not be confused with Marcus Junius Brutus*, one of the assassins of Julius Caesar*.

A bust of *Junius Brutus,* height 25ins., was supplied by Hoskins & Grant* in 1774 and reproduced in basaltes.

Brownsword, Henry. *Painted Queen's ware dish, signed. 9ins. in diameter.* Zeitlin Collection.

Brutus, Marcus Junius (85?-42B.C.)

As a young man Brutus fought on the side of Pompey against Caesar*, but after the battle of Pharsalia he was pardoned and shown many marks of confidence and favour. Persuaded by Cassius to join in the plot to assassinate Caesar, Brutus retired to Macedonia. The combined forces of Cassius and Brutus were defeated by those of Octavian and Antony at Philippi in 42B.C., and Brutus committed suicide. He should not be confused with Lucius Junius Brutus, first Consul of Rome.

A bust of Brutus was supplied by Hoskins & Oliver* in 1774, and reproduced, height 25ins., in basaltes in that year.

Brutus, Marcus Junius. *Black basaltes portrait medallion of Marcus Junius Brutus, probably from a medal by Warin. First listed in the 1773 Catalogue.* Dwight and Lucille Beeson Collection.

Bryan, Sir Arthur (b.1923)

Chairman and Managing Director. Born in Stoke-on-Trent and educated at Longton High School, Arthur Bryan served in aircrew with the RAFVR during the Second World War. In 1947 he joined Wedgwood, spending the following two years in the production, design and administration departments at Barlaston* before joining the sales department. In 1950 he was appointed assistant London Manager, and three years later succeeded Felton Wreford as London Manager. In 1955 he was appointed General Manager of the Wedgwood Rooms*, a pioneering retail sales organisation started in 1953. In 1959 he was appointed General Sales Manager for all markets and in the following year moved to New York as President of Josiah Wedgwood & Sons, Inc. of America. His period as President was notable for a substantial increase in exports to the United States and, on the retirement of F. Maitland Wright and Norman Wilson* in 1963, Arthur Bryan was appointed

Managing Director of the parent company. He was the first chief executive of Wedgwood to be appointed from outside the family.

When Josiah V* retired in 1967, Arthur Bryan succeeded him as Chairman. Earlier in that year the company's shares were introduced for the first time to the London Stock Exchange.

During the first three months of 1966 Wedgwood had embarked on a policy of expansion, acquiring the businesses of William Adams*, Royal Tuscan (now Wedgwood hotelware), and Susie Cooper*, and forming the Wedgwood Group*. The Group's size was soon more than quadrupled by the acquisitions of Coalport, Johnson Brothers, J. & G. Meakin, Midwinter, Crown Staffordshire, and Mason's Ironstone, as well as the considerable expansion of the Wedgwood factory at Barlaston. Diversification was achieved by the addition of King's Lynn Glass (now Wedgwood Glass), Galway Crystal, Merseyside Jewellers (makers of jewellery mountings), and Precision Studios (specialised producers of ceramic decorative materials). The Group has formed a retail division through the acquisition of important London china and glass shops in the West End — Gered of Piccadilly and Regent Street, and Goldsmiths & Silversmiths Assn. at Oxford Circus.

During the first fifteen years of Arthur Bryan's tenure of office as chief executive, Wedgwood grew from a family firm employing 2,400 people to a group of companies with more than 10,000 employees in the United Kingdom. By 1977 the Group's twenty factories accounted for twenty per cent of the British ceramic industry's output and twenty-five per cent of its exports. Nor was expansion confined to the acquisition of other companies; plans were put in hand to complete by the end of

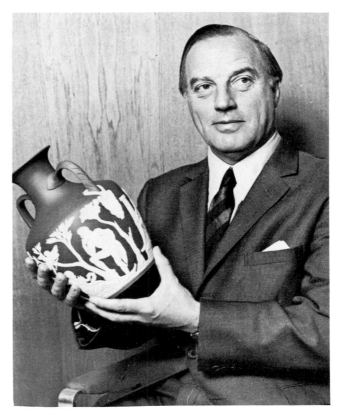

Bryan, Sir Arthur. *Chairman of Josiah Wedgwood & Sons Ltd., and of the Wedgwood Group.* Photo: Wedgwood.

1980 a £9.5 million development programme to increase production capacity by about twenty-six per cent.

This remarkable expansion was successfully undertaken at a period of industrial unrest and widespread commercial stagnation. Appointed Her Majesty's Lord Lieutenant of Staffordshire in 1968, Arthur Bryan was knighted for services to export in 1976.

Bubby Pot

A patent baby feeder* invented c.1777 by Dr. Hugh Smith and known as 'Smith's Bubby Pot'. Made by Wedgwood in plain or transfer-printed creamware.

Bulb Pot

See: Root Pot.

Burch, Edward, RA (1730-1814)

Burch was originally a waterman who was accepted into the Royal Academy school in 1769, and was elected a member two years later. Most of his work was as a gem engraver and modeller in wax (see: Gems). He exhibited at the Academy from 1771 to 1808, and at the Society of Artists, showing engraved gems, models in wax, and sulphurs*. He modelled for Wedgwood from 1788 to 1790.

Wedgwood subjects include:

George III, portrait medallion after the Academy Prize Medal entry, 1785.

Horses, nineteen models of single horses, including *Cleopatra* and *Dingannon.*

The Virgin (Virgo, sixth sign of the Zodiac*).

Burch, Edward. *Jasper button ornamented with relief of Burch horse (first on the centre line, right). 1½ ins. in diameter. c.1790.* Wedgwood.

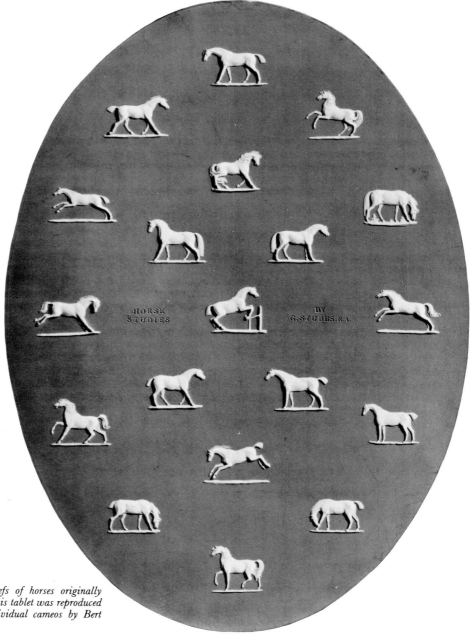

Burch, Edward. *Nineteen reliefs of horses originally modelled by Burch after Stubbs. This tablet was reproduced as a single composition from individual cameos by Bert Bentley.* Wedgwood.

Busts. *Black basaltes bust of Mark Antony, sometimes incorrectly known as* Terror. Zeitlin Collection.

Busts. *Black basaltes bust of Sir Isaac Newton after the 1718 ivory by David Le Marchand.* Zeitlin Collection.

Busts. *Black basaltes bust of Joseph Addison. 14½ ins. high. Impressed mark 'WEDGWOOD & BENTLEY'. c.1777.* Dwight and Lucille Beeson Collection.

61

Oval creamware plate with moulded and pierced rim, enamelled in rose-purple in the style generally associated with James Bakewell, though there is some evidence that similar painting was done by several others at the Chelsea Decorating Studios. c.1772. Reilly Collection.

Veilleuse of the type known as Veilleuse-théière or Veilleuse-tisanière (the upper part being a teapot), showing the aperture in the pedestal for the godet, which held a wick floating in oil to supply a low heat. c.1790. Photo: Authors.

Plate, painted with an unnamed view, from the Frog service made to the order of the Empress Catherine II of Russia in 1773-74. The service of 952 pieces was intended for the palace of Chesman at La Grenouillière (the place of frogs), and takes its name from the frog crest or emblem painted on the border. Wedgwood.

Burdett, Peter Perez (fl.1755-1780)

Engraver, painter and cartographer, of Old Hall Street, Liverpool. Towards the end of 1771 Burdett developed a method of engraving (a technique for transferring aquatint decoration to pottery and porcelain) which Wedgwood described as "the full and complete effect of painting in one colour." He also provided Wedgwood, who saw him in Liverpool, with an improved method of edging plates in colour. Burdett set off for London, to the Chelsea Decorating Studio*, but he was dissatisfied with his treatment there and eventually departed, after writing a series of acrimonious letters. Wedgwood paid him for some paintings of dead game, later copied by Ralph Unwin*. Burdett exhibited six engravings in the Society of Artists exhibitions between 1773 and 1779.

Burton, William (1863-1941)

Ceramic chemist and author. After a short period as a schoolmaster in Manchester, Burton obtained a scholarship to the Royal School of Mines. In 1887 he joined Wedgwood at Etruria* as a chemist, remaining for five years and making some important experiments in lustre* decoration which laid the foundations for the work of Daisy Makeig-Jones*. With his brother, Joseph, he managed the Pilkington Tile & Pottery Co. until his retirement in 1915, and it was largely due to his research and experiments that Pilkington's Lancastrian Pottery was able to produce a superb range of ornamental lustre. He wrote a number of books on the history and manufacture of pottery, including *Josiah Wedgwood and his Pottery*, 1922.

See: Fairyland Lustre.

Busts

The popularity of portrait busts in neo-classical England, and in Europe generally, was no doubt influenced by the growing interest in Roman portraiture. To the Romans belongs the credit for making the bust a statement about a particular human being, and not one about human beings in general, as in the case of Greek sculpture. The Romans also succeeded in making drapery a special characteristic of their sculpture, and it is by considering points such as this that one can sometimes assign Wedgwood's subjects to their Greek or Roman sources. The presence of a large number of Greek craftsmen in the Rome of the Caesars, however, makes the task somewhat more complex, and a useful exercise in connoisseurship.

Most of Wedgwood's portrait busts were in the black basaltes* body, imitating the appearance of Roman bronze heads and busts, and it is to this that they owed some of their popularity. There are also busts in the *rosso antico** and white terracotta* bodies, but these are relatively few, probably because it was well known that the Romans preferred bronze for portraiture. Busts were very occasionally made to special order, or for a special purpose, in white jasper or the waxen body. An example is the white jasper bust of Voltaire on a black basaltes pedestal to mark the great man's death. The well known Mark Antony (sometimes mistakenly referred to as *Terror*), which is an obvious pair to Cleopatra, is another white example which also occurs as a medallion.

Wedgwood began to give serious attention to busts in 1770, buying moulds and casts from Hoskins & Oliver*. This he found very expensive, and apparently bought some casts from Oliver in 1771 with the intention of making his own moulds. In February 1771, he wrote to Bentley that Oliver's casts were no use to make a mould from, and asked if Bentley could borrow some good bronze or marble busts for the purpose, suggesting an approach to Lord Rockingham and Lord Bessborough. Later he suggested that busts from the Academy would be better for his purpose, and more novel than anything to be obtained from the seller of casts.

It is easy to see why Wedgwood was charged heavily by the plaster sellers for their goods and services — the heads and moulds they sold him were being used to make a product which was both better and less vulnerable than their own, and the effect of the new product on their sales must have been considerable. Wedgwood was obtaining moulds and casts in large quantities, both from Hoskins and from John Cheere*. Surviving invoices from the former for 1774 and 1775 alone list fifty-six busts. In August 1774, Wedgwood wrote: "We are going on very fast with the busts, having four of our principal hands constantly employed on them...Hackwood bestows a week upon each head in restoring it to what we suppose it was when it came out of the hands of the statuary." A month later he wrote to Bentley: "The busts will employ Hackwood for a year or two before our collection is tolerably complete, and I am much set on having it so, being fully persuaded they will be a capital article with us...They are infinitely superior to the Plaister ones we take them from." Later in the same letter he remarks: "We now have about 14 busts repaired but what are they to the collection we ought to have?" By November, 1774, he was writing to Bentley on the subject of busts: "We should aim at procuring some *Maiden Ones* — I mean from Gentlemen's collections which have not yet found their way into the Plaister shops..."

The bust of Homer proved very popular, and this model was later made elsewhere in Staffordshire in a smaller version of glazed and painted earthenware. We may reasonably infer from the letters to Bentley that inquiries from London for busts of all sizes were frequent, but it was not always possible to identify the portrait with accuracy. In May 1777, Wedgwood confirmed that the only bust of Solon they had was one they called Demosthenes — "Mr Cox says it was called Solon when it first came from London in Plaister, and continues under that name in our Catalogue. We shall send you one or two of these."

An order for 105 busts came from Dublin in November 1778, and Veldhuysen*, Wedgwood's agent in Amsterdam, sent an order for eight busts, and seventy portrait medallions*, which was followed a few months later with an order for seventy busts of various sizes. By 1780 a number of Dutch subjects had been added to the busts available. Grotius (20ins. high) appears in the 1779 Catalogue, and Oldenbarneveldt seems to have been made by 1780. Advised by Egbert de Vrij Temminck, the Amsterdam Burgomaster, the Dutch group had received the addition of portraits of Boerhaave, de Ruyter, Hein, Hogerbeets, Kortenaar, the de Witt Brothers, and members of the Dutch Royal Family, as well as Temminck himself, by 1789. Portrait medallions also exist of these men.

Despite his hankering to break into the rigidly controlled and protected French market Wedgwood did not make many busts of French notabilities — only Voltaire, Rousseau, and Montesquieu, all three of whom were well known in 18th century England. Montesquieu was a member of the Royal Society, and all three held anti-Christian views. This is in contrast to the series of portrait medallions, where the number of French portraits is large, and Wedgwood also issued a set of the Kings of France, from Pharamond to Louis XVI.

An analysis of the 1779 Catalogue, the last issued by Wedgwood & Bentley (the latter died in 1780), shows nine busts, 25ins. high, of which eight are classical and one (Lord Chatham) modern; seven are 22ins. high, of which five are classical and two (Palladio and Inigo Jones) are modern and were, no doubt, intended as a pair; nine are 20ins. high, of

Right: **Buttons.** *Jasper buttons. Above: Hercules with his club and the skin of the Nemean lion. Right: Apollo standing between a lyre and a sacrificial tripod.* Wedgwood.

Left: **Butterfield, Lindsay.** *Vase designed in the art nouveau style, c.1910.* Buten Museum.

which three (Rousseau, Swift, and Grotius) are modern; six are 18ins. high, of which only the Venus de Medici is classical; there are three classical busts 16½ ins. high; thirty-one are 15½ ins. high, of which only thirteen are classical; one (Cicero) is 11½ ins. high; four moderns, including Voltaire, are 10ins. high; four classical subjects are 8ins. high; four moderns are 7ins. high; four, including another version of Voltaire, 4½ ins. high; and three moderns (Voltaire, Rousseau, and Montesquieu) and two classical, 4ins. high. This is a total of eighty-three subjects, although the Madona (*sic*) — 15ins., is entered twice, and there may only have been eighty-two. Missing from this list are large busts of Bacchus, Ariadne, Alexander, and Sterne. Not only are these in the old pricing book (which sets out the price to be paid to the repairer for moulding and preparing for firing) but Barnard *(Chats on Wedgwood)*, states that when he wrote in 1934 part of the moulds were still at Etruria. Of these busts, only one, that of Sterne, appears to survive, and this is in the earthenware biscuit body. There are also two 4½ -inch heads of Ariadne and Bacchus listed in 1779. As Barnard points out, the appearance in the pricing book makes it certain that the large Bacchus, Ariadne, and Alexander were made, since nothing was entered in this book until manufacture was started.

Basaltes busts were again popular in the 1850s, some reissues, and some the work of the sculptor, Edward Wyon*, who modelled John Bunyan, Field Marshall Sir Colin Campbell, Lord Palmerston, the two Stephensons, Tennyson, James Watt, and John Wesley.

In modern times busts of H.M. Queen Elizabeth II, H.R.H. The Duke of Edinburgh, the Prince of Wales, Sir Winston Churchill and Franklin Roosevelt have been made in basaltes, most after models by Arnold Machin*. The last two were also produced in Queen's ware.

See: Carrara Ware.

Buten Museum of Wedgwood

Founded in 1957, the Buten Museum of Wedgwood in Merion, near Philadelphia, is the only museum (outside the Wedgwood Museum* at Barlaston) dedicated entirely to the products and history of the Wedgwood firm. Starting from the modest purchase of a 1930 'silver' lustre (see: Platinum lustre) jug during a visit to Montreal in 1931, Harry M. Buten and his wife, Nettie, assembled a remarkable private collection of some 3,000 examples of Wedgwood wares of all periods. At a time when wares of the Victorian period were despised or neglected, the Butens had the foresight to collect fine and representative pieces, and the Museum collection of some 10,000 exhibits now contains the most comprehensive range of Wedgwood to be seen anywhere in the world.

Since the founding of the Museum, the cornerstone of which was the Buten's private collection, the number of exhibits has been more than trebled, and membership of the Museum exceeds 2,000. Museum publications include several books by Harry Buten (see bibliography) and reprints of standard works on Wedgwood which have long been out of print.

The Museum's Director is now Harry and Nettie Buten's son, David, a graduate of Wharton School, University of Pennsylvania, who serves on the board of directors of many cultural organisations.

Butterfield, Lindsay Phillip (1869-1948)

Nephew of the architect, William Butterfield; studied at Lambeth School of Art, Lambeth, 1887; apprenticed as architect to his cousin, Philip Johnstone, 1889, and studied at the National Training School, South Kensington, becoming a freelance designer in 1894. In 1909 he became a founder member of the Design Club, a free association of industrial designers and progressive manufacturers which included Wedgwood and Liberty's of Regent Street, London, among its members. For Wedgwood he designed a small number of ornamental vases and bowls, enamelled in bold colours with designs in the art nouveau style. These, known as Lindsay Ware, were backstamped with the name, Lindsay, within a cartouche of leaves. Lindsay ware appears to be extremely rare and was probably made in very small quantities.

Butterfly Lustre

See: Ordinary Lustres.

Buttons

The 18th century was the great age of lavish buttons. More decorative than useful, they were made in gold, silver, copper, brass, cut steel, pinchbeck*, French *passementerie,* glass, porcelain, ivory and bone. They were worn more by men than women, and their size and brilliance reflected the taste of pre-Revolutionary France for the display of luxury. They were regularly made in sets, varying in number from five to thirty-five, and even larger sets were custom-made for particularly splendid garments.

Wedgwood's jasper* cameos* were specially well suited to this purpose, and his friendly business connection with Matthew Boulton* provided a ready source of cut-steel mounts*. In 1775, as soon as he was 'absolute' in his jasper, Wedgwood sent a quantity of cameos to Boulton's Soho (Birmingham) works for mounting in cut steel as buttons. Even earlier, some white body cameos, the backgrounds coloured in enamel, had been mounted under glass with plain metal rims and backs. These are extremely rare. Lapel buttons, with a miniature replica of the Portland* vase in relief on various coloured jasper grounds, have been made since the 1950s, principally to be worn by Wedgwood's staff at trade shows and exhibitions.

Byerley, Thomas (1747-1810)

The son of Josiah I's elder sister, Margaret, Tom Byerley had early ambitions to be a writer or an actor but lacked the necessary application for success in either career. Nor were his ambitions approved by his mother or his uncle. In June 1768, he was helped by Wedgwood to emigrate to America where, after some abortive ventures in other directions, he settled in New York as a schoolmaster. In 1775 the outbreak of the War of Independence persuaded him to return to England. Josiah gave him a job as a clerk, and he became Clerk to the Committee of Potters. His knowledge of French enabled him to translate and compose Wedgwood's correspondence with French customers, and he became a useful salesman and debt collector. When Josiah decided to have his children taught at home it was Byerley who instructed them in Latin, English, French, writing, accountancy and drawing.

After the death of Bentley* in 1780, Byerley was entrusted with the management of the London showrooms*. He married Frances Bruckfield of Derby, and became the father of a numerous family.

In 1787-88 Byerley visited Paris, and two years later he accompanied Josiah II* on an extended tour of the Continent where they displayed, for the first time outside England, a copy of the Portland* vase. During their stay in The Hague, they enjoyed the assistance of Sir William Eden (Lord Auckland*). Their travels also took them to Germany, Switzerland and France.

In 1790 the partnership of Wedgwood, Sons & Byerley was established (see: Proprietors of Wedgwood) and Josiah I began gradually to retire from the business. For several years after Josiah's death in 1795 Byerley was left in charge of the factory and it has been suggested that his inexperience was responsible for the firm's decline at this time. That he was a poor manager is scarcely to be doubted, but the firm was also severely affected by war in Europe and social unrest at home which depressed industry and commerce, and the indiscipline of factory employees, attributable partly to the influence of the French Revolution, had been evident for some years before Byerley found himself suddenly in charge. The absence of Josiah's sons, John* and Josiah II, who preferred the country to the Potteries, was as much to blame as Byerley's inadequacy.

Byres, James (1734-1817)

Scottish architect (though none of his designs appears ever to have been built) living in Rome from c.1756. In 1764 he began a new career as antiquarian, and showed the historian, Edward Gibbon, the sights of Rome. Later in the same year he made his first major purchase — a ''Picture of the Assumption by Poussin'' (now in the National Gallery of Art, Washington) — for Lord Exeter. Sixteen years, and many guided tours, later, Byres had become respected as ''a gentleman of probity, knowledge, and rare taste.'' He had also made the acquaintance of Sir William Hamilton*. In 1780 Byres bought the Barberini (later Portland*) vase from Donna Cornelia Barberini-Colonna and had no difficulty in selling it to Hamilton for £1,000. For the next ten years he was profitably employed in his dual professions of antiquarian and dealer, crowning his career by the acquisition and illegal export from Italy of Poussin's *Seven Sacraments,* which he sold to the Duke of Rutland. In 1790 he retired to the family estate of Tonley, in Aberdeenshire, where he died at the age of eighty-three.

Byerley, Thomas. *Portrait medallion in jasper of Thomas Byerley (1742-1810), modelled by William Theed in 1810.* Wedgwood.

Byres, James. *Jasper portrait medallion of James Byres modelled by James Tassie in 1779.* Scottish National Portrait Gallery.

C

Cabaret à Deux

The *cabaret à deux,* a set comprising two cups and saucers, cream jug, sugar box, and either a teapot or a chocolate pot on a tray, was probably the largest group of jasper teaware* made during the 18th century. The interiors and rims of cups were often lapidary polished*, but it is clear that these sets were intended for 'cabinets' and not for use. Similar sets were made by both French and English porcelain factories.

Cabinet Pieces

Term applied to apparently 'useful' wares intended solely for ornament, and particularly to jasper teaware* and coffee ware (the hollow ware* with unglazed interiors) made in the 18th century. Such pieces were finely ornamented and often engine turned*, with lapidary polished* rims (and sometimes also interiors) of cups. 'Cabinet' jasper of this type was made until the last quarter of the 19th century and some of these late pieces are of excellent quality, though the jasper body is more granular than that of the first period.

Cadell, Thomas (1742-1802)

London publisher; partner with Andrew Millar in The Strand, London, and took over the business in 1767. Alderman of London 1798, and Sheriff 1800-1801. Wedgwood obtained several important books from him, including the second and third volumes of Sir William Hamilton's* *Etruscan Antiquities.* His provision of prints for landscapes used for the Frog* service, and the misprinting of his name as 'Cedell', has led to the erroneous statement that he was a painter employed at the Chelsea Decorating Studio*.

Cades, Giuseppe (1750-1799)

Often identified as a modeller employed by Flaxman* and Webber* in Rome, Cades was a sculptor and gem engraver, whose signed gem, *The Sale of Erotes,* a subject copied as a cameo by Wedgwood, was inspired by a mural painting now in the Naples Museum. The subject was well known and popular during the second half of the 18th century, and Wedgwood may have obtained a glass paste gem from Tassie* to use as his model. Cades was partly responsible for 18th century decoration to the Borghese Palace, Rome.

See also: Borghese Family.

Caesar, Julius. *Jasper portrait medallion of Caius Julius Caesar, said to have been modelled by John Flaxman Junior in 1776. National Museum of Wales.*

Cabaret. *Solitaire with one cup and saucer, à deux with two. Tray, Brewster teapot, creamer, sugar basin, and tea bowl and saucer ornamented with Lady Templetown's* Domestic Employment *and* Poor Maria, *modelled by Hackwood. All pieces except the tray are also engine-turned. c.1784. Wedgwood.*

Caduceus

The herald's wand, or staff, carried by Hermes (Mercury*) in his rôle as messenger of the gods. In addition he wears a winged helmet, and has wings on his heels. The caduceus is sometimes used by itself as an ornament, when it commonly stands in place of Hermes.

Caesar, Caius Julius (106-44 B.C.)

Dictator and general. Caesar courted the favour of the people, and in so doing attained the highest offices of State. Crassus, Pompey, and Caesar entered into an agreement to divide the State between them. Pompey became jealous of Caesar's military successes, and in 49 Caesar was called upon by the Senate to disband his army. Instead, he crossed the river Rubicon, the southern boundary of his command, and marched on Rome. Pompey's army deserted to Caesar, and Pompey and his associates withdrew to Greece. Caesar followed and defeated him at Pharsalia in 48. Pompey fled to Egypt, and was murdered there. Caesar pursued him, and placed Cleopatra* and her brother, Ptolemy, on the throne. He had a son, Caesarion, by Cleopatra. When Caesar returned to Rome in triumph in 45 Marc Antony offered him the royal crown, but Caesar refused it. The action was used by Cassius, a bitter enemy of Caesar's, to foment a conspiracy among members of the aristocratic party to assassinate Caesar, who fell at the foot of Pompey's statue on the 15th March, 44 B.C.

Wedgwood subjects:
Portrait medallion by Flaxman*, 1776.
Bust supplied by Hoskins & Grant, 1779. Not listed in the Catalogues after that date.

Calcining

The process of heating a substance like flint* or ox bones (see: Bone ash) until it can be reduced to powder.

'Caledonian Boar'

The Calydonian Boar is thus misspelt in the 1779 Catalogue, and in one of Wedgwood's letters.
See: Meleager.

Calendar Plate

Queen's ware Calendar plates were introduced by Wedgwood in 1971. The first of the series was decorated with the signs of the Zodiac*.

Calendar Tiles

Rare Queen's ware rectangular tiles printed with a calendar on one side, and on the other side a decoration which is usually an illustration in monochrome of a subject from Boston (Mass.). Single tiles could be used as calendars or for wall decoration, since they were pierced for hanging, and they could also be employed as teapot stands. The mark is 'WEDGWOOD COPYRIGHT JONES, McDUFFEE & STRATTON', and the year and the name of the subject. The firm were Wedgwood's United States representatives for commemorative ware*. Calendar tiles were produced from 1879 to 1929.

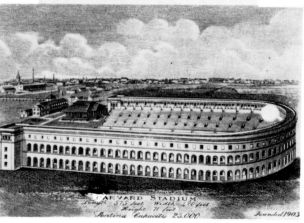

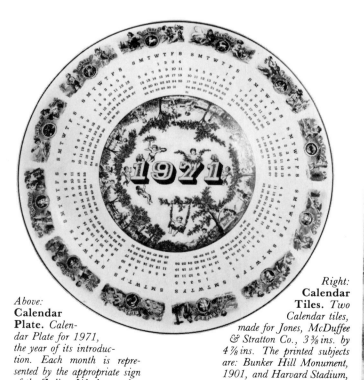

Above:
Calendar Plate. *Calendar Plate for 1971, the year of its introduction. Each month is represented by the appropriate sign of the Zodiac. Wedgwood.*

Right:
Calendar Tiles. *Two Calendar tiles, made for Jones, McDuffee & Stratton Co., 3⅜ ins. by 4⅞ ins. The printed subjects are: Bunker Hill Monument, 1901, and Harvard Stadium, 1907. Sotheby's Belgravia.*

Caligula, Caius Caesar (A.D.12-41)

Roman Emperor A.D.37-41. Born in A.D.12, the son of Germanicus and Agrippina, Caligula was always called Caius by his intimates. The name 'Caligula' was given to him by the Legionaries as a small boy when he frequented their camps in Germany because he wore small *caligae*, or soldier's boots. He succeeded to the Imperial power on the death of Tiberius. As the son of the popular Germanicus he was greeted with enthusiasm, but after a serious illness he became insane and his cruelty pathological. He had a temple built to himself, and mounted an expedition into Gaul for no other reason than to replenish his treasury by plunder and extortion. He was assassinated in A.D.41, with his wife and daughter.

Wedgwood subject:
Portrait in the series entitled *The Twelve Caesars*.

Cameo

A term originally applied to gems* carved in low relief during the Greek and Roman period, and later extended to small objects similarly carved, especially those of natural laminated material providing a background of contrasting colour to the relief (e.g. shell cameos). The word *cameo* actually means decoration in relief, irrespective of size, but by general usage it has become more or less confined to small objects of this kind, the larger being described as medallions*, plaques* or tablets*.

Antique gems were avidly collected during the 18th century, and Wedgwood was able, on a number of occasions, to make use of existing collections as a source of designs for his own cameos and intaglios*. Impressions of intaglios were taken in a mixture of sulphur and wax, and cameos could be cast in the normal way. Many such casts were made by James Tassie* for reproduction in his glass paste, and Wedgwood bought moulds from him. Wedgwood also employed gem engravers, among whom the most important was probably Edward Burch, RA*.

In his 1779 Catalogue of Ornamental Ware Wedgwood refers to his cameos as fit for rings, buttons, lockets, bracelets, inlaying into fine cabinets, writing tables, bookcases, etc. His sources, he freely acknowledges, were the nobility and gentry in possession either of the original gems, or of fine impressions of gems in foreign collections (e.g. the Duke of Marlborough and Sir Watkin Williams Wynn*). The cameos were first made in basaltes or in 'waxen biscuit' with grounds enamelled in different colours, and later in jasper with blue or brown grounds. The jasper cameos were said to be like those of natural stone, and to admit of the same polish. Subjects listed in Wedgwood's catalogues included Egyptian mythology; Greek and Roman mythology; philosophers; the Trojan war; Roman history; illustrious men; and an appendix of recent additions, some of which would be better described as portrait medallions*.

At this time Wedgwood & Bentley advertised their willingness to make likenesses of their patrons, families and friends, in the form of jasper cameos in sizes suitable for rings, lockets, seals or bracelets from waxes or engraved stones, either in cameo or intaglio. The wax model for a portrait suitable for a ring, seal or bracelet cost three guineas. For the jasper copies ("black and Blue Onyxes") either cameo or intaglio, the sum of 5s. was charged in lots of not less than ten. Cameos for rings were the same price, and those for bracelets, 7s. 6d. These also were sold in lots of ten or more. Portrait medallions could be made on similar terms, the cost of a medallion from three to six inches in diameter being from three to five guineas.

Nearly all cameos were of jasper or 'waxen biscuit' with or without enamelled backgrounds. Double cameos — two cameos fused back-to-back and thus ornamented on both sides — were also made. These are unmarked. Cameos were made

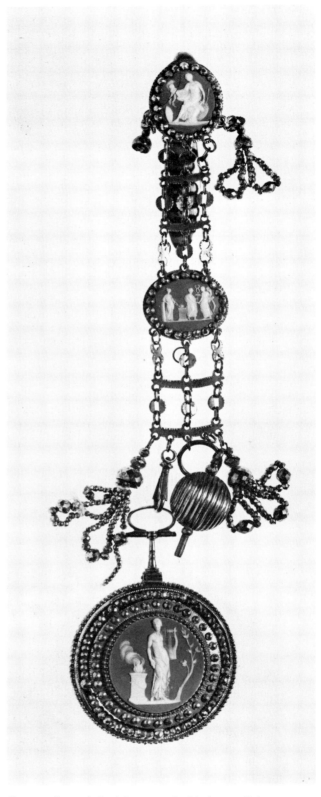

Cameo. *Cut-steel chatelaine mounted with three small jasper cameos. c.1785.* Wedgwood.

in both solid jasper and jasper dip*, and many had bevelled and lapidary polished* edges. They were mounted in cut-steel mounts*, silver, pinchbeck* or gold by such firms as Boulton* & Fothergill* and Boden & Smith*. Subjects specially designed included cameos of horses by Edward Burch after George Stubbs*. Specimens exist of cameos with yellow, brown, green, black, blue and lilac grounds, but only those with blue grounds are commonly found, and the experimental yellow is extremely rare. Also rare are early cameos of more than two colours, though small quantities were made during the 19th century and again in 1959.

The manufacture of cameos was started in 1771 and was well established by the spring of 1772, when Wedgwood wrote of a variety of gems in the "bisket oven." Jasper cameos date from 1775. In 1773 Wedgwood supplied Boulton & Fothergill with plain white cameos which they set under glass into the lids of small boxes. The cameo grounds were painted in water-colour.

Objects decorated with Wedgwood cameos included *chatelaines,* combs, clock pendulums, clock cases, watch cases, snuff boxes, patch boxes, *étuis,* work boxes, writing desks, toothpick cases, metal vases and urns, metal lamps, metal boxes, coach panels, buckles, bracelets, lockets, buttons, rings, brooches, sword hilts, opera glasses (monocular* and binocular), scent bottles, watch keys, and *papier mâché* made by Henry Clay* of Birmingham and others. Cameos were also used to ornament vases and some rare three-colour jasper cabinet pieces*.

Cameograph Company

A company specialising in the production of bas-reliefs* and sculpture multiplied by a process of machine carving. Harry Barnard*, who modelled fifty-four medallions and six busts for the Cameograph Company, described the process as "wonder-ful. . .and quite satisfactory for a foundation, but in translating it into such a material as our Jasper it required more work upon it which was entrusted to me." The medallions reproduced in jasper* have a curiously flat appearance in comparison with those cast from moulds. They include portrait medallions of Edward VIII as Prince of Wales, George V, and George VI as Duke of York, all c.1925.

Camera Obscura

Optical apparatus consisting of a box with an open side, over which a black curtain is hung. Fitted into the box at the top is a convex lens (mounted on bellows to allow of focusing) above which is an adjustable angled mirror. The object to be copied is reflected in the mirror, and the image passes through the lens to form a picture on the white paper placed on the viewing table at the base of the box. The image appears the right way up but reversed. With his head under the curtain, any copier may trace over the outline of the image, but it required a professional draughtsman's technique to produce anything resembling a work of art. The invention of the camera obscura is often attributed to Giovanni Battista della Porta in 1569, but the principle was well known and employed many years earlier. It was extensively used by the artists employed by Wedgwood to obtain "real views" for the the Frog* service and by Thomas Daniel(l)*. Thomas Wedgwood* was the first to make use of the camera obscura in photographic experiments in 1794.

Campana

A vase shape derived from the Greek krater. It is of inverted bell shape, with side handles low down on the shoulders. Originally made in ancient times, it was popular towards the end of the 18th century and during Empire (Regency) times. The porcelain factories used it primarily as a vehicle for fine paintings, and Wedgwood employed the shape extensively for basaltes* and jasper* vases. The vase 43, which is a campana shape is still produced in jasper.

Campana. *Black basaltes krater of depressed Campana shape in the form of a bough pot, enamelled with Oriental flowers, c.1810. The same shape occurs in ornamented basaltes, in encaustic painted basaltes, and (generally with a square plinth) in white smear glazed stoneware with coloured ornaments. The bowl is fitted with two interior lids (one pierced) and was intended for alternative use as a pot pourri vase. The same shape appears in the Spode Shape Book for 1820 described as a "Pot-Pourri Bowpot."* Sotheby's Belgravia.

Canal, Trent & Mersey

A considerable obstacle to the expansion of the pottery industry in Staffordshire was the state of communications between London and Liverpool. Roads were hardly more than cart tracks, impassable in winter, and the pack horse was widely used to transport both raw materials and the finished product. Wedgwood, already connected with a scheme for constructing turnpikes (toll roads) as early 1760, supported a scheme in 1765 for connecting the rivers Trent and Mersey by a canal, which would have the effect of linking the Potteries with Liverpool and Hull. Eventually, with its branches, it linked the Potteries with the rest of England.

In 1766 Wedgwood was appointed Treasurer to the Proprietors, contributing £1,000 towards the cost. The scheme had been proposed as early as 1755, and surveying of the route began in 1762. Constructional work was started at Brownhills, between Burslem and Tunstall, in 1766 with a celebration which included an ox roasted whole. The engineer of the project was James Brindley* on behalf of the Duke of Bridgewater*, who was the leading spirit. Brindley died in 1772, five years before the completion of the work. The new canal was ninety-three miles long, there were seventy-five locks to be negotiated, and at its highest point it traversed a tunnel 2,880 yards long at Harecastle. It passed through the Etruria estate, with a branch alongside the factory, and the waterway now runs through the Barlaston* estate. In a letter to R.L. Edgeworth* in 1786 Wedgwood estimated the whole cost at £3,000,000, or between £700 and £800 a mile. By these means the cost of transportation was reduced from 10 pence to 1¾ pence per mile per ton for raw materials. A pamphlet setting out the advantages of the scheme and the savings to be anticipated, was produced by Wedgwood with the help of Erasmus Darwin*, Bentley* being responsible for the final draft. The bicentenary of the Canal's completion was celebrated at Barlaston by a rally staged by the Trent & Mersey Canal Society in 1977.

Canarsac, Lafon de (1821-1905)

Paris manufacturer of porcelain who, in 1854, invented a technique of using photographs for ceramic decoration. He was awarded a medal for his exhibit at the London International Exhibition of 1862, and the Victoria and Albert Museum has a cup and saucer acquired at that time.

See: Photolithography.

Candlesticks

Among the earliest objects made by Wedgwood, candlesticks exist in a wide variety of shapes and in all the ceramic bodies produced by the firm since 1760. Early examples of green glaze*, tortoiseshell* ware and variegated* ware candlesticks have survived. Although many of the shapes are elegant enough to be considered as purely ornamental, all appear to have been intended for use. In general, candlestick shapes followed closely the designs for silver, and a knowledge of English and Continental silver is often useful in dating them. Among the forms produced during the lifetime of Josiah I* are the following:

Cassolettes*.

Chamber candlesticks (chambersticks) — short-stemmed candlesticks provided with loop carrying handles, and usually with cone-shaped snuffers, designed to light the owner to bed.

Dolphin*.

Figure (e.g. *Ceres** and *Cybele**).

Griffin*.

Laurel leaf, a moulded relief pattern of overlapping leaves covers the entire body of the candlestick.

Pillar, simple tall pillar shapes, often in turned jasper dip*.

Reading, turned, flared bell-shape.

Rustic, figures of boys by Hackwood.

Sphinx*, candleholders sprouting somewhat oddly from the head of the figure, occur on both the seated and the crouching sphinx models in basaltes*, basaltes and *rosso antico** and jasper*.

Triton*.

Above: **Candlesticks.** *Solid marbled candlesticks, the nozzles supported by three sphinx monopodia. Originally produced during the Wedgwood & Bentley period in black basaltes, and later in jasper, this shape was reproduced in the 19th century in various bodies with varying aesthetic appeal. 6¾ ins. high. Date code for 1864.* Christie's.

Right: **Candlesticks.** *Pair of silver-pattern marbled candlesticks, 6¼ ins. high. c.1845.* Nottingham Castle Museum.

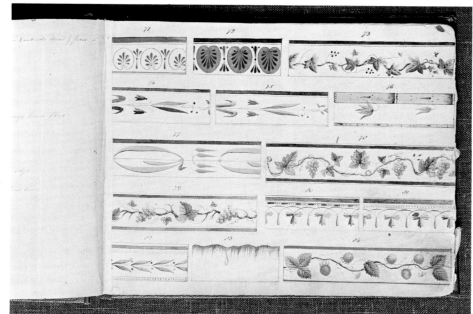

Colour Plate V

Right: Page from the first Pattern Book (copied c.1810 from the original started c.1769) showing typical hand-painted border patterns of the period. Wedgwood.

Below: Page from the Pattern Book showing the original designs for the 'Dogs of Fo' (Chinese Tigers) pattern, c.1814, and a modern reproduction teacup and saucer of the same bone china pattern. Wedgwood.

Candlesticks. *Pair of silver-pattern candlesticks, similar to shape No.14 in the first Queen's ware catalogue, covered with a green glaze.* City Museum, Stoke-on-Trent.

Candlesticks. *Canopic vase-candlestick in black basaltes, 9½ ins. high, Wedgwood & Bentley period.* Laver Collection.

Candlesticks. *Pair of table candlesticks: the left hand figure is Minerva with a shield bearing the head of Medusa; and the right is Diana, goddess of the chase, with a hound, 13¾ ins. high.* Wedgwood.

Above: **Cane Ware.** *Tureen of enamelled cane ware with rare cow finial. c.1790.* Buten Museum.

Right: **Cane Ware.** *Pot-pourri vase painted with a fêng huang (phoenix) and Oriental flowers. c.1820.* Wedgwood.

Cane Ware

Vitreous biscuit or dry body* prepared from local marl. Production dates from 1770, when Wedgwood refined the clays used by Staffordshire potters for traditional brown wares to make a new tan-coloured body which he called 'Cane'. The colour varied considerably, from a rich tan-yellow to buff, the darker shade being used for 'Bamboo'* in imitation of earlier Chinese wares.

Next to jasper and basaltes, cane was Wedgwood's most important ornamental body, besides being used for a wide variety of 'useful'* wares, but it was not until some years after Bentley's* death that Wedgwood overcame difficulties in production. He wrote to Bentley in September 1779: "Our present cane colour body is very imperfect. It has a coarse speckled appearance if examin'd with attention. Is very porous & apt to stain. I have not yet been able to give it a porcelain texture, & preserve its color..." Three weeks later he sent statuettes of Voltaire and Rousseau to London, but wrote, "you will find them so much discoloured in burning as to stand in need of a wash of paint. We cover'd them close in burning, knowing how apt this body is to turn brown, but in vain...I hope to overcome this evil but it must be with a new body, the present is incorrigible." A letter from Josiah II* to his father in

1783 refers to trials of a new cane body, and it appears that this was perfected soon afterwards. The resulting body was fine grained and would stand up to being thinly potted and engine-turned* on the lathe. Further decoration was added in the form of relief ornaments, encaustic painting*, and enamelling in blue, green or red. Applied ornament was often in a contrasting colour, the most popular being green, lilac, blue, chocolate and white.

A rather coarser cane body was also used for pastry ware* and game pie dishes*. In the 1820s and 1830s smear-glazed* cane ware was introduced in both cast and turned shapes and with moulded or applied decoration.

The cane colour later inspired the production of *Honey-Buff* Queen's ware tableware for Heals in 1930, and *Harvest Moon* on the Barlaston shape* in the 1950s. In 1975 Wedgwood introduced primrose jasper in bamboo shapes and with white prunus blossom* or Egyptian terracotta colour reliefs. This closely resembles the palest cane, but the composition of the body is easily distinguished as different.

Cane ware was copied in the 18th and 19th centuries, notably by the Spode*, Davenport*, Liverpool. Herculaneum*, E. Mayer*, and Turner* factories.

Cane Ware. *Bough pot in the form of a Greek kylix, flanked by a pair of canopic vases decorated with Egyptian motifs in rosso antico and fine gilding.* Zeitlin Collection.

73

Canephoros
Figure of a woman with a basket on her head used for the same purpose as the caryatid*.

Canisters
An early name for a short, wide container with a bottle-shaped neck which, filled with tea, was an essential part of the 18th century 'tea-equipage'. Canisters were of silver and porcelain, and they were made by Wedgwood in jasper, black basaltes, and Queen's ware.
See: Tea Caddy.

Canopic Jars
A set of four jars in which the ancient Egyptians preserved the viscera of the deceased, usually for inhumation with the mummy. They were made at the Egyptian city of Canopus. Jars similar in style were employed for funerary purposes by the Etruscans as cinerary urns. The term 'Canopic vase' was used by Wedgwood for a human-headed vase in the Ptolemaic style after an illustration in Bernard de Montfaucon's* *L'Antiquité Expliquée,* Paris, 1722, which was in Josiah Wedgwood's library.

Canova, Antonio (1757-1852)
Neo-classical* sculptor, who lived in Rome from 1781. He went to Vienna in 1797 during Napoleon's invasion of Italy, but accepted Napoleon's invitation to Paris in 1802, and carved portraits of the Emperor and some of the Bonaparte family. In 1816 he was ennobled by the Pope for his part in ensuring the return to Italy of art treasures looted by the French armies. Canova greatly influenced the neo-classical style in his day.

Two statuettes after Canova were made by Wedgwood — *Creugantes* and *Damoxenes,* both boxers.

Cans
See: Coffee Cans

Car
A waste product of coal mining used in Staffordshire for colouring clays employed in the manufacture of pottery.
See: Black Egyptian.

Carocchi, Fabbri & Co. (Gubbio, Italy)

Makers of reproductions of Italian *maiolica* established about 1857. According to Marryat *(Pottery & Porcelain)* a young man named Luigi 'Parocci' (undoubtedly Carocchi), who was a pupil of the chemist, Professor Angelico Fabbri, rediscovered the method of producing the lustre of Maestro Giorgio Andreoli, not only the early ruby colour, but other, "more rare tints". On the 13th April, 1857, twenty plates thus decorated were exhibited in Gubbio, which were taken for genuinely early ware by those who saw them. It was this secret process which Pietro Gaj* offered to sell to Wedgwood in 1862.

See also: Gubbio Lustre: Lustre Decoration.

Carrara Ware

Wedgwood's name for Parian*, introduced at Etruria about 1849, and named after the celebrated white statuary marble from the quarries at Carrara in Northern Italy. The name did not become widely accepted, and the term 'Parian' is more commonly used to describe the wares of all factories. Many of Wedgwood's earlier busts and figures were reproduced in Carrara ware, and others, by or after work by Beattie*, Carrier de Belleuse*, F.M. Miller* and Wyon* were modelled specially for the new body.

The following Wedgwood subjects, of which the first twelve were exhibited in 1851, are listed as being in production on 1st October, 1859:

FIGURES

Christ on the Mount, height 15ins.
Madonna, height 13ins.
Madonna on pedestal, height 15ins.
Diana, 8⅞ins. by 9½ins.
Ariadne, 8⅞ins. by 9½ins.
Mercury by Pigalle*, height 17ins.
Venus by Pigalle, height 18ins.
Crouching Venus, height 13ins.
Sterne's* *Poor Maria,* height 12½ins.
Cupid, height 24ins.
Venus and Cupid, height 27ins.
Infant Hercules, 20ins. by 17ins.
Morpheus, 18ins. by 24ins.
Faun with Infant Bacchus, height 18ins.
Eros and Euphrosyne, height 22ins.
Greek Flute Player, height 14ins.
Faun and Goat, height 23½ins.
Broken Heart, height 12¼ins.
Strawberry Girl, height 15ins.
England ⎫
Ireland ⎬ by Beattie, height 13ins.
Scotland ⎭
Wanderer (female figure), height 18ins.
Spring ⎫
Summer ⎬ height 10ins.
Autumn ⎬
Winter ⎭
Infant Bacchus, height 13ins.
Triton candlesticks, height 11ins.
Cupid, height 7½ins.
Psyche, height 7½ins.
Venus, height 9½ins.
Cleopatra, height 9½ins.
Water Nymph, height 9ins.
Innocence, height 12ins.
Forget-me-not, height 9ins.
Cupid with Bow, height 9ins.
Nymph at the Fount, 10½ins. by 11½ins.

Nubian Water Carrier by Wyon*, height 9½ins.
Hope by Wyon, 9½ins. x 9½ins.
Grape Gatherer (male), height 10ins.
Grape Gatherer (female), height 10ins.
Shakespeare, height 17½ins.
Milton, height 17½ins.
Hiawatha, height 20ins.
America, height 4½ins.
Faun with Flute, height 17ins.
Faun after Clodion*, height 15ins.
Bacchante after Clodion, height 15ins.
Satyr after Clodion, height 14½ins.
Bacchus
Apollo
Mercury
Antinous

GROUPS

The Sacrifice (Abraham offering up his son Isaac), by Beattie, 24ins. by 14ins.
The Interpretation (Joseph before Pharaoh), by Beattie, 20ins. by 16ins.
Finding of Moses by Beattie, 19½ins. x 15ins.
Isaac and Rebekah by Beattie, 21½ins. by 18ins.
Cupid and Psyche, 12½ins. by 12½ins.
Oberon by Wyon, 21ins. by 13ins.
Titania by Wyon, 21ins. by 13ins.
Venus and Cupid, 21ins. by 12ins.
May-Day, 10ins. by 9ins.
Boy and Goat, height 8ins.
The Surprise, height 13ins.
Charity ⎫ 15ins. by 18ins.
Faith ⎬ set by Carrier de Belleuse* height 18ins.
Hope ⎭ height 18ins.
The Marketer

BUSTS

Byron by Wyon, height 15ins.
Moore by Wyon, height 15ins.
Scott by Wyon, height 15ins.
Burns by Wyon, height 14ins.
Shakespeare by Flaxman*, height 14ins.
Milton by Wyon, height 14ins.
Bunyan by Wyon, height 14ins.
Wellington by Wyon, height 15½ins.
Colin Campbell by Wyon, height 16ins.
Havelock by Wyon, height 15ins.
George Stephenson by Wyon, height 15ins.
Robert Stephenson by Wyon, height 15ins.
James Watt, by Wyon, height 15ins.
Venus, height 14ins.
Washington, height 19½ins.
Pope Pius IX, height 10ins.
Sir Isaac Newton, height 9ins.
Wesley, height 9ins.
Christ after Michelangelo, height 3ins.
Locke, height 3ins.
Sir Walter Raleigh, height 4ins.
Lord Palmerston (two sizes), 15ins. and 10ins.

MISCELLANEOUS MODELS

Spill vase, *Bonfire,* 4½ins.
Spill vase, *Muses,* 4ins. and 3ins.
Candlesticks, *Oak and Vine,* 10ins.
Butter cooler, *Sunflower.*
Beehive honey pot.
Sleeping Boy, on pedestal.

Carrier de Belleuse, Albert Ernest (1824-1887)

French sculptor and modeller for porcelain who studied with the École des Beaux-Arts, Paris (1840). He established a large studio for sculpture and ornamental work, where one of his assistants was Auguste Rodin. He reproduced statuary, in small and large sizes, and made many pastiches for decorative purposes, usually signed. He worked for a number of English factories, including Minton*, Copeland, Brownfields and Wedgwood. For Wedgwood he modelled a figure called *Charity* shown at the Great Exhibition of 1851. In 1870 he was appointed art-director at Sèvres*.

Caryatid

Figure of a woman used in architecture in place of a column to support an entablature. Caryatids are the female form of Atlantes (see Atlas). They occur in classical ornamental design, and Wedgwood used them to provide supports for a small number of fine basaltes tripod vases of the Wedgwood & Bentley period.

Cassandra

Daughter of Hecuba and Priam, King of Troy, and desired by Apollo*. He was ready to confer on her the gift of prophecy if she would promise to comply with his desires, but when she received the prophetic power she was no longer willing to fulfil her promise, and Apollo decreed that no one should believe her prophecies. After the fall of Troy, which she had foretold with irritating perseverance, Cassandra became part of the share of Agamemnon, who took her to Mycenae. There she was murdered by Clytemnestra and subsequently deified.

Two Wedgwood medallions are generally listed:

Cassandra, 7¼ins. by 4½ins., modelled by John Bacon*, and included in the 1773, 1774, 1777, 1779 and 1787 Catalogues*.
Cassandra grasping the Palladium, which appears only in the 1788 (French) Catalogue.

From the Catalogue description and the surviving examples, it is plain that these are one and the same. The medallion, described as taken from a gem in the collection of the French King (Louis XVI), was more probably copied from an antique bas-relief* now in The Louvre.

Cassolette

A covered vase to contain perfumed substances for scenting a room. It has holes pierced in the shoulders, and usually in the cover also. Some mounted vases have had a pierced metal band added between the mouth and the cover, thus changing them into cassolettes or pot-pourri vases*. Boulton* called vases of this kind 'essence pots' or 'essence vases'. They were made also by Wedgwood, although Wedgwood's productions, being ceramic ware, are more likely to be pot-pourri vases, the essential difference between the two being that the cassolette contains dry ingredients and the pot-pourri vase liquid.

See: Pastille Burner.

Caster

See: Cruet Set.

Casting

The process of using a mould or moulds to duplicate an existing model by pouring in a liquid which later sets or hardens. The moulds are usually of fired clay or plaster of Paris. Plaster moulds are commonly used for slip casting* because they readily absorb a good deal of moisture from semi-liquid clay. Fire-clay moulds are more commonly employed for press moulding*, although plaster moulds may be used for this purpose.

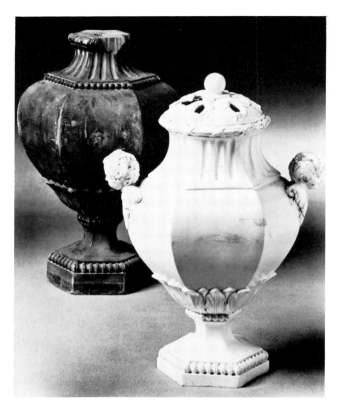

Casting. *Wooden block mould carved by John Coward and an example of a creamware vase cast from it. c.1770.* Wedgwood.

Every cast begins with an original model from which a mould is taken. This may be modelled for the purpose in clay or wax, or it may already exist in marble, bronze, or wood. Moulds have usually been made of plaster of Paris since about 1745. This is a fine powder which, when mixed with water, forms a plastic substance varying in consistency from dough to thin cream according to the amount of water added. In this state it will take on the shape of anything with which it is brought into contact and, after an interval which varies from five to thirty minutes according to the type of plaster being used, it becomes rigid. At the same time a certain amount of heat is generated, and there is a slight increase in size.

To take moulding an ordinary portrait bust as an example, the workman first decides how many pieces will be necessary, and this largely depends on the complexity of the model. A clean-shaven bald man requires fewer pieces than a woman with an elaborate *coiffure,* and a bearded man can cause distinct difficulties, since the pieces of the finished mould must draw away from the model without damaging the surface, or themselves being damaged. There are several ways of overcoming these difficulties, either by modifying the model and trimming the cast afterwards, or by multiplying the number of pieces in the mould. As each piece of the mould is finished the edge is notched so that it fits accurately into the next piece, and when all the pieces have been made they are put together and a strong outer case cast over them. Each piece, as it is made, is oiled to prevent it from adhering to the next one. The next step is to remove the outer case, and then the inner pieces from the model, and then to put them all together again, this time with a hollow interior. They are now ready for use to cast either a block mould, from which working moulds of the same kind can be cast, or to cast the objects themselves in slip. A plaster block mould can be made hollow by pouring in liquid plaster, swilling it round, and then pouring it off, repeating the process until the cast is thick enough or the plaster is beginning to set. In the case of a slip cast, the slip is poured in and left until a layer of sufficiently firm clay has adhered to the walls, after which the surplus is poured off and the remainder left to harden and shrink away from the mould. The operations of making the moulds and taking casts in plaster are highly skilled; the making of slip casts is less so.

Moulds intended to be used for press moulding are, of course, open, and not closed. A bust is usually divided into the front (in one or more pieces) and a comparatively shallow back, and a somewhat stiffer ceramic body is applied by hand pressure. The two halves of the object, after extraction, are luted together, using slip as an adhesive, and the mould seams and minor blemishes are removed by hand (a process known as fettling*).

Moulds for figures are made by dissecting the original model into parts, which are moulded and cast separately. The parts are then joined together, ready for firing by a repairer. Elsewhere (e.g. James Hoskins*) notes will be found of certain busts bought ready made which were later worked on by various modellers, usually Hackwood* or Keeling*. These, no doubt, were some of the tasks they performed. At first Hoskins (and no doubt Mrs. Landré* and Richard Parker*) supplied Wedgwood with moulds, but later models in plaster were sent from which Wedgwood made his own moulds. These people often obtained permission to take casts from objects in marble, bronze, etc. in private collections, and Josiah Wedgwood also acknowledges similar permissions in his catalogues.

See also: Processes of Manufacture; Repairers.

Castleford Ware
Fine stoneware, mainly teapots and jugs, made at Castleford (nr. Leeds), c.1800-20 and decorated in low relief, often with coloured ornament, in a manner inspired by Wedgwood's jasper. Similar 'Castleford type' jugs, particularly those with hunt scenes and classical figures in relief on coloured grounds, were made by several manufacturers in the early 19th century, notably Spode*, John Turner* and Ridgway.

Casting. *Block mould for a salt-glaze sauce boat made at the Ivy House Works.* Wedgwood.

Catalogues
The first Catalogue, devoted to ornamental ware, was issued by Wedgwood & Bentley in 1773. This, with only sixty pages, was much smaller than any of the subsequent editions. The first Queen's ware Catalogue, very well illustrated, appeared in the following year, and a French translation of the Queen's ware Catalogue presumably belongs also to 1774. A French edition of the Catalogue of Gems seems to have been issued in that year. The Queen's ware Catalogue, first suggested by Wedgwood in November, 1773, was illustrated with nine plates engraved by John Pye*.

The first edition of the Ornamental Catalogue in 1773 was followed by subsequent editions in 1774, 1777, 1779, 1787, and 1788. Each new edition was enlarged by including objects produced for the first time since the publication of the previous one, and this is sometimes almost the only way of dating specimens reasonably closely, although this method can only be used to estimate the earliest possible date of a specimen. The 1774 edition had an additional category inserted — the "fine white terracotta" which was a precursor of jasper. By the 1777 edition this had become "a white porcelain bisque . . . possessing the general properties of the basaltes," and in 1779 "a white waxen Biscuit ware, or Terra Cotta, capable of bearing the same Heat as the Basaltes." There was a reissue of the 1774 Catalogue in 1775 to mark the removal of the showrooms* from Great Newport Street to Greek Street, Soho, London, W.

The Ornamental Catalogue was divided into twenty headings with subsections (see: Ornamental ware). The bodies employed for this purpose were divided into four categories — black basaltes* (the term was first used in the 1773 Catalogue), jasper* (from 1777), a white waxen biscuit, and a terracotta (i.e. an earthenware) "resembling porphyry, jasper, and other beautiful stones," the latter category including the "Pebble' vases (see: Vases, creamware).

The Catalogues of 1773 and 1774 were printed by Joseph Cooper* of Drury Lane, London, who also printed the Catalogue (in French) of the Frog* service when it was exhibited in Greek Street* in 1774. This listed and identified the source of each painting.

The 1817 Creamware Catalogue had the distinction of being illustrated by William Blake*, whose name appears on some of the plates. Blake had previously engraved the Portland* vase for Erasmus Darwin's *Botanic Garden* (1791), and reputedly plates for a Queen's Ware Catalogue of 1781-83, but this is unconfirmed.

For information about the Auction* Sale Catalogue of 1781, see the separate entry above. Listed hereunder are some of the more important Catalogues relating to Wedgwood wares, and collections of interest to the student:

Catalogue of Cameos, Intaglios, Bas Reliefs, Medallions . . . joint property of Mr. Wedgwood and Mrs. Bentley which are to be sold by Auction by Messrs. Christie & Ansell, 1781.

Catalogue of works on Queen's ware painted for Messrs. Wedgwood by the late Emile Lessore. On exhibition at Messrs. Mortlock's galleries, London, 1876.

Catalogue of a Loan Exhibition of the Works of Josiah Wedgwood at the Liverpool Art Club. Compiled by Charles T. Gatty, 1879.

Catalogue of a Collection of Wedgwood Ware formed by Mr. William Bartlett. Liverpool, 1882.

Catalogue of Old Wedgwood Ware: Handbook of the Collection formed by Richard and George Tangye. Frederick Rathbone, London, 1885.

A CATALOGUE,

Of the different Articles of QUEEN's WARE, which may be had either plain, gilt, or embellifhed with enamel Paintings, manufactured by JOSIAH WEDGWOOD, Potter to her MAJESTY.

A SERVICE of QUEEN's WARE, of a middling Size, with the loweft *wholefale Price*, at Etruria, in Staffordfhire.

							s.	d.		£.	s.	d.
	2	Oval Difhes,	—	19 Inches	—	—	2	6	—	0	5	0
	2	Ditto	—	17	—	—	—	1	6	—	0	3	0
	2	Round Difhes	—	17	—	—	—	1	6	—	0	3	0
	2	Ditto	—	15	—	—	—	1	0	—	0	2	0
	4	Oval Difhes	—	15	—	—	—	1	0	—	0	4	0
	4	Ditto	—	13	—	—	—	0	8	—	0	2	8
	4	Ditto	—	11	—	—	—	0	5	—	0	1	8
	4	Round Difhes	—	11	—	—	—	0	5	—	0	1	8
	4	Covered Difhes	—		—	—	—	2	0	—	0	8	0
*Fig. 3, 24, 27.	2	Terrines for Soup	—	—	—	—	7	0	—	0	14	0
Fig. 13.	2	Sauce Terrines	—	—	—	—	2	0	—	0	4	0
Fig. 10, 11, 12.	4	Sauce Boats	—	—	—	—	0	5	—	0	1	8
Fig. 25.	2	Salad Difhes	—	—	—	—	1	4	—	0	2	8
Fig. 6 & 33.	6	Salts	—	—	—	—	0	4	—	0	2	0
	2	Muftard Pots	—	—	—	—	0	4	—	0	0	8
	4	Pickle Difhes	—	—	—	—	0	3	—	0	1	0
	6	Dozen flat Plates	—	—	—	—	2	6	—	0	15	0
	2	Dozen Soup ditto	—	—	—	—	2	6	—	0	5	0

						£.	s.	d.
This Service plain, No.	comes to	—	—	—	—	3	17	0
The fame enamelled, according to the Patterns, No.		—	—	—				
Ditto	Ditto	—	— No.	—	—			
Ditto	Ditto	—	— No.	—	—	—		
Ditto	Ditto	—	— No.	—	—			

N. B. Any of thefe Articles may be left out, or changed, as is moft agreeable ; or others may be ordered from the following Catalogue, and the Price will vary accordingly.

---

* It being impoffible to inclofe Patterns of the Terrines and feveral other Articles, in the Pattern Box; and the Names giving but a very imperfect Idea of the Forms, it has been thought proper to have Prints engraved of fome of the principal Pieces, which will fhew the Forms better than could be done by any written Defcription.

Catalogues. *Facsimile page from the Queen's ware Catalogue of 1774. The difference between the prices then and those of today is a measure of two centuries of progressive currency debasement.* Wedgwood.

Catalogue of a collection of plaques, medallions, vases, figures, etc., in coloured jasper and basaltes produced by Josiah Wedgwood, FRS, at Etruria in the County of Stafford, 1760-1790, the property of Arthur Sanderson, Esq. Frederick Rathbone, London, 1901.

Catalogue of the Wedgwood Museum at Etruria, Staffordshire, Frederick Rathbone. Josiah Wedgwood & Sons, London, 1909.

Catalogue of a Wedgwood Collection, Art Institute of Chicago. Frank W. Gunsaulus, Chicago, 1912.

Exhibition of Replicas of Eighteenth century sculptured portrait miniatures: Wedgwood's portrait medallions of Illustrious Moderns. Harry Barnard, 1922.

Chinese Porcelain and Wedgwood Pottery. Catalogue of the Collection in the Lady Lever Art Gallery, Port Sunlight. Vol. II. R.L. Hobson, London, 1928.

Catalogue of an exhibition of Old Wedgwood from the bequest of Grenville Lindall Winthrop, Jean Gorely and Mary Wadsworth. Fogg Museum of Art, Cambridge, Mass., 1944.

Wedgwood, John M. Graham II and Hensleigh C. Wedgwood, Brooklyn Museum, 1948.

Early Wedgwood Pottery. Josiah Wedgwood & Sons, Barlaston, 1951.

Exhibition at Kenwood House, Iveagh Bequest. London, 1954.

Catalogue of a special Exhibition of Wedgwood's Heads of Illustrious Moderns. Compiled by Vivian J. Scheidemantel, Art Institute of Chicago, Department of Decorative Arts, 1958-59.

Catalogue of the Wedgwood Bicentenary Exhibition, 1759-1959. Introduction by Arthur Lane. Victoria and Albert Museum, London, 1959.

The Emily Winthrop Miles Collection, Jean Gorely and Maria D. Schwartz. Brooklyn Museum, 1965.

Eighteenth century Wedgwood at the Paine Art Centre. Oshkosh, 1965.

Wedgwood at Woburn. An exhibition of early Wedgwood held at Woburn Abbey. With an introduction by Bruce Tattersall, 1973.

Wedgwood Portrait Medallions: An Introduction. Catalogue of the Exhibition held at the National Portrait Gallery. Robin Reilly, London, 1973.

Stubbs & Wedgwood. Unique alliance between Artist and Potter. With an Introduction by Basil Taylor, Tate Gallery, 1974.

Mr. Wedgwood. An exhibition. Nottingham Castle Museum, 1975.

Wedgwood Portraits and the American Revolution. National Portrait Gallery, Smithsonian Institution, 1976.

Josiah Wedgwood: The Arts and Sciences United. Science Museum, London, 1978.

Cathcart, Charles, 9th Baron (1721-1776)

Lieutenant-General. As British envoy to the Court of the Empress Catherine II*, he was instrumental in introducing Wedgwood wares into Russia. In January, 1768, Wedgwood wrote to Boulton*: "I have waited upon Ld Cathcart, the Ambassador appointed for Russia, to bring about the plan we settled of introducing my manufacture at the Court of Russia ... The Ambassador, but particularly his Lady, came into my measures with the utmost readiness ... His L^dship has now ordered a large service, plain, to take with him." Cathcart also ordered a crested service. During the following three years Lord Cathcart proved himself to be a magnificent commercial ambassador for Wedgwood. Through his influence large orders were obtained from the Russian nobility, and, more important, the Empress was induced to adorn her palaces with vases and tablets. Although Cathcart had returned to England before the great Frog* service was ordered, it was undoubtedly to him that Wedgwood owed the Empress Catherine's patronage.

Catherine II (The Great) 1729-1796

Empress of Russia, born at Stettin, the daughter of the Prince of Anhalt-Zerbst; married Peter, heir to the Russian throne, in 1745. Her husband reigned as Peter III for only a few months before he was murdered, and their son, who became Paul I, was also assassinated. Catherine, a clever and ambitious woman, too often frustrated her own plans by promoting one or other of her many lovers to high office. She made extensive purchases of French decorative art, patronising the *ébéniste*, David Roentgen, and the Sèvres porcelain factory. She bought Sir Robert Walpole's picture collection, and ordered Queen's ware services (the Husk* service and the Frog* service) from Wedgwood. For the palace at Tsarkoë Selo (Saint Petersburg) the Scottish architect, Charles Cameron, designed three suites of apartments for the Empress which were decorated with Wedgwood jasper plaques in some of the rooms, including the Empress's bedroom. Unfortunately this palace was destroyed during the siege of Leningrad, 1941-43.

Wedgwood, whose judgement was no doubt coloured by purely commercial considerations, described Catherine as "a Woman of sense — fine taste and spirit." The portrait listed in the 1773 Catalogue was probably a small basaltes medallion. By 1777 two jasper portraits had been produced, but were not included in the Catalogue of that year. One is adapted from a

Catherine II. *Portrait medallion in jasper of the Empress Catherine II (The Great). First recorded in the Oven Book entry for 21st August, 1777.* Brooklyn Museum, Emily Winthrop Miles Collection.

coronation medal by T. Ivanov of 1762, and another from a medal by the same hand of 1774. A head of Catherine wearing the helmet of Minerva* was modelled by Maria Feodorovna* in 1782. A black basaltes tablet, impressed on the reverse with the inscription 'CATHERINE II REWARDING ART AND PROTECTING COMMERCE', attributed to Flaxman c.1785, shows the Empress, somewhat flatteringly, as Minerva.

Catherine Shape
A Queen's ware shape introduced in 1770 and used for the Frog* service. The plates have a uniform wavy edge. The shape was also employed for other purposes (e.g. three plates printed and painted with Fable subjects by Guy Green* in the British Museum) and has since become a popular tableware shape, particularly on the Continent.

Cato, Marcus Porcius (234-149B.C.)
Statesman, often called Cato the Censor, or Cato the Elder. The consistent champion of an anti-Carthaginian policy, he was largely responsible for forwarding the Third Punic War. He should not be confused with his great grandson of the same name, who was one of the principals of the aristocratic party in opposition to Julius Caesar*. The bust of Cato the Elder, height 20ins., was reproduced in basaltes after a model supplied by Oliver & Hoskins* in 1774.

Caudle Set
Caudle in the 18th century was a kind of warm alcoholic gruel made from wine or ale blended with eggs, bread or oatmeal, sugar and spices, and was generally intended for the nourishment of invalids. Caudle was served in covered cups with one or two handles and a conforming saucer, both of which were well decorated. Josiah Wedgwood presented a caudle and breakfast service (the composition of which is not recorded) to Queen Charlotte*. The date of this presentation is uncertain, but it is believed to have been made shortly after the birth of George, Prince of Wales, in August 1762. No reliable evidence exists as to the decoration of this creamware service, but it is reputed to have been ornamented with raised (probably sprigged*) flowers and enamelled by Daniel Steele* and Thomas Daniel(l)*.

Cauliflower Ware
Cream-coloured ware naturally modelled and coloured in imitation of the cauliflower — usually a teapot, coffee pot, a covered bowl, or a tureen. The lower part was modelled to represent the leaves and covered with a green glaze; the flower head was cream or yellow. Ware of this kind was made by Josiah Wedgwood c.1759 onwards, and is a good example of a Wedgwood production in the rococo style.

Cawk
Local term for a mineral found in Derbyshire which is principally barium sulphate*, an essential ingredient of jasper*.

Caylus, Comte de (1692-1765)
Ann-Claude-Phillippe de Tubières
A collector of antiquities who wrote an important work on classical and Egyptian art, *Recueil d'Antiquités Égyptienne, Étrusques, Grecques, Romaines, et Gauloises,* published in five volumes between 1752 and 1755. With Winckelmann* and Sir William Hamilton*, the Comte de Caylus may be regarded as one of the architects of the neo-classical* style. Wedgwood possessed the *Recueil,* and quotes it from time to time in his letters (e.g. Wedgwood to Bentley, 13th October, 1770, referring to an advertisement for encaustic vases: "Could you not weave in Count Caylus's lamentation that no Artist had then been able to imitate the Antient Etruscan Vases?").

Cauliflower Ware. *Teapot in the form of a cauliflower, decorated with green and yellow glazes, c.1763.* Wedgwood.

Ceiling Rose

A ceiling rose with a central hole to be used in conjunction with a light fixture was made by Wedgwood at the end of the 19th century of black jasper with white reliefs. A specimen in the Buten Museum* is dated 1896.

Celadon

A glaze of varying shades of green covering Chinese stoneware of the Sung dynasty (960-1280) and later. A modified green, similar in shade, was employed by the Chinese as a porcelain ground colour in the 18th century. The word is probably a corruption of Saladin (Salah-ed-din), the Saracen Sultan of Egypt in the 12th century, who was especially fond of this ware. Wedgwood applied the term 'Celadon' to a self-coloured, sea-green earthenware introduced in 1805. It was the first of the stained clay 'coloured bodies'* to be introduced during the 19th century, and these were among the most important technical developments of the period.

Cellini, Benvenuto (1500-1571)

Italian sculptor, goldsmith, and medallist whom Michelangelo called "the greatest sculptor in the world." Cellini is also well known for his swashbuckling *Memoirs* written about 1560, and his *Treatise* on the goldsmith's art is of considerable importance. His 'Perseus' is in the Loggia dei Lanzi, Florence, his 'Nymph of Fontainebleau' is now in the Louvre, and a gold salt made for François I is in the Kunsthistorisches Museum, Vienna. Apart from these, almost nothing has survived which can be certainly attributed. A Wedgwood plaque, the *Downfall of the Giants,* of which an example is in the Buten Museum*, was taken from a silver plaque attributed to Cellini. It must be remembered, however, that there were many more attributions to Cellini in the 18th and 19th centuries than have stood the test of time. The source of the Buten plaque is more likely to have been Guglielmo della Porta*.

Celtic Ornaments

Designs by Daisy Makeig-Jones* adapted from ornamental motifs in the 6th-century *Book of Kells,* of which Wedgwood procured an expensive reproduction in 1916. Three patterns, which she named *St. Chad's* and *Lindisfarne* (produced in two versions), were designed for Queen's ware tableware, but the *Celtic Ornaments* designs were principally on bone china* tea-ware and coffeeware and for bone china ornamental pieces. Mother-of-pearl lustre glazes were often applied over the ornamental wares, sometimes over a matt blue ground. Bone china patterns, most of which occur in several versions, include *Tyrone, Celt, Armagh, St. Chad's,* and *Gothic Circles.*

See also: Fairyland Lustre; Lustre Decoration; Ordinary Lustres.

Centaur

Mythical being which was half-horse and half-man. Centaurs lived in a region of Mount Pelion and were said to be the off-spring of Ixion and a cloud. Their conflict with the Lapiths is sometimes depicted in art. No doubt the legend grew from the contacts of settled peoples with nomadic tribes who were rarely out of the saddle. Chiron was a centaur famous for his wisdom. Jason, Peleus, and Achilles* were his pupils, and Hercules* was his friend.

Centaurs figure in three of the Herculaneum* subjects listed as nos. 51-65 of Class II in the Wedgwood Catalogues from 1773. These are:

Centaur with Bacchante on his back.
Female Centaur with a child on her back.
Centaur teaching Achilles the Lyre.

All were produced in white terracotta or basaltes (and later in

jasper), some with coloured grounds and often with frames of the same material. They measure 11½ ins. in diameter without frames. A smaller medallion, *Perseus and Centaur,* 3¾ ins. by 3ins., is no. 74 in the Catalogues.

Centrepiece

See: Grand Plat Menage.

Ceracchi (Cernachi), Joseph (Giuseppe) (1751-1801)

Ceracchi arrived in England in 1773 and was employed by Robert Adam*, and also by William Chambers*. After working in Vienna, Italy and Prussia, he left for America in 1790, returning to Europe in 1795. His part in a plot against the life of Napoleon was discovered, and he was executed in 1801. He modelled a portrait of Dr. Priestley* in 1779 for Wedgwood's series of *Illustrious Moderns*.

Ceres

Roman name for Demeter, the goddess of agriculture and the fruits of the earth. The sister of Zeus (see Jupiter) and mother of Persephone (see Proserpine), Demeter is usually represented wearing a garland of ears of corn, and holding in her hands ears of corn, a torch, or a basket. The Romans celebrated a festival in her honour, and her cult was of considerable political importance. The earliest reference to a Wedgwood model is in an invoice from Theodore Parker* for two figures ("1 Large") dated 1769. A statuette 17ins. high is listed in the 1787 Catalogue*, but no other figures of this subject appear in Wedgwood catalogues. Three more are known: a seated figure; and two standing figures modelled as candlesticks as pairs to others of Cybele*. All have been attributed to Flaxman*, but at least one pair of the candlesticks exists bearing the scratch mark associated with Keeling*, and it has also been ascribed (though with less confidence) to Tebo*. This latter pair, of two female figures (without attributes*), is probably Keeling's work, and there is good reason to suppose that they have been wrongly identified. The more sophisticated figures, with the traditional attributes of a lion and a sheaf of corn, are more in keeping with Flaxman's work. The tablet

Celtic Ornaments. *Tyrone pattern, one of the range of Celtic Ornaments designed by Daisy Makeig-Jones and derived from a reproduction of the 6th-century* Book of Kells. *Buten Museum. Photo: Una des Fontaines.*

Sacrifice to Ceres is also attributed to Flaxman, c.1779, but may be a somewhat later work by Webber*. A medallion measuring 4ins. by 3ins. is listed in all the Catalogues from 1773, and a small cameo, titled *Ceres* but based on a Tassie* gem, *Demeter searching for Persephone,* is listed in 1787. Also recorded is a head of Ceres, diameter 8ins., again attributed to Flaxman, but without supporting evidence.

Chamber Pots

As well as the *bourdalou*, or coach pot, Wedgwood made chamber pots, but he did not regard them as anything more than wares of the plainest domestic utility requiring very little adornment. We do not therefore, find anything like the superbly painted specimens from Meissen* or Sèvres*, or the

Ceres. *Solid blue and white jasper figure of Ceres carrying ears of corn with a sheaf by her side. 11½ins. high. One of a pair of candlesticks attributed to Flaxman, c.1785. See also Cybele.* Wedgwood.

examples of robust *grivoiserie* which came mainly from the Sunderland potteries, all of which are now eagerly sought collectors' items.

Early chamber pots are comparatively small because they were kept in a special cupboard in the sideboard, ready for use by after dinner drinkers. Chamber pots of a larger size for bedroom use seem to have been a 19th century addition to the toilet ewer and basin because these things are not illustrated *en suite* in the early shape books. The upper part of the house was served by what the English euphemistically called a 'commode' (actually a decorative chest of drawers for the drawing room), the French equivalent term being *chaise percée*. Wedgwood made pans for these in standard sizes. They were in the form of a truncated cone, and are undecorated.

Wedgwood production of chamber pots is immortalised in a note to *The Rolliad* (*Probationary Odes* VI), published in 1795 as a political attack on William Pitt the younger: ''I am told, that a scoundrel of a potter, one Mr Wedgewood [*sic*], is making 20,000 vile utensils, with a figure of Mr Pitt in the bottom; round the head is to be a motto,

We will spit

On Mr *Pitt*

and *other such* d-md rhymes, suited to the uses of the different vessels.''

Chambers, Sir William (1726-1796)

Born in Stockholm of an English father, William Chambers became a supercargo for the East India Company, and travelled to China in this capacity, where he studied native art and architecture at first hand. Later he visited Italy, and became one of the last of the Palladians in a neo-classical* world. He published his influential *Treatise on Civil Architecture* in 1759. This followed his *Designs for Chinese Buildings, Furniture, &c.* of 1757, which is remarkable for its faithfulness to its source of inspiration at a time when English designers prided themselves on the fact that their Chinese ornament was their own invention. Chamber's *Dissertation on Oriental Gardening* was very influential in its effect on the Romantic aspects of the neo-classical style, and on landscape gardening in particular. His best known work in architecture is Somerset House. He also designed the Pagoda in Kew Gardens. A view of the Kew Pagoda and Footbridge was employed as one of the painted designs on the Imperial Russian (Frog*) Service. Sir William became architect to George III, and he, the King, and Horace Walpole agreed on the subject of the brothers Adam*, which may be summed up in Walpole's words: ''from Kent's magnificence we are dwindled to Adam's filigree.'' It was Sir William and Sir Joshua Reynolds* who recommended Henry Webber* to Wedgwood as a modeller.

Chambers was a figure of some influence and considerable pomposity whose favour Wedgwood sought to gain by flattery. In this he was not entirely successful: his productions in jasper were altogether too close in style to 'Adam's filigree' for the taste of Chambers. A portrait medallion of Sir William was modelled by Charles Peart* in 1787.

Champagne

A pale cane-coloured body introduced in 1930.
See: Coloured Bodies.

Champagne Glaze

Deep cane-coloured glaze introduced in 1930.
See: John Skeaping.

Champion Richard (1743-1791)

Porcelain manufacturer of Bristol who used Cornish feldspathic rock (growan stone) and china clay (kaolin). The enterprise was started by William Cookworthy in Plymouth in 1768,

Chambers, Sir William. *Jasper portrait medallion of Sir William Chambers (1723-96), modelled by Charles Peart in 1787.* Scottish National Portrait Gallery.

and transferred to Bristol in 1772 with Champion as manager. The formula was patented in 1768, and the patent conferred a monopoly of Cornish materials. In 1773 Champion bought both factory and patent, and in 1774 applied for an extension of the latter for another fifteen years. The Staffordshire potters, led by Wedgwood, excluded from the Cornish materials, petitioned the House of Lords. Rather than face the uncertainty, delay, and expense that would otherwise have occurred, Champion compromised and amended his specification to refer to the use of Cornish clay and stone only for the manufacture of porcelain. By 1781 Champion was bankrupt and turned to Wedgwood for assistance. The latter, no longer interested in porcelain manufacture, helped Champion to sell his patent to a company of Staffordshire potters. Champion procured a position as Deputy-Paymaster to the Forces, and in 1784 he emigrated to South Carolina, where he died.

See: New Hall Factory.

Charlotte Mourning at the Tomb of Werther

A late 18th century decorative subject derived from Goethe's sentimental best-selling romance, *The Sorrows of Young Werther**. It depicts a young woman, Charlotte, standing by, or kneeling in front of, a column surmounted by an urn containing the ashes of her lover, who committed suicide for her sake. The subject was used by Wedgwood for a jasper relief designed by Lady Elizabeth Templetown* in 1787 and modelled by Hackwood* in 1790.

Charlotte, Queen (1744-1818)

Consort of George III, to whom she bore fifteen children, Charlotte Sophia was the daughter of the Duke of Mecklenburg-Strelitz. She took a keen interest in pottery and porcelain, and ordered an important porcelain service from the

Chelsea Porcelain Factory* in 1763. Josiah Wedgwood presented her with an enamelled creamware* breakfast and caudle* set about 1762, and in 1765 she ordered from Wedgwood a tea and coffee service for twelve. This included matching candlesticks*, melons* and fruit baskets, and was decorated with raised flowers in green on a gold ground. The production of this service, and in particular the gilding, caused Wedgwood considerable difficulty and anxiety, but it was safely completed and delivered before the end of the year. The Queen was sufficiently pleased with it to order a creamware dinner set and to permit Wedgwood to style himself 'Potter to Her Majesty'. Shortly thereafter he named his creamware 'Queen's ware'*, and the Queen's shape was also named after her. None of the teaset appears to have survived. Other orders received from St. James's Palace (probably at the instigation of Queen Charlotte) included jasper vases and girandoles, toy teasets, dairy ware* and dog pans.

Queen Charlotte's portrait appears in at least three engraved versions on Wedgwood creamware or Queen's ware teapots; and no less than seven different portrait medallions were modelled between 1772 and 1789, three of them by Hackwood*.

See also: Deborah Chetwynd.

Chatelain, Jean Baptiste Claude (1710-1771)

Draughtsman and engraver; born in Paris; served as an officer in the French Army. Views by his hand were used in the decoration of the Frog* service, but he was not himself employed at any time by Wedgwood, either in London or at Etruria. Chatelain died two years before the service was painted.

Charlotte, Queen. *Portrait medallion in jasper of Queen Charlotte, consort of George III, remodelled by Hackwood in 1776 from a wax portrait by Isaac Gosset in the Victoria and Albert Museum.* Wedgwood.

Chatelaine

Ornamental clasp worn at a woman's waist, with a chain from which were suspended keys, *etuis,* watch, etc. Wedgwood's jasper, mounted in metal, was sometimes employed for the clasp and for some of the ornamental objects suspended from it.

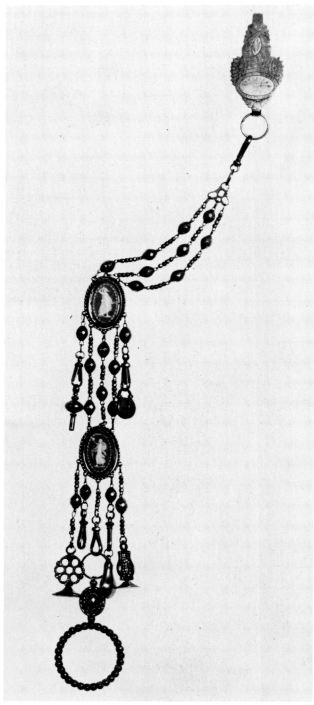

Chatelaine. *Cut-steel chatelaine, or fob chain, for a gentleman, mounted with two double-sided jasper cameos. Several seals, an eyeglass, a miniature padlock and chain were attached to the chatelaine which, in turn, was attached to the waist. c.1785.* Wedgwood.

Cheere, John (1709-1787)

Younger brother of the celebrated sculptor, Sir Henry Cheere. John Cheere took over John Nost's yard near Green Park, London, together with Nost's moulds for lead figures, in 1737. He enjoyed considerable esteem as a purveyor of statuary in lead and plaster, and he always kept a large stock for the inspection of his customers. A contemporary (1772) description of Cheere's yard compares it to ''a country fair or market, made up of spruce squires, hay makers with rakes in their hands, shepherds and shepherdesses, bagpipers and pipers and fiddlers.'' These garden ornaments would have been painted, in the fashion of the day, in naturalistic colours. More important to Wedgwood were his portrait busts*, adapted from the antique or from the work of such eminent sculptors as Coysevox (Prior), Roubiliac* (Pope), Rysbrack* (Milton) and Scheemakers* (Dryden). He supplied Wedgwood with busts of Plato*, Homer*, and Aristotle* in 1774, and one of Shakespeare on which Hackwood* worked in the following year. Cheere appears to have invented his own method of 'bronzing' his statues and busts, which are nearly black with a smooth and subtle polish. In several reference books relating to Wedgwood wares his name is erroneously given as John Cheese.

Cheese Dish

Flat dish with shaped cover for storing and serving cheese. Those dishes with a sloping rectangular cover are for serving a wedge-shaped piece of a cheese, like Cheddar or Cheshire. The large jasper or cane ware dishes with cylindrical covers are for serving a whole Stilton cheese.

Cheese Hard

See: Leather Hard.

Cheese Dish. *Cane ware dish for a whole Stilton cheese: a cylindrical engine-turned cover on a footed dish. c.1790.* Reilly.

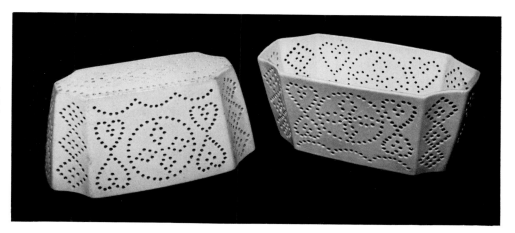

Cheese Mould. *Also known as curd mould. Creamware strainer in the form of a cheese mould for separating the whey from the curd. c.1790.* Buten Museum.

Cheese Mould (Curd Mould)

A mould of cream-coloured ware with pierced sides for making cheese. It was used with a lining of cheese cloth. Cheese moulds of this type were made by Wedgwood.

Chelsea Decorating Studio

Towards the end of 1769 the Wedgwood & Bentley partnership acquired a house in Chelsea for the purpose of enamelling undecorated ware sent from Etruria for the purpose. In 1770 Bentley began to reside in the firm's rooms at Great Newport Street and Wedgwood travelled to London in 1769 to oversee the installation of enamelling kilns at Chelsea. For a time Wedgwood's attention was focused on printing and painting, although Bentley resisted the introduction of outline transfer prints. Painters were sent from Staffordshire to London, and new painters were sought in Liverpool and Birmingham, and among the fan painters and japanners. Wedgwood wrote: "Give my respects to Mr. Rhodes*, and tell him that if any man who offers himself is *sober* he must make him *everything else.*" The studio was occupied with, among other tasks, encaustic painting* on vases, and in 1773-74 the painters were principally engaged on the Frog* service. When finished the service was displayed at the new showrooms at 12, Greek Street, Soho, London. A twenty-one year lease of these premises had been acquired in 1774 to replace the Great Newport Street showrooms and the Chelsea Decorating Studio, with living accommodation for Bentley and his wife which enabled him to supervise the whole of the London enterprise.

See: Showrooms.

Chelsea Decorating Studio. *Plate from the Frog service painted with a view of a road leading to 'a Gothique ruin.'* Wedgwood.

Chelsea Porcelain Factory

The first English porcelain factory, founded by Nicolas Sprimont and Charles Gouyn, both of Huguenot origin, in 1745 or earlier. The wares fall into three well-marked periods. The first is known as the triangle period from the mark employed, when the principal source of inspiration was French rococo silver; the second as the raised and red anchor period (1750-56), when the primary influence was that of Meissen; and finally the gold anchor period, from 1756 onwards, when the styles of Vincennes-Sèvres were fashionable. Chelsea made the finest quality porcelain of any factory in England during its lifetime, and at its best the body approached that of Sèvres.

In 1769 the factory was advertised for sale with all the plaster moulds, models in wax, lead, or brass, kilns, mills, and iron presses. Wedgwood wrote to Bentley: "The Chelsea moulds, models, &c. are to be sold . . . There's an immense amount of fine things." In July 1769, he wrote: "Pray inquire of Mr. Thomas [Sprimont's manager] whether they are determined not to sell less than the whole of the models &c. If so, I do not think it would suit me to purchase. I should be glad if you would send me further particulars of the things at Chelsea."

The undertaking was eventually purchased by William Duesbury* of Derby who continued it until 1784, largely as a decorating studio for the Derby* factory.

It has been suggested, mainly on stylistic grounds, that Chelsea engaged painters from Meissen* during the 1750s. There are one or two painters with German-sounding names, recorded as working at Wedgwood & Bentley's Chelsea Decorating Studio who may have been taken on in 1769 when the porcelain factory closed.

Cherokee Clay

In 1745 William Cookworthy*, a Plymouth pharmacist, chemist, and Quaker, received a visit from a Huguenot colonist from Virginia, one Andrew Duché, who brought samples of porcelain clay from America, which was called by the Indians, according to the Bow* patent specification, *unaker*. Cookworthy considered this clay to be equal to the 'Asiatic' (i.e. to that of China). He was a trustworthy observer who had, no doubt, seen Chinese clay, and may have had samples with which to compare it. It is probable that some of the Chinese porcelain imported into London, especially the so-called Nankin or blue and white export porcelain, was packed in powdered porcelain clay. Documentary evidence of this kind of packing exists, and white porcelain clay deposits have been found in association with porcelain in the wreckage of a Spanish galleon. It does, however, seem to be a factory method of packing, where porcelain clay would be plentiful, rather than one likely to be employed by the Canton enamelling shops, where much Chinese export porcelain was painted. Cookworthy mentioned in his letter of May 1745, that his visitor estimated he could import the porcelain materials into England at £13 a ton, but that he did not propose to undercut the Company (i.e. the East India Company), who were also importing china clay, possibly as hair powder.

Wedgwood certainly knew all about this clay by September 1766, when it would appear that Captain Vigor, sailing into Liverpool, brought information about American clays which Bentley, then in Liverpool, passed on to Wedgwood. The latter replied that import must depend on quality and price.

Late in 1764 specimens of porcelain made from this clay arrived in Bristol from Georgia. "The material", wrote the *Bristol Journal,* "appears to be good, but the workmanship is far from being admired." In 1765 samples of this clay for testing arrived in Bristol, some of which went to Champion*, and some was sent to the Worcester Porcelain Factory*. Nothing

appears to have been done with it.

In 1767 Wedgwood in London wrote to Bentley in Liverpool that he had met Thomas Griffiths, the brother of their mutual friend, Ralph Griffiths*, who had resided for many years in South Carolina. He discussed the pros and cons of a proposal to finance a journey to America to buy Cherokee clay and ship it back. Eventually the decision was made, and sixteen years later, in a letter to W.G. Constable, Wedgwood recounted the outcome: "I was so delighted with this beautiful raw material that I was determined upon sending an agent to the spot to . . . procure me some of the clay . . . With much difficulty he procured me about six tons at the expense altogether of about £500, but . . . there was no hope of any future supply upon such terms as could be complied with by any manufacturer." Later, in this letter, he stated that this clay was the basis of his 'biscuit porcelain' (probably jasper was intended).

In December, 1777, he wrote to Bentley: ". . . it may not be a bad idea to give out that our jaspers are made of Cherokee clay which I sent an agent into that country to procure for me, and when the present parcel is out we have no hopes of obtaining more, as it was with the utmost difficulty the natives were prevailed upon to part with what we now have. . . His Majesty should see some of these large fine tablets and be told this story first, as he has repeatedly inquired what I have done with this Cherokee clay. . . A portion of the Cherokee clay is really used in all the jaspers, so make what use you please of this fact. . ."

On the 12th June, 1950, a marker was placed on Highway 28, five miles north of Franklin, North Carolina, to mark the position of the pit from which the clay was dug. The discovery of Cornish china clay, and relaxations in the terms of Champion's patent, made it unnecessary to continue seeking sources of supply so far afield as North America and China.

See: John Bradby Blake; Sydney Cove Medallion.

Cherry Blossom

See: Prunus Blossom.

Chert

A type of quartz which occurs in limestone. It is coarser than flint, and more brittle, and it is found in several colours — grey, brown, yellow, red and white. It is used as a pulverising agent in certain types of grinding mill. Wedgwood employed chert from Derbyshire for this purpose as a substitute for granite which he found was the cause of black specks in the pulverised material.

Chessmen

Chessmen have been a popular product in jasper, basaltes, and Queen's ware since the 18th century. A set was designed by John Flaxman in 1785, and the original drawing is in the Museum at Barlaston. Some of the waxes have also survived, but only the Queen is in an undamaged state. She has always been regarded as a portrait of Mrs. Siddons in the role of Lady Macbeth. One hundred and thirty sets were sold between 1785 and 1795, and variations in colour were employed. Dark blue, lilac, and green dip bases are provided for some of the white jasper pieces.

A set of chessmen was designed by Arnold Machin*, in 1938 and produced in several bodies — basaltes, jasper, Queen's ware, and bone china from about 1940 onwards.

Chessmen made in the 18th century, and reproductions of Flaxman's designs made in the 19th century (about 1865), are now rare, and even odd pieces have become difficult to find.

Chessmen. *Ink and wash design by John Flaxman for set of chessmen, signed. Flaxman charged six guineas for the drawing.* Wedgwood.

Chessmen. *Part of the set designed by Arnold Machin in 1938.* Wedgwood.

Chessmen. *Figure of a King from Flaxman's chess set. Solid blue jasper, 3½ ins. high.* Wedgwood.

Chestnut Basket

A pierced basket with a domed pierced cover and a conforming stand, often inspired by contemporary silver, made by Wedgwood in cream-coloured ware and illustrated in the first Queen's Ware Catalogue (c.1770-80). Also called an orange basket. Similar baskets were made of creamware at Leeds, and of porcelain at Worcester.

Chetwynd, Deborah (fl.1745-1780)

Third daughter of William Richard ('Black Will') Chetwynd, Master of the Mint and, from 1767, 3rd Viscount Chetwynd. 'Deb' Chetwynd held an honorary appointment at Court as Seamstress and Laundress to Queen Charlotte*, and was instrumental in obtaining for Wedgwood his first royal orders. As a native of Staffordshire, she was glad to promote Wedgwood's interests. In gratitude, Josiah paid her the graceful compliment of naming a fine engine-turned and gilt creamware* vase (c.1766-67) the Chetwynd vase.

On the death of her father in 1770, Deborah Chetwynd decided to commission a monument to his memory, to be placed in Ashley Church, Staffordshire. At her request, 'Athenian' Stuart* designed an austere inscribed slab surmounted by a cornice and arch. Wedgwood supplied a basaltes* vase, fluted on the lower half of the body, with tall scrolled handles. From correspondence surviving at Barlaston, it is clear that Miss Chetwynd was not satisfied with the design of the vase, but the substance of her complaint seems not to have been committed to paper.

Ch'ien Lung, Emperor (1736-1796)

An Emperor of the Chi'ing dynasty during the reign of whom the export trade in porcelain with Europe and America considerably increased in quantity and variety. In 1793 Lord Macartney (British Ambassador to the Imperial Court) in the course of a well known interview with the Emperor, who commended George III for his loyalty and fidelity, presented Chi'ien Lung with various articles of Western manufacture, including Wedgwood's Queen's ware, which much impressed

this royal connoisseur. The Emperor had these Wedgwood vessels copied in porcelain at the Imperial factory, and cream-ware shapes sometimes occur in export porcelain thereafter which may have been derived from this source, or from ware sent to China as patterns by merchants placing orders.

Children's Story Series

A series of colourful Queen's ware plates decorated with transfer-printed* subjects of a kind likely to appeal to small children. The first, dated 1971, is *The Sandman,* after Hans Andersen.

Chimaera

Fabulous monster with the front part of a lion, the middle part of a goat, and the hinder part of a dragon. It breathed fire, and was named after the volcano of Chimaera in Lydia. It was eventually killed by Bellerophon*. A *Chimerae (sic)* is believed to have been modelled by Josiah Wedgwood. No example of this appears to have survived. The chimaera illustrated by Meteyard (*Life of Wedgwood,* Vol.II, Fig.42) is a hawk-faced griffin.

Chimney Piece

The chimney piece as a decorative focal point of the room dates from medieval times, and those in the larger country houses during the 17th and 18th centuries were often especially ornamental and imposing. Wedgwood began providing plaques and tablets for the decoration of chimney pieces, particularly those of wood, before the introduction of jasper. The earliest work of this kind was in basaltes*, what Wedgwood called "waxen porcelain bisque" (usually with a coloured background to the relief ornament), and terracotta. In 1772 Wedgwood provided encaustically painted basaltes tablets for a chimney piece in the house of Sir Watkin Williams Wynn* in Saint James's Square, London, when it was remodelled and redecorated by Robert Adam*. These tablets were made to designs furnished by Adam which are now in the Soane Museum. In the same repository are other Adam drawings for chimney piece ornaments which appear to have inspired Wedgwood designs. In 1775 we find Wedgwood inquiring from Bentley* whether an order for tablets was to be of 'fine white' composition or the cream-coloured body. 'Fine white' seems to refer to the 'waxen white' body which preceded the discovery of jasper.

Tablets and plaques made for decorating chimney pieces were oval or rectangular, and these had to be of definite proportions. Throughout 1776 Wedgwood experienced difficulty in making jasper tablets. They were prone to a

Chestnut Basket. *Decorative silver-pattern Queen's ware basket, shape No.32 in the first Cream Colour Catalogue ("Pierced Chestnut or Orange Basket").* Wedgwood.

Children's Story Series. The Sandman, *after Hans Christian Andersen, transfer-printed on Queen's ware. The first issue in the series, 1971.* Wedgwood.

Chimney Piece. *A chimney piece decorated with Wedgwood plaques shown at the International Exhibition of 1867. Flanking it are two red-figure vases of a type popular at the time for library decoration. Paris Exposition Universelle, 1867. Art Journal Catalogue.* Photo: Wedgwood.

number of defects, of which the most serious was the development of firecracks* during cooling.

In 1777 Sir Roger Newdigate (who lived at Arbury, not far from Nuneaton, which he 'gothicised' in the Strawberry Hill manner in 1780) gave Wedgwood permission to take casts from marbles and plaster casts which he had collected in Italy. These were listed in the 1779 Catalogue, in which Wedgwood refers to ''The large Cameo Pictures and Tablets for chimney-pieces, in blue and white jasper, [which] have been brought to their present Degree of Perfection with much Labour and Expence to the Artist, and may with Propriety have a place amongst the first Ornaments the Arts have produced.''

In the autumn of the same year Wedgwood succeeded in making large jasper plaques, and tablets measuring 14ins. by 5½ins. Probably the latter were first employed for the centre of the frieze of a chimney piece at Longton Hall, not far from Etruria*, which was then being rebuilt. The architect was the same Mr. Gardner who had worked on Etruria for Wedgwood in 1769. The Longton chimney pieces are now in the Lady Lever Art Gallery.

By 1778 Wedgwood was putting in hand the task of translating some of the earlier subjects made in basaltes or the white body into jasper, among them *The Dancing Hours**. Ornamental chimney pieces were becoming fashionable among a class which could not afford the carved marble of the great houses, and such men as Boulton* were making die-stamped ornament

which, attached to wooden carcase-work and painted over, looked very much like carved wood. Wedgwood discussed the provision of tablets, friezes, and so forth with Boulton's partner, John Fothergill, without arriving at any conclusion. Wedgwood was disturbed by the thought that Boulton's might copy some of his subjects in die-stamped metal if they were given an opportunity, and he preferred to travel to London to discuss his new manufacture with architects, builders, and cabinet makers. Here he met competition in the form of Coade* of Lambeth, the most successful of the metropolitan makers of artificial stone, who made tablets, friezes, medallions, and complete chimney pieces, as well as busts and figures, for interior and exterior use. Among the modellers who worked both for Mrs. Coade and Wedgwood were Bacon*, De Vaere*, Rossi, and Flaxman*. Some architects and builders seem to have preferred Coade to Wedgwood. This surprised the latter, because he rightly considered Mrs. Coade's products to be much coarser than his own. In the case of London builders, the reason was probably that they could see a larger selection at Mrs. Coade's Lambeth premises than at Wedgwood's showrooms, and that her products were cheaper. To meet this competition Wedgwood offered cheap terracotta plaques painted to match the decoration of the room.

Complete suites of ornamental jasper for chimney pieces, with vertical tablets for the jambs, as well as horizontal tablets for the frieze, were introduced in 1786, but they have seldom been preserved intact.

Some marble chimney pieces inset with jasper plaques and tablets have survived, even though the houses for which they were originally made have long since been demolished, and there are several examples in the Lady Lever Art Gallery at Liverpool. To judge from such evidence as the listings in the 1787 Catalogue, the demand for chimney piece ornaments continued unabated at least until Josiah I's death, after which it seems to have fallen away rapidly.

Among the subjects employed in the decoration of chimney pieces the *Marriage of Cupid and Psyche* was particularly popular. *The Apotheosis of Homer,* the *Sacrifice to Flora,* the *Triumph of Bacchus,* the *Choice of Hercules,* the *Birth of Bacchus,* and *The Dancing Hours* were all used for this purpose, and many of those tablets and plaques now appearing on the market were once part of a chimney piece since demolished.

During the 19th century many chimney pieces were destroyed to extract the tablets and plaques for display in collectors' cabinets. It is also likely that Wedgwood tablets and plaques are still *in situ* in the chimney pieces of old houses, hidden under layers of paint and whitewash, or by panelling. Paint has the effect of blurring the sharpness of the modelling to a point where the actual nature of the work is difficult to recognise unless it is examined with unusual care.

Chinoiserie
Fantasy Chinese scene invented by a European designer, but usually based in a general sense on a Chinese prototype. Decoration of this type with a strong fantasy element was especially popular at Meissen* during the 1720s and 1730s. This later inspired early porcelain decoration in England. The Willow* pattern is a true *chinoiserie* since it is a European invention. *Chinoiseries* in low relief occur as decoration on some of Wedgwood's early creamware, and *chinoiserie* designs were among the earliest patterns for underglaze blue prints* in 1805-10.
See: The Ladies' Amusement; Jean Pillement.

Chintz
Decorative motif enamelled on early creamware.
See: David Rhodes.

Chisholm, Alexander (1723-1805)
Chemist, and assistant to Dr. William Lewis of Kingston-upon-Thames who was practical chemist to the Society of Arts and author of a number of scientific works; employed by Wedgwood in 1780 as his secretary and chemical assistant, and as tutor for the children. In Tom Wedgwood* especially Chisholm found an apt pupil, who took great interest in chemistry. Chisholm was also chief works chemist until his retirement.

Chitqua (c.1750-1796)
A Chinese artist who arrived in England from Canton in 1769, returning three years later. He exhibited at the Royal Academy in 1770, in which year he modelled a portrait of Josiah Wedgwood. This bust (probably modelled in clay) has since been lost, but Chitqua was noted for his ability to achieve a striking likeness of the sitter. He committed suicide by taking poison.

Chocolate Cup
A covered cup, the saucer having a deep well into which the foot of the cup fits. It is often described as a *trembleuse* cup and saucer, since it was convenient when held in a trembling hand. Often made as cabinet pieces * in jasper*, most cups of this kind were made with two handles opposite to each other. The first London chocolate house was opened in 1657, and the *trembleuse* cup and saucer for the service of chocolate seems to have been made in England in porcelain from about 1755, and somewhat earlier in France. Wedgwood made this type from about 1785 for a variety of purposes, in addition to the service of chocolate; for instance, it was used in the 19th century for the service of ice cream.

Choiseul-Amboise, Duc de (1719-1785) Étienne-François
Minister of Louis XV who reorganised the army and the navy, developed trade and industry, and made himself popular by opposing the Jesuits. He enjoyed the patronage of Mme. de Pompadour, but Mme. du Barry succeeded in alienating him from the King. Wedgwood had written to Bentley in September 1769, of the possibility that they might "conquer France in Burslem," and before he went into retirement at Chanteloup in 1770, Choiseul received a letter from Josiah Wedgwood which accompanied the gift of a box containing "an assortment of urns and Vases in the Antique taste." Wedgwood went on to admit that, being earthenware, it was not comparable to the wares of Sèvres and Sceaux (*sic*), and that he knew it was "counterband" in France (i.e. prohibited by Royal Edicts in favour of the Sèvres factory, in which the King was the principal shareholder). Moreover, continued Josiah, he did not send it in the hope of opening trade in cream-coloured ware between France and England, but all the other crowned heads of Europe enjoyed creamware, and surely the rigours of the law could be relaxed, in this as in other matters, in favour of the nobility of France. If Choiseul replied to this disingenuous approach his answer has not survived, but French nobility at the time paid very little attention to Royal Edicts of this kind, and had they wanted creamware, no doubt they could quite easily have procured what they wanted. In fact, the Pont-aux-Choux* factory had been making creamware in the English manner for some time when this letter was written, and others followed. These, of course, competed with the faience factories, not with those making porcelain.

Cholerton, Herbert A.
Artist, armorial painter, and gilder, employed by Wedgwood, 1901-55. Cholerton decorated a bone china service ordered by Theodore Roosevelt for the White House in 1902. It is painted in gold with the seal of the United States.
See: White House Service.

Christie, James, The Elder (1730-1803) (Christie's)
Auctioneer in Pall Mall, London, 1766-1803, and founder of the famous firm of Christie, Manson & Woods. Wedgwood referred to him as "Mr Christy". In Wedgwood's day the firm was Christie & Ansell (Robert Ansell, partner 1777-84). The firm was responsible for the valuations of the properties of Sir William Chambers*, Sir Joshua Reynolds* and Johann Zoffany, and for the valuation and attribution of the Houghton pictures sold to Catherine II* of Russia in 1778.

By 1780, when Bentley* died, the firm's reputation was firmly established, and Christie & Ansell were the natural choice to act as auctioneers for the joint stock of ornamental* wares belonging to the Wedgwood & Bentley partnership. The sale was held in 1781, and the priced catalogue which survives in Christie's archives is one of the most valuable of existing records of Wedgwood & Bentley period production.

James Christie was described by a contemporary as "courteous, friendly and hospitable in private life — held in great esteem by his numerous friends among whom there were many of high rank."

Christmas Plates

Pale blue and white jasper* plates, 8ins. diameter, with centre relief ornament of a famous British scene or building and holly-leaf border. The first Christmas plate was produced in 1969, with a centre bas-relief view of Windsor Castle.

Subsequent designs have been as follows:

1970 Trafalgar Square.
1971 Piccadilly Circus.
1972 St. Paul's Cathedral.
1973 Tower of London.
1974 Houses of Parliament and Westminster Bridge.
1975 Tower Bridge.
1976 Hampton Court.
1977 Westminster Abbey.
1978 The Horse Guards.

In 1978, also, a limited edition of 10,000 plates in three-colour jasper (Portland blue, pale blue and white) was issued. This featured ten miniature bas-reliefs of the scenes used for each annual plate since 1969 (centre decoration: Windsor Castle) with a gold inscription.

Pale blue and white jasper Christmas mugs with similar ornaments have been issued since 1971.

Above: **Christmas Plates.** *Jasper Christmas Plate for 1969, the year of introduction. Holly-leaf border, ornamented with a view of Windsor Castle. Limited edition. Wedgwood.*

Above right: **Christmas Plates.** *Following the outstanding success of the Christmas plates, introduced in 1969, Wedgwood began, in 1971, a series of Christmas mugs. The first, in jasper, is ornamented with a view of Piccadilly Circus. Wedgwood.*

Right: **Christmas Plates.** *Tenth anniversary Christmas plate ornamented with reliefs from the previous issues. 1978. Wedgwood.*

Chrome Green

The first of the chromium colours to be introduced, c.1795, chrome green is derived from chromium oxide. It yields an opaque colour, variable in shade and more yellow in appearance than copper green, which inclines to blue. It has been popular with manufacturers since the beginning of the 19th century.

Chrysanthemum Pattern

Flowers in the *famille rose** style painted in enamel colours on black basaltes ware and red ware (terracotta or *rosso antico*), c.1804-15 or in print and enamel patterns on pearl* ware. Objects decorated in this style included tea and coffee ware, flower vases, bulb pots, candlesticks and inkstands.

Churchill, Sir Winston Leonard Spencer (1874-1965)

A Queen's ware bust 8ins. high was modelled for Wedgwood by Arnold Machin*. There is also a jasper* portrait medallion. For the centenary of his birth on the 30th November, 1974, Wedgwood issued a black basaltes bust 6¾ins. high, reproduced from the model by Arnold Machin in a limited edition of 750 copies. At the same time a pale blue and white jasper portrait medallion, and a Wedgwood glass cameo goblet, were issued, both in limited editions of 1,000. In addition, jasper sweet dishes, and gold inscribed black basaltes plates, bear bas-relief* portraits.

Churchyard Works

The works were first occupied in 1656 by Josiah Wedgwood's great grandfather, and were inherited by his eldest brother in 1739. Josiah served his apprenticeship there from 1744, and, after his brother's death in 1773, took over the mortgage of the Churchyard Works himself, later letting them to his cousin, Joseph Wedgwood.

Cicero, Marcus Tullius (106-43B.C.)

Roman orator and statesman; elected consul in 63B.C. As a statesman he was remarkable only for his ineptitude and habitual errors of judgement. ''I have,'' he wrote sadly, ''behaved like a perfect ass.'' Some years after the murder of Julius Caesar, he became the acknowledged leader of the republican party and attacked Mark Antony in his famous series of fourteen orations known as the *Philippics*. Antony had him killed in 43B.C. His extensive letters and philosophical writings have in great part survived.

His portrait is included in Wedgwood's lists of cameos and intaglios. A basaltes bust, about 20ins. high, was produced in 1775 from a cast supplied by Hoskins & Grant*, probably from an original model by John Bacon*.

Churchyard Works. *View of the Churchyard Works, Burslem, with two bottle kilns to the left.* Photo: Wedgwood.

Colour Plate VI

A page from Josiah Wedgwood's Experiment Book with a tray of early jasper trial pieces, each marked with a coded description of materials and firing method. Wedgwood.

Cipriani, Giovanni Batista (1727-?1788)

Painter, designer and engraver, born in Florence. He removed to London in 1753, and worked there for the rest of his life, becoming a member of the Royal Academy. He designed and painted ceilings for Robert Adam*, and collaborated with Bartolozzi*, who produced sensitive engravings of much of his work. Cipriani's designs were reproduced by Wedgwood using Bartolozzi engravings for both encaustic painting* on basaltes tablets* and for jasper bas-reliefs. The subjects include: *Cupids and Goat (Sacrifice to Hymen),* and *The Four Seasons.*

An encaustic-painted tablet after Cipriani is in the British Museum.

Citharist

The Crowning of a Citharist.
A Victorious Citharist.

See: Apotheosis of Homer.

Clam Dish

A 19th century dish with six clam-shaped depressions round the centre well which was used for sauce. Made of Queen's ware towards the end of the 19th century. A majolica* specimen in the Buten Museum* is dated 1897.

Clark, Esau

Merchant. Wedgwood's agent in Dublin from 1778. Josiah described him as having "the character of a timerous [*sic*] but very safe and good man."

Classicism

Classical art is based on the principles of ancient Greek and Roman art and architecture, particularly in such aspects as mathematically-expressed rules of proportion by which the parts were related to the whole, both in the elements of a building and in the measurements of the human body. This necessarily led to certain conventions in the representation of the subjects of classical art, and one of its principal manifestations was a well-marked symmetry in ornament, both in form and disposition. Asymmetry, deliberate departures from symmetry, marks most forms of non-classical art, for instance, the rococo*, Gothic, and some Oriental styles, notably Japanese. In the case of the latter, asymmetry is elevated to a guiding principle. A Roman temple was always built to a fixed plan laid down before the foundations. The height, diameter, and spacing of columns adhered to rules which were first enunciated by Vitruvius sometime after 46B.C. He wrote a poor treatise on architecture, much of it borrowed from Greek sources, which survived when other, better, books failed to do so. Gothic churches adhered to no fixed plan, and were often drastically altered during the course of construction. Gothic had no system of proportion, although an English rural architect, Batty Langley, attempted to impose one in the 18th century, without success.

Classical art is European mainstream art, although from time to time other, non-classical, styles arose, such as Gothic (12th to 16th centuries) which re-echoed some aspects of Islamic architecture in such features as the pointed arch and the arcade, and became widespread in northern Europe, even invading the northern towns of classical Italy.

The decay of Gothic art was followed by the rebirth of classicism, referred to as the Renaissance. Classical principles, and the vocabulary of classical ornament, were revived with some significant differences. The model for the Renaissance artist was Rome; for the neo-classical* artist it was often Pompeii* and Herculaneum*, provincial rather than metropolitan, and for the later Empire style the model was Greek rather than Roman. Roman classicism was, of course, heavily influenced by Greek and Etruscan art, and the work of the Etruscans, including their later pottery, was much influenced by Greece.

Neo-classicism, dating from the middle of the 18th century, followed an interregnum represented by some aspects of the baroque style, the rococo style, and the early influence of China and Japan, as well as a brief Gothic revival shortly before mid-century. With the close of the Empire period (a style marked by a return to Grecian and metropolitan Roman models) about 1830, the eclecticism of the 19th century started. This was a view of art which assumed that one style was as good as another, and all could be mixed freely, which led to such solecisms as Minton's classical vase on a Gothic arcaded pedestal. Classicism then tended to become one style among many, but it was a style to which Wedgwood largely remained faithful, and it accounts for the fact that although the factory produced some wares the design of which was no better than that of many of its competitors, a good deal of work, especially Queen's ware, was far ahead of its time in qualities of design, and its classical bias accounts to a great extent for its continued popularity in the United States, where classical styles (such as the Federal style) have always dominated the scene.

See: Gothic Revival; Neo-classical Style; Romantic Style.

Cleopatra. *Jasper portrait medallion of Cleopatra attributed to William Hackwood, 1775. Similar to a wax in the Victoria and Albert Museum, and modelled as a pair to the portrait of Mark Antony.* Dwight and Lucille Beeson Collection.

Clay

Hydrated silicate of aluminium formed from the decomposition of feldspar. Kaolin, or china clay, is white burning, but most other clays burn from light brown to red due to the presence of iron as an impurity. A few clays are grey after firing. Clays, of course, may be coloured by the addition of the metallic oxides, such as cobalt and manganese, normally used as pottery colours. Clay is plastic when it contains water. It shrinks and becomes hard when dry, and can be reduced to a fine powder when in this state. Dry clay can be reconstituted by the addition of water, but, if it is fired, point-to-point attachment of the particles takes place, and this state is irreversible. Although clays can be fired to this state at a comparatively low temperature, they are also refractory, and will only fuse at about 1600°C, a temperature above that of feldspar and the fusible rocks (such as barium sulphate) used in the manufacture of fine stonewares and porcelain. Clay is commonly found with various impurities, most of which need to be removed before it is fit for use in the manufacture of pottery.

Clay, Henry (fl.1750-1802)

Japanner, of Newhall Street, Birmingham, who took out, in 1772, a patent for the manufacture of 'panels from paper of several thicknesses dried in a hot stove for furniture etc.', a product which he called 'paper ware' to distinguish it from 'true' *papier mâché* produced from pulped paper. Highly varnished panels of Clay's paper ware were used for trays, tables, cabinets, screens, bookcases and chairs as well as for smaller decorative objects which were often inset with Wedgwood jasper cameos* or medallions. Clay retired from business in 1802, and his firm was taken over, in 1816, by Jennens & Bettridge.

Cleopatra

The eldest daughter of Ptolemy Auletes. Her father appointed her co-heir with her brother, Ptolemy, whom she was to marry according to the custom of the Egyptian royal house. She acceded in 51B.C., but was expelled by her brother's guardians. She at once appealed to Julius Caesar, who replaced her on the throne. By him she had a son, Caesarion. After Caesar's death she met Marc Antony, and accompanied her lover to the battle of Actium in 31B.C.; by withdrawing her fleet from the battle she undoubtedly sealed Antony's fate. She opened negotiations with Augustus, and caused rumours of her death to be spread abroad. Antony, hearing these, stabbed himself, and, overcome by remorse, Cleopatra poisoned herself with the bite from an asp. After her death Caesarion was executed by order of Augustus.

Wedgwood subjects:

Cleopatra, Bust, height 8ins., attributed to Hackwood*, 1777.

Cleopatra (dying), ¾-face 'portrait' medallion, modelled by Hackwood, 1775. Possibly the 'figure', a cast of which was obtained from Hoskins & Grant* in the same year.

Cleopatra before Augustus, Sepia-painted creamware plaque, 13½ ins. diameter, from a print by Thomas Burke (1749-1815) after Angelica Kauffmann*.

Cleopatra on a Rock, basaltes figure, 8ins. Reproduced as late as 1913 from an earlier uncatalogued model.

Clock Cases

The fashion for elaborately decorated clock cases inspired by contemporary French styles arose during the last quarter of the 18th century. Many of these were made from gilt metal and alabaster, often with the addition of ceramic ornament. Among the most common ornaments were Sèvres* porcelain and Wedgwood jasper medallions, and a fine clock by Benjamin

Clock Cases. *Clock case of pearl ware and brass with French type movement, 1888.* Buten Museum.

Vulliamy* embellished in this manner is in the British Museum. Vulliamy also made clocks the ornamental cases of which were mounted with biscuit porcelain figures made at Derby*, and it is now known that white jasper figures by Wedgwood were used for the same purpose. Mounted in this manner, the difference between biscuit porcelain and white jasper figures is not immediately apparent. In the case of the latter, the mark is on the sole of the foot and may be seen only when the figure is detached from its mount.

Wedgwood had seen in 1776 the profitable business being done by Boulton* in French-style ormolu* clocks, and he wrote to Bentley* in July: "...You remember a poor Venus weeping over the tomb of Adonis — A Time-piece. How many would you think they have sold of this single group? 200 at 25 guineas each, including the watch." No doubt, too, he had seen something of the porcelain clock cases being produced by Sèvres, one form of which, in an oviform vase, either had the conventional dial attached to a movement inset into the body, or the more unusual form of hours on a ring encircling the vase and a pointer which moved round it. There is evidence that Wedgwood experimented with the adaptation of vases for this purpose. He also experimented with watch stands, four being sent to London in 1774, and a black basaltes urn with watch stand marked 'WEDGWOOD & BENTLEY ETRURIA' is in the Brooklyn Museum. Several of the porcelain factories made watch stands, intended to be placed on the bedside table so that the watch might be used as a timepiece at night, but none of them ever produced a thoroughly satisfactory model. An exceptionally fine jasper clock case showing *Peace destroying the Implements of War* (probably to celebrate the Treaty of Amiens in 1802) is in the collections of the Merseyside Museums.

During the late 19th century and the early years of the 20th small clock cases were made in both jasper and basaltes, and similar models have been produced in jasper since 1965.

Clock Cases. *Three-colour jasper clock case, blue figures and green borders on white ground, c.1905, the form based on the popular marble clocks of the period.* Sotheby's Belgravia.

Clodion, Claude Michel (1738-1814)

French sculptor, born Claude Michel, in Nancy, later assuming the name Clodion. At the age of sixteen he moved to Paris, where he studied under L.S. Adam, a relation of his mother's, and Pigalle*. After nine years in Rome, executing commissions for the Empress Catherine II* and other patrons, he returned to Paris, but his work — generally small terracotta figures and bas-reliefs* of nymphs and satyrs treated with frank sensuality — did not recommend him for recognition by the Academy until 1793, when he became an Associate. Later he successfully changed his style to conform more closely to the fashion for Greek sculpture, and worked on the Calonne de la Grande Armée and the Arc de Triomphe de Carrousel. In 1798 he returned to Nancy and provided models for the Niderviller porcelain factory.

Wedgwood bas-relief subjects which appear to have been copied or adapted from Clodion's original work include:
Bacchante, figure
Danae, figure
Faun, figure
Bacchanalian Sacrifice, tablet 21ins. by 9ins. Modelled prior to 1773.
Bacchanalian Triumph, tablet 21¼ins. by 9½ins. Modelled prior to 1773.

The *Wine* and *Water* ewers are also said to have been adapted from original models by Clodion.

Coach Pot
See: Bourdalou.

Coade Stone
Although Coade's Artificial Stone Works in Lambeth was not the first to manufacture artificial stone in London, it was the largest. Founded in 1769, the manufactory was situated at Pedlar's Acre, and it was managed by Mrs. Eleanor Coade, in partnership with her daughter and John Sealy, her cousin. Several modellers and sculptors worked alike for her and for Wedgwood, including Voyez*, De Vaere*, Rossi and Flaxman*. The works closed in 1836.

Coade's success was due largely to the secret composition of the artificial stone. This was a ceramic stoneware, and infinitely superior to modern cement compositions. It was also fine textured and creamy white in colour (though it could be tinted to produce shades of yellow, grey or pink to tone with the stone or brick of buildings), and thus better suited to classical ornament than the later red terracotta so popular with Victorian architects.

Coade competed with Wedgwood very successfully in the sale of chimney piece ornaments, possibly because articles of similar appearance and durability could be produced at lower cost. Certain of Wedgwood's tablets and plaques, including one version of the *Bacchanalian Triumph,* were made also by Coade, but it is not certain which of the models is the earlier.

Coalport
Porcelain factory established in 1795 by John Rose, previously an apprentice at the Caughley pottery, which he acquired in 1799. From 1798 Rose was one of the pioneers of the manufacture of bone china*. At first this was marred by uneven quality and iron specks, but by 1820 Rose had achieved a fine white body with creamy translucency. In 1820 he introduced a hard transparent leadless glaze. During the 19th century the firm's china became particularly notable for flower-encrusted rococo* shapes, and for reproductions or copies of large and magnificent Sèvres* and Meissen* vases of a century earlier. A small quantity of Parian* was made from about 1845. In 1967 the firm was acquired by Wedgwood as part of the Wedgwood Group*.

Cobalt Oxide
The most commonly used colouring oxide, yielding a distinctive blue which is used underglaze, onglaze, for colouring glazes, and for staining slips and bodies. It appears to have been employed first in Persia about the 10th century, and it was known in China about a century later. Wedgwood used it particularly for colouring jasper. Cobalt oxide was used in the form of smalt*, and it was both scarce and expensive in the 18th century. In April 1777, Wedgwood complained to Bentley that he was having to pay 36s. a pound, a very considerable sum, and soon afterwards he introduced jasper dip*. By the end of that year the price had risen to three guineas. At this time the best cobalt came from deposits in Saxony, but very little was exported through normal channels, and smuggling was rigorously suppressed. Earlier, Wedgwood had written to Bentley that a man had been hanged in Prussia for engaging illegally in this trade.

Cockpit Hill
See: Derby.

Coconut Vase
The mounting as vases of such natural objects as nautilus shells in gold and silver had been customary for several centuries in Wedgwood's day, and the making of vases from mounted coconut shells was not at all uncommon. The Victoria and Albert Museum has one such vase mounted in silver gilt which is inset with two jasper medallions of classical subjects, one of the *Three Graces* (see: Graces), and the other of *Omphale*, Queen of Lydia.*

Codes and Formulae

Stealing manufacturing secrets was a well-established commercial practice in the 18th century. All manufacturers who employed new or significantly improved techniques were compelled to guard against industrial spies, and Wedgwood was already taking precautions against them during his partnership with Thomas Whieldon*. This partnership was undoubtedly offered to Wedgwood because, even as early as 1754, he had achieved a reputation for research which led to useful improvements and developments in the ware itself, and in manufacturing processes. Wedgwood was able to insist that any improvements that he introduced should remain his property which he was not bound to share. His *Experiment Book* belonging to the end of this period survives in the Wedgwood Museum at Barlaston, and it records how he was induced to try "for some more solid improvements as well in the *Body*, as in the *Glazes*, and *Colours*, and the *Forms*. . ." He formulated an elaborate code to express the different degrees of heat to which trial pieces had been subjected. GO meant gloss (glost) oven, and BO, the biscuit oven. The letters B, M, or T prefixed meant Bottom, Middle, or Top, so TBO meant top of the biscuit oven (not to be confused with T° which is the mark of Mr. Tebo*). Experiments were ranged in classes and sections, the first, second, or third class being indicated by one, two, or three dots respectively, and the appropriate section by a figure. One of the formulae, set out numerically, is characteristic:

$$\frac{7 \qquad 3 \qquad 17 \qquad 33}{120 \qquad 30 \qquad 9}$$

This is the seventh experiment on the first page. The numbers above the line, which are in red, indicate the materials; those below the line, in black, are quantities. This is the formula for a copper green glaze to be used on cream coloured biscuit, and it is dated March 23rd, 1759. The date makes it very doubtful that Wedgwood ever used this glaze while he was working with Whieldon, since the partnership was dissolved in April, 1759, and his cousin, Thomas*, agreed to serve him for six years as a journeyman from 1st May.

Despite Wedgwood's efforts to keep his manufacturing secrets from others, they were acquired by his rivals. He took out only one patent — for encaustic painting* — and James Neale* and Humphrey Palmer*, who were responsible for infringing it, proved of how little value a patent could be in the 18th century when others were sufficiently unscrupulous as to disregard it. Wedgwood eventually compromised, and withdrew his action for damages. After this experience he lost confidence in patents, and relied even more upon secrecy.

This became specially marked when the trials for jasper were nearing success. He conducted his researches in his home, Etruria Hall, in cellars reached by a trapdoor in the floor. An outside door to the cellars was reached down a flight of steps, and the path to it was concealed behind high brick walls. The experimental materials were delivered without the knowledge of anyone but a few trusted employees.

In the autumn of 1774 Wedgwood journeyed into Derbyshire in search of minerals. Here he discovered cawk* or barium sulphate* (74 in Wedgwood's code, and called 'radix jasperini* in his letters to Bentley) which proved superior to the 'spaith fusible' (see: Spath) with which he was experimenting. Even in 1776, when jasper was an accomplished fact, Wedgwood was still experimenting with radix jasperini, this time in the manufacture of porcelain. At the end of a long letter to Bentley, dated 24th June, dealing principally with the behaviour of a variety of materials used in the manufacture of porcelain, a process which he analyses with remarkable insight into contemporary practice at home and abroad, he writes: "I am sending you some Pitchers [i.e. trials] of 74 Porcelain, and beg you will let Mr. Rhodes* try his skill in glazing them." It is evident that by this Wedgwood meant porcelain made with barium sulphate replacing the feldspar used by Champion*. Had he proceeded with it successfully, this would have produced a porcelain that would not have infringed Champion's patent (limited to Cornish materials, and, after the renewal of the patent, only in specified quantities).

In December 1777, Wedgwood wrote to Bentley about supplies of radix jasperini: "It will come cheaper to us from London by way of Liverpool than from Hull. Suppose you write to Mr. — : That you are in hopes of opening an exportation trade for it, and that he may be preparing at his leisure 50 or 60 barrels of 240lbs each, weighed exclusive of the cask, and you will give him directions what Port they must be sent to as the Merchant does not yet know from whence he can best ship them for the intended Market... I think we may manage without any third party being in the secret, and I wish you would burn, or lock up safe, this and all of my letters which mention this article."

When, in 1775, Wedgwood wanted some ground glass, probably for experiments in the making of frit porcelain, he wrote to Bentley: "I must have some before I can proceed, and I dare not have it the *nearest way,* nor undisguised, though I could only wish to have it pounded and put through a coarse hair sieve, but even this I would not have done with your people, nor have them see it at all. Could not Mr. More* get some poor man to work upon it in some of the uninhabited buildings of the Adelphi?."

These precautions may seem excessive, but Wedgwood suffered a great deal from the imitation of some of his wares, and from the pirating of his designs. He was not the kind of man who wished to keep a monopoly of his innovations and improvements, however, even had it been possible. He was content to keep ahead of the competition, provided no one tried to pass off his wares as Wedgwood (as in the case of Voyez*), or make exact copies, or use the Wedgwood mark. Wedgwood's wares were always more expensive than those of his competitors, but they rarely approached him for quality allied to persuasive salesmanship, and he relied on these to maintain his lead.

The affair of Palmer and the infringement of the encaustic patent ended in Wedgwood agreeing to share the patent with his neighbour on payment of a sum of money, and the two men shook hands on the settlement. It was a matter which speedily became less important with the waning of the vogue for this type of ware. Palmer had copied Wedgwood's wares from the first and he succeeded in producing a basaltes which even Wedgwood admitted was "very good."

John Turner*, one of Wedgwood's friends with whom he visited Cornwall in 1775 in search of supplies of china clay and china stone, imitated both basaltes and jasper (although he did not use the same substances as Josiah in his versions of the latter), but he was unable to achieve the same quality of design, and he did not use classical subjects to the same extent. Adams* of Greengates made jasper from about the middle of the 1780s in several colours, as well as basaltes and cane ware. Some of his subjects were copied from Wedgwood, but original work was done and is attributed to Joseph Mongenot*. Following Wedgwood's lead, Palmer, Turner, and Adams all used an impressed mark.

Before the end of the century, copying Wedgwood had become a growth industry, not only in Staffordshire, but throughout Europe, and during the last quarter of the 18th century he occupied the position of influence as arbiter of taste in the manufacture of pottery that Meissen and Sèvres had held earlier in the century. By this time codes, and elaborate precautions to maintain secrecy, were becoming less vital than they had been at the outset, when Wedgwood's success depended to some extent on a chance to exploit his improvements and innovations undisturbed for a few years, but he had attracted the attention of foreign industrial spies who endeavoured to gain access to the works to copy machinery, or to view processes.

During the 19th century, when it became fashionable to adulate men like Josiah who, by hard work, strength of character, and sheer business acumen built up a large and thriving business, using secret processes to do so, another section of society considered that manufacturing secrets should be public property, and used for more general benefit. William Evans, who wrote *The Art & History of the Potting Business* in 1846, made this clear in his first paragraph: ''Time was, when most of the Handicrafts of this country were secrets, confined to the possession of those whom Fortune, or Capital had placed in the position of EMPLOYERS. Few amongst the working, or operative class, could boast of a knowledge of the ingredients or processes, by which the most beautiful articles of British Manufacture have been wrought into existence. Indeed, it has been a matter of legal prosecution for an apprentice or adult mechanic, having discovered some of the *secrets* of his profession, to divulge the same in opposition to the expressed wish or sanction of his employer. This state of mental darkness is fast passing away, and the secrets of Operative Industry are becoming as generally known as a Cheap Press and more liberal institutions can make them. Working men no longer remain the mere physical manipulators of the craftily compounded materials of hidden processes and hoarded up recipes. They feel. . . that they have the *right* to know the component parts of all that passes through their hands.'' No doubt foreign buyers were still as eager to buy as the workmen would have been to sell had they been in a position to do so. One can only feel surprise at the naïvety of the disgruntled William Evans.

Nevertheless, manufacturers still have their secrets, it is still illegal for an employee to disclose them, and industrial spies are even more numerous and ruthless than they were in the 18th and 19th centuries. The difference, today, is that they are more likely to be employed by governments than by rival manufacturers.

See: Spies, Industrial.

Coffee Biggin

Forerunner of the filter-method coffeepot, and made in Queen's ware and drab ware, c.1850-80. The biggin consists of a standard teapot and a cylindrical cup (without handle), shaped and perforated at the base. The cup rests in the open top of the teapot, the teapot lid being used as a cover for the whole. Coffee, made by pouring boiling water onto the measured grounds in the cup, drips slowly into the pot below. The cup is then removed, and the lid replaced on the teapot.

Coffee Cans

Straight-sided cylindrical cups, about 2½ ins. high, for the service of coffee. The shape was copied from Sèvres by a number of English factories for cups of exceptional quality intended to be displayed in cabinets. They date from the last quarter of the 18th century. Wedgwood made them in white jasper* decorated with reliefs in several colours, in solid-colour jasper, and jasper dip*. A large size can made in porcelain at Derby was always described as a 'breakfast can', and for these no saucers were provided. In 1773 a letter from Wedgwood to Bentley records the preparation of coffee cans for the Turkish market, and no doubt these were of Queen's ware*. The German *Turkenköpgen,* staple articles of trade with the Meissen and Nymphenburg factories, were tall cups with small handles. Meissen adopted a special mark for wares destined for Turkey. Although other shapes have been introduced, the can shape (in a smaller size than that produced for display in cabinets) has remained the most popular for coffee sets in bone china*, Queen's ware, basaltes* and jasper.

Coffee Cans. *Straight-sided jasper coffee can and saucer, finely ornamented with the* Dancing Hours *and intended as a 'Cabinet piece,' with a richly festooned jasper teapot c.1790.* Photo: Wedgwood.

Cold Painting

Painting in unfired colour, a practice quite common at some of the early porcelain factories during the first years of their existence. In England enamelling on porcelain was not practicable until about 1750 when William Duesbury*, later proprietor of the Derby factory, had an enamelling studio in London. Wares decorated in 'cold' colour (oil paint or coloured varnish) are now usually white after years of washing and handling, although slight traces of paint sometimes remain. There is no record that Wedgwood ever employed 'cold' colour for anything but experimental work. The background of early white cameos was painted with watercolour independently, and, more rarely, by Wedgwood also. Other wares, mostly vases, painted in this way do exist, although they are very rare. They are the work of amateur painters, usually ladies. A letter to the factory dated 1st March, 1796, will explain the position: "The Marchioness of Blandford wishes you to send (along with the things already bespoke) a small vase for Lady's [sic] to paint on. What her ladyship means is made of a white composition."

Coloured Bodies

Coloured wares obtained by mixing colouring oxides or ochreous earths with the clay. Wedgwood's research was encouraged by the success of cane ware* and the development of coloured jasper. The majority of Wedgwood's coloured bodies, and the most successful, were of Queen's ware. The first, a grey green which was named *Celadon*, was introduced in 1805. *Drab* ware* in tableware shapes was produced at about the same time, and *Lavender* followed in 1850. Wedgwood's coloured bodies, produced in traditional shapes*, were probably the most important technical development at the factory during the 19th century, representing a return to the appreciation of pure form at a time when excessive ornament

Commemorative Ware. *Queen's ware jug commemorating the death of Thomas Carlyle in 1881. Backstamp of John Mortlock.* Private Collection.

Commemorative Ware. *Pearl ware mug decorated with diaper design in red and hand-painted Chinese flowers, with printing in red, made to commemorate the Golden Jubilee of George III, 1810.* Wedgwood.

was the fashionable vice of designers and manufacturers. Their appeal was ageless and they remained for more than 150 years among the most popular of Wedgwood's productions. Several new colours were introduced in the 20th century, including *Champagne, Honey-Buff* (for Heal's, 1930), *Windsor Grey* (1953), and *Cane* (1957). *Drab* ware is still produced for Tiffany's, New York. Two-colour clay bodies were introduced in 1936 with the production of *Summer Sky* (lavender and cream colour) and *Wintergreen* (celadon and cream colour), and these were reintroduced in 1952. They were superseded in 1955 by *Summer Sky* and *Barlaston Green* on Barlaston shapes*, and to these were later added *Harvest Moon* (cane and cream colour), *Moonlight* (Windsor grey and cream colour), and *Havana* (brown and cream colour). Trials were also made with a terracotta colour, but it did not prove popular in the two-colour form and it was rapidly withdrawn. *Alpine Pink*, a pink-stained bone china* body, was introduced in 1936 and made again during the late 1950s in tableware and a range of Nautilus* and other shell shapes. Some trial pieces were also made in grey bone china.

Combed Ware

See: Marbling.

Commemorative Ware

Throughout its history the Wedgwood firm has made wares in celebration of popular heroes and historical events. Typical examples are the 'Death of Wolfe'* teapots and jugs, c.1778, and the Wolfe bicentenary jugs and trays of 1959; the medallions celebrating George III's* recovery from his illness in 1789; the 'German cameos'*; the Bastille medallion*; and in recent times the American Independence Series* of 1976. In

Commemorative Ware. *A commemorative bowl marking the tercentenary of Harvard University. Made for Jones, McDuffee & Stratton Co., 1936.* Wedgwood.

Commemorative Ware. *Queen's ware plate decorated with a print of the United States Naval Academy in 1858. Issued by Jones, McDuffee & Stratton Co., in 1935.* Wedgwood.

broad terms, many of the Illustrious Moderns* portrait medallions* and the modern Christmas* plates may be classified as commemorative, but the description, Commemorative Ware, is properly applied only to those 'named views' commissioned by Jones*, McDuffee & Stratton.

Comport
A form of dessert dish on stand (somewhat resembling a *tazza*) made by Wedgwood in cream-coloured ware in the 18th century, and especially popular during the 19th century, when 'tall' and 'low' comports were essential parts of bone china and earthenware dessert services.

Compotier
A bowl or deep dish, often on stand, for serving *compôte* (cooked whole fruit). Wedgwood have also used the term to describe small shallow bowls in various shapes and patterns suitable for serving nuts, olives, etc.

Conceit
A ceramic object in the form of a round cake used for the decoration of the dinner table when flour for real cakes was scarce. Made by Wedgwood in cane ware* and white jasper* early in the 19th century.

See: Pastry Ware; Game-Pie Dish.

Conchology
The science of the study of shells. The collecting of exotic shells was a fashionable 18th century pursuit, and Josiah Wedgwood was an avid shell collector. In 1778 he wrote to Bentley, then on holiday in Margate, asking him to search the beach and rummage in chalk pits for specimens. The rococo style of mid-century made much use of shells as decorative motifs, especially in the design of porcelain*. Shell forms also decorated Wedgwood wares. Flaxman's *Triton* is grasping a whorled shell, often erroneously called a cornucopia, which

Commemorative Ware. *The Olympic Plate, an example of modern commemorative ware, made in a special edition to celebrate the Olympic Games at Montreal, 1976.* Wedgwood.

Conceit. *Pair of cane ware conceits, c.1800-10.* Buten Museum.

Conchology. *Two vessels from the dessert service in Queen's ware based on the Nautilus shell. The border is No.384 from Josiah Wedgwood's first pattern book. c.1798. Wedgwood.*

Below: **Conchology.** *Bone china vase in the form of shells upheld by branches of coral. A typical rococo theme again popular in the second half of the 19th century. c.1885. Wedgwood.*

acts as a candleholder. Shell shapes occur in bas-reliefs, in the decoration of Queen's ware patterns, and in moulded shapes for tablewares. The popular Nautilus* service of 1769/70 was designed by Josiah Wedgwood as a dessert service, and is still in production. It consists of a cream bowl, a centre bowl, and plates. After 1805 it was made in Moonlight lustre*, and it has since been made in creamware, Alpine pink*, bone china*, and Moonstone glaze*.

Concordia

A Roman goddess with several temples in Rome. She personified harmony and agreement. She is usually represented holding a cornucopia in one hand and an olive branch in the other.

Wedgwood subject:

Sacrifice to Concordia, medallion, height 10ins. Modelled by Webber*, c.1786, as a companion to his *Sacrifice to Hymen* (see: Sacrifice).

Cookworthy, William (1705-1780)

See: Richard Champion; Cherokee Clay.

Cooper, David (fl.1770-1773)

Cooper, a good flower painter, was hired for three years in May 1770, at 13s. per week in the country and 16s. at the Chelsea Decorating Studio*.

Cooper, Joseph (fl.1770-1780)

Printer of Drury Lane, London, who printed Catalogues for Wedgwood, and was, for a time (1772-77) in partnership with Du Burk* of Amsterdam.

Cooper, Nathaniel (fl.1769-1774)

Painter at Chelsea Decorating Studio* of encaustic* vases, who worked on the Husk* service, and painted inside borders and frogs on the Frog* service.

Cooper, Susie, OBE, RDI (b.1903)

English ceramic designer; studied at Burslem Art School from 1922; from 1925, designer for A.E. Gray & Co., Hanley; noted for abstract designs in styles influenced by art nouveau and art deco. In 1932 she established her own company, using the mark of the deer, and during the 1930s she worked principally on bone china. In 1966 her company was one of the first acquisitions by Wedgwood in the formation of the Wedgwood Group*. She is now one of Wedgwood's leading designers, and executed successful commissions for the Queen's Silver Jubilee in 1977. A retrospective exhibition of her work was held at Sanderson's Showrooms, Berners Street, London, in 1978.

Copeland

See: Spode.

Coriolanus

Originally Gaius Marcellus, he was surnamed Coriolanus to commemorate the heroism he displayed during the siege and capture of the Volscian town of Corioli. His arrogance made him many enemies however, and in 491B.C. he was exiled, taking refuge among the Volscians. Their King appointed him general of the army, and in 489 Coriolanus led his command to within a short distance of Rome. Here he was visited by many distinguished Romans, who implored him to spare the city, but he would listen to none, until a deputation of Rome's noblest matrons, including his mother, Veturia, and his wife, Volumnia, accompanied by his two small children, came to plead with him. He relented and turned away from Rome, returning to live with the Volscians.

Wedgwood subjects:

Veturia and Volumnia entreating Coriolanus, tablet 6ins. by 9¾ins., by Flaxman*, 1784. Erroneous variations on this title include: *Coriolanus with his wife and mother persuading him to return* [sic] *to Rome,* and *Octavia* [sic] *and Volumnia, entreating Coriolanus.*

Volumnia, Mother [sic] *of Coriolanus,* medallion by Flaxman, after a print (d'Hancarville* II. pl.26).

The history of Coriolanus does not seem to have been well known at Etruria.

Cornish Journey

In May 1775, Josiah Wedgwood and John Turner*, accompanied by Thomas Griffiths (who had been Wedgwood's agent in South Carolina for the purchase of Cherokee clay*), set out on a journey of exploration into Cornwall on behalf of the Staffordshire potters. Wedgwood kept a journal of his travels which was reprinted in the *Proceedings of the Wedgwood Society of London,* Nos. 1 and 2. The object of the journey was to find and assess deposits of minerals, such as china clay and feldspathic rock, likely to be of use in the pottery industry. Wedgwood paid a visit to the source of the Worcester factory's supplies of soaprock near the Lizard and took samples, and, not far away, he found the site from which Chaffers' Liverpool factory drew supplies. By June 11th, 1775, the travellers had acquired the rights to deposits of minerals sufficient for their purpose, and Griffiths was left behind to supervise the conclusion of the arrangements. A travelling companion, Henry Tolcher of Plymouth, possessed a cobalt mine. Wedgwood proposed the setting up of a joint stock company to carry out experimental work on behalf of those potters and subscribers who opposed Champion's* porcelain Bill, but no agreement was possible, and Wedgwood felt free to continue experiments with the Cornish materials alone.

Cornish Metal Company

A company formed to exploit Cornish metal deposits. Josiah Wedgwood was a shareholder, with Matthew Boulton*, James Watt*, and Richard Arkwright. A letter from Wedgwood to James Watt dated 17th September, 1785, discusses payment for shares.

Cornish Stone

A mineral rich in feldspar used in the manufacture of porcelain, bone china, and fine stonewares. Also called moor stone or growan stone.

Cornucopia

Pl. Cornucopiæ. A horn of plenty. This is symbolic of Happiness, Concord, and Fortune, and takes the form of a drinking horn *(cornu)* filled with corn and fruit, the two kinds of nourishment essential to man. The goddesses, Fortuna and Ceres* (Demeter), are often represented with a cornucopia spilling out fruits and corn.

Coronation Pattern

Bone china border pattern designed by Cecily Stella 'Star' Wedgwood* in 1937. Three white plumes are outlined with platinum lustre on a ground of onglaze red, (pattern number W3369).

Coupe Shape

Rimless plates and dishes introduced in 1955 for bone china* tableware patterns and principally designed for the Savoy Hotel, London, and for export to the United States. Teamed with Savoy shape hollow ware*, it became extremely popular in a period when form and decoration were strongly influenced by the simplicity of Scandinavian design. The lack of a plate rim, however, did not conform to English eating habits (providing no dry surface for salt or mustard) and the Coupe shape achieved wide popularity in Britain only for teaware and coffeeware.

Coward John. *Carved wood block moulds probably by John Coward.* Wedgwood.

Coward, John

Woodcarver, said to have worked for the brothers Adam*, who was engaged by Wedgwood in 1768 to repair defective vases, and to make wooden models for new vases, some of which are now in the factory museum. Although most of the vases so treated were of basaltes ware, some cream-coloured vases also underwent the same treatment to make them saleable. Coward's work included the making of wooden covers, providing wooden bases to which the body of the vase could be attached, and carving handles to replace those which had been broken. The collector should remember, however, that not every vase with a wooden base or handles was refurbished by Coward. In addition to this work on vases, Coward also carved or sketched designs for tableware pieces.

The following subjects are by or attributed to Coward:
Basket (drawing), 1768.
Candlesticks (sketches), 1768.
Compôtier stand (pearwood model in Wedgwood Museum).
Crossed ribbons 'to a neat small tray in mahogany' (carving), 1769
Hexagonal Pot-Pourri vase, 1765 (pearwood model in Wedgwood Museum).
Queen's Arms, 1768.
Somnus (Sleeping Boy), from a cast by Hoskins & Grant.
Soup tureen and ladle (pearwood model in Wedgwood Museum).

Cox, William (fl.c.1763 onwards)

Warehouseman and book keeper, London and Burslem. Cox was sent to London in November 1767, to take charge of the showrooms in Charles Street, Grosvenor Square. In June 1768, an assistant was hired in Staffordshire and sent to London to help him in the removal to Great Newport Street. At this time it was necessary for Wedgwood to press continually for money to be remitted from London to Burslem, and Cox's book keeping, although honest, was far from accurate. In August 1768, Wedgwood wrote to Cox warning him that their new designs were being pirated by other Staffordshire potters, pin-pointing the china dealers, Caravalla and Fogg, as the two principally responsible. Cox was instructed to watch for anyone repeatedly buying a few pairs or single articles of the new patterns. In November 1768, Wedgwood in London wrote to Bentley, then staying in Burslem: "Mr Cox is as mad as a march Hare for Etruscan Vases; pray get a quantity made or we shall disgust our good customers by disappointing them in their expectations," and in April 1769, writing from Burslem: "I had a piteous letter last night from Mr Cox — not a vase scarcely of any sort to sell, Blue Pebble* and Marbles [see: Marbling], all gone." By December 1769, Cox's deficiencies as a book keeper caught up with him, and Wedgwood wrote to Bentley: "I am much concerned to find so many more blunders in Mr Cox's Cash account, and as I am daily suffering in so tender a point as that of my Character for Honesty, and all through his neglect, I could not help reproving him very severely for it . . . I insist on his doing nothing but assist in clearing up the Books . . . and till this work is finished I beg you will not send out any more bills, unless such as you are certain are not paid . . . It is equitable and just that he [Cox] should rather lose his Character as a book-keeper which he has deserved to do, than that I should lose mine for Honesty, which I have never forfeited . . ."

In 1773 we find Wedgwood writing, apropos of Cox: "These all-sufficient men create one a vast deal of plague and trouble." On an occasion when Cox sent some large white cameos to Boulton* and charged him only eighteen pence apiece, he added "I do not know how or in what way to

contradict what he has done without appearing foolish upon the occasion."

Crabstock (Crabtree)

Type of spout and handle moulded in relief to represent the gnarled branch of a crab apple tree. A teapot with a crabstock spout usually has a conforming handle. Also sometimes called 'rustic', the type was first introduced on salt glazed* wares c.1745 and is also to be found on early red ware and glazed black ware. It was the first type of spout to be adopted for Staffordshire, Yorkshire, Liverpool and Derby creamware, and was made by Whieldon* and by Wedgwood at Burslem.
See: William Greatbatch; Rococo.

Crabstock. *Black-glazed teapot of the type associated with Jackfield, decorated with vine leaves, grapes, and a bird finial. Crabstock handle and spout. Unmarked. Wedgwood.*

Craft, William Hopkins (c.1730-1811)

Partner with David Rhodes* in 1769-70, and worked with him at the enamelling studios at Newport Street and Chelsea Decorating Studio*. Wedgwood wrote to Bentley in September 1769: "It must be yours and Mr. Croft's [*sic*] care to collect and make the painters; perhaps you may get some better hands from the Fan Painters if that business is carried on now . . . than from among the China men [e.g. from Bow, Chelsea, or James Giles*]." Craft certainly painted encaustic vases* but, from about 1771, he appears to have worked as an independent enameller and executed a number of fine portraits and plaques, including one of David Garrick.

Crane, Walter (1845-1915)

Artist, designer, book illustrator, writer and lecturer, born in Liverpool. An associate of William Morris, Crane was one of the leading figures in the Arts and Crafts movement, and first President of the Arts and Crafts Society, founded in 1888. With Kate Greenaway* and Ralph Caldecott*, he was one of the three 'Academicians of the Nursery': influential artists whose work as contemporary illustrators of children's books made their names household words. Strongly influenced by the Pre-Raphaelites, Crane's illustrations relied upon decorative design, of which purity of line and charm of colour were essential ingredients. To modern taste the technique may appear admirable but the overall effect faintly sickening. Among his many distinctions, Crane was the inventor of 'Mr Michael Mouse', a recognisable antecedent of Disney's immortal character. More formally, Crane was a member of the Royal Watercolour Society (1902), Director of Design at the Manchester Municipal School (1893), Art Director at Reading University College (1896) and Principal of the Royal College of Art (1898).

Crane designed for Minton c.1870, for Wedgwood, 1867-88, for Maw & Co. and for the Pilkington Tile & Pottery Co. His designs for Wedgwood include the tournament border for a chess table (1870), and the decoration of a number of vases (e.g. *Ambition,* 1870, and *Seven Ages of Man,* 1867) and jugs (*Knowledge,* 1888).

Crazing
A network of surface cracks on the glaze of pottery or porcelain, usually the result of an unintended disagreement between the shrinkage rates of glaze and body during the cooling stage, but sometimes caused by later reheating in a domestic oven, when the cracks are often badly discoloured. Particles of dirt or grease are inclined to collect in these glaze cracks and cannot be removed by washing, and the passage of time makes them more obvious, especially in the case of useful ware. Chinese potters were able to control crazing to a notable extent, and it was employed as a decoration on some of the finest wares. Crazing appears on some early creamware and frequently upon mid-19th century pieces. It is often the result of re-heating.

Crealock, Henry Hope (1831-1891)
Soldier, artist and author; served in the Crimea, in China, in India, and in the Zulu war, 1879; retired with the rank of

Lieutenant-General, 1884. He sketched many scenes in the Indian Mutiny and the Chinese campaign, and during the Zulu war, for the *Illustrated London News.* He also illustrated Whyte-Melville's *Katerfelto,* 1875. His *Deer-Stalking in the Highlands of Scotland,* profusely illustrated with his drawings, was published posthumously in 1892.

Several of his illustrations, which are signed, have been identified on Wedgwood Queen's ware, printed by a photographic process. These have led to the conclusion being incorrectly drawn that he was the inventor of the process rather than the artist.

Cream-Coloured Ware (Creamware)
Wedgwood's creamware, known from 1765 as Queen's ware*, was a development of the traditional cream-coloured ware of Staffordshire, the invention of which is generally ascribed to Astbury, c.1725; but Wedgwood's refinement of this body and glaze was so entire that he is justifiably considered to have created a new form of earthenware. Unlike potters who had traditionally whitened their wares by adding tin oxide to the covering lead glaze, Wedgwood produced a fine, durable ware that was white bodied, owing its colour primarily to the introduction of Cornish china clay and china stone into the body. Wedgwood's earliest creamware was buff coloured, but the shade was considerably paler by 1763, and five years later the transformation in the body and glaze, which made Wedgwood's Queen's ware the most important development in the history of English pottery, was complete. Before Josiah died, in 1795, he saw his Queen's ware copied all over Europe,

Above: **Crane, Walter,** *Vases decorated with figures emblematic of the arts of Music and Painting. Queen's ware.* Wedgwood.

Right: **Crealock, H.H.** *Typical stag subjects, photographic prints on Satsuma shape.* Wedgwood.

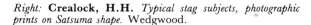

where he had achieved what at one time amounted almost to a monopoly of the earthenware tableware trade. If jasper* may be said to be Wedgwood's greatest invention, his refinement of creamware was his most influential achievement.

Decoration of early creamware was by painting with enamel colours (see: David Rhodes), transfer printing (see: John Sadler), moulding, piercing, and decorating with coloured glazes to imitate semi-precious stones. The tortoiseshell* effect was achieved by dusting the surface with manganese and copper before the glost (glaze) firing.

Manufacturers on the Continent started to make cream-coloured ware before 1775, but not on a large scale until the end of the century. It was known as *faience-fine, faience anglais,* and *terre de pipe anglaise* in France, *Steingut* in Germany, *terraglia* in Italy, and *flint porslin* in Scandinavia.

See: Crystalline Ware; Variegated Ware; Anne Warburton.

Cream-Coloured Ware. *Bough-pot of turned and enamelled creamware, c.1790. Similar pieces in various colours are of the Wedgwood & Bentley period. Buten Museum.*

Cream-Coloured Ware. *An early creamware teapot embossed with fruit and leaves in a basket. Below the handle is an example of blind basketwork.* Authors.

Cream-Coloured Ware. *Two teapots. Left, transfer-printed with group from Benjamin West's* Death of General Wolfe, *c.1776. Right, enamelled with a Chinese scene, c.1770.* Wedgwood.

Cream-Coloured Ware. *Creamware dinner service with painted border pattern No. 92, showing typical tureens, compotier, sauceboat and stand, and plates. c.1790.* Wedgwood.

Cream-Coloured Ware. *Creamware teapot of bamboo form with enamelled decoration and bail handle. 5¼ ins. high. 1871. Sotheby's Belgravia.*

Cream-Coloured Ware. *A group of kitchen ware, c.1850.* Wedgwood.

Cream-Coloured Ware. *Gilded creamware centrepiece in the form of two putti supporting an urn beneath which lie various garden implements. Probably modelled by Protât, this centrepiece also exists in majolica glazes, and in an enamelled version painted by Lessore. 9¼ ins. high.* Zeitlin Collection.

Cream Cooler

Ovoid-shaped Queen's ware vessel with lid and two handles, designed as part of Wedgwood's dairy* ware. An example decorated with the Bedford Grape pattern, apparently ordered by the Duke of Bedford for his dairy at Endsleigh, Devon, in 1822, is in the Buten Museum*.

Cream Pans

Large, flat, oval pans or dishes with a lip at one end for pouring, made in cream-coloured ware, cane ware* and, in the 19th century, lavender* ware. They were made for use in dairies, for the separation of cream.

Cream Skimmer

A flat, perforated implement for removing cream from the surface of the settling* pan, made of Queen's ware in the 18th century. A large flat spoon or ladle of Queen's ware, with a turned-over end to the handle, was also employed for the same purpose.

Cream Ware

See: Cream-coloured Ware.

Creil (Oise)

A factory was founded at Creil in 1793 to make *faience-fine* (creamware) and other English type wares, including basaltes. It merged with Montereau, a factory originally founded in 1774 by English potters, early in the 19th century. A good deal of cream-coloured ware* decorated with transfer-printing, an unusual technique on Continental wares, was made at Creil, and topographical prints of English country houses titled in French were popular, perhaps inspired by memories of the Frog* service. The pottery chemist, Saint-Amans, who had spent more than twenty years in England studying the industry, made soft-paste porcelain in the English manner about 1820.

Cream Cooler. *Cream cooler and cover in the form of an urn, the finial in the shape of a recumbent cow. Decorated with a crest of a dragon's head erased and monogram. 11ins. high. c.1800.* Liverpool Museums.

Cress Dish

Circular or rectangular Queen's ware pierced dish, standing on four pointed feet, and often provided with a conforming slightly dished plate, to be used for draining cress or salads. The rectangular shape appears in the 1817 (Blake*) Catalogue*. Cress dishes were painted to match contemporary Queen's ware patterns.

Crewe, Miss Emma (fl.1787-1818)

Of Crewe Hall, Cheshire, daughter of the Whig hostess, Frances Anne Crewe*, and John, later Baron Crewe. Amateur artist, designer, and modeller for Wedgwood from 1787 to 1818. Miss Crewe's designs are not unlike those of Lady Templetown*, with whose work they have been confused.

The following bas-relief* subjects are generally assigned to her:

Bacchanalian Children.
Children.
Maternal and Infant Groups.
Maternity.
Reading.
The Young Seamstress.
The Sewing Lesson.
The Spinner.
Springtime.
The Domestic Employments series (e.g. a small girl sewing or spinning.) Also attributed to Lady Templetown.

These designs appear on medallions of various sizes, and also on vases, teapots and smaller jasper pieces.

Crewe, Mrs. Frances Anne (d.1818)

Married John Crewe, created Baron, 1806. A fashionable beauty who was a friend of Fox, Burke, and Sheridan. Her son's portrait was modelled by Hackwood* in 1771. Wedgwood wrote to Bentley in September 1771: "... Hackwood has been three times at Crewe by Mrs. Crewe's particular desire to model the head of her son and heir." This may have been the origin of Wedgwood's decision to model contemporary portraits, but this particular medallion does not appear to have survived.

Croft or Crofts, W.

See: William Hopkins Craft.

Cruet Set

A set generally comprising a footed stand with space for two to six containers (cruets) for oil, vinegar, salt, mustard, pepper and sugar. Cruets with pierced covers are properly known as casters. Plate 6 of Wedgwood's first Cream Colour Catalogue of 1774 illustrates an "oil cruet" — a stand with looped handle and two stoppered bottles — and "Oil and Vinegar Stands, containing from two to six Cruets" are described in the text. The 1817 Catalogue, engraved by William Blake* illustrates five sets, four of which have decorative pierced stands.

Crystalline

The name given by Wedgwood to his variegated* and marbled wares in imitation of natural stones. These included the colours described as porphyry*, granite*, Egyptian pebble, agate*, black marble, jaune antique, and serpentine.

Crystalline glazes are those partially devitrified glazes in which some crystallisation is apparent (e.g. aventurine glaze*).

Crystalline. *Vase simulating porphyry, with snake handles and an applied relief medallion portrait of Raphael. Wedgwood.*

Cruet Set. *Queen's ware cruet set, 7½ ins. high, 6¾ ins. diameter, the five containers set in a circular pierced stand with moulded scrolls and three splayed feet. This shape appears as No.781 in the 1817 Catalogue engraved by William Blake. Sotheby's.*

Cullet

Broken glass added to the other ingredients in the crucible before heating to promote fusion. Cullet was also used by the potter. In the 18th century it was powdered and mixed with the other substances employed to make artificial porcelain*, forming part of the fusible ingredients of the body. In 1775 we find Wedgwood writing to Bentley asking for scraps of London crown glass to be obtained for him. He also requested Bentley to ask Mr. More, Secretary of the Society of Arts, to get some poor man to work secretly on reducing it to a powder which could be "put through a coarse hair sieve." The letter suggests either that he may have been experimenting with 'soft' porcelain or was engaged in making his own enamel colours. Parian* bodies, first made in the 19th century, are composed of about 70 per cent of feldspar and 30 per cent of china clay, to which is added a small quantity of cullet. This helps to give this type of porcelain its satin surface and glass-like body.

See: Carrara Ware.

Cupid

Cupido, or Amor, the Roman god of love identified with the Greek Eros. Cupid was the son of Venus* by either Mars*, Jupiter* or Mercury*. He is usually represented as a boy, often winged, with arrows in a golden quiver, and torches. Sometimes he is blindfold, and he frequently accompanies Venus. When depicted with Psyche* he is usually an adolescent rather than a child. There is a notable series of Cupids engaged in various crafts in the House of the Vetii in Pompeii and this has frequently been used as inspiration for decoration.

Cupids, *putti* and 'bacchanalian boys' were among the most popular and frequently used subjects of decoration and ornament in the 18th century, and Wedgwood reproduced numerous designs by Beauclerk* and Templetown*, many of them modelled by Hackwood*. Others were original models by Flaxman* or Webber*, or remodelled from casts supplied by Hoskins & Grant*. Cupids, in various forms, also appear in the compositions of many of the larger bas-reliefs* for tablets*. In the 19th century, such painters as Lessore* and Henry Brownsword*, and the modeller and designer, Hugues Protât, made frequent use of Cupids as decoration.

Cupid. *Group of Cupids by Emile Lessore.* Wedgwood.

Principal Wedgwood subjects include the following:

Autumn and *Winter*, Cupid figures emblematic of autumn and winter with tree trunks in the form of candlesticks. Modelled by Hackwood, c.1785 ('Rustic Candlesticks').

Cupid and Psyche, basaltes group on oval base, height 12ins. Source unidentified, c.1820.

Cupid and Hymen, medallion 3¼ ins. by 5ins. Cast supplied by Hoskins & Grant, 1774.

Cupid and the infant Mercury, tablet 5½ ins. by 10⅝ ins. (also in smaller sizes on oval medallions) from a model probably made in Rome c.1787 after the relief on a sarcophagus now in the Capitoline Museum.

Cupid Inflaming the Mind, medallion 3¼ ins. by 5ins. Cast supplied by Hoskins & Grant, 1774.

Cupid on a Lion or *The Power of Love*, medallion 4⅛ ins. by 3¼ ins. Modelled by Flaxman, 1776, possibly after a sardonyx in the Medici collection.

Cupid menaçant ('Cupid sitting pensive'), figure, height 8ins., after the marble, 1757, by Falconet*. This figure was reproduced in Sèvres* biscuit porcelain in 1758, and was supplied to Wedgwood, probably in the form of a cast (with the matching figure of Psyche*), by Flaxman Senior* in 1781.

Cupid drawing his dart, medallion by Webber*, c.1782.

Cupids as Four Seasons, tablet by Flaxman, 1777, from casts supplied by Flaxman Sr., 1775. Also used singly as ornament for flower pots and medallions.

Cupids at Play, two bas-reliefs designed by Flaxman specially for the decoration of teapots, but also used on other pieces in various sizes.

Cupid shaving his bow, medallion, first catalogued in 1773, 3ins. by 2¼ ins., and smaller sizes down to 1¼ ins by 1ins., after the painting by Parmigianino (previously attributed to Correggio).

Cupid sharpening his arrows) pair of circular medallions, 5ins.
Cupid stringing his bow) in diameter, c.1784.

Cupid watering the swans, bas-relief used for the decoration of vases and also for medallions, 4¼ ins. by 9ins., first listed 1787. After a design by Le Brun* (pair to *Venus in her car*).

The Marriage of Cupid and Psyche, see separate entry.

Sacrifice to Love, tablet 9½ ins. by 21ins. and 10½ ins. by 25ins., attributed to Flaxman, c.1778.

Sacrifice to Eros, tablet, 11ins. by 22ins., similar in composition to *Sacrifice to Love* but fewer figures. Possibly the work of Webber, c.1787.

Sacrifice to Cupid, tablet, probably misnamed, showing Cupid on a pedestal flanked by Diana and other goddesses. Attributed to Flaxman.

Sale of Erotes (Cupid Market), medallion attributed to Hackwood, after a wall painting now in the Naples Museum, possibly by way of a gem by Cades*.

Seven Cupids, set of four very large medallions, 13ins. by 10¾ ins., showing the emblems of Fire, Air, Earth and Water. From casts supplied by Hoskins & Grant, 1774.

Venus and Cupid (Selene visiting Endymion), see: Diana.

Venus in her car, (drawn by swans, with attendant Cupids, etc.), medallion 4¼ ins. by 9ins., c.1787, after a design by Charles Le Brun (companion to *Cupid watering the swans*).

Winged Cupid upon a Swan, medallion 2¾ ins. by 2½ ins., by Flaxman.

See also: Bacchus ('Bacchanalian Boys'); Hymen; Somnus; Venus.

Curd Mould

See: Cheese Mould.

Cupid. *Pair of vases, of solid grey-green and white jasper,* Cupid with Bird's Nest *and* Cupid with Butterfly, *the bases ornamented with oak leaves, the tree trunk with acanthus foliage. 8 ½ ins. high. c.1785.* Dwight and Lucille Beeson Collection.

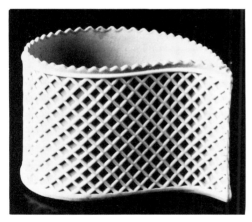

Above: **Custard Cups.** *One of a set of jasper custard cups ornamented with lattice-work, the cup of teardrop or lozenge shape, c.1785.* Wedgwood.

Right: **Custard Cups.** *Set of four blue and white jasper custard cups with covers on a square tray, c.1784, and a large oval jasper tray.* Wedgwood.

Custard Cups

Small covered cups of jasper with lapidary polished interiors usually made in sets of four on an octagonal tray. A particularly rare type is the covered can shape (see: Coffee Cans), or the uncovered pear or tear shape (sometimes described as 'comma') made in solid-colour jasper with white jasper lattice-work decoration. These were made c.1780-90. Custard cups were also made in cream-coloured ware and illustrated in the 1774 Catalogue*. It is very unusual to find a complete set.

Cut-Steel Mounts

Many of Wedgwood's cameos*, seals*, and plaques* were mounted in cut steel as jewellery at the Soho (Birmingham) factory of Boulton* & Fothergill. Similar wares were sent by Adams* of Tunstall to Thomas Low of Sheffield.

Steel was cut, chiselled, and filed into facets which, when brightly polished, reflected the light, and provided a substitute for marcasite that was more durable and less prone to damage. Small objects of cut steel were first made in the 17th century as a cottage industry at Woodstock, and Wedgwood may have seen work of this kind when he visited Blenheim Palace. He was at Blenheim in December 1770, and on the same journey he went on to Birmingham and saw Matthew Boulton. It is interesting to speculate whether it may not have been at this time that Wedgwood first had the idea of having his wares mounted in cut steel, but it was not until five or six years later that he was able to produce jasper cameos for this purpose. A great variety of objects was made in this way — buckles, buttons*, necklaces, bracelets, sword hilts*, chatelaines*, etc.

Cutts, John (1772-1851)

Landscape painter at the Pinxton (Derbyshire) porcelain factory. In 1812 he began to decorate sample wares for Wedgwood painting flowers and landscapes on bone china*. In 1813 Josiah Wedgwood II's opinion was "he will not suit as a flower-painter, and probably not as a landscape painter." To paint the fifty-one pieces of a teaset with flowers (pattern No.673) he took twelve days at 5s. a day. He seems to have left Wedgwood in 1816 to set up as an enameller and gilder in Hanley, taking his sons into partnership, and by 1842 the firm of John Cutts & Sons was employing fifty people. Much of his work is not positively identified, but he was responsible for the following landscapes on Wedgwood's bone china:

Alder Valley, Derbyshire.
Brockenhurst, Hampshire.
Brookhill, Nottingham.
Cottage at Pinxton, Derbyshire.
A view in Cumberland.
Dovedales, Derbyshire.
Longley Park, Kent.
Nottingham Castle.
Paddington, Middlesex.
Saltram, Devonshire.
Ullswater, Cumberland.

Cut-Steel Mount. *Cut-steel and jasper bead buckle framing a jasper medallion of* Poor Maria *after a design by Lady Templetown. 3½ ins. high. c.1785.* Wedgwood.

Cutts, John. *Sugar box from a bone china tea service painted by John Cutts, c.1815.* Wedgwood.

Cybele

Roman name associated with the ancient Greek goddess Rhea, mother of Zeus (Jupiter*), and known as 'Mother of the Gods'. From the orgiastic nature of the rites accompanying the worship of Cybele, her name became associated with that of Dionysus (Bacchus*). The lion was sacred to her, and in art she is usually represented seated on a throne, with a garlanded crown, and attendant lions. The figure of Cybele holding a cornucopia* surmounted by a candleholder was modelled c.1785 as a pair to one of Ceres*. Both are usually attributed to Flaxman. A pair of similar candlestick figures, but without the lion and cornsheaf attributes of the goddesses, was modelled at least ten years earlier and is attributed to Keeling*. These latter figures are generally, but erroneously, described as Ceres and Cybele.

Czechoslovakia

Czechoslovakia includes the former kingdoms of Bohemia and Moravia, as well as Slovakia. In the second half of the 18th century the principal ceramic bodies competing for attention in Central Europe were *faience* and porcelain, but earthenware in the English manner (i.e. creamware; in German, *Steingut*), was beginning to be popular. The *faience* factory at Holiĉ (Holitsch) had been making white and cream-coloured earthenware since 1786, and soon afterwards factories at Byotrice, and at Hranice in Moravia, were also imitating it. Probably the wares of Prague, founded with a privilege by Carl Hunerle and J.E. Hübel, and those of Týne-nad-Sazavon, both founded in 1793, came nearest to Wedgwood designs. Among the porcelain factories to imitate Wedgwood products may be numbered Karlovy Varỳ (Karlsbad), Slavkov (Schlaggenwald), Klasterac (Klosterle), and Brezová (Pirkenhammer). The place names in German, likely to be more familiar to English-speaking readers, are bracketed. Wares made at Vranov-nad-Dyji, a factory operating from 1799 to 1882, which are in the style of Wedgwood are preserved at Vranov Castle. The factory imitated Wedgwood relief decoration, producing jasper in light blue and light brown, including a light blue relief on a brown ground, pierced creamware, excellent fruit and flower painting, and transfer printing, much of it utilising copper plates by the engraver Josef Doré. Colours used for printing were blue, green, rose, brown, and grey, and subjects include landscapes, architecture, and hunting scenes.

Cybele. *Solid blue and white jasper figure of Cybele crowned, with attendant lion. 11 ½ ins. high. One of a pair of candlesticks attributed to Flaxman, c.1785. See also Ceres.* Wedgwood.

Da Bologna, Giovanni (1529-1608)

Giovanni (Gian) da Bologna was born Jean Boulogne at Douai and passed most of his working life in Florence. He was one of the most noted of Mannerist sculptors, and small bronzes, and reductions of his large works, were made in considerable quantities. In addition his pupils and studio assistants produced work in his style. These works were drawn upon by European porcelain factories, and Wedgwood modellers used them as a source of inspiration. Six small medallions "by John of Bologna", the subjects of which are not described, are listed in the 1777, 1779 and 1787 Catalogues*.

Daguerre, Dominique (fl.1770-1795)

Marchand privilégié de la cour. Associated before 1778 with the dealer, Simon Poirier. Mainly he dealt in furniture, from premises in the rue Saint-Honoré, Paris. Daguerre supplied the French Court, the Prince of Wales (later Prince Regent and King George IV), and the Duke of Northumberland. In June, 1787, he was Wedgwood's agent in Paris, but he retired to England in 1793 and was succeeded in Paris by Martin Eloi Lignereux.

Dairy Ware

Cream-coloured ware for dairy use. It includes cream steins, cream ladles, milk pans, settling pans*, skimmers*, etc. Some dairy wares are plain, others are painted freehand with border patterns in monochrome or colour. Specimens survive from the 18th and early 19th centuries, one of the most complete being at Althorp, Northamptonshire. Like the dairy ware made for Queen Charlotte, the Althorp set, made for the Countess Spencer in 1786, is decorated with a painted border of ivy leaves. Wedgwood also supplied the matching tiles* for the dairy at a price of tenpence each. Plain tiles were priced at threepence. An order from the duc d'Orléans for cane-coloured ware for his dairy at Raincy is preserved in the Wedgwood archives, but none of this seems to have survived.

Dairy Ware. *Cream cooler and cover (Shape No.1109), made for the Endsleigh Dairy, decorated with the Bedford Grape pattern, c.1822.* Buten Museum.

Colour Plate VII

Oval frame of twenty-five jasper cameos, illustrating the variety of colours and including an interesting trial piece of green on black. Among the cameos are three versions of the Slave medallion, 1787, Aesculapius centre, and two of Apollo with his lyre. Wedgwood. Photo: Reilly/Charles Letts.

Dancing Hours. *Removing the plastic clay body from a pitcher mould to make one of the* Dancing Hours *figures.* Photo: Wedgwood.

Dancing Hours. *Putting one of the component figures of the* Dancing Hours *into position on a modern bowl. The technique has varied little since the 18th century.* Photo: Wedgwood.

Dalmazzoni, Angelo (fl.1787-1795)

Italian modeller employed in Rome from 1787 to 1795, at first under the direction of Flaxman* and Webber*, but subsequently as chief modeller for Wedgwood in Italy. None of his work has been identified with certainty. The following subjects have been variously attributed to him:

Achilles and the daughters of Lycomedes, tablet, now attributed to Pacetti*.

Nereides,* tablet also attributed to Webber*.

Priam begging the body of Hector from Achilles, tablet, now known to be the work of Pacetti. A second version was modelled by Flaxman.

Roman Procession,* tablet, also ascribed to Pacetti.

See: Achilles.

Dancing Hours, The

The best known of jasper relief subjects which is still used today. It was originally modelled by John Flaxman*, and remodelled with some alteration to the drapery by Hackwood in 1802. The companion tablet is the *Birth of Bacchus,* modelled by Flaxman in 1782. The original version of *The Dancing Hours,* a tablet intended for chimney pieces*, measured 15⅜ ins. by 5⅞ ins., but the subject has since been employed for many purposes, and made in many sizes. It may even be found ornamenting salt cellars and teapots.

The first mention of the subject is in a letter from Wedgwood to Bentley in April 1778, and in the same letter the name of Sir Lawrence Dundas is mentioned as the purchaser of a tablet called the *Sacrifice to Flora.* Sir Lawrence owned Moor Park, Hertfordshire, in which there was a chimney piece of white marble which came from the Villa Borghese in Rome, and is now in the Lady Lever Art Gallery. This has a frieze depicting nine dancing girls, alternately facing inwards and outwards, carved in relief against a background of lapis lazuli*. It was based on a late Greek relief of the 1st or 2nd century B.C. now in the Louvre, formerly in the Villa Borghese (see: Borghese Family), and sold in 1806 to Napoleon I by Count Camillo Borghese. The five girls, like those of Flaxman's version, are lightly draped. That Flaxman originally modelled them naked is no more than a legend. The girls are dancing against a back-

ground of Corinthian pilasters and the relief measures 74cm by about 2m. The mould of the Flaxman version no longer exists; the somewhat more decorous version usually seen is the work of Hackwood. This relief was well known to the *cognoscenti* in former times. At one time it was regarded as a Bacchanalian procession, and the present name dates from the 18th century.

Daniel(l), Thomas (fl.1750-1765)

Painter employed by Wedgwood in 1762 when, in association with Daniel Steele*, he painted the raised flowers on a caudle set* and breakfast set presented by Wedgwood to Queen Charlotte*. He has sometimes been identified with the Thomas Daniell, RA (1749-1840) who, with his nephew,

Dancing Hours. *Black basaltes punch kettle with bail handle and finial in the form of a bunch of grapes, ornamented with the* Dancing Hours. Wedgwood.

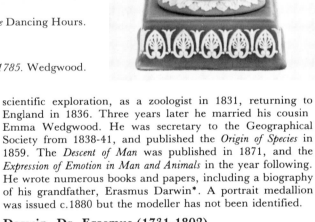

Above: **Dancing Hours.** *Jasper open salt cellar ornamented with figures of the* Dancing Hours. *Inlaid white jasper line at rim. 1785.* Wedgwood.

Right: **Dancing Hours.** *Jasper urn ornamented with the* Dancing Hours. *1785.* Wedgwood.

William, became celebrated as a painter of landscape and published several magnificent books of aquatint views, including *Oriental Scenery* (1808). No evidence has been found to support this identification, but Daniell told Joseph Farington that he came to London, apprenticed to a coach painter, at the age of fourteen (1763). It is almost inconceivable that Wedgwood should have employed a fourteen-year-old apprentice for work of such importance, and it therefore seems certain that another Daniell was Wedgwood's employee. A likely candidate is the father of Henry Daniel, Spode's enameller. Born c.1739, Thomas Daniel is credited by Simeon Shaw (1837) with being the finest enameller in Britain, and, as late as 1808-11, he was supplying colours to Wedgwood and Byerley*.

Daphne
Daughter of the Thessalian river-god, Peneus, Daphne was pursued by Apollo* and prayed for help. As he was about to seize her she was changed into a laurel which, thereafter, was Apollo's favourite tree. A bas-relief* of *Apollo and Daphne* ('Apolow & Dafnee') was supplied to Wedgwood in 1769 by Mrs. Landré*; Bacon* is believed to have modelled a statuette in the same year; and Webber* modelled Apollo and Daphne 'as a beaupot' (bough pot) c.1785.

Darwin, Charles Robert, FRS (1809-1882)
English naturalist, son of Robert Waring Darwin* and Susannah Wedgwood; educated at Shrewsbury, Edinburgh University, and Christ's College, Cambridge. He embarked on H.M.S. *Beagle,* bound for South America on a voyage of scientific exploration, as a zoologist in 1831, returning to England in 1836. Three years later he married his cousin Emma Wedgwood. He was secretary to the Geographical Society from 1838-41, and published the *Origin of Species* in 1859. The *Descent of Man* was published in 1871, and *Expression of Emotion in Man and Animals* in the year following. He wrote numerous books and papers, including a biography of his grandfather, Erasmus Darwin*. A portrait medallion was issued c.1880 but the modeller has not been identified.

Darwin, Dr. Erasmus (1731-1802)
Scientist, poet and physician, educated at St. John's College, Cambridge and Edinburgh University. Darwin was a doctor of medicine who practised at Lichfield. He declined an appointment as physician to George III*. His literary reputation rests on a long poem, *The Botanic Garden,* published in two parts in 1789 and 1791. Written in decasyllabic rhymed couplets of stupefying dullness, it is nevertheless a monument to scientific interest in nature. He was twice married. Robert Waring Darwin*, his son by his first wife, married Susannah Wedgwood (Josiah I's daughter 'Sukey'), and one of their children was Charles Darwin, who married his cousin, Emma Wedgwood. By his second wife, Erasmus Darwin became grandfather of Francis Galton. Darwin was a member of the Lunar Society*, and Wedgwood's "favourite Aesculapius." His portrait by Joseph Wright* of Derby, 1770 (now in the National Portrait Gallery, London) was copied for a jasper portrait medallion (attributed to Hackwood*) in 1780, and a similar portrait was painted in enamel on Wedgwood biscuit* Queen's ware* by George Stubbs* in 1783.

Darwin, Dr. Erasmus. *Jasper portrait medallion of Dr. Erasmus Darwin, modelled by Hackwood after the portrait by Joseph Wright of Derby. Produced early in 1780.* Wedgwood.

Darwin, Dr. Erasmus. *Portrait by George Stubbs, painted in 1783 on a Queen's ware plaque.* Wedgwood.

Darwin Mug, The

This Queen's ware mug was commissioned by the Wedgwood Collectors' Society as a companion piece to several other specially commissioned Queen's ware objects decorated with historical designs. It is 6¼ ins. high and 3¼ ins. in diameter. The decoration is the *Water Lily* * pattern. A service of this pattern was in the possession of Erasmus Darwin*, and the *Water Lily* service has sometimes been more definitely connected with him by being called the *Darwin Service* without any very good reason.

Darwin, Dr. Robert Waring (1766-1848)

Third son of Erasmus Darwin* by his first wife. He married Susannah Wedgwood, his cousin, in 1796, and Charles Darwin* born in 1809, was among their children. In the year of his marriage Robert Darwin moved to Shrewsbury, where he formed a large collection of Wedgwood ware which included a first issue Portland* vase (now in the British Museum). Many years later Eliza Meteyard* visited the Darwins' house, and it was probably there that she first formed her abiding interest in Wedgwood.

Robert Darwin kept an account with Wedgwood and bought considerable quantities of both useful* and ornamental* wares. Recent research by Mrs. Una des Fontaines has shown beyond reasonable doubt that the famous 'Darwin' Water Lily* service was neither made for Erasmus Darwin nor presented to his son on the occasion of his marriage, but chosen on advice from Josiah II* and purchased by Robert Darwin in 1807.

Darwin Mug. *Made in memory of Charles Darwin and decorated with the Water Lily pattern in blue. No. 33 of the Special limited editions produced for the Wedgwood Collectors' Society.* Wedgwood.

Jasper portrait medallion of George Washington on a rare yellow ground, 3¼ ins. by 2¼ ins. c.1778. This portrait was taken from a medal designed by Voltaire and struck in Paris in 1777. Examples exist erroneously impressed 'CHATHAM', including a quantity reproduced c.1879. Eugene D. Buchanan Collection.

Grey jasper portrait medallion of Gustavus III, King of Sweden, with bevelled and polished frame. c.1778. 4ins. by 3¼ ins. Eugene D. Buchanan Collection.

Green jasper dip portrait medallion of Josiah Wedgwood's brother-in-law, William Willet, modelled by Hackwood in 1776. Of this portrait Wedgwood wrote: ''A stronger likeness can scarcely be conceiv'd.'' It is signed 'W.H.' on the truncation. 4ins. by 3¼ ins. Wedgwood.

Brown jasper dip portrait medallion of Admiral Keppel modelled in 1779. This example appears to be unique, since no other 18th century portrait medallion in this colour is recorded. 4ins. by 3¼ ins. Private Collection.

Dassier

I. Dassier et cie, J. Dassier et cie. Swiss partnerships of medallists and engravers. The partners were I. Dassier, Jean Dassier (1676-1763) and Antoine Dassier (1718-80). There seems to be no evidence to support the suggestion that the Dassiers were connected with the English Mint. Jean Dassier, who produced numerous medals of famous characters in history, worked in a style that became more or less international.

Wedgwood cast many of the Dassier medals in basaltes* and also used Dassier models for his series of heads of the Popes, Kings and Queens of England, and the Roman History portraits (provided as sulphurs* by Tassie*). Several of the portrait medallions of *Illustrious Moderns** have also been ascribed to the Dassiers, but without sufficient evidence. The following *Illustrious Moderns* are from Dassier medals:

Philip Dormer Stanhope, Earl of Chesterfield.
Abraham Demoivre.
Cardinal Fleury.
Martin Folkes.
Sir Andrew Fountaine.
Louis XV.
Francesco Scipio di Maffei.
John Churchill, Duke of Marlborough.
John, 2nd Duke of Montagu.

Davenport Factory (Longport, Staffs.)

Manufactory of earthenware, stone china, and porcelain founded in 1794 by John Davenport. He retired in 1838, when the business was continued by his sons. They specialised in well-painted table services and vases, especially those decorated with bold Japan patterns. Painters who worked there include Daniel and Edwin Steele, James Rouse, and Jesse Mountford. Under John Davenport's direction, the factory produced fine creamware*, green glaze* leaf dessert plates, white stoneware, black basaltes*, and cane ware* (including pastry ware*) in imitation of Wedgwood's productions. The creamware table services, in particular, were decorated with simple, well-painted border patterns in typical Wedgwood styles.

Davies, Oscar (fl.1920-1950)

English potter, established the Roeginga Pottery at Rainham, Kent, in association with his wife, Grace Barnsley*. He patented a combined milk and coffee pot produced by Wedgwood, c.1935, as part of a Queen's ware coffee set. It was decorated by Grace Barnsley.

Davis, E. (fl.1903-1932)

Engraver; worked for Wedgwood between the above dates. Erroneously stated to have been responsible for the statue of Josiah Wedgwood at Stoke railway station.
See: Edward Davis.

Davis, Edward (1813-1878)

Sculptor, a native of Carmarthen, he studied at the Royal Academy Schools and exhibited at the Academy 1834-77. A marble group, *Venus and Cupid,* shown at the Great Exhibition of 1851 is now in the Salford Art Gallery, and a figure of *Rebecca* was included in the International Exhibition, London, 1862. A bronze figure of Josiah Wedgwood by Davis was finished in 1860 and placed near the entrance to Stoke-on-Trent railway station. A copy of this figure was cast in bronze in the 1960s and now stands at the main entrance to the Barlaston* factory.

Davy, Sir Humphrey, FRS (1778-1829)

English natural philosopher, educated at Penzance Grammar School; he superintended the laboratory of the Bristol Pneumatic Institution, visited London in 1799, and was appointed director of the chemical laboratory of the Royal Institution in 1801. In 1802 he was appointed Professor of Chemistry. In 1803 Davy became Fellow of the Royal Society of which he was President in 1820. He was knighted in 1812, and created baronet in 1818.

Davy collaborated with Josiah I's youngest son, Tom*, in the invention of an early photographic process by which the latter succeeded in reproducing images by the action of light on paper sensitised with silver nitrate. They were, however, unable to fix the images, which faded when exposed to light.

Davy, Sir Humphrey. *Commemorative mug with portrait of Sir Humphrey Davy, 1978.* Wedgwood.

De Morgan, William Frend (1839-1917)

Designer and studio potter. Attended the Royal Academy Schools. He first worked in stained glass, and later turned his attention to coloured glazes and the use of lustre* as pottery decoration. He started by decorating ware bought in white from outside sources, and several large Wedgwood dishes (with impressed marks) have been observed decorated with lustre in characteristic De Morgan style. He is also known to have decorated Wedgwood black basaltes tiles. He opened his own pottery in Chelsea in 1872 which he later transferred to Merton Abbey, Surrey. From 1888 he was in partnership with the architect, Halsey Ricardo*, at the South End Pottery, Fulham West London.

De Shoning (Shonen, Shonnings, de Shonen)

The spelling is not consistent in the surviving letters. A friend of Thomas Bentley*, who helped to sell Queen's ware* to the German princes. Parcels of ware were sent to them in the speculative hope of promoting sales. The first attempt was made in September 1771. *Steingut,* the German equivalent of creamware which was copied from Wedgwood's Queen's ware, dates from this period or a little later.

De Morgan, William. *Wedgwood cream-ware dish, diameter 9ins., painted with lustre pigment (obverse and reverse) by Charles Passenger. Signed.* Zeitlin Collection.

De Vaere, John

Also Devaere and De Vere. Born in France, de Vaere attended the Royal Academy schools in London in 1786. On Flaxman's* recommendation he was commissioned by Wedgwood to make portrait medallions. Until 1790 he assisted Flaxman and Webber* in Rome, and became chief modeller in the ornamental department in succession to Webber when, in 1794, the latter left the factory. De Vaere appears to have gone to Flanders in 1810.

Wedgwood subjects by or attributed to De Vaere include:

Achilles * *and the daughters of Lycomedes* (sometimes called *Achilles in Scyros*), tablet, c.1790. (See also: Pacetti.)

Admirals Nelson, Duncan, Howe and St. Vincent, portrait medallions, 1798.

Allardyce, Alexander, portrait medallion, 1798.

Borghese (Campaña) Vase, the reliefs retouched by Flaxman.

Judgement of Paris *, tablet, c.1790.

Orestes * *and Pylades* (prisoners on the shores of Scythia), tablet.

Proserpine, bas-relief, 1788.

De Wilde, William (fl.1777)

Modeller who executed commissions for Wedgwood. None of his work has been identified.

Death of a Roman Warrior

One of Wedgwood's earliest large basaltes tablets* (listed in the 1773 Catalogue*), measuring 11ins. by 20ins., this subject would be more accurately titled *The Death of Meleager*. The central group derives from a Greek marble relief in the Capitoline Museum, but certain alterations have been made, some of which were necessary restoration, and others artistic 'improvements'. Two of the figures, one of which is copied from Bartoli and Bellori (*Admiranda Romanarum Antiquarum*, 1693) appear also in the later group, *Roman Procession*.

Death of Meleager

See: *Death of a Roman Warrior*.

Decalcomania (Decal)

See: Transfer Printing; Lithography.

Della Robbia Ware

Tin-glazed terracotta made in Florence, Italy, by Luca Della Robbia, his nephew, Andrea, and the latter's four sons,

De Vaere, John. *Jasper portrait medallion of Horatio, Viscount Nelson, modelled by John De Vaere in 1798. This portrait, one of the set of four of great admirals (the others were Duncan, Howe, and St. Vincent) by De Vaere, was used in a smaller version to decorate the base of the figure* Britannia Triumphant. Wedgwood

c.1438-1520. Their models were often bas-reliefs* or figures of *putti* or *amorini*, usually in white on a blue ground, but sometimes with touches of green, maroon and yellow. Hackwood* modelled a number of small figures after Della Robbia for Wedgwood c.1785.

See: Infant Reclining Figures.

Demeter

See: Ceres.

Democritus

Greek philosopher, born in Thrace about 460B.C. Noted for his cheerfulness and optimism, he was known as the 'Laughing Philosopher'. A bust of 'Democrates', height 12½ins., was supplied by Hoskins & Grant* in 1775, and is thought to have been finished by Keeling*. It does not appear in Wedgwood's Catalogues* until 1779.

Demosthenes (c.384-322B.C.)

The great Athenian orator. He used his eloquence to warn the Athenians against the intentions of Philip of Macedon. He poisoned himself in 322. Sixty of his orations have survived.

A bust of Demosthenes, height 22ins., was produced by Wedgwood in basaltes, after a cast supplied by Hoskins & Grant* in 1775.

Denby, Charles (fl.1760-1780)

Painter and modeller, formerly of Derby, employed at the Chelsea Decorating Studio* from 1770. In September, 1769, Wedgwood wrote that he had hired Hackwood, "an ingenious Boy," as a modeller, and "with Denby and him, I shall not want any other constant modeller at Etruria." In May 1770, however, Denby was dispatched to London as a painter, so great was Bentley's need of skilled hands. Wedgwood wrote of him: "He applys close to business, has a delicate modesty in his manners, and I think will be an agreeable and useful assistant to us in a little time... he is really *learned* in the Anatomy and the drawing of a human figure."

Dent, Catherine (fl.1769-1774)

Painter at the Chelsea Decorating Studio*, responsible for borders on the Frog* service.

D'Entrecolles, Père (fl.1690-1722)

Jesuit missionary in China who sent descriptions of porcelain manufacture to Europe in 1712 and 1722, as well as samples of china clay (kaolin) and feldspathic rock (pai-tun tzŭ or petuntse). His letters were published in 1717 and 1724 as *Lettres édifiantes et curieux,* and they circulated widely among European potters. Undoubtedly they were known to Wedgwood.

Dentures

Josiah Bateman, Wedgwood's travelling salesman, wrote from Plymouth in February 1815, enclosing an order from a Mr. Eardley for "A set of teeth enamelled china to pattern...a quantity will be wanted as they are for a respectable dentist." No record of a reply is to be found, nor do Wedgwood appear to have made artificial teeth. A British patent for dentures was granted to a French *emigré*, Nicolas Dubois de Clemant, in 1793. The difficulty experienced in making porcelain dentures, as distinct from teeth, was the one-sixth shrinkage rate of porcelain, which made accurate fitting virtually impossible. In the 1780s the introduction of a heavily fluxed porcelain paste which could be fired at a much lower temperature than usual, and which shrank far less, was employed in France by de Clemant, and after his migration to London. The firing temperature was measured with Wedgwood's pyrometer* at 12-25° instead of the customary 72-75°. This porcelain paste was supplied by Wedgwood, and Turner*, who had evolved a similar paste, refused supplies to de Clemant on the ground that he had a previous agreement with another dentist.

In 1813 Wedgwood began to supply pastes to another dentist, Joseph Fox, who used them very successfully. After 1830 dentures were only made by specialist firms, and were no longer included among the products of the general potter.

See: Joseph Bramah.

Derby

Creamware was made at a small factory founded about 1751 and situated at Cockpit Hill, Derby, which lasted until 1770. Specimens are rare, but an example in the British Museum is transfer printed* and inscribed 'Radford sculpsit DERBY Pot Works.' One of the proprietors named John Heath, a banker, was connected with the foundation of the porcelain factory in 1756.

Perhaps as early as 1745, but certainly by 1750, a small quantity of porcelain was being made at Derby by Andrew Planché. The accounts of William Duesbury*, who at this time had an enamelling studio in London, refer to the enamelling of figures from Derby in 1753. This porcelain was made by Planché at Cockpit Hill. In 1756 an agreement was drafted, but never signed, between John Heath, banker, William Duesbury, enameller, and Andrew Planché, china maker, for

Death of a Roman Warrior. *Black basaltes tablet, 20ins. long. The subject, known as* Death of a Roman Warrior, *but more accurately the* Death of Meleager, *is largely an 'improved' version of a Greek marble relief in the Capitoline Museum. c.1782.* Wedgwood.

organising a new porcelain factory at Nottingham Road, Derby. Duesbury, however, emerged as sole proprietor, and during the years 1756, 1757, and 1758 the products of the factory were advertised as 'Derby, or the second Dresden'. The Longton Hall factory was bought by Duesbury in 1760, who gained control of the Bow Porcelain Factory* in 1762, and of the Chelsea Porcelain Factory* in 1770. Derby specialised in figures (in biscuit* after about 1770) and fine quality enamel painting in the 18th century. 'Japan' patterns became a speciality towards the end of the century. Richard Holdship went from Worcester to Derby in 1764 and took the process of transfer printing with him. Rare examples of both Derby porcelain and Cockpit Hill creamware bear transfer prints signed with an anchor, assumed to be the rebus of Richard Holdship, the same mark occurring on earlier Worcester porcelain in conjunction with the signature of Hancock*. The Derby factory closed in 1848; the modern factory was founded in 1878.

No doubt Wedgwood and Duesbury were acquainted, but they do not seem to have been in contact, probably because their products and problems were so vastly different. Wedgwood, however, refers on a number of occasions to painters who had been at Derby applying for work. He rarely engaged one. Modellers who worked for both Duesbury and Wedgwood include John Bacon* and Pierre Stephan*.

Dere, John (fl.1765-1780)
Landscape painter of Newport Street, London. A number of his views of Staffordshire were copied by Wedgwood for the Frog* service.

Devis, Anthony (1729-1817)
Landscape painter particularly in watercolour; received a Premium from the Royal Society of Arts in 1763; exhibited at the Royal Academy, 1772 and 1781; supplied views for the Frog* service. Wedgwood wrote to Bentley, in November 1773: "I asked [Lord Stamford's] permission to add some views from Enville to our list. He told me... he had ten or a dozen colour'd sketches taken by an Eminent hand, and I should be welcome to have them copied, and he thought that if we would apply to the person who took them he could furnish us with a great variety more, as he was particularly fond of taking such sketches... and had travelled over a good part of England and Wales for that purpose. His name is Devis, and he lives in Lambs Conduit Street." There is no evidence to support the statement that Devis was employed at the Chelsea Decorating Studio*.

Devitrification
Glass is a super-cooled liquid which is amorphous in structure. Glazes are a kind of glass. Devitrification takes place when the substance is cooled in such a way that it begins to lose its amorphous structure, with the formation of crystals. Crystalline glazes were introduced in the last quarter of the 19th century at Meissen and several other European factories. In the 18th century the French chemist, Réaumur, made a porcelain substitute from completely devitrified glass.
See: Aventurine Glaze.

Devoto, John (fl.c.1750-1780)
Artist in watercolour, who was employed, with Unwin* and Catherine Willcox*, in the encaustic painting* of tablets and Herculaneum Subjects*.

D'Hancarville, Baron Pierre (fl.1760-1790)
Pierre Germain Hugues, a French adventurer, who assumed this title. As an antiquarian and art historian of some repute, he published, in 1766-67, *Collection of Etruscan, Greek and Roman*

Antiques from the Cabinet of the Honble William Hamilton, a sumptuous work in four volumes lavishly illustrating Hamilton's collection. It is described, with Staffordshire brevity, as 'Hambleton's [sic] Etruscan Antiques' in the list of books belonging to Wedgwood and Bentley in 1770, and many of Wedgwood's black basaltes vase shapes, and their 'Etruscan' decorations, were copied from it, although Wedgwood considered that the illustrations were superior to the originals. ''Mr. Hambleton,'' he wrote to Bentley in 1770, ''...has flattered the old pot-painters very much.'' Later, in 1785, the Baron published a highly inaccurate work entitled *Recherches sur l'Origine, l'Esprit, et les progrès des Arts de la Grèce.*

Diana. *Jasper coffee pot ornamented with a figure of Diana with stag and attendant.* Wedgwood.

Diana
Roman name for Artemis, the daughter of Zeus and Leto, and twin sister of Apollo*. She was a goddess who delighted in the chase and is usually depicted carrying a bow and quiver. She is also identified with Selene, goddess of the Moon, in love with Endymion*, and is sometimes shown with a crescent moon on her forehead. Unlike most of the inhabitants of Olympus she was noted for her chastity. She slew Orion because he attempted to violate her, and Actaeon was changed into a stag because he saw her bathing.
Wedgwood subjects:
Diana (seated), figure for a candelabrum. Modelled as a pair to *Minerva** by Henry Webber*, c.1790.
Diana the Huntress, cameo modelled by Hackwood, 1774.
Diana visiting Endymion,* tablet 8½ ins. by 27½ ins., modelled by Flaxman* from the bas-relief of *Selene and Eros visiting Endymion* on the Sarcophagus of Gerontia in the Capitoline Museum, Rome.
Diana and Actaeon, plaque, modelled by Alec Miller*, 1906.

Dice Pattern. *The dice pattern on this three-colour coffee can is produced with the aid of the engine-turning lathe, the lathe cutting through the dip to the white ground beneath. It is further decorated with applied quatrefoils and running laurel borders. c.1880. The jasper vase behind, which has the same pattern on the shoulder and near the base, is also ornamented with a figure of Apollo. Relief ornaments were commonly adapted to a variety of purposes.* Photo: Wedgwood.

Dice Pattern

1. A jasper pattern produced on the engine-turning lathe*, the chequered effect being obtained by cutting through a coloured dip* to a contrasting ground (usually white) at regular intervals. More rarely, coloured squares were separately applied, but this was too laborious and costly a method for regular production, and the resulting pattern was uneven. The dice pattern is found most frequently on vases, trophy plates*, cassolettes*, tobacco jars, and coffee cans.
2. A decorative pattern on jasper ware consisting of parallel vertical stripes. Alternating stripes are decorated with trailing flowers and chequered light and dark squares with applied coloured rosettes.

Dilettanti Society, The

A social club founded in 1734 in London which had as its purpose the study of classical art. The members provided funds for visits to ancient sites, especially to Greece, for the purpose of collecting detailed descriptions and drawings which were later published in several volumes. Both 'Athenian' Stuart* and Nicholas Revett were members. Another member was

Charles Townley (1737-1805), collector of antiquities and Trustee of the British Museum, whose collection of classical sculpture was bought by the Museum when he died. His jasper portrait medallion was made about 1785. It is marked 'Mr. Townley' below the truncation on some examples.

Dimcock, Thomas (fl.1760-1780)

Painter employed by Wedgwood in 1770 and believed to be responsible for the dessert services painted with naturalistic flowers in purple monochrome, marked with the letter 'D'.
See: Thomas Green.

Dimpled Jasper

See: Granulated Jasper.

Diomedes

King of Argos, who went to Troy with eighty ships. He enjoyed the protection of Athene*, and fought against Hector* and Aeneas*, the great warrior heroes of the Trojans. Diomedes and Ulysses* carried off the Palladium*, which protected Troy while it remained within its walls. Hackwood* modelled a tablet, *Diomedes gazing at the Palladium* (length 8ins.) c.1778, and he again took Diomedes as a subject in 1796. Other versions are:
Diomedes carrying away the Palladium, medallion, 3ins. by 3ins., after a model by Bacon* (from a gem engraved by Dioscorides) first catalogued in 1773.
A second model, by Flaxman*, of the same subject, 3¾ ins. by 2¾ ins., appears in the 1777 Catalogue*.

Dionysus

See: Bacchus.

Dip

The process of covering solid colour jasper (generally white or pale blue) with a darker jasper slip*. Some jasper pieces are dipped on one side only, some on both, with the ground colour showing at the edges. Jasper dip was introduced as early as 1777, when the rising price of cobalt oxide* made the cost of staining solid jasper prohibitive. Solid jasper was reintroduced in 1854 and jasper dip was gradually withdrawn from general production. It continued in use, however, and is still used, for the production of bowls and vases which rely for their decoration on the effect produced by engine turning. On some late 19th century ware the dip was brushed on or sprayed.

See: Bas-relief Ware; Jasper.

Documentary Pieces

Specimens of ware which cast light upon a factory's history are described as 'documentary'. These include fragments discovered during the excavation of a factory site, examples of ware which have impeccable provenance (such as those which are recorded as owned by successive generations of a potter's family), and pieces which bear modellers' or artists' signatures, or dates, or informative inscriptions. Josiah I took active steps to prevent his modellers from signing their work after he discovered Hackwood's* signature on portrait medallions*, and signed pieces of 18th century Wedgwood are therefore rare. The signatures of later artists such as Lessore*, Brownsword* and the Powells*, however, often appear in the decoration or on the base of the piece, and Daisy Makeig-Jones* hid her initials skilfully among the complicated decoration of some of her Fairyland Lustre* bowls and vases.

Creamware jugs sometimes bear inscriptions to individuals or to groups or associations (for example volunteer regiments) and these are often dated. Such inscriptions on early jasper or black basaltes wares are extremely rare.

Documentary Pieces. *A black basaltes documentary vase and cover of shield shape with ribbed loop handles and splayed foot, the obverse decorated in red encaustic with two figures, and the reverse with the inscription 'W.M. MOSELEY. 1788' and elaborate foliate scrolling. The cover is also decorated in red with formalised foliate patterns. 9¾ ins. high. Sotheby's.*

Dod

A die through which a strip of clay is extruded in a desired form and size. After extrusion the strip is cut off and bent to the required shape. The technique is often used for making handles, which are then luted on.

Dolphin

French: *Dauphin*. Sea-mammal venerated in ancient times, and then, as now, protected from persecution. Representations of dolphins appear occasionally on antique coins and terracottas, in Pompeian wall paintings, and on the furniture and pottery of the Greeks and Romans. The title 'Dauphin' was taken by Guigo IV of Viennois in 1140 and surrendered to the family of Valois two hundred years later on condition that it should belong to the heir to the French throne. This explains the frequent appearance of the dolphin in French decoration, but it was also popular in Italy and England. Dolphins are used as supporters for Wedgwood tripod vases (particularly for the tripod pastille burners*); and the well known dolphin candle-sticks*, which have been produced until the present day in basaltes*, Queen's Ware*, and majolica* glazes, are believed to have been modelled by Josiah Wedgwood himself. A Dolphin pattern on bone china, confined to 10-inch service plates, was designed in 1955 by Laurence Whistler*.

Doncaster, Samuel (d.after 1841)

Engraver of Burslem; worked for Wedgwood, 1806-11.

Dolphin. *Large black basaltes pastille burner mounted on triple dolphin supports. 12ins. high. 18th century.* Wedgwood.

Door Furniture

Finger plates, key escutcheons, door and drawer knobs were all made by Wedgwood, Turner*, and other 18th century potteries, but in the 19th century their manufacture tended to be concentrated among a few specialist factories. 18th century examples of Wedgwood door furniture are extremely rare.

See: Bell Pulls.

Downing, William

Engraver of Hanley; worked for Wedgwood, 1806-11.

Drab Ware

Drab-coloured stoneware (a distinctive greenish brown) covered with a salt glaze* was being produced in Staffordshire in the 1740s. It was employed particularly for domestic articles — teapots, coffeepots and jugs — often with a wash of white slip* applied to the interior, white clay handles, spouts and knobs, and applied decoration of trailing leaves. Two forms of drab ware were introduced by Wedgwood between 1800 and 1820. The first, a dry body* stoneware, was used mainly for decorative wares and ornamented with applied reliefs in blue, white or chocolate. Drab stoneware reliefs were also occasionally used to ornament cane ware*. The second, a glazed earthenware varying in shade from a pale coffee colour to dark olive, was generally employed for tableware, though it is occasionally to be found, with gilding, in the form of small vases and inkstands. The interiors of hollow pieces for table-ware were often brightened with a contrasting wash of robin's-egg blue. The drab colour was achieved by a mixture of manganese and nitre (potassium nitrate) with the addition of blue stain to the glaze to deepen the shade.

Neither version of drab ware ever won wide popularity, but the quality of potting and decoration is generally excellent. Production of drab ware appears to have ceased about 1860, but it was reintroduced in the 1970s for Tiffany's, New York.

Drab Ware. *A pot-pourri vase, a jug, and a bowl with robin's-egg blue interior. The bowl and jug are glazed inside and lightly gilt. Early 19th century.* Photo: Wedgwood.

Dragon Lustre. *Vase of Chinese mei ping shape decorated in lustre with colours.* Wedgwood.

Dragon Lustre

Type of lustre decoration devised by Daisy Makeig-Jones*.
See: Fairyland Lustre; Ordinary Lustres.

Drainer (Strainer)

A flat, pierced, false bottom to rest on a large platter, principally for draining boiled or steamed fish. They were also made with small feet to stand in large meat dishes, the surfaces of which were sloped towards a scooped well for the collection of juices. The making of drainers in the 18th century was a skilled operation, and it is worthy of note that, when Wedgwood was finding difficulty in making flat jasper tablets, he brought in a maker of drainers from the useful works.

Dresser, Christopher (1834-1904)

Designer, writer and botanist, born in Glasgow. Dresser studied at the London School of Design, and also at Jena University, where he obtained a Doctorate of Philosophy. In 1862 he published *The Art of Decorative Design.* He lectured on design and published a number of articles on the subject, producing also designs for domestic silver and metalwork, textiles, glass and furniture. He was an enthusiastic collector of Japanese art and was among the earliest of western visitors to Japan (1876). In 1883 he published *Japanese Architecture, Art and Art Manufactures* which established his reputation as an Orientalist, and he also made a study of South American art. In 1880 he became Art Designer and Art Superintendent of the Linthorpe Pottery, Middlesbrough, and he was Art Editor of *Furniture Gazette.* His work is characterised by simplicity of style and a concentration on practicality without loss of form.

Dresser's facsimile signature appears on a variety of wares in styles described as Egyptian, Moorish, Indian, Chinese, Japanese, Peruvian and Celtic, usually slip cast* with embossed or impressed designs decorated with coloured glazes. In the 1890s, Dresser supplied designs for William Ault's Art Pottery.

Few signed vases designed by Dresser for Wedgwood have been identified, one of which is now in the Wedgwood Museum*, but there can be little doubt that more are unrecognised.

Drum

A cylindrical pedestal on which is placed a lamp, vase, figure, candelabrum of glass with prismatically cut drops, etc. Drums for these purposes were nearly always of basaltes or jasper, sometimes mounted in ormolu, and were made in the last decades of the 18th century. Drums were adapted, with domed lids, to form tobacco jars.

Dry Bodies

Non-porous, unglazed stonewares, usually made by adding colouring oxides to local clay. Wedgwood dry bodies include jasper*, basaltes*, cane ware*, *rosso antico*, drab ware* and terracotta. Dry bodies were used for a wide variety of objects, both useful and ornamental, and were decorated by engine turning, enamelling, or with applied ornament, often of a contrasting colour. The interior of hollow ware pieces intended for use (cups, teapots, coffeepots, etc.) were glazed to prevent staining.

Dresser, Christopher. *Spill vase, the decoration designed by Christopher Dresser. Signed.* Wedgwood.

Dumb Waiter. *Bone china breakfast service decorated with panels of Oriental flowers within bands of dark blue and gold on a matching revolving circular tray, or 'dumb waiter', 14ins. diameter. c.1880.* Christie's.

Du Burk (fl.1760-1777)

Merchant; at one time Wedgwood's agent in Amsterdam; first mentioned in April, 1769, as purchasing £50 worth of vases. Wedgwood had doubts about his financial integrity in the year which followed as payments continued to be delayed. A partnership entered into between Joseph Cooper* and du Burk at the end of 1772 may have been evolved as a way of protecting Wedgwood & Bentley's interests in Amsterdam. In May, 1776, it was decided to send Ben Mather* to take stock prior to a dissolution of the partnership between Cooper and du Burk, and Mather reported that du Burk had been selling stock without accounting for the money received. In 1777 du Burk was imprisoned and a settlement negotiated. In June of the same year Wedgwood was fortunate in finding a new outlet in Amsterdam, L. van Veldhuyson*.

Du Roveray, J.P. (fl.1760-1780)

A London merchant of Swiss extraction with whom Wedgwood first established a connection in 1775. Du Roveray exported to the Continent, and was noted for writing lengthy letters. On his mother's side he was related to the Dassier* family, and offered to help Wedgwood obtain medals.

Duesbury, William (1725-1786)

Son of a tanner; born at Cannock, Staffs; proprietor of a London decorating studio, 1751-53; proprietor of the Derby* porcelain factory founded in 1756. He probably controlled the Bow Porcelain Factory* in East London from 1762 and had a financial interest in the studio of James Giles* after 1770 in which year he bought the Chelsea factory*. The Derby factory was especially noted for the quality of its biscuit figures and enamel painting. Wedgwood's white jasper figures used as ornament for Vulliamy* clocks are almost indistinguishable from Derby's biscuit figures and were evidently inspired by them.

Dumb Waiter

A revolving circular tray, 'Dumb Waiter' or 'Lazy Susan', 18¾ins. in diameter, decorated with *Oriental Flowers* pattern, with a matching breakfast set, was sold at Christie's* in October 1973. The set was of bone china*, c.1880. Another bone china tray with matching tableware is in the Wedgwood Museum*.

Dummy Ware

Another name for pie-crust ware*.

Duquesnoy, François (1594-1643)

Born in Brussels, Duquesnoy lived in Italy from 1620 onwards, and assisted Bernini with the St. Peter's, Rome, *baldacchino*. He became known by the sobriquet, *Il Fiammingo* (The Fleming). He adhered mainly to the classical tradition, and his work was notable for bronzes of *putti* — small boys in various guises and engaged in various occupations — which were a favourite form of Roman decoration, a particularly famous example being the 'Cupids as Craftsmen' painted on the walls of the House of the Vetii at Pompeii*. The much-reproduced fountain figure, the *Manaken-pis* in Brussels, is Duquesnoy's work. Most of the 18th century porcelain factories, including Sèvres, owed models of *putti* to his inspiration, and forty figures of *Sleeping Boys** after sketches by Duquesnoy were made in Vincennes porcelain for the King of France in 1755. A dated *Somnus** figure was produced in white porcelain by the Chelsea Porcelain Factory* in 1746. Duquesnoy's bas-reliefs* of boys were reproduced also in ivory, bronze and plaster. Wedgwood reproduced both figures and bas-reliefs in basaltes* and jasper*.

The following subjects are after Duquesnoy:

Bacchanalian Boys, a set of six tablets, 6ins. by 8ins., casts of which were supplied by Mary Landré in 1769. These include *Boys playing with a Goat, Boys as Musicians, Silenus and Boys,* and *Feast of Bacchus.*

Five models of Sleeping Boys (often called *Somnus*), also probably supplied by Landré.

Dwight, John (c.1637-1703)

M.A. of Christchurch, Oxford, who took out a patent in 1671 for "the mistery of transparent earthenware, commonly known by the name of porcelane in China, and of stoneware, vulgarly called Cologne ware." From other sources we know that 'red porcelain' was a term commonly employed to describe Yi-Hsing stoneware*, and some of Dwight's white (or drab coloured) stonewares are translucent in parts where they are thin enough. Dwight established himself at Fulham, where he made some extremely distinguished figures. He also made bellarmines which are often difficult to distinguish from those made in Cologne. In 1690 Dwight started an action, alleging infringement of his patents, against the Elers brothers*, and Aaron, Thomas, and Richard Wedgwood. The Wedgwoods were probably, like the Elers, making red stoneware. Dwight is said by Eliza Meteyard* to have died in 1737, which is inaccurate.

Dysart Glaze

See: Glaze.

Dysart Green

The Victorian architect, Halsey Ricardo, a connection of the Wedgwood family and partner to William De Morgan*, remodelled Lord Dysart's house at Buckminster Park, Leicestershire, which has since been demolished. Ricardo's work included extensive redecoration utilising Wedgwood jasper plaques for chimney pieces and mural decoration. Among them were plaques with a specially developed 'Dysart Green' used as a background.

Dysart Ware

A type of Queen's ware made c.1876 at the suggestion of Lord Dysart. It was covered with a deep cream or yellow glaze owing its colour to vanadium but was otherwise undecorated.

Duquesnoy, François (Il Fiammingo). Pair of blue and white jasper plaques of Drunken Silenus and Bacchanalian Boys, 7⁷/₁₆ins. by 5⁹/₁₆ins. Impressed mark 'WEDGWOOD & BENTLEY' c.1778 Dwight and Lucille Beeson Collection.

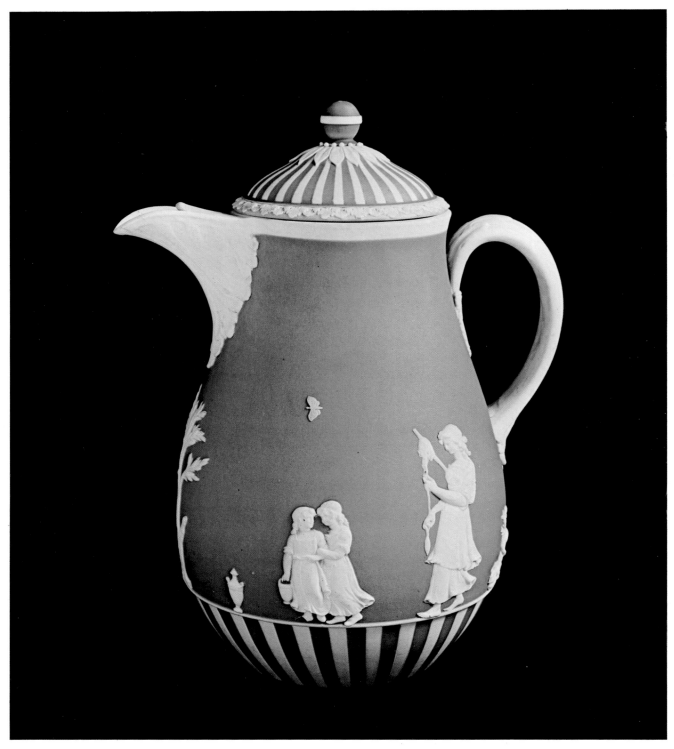

Colour Plate IX

Blue and white jasper dip coffee pot, height 8ins., with engine-turned decoration to the lower part of the body and the lid. This is a particularly fine example of a jasper 'Cabinet' piece, showing fine, even, engine-turning, crisp relief decoration, beautifully modelled acanthus terminals to the spout and handle, and a form that is at once sturdy, practical and elegant. c.1783. Wedgwood. Photo: Reilly/Charles Letts.

Earthenware

An English term for all factory-made pottery which is not vitrified. It therefore excludes stoneware and porcelain. Since earthenware is porous it requires a glaze. The finest quality earthenwares are white, or near white, and since the middle of the 18th century have contained calcined flint*. Wedgwood's Queen's ware belongs to this class. Earthenware of the type made by Wedgwood is usually called *faience-fine* in France and *Steingut* in Germany. In both countries earthenware inspired by Queen's ware was made from the last decades of the 18th century.

Eastern Flowers

Oriental-style pattern of the *famille rose** type, designed by G. Allen in 1845. First produced with overglaze enamel and lustre decoration* on Queen's Ware, it was reintroduced in 1954 as an underglaze lithograph pattern in muted shades of brown, yellow, pink and green.

See also: Lithography.

Eastwood, Hanley, Staffordshire

Earthenware manufactory owned by William Baddeley*. He made creamware, cane ware, Egyptian black, and other wares inspired by Wedgwood during the last quarter of the 18th century and the early years of the 19th. He employed the impressed mark 'Eastwood'.

Edme Shape. *Examples of the popular Edme shape on Queen's ware, introduced by John Goodwin.* Wedgwood.

Ecuelle

The French for a lidded shallow bowl, usually with two handles level with the rim, and a conforming stand. Shapes in English pottery and porcelain were based on silver or Continental porcelain shapes. *Ecuelles* were generally used for soup. Wedgwood's jasper *écuelles*, made in the 1780s and 1790s, had unglazed interiors and were therefore probably intended as 'cabinet' pieces. They were produced, until recent times, in Queen's ware* and bone china* to match dinnerware patterns and also occur more rarely in glazed drab* ware.

Eden, Sir William

See: Auckland.

Edgeworth, Honora Sneyd (d.1780)

Daughter of Ralph Sneyd of Lichfield; the second wife of the author, R.L. Edgeworth*, who was a close friend of Josiah Wedgwood. Wedgwood, who stayed with the Edgeworths in 1777, described her as "a very polite, sensible, and agreeable lady... with a considerable share of beauty." After her death in 1780, Edgeworth wrote to Wedgwood asking for her profile to be made in jasper. This was modelled, probably by Flaxman*, "from a profile by Mrs. Harrington [the well known artist in silhouette] and an excellent picture by [John] Smart." The field below the truncation is impressed 'HONORA EDGEWORTH O B 1780', and the portrait is one of the few to have been produced on the rare brown jasper ground.

Edgeworth, Honora. *Jasper portrait medallion of Honora Sneyd Edgeworth. Modelled in 1780 by John Flaxman at the request of Richard Lovell Edgeworth.* Victoria and Albert Museum.

Edgeworth, Richard Lovell (1744-1817)

English author; educated Trinity College, Dublin, and Christ's College, Cambridge; friend of Anna Seward, Erasmus Darwin*, and Josiah Wedgwood. His principal publications were on educational and mechanical subjects. He was four times married, and father of Maria Edgeworth, the novelist, by his first wife. In his later years, after the death of Bentley, Wedgwood's friendship with Edgeworth was fairly close, and Edgeworth submitted many ideas for Wedgwood's approval. The earliest instance appears to have been in 1777. In 1782 Edgeworth committed what was then an illegal act by marrying his deceased wife's sister and went to live on his estates in Ireland. He and Wedgwood then corresponded on current affairs, on which they held, for the most part, divergent views.

See: Honora Sneyd Edgeworth.

Edme Shape

A ribbed Queen's ware shape, introduced in 1908 for Pannier Frères of Paris, which has been for more than seventy years one of Wedgwood's most popular tableware shapes.

Egg-and-Dart Border

A border pattern of alternating ovoid and dart-like forms.

Egg-and-Tongue Border

Border pattern consisting of alternating ovoid and tongue-shaped forms.

Egg Beater

A small cylindrical covered vessel of cream-coloured ware to the inner walls of which are attached a number of spikes. Used to beat an egg by shaking. Made in the 18th century, specimens are now very rare.

Egg Border

A border of adjacent ovoid motifs cut in half horizontally.

Egg-cup Stand

A circular tray on a stem foot pierced with holes for holding egg-cups, usually with a tray *en suite* for spoons. Made in cream-coloured ware by Wedgwood, and also at Leeds.

See: Egg Stand.

Egg Separator

A shallow dish with a recessed cover. The cover is pierced with a number of holes to permit the white of the egg to pass through it, thus separating the yolk from the white. Made by Wedgwood in cream-coloured ware.

Egg Stand

A horizontal flat disc on a low foot pierced with holes of sufficient size to hold an egg. Made by Wedgwood in cream-coloured ware.

Egyptian Black

See: Black Egyptian.

Egyptian Collection 1978

Limited editions of figures, plates, and plaques in terracotta and black jasper, terracotta and primrose jasper, and gilded basaltes. The Sphinx* figures and Canopic* vases were reproduced from 18th century models.

Sphinx couchant, terracotta on black jasper, height 4ins. (Edition 250); gilded basaltes (Edition 100).

Sphinx sitting, terracotta on black jasper, height 8¾ins. (Edition 250); gilded basaltes (Edition 100).

Canopic Vase, terracotta on black jasper, height 9¾ins. (Edition 500); terracotta on primrose jasper (Edition 500); gilded basaltes (Edition 50).

Beloved of the Great Enchantress, miniature plaque, gilded basaltes, 4½ins. by 4ins. (Edition 3,000).

Lord of the Diadems, plaque, gilded basaltes, 8ins. by 8½ins. (Edition 250).

Lord of the Two Lands, plaque, gilded basaltes, 15ins. by 8½ins. (Edition 250).

Trophy Plate, Egyptian motifs and Zodiac signs encircling a profile portrait of Tutankhamun in terracotta on black jasper (Edition 500).

Trophy Plate, similar motifs encircling a profile portrait of Ankhesenamun in terracotta on primrose jasper (Edition 500).

Egyptian Taste

Although most of Wedgwood's decorative products were inspired by Greek and Roman sources, examples of Egyptian influence also occur. Most of these motifs look as though they

Egg Beater. *Creamware egg beater, shown with cover removed. The egg is broken into the lower part, the cover replaced, and the whole shaken, the projecting spikes blending yolk and white. Buten Museum.*

had been taken at third-hand, from a book illustration by way of Greece. Between 800 and 700 B.C. Greek art entered an 'Orientalising' phase in which Egyptian and Near Eastern motifs were employed extensively, and were sometimes copied so closely that the true origin may be in doubt. A number of Wedgwood models come from sources of this kind, possibly taken from Montfaucon* or later vase paintings. The Canopic* inkstand, which is boat shaped, is decorated with lotus flowers and scarab beetles. It has a griffin's* head at the prow, which is Greek and not Egyptian, and a not very convincing crocodile's head at the stern. The Canopic jar in the centre has only a superficial resemblance to Egyptian jars of this kind, and is probably derived from a book illustration of mid-18th century date. The whole is a pastiche of Graeco-Egyptian motifs put together from various sources at Etruria.

Egypt was a very exotic taste during the 18th century, and it was not until Napoleon's Egyptian Campaign and the subsequent publication of a work on the monuments of Egypt by the Baron Vivant Denon, and the work of Belzoni (who organised an exhibition of Egyptian antiquities in London in 1821) and others, that any serious interest was taken in the subject. Wedgwood's 'hieroglyphic' decoration dates from this period.

Electricity and Pottery Decoration

It is evident from a letter written to Bentley* in 1766 that Wedgwood had been invited by his friend to make his first contribution towards the cost of the experiments of their mutual friend, Dr. Joseph Priestley*. It seems that Priestley thought it might be possible to adapt electricity to the decoration of pottery. Wedgwood replied in mock-rhetorical vein: "Heavens once dreaded bolt is now called down to amuse your wives and daughters — to decorate their tea-boards and baubles!" Nothing, however, seems to have come of it. It is difficult to think what the process might have been, unless Dr. Priestley was anticipating Elkington* by seventy years and experimenting with the electrical deposition of metal.

Egyptian Collection. *Canopic vase and bowl, ornamented in terracotta on black, and Trophy plate with central portrait of Ankhesenamun in terracotta on primrose jasper, from the Egyptian Collection, 1978.* Wedgwood.

Egyptian Taste. *An 18th century black basaltes inkstandish in the Egyptian manner. It is in the form of a ship with a griffin's head at the bow and a crocodile's head at the stern. Amidships, a canopic vase is flanked by circular inkwells.* Wedgwood.

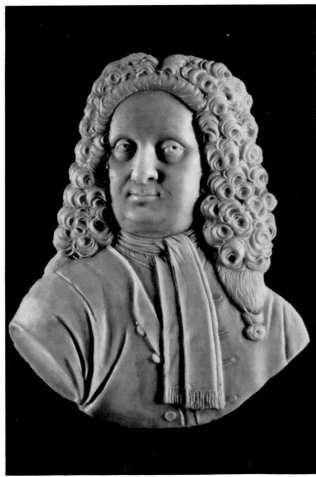

Elers, John Philip. *Wax portrait medallion of J.P. Elers modelled by Hackwood, 1777.* Formerly Reilly Collection.

Elers, John Philip and David (fl. 1688-1710)

Originally silversmiths; believed to have been salt glaze* potters at Cologne (Rhineland). They are mentioned by Dr. Martin Lister in 1699 as "two Dutch [Deutsch] men brothers... who wrought in Staffordshire... and were not long since at Hammersmith [W. London]." The Elers brothers made red stoneware* at Bradwell Wood, and other types of ware are doubtfully attributed to them. Apparently they left for Dublin in 1700, and there is no further record of their activities. A portrait medallion of J.P. Elers, modelled by Hackwood*, was produced in 1777. The original wax model (Reilly collection) was exhibited at the National Portrait Gallery, London, in 1973.

Elers, Paul (1700-after 1777)

Son of John Philip Elers*. He corresponded at length with Wedgwood in 1777 on the subject of the wares made by his father and uncle, making extravagant claims on their behalf, which Wedgwood rebutted in a long letter to Bentley in July. At Paul's request, Hackwood modelled the portrait of John Philip, and, in a letter of 19th July, 1777, Wedgwood relayed a demand for "about half a dozen more of the Portraits, for his friends are pretty numerous." R.L. Edgeworth's* first wife was Elers' daughter.

Elkington & Sons (Birmingham)

Silversmiths, founded in the 1830s by G.E. Elkington (1801-65) and his cousin, Henry Elkington (c.1810-52). The firm developed a process of electro-plating on base metal, usually nickel silver (EPNS), and a process of making reliefs and models in the round by the electric deposition of metal (electro-typing). They also made mounts of silver for the embellishment of pottery and porcelain. When George Elkington died in 1865 the firm employed over 1,000 workmen, occupying much the same position in the 19th century as Boulton had done in the 18th. During the latter half of the 19th century Elkington produced EPNS mounts for Wedgwood jasper biscuit barrels, match holders, salad bowls, etc., some of which bear the name 'Elkington' impressed with the Wedgwood mark in the clay body, indicating that they were supplied to, and marketed by, Elkington.

Elysian Fields

According to Homer*, a land lying to the West, where there is neither cold, nor snow, nor rain. Favourites of the gods passed there without dying first. According to the Roman poets, Elysium is part of the Lower World whence pass the souls of the favoured dead.

Wedgwood subject:
Pleasures of the Elysian fields, tablet, attributed to Angelini*, c.1790.

Embossed Queen's Ware. *Edme vases with applied, or embossed, vine-leaf decoration in a contrasting colour. Tablewares ornamented in this manner, in various colours, were introduced in 1902, but the original vine relief was modelled by Hackwood. Wedgwood.*

Émail Ombrant

French term for a form of pottery and porcelain decoration, suitable only for flat dishes and plaques, developed in 1842 by the Baron du Tremblay from the lithophane*. The design was deeply impressed in the centre, which was then flooded with coloured glaze (generally green or brown), light and shade being defined by the varying depth of the design. Table and dessert services decorated in *émail ombrant* from the Rubelles factory were awarded a Gold Medal at the Great Exhibition of 1851. Wedgwood acquired the process under licence from Rubelles in 1873, employing it largely for earthenware plates and dishes of the majolica* type.

Encaustic Painting.
Black basaltes spill vase decorated with encaustic painting. Wedgwood.

Encaustic Painting.
Cup and saucer with encaustic painting of an owl, c.1770. Unmarked, but decorative pattern on both cup and saucer are from Wedgwood's pattern book, copied from Hamilton and D'Hancarville. Dwight and Lucille Beeson Collection.

Embossed Queen's Ware

Tableware and ornamental wares of cream-coloured Queen's ware or coloured bodies* ornamented by hand with relief vine decoration in a contrasting colour. Colour variations include lavender on CC (cream-colour), CC on lavender, celadon on CC, CC on celadon, CC on Windsor grey and pink on CC, and the tablewares were produced on traditional* and shell edge* shapes. Introduced in 1902, and particularly popular in the USA, the style and ornament was based on the Hackwood Vine* designed by William Hackwood for bone china* in 1812.

Encaustic Painting

Developed by Josiah Wedgwood mainly for the purpose of imitating Greek and Italian vases in the red-figure style. The surface of the colours is matt rather than glossy, and they are smooth and durable. They were applied in the usual way, with a brush, and the palette, although limited, consisted of several contrasting colours, as well as red and black, more or less the full range occurring on some rare basaltes* tablets intended to be inset into chimney pieces*. Wedgwood patented encaustic colours in 1769 (see: Bronzed Basaltes), but the patent gave little protection against infringements by his competitors, and he never bothered to patent anything else.

Wedgwood lavished a great deal of time, skill and expense on his copies of antique* vases, and the failure rate was high. The painting was, as might be expected, lifeless and stilted in comparison with the free and vigorous style of most of the originals. Wedgwood's own description refers to "Vases and encaustic paintings where every succeeding Vase and every Picture is made, not in a Mould, or by a Stamp, but separately by the Hand, with the same Attention and Diligence [as the first model]." A list of the patrons who possessed these red-figure vases, referred to by Wedgwood as "painted Etruscans," included George III* and Queen Charlotte*, Catherine II* of Russia, and the Kings of Poland, Prussia,

Encaustic Painting. *Group of black basaltes teapots and a creamer encaustically painted. The creamer, although technically a piece of 'useful' ware, is evidently a 'Cabinet piece' and therefore considered as ornamental since it is marked 'Wedgwood & Bentley'.* Photo: Paine Art Centre.

Plate X

Left: Pale grey-blue jasper medallion, with darker blue dip and white bas-relief of Ganymede and the Eagle, *height 7ins. Modelled c.1778.* Nottingham Castle Museum. Photo: Reilly/Charles Letts.

Below: Dark blue jasper dip medallion, 8ins. by 11¾ins. with bas-relief of The Marriage of Cupid and Psyche. *The subject was taken from a Graeco-Roman sardonyx then in the possession of the Duke of Marlborough. c.1785.* Nottingham Castle Museum. Photo: Reilly/ Charles Letts.

Encaustic Painting. *Solitaire or early morning tea set in caneware with bamboo moulding and encaustic painting in blue and red. c.1792.* Wedgwood.

Sweden, and Portugal, followed by an impressive list of Grand Dukes, Electors, Princes, Dukes, Marquesses, Barons, Landgraves, etc., in descending order, which is excellent testimony to the widespread nature of the interest in the subject.

Included in this category of basaltes vases with encaustic painting are the First Day's vases* of 13th June, 1769. The painting of these, and much else besides, was done at the Chelsea Decorating Studio* under Bentley's supervision. Among those artists who painted tablets, using a wider palette of colours, were Unwin*, Mrs. Wilcox*, and, from 1784, Aaron Steele*.

Manufacture of these vases began in 1768, and for a time they were in considerable demand. The source of many of the designs was Sir William Hamilton's* collection, lately sold to the British Museum. They were advertised as suitable for standing on chimney pieces, cabinets, bookcases, etc., and were from 6ins. to 20ins. high. Cabinets and bookcases in the 18th century were often designed with a broken pediment and a special stand in the centre for a bust or vase, and Wedgwood made both for the decoration of gentlemen's libraries.

Apart from copies of Greek vases and decorative tablets, and small medallions, encaustic painting occurs on basaltes teaware, on candlesticks, and on rare examples of cane ware*. The style of red and black decoration was also adapted for the borders and centre motifs of tableware, and these patterns were known as 'Etruscan'. A letter written from Paris in February 1788, testifies to the popularity of this style of tableware decoration in France.

Encaustic Painting. *Pair of vases, 12¼ ins. high, painted in yellow and iron red with white borders. c.1840. The subjects are* Ganymede and the Eagle, *and* Bacchus and Panther. Sotheby's Belgravia.

Encaustic Painting. *Important black basaltes plaque, 8ins. by 13½ ins., painted in encaustic colours of flesh tones and brown, with a central design of the American eagle within a wreath of bound laurel flanked by acanthus scrolls. Intended to be set in a chimney piece, this plaque may have been produced to celebrate American victory in the War of Independence, c.1784.* Christie's.

135

Engine-Turning Lathe. *The engine-turning lathe being used to cut in a curved pattern.* Wedgwood.

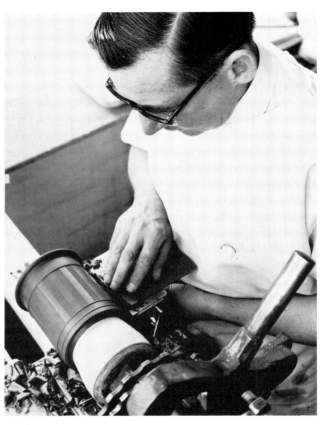

Engine-Turning Lathe. *Engine-turning a vase to produce slightly raised bands, the vase moving alternately towards and away from the cutting tool at predetermined intervals. The operation calls for special skill since the cutting tool is hand-held.* Wedgwood.

Engine-Turning Lathe. *The modern engine-turning lathe copied from the 18th century lathe still in use.* Wedgwood.

Engine-Turned Decoration. *Two engine-turned creamware vases, c.1780.* Wedgwood.

136

Endymion

A youth renowned for his beauty, he was perpetually asleep on Mount Latmos. It was generally thought that Selene (the Moon) had put him to sleep so that she could kiss him without his knowledge.

Wedgwood subjects.

Endymion (asleep) on Latmos, tablet attributed to Pacetti*, c.1789.

Diana (Selene) visiting Endymion, tablet, 8½ ins. by 27½ ins.

See: Diana.

Engine-Turning Lathe (Engine-Turned Decoration)

The engine-turning lathe is similar in general principles to the simple lathe*, but it has an eccentric motion which enables a variety of repetitive patterns to be cut with it, the more elaborate of which are cut with the aid of a guide tool termed a rosette. Wedgwood wrote in May 1767, of negotiating to buy a lathe fitted with rosettes from Matthew Boulton. Engine turning is carried out on unfired pottery dried to leather* hardness. It is used for fluted, diced, and similar patterns, some so intricate that the lathe has to be turned very slowly by hand. Josiah saw the engine-turning lathe at work in Matthew Boulton's Soho factory in 1763, and installed his own in the same year. It has been in use ever since.

It proved to be impossible to adapt this type of lathe to electrical motive power, and when the demand for wares decorated in this way grew too great in 1976 the decision was taken to copy the two-hundred-year-old machine. This was done, apart from some specialist castings, by Wedgwood's engineering staff, and assembled by Arthur Ward, a fitter, and George Hughes, a pattern maker, who, between them, had seventy-four years' experience at the factory. The new machine, almost the twin of the old one, can work at speeds of between 4 and 550 revolutions per minute.

Engine turning is a highly skilled operation both for the turner and his assistant, a fact to which Josiah's letters consistently testify. Engine-turned patterns of the highest quality were never successfully imitated by Wedgwood's contemporaries in the 18th century.

Englefield, John (fl.1769-1774)

Painter at the Chelsea Decorating Studio* who worked on the Frog* service.

Epergne

See: Grant Plat Menage.

Epicurus (342?-270B.C.)

Greek philosopher, who taught that peace of mind arising from a cultivation of the virtues is the highest good. This precept was later misinterpreted, some of his followers suggesting that he had held the highest good to be happiness, thus opening the way for sensual enjoyment. A bust of Epicurus, supplied by Hoskins & Oliver* in 1774, was worked on by Hackwood* and reproduced, about 25ins. high, in basaltes.

Erasmus Darwin Service

A popular, but erroneous, name for the Water Lily* pattern.

Eros

See: Cupid.

Engine-Turned Decoration. *Ewer of black basaltes, based on the Greek oenochoe, engine-turned and marked 'Wedgwood & Bentley'. 11ins. high. c.1778. Dwight and Lucille Beeson Collection.*

Etruria (also Tuscia)

Called by the Greeks, Tyrrhenia; an area of central Italy inhabited by the Etrusci (or Tusci), who were probably of Pelasgian origin. The Pelasgians were the original inhabitants of Greece. The Etruscans were a highly civilised people from whom the Romans learned a great deal about the arts, and religious and social organisation. They became subject to Roman power in 283B.C., received the Roman franchise in 91B.C., and were completely Romanised by the time of Augustus.

Etruria Factory. *An old photograph of the Etruria factory from the canal.* Wedgwood.

Etruria Factory, Staffordshire (1769-1940)

The opening of the Etruria factory on the 3,000 acre Ridgehouse Estate marks the beginning of the production of ornamental wares by the Wedgwood & Bentley partnership. The deeds of partnership were signed on the 10th August, 1769. It continued until Bentley's death in 1780. Jasper was

Etruria Factory. *Potter's throwing wheel from the Etruria factory, reputed to be one of the first used by Wedgwood. The motive power was supplied by an assistant turning the large wheel. This type of wheel would have been used for throwing the First Day's Vases in 1769.* Photo: Wedgwood.

first produced in 1775, jasper dip in 1777, cane ware from 1770, *rosso antico* from 1776, and pearl ware from 1779. Creamware, and useful wares generally, were made at Etruria from 1772, when the Brick House* works were closed. Production was started at Barlaston* in 1940, but due to the Second World War the building of the new factory was not completed until 1949, when all production of Wedgwood at Etruria ceased. Josiah Wedgwood resided at Etruria Hall nearby.

Etruria Hall

The residence of Josiah Wedgwood built on the Ridgehouse Estate at a cost of £22,000. The architect was Joseph Pickford of Derby, a former plasterer who had built the Soho factory for Matthew Boulton*, and who was also responsible for the design and building of the Etruria factory, Bank House (built nearby for Bentley at a cost of £16,000 and never occupied by him), and the necessary workmen's cottages. Etruria Hall was enlarged in 1780. Bank House was demolished early in the 19th century.

Nothing remains of the interior ornament of Etruria Hall, and its drawing-room ceiling, reputedly painted by William Blake, now bears no trace of its erstwhile decoration.

The family left the Hall after the death of Josiah in 1795, and when Josiah II* died in 1844 the whole of the estate, including the factory, was put up for auction. The contents of the Hall, which included paintings by Joseph Wright* and Stubbs* were distributed among members of the family. The factory did not reach the reserve price and was retained. The Hall was sold, and later became the offices of the Shelton Iron & Steel Company.

Etruscan Patterns

Queen's ware tableware patterns enamelled in red and black in imitation of the decorative motifs found on Greek and Italian vases in the red-figure style. These patterns appear to have been a development from the popularity of encaustic* painted vases, and they were particularly popular in Paris.

Etruscan Pottery

Much ancient Etruscan pottery was inspired by the wares of contemporary Greece, and some of the finest examples of Greek wares have been found in Etruscan tombs. Later, Roman potters also copied contemporary Greek wares.

Etruria Factory. *View in the Throwing Room, Ornamental Works, Etruria. From an engraving.* Photo: Wedgwood.

Etruria Hall. *Large oval platter from the Frog service painted with a view of Etruria Hall, with the Trent and Mersey canal in the foreground. 1773-74.* Photo: Wedgwood after Williamson.

Collections of vases of this kind were made in the 18th century, notably by Sir William Hamilton*, Ambassador to the Court of Naples, who subsequently sold his vases to the British Museum. Josiah Wedgwood copied some of Sir William's undecorated ware, as well as vases in the red-figure style*. At the time the subject of ancient pottery had not been very seriously studied, and anything found in Italy was regarded as Etruscan or Roman without very obvious evidence to the contrary. The Etruscan *bucchero nero* ware, a black pottery with moulded or incised ornament dating from the 8th century B.C., was also recovered from tombs, and may have inspired some of the 18th century black wares.

Etruscan Vases

Black basaltes vases made by Josiah Wedgwood and painted with encaustic* enamels with decoration in the classical red-figure style, using mainly red and white pigments on a black ground. Most 'Etruscan' vases are closely copied from ancient sources.

True red-figure decoration executed by ancient Greek and

Italian potters was the result of using a red-burning clay for the vase, reserving the figures by covering the remainder of the red surface with a very fluid black slip*. The secret of this fluid slip was supposed, by the 18th century, to have been lost. It was achieved by adding urine or stale wine lees as a spreading agent, much in the same way as the water colourist adds ox gall to his washes of colour. There does not seem to be any evidence that Wedgwood ever experimented with the production of red-figure vases using the ancient technique of black slip on a red ground, but the Buten Museum* possesses a very rare example of a *rosso antico** krater* in which the red figures have been achieved by painting the remainder of the surface with black enamel, which took the place of the Greek slip. It is evident, therefore, that Wedgwood fully realised that his 'Etruscan' vases were attaining by different means an effect comparable with ancient work, and that he interested himself to some extent in reproducing the ancient ware more closely. The authors do not know of a Wedgwood example of black-figure painting — the earlier type of Greek vase in which the figures were painted in black slip on a red ground — but copies of Greek pottery thus decorated were made elsewhere in the 19th century.

Exotic Birds
During the 1760s and 1770s the porcelain factories, especially Worcester* and Derby*, made frequent use of exotic birds as painted decoration. These had first been employed at Meissen*, but the Sèvres* factory developed the style and made it fashionable, taking their subjects from one or another of the popular private aviaries of the day. In London the independent decorator, James Giles*, also painted similar birds in a characteristic style which W.B. Honey christened 'dishevelled birds'. Some comparatively rare Wedgwood creamware is painted with birds of this kind in vignettes, probably at the Chelsea Studio, but somewhat more frequent are the transfer-prints on creamware by Sadler & Green*. These, first produced about 1775, are called 'Liverpool birds', but they are very similar in style to birds painted at Worcester by a M. Soqui, reputed to have come from Sèvres about 1770.

Experiment Book
The manuscript record, begun during Josiah Wedgwood's partnership with Whieldon* (1754-59), in which he kept details of his experiments for the improvement of bodies and glazes. The Experiment Book preserved in the Wedgwood Museum*, a fair copy of the original, is in the handwriting of Alexander Chisholm* and was made c.1782, and the introduction was probably written by Josiah at that time. An incomplete draft of this exists, however, in an earlier version partly in his own hand. In his introduction Josiah wrote:

"This suite of experiments was begun at Fenton Hall in the parish of Stoke-on-Trent, about the beginning of the year 1759 in my partnership with Mr. Whieldon, for the improvement of our manufacture of earthenware, which at the time stood in great need of it, the demand for our goods decreasing daily, and the trade universally complained of as being bad and in a declining condition.

"White Stone Ware was the principal article of our manufacture, but this had been made a long time and the prices were now reduced so low, that the potters could not afford to bestow much expense upon it or make it so good in any respect as the ware would otherwise admit of. And with regard to Elegance of form, that was an object very little attended to.

"The article next in consequence to Stone Ware was an imitation of Tortoiseshell. But as no improvement had been made in this branch for twenty years, the country was grown weary of it... and something new was wanted to give a little

spirit to the business.

"I had already made an imitation of Agate, which was esteemed beautiful and a considerable improvement, but people were surfeited with wares of these variegated colours. These considerations induced me to try for some more solid improvements as well in the Body as the Glazes, the Colours, and the Forms of the articles of our manufacture.

"I saw the field was spacious and the soil so good, as to promise an ample recompense to any who should labour diligently in its cultivation."

The experiment numbered as seventh in the Book is for Wedgwood's Green Glaze*. Wedgwood left Whieldon and set up on his own account in May 1759, but it is clear that he did not sever his connection with him since a page of the Experiment book dated 28th March, 1760 is headed "at Fenton."

See: Codes and Formulae.

Extrusion
The process of forcing plastic clay through suitably shaped forms to produce rods of uniform section which may be cut off in desired lengths for the production of handles, strips for twig baskets*, etc.

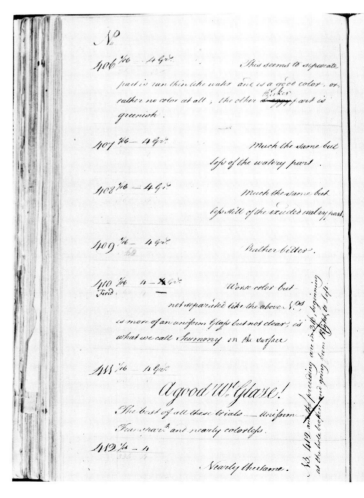

Experiment Book. *A page from Wedgwood's Experiment Book, coded formulae on the left, the result of firing trials on the right.* Wedgwood.

Fairyland Lustre. *Octagonal bowl decorated with Fairyland Lustre* Poplar Trees *design by Daisy Makeig-Jones.* Wedgwood.

Faience-Fine

Also *faience-fine d'Angleterre.* French name for English cream-ware, notably that of Wedgwood and Leeds, and wares in this style.

See: Creil.

Fairyland Lustre

The name given by Daisy Makeig-Jones* to a large range of ornamental lustre wares produced, from her designs and under her supervision, from November 1915. These designs, combining the use of bright underglaze colours (occasionally with onglaze enamel highlights), painted-on commercial lustres, and finally gold-printing, with fantastic and often grotesque figures, scenes and landscapes, followed immediately upon the successful Ordinary Lustres*, first introduced in the autumn of 1914. The production of these two new forms of decoration enabled Wedgwood, for the first time, to compete with the great porcelain manufacturers — Minton*, Crown Derby*, Coalport* and Worcester* — in the production of ornamental bone china*.

The Fairyland Lustres fall into three main categories: Queen's ware* plaques, 16ins. by 11ins. (pattern numbers with 'F' prefix); bone china plates, 10¾ ins. in diameter ('W' prefix); and bone china ornamental pieces (vases, bowls, plaques etc.; 'Z' prefix). The method chosen for the numbering and identification of the many different shapes and patterns was unfortunately one of remarkable complexity. The six 'F' and eleven 'W' prefix pattern numbers are comparatively straightforward; but the 'Z' prefix numbers were often 'comprehensive', the same number covering a wide diversity of shapes, sizes and designs which had in common no more than a recognisable style of decoration or a particular combination of enamel colours. The resulting confusion has been patiently disentangled by Una des Fontaines, whose splendid *Wedgwood Fairyland Lustre* is essential to any serious collector.

Fairyland Lustre was produced by Wedgwood from 1915 until 1931, but demand declined after 1929, and only one pattern (a new colour version of an existing design, concocted by Victor Skellern* in 1935, to meet a particular order) was added after the retirement of Daisy Makeig-Jones in 1931. The order, given by Josiah V*, for the destruction of all the copper plates, was not obeyed, and these were discovered by Una des Fontaines in the engravings store at Barlaston. Two reproductions have been made in recent years: a plaque, *The Enchanted Palace,* issued in a limited edition of 250 in 1977; and an octagonal bowl, produced in 1979.

Neglected for some thirty years, Wedgwood's Fairyland Lustre has enjoyed an impressive revival in popularity and is much sought-after by collectors. The consequent rise in prices at auction has led to the appearance of lustre pieces, made during the twenties in imitation by other factories without any intention to deceive, but now bearing spurious Wedgwood and Portland vase marks*, replacing genuine marks which have been removed by grinding. The surface damage done to the base of the object by grinding, the poor quality of the printed mark, and the evidence of reglazing or varnishing, are all obvious to the eye and should deceive no one.

The pattern numbers listed on the next page were painted on the base of Fairyland Lustre pieces by the paintresses who had decorated them, and their appearance, with the authentic Wedgwood marks, is a valuable aid to identification. They are not, however, infallible.

Fairyland Lustre. *Plaque, 10ins. high,* Torches, *pattern No. Z5331, painted in colours and lustre by Daisy Makeig-Jones. Signed.* Zeitlin Collection.

QUEEN'S WARE PLAQUES

F3078)
F3080) *The Stuff that Dreams are made of* [sic]
F3081)
F3082) *Imps on a Bridge and Tree House*
F3083)
F3084) *Bubbles*

BONE CHINA PLATES

W556	*Roc* centre, *Flaming Wheel* border
W557	*Firbolgs* centre, *Gnome* or *Imp* border
W558	*Roc* centre, *Twyford* border
W559	*Roc* centre, floral diaper border
W560	*Roc* centre, *Gnome* or *Imp* border
W561	*Si Wang Mu* centre, *Flame* border
W607	*Imps on a Bridge and Tree House*
W608	*Imps on a Bridge and Tree House*
W609	*White Pagodas, Gnome* or *Imp* border
W610	*White Pagodas,* triangular masks border
W1050	*Roc* centre, fruit and flower border
	White Pagodas, Pebble and Grass border (unrecorded in design books)
Z5501	*Goblins,* on *Bubbles* background

(All the above plates are 10¾ ins. in diameter with the exception of Z5501 which is 9½ ins.)

BONE CHINA ORNAMENTAL VASES, BOWLS ETC.

Z4935	*Poplar Trees*
Z4968	Comprehensive pattern number (long line)
Z5125	Comprehensive pattern number for octagonal bowls: *Dana* panels
Z5157	*Candlemas*
Z5200	*Firbolgs* and *Thumbelina*
Z5217	*Angels* or *Geisha* and *Running Figures*
Z5219	*Firbolgs* and *Thumbelina*
Z5228	*Willow Fairyland*
Z5247	*Firbolgs* and *Thumbelina*
Z5252	*Woodland Elves* IV (*Big Eyes*)
Z5257	*Bubbles* (3 versions)
Z5275	*Red Firbolgs*
Z5331	*Torches*
Z5346	*Firbolgs*
Z5348	Coral and Bronze
Z5349	Coral and Bronze
Z5360	Comprehensive pattern number: Flame Fairyland (long line)
Z5366	*Bifrost*
Z5367	*Goblins*
Z5391	*Imps on a Bridge and Tree House*
Z5392	*Imps on a Bridge and Tree House*
Z5404	Coral and Bronze
Z5406	Coral and Bronze
Z5407	*Willow Fairyland*
Z5443-6	Various Fairyland patterns, borders and centres on *Daventry* shape (footed) bowls
Z5454	*Bird in a Hoop*
Z5461	*Candlemas*
Z5462	*Moonlight Fairyland* (various designs)
Z5463	*Bubbles*
Z5464	*Willow*
Z5481	*Sunset Fairyland* (various designs)
Z5442	Comprehensive pattern number

BONE CHINA PLAQUES

Z5154)
Z5155)
Z5287) *Elves in a Pine Tree*
Z5288)

Z5156)
Z5158)
Z5279) *Picnic by a River*
Z5280)

Z5292) *Elfin Palace*

Falconet, Etienne-Maurice (1716-1791)

French sculptor, whose work belongs to the early days of the neo-classical* style. A favourite of Mme. de Pompadour, he went, after her death in 1764, to Russia where he executed the colossal equestrian statue of Peter the Great at St. Petersburg. His most famous work is undoubtedly *La Baigneuse,* a standing nude exhibited at the Salon in 1757, and later copied in porcelain by a number of factories.

Two Wedgwood subjects are derived from this source:

Psyche, figure, height 8ins. The source is Falconet's marble (1757) which was copied in Sèvres* biscuit porcelain (1761). The model was supplied by John Flaxman, Senior* in 1781 and was produced in basaltes intermittently until the 1920s.

The companion figure of *Cupid Menaçant* (Cupid Threatening or Menacing), more convincingly described as *Cupid Sitting, Pensive,* was first produced by Sèvres in 1758.

Famille Rose

Chinese decoration distinguished by the use of an opaque enamel ranging in shade from pink to a purple-rose. The pigment, a crimson-purple discovered by Andreas Cassius of Leyden, Holland, before 1673, was introduced into China by Jesuit missionaries c.1685, appearing on Chinese porcelain before the end of the century. The finest *famille rose* porcelain was produced during the reign of Yung Chêng (1723-35). Thereafter it was exported in large quantities to Europe and the quality declined. The colour was developed at Meissen*, and at other German and French factories, particularly for porcelain decoration in the Chinese manner. In 1810 Wedgwood introduced a range of teaware, coffee ware, inkstands, flowerpots and ornamental pieces in black basaltes and *rosso antico** enamelled in this style of decoration.

Feather Edge. *A moulded feather-edge shape of the typical Wedgwood type. Queen's ware plate transfer-printed with the* Tea Party. *Wedgwood.*

Faun (Faunus)

Ancient minor Italian deity who protected agriculture and flocks. He later became identified with another rustic god, the Greek Pan*, and is similarly represented with goat's hooves and horns. Fauns may be defined as half-men half-goats with short horns, and may be identified with the Greek satyrs. Female fauns are referred to as fauna.

Wedgwood subjects:

Faun, figure, height 10¾ins., c.1773-74, attributed to Flaxman*, but more probably from a cast supplied by Flaxman Senior*.

Faun Running, figure, height 17ins., after Clodion*. Late 19th century (basaltes and Queen's ware). Pair to *Bacchante*.

Faun with Bacchus, group, height 17ins. Late 19th century.

Faun with Goat, figure, height 21ins., after Sansovino.

Faun with Flute, figure, height 17ins. Late 19th century.

Fauns Sacrificing, tablet, 8½ins. by 15ins., by Flaxman, 1777.

Faun with three Spartan Bacchantes, medallion by Pacetti*, c.1787.

Fauns (two), medallion by Angelini*, c.1787.

Fauns (two), Flaxman, 1776.

Piping Faun, medallion 4ins. by 3ins., 1773.

Piping Faun, medallion 4ins. by 3¾ins., by Flaxman, 1776.

Set of *Four Fauns*, medallions 9ins. by 7ins., representing childhood, adolescence, maturity and old age, 1773.

Faustina (fl.c.125-176)

Wife of the Emperor Marcus Aurelius Antoninus, noted for licentiousness. She intrigued with Avidius Cassius to replace her husband as emperor, and died, perhaps by her own hand, during his expedition to suppress a revolt.

Wedgwood subjects;

Faustina, bust, reworked by Hackwood* from a plaster cast obtained from Hoskins & Grant*, 1774.

Apotheosis of Faustina, attributed to Pacetti*, c.1787.

Faustina, portrait medallion, 1779.

Feather Edge

A moulded border decoration consisting of repeated feathery forms with barbs disposed diagonally to the edge. Its characteristics differ according to factory of origin. Wedgwood 'feathers' have seven barbs with a space between the third and fourth.

Federal Style

American term for the neo-classical style*. It includes the Empire and Regency aspects of neo-classicism, and refers particularly to the production of the craftsmen and cabinet makers of Boston, New York (e.g. Duncan Phyfe), Philadelphia and Salem during the period 1789-1812.

Feeding Bottle

A boat-shaped bottle completely enclosed except for a spout at one end and a hole in the top through which it was filled. Made for feeding infants and invalids. Wedgwood produced feeding bottles in Queen's ware, and occasionally in other bodies (e.g. cane ware*, drab* and coloured bodies*).

Feeding Cup

Type of spouted cup, partly covered, for feeding infants and invalids. They were made of cream-coloured ware, either plain or transfer printed.

Feeding Jug

Spouted jug or vessel for feeding invalids.

Ferrara Pattern

Transfer-printed pattern engraved by William Brookes* in 1832 and printed in dark blue, and brown. A purple version was introduced some years later. It depicts an Italian harbour

Ferrara Pattern. *Underglaze blue transfer-printed Ferrara pattern with deep floral border. First produced in 1832 from engravings by W. Brookes.* Wedgwood.

scene with the castle of the Dukes of Este to the left, a canal which connects the harbour with the river Po, and a group of shipping which was taken from a set of engravings published in 1832 under the title *Lancashire Illustrated*.

Festoon

A garland of flowers, fruit, leaves, or drapery supported at either end, and hanging in a natural curve. The motif is also known as a swag. Wedgwood used festoons in painted or moulded form, and they are a common neo-classical decorative feature. In a letter to Bentley of December, 1767, Wedgwood wrote: "We shall want many of this branch [Modellers] to work festoons and other ornaments upon Vases, free, without moulds, which Boys may be taught to do at moderate expense, and they will look infinitely richer than anything made out of moulds. Mr. Pickford has a Plaisterer who can do this sort of work in miniature (the size we shall want) and he will lend him to me to instruct some Pupils when I have any forward enough to put under him."

Festoon. *Three-colour jasper teapot, c.1790, ornamented with festoons dependent from rams' heads with ribbon-ties below a Vitruvian scroll frieze.* Hove Museum.

143

Fettling

The process of finishing a vessel before firing by removing cast and seam marks and other blemishes with the aid of a metal tool. The presence of cast and seam marks on pottery and porcelain is evidence of poor quality control, and, if very pronounced, is due to the use of worn working moulds (see: Moulds). Such seams do not occur on wares thrown on the wheel, but other blemishes need removal before firing.

Fiammingo, Il ('The Fleming')

See: François Duquesnoy.

Figures

The production of figures was never particularly favoured by Wedgwood, who considered that while his workmen were sufficiently occupied without them figures were better left to others. Bentley, if we can judge from Wedgwood's letters, did not favour the kind of figures made by the porcelain factories, which was probably the reaction of a fervent neo-classicist to a largely rococo concept. Wedgwood's objections seem to have been more on account of technical difficulties. On the 19th November, 1769, he wrote: "If there were any such thing as getting a sober figure-maker to bring up some Boys I should like to ingage in that branch. Suppose you inqre at Bow; I despair of any at Derby*."

The actual modelling in wax or clay was probably the least of Wedgwood's difficulties. He could easily have found modellers in London to do the work. The need was for workmen who could dissect the models, mould the various parts, cast them, put them together again, prop them for firing, and see them through the kiln. Repairers*, as these operatives were called, were not very numerous, and we find Wedgwood eagerly hiring one of them, Mr. Tebo*, in 1774, only to be disappointed that this repairer and modeller, who had worked at Bow in the early years, could not produce the kind of figures he required. Wedgwood thought Tebo incompetent, when he was really a rococo workman accustomed to porcelain, who was too set in his ways to change. Had Wedgwood succeeded in tempting other figure makers from Bow or Derby no doubt the verdict would have been the same. Wedgwood had to find his own workmen capable of working in the neo-classical* style to his exacting standards and train them himself.

In the 1770s, when Wedgwood was beginning to take the subject of figure modelling seriously, a considerable change was occurring in the industry as a whole. In 1752 J-J. Bachelier, art director at the factory of Vincennes (later to become the Royal factory of Sèvres*), introduced the use of white unglazed porcelain for figure work. These biscuit* figures were highly successful. In England the manufacture of biscuit porcelain figures was taken up at Derby, already specialising in figure making, and it was an obvious temptation to Wedgwood to enter this market with his so-called 'white terracotta'. This material was particularly suitable for figures in the neo-classical style. The influence of the white marble statuary being excavated at Pompeii* and Herculaneum*, that led to what André Malraux has well called the 'white world' of neo-classicism, still prevails in the popular conception of ancient civilisations.

Derby charged more for their biscuit figures than for their glazed and painted ones. Although the latter required more work, the glaze and enamelling covered many minor faults which would not have been accepted by the purchaser of a biscuit figure. Wedgwood had not developed the glazed and painted figure, and his models were unsuitable for this treatment. Imperfect wares, unless he was prepared to sell them as second quality, were wastage. Although, like all 18th century manufacturers, Wedgwood had his share of wares which had

Figures. *Black basaltes figure of Mercury, 12¾ ins. This figure, first catalogued in 1779, was modelled by Flaxman in 1777. The example illustrated belongs to the 19th century.* Sotheby's.

suffered some defect in manufacture, and therefore had to be sold as 'seconds', he nevertheless appreciated the harm that this did to the finer quality ornamental wares, and did not venture, without much forethought, into fields where 'seconds' were apt to be greater than average.

In 1770 and 1771 Wedgwood and his partner, Bentley, were giving a great deal of attention to the making of portrait busts* which were in demand for the decoration of libraries and galleries. Working on these busts in 1774 was William Hackwood*, hired in 1769, and in July 1774, Wedgwood wrote: "We are going on with the Busts, but ... whilst this business continues, we have no body to work at the Statues." We find a later reference to two Muses "model'd Statue size" from which we may reasonably infer that some extremely large figures were being attempted. The Wedgwood & Bentley Catalogue of 1779 lists several such figures: *Neptune*, 2ft., in height; *Triton*, 2ft. in height; *Polyphemus*, 19ins. by 16ins; *Morpheus*, a reclining figure 25ins. long, and the *Infant Hercules with the Serpent*, 20ins. high by 21ins. broad. These appear to be the largest figures made by any English factory during the 18th century, *Neptune* and *Triton* being three inches taller than Chelsea's* *Una and the Lion*. An Elephant 16½ ins. long by

Figures. *Wedgwood & Bentley period black basaltes figure of Voltaire, 11½ ins. high. This figure was also made in cane ware, but examples are extremely rare. It is thought to have been modelled by William Keeling. Sotheby's.*

14ins. high must have been an impressive beast, but no example is known and the mould has not survived.

The earliest figures go back to 1769, and include sphinxes*, tritons*, and lions. No lion seems to have survived, but no doubt it was one of the two models (i.e. standing or reclining) popular with the porcelain factories and taken from Renaissance sources. They were made from the terracotta* body by Boot*, who modelled for Wedgwood from 1769 to 1773 and was responsible for lions, tritons (figures and candlesticks*), and sphinxes (see: Egyptian taste). During the 1770s basaltes was employed as material for figure making on a fairly large scale, Wedgwood's object being to provide a chimneypiece* garniture which would be a mixture of figures and vases, instead of the customary combination of beakers and vases. To a lesser extent, jasper and cane ware* were also employed for figure making, although specimens are rare.

The moulds for the large figures (Wedgwood's 'Statues') were bought in 1770 from a London supplier of models and plaster casts, James Hoskins* of St. Martin's Lane, London. From 1769 to 1773 Hoskins was associated with Oliver in the firm of Hoskins & Oliver and later with James Grant as Hoskins & Grant. Hoskins supplied Wedgwood with both moulds and casts from 1769 to 1779. Hoskins & Oliver charged £5 for a "Mould for the Morpheus for pressing, cutting the model in pieces, and joining it together again after it was moulded." From this it is clear that Hoskins undertook to dissect the figure and mould its components, and obvious, too, that the moulds were used to take 'squeezes', and that slip casting* was not used. Production moulding and repairing*, of course, had to be done at Etruria, and probably between 1769 and 1773 the repairer was Boot.

Hoskins supplied the moulds for these figures, but the question remains: who supplied the models? In 1769, Peter Swift, Wedgwood's London agent, wrote to Etruria: "Mr Bacon brot. a model of *Apollo* and *Daphne* which I have got a cast of. He asks for your future instructions..." John Bacon*, of course, supplied Wedgwood with a good many models which are noted under his name. Among those which have been attributed to his hand are a *Triton* and a *Neptune* of 1769, and *Polyphemus*. The assumption that Bacon modelled some or all of these figures for Wedgwood, and that Swift arranged for Hoskins to cast them from the original clay, is a reasonable one, especially in view of the latter's later work for Etruria.

Theodore Parker* (modeller and supplier of plaster casts) worked for Wedgwood from 1769 to 1774. According to the Archives he modelled "statues of Flora, Seres [Ceres], Spencer, Hercules, Juno, Prudence, Milton, Shakespeare, a boy [on] a couch, and three doggs." Richard Parker* of London, modeller and maker of plaster casts, supplied Wedgwood with both casts and models from 1769 to some time after 1774. In the latter year he modelled a Zingara* figure, a Vestal*, and a pug dog*.

Hoskins supplied numerous moulds for busts as well as for figures. The figures are either unknown today, or are exceedingly rare, although they appeared in several catalogues (1773 and 1779, for instance). Probably very few were made in the first place, after which the moulds were stored, and the figures listed, in the hope of more orders for which the moulds were available.

The Wedgwood & Bentley Catalogue of 1779 includes the following, apart from the figures already quoted:

Ceres, a girl sitting.
Ganymede, from the Florentine Museum. 12ins.
Bacchus, after Sansovino. 11ins.
Bacchus, after Michelangelo. 11ins.
Egyptian Lions, from the Capitol (i.e. from the collection in the Capitoline Museum, Rome), 8½ ins. by 8ins.
Five Boys, from Il Fiammingo.
Egyptian Sphinxes*, a pair 6ins. long.
Sitting Sphinxes with nozzles, to hold candles. 10¾ ins.
Grecian Sphinxes, a pair 12ins. long.
Grecian Sphinxes, a pair 5ins. long.
Egyptian Sphinxes with the Lotus, to hold candles. 6ins. long.
Griffin, with nozzles to hold candles, 13ins. by 7ins.
Elephants, 16½ ins. long by 14½ ins. high.
A pair of *Tritons*, from Michelangelo, 11ins. high.
Bacchus, a statue 10¾ ins. high.
Fawn [sic], a statue 10¾ ins. high.
Two pug dogs*.
Apollo, a statue, 11ins.
Venus de Medici, 10½ ins.
Mercury, 11ins.
Voltaire* ('Mr de Voltaire'), 12ins.
Venus rising from the sea (upon a pedestal richly ornamented with figures [representing] the *Seasons*), 6½ ins.

Rousseau does not appear in the above list although modelled in 1779, probably too late for inclusion. This figure is attributed to Keeling*.

145

To this list may be added a number of other figures, like the jasper triton supporting a shell, which is a candlestick by Flaxman*, the pair of 'Rustic' candlesticks modelled by Hackwood, and Flaxman's jasper candlestick figures, *Cybele* and *Ceres,* which were made after 1779.

This section is mainly concerned with free-standing figures, but it would be incomplete without reference to figures employed for other purposes. Wedgwood found that figures were becoming less popular, and after Bentley's death in 1780 he tended to limit their use to the decoration of wares otherwise useful, such as candlesticks* and lamps*, or as paperweights, or as part of the ornamentation of vases — for example, the wine and water ewers, or a tripod basaltes incense burner with applied female grotesques.

A class of figure not hitherto discussed is those white figures made towards the end of the 18th century for Vulliamy*, who used them for decorating clocks. The mark is impressed where necessary on the sole of the foot, and can be seen only when the figure is removed from the clock case*. How numerous these figures may have been is not on record, and figures of this kind mounted on Vulliamy's clocks may sometimes be mistaken for Derby* biscuit figures. Derby were, at one time, thought to be Vulliamy's only supplier.

There is no documentary evidence that any creamware or pearl ware* figures were made during the lifetime of Josiah I, but a number of such figures exist, including those of *Faith, Hope,* and *Charity,* and a bust entitled *Sadness* (after a painting by Sassoferrato) all bearing the Wedgwood mark impressed. These are all recognisable in the style of the Wood family of Burslem and may have been made by them to the order of Wedgwood. They are probably the work of Enoch Wood*, whose elder brother, William* was a modeller at Etruria*.

During the 19th century figures continued to be modelled by such sculptors as Beattie*, and when Parian* porcelain was introduced for figure work Wedgwood produced Carrara* in competition. Nevertheless, in this period also figures did not

Finial. *Creamware coffee pot enamelled with bouquets of flowers and scattered sprigs in iron-red, lilac, yellow and green. 9¼ ins. high. The simple loop handle, domed cover, and pierced ball knop or finial are all characteristic of creamware pieces c.1765-75. Sotheby's.*

assume the same importance in the factory's productions as other wares, and specimens are distinctly rare. Decorative objects like the 'Majolica' *Dolphin,* the design inherited from the 18th century, occur occasionally. The 20th century has seen the well known figures by John Skeaping*, and Arnold Machin*.

There was, also, a series of basaltes animals and birds, modelled by Hubert Light between 1912 and 1920; and small statuettes (7ins.-8½ ins.) of Charles I, Cromwell, the Lady of the Lake, Olivia, Roderick Dhu, and the Vicar of Wakefield were produced in basaltes, c.1910.

See: Busts; Half-figures and Busts.

Filter

Large cylindrical vessel with a cover and spigot, containing a porous stone filter for the purification of water. Filters were made from the 1830s in large sizes of about five-gallon capacity for kitchens, and in smaller sizes for the table. They were usually of plain brown stoneware, often decorated with the royal coat of arms in relief, and are particularly associated with Doulton. A particularly fine and decorative Wedgwood jasper filter, 15ins. high, is in the Buten Museum*. It is marked 'Spencer's Patent Purifying Magnetic Filter' and was made in 1887.

Finger Vase (or Five-Finger Vase)

Vase with five flower holders arranged in a fan shape. Made in porcelain at Vienna, and of tin-glazed earthenware at Delft, they were also produced in 18th century creamware by Wedgwood and Leeds*. They have been reproduced intermittently by Wedgwood during the 19th and 20th centuries. Sometimes called a quintal flower vase.

Filter. *Spencer's Patent Magnetic Purifying Filter. Jasper, 15ins. high. 1887.* Buten Museum.

Finial

The terminal ornament of an object, but used particularly of a decorative handle or knop on the cover of a vase, teapot, coffeepot, covered bowl or tureen. Finials have been made in a great variety of forms, including figures, animals, flowers and fruits (especially the pineapple, the pine cone, and the acorn) and they are characteristic of their period and style: for instance, flowers and certain fruits, like the lemon, are typically rococo*, pineapples and acorns characteristic of neo-classicism*, and sphinxes* of the Empire of Regency styles. Knops particularly associated with Wedgwood are the widow* finial and the oval and round plumes; but animals, figures, fruit, flowers, vegetables and acorns are among those which occur on pieces of 18th and 19th century design. Rare finials of the Whieldon-Wedgwood* and Ivy House* periods include a bird in flight, a conch shell and a recumbent sheep.

Fire Speckling

Minute pieces of carbon or other material embedded in the glaze either during the original firing, or as a result of refiring to add enamel or transfer-printed decoration. Fire speckling often accompanies refiring which takes place at a considerable time after manufacture, and glaze which has been enamelled at a later date to enhance the value of a plain piece very often suffers in this way. At one point, however, Sadler & Green complained to Wedgwood that they were having trouble of this kind in firing printed ware, and suggested that the cause might be dampness in transport. The presence of this fault cannot be regarded as a certain indication of faking or redecoration at a much later date, and it should be considered in conjunction with the nature of the decoration.

Fireclays

Very refractory clays able to withstand extremely high temperatures without fusing. Clays of this kind are used in the making of saggars and kiln furniture generally.

Firecracks

Firecracks must be carefully distinguished from cracks due to damage which usually have a depressing effect on value unless a specimen is extremely rare. Firecracks are always slightly wider at one end, and are usually due to faulty design. The thicker parts of an object take up heat in the kiln more slowly than the thinner parts, and give it off more slowly during cooling. Unless this has been taken into account in the design, tensions are created which lead to the opening of firecracks, or to distortion. Firecracks are not, by themselves, a good reason

Firecracks. *Jasper Sphinx couchant with a candleholder between its wings. Well marked firecracks appear at the junction of the left paw with the body, just in front of the back paw which separates the body from the base, and in the region of the neck. The difficulties here apparent may have been the reason for later placing the candleholder on the head.* Liverpool City Museums.

for rejecting a specimen.

The term 'age crack' sometimes used is undesirable, because it does not define the nature of the crack, and leaves in doubt whether it is due to firing or later damage. No cracks occur as the result of age, so the term is, in any case, incorrect.

Firecracks are rare in any but 18th century work, and then only in early specimens as a general rule. In Wedgwood they are most frequent in basaltes, and they are sometimes to be found in early basaltes wares filled with some kind of bituminous substance to make them fit for sale.

Firecracks occur occasionally in early jasper tablets, but are rarely seen even in early creamware. Writing to Bentley in September 1776, referring to a jasper tablet, Wedgwood said: "...we have done with the cracking which teized [sic] us so much in former compositions, and only want a proper fire to make us absolute."

Firecracks sometimes occur today in the early stages of the production of new models, but they are usually eliminated by modifying the design before manufacture starts.

First Day's Vases

The manufactory of ornamental ware was removed to Etruria in 1769, and on the 13th June Bentley* came from Liverpool for an inaugural pot-making ceremony. He supplied the motive power for a wheel on which Wedgwood threw six copies of an 'Etruscan' vase in black basaltes. After firing, these vases were sent to London for decoration, where they were painted by David Rhodes*, probably assisted by William Craft*, in red encaustic enamel in imitation of ancient red-figure vases. The subject was *Hercules in the Garden of the Hesperides* on one side, and on the other, the following inscription:

'June XIII   M. DCC LXIX
One of the First Day's Productions
at
Etruria Staffordshire
by
Wedgwood & Bentley
Artes Etruriae Renascuntur'
(The Arts of Etruria are reborn)

The figures were taken from Hamilton's *Etruscan Antiquities* Vol. 1, Plate 129.

Fifty replicas were issued in 1930 to mark the bicentenary of Josiah Wedgwood's birth. These bear an inscription which gives the date of his birth (1730) and death (1795). The works at Etruria were closed finally on the 13th June, 1950, one hundred and eighty-one years after opening, and to commemorate the event six Last Day's Vases were produced.

Fish Lustre
See: Ordinary Lustres.

Fish-Tail Ewer
Ewer with a handle in the form of a scaled fish tail which curves in a semi-circle from centre to shoulder. There is a mask below the handle, and another below the spout, as well as festoons*, and a key fret* around the rim. The model, apparently in production in 1770, and often attributed to Flaxman, was inspired by a drawing in Stella's* *Livre de Vases aux Galeries du Louvre.* Wedgwood referred to them as 'Stella's ewers' in a letter to Bentley defining the difference between useful and ornamental wares of 3rd September, 1770. A French *faience* pot and cover with a similar handle is in the Victoria and Albert Museum.

Fish Trowel
A flat, trowel-like implement with a pierced blade and a handle, used for the service of fish, and made by Wedgwood

during the 18th century in cream-coloured ware. The shape is fairly common in silver, but pottery specimens are rare.

Flatware
Term applied to saucers, plates, round and oval dishes, platters, and trays. These wares are apt to warp in the kiln unless carefully placed.

Flaxman, John, RA (1755-1826)
English sculptor, draughtsman, and designer; the son of a modeller and maker of plaster casts at New Street, Covent Garden, London. Young Flaxman suffered from ill health in his early years, and his family were extremely poor. At first he was unable to walk, and passed his time sitting in his father's shop, drawing and learning to read. He was befriended by a local clergyman, who lent him books and taught him Latin and Greek. He started to model in wax and clay at an early age and showed great promise. As he grew older he was able to walk on crutches and, to relieve straitened family circumstances, he began to help his father. At the age of twelve he won the first prize of the Society of Arts for a medal, and soon afterwards enrolled at the Academy Schools. He first exhibited at the Academy in 1770, at the age of fifteen, and had come to the notice of Josiah Wedgwood by 1771, probably because some of the work attributed to his father was discovered to be by his hand. Wedgwood wrote to Bentley* regarding the visit of a

Flaxman, John, RA. *Detail from the portrait by George Romney.* National Portrait Gallery, London.

148

Mr. Freeman in that year: "He is a great admirer of young Flaxman, and has advised his father to send him to Rome... Mr Freeman says he knows young Flaxman is a coxcomb, but does not think him a bit the worse for it, or the less likely to be a great Artist." The earliest surviving bill for work done by the Flaxmans is dated March 1775, for the modelling of a pair of vases at three guineas, and a number of bas-reliefs* at 10s. 6d. each. The younger Flaxman did not set up his own establishment until 1782, when he married Ann Denman (a course of action that Sir Joshua Reynolds told him had "ruined him for an artist") and rented a small house in Wardour Street, London.

Early in 1784 Flaxman was designing ceilings and cornices for Wedgwood's drawing room at Etruria Hall and, although it is not certain that these were used, it is probable that they were, since the room, which is thought to have been painted by William Blake*, became a showpiece for visitors. At this time he was modelling the bust of Mrs. Siddons, a number of important portrait medallions*, and the first ceramic set of chessmen* to be made in modern Europe.

Three years later he went to Rome, where he remained until 1794. Partly subsidised by Wedgwood, who needed a supervisor for the designers and modellers he was employing there to copy antique friezes, Flaxman worked also on his own account, making a substantial reputation for himself not only as a sculptor but even more particularly as the illustrator of the *Iliad,* the *Odyssey,* the works of Dante, and the tragedies of Aeschylus, for which engravings from his drawings were made in Rome. He made the acquaintance of Canova*, who became his friend and one of his most fervent admirers.

After seven years in Italy, Flaxman returned to London and rented a house in Buckingham Street, Fitzroy Square, where he lived for the rest of his life. He devoted himself largely to monumental sculpture, but he maintained a friendly connection with the Wedgwoods and did a small amount of work for them. He also supplied important designs for Rundell, Bridge & Rundell, silversmiths to the Prince Regent. Sir Richard Westmacott, who followed him as Professor of Sculpture at the Academy, spoke of him as "the greatest modern sculptor." He was elected a Member of the Royal Academy in 1800.

Wedgwood's production in the 18th century would have looked very different without the work of Flaxman. He modelled not only bas-reliefs for tablets*, medallions and cameos*, but important portrait medallions, figures, chessmen, and vases, and almost anything requiring invention and artistry beyond the scope of modellers employed at the factory. The relationship between Flaxman and Josiah I provides an interesting illustration of the friendly working association between artist and manufacturer. Flaxman accepted Wedgwood's criticisms and suggestions, adapting his techniques to reproductive processes and benefiting from the disciplines imposed by them.

Flaxman was the most complete and the most consistent artist employed by Wedgwood in the 18th century, and, with the single exception of Hackwood*, he was also the most prolific. There has thus been some temptation to attribute to him all of Wedgwood's finest models. The list that follows is not definitive, but it includes the most important works which can be definitely or reliably attributed to Flaxman:

BUSTS

Fothergill*, Dr. John, 1781.
Rousseau*, Jean-Jacques, 1781.
Siddons, Sarah, c.1783-84.
Sterne*, Laurence, 1781.
Wedgwood, Josiah, marble bust in the Memorial Institute, Burslem.

FIGURES

Apollo, 11ins., 1777.
Ceres, seated.
Ceres, standing (attributed), figure for candlestick.
Cybele, standing (attributed), figure for candlestick.
Day, 1776.
Flora, seated, 1781.
Mercury (standing leaning on a tree stump), 11ins., 1777.
Venus rising from the sea (on *Seasons* pedestal), 1777 (attributed).

PORTRAIT MEDALLIONS

Banks*, Sir Joseph (3), 1775 and 1779.
Banks, Lady, 1779.
Boerhaave, Hermann, 1782.
Buchan, Dr. William, 1783.
Caroline, Princess of Wales (attributed), 1796.
Cats, Jacob (attributed), 1785.
Queen Charlotte* (attributed), c.1789.
Chatham, William Pitt, 1st Earl of, 1778.
Coligny, Louise de (attributed), c.1784.
Cooke, Captain James (2), 1777 and 1784.
de Ruyter, Michel, 1782.
de Witt, Cornelis, c.1782.
de Witt, Jan, c.1782.
Devonshire, Georgiana, Duchess of, 1782.
Edgeworth*, Honora Sneyd (attributed), 1780.
Ferdinand I, King of the Two Sicilies, 1781.
Flaxman, John (aged 14).
Flaxman, John, c.1787-94.
Flaxman, Mrs. Ann, c.1787-94.
Fothergill, Dr. John (attributed), c.1778-79.
Fox, Charles James (attributed), c.1790.
Franklin, Governor William (attributed), 1784.
Franklin, William Temple, c.1783.
George, Prince of Wales, later George IV (2).
Goethe, Johann Wolfgang von (attributed), c.1790.
Gustavus III, King of Sweden, 1784.
Hastings, Warren, 1784.
Hein, Peter, c.1782.
Herschel, Sir William (attributed), c.1781.
Hogerbeets, Rombout (attributed), c.1782.
Johnson, Samuel, 1784.
Julius Caesar*, 1776.
Kemble, John Philip (attributed), 1784.
Kortenaer, Egbert Meeuwszoon (attributed), c.1782.
Lever, Sir Ashton, 1781.
Liverpool, Charles Jenkinson, 1st Earl of, 1784.
Maria I, Queen of Portugal, 1787.
Meerman, Comte Johann, 1786.
Meerman, Anne, Comtesse, 1786.
Paul I, Emperor of Russia, 1782.
Pitt, William, the Younger, c.1787.
Reynolds*, Sir Joshua, c.1782-87.
Siddons, Sarah, 1782.
Solander*, Dr. Daniel Charles, 1775.
Victor Amadeus II, King of Sardinia, Duke of Savoy, 1788.

SMALL PORTRAITS

English Poets, set, 2ins. by 1¾ins., 1777.
Kings of England, part of the set of 36.

BAS-RELIEFS

Apollo (flanked by a tripod and his lyre on a pillar), cameo, 1775.
Apollo and Nine Muses. See separate entry under Muses.
Apotheosis of Homer (*Crowning of a Citharist* or *Homer and Hesiod*), bas-relief, 1777, adapted to Homeric Vase*, 1786.

Apotheosis of Virgil, 1785.
Ariadne, head, 1775.
Ariadne drawn by panthers, with Pan etc., c.1777.
Autumn, head, 1775.
Bacchanalian Triumph, remodelling (attributed).
Bacchus, head, 1777.
Birth of Bacchus (companion-piece to *Dancing Hours*), c.1788-90.
Blind Man's Buff (designed specifically for the decoration of teapots), 1782.
Boys playing marbles (designed for the decoration of teapots), 1782.
Ceres, head (attributed).
Citharist, see: *Apotheosis of Homer**.
Commercial Treaty with France, 1787.
Conquered Province, 1775.
Coriolanus with his wife and mother persuading him to return [sic] to Rome (they were in fact, persuading him to stay away), see below: *Veturia and Volumnia*.
Cupid riding on a Lion (The Power of Love), 1776.
Cupid seated under a tree.
Cupid with Wreath, 1787.
Cupids with Goat, see below: *Sacrifice to Hymen.*
Cupids with festoons of Laurel.
*Dancing Hours**, 1775. See separate entry.
Diana visiting Endymion, 1787.
Diomedes carrying away the Palladium, c.1776.
Fame.
Farnese Hercules, 1776.
Fauns sacrificing, 1777.
Figure [male] with greyhound, c.1776.
Flora, head, c.1776.
Hebe and the Eagle, c.1777.
Hercules, 1776.
Hercules and the Erymanthean Boar, 1775.
Hercules binding Cerberus, 1775.
Hercules in the Garden of the Hesperides, 1787.
Hercules strangling the Nemean Lion, 1775.
Hippocrates, c.1782.
Hope, 1775.
Hygeia, c.1775.
Indian Bacchus, 1776.
Isis, head, 1776.
Juno, standing with sceptre, 1775.
Jupiter with thunderbolt, 1775.
Justice, 1775.
Marriage of Cupid and Psyche. See separate entry.
Medea, 1776.
Medea rejuvenating Jason's father, 1776.
Medusa, head, 1776.
Meleager, 1775.
Mercury, bust, height 18½ ins., from a model exhibited at the Royal Academy, 1782.
Mercury joining the hands of Britain and France (Webber's* design), 1787.
Mercury with caduceus (attributed).
Minerva, 1775.
Muses, see separate entry.
Muses watering Pegasus in Helicon (attributed).
Omphale with the club of Hercules, cameo, 1776.
Omphale in Lion's skin, cameo, 1776.
Pan, head (pair to *Syrinx** below), 1776.
Peace preventing Mars from breaking open the doors of the Temple of Janus, 1787.
Perseus and Andromeda, c.1776.
Piping Faun, 1776.

Sacrifice to Ceres (also attributed to Webber), c.1779.
Sacrifice to Cupid (attributed).
Sacrifice to Hymen, 1778.
Sacrifice to Love, 1778.
Sacrifice to Pan, 1778.
Sappho, 1775.
Seven Cupids (playing music, dancing etc.), c.1785.
Shell Venus, 1781.
Silenus and Boys, 1776.
Sophonisba, 1776.
Spring, head, 1775.
Summer, head, 1775.
Syrinx, head, (pair to Pan* above), 1776.
Triumph of Cupid (two versions), 1782 (designed for the decoration of teapots).
Triumph of Silenus, c.1778.
Triumph of Venus (attributed), 1777.
Venus bound by two Cupids, 1790.
Venus captive.
Vestal, c.1777.
Veturia and Volumnia entreating Coriolanus, 1784.
Volumnia (wife of Coriolanus) after d'Hancarville* II. pl.26.
Vulcan with Mars and Venus in a Net, c.1778.
Winged Cupid upon a Swan.
Winter, head, 1775.

OTHER WORK OF IMPORTANCE
Borghese Vase, finishing work by De Vaere*.
Frog (Catherine) Service*, models of new tableware shapes, including vegetable tureen.
Chessmen, 1783-85.
Flower pots, two modelled in 1785.
Homeric (Pegasus) Vase and Pegasus finial, c.1785.
Wine and Water (*Satyr* and *Triton*) ewers, 1775, after antique models and perhaps supplied as casts by Flaxman Senior.
See also the list of work attributed to John Flaxman Senior, some of which may have been, either wholly or in part, the work of his son.

Flaxman, John, Senior (1726-1795)
Modeller and maker of plaster casts; employed as modeller by Louis-François Roubiliac* and Peter Scheemakers* (1691-1781), and subsequently supplied plaster casts of busts

Flaxman, John, RA. *Jasper portrait medallion of John Flaxman, RA. A self-portrait thought to have been modelled, with the portrait of his wife, when he was in Italy between 1787 and 1794.* Wedgwood.

Colour Plate XI

Right: Tea Caddy. Tortoiseshell and ribbed ivory tea caddy, height 5¾ ins., inset with gold-mounted blue and white jasper cameos. c.1800. Nottingham Castle Museum. Photo: Reilly/Charles Letts.

Below: Two chambersticks in green and blue jasper dip, height 3½ ins. and 2¼ ins., and a solid blue jasper 'reading' candlestick, height 5½ ins. The green chamberstick is provided with a loop to hold a snuffer. Chambersticks c.1810; 'Reading' candlestick c.1790. Nottingham Castle Museum. Photo: Reilly/Charles Letts.

Flora. *Large blue and white jasper tablet,* Sacrifice to Flora, *also known as* Offering to Flora, *length 18ins., modelled by William Hackwood in 1777.* Wedgwood.

and figures to Wedgwood, some of which may have been from his own original models. The elder Flaxman was probably supplying Wedgwood with casts as early as 1771, since in February of that year Wedgwood wrote to Bentley: "Concerning busts, I suppose those at the Academy are less hackneyed and better in general than the Plaister shops can furnish us with; besides it will sound better to say — This is from the Academy, taken from an original in the Gallery of &c. than to say we had it from Flaxman." The earliest surviving invoice from Flaxman, however, appears to be that of 25th March, 1775, and it is receipted by John Flaxman* Junior on behalf of his father.

The work of the elder Flaxman for Wedgwood has become inextricably confused with that of his son. The younger Flaxman was employed by Wedgwood in 1775, and had won the Gold Medal of the Society of Arts at the age of fourteen. It is certain that he helped his father even earlier, and there is good reason to suppose that some of the casts and models on the earliest invoice are his work. Thus, even the famous *Wine* and *Water* ewers, invariably attributed to the younger Flaxman, may have been casts supplied by his father. It has become acceptable to assign to Flaxman Senior the bas-reliefs* of *Melpomene, Thalia, Terpisichore, Euterpe, Sappho, Apollo, Bacchus, Ariadne,* the *Four Seasons, Jupiter, Juno, Minerva, Justice, Hope,* and the set of three bas-reliefs depicting *Hercules and the Nemean Lion, Hercules and the Calydonian Boar,* and *Hercules and Cerberus,* all of which appear on the 1775 invoice signed by the younger Flaxman for his father. For some reason it is considered less acceptable to assign to the elder Flaxman the *Wine* and *Water* ewers on the same invoice. Since both Flaxmans were modellers and makers of casts, this problem is unlikely to be finally resolved.

Flemish Ware

An earthenware of variable colour between grey-green and bluish-sage which in shapes, glaze textures, and finish is similar to the drab* and lavender* bodies. It was introduced c.1870 but appears to have been withdrawn after only a few years, probably because of unacceptable variations in colour.

Flint

A kind of silica in the form of quartz crystals in combination with molecules of water. When it is calcined at about 400°C it can easily be crushed and powdered. It was employed by Wedgwood in both cream-coloured ware and pearl ware, helping to confer additional strength, freedom from warping, and lightness of colour.

Flint Ware

Term for salt-glazed stoneware* which contains flint*.

Flora

Roman goddess of flowers and spring. The half-length figure of the goddess appears in relief on salt-glaze* wall vases in the form of cornucopiae*, probably modelled by William Greatbatch* for Whieldon* or Wedgwood (though similar models were made at Leeds). A seated figure of Flora was modelled in 1781 by John Flaxman*, and to him is also attributed a head of the goddess. A statue of Flora was also supplied by Theodore Parker* in 1769, and this is probably the figure which later appeared in jasper* with the same artist's figure of Ceres*. The relief *Sacrifice to Flora* was modelled by Hackwood in 1777.

Florentine Pattern

Wedgwood's most popular and successful bone china* tableware pattern, introduced c.1880 and redesigned by Victor Skellern* in 1935. The border of grotesques* has its source in Urbino maiolica. The pattern exists in a great variety of colours — green, turquoise, dark blue, coral and yellow enamel over an outline print — and as a gold print (latterly silk-screen*) on white, ivory, dark ('Arras') green, ruby, and dark ('Mazarine') blue grounds.

Flötner, Peter (c.1485-1546)

A Swiss bronze sculptor who was working in Nürnberg in 1522. His work suggests that he had spent some time in Italy. Bronzes by him are rare, and are often doubtfully attributed. A Wedgwood subject, *Terpsichore* (see: Muses) is thought to have been derived from this source.

Flute and Wreath Pattern

See: Lag and Feather pattern.

Folgham, John (fl.1780-1790)

Case and cabinet maker of 81, Fleet Street, London. Folgham appears to have made cases and cabinets for housing cameos and intaglios, and boxes for chessmen. It is also probable, to interpret a letter he wrote to Byerley in 1788, that he was selling Wedgwood's chessmen ready boxed.

Follot, Paul (1877-1941)

French interior designer who worked in the art nouveau and art deco styles. He specialised in luxury furniture, and during the 1930s was co-director with Chermayeff of Waring & Gillow's French furniture department. Before this he had been director of the Pomona workshops of Bon Marché, Paris. For Wedgwood he designed the *Sylvia* pattern in grey and platinum on bone china in 1922.

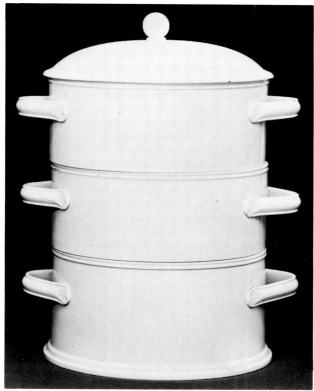

Food Carrier. *Three-tier food carrier in Queen's ware. 18th century.* Wedgwood.

Fonts

Wedgwood is known to have made four baptismal fonts. All are of basaltes*, and two of the four were made for the Whitbread family. A third was made for a church with which the Whitbreads had connections. Samuel Whitbread, founder of the famous firm of brewers, and father of the Whig politician, was an enthusiastic buyer of Wedgwood wares, and relations between him and Josiah I were cordial, despite a sharp letter of rebuke which followed the discovery of an error in Wedgwood's handling of one of his orders.

The first font was made in 1778 for the church of Essendon, Hertfordshire. It is in the form of a large footed bowl, 22ins. diameter and 14ins. high. The lip is finished with a border of banded reeds, similar to the inner moulding of frames* used for the Herculaneum Subjects*, and the body of the bowl is ornamented with simple festoons of folded drapery suspended from rings attached to a turned bead. This was presented to the church in the name of Samuel Whitbread's daughter, Mary. Five years later her half-sister, Harriet, presented a similar font to the church of Cardington, Bedfordshire, and a third of the same shape appears to have been made for Melchbourne, Bedfordshire, in 1788 (probably the example now in the Buten Museum*). The fourth, a smaller and shallower font, 16½ ins. diameter and 11ins. high, was presented by Josiah I to the church of Moreton Say, Shropshire, in 1788. It was subsequently bought from the church by Sir Joseph Dalton Hooker*, and is now in the Lady Lever Art Gallery, Port Sunlight.

Each of these fonts was originally supplied with a basaltes pedestal, about 10ins. high, ornamented in relief with a design of bell flowers and acanthus leaves. This served as a pedestal for the font itself, and also as a pedestal, inside the font, for the

silver-gilt bowl of kylix form which held the holy water for a christening service.

It is probable that more Wedgwood fonts, now used for secular purposes, exist unrecognised.

Food Carrier

A utensil consisting of several flat-bottomed bowls with handles which fit into one another, the bottom bowl containing hot water, the top one with a cover. Used for keeping food warm, the type was made by Wedgwood in cream-coloured ware. It may originally have been inspired by Chinese porcelain, where food warmers of this type are well known.

Food Warmer

Also called a *veilleuse* and, in the 18th century, a night lamp, this is a composite creamware utensil of several pieces, usually about 12ins. high. It consists of a cylindrical pedestal, into the top of which is fitted a flanged bowl. The pedestal rests on a base, and immediately above the base is an arched opening for the insertion of a small lamp *(godet)*. The pedestal is pierced with holes to allow a free circulation of air, and the bowl has a cover. When the bowl is intended to be filled with water, and to heat another bowl fitting into it, then it is a *bain marie*. With a teapot it becomes a tea warmer, or *théière*. The 1774 Catalogue has the entry "Night-lamps, to keep the Liquid warm all night."

18th century Wedgwood food warmers were of plain cream-ware, but specimens decorated in underglaze blue* transfer printing have been noted dating from about 1840.

Foot Bath

A deep basin, usually oval in shape and with two lateral handles, used for washing or soaking the feet. Until about 1820 the sides were vertical, sometimes with hooped bands or moulded decoration. Later examples had curved sides and more ornate handles. Shapes 1331 and 1332 in Wedgwood's first shape drawing book illustrate two leg pans with vertical sides. The 1880 Catalogue of Shapes illustrates shape 1331 and another with curved sides, No.2139 Chatsworth shape, both described as foot pans.

From about 1820 Wedgwood made foot baths with under-glaze blue* transfer-printed decoration, and these were also produced by many other Staffordshire pottery manufacturers. Today they are much in demand as *jardinières*.

Foot Bath. *Oval pearl ware foot bath (leg pan), 19ins. long, decorated with underglaze blue print of the Water Lily pattern, c.1810-20.* Buten Museum.

Foot Pan
See: Foot Bath.

Ford, G.
Engraver who worked for Wedgwood, 1842-43.

Fothergill, Dr. John, FRS (1712-1786)
Quaker physician; MD, Edinburgh; FRS, 1763; Fellow of the Royal Society of Medicine in Paris, 1776. At Upton, Essex, Fothergill possessed one of the finest Botanical Gardens in Europe, a collection of shells and insects, and one of natural history drawings. The drawings were eventually bought by Catherine II* of Russia. His portrait by Hogarth is at the College of Physicians, and Wedgwood produced a jasper medallion which was listed in the 1779 Catalogue, probably taken from a Medical Society medal of 1773 by Lewis Pingo (see: Thomas Pingo). Wedgwood and Dr. Fothergill corresponded from about 1766 and he was one of the inner circle of friends who knew of Wedgwood's experiments towards the invention of jasper. In 1776 Wedgwood refers to a formula probably intended for bronzing frames and mounts which had been given to him by Fothergill.

Fothergill, Dr. John. *Jasper portrait medallion, probably from a Medical Society medal by Lewis Pingo dated 1773 and first listed in the 1779 Catalogue.* Reilly.

Fox's Patent Milk and Soup Pan
A pan for separating two liquids of different densities, such as milk from cream, or soup from fat. It has two pouring lips, one below the other, the lower of the two being connected by a hole with the bottom of the pan. By tilting the pan to an angle sufficient to allow the liquid to flow only from the lower of the two pouring lips, the liquid in the lower part of the vessel may be drawn off, leaving behind that floating on its surface. It is illustrated in the 1880 Shape Book. The principle is the same as that of the French porcelain gravy-boat made to separate gravy from fat.

Frames
Josiah Wedgwood expressed his opinion of ceramic frames in a letter to Bentley* dated 8th January, 1775: "I think it impossible for us to make any frames of *pottery*, however fine or coloured, that will not degrade the gem or picture." Few collectors of old Wedgwood would agree with this view, and it is a surprising one to come from a potter who had already made frames of splendid quality for plaques and medallions.

Among the earliest Wedgwood frames were those made for the Herculaneum Subjects*. These were produced in circular or oval shapes and in three patterns: an inner border of reeds bound with crossed straps within an outer frame of fluted cavetts; a similar double border without the crosssed straps; and a wide concave or 'dished' inner border of cavetts within an outer band of laurel. These were made in basaltes or white terracotta, sometimes gilt, by 1772, and later in jasper. Large portrait medallions, and the plaques after Guglielmo della Porta* were among the subjects similarly framed. These plaques and medallions, intended "for inlaying. . . in the Pannels of Rooms" and as "Tablets for Chimneypieces" were seldom marked, and the frames were "modelled and burnt together with the bas-reliefs."

Later, Wedgwood experimented with frames made separately, and this allowed for the use of differert colours and bodies. The most effective were probably those made in *rosso antico* * with black reliefs, or the basaltes frames for blue and white jasper medallions, but they were never made in large quantities and are now extremely rare. In the 19th and 20th centuries, simple laurel frames for portrait medallions have been made in basaltes and jasper.

Fratoddi
Modeller in Rome* in 1787 under Flaxman* and Webber*.

Frederick The Great (1712-1786)
King of Prussia, son of Frederick William I of Prussia and Sophia Dorothea, daughter of George I of England. Frederick was an able and enlightened ruler, who laid the foundations of Prussia's future greatness. He wrote extensively on political matters and philosophical subjects, and was extremely popular in England, especially during the Seven Years' War (1756-63). The resource, courage, and genius he displayed during his military adventures earned him the sobriquet of 'the Great.' During the Seven Years' War he occupied the Meissen* factory, and after the War he acquired the Berlin porcelain factory which he had previously patronised.

There are three portrait medallions — an oval of about 1779 from a medal (which also exists in circular form) and a small medallion reversed from the first mentioned, produced before 1780. A third was produced c.1779-80. All were marked 'Wedgwood & Bentley'. An unmarked black basaltes bust, erroneously described as Frederick the Great, was sold at Christies* on 8th July, 1969. It is, except for the pedestal, identical to a marked Turner* white jasper bust of Voltaire* after Houdon*. No Wedgwood bust has been discovered and none is listed in Wedgwood's Catalogues*.

A transfer-printed portrait of Frederick the Great, after the portrait by Antoine Pesne and engraved by W.W. Ryland, appears on a creamware teapot, first mentioned by Wedgwood in 1763. From Josiah's correspondence with Sadler*, who supplied the engravings and printed the ware, it is evident that two sizes of teapot were engraved, and there may also have been a mug and a jug. The 'King of Prussia' was a popular print on Battersea enamel and on Worcester* porcelain.

French Commercial Treaty, 1786

As early as 1772 Josiah Wedgwood was seeking to influence English politicians to negotiate a trade treaty with France. An early attempt to enter the market is discussed in the entry relating to the Duc de Choiseul-Amboise*, and since that time Wedgwood had neglected no opportunity of achieving his aim, issuing catalogues in French, and maintaining whatever commercial connections with France were possible. Catalogues in French, of course, were not wholly directed to France. At the time French was the language of the Court in Germany and Russia, where Wedgwood found fewer obstacles to trade. Trade in pottery and porcelain with France was exceptionally difficult, since the import of both was prohibited. The earliest French porcelain factories, and many of the *faience* potteries, had been established with the aid of the aristocracy. Louis XV had, through Mme. de Pompadour, assisted in the founding of the Sèvres porcelain factory, and after 1756 was the principal shareholder. A number of Edicts had been promulgated in favour of the factory, prohibiting the manufacture of porcelain elsewhere, and even limiting the *faience* factories to painting in blue only, polychrome decoration being reserved for Sèvres. Even during the lifetime of Louis XV these Edicts were, to some extent, disregarded by factories under the patronage of members of the royal family. Chantilly for example was owned by the Prince de Condé, and *faience* factories were apt to add more colour to their palettes according to their distance from Paris. It was not until the accession of Louis XVI in 1774, however, that restrictions were noticeably eased. Even so, most of the small porcelain factories which grew up in and around Paris especially were still under the protection of members of the royal family and the aristocracy, including one patronised by Marie-Antoinette. Only the factory at Pont-aux-Choux*, Paris, made earthenware in the manner of Wedgwood, although one or two small factories started by Englishmen, such as the Leigh* brothers at Douai, copied the creamware of Wedgwood and Leeds. An Edict reviving former prohibitions was promulgated in 1784, but by 1787 this had dwindled in force to a point where French factories were only forbidden to copy the products of Sèvres without permission from the King. That these prohibitions were understood by Wedgwood may

French Commercial Treaty, 1786. Mercury uniting the hands of Britain and France. *Blue and white jasper plaque, 9ins. by 9⅝ins. 1787.* Christie's.

French Commercial Treaty, 1786. *Original block mould for the plaque.* Wedgwood.

be seen from his letter to Choiseul in which he refers to English creamware being contraband in France, but his own understanding of the market seems to have been deficient because, in a letter of 30th June, 1786, to William Eden (Lord Auckland*), he does not seem to have grasped the true difference between *poterie* and *fayence*. The proposed duty on *poterie* was 1 livre 8 sols, and on *fayence,* 20 sols per 100 lbs. (French currency at the time was divided into Livres, Sols, and Deniers, the origin of the English £.s.d.)

Faience is tin-enamelled ware (the same as *delft* or *maiolica*), a type of ware never made by Wedgwood. *Poterie* is lead glazed earthenware, such as creamware, also called in France *faience-fine* or *faience anglaise*. A low-fired ware covered with a transparent glaze falls into this category, but true *faience* is excluded. Stoneware is *grès,* and the term *porcelaine* admits of no mistake.

Wedgwood, however, regarded the difference between *poterie* and *fayence* as residing in the decoration. The difficulty may have been one of translation, since similar errors are made by modern translators. Also Wedgwood had never even displayed an interest in tin-enamelled ware, apart from attempts to recruit painters from this source. Eventually the difficulties were settled to the satisfaction of the Staffordshire potters by the imposition of an *ad valorem* duty of twelve per cent.

The Treaty was signed in September 1786, and was ratified by Parliament in the following year. In 1786 Wedgwood wrote to Flaxman* discussing medallions to commemorate the event, which, he suggested, should be scrupulously impartial. Writing to William Eden on 16th June, 1787, Wedgwood refers to an agreement he had concluded with Dominique Daguerre*, a furniture dealer of Paris who supplied the Court, and a merchant named Sykes* of Paris and Bordeaux. He sent them "a considerable assortment", saying "I have refused many other correspondents..." Two medallions were modelled to commemorate the Treaty; one showed Mercury as

the god of Commerce joining the hands of Britain and France, and the other was *Peace preventing Mars from bursting open the Temple of Janus.*

See: Catalogues; French Ware; Sèvres.

French Revolution

In common with many Englishmen of liberal opinions and Whig persuasion, Josiah Wedgwood warmly welcomed the French Revolution. He wrote, on 29th August, 1789: "I have no fears, as an Englishman, from the French nation obtaining their liberty, but join... in the truly liberal sentiments that the diffusion of liberty through any nation will add to the security and happiness of the neighbouring ones." Later, as the mindless violence of the revolutionaries became apparent, he changed his mind. Meanwhile, however, he hastily adapted the Sydney Cove* medallion to the requirements of the moment, endowing the figure of *Peace* with a staff surmounted by the Phrygian cap of revolution, and hanging the French King (not too subtly symbolised by a shield bearing the royal *fleur-de-lis*) from a pillar. This thinly disguised political medallion occurs in at least two versions.

French Revolution. *France greeted by Athene, goddess of Wisdom, in the presence of Fortuna standing on an altar. 1789.* Wedgwood.

French Ware

In the early months of 1765 Josiah Wedgwood wrote to his brother, John, that he was about to attempt "the French ware" in earnest, but a month later he wrote again saying that he did not intend to make the French white ware at Burslem, but was considering more convenient premises elsewhere for the purpose. It is difficult to be sure exactly what he meant by 'French ware', but it is evident that it was white, and a great deal of French porcelain, apart from that made at Sèvres, was white, or very sparsely coloured. This was because colouring was forbidden to any but the Sèvres factory by Royal Edict, although these Edicts were somewhat relaxed after the death of Mme. de Pompadour in 1764. The reference might have been to the porcelain of Saint-Cloud or Mennecy, which Wedgwood

French Revolution. *Two medallions, one hastily adapted from the Sydney Cove medallion, to celebrate the French Revolution, which was at first applauded by liberal opinion in England. The figure of Peace, now perhaps intended as Fortuna or Concordia, is provided with a staff surmounted by the Revolutionary Phrygian cap, and a shield bearing the royal fleur-de-lys (representing Louis XVI) is symbolically hung from a pillar or discarded against it. These medallions provide admirable examples of Wedgwood's commercial opportunism. 1789-90. Wedgwood.*

could have seen, since specimens were not uncommon in England; or it is possible that *faience* (tin-enamelled ware) was intended. This, too was either decorated in blue, or sparingly in enamel colours, since the *faience* factories were subject to the same Edicts. Wedgwood eventually produced a white body (pearl ware) but it is doubtful if this is what he meant. It seems most likely that he was referring to porcelain. For years Wedgwood harboured an ambition to make porcelain, and when he perfected black basaltes he referred to it as his "black porcelane." From his later letters to Bentley* it is obvious that not only had he studied the problems of porcelain manufacture in considerable detail, but he was well aware of the difficulties of making the kind of porcelain then being produced by most English factories, apart from Bristol. Here he could, no doubt, have succeeded, but Richard Champion's* patent stood in his way, and by the time Champion was willing to sell his patent Wedgwood had successfully produced his jasper ware and was no longer interested. Bentley, in particular, was very apprehensive of infringing this patent, and urged his partner not to allow jasper to be fired at a temperature which would make it translucent. Some examples of 18th century jasper do, in fact, possess this property.

Fret

A decorative border pattern of continuous repetitive form made by short lines of equal length meeting, usually, at an angle of 90° or occasionally at a slightly greater or lesser angle. Fret patterns are either painted, printed, or incised, and occur as decoration on both classical and neo-classical pottery, as well as in Chinese decorative art. They are also sometimes referred to as *meanders*.

Frog Service

A service made to the order of Catherine II* (the Great) of Russia in 1773-74. It was intended for the Palace of Chesman at La Grenouillière (the place of frogs) near Petrodvorets, and each piece bore the crest of a green frog. According to Bentley* the service comprised 952 pieces of Queen's ware worth £51 in the undecorated state. It was hand-painted in a mulberry-coloured enamel (which Bentley described as "delicate black" and Mrs. Delaney as "a purple") with 1,244 "real Views of Great Britain", all different. Dr. Williamson (*The Imperial Russian Service*, 1909) gives a total of 760 pieces and 1,282 views, but Bentley's figures are confirmed by the inscription preserved on the base of a monteith* on show in the Hermitage Museum, Leningrad, where the service is now displayed. The manufacturing cost of this service is believed to have been approximately £2,600, but the records are not clear. The price received was only £2,700, and the eventual profit accruing to Wedgwood was therefore negligible. At the outset, Wedgwood considered that two to three years would be needed to complete the order; in fact it was finished in less than twelve months.

The investment involved was substantial, and there was a considerable risk, which did not escape Wedgwood, that the service might never be paid for — a difficulty later experienced by the Sèvres* factory when they supplied an expensive service to the same patron. There was also the important consideration that much of the partners' time and the output of the Chelsea Decorating Studio* would be swallowed up by this order to the detriment of normal production.

This important commission came to Wedgwood through Alexander Baxter, the Englishman acting as Russian consul in London. Lord Cathcart*, who had originally introduced Wedgwood's wares into Russia when he was ambassador to Catherine's Court, played no part in obtaining this particular order, which was the second tableware commission received from this source (see: Husk Service).

The decoration of the Frog service was much more ambitious than anything Wedgwood had hitherto attempted. The painting was done at the Chelsea Decorating Studio, and it demanded the finding and training of additional painters. Each piece was to be painted with an important English landscape, a country house, or some well-known landmark. In

Frog Service. *Glacier from the Frog service with three 'widows' grouped to form the finial. 1773-74.* Photo: Wedgwood.

Frog Service. *Cup and saucer from the Frog service. The wide interior border does not appear on other pieces. 1773-74.* Wedgwood.

Frog Service. *Tureen, the cover painted with a view near Ludlow Castle, Shropshire. 1773-74.* Photo: Wedgwood.

159

Frog Service. *Trial, without the 'Frog' crest. The interior of a square compôtier, painted with a view of Stoke Gifford in Gloucestershire. 1773.* Wedgwood.

April 1773, Wedgwood found it necessary to travel to London to discuss the project, and wrote to Bentley: "Dare you undertake to paint the most embellish'd Views, the most beautiful Landskips, with Gothique ruins, Grecian Temples, and the most Elegant Buildings, with hands who have never attempted anything except Huts and Windmills upon Dutch Tiles at three-halfpence a dozen?" He estimated the total costs at £3,000-£4,000. To reduce these he rejected the first trial specimens in polychrome enamels and adopted instead the "rich mulberry purple" for the views. The use of monochrome enamel not only demanded less skill from the painters and reduced the number of firings in the muffle kiln*, but also made it easier for the views to be copied directly from prints. Nevertheless, the complicated inner borders of the dinner-service pieces, and the intricacy of the painting of the cups, could not be simplified and the whole project remained both formidable and expensive.

By July 1773, Wedgwood was getting to grips with the problem of finding twelve hundred views, heartened by an agreement with the Empress on the subject of cost and finance. In his letter to Bentley at that time he proposes to have some real views taken of Trentham, Booth, Swinnerton, Shugborough, Ingestre and other places in the vicinity of Etruria*. He sent draughtsmen all over the country to obtain "real views of real places" using a *camera obscura*, ransacked the print shops, and applied to his friends and patrons for the loan of books of views. "Pray have you Wilson's views of different places in Wales?" he asked Bentley, "If you have not, Mr. Sneyd* will lend them us... There is another source for us besides the published views and the real parks and gardens, I mean the paintings in most Nobleman's and Gentlemen's houses of real views which will be sketched from by some of our hands at less expense than we can take real views, but I hope prints may be picked up to go a great way, or we shall be sadly off, *as they are to be number'd and nam'd.*" The

authors' italics draw attention to Wedgwood's reference to the naming and numbering of views, a new departure in ceramic decoration. Topographical painting on pottery and porcelain achieved wide popularity soon after the completion of this service, and among the porcelain factories it formed a distinct category referred to as 'Named Views'. It is also interesting to recall that the Creil* factory of northern France early in the 19th century made creamware services decorated with transfer prints of the seats of English noblemen.

In June 1774, Wedgwood & Bentley's new showroom opened in Greek Street*, Soho. Wedgwood journeyed to London for the occasion, and wrote to Richard Wedgwood (his father-in-law) at Etruria on 31st May: "At last we have fitted up our new Rooms at Greek Street so far as to be able to set out the Russian service with some Vases &c, to be seen there, and tomorrow we advertise and open them for that purpose." Mrs. Delaney confided to her diary: "I am just returned from viewing... the Wedgwood Ware that is to be sent to the Empress of Russia. It consists, I believe, of as many pieces as there are days in the year, if not hours. They are displayed at a house in Greek Street, Soho, called Portland House; there are three rooms below and two above filled with it, laid out on tables, everything that can be needed to serve a dinner..." Wedgwood suggested closing the exhibition after 8th July, but before this was done it was visited by Queen Charlotte*. Sample plates painted in polychrome and monochrome exist outside Russia, some of which lack the frog crest.

The following artists are believed to have been employed on the decoration of the service:
Armstrong, S.; Bakewell, J.*; Barrett, J.: Cooper, D.; Cooper, N.; Dent, Miss C.; Englefield, J.; Glisson, Miss; Glover, T.; Henshaw, W.; Hutchins, T.; Isaacs, Miss; Linley, J.; Mence, W.; Mills, Miss A.; Mills, T.; Pars,* Miss; Quirk, W.; Roberts, Miss A.; Roberts, Miss G.; Roberts, J.; Seigmund, G.; Shuter, W.; Simcock, T.; Simons, G.;

Thomas, W.; Unwin,* R.; Vitalba (or Nitalba); Wallace, N.; Willcox,* R.; Willcox,* Mrs. C.. The work was supervised by David Rhodes*, and pieces of the service, which did not already exist in acceptable form, were modelled by Flaxman*.

Fruit Lustre
See: Ordinary Lustres.

Frye, Thomas (1710-1762)
Irish portrait painter, miniaturist, and engraver in *mezzotinto*. A Quaker, born in Dublin, he took out a patent for the manufacture of porcelain in 1748, specifying the use of Cherokee* clay. He was also the first to use calcined* bones (bone ash) in porcelain manufacture. Until 1762 he was the manager of the Bow* Porcelain Factory. His daughter, Catherine, married Ralph Willcox*, and was employed by Wedgwood at the Chelsea Decorating Studios*.

Fumigating Ribbon Holder
A container in blue and white jasper for holding a volatile fumigating liquid which evaporated from a wick protruding through a slot in the cover. Like the earlier pot-pourri vase, it operated on the principle of replacing an unwanted smell with one which was stronger and more tolerable. Impressed mark: 'WEDGWOOD. PIESSE & LUBINS FUMIGATING RIBBON,' c.1892.

Furniture, Ornamental
The use of inset painted porcelain plaques for the decoration of furniture started in France in the 1760s, when Sèvres* porcelain plaques were first employed for the purpose, as well as for the tops of small tables. The use of Wedgwood ware as furniture decoration must have started in the 1770s. In February 1774, in a letter to Bentley, Wedgwood refers to those encaustic paintings and cameos which had been inset into furniture, and he suggests engravings of them, with the owner's permission, ''to show *what might* be executed in the same stile.'' There is no record that this suggestion was put into practice. Furniture dating from the 18th century decorated with encaustic painted basaltes, early biscuit, and jasper certainly exists, and most examples are in the Adam style veneered in satinwood. English furniture predominates, but the Metropolitan Museum, New York, has a very rare *sécretaire à abbatant* by the *ébéniste du roi*, Adam Weisweiler*, better known as a maker of such small pieces as occasional tables, in which he has replaced the customary small Sèvres plaques with Wedgwood jasper medallions surrounding a large central porcelain flower plaque. One of the medallions employed dates this piece certainly to after the Anglo-French Commercial Treaty of 1786 (see: Auckland), at a time when English design was fashionable in Paris. By this time Sèvres were making wares inspired by Wedgwood's jasper, using a blue body devised for them by Josse of the Faubourg Saint-Denis, but from surface appearance, general style, and treatment of the classical subjects employed it should not be difficult for anyone accustomed to old jasper to distinguish French work. There are excellent examples in the Victoria and Albert Museum.

The term 'Adam style' is, of course, a generic term for neo-classical furniture. Individual makers using Wedgwood as furniture decoration included Hepplewhite, Gillow, Ince & Mayhew, and Seddon. Sheraton was a designer who employed Wedgwood to decorate some of his furniture, including pianofortes, and both Sheraton and Hepplewhite chairs are known inset with Wedgwood medallions. No doubt unrecorded specimens of all kinds exist. On the other hand, a certain amount of caution is necessary with unrecorded examples: for instance, a cabinet inset with portrait medallions of George III and Queen Charlotte which, when removed for inspection, proved to be reissues of the 1920s by A.H. 'Bert' Bentley*. These had been fitted in recent times, possibly to replace the original medallions removed by an over-enthusiastic collector.

When Josiah II* was in Holland in July 1790, he wrote to

Furniture, Ornamental. *Cabinet, of "the highest Art-character" by Lamb of Manchester inset with Wedgwood medallions, plaques, and tablets, and inlaid with various exotic woods. London Exhibition, 1862.* Photo: Wedgwood.

161

his father that he had been endeavouring to find cabinet makers and inlayers who would be prepared to use jasper medallions and cameos, and a Dutch *secretaire* is recorded thus decorated.

In the 1850s the architect, Gottfried Semper*, designed a cabinet which, like Weisweiler's, had a central porcelain panel surrounded by small rectangular Wedgwood tablets. This was shown in the Paris Exposition of 1855. Wright & Mansfield* produced a large satinwood cabinet in the Adam style decorated with coloured wood marquetry and Wedgwood medallions which was highly commended at the Paris Exposition Universelle of 1867. During the 19th century objects of this kind were often made as a kind of *chef d'oeuvre* for one or other of the popular International Exhibitions, and some, as in the case of the Semper cabinet, were the object of commercial reproduction afterwards. For more popular taste in the 19th century, Wedgwood cameos were set in the various pieces comprising desk or writing sets, generally of excellent quality and veneered in walnut or amboyna.

In addition to decorative medallions and cameos,

Wedgwood also made knobs, escutcheon plates, handles, etc. of jasper.

It is possible to find Queen's ware tiles* used to decorate furniture c.1880: for example, 8ins. by 8ins. painted tiles inset into a bamboo table of an Arts and Crafts type.

See also: John Broadwood; Papier Mâche.

Fürstenberg (Brunswick)

A factory founded in 1747 by Duke Carl I of Brunswick. It flourished especially between 1770 and 1814, and is still in existence. From 1794 to 1814 the director was Louis-Victor Gerverot*, and Wedgwood products were copied during this period. Biscuit porcelain reliefs in oval frames, sometimes with a lavender blue ground and inspired by Wedgwood's jasper, were produced by the modeller, Schubert, copied from cameos and gems in the Ducal collection depicting Greek poets, philosophers, and statesmen. Gerverot added black basaltes to the production in 1796, and some small busts were made. The biscuit body was improved and used for many new models in the Empire style from 1805.

Furniture, Ornamental. *Cabinet in the Adam style ornamented with Wedgwood medallions. Made by Wright & Mansfield of London for the 1862 Exhibition, it was bought by the Victoria and Albert Museum in 1867.* Victoria and Albert Museum.

162

G

Gaj, Pietro (fl.1850-1870)

Italian sculptor working for the pottery manufacturers, Carocchi*, Fabbri & Co. of Gubbio, who specialised in copies of Hispano-Moresque ware and Italian *maiolica*. In 1862 he visited England in connection with the International Exhibition and, while there, offered the secret of the Gubbio* ruby and yellow lustres to Wedgwood. His formulae could not be made to work and Wedgwood refused to pay him anything after the first instalment. Three experimentally decorated *tazze* in the Gubbio style are in the Wedgwood Museum*.

See: Lustres.

Game-Pie Dish

A covered bowl, oval or circular, modelled and coloured to resemble piecrust. These dishes were made of cane ware* with leaf or floral decoration in relief around the bowl and on the flat cover, and often with a hare or cauliflower handle. They were produced in fairly large quantities during the early years of the 19th century when flour was scarce. The following passage is taken from Captain Jesse's *Life of Beau Brummel* (1844): ''The scarcity two years after Brummel's retirement, viz. in 1800, was so great that the consumption of flour for pastry was forbidden in the Royal Household, rice being used instead. The distillers left off malting...and Wedgwood made dishes to represent piecrust.''

In 1850 Wedgwood introduced a glazed stoneware which could be used for cooking meat or game in the oven. A dish, or 'liner', of this ware was then placed inside the warmed game pie dish to be brought to the table. These pie dishes with liners were produced in four sizes, the largest being supplied in quantity to the university colleges. After about 1840 the relief decoration was moulded in one piece with the body, not sprigged* as on earlier examples. Similar dishes were made by other manufacturers, including Spode*.

See also: Piecrust Ware.

Game-Pie Dish. *Cane ware game-pie dish with rabbit finial made during the flour shortage to simulate pastry. c.1805.* Wedgwood.

Ganymede

A youth, the most beautiful of mortals, who was carried off by Zeus, in the form of an eagle. He became cup bearer to Zeus and lived among the gods on Olympus. He is usually represented in art as a naked youth accompanied by an eagle.

There are three Wedgwood subjects:

Ganymede, figure, height 12ins., modelled after the statue in ''the Florentine Museum''. This has been attributed to Flaxman*, but its appearance in the 1773 Catalogue makes this unlikely. It is possible that the figure was taken from a model or cast supplied by John Flaxman, Senior*.

Ganymede and the Eagle,* tablet, 6¼ins. by 5ins., modelled c.1778.

Jupiter and Ganymede, tablet, 3ins. by 6ins. Listed in the Ornamental Catalogues from 1773.

Ganymede and the Eagle

Listed as no.225 in Wedgwood's 1779 Catalogue* and certainly in production in 1778. The source of this tablet is the subject of controversy, the origin of the design being ascribed to a Roman sardonyx in the Marlborough collection and to a relief illustrated in Bartoli and Bellori (*Veterum Sepulcra,* Rome 1728). It is probable that Wedgwood's immediate source was a glass-paste gem by Tassie*.

Garbe, Louis Richard, RA, FRBS (1876-1957)

Sculptor of figure and animal subjects. Born in London and studied at the Central School of Arts and Crafts and at the Royal Academy Schools. He exhibited subjects in marble and bronze at the Royal Academy from 1908, and was elected a member of the Royal Academy in 1936. He was Professor of Sculpture at the Royal College of Art 1929-46. Two figures, *Boy on a Shell* and *Syren,* were reproduced by Wedgwood in about 1938.

Garbett, Samuel (fl.1745-1786)

Manufacturer of industrial chemicals in Birmingham, who established a laboratory with Dr. John Roebuck, chemist and Fellow of the Royal Society, in 1745. Influential in business affairs in the Midlands, and acquainted with Matthew Boulton*, Garbett was also in touch with Wedgwood on a variety of matters ranging from canals to the French Trade Treaty of 1786.

Garniture de Cheminée

The French for a set of vases, or ornaments, to decorate the shelf of the chimney piece*. The number varied — three, five or seven, but five was the more usual. The Chinese *garniture,* which became standard in the 18th century with English factories, included a central baluster-shaped covered vase, two smaller vases of the same shape, and two beaker-shaped vases. They were decorated *en suite.* Variations on the theme include three figure groups, one central group and a flanking smaller pair. Other *garnitures* include the *garniture de table,* a set of vases or ornaments made for a side-table in a reception hall or a *Salon,* or a *garniture de toilette,* a set of perfume bottles, powder boxes, ring stands, etc., for a dressing table.

Gaugain, Thomas (1748-c.1805)

French engraver, who lived in England from his youth. He exhibited at the Royal Academy, 1778-82, and executed numerous engravings after such artists as Reynolds*, Morland, Northcote and Maria Cosway. He supplied Wedgwood with engravings c.1790-1800.

Above: **Garniture de Chiminée.** *Three-piece cane ware garniture de cheminée, comprising a set of two small flower pots, 3 ¼ ins. wide, and a centre flower pot, 6 ¼ ins. wide, ornamented in relief with figures of cupids on enamelled blue grounds with gilt frames and blue and white enamelled swags. The interiors are glazed. c.1790.* Christie's.

Left: **Garniture de Cheminée.** *Black and white jasper dip vases with white Etruscan scroll handles, the feet and plinths attached with screws and nuts, c.1790. This shape was made in two sizes, 12ins. and 10ins., to be used as a garniture of three, the taller in the centre.* Wedgwood.

Gelatine

A jelly-like substance sometimes used in transfer printing. It is also employed as a method of multiplying plaster casts, the moulds being made with an inner surface of flexible gelatine which can be pulled off the casts without damaging them. Gelatine will not usually take such fine detail as either plaster or fired clay.

See: Bat Printing; Casting; Transfer Printing.

Gems

Precious or semi-precious stones carved in cameo* or intaglio* were made from ancient times. Greek temple inventories dating from 400B.C. record gold and silver rings set with seals of this kind, and by the 1st century B.C. gem-collecting was an established enthusiasm in Rome. Julius Caesar, for instance, presented six cabinets to the temple of Venus, and Pliny the Elder records that the manufacture of false gems in glass paste and other materials was on a very large scale, so scarce had genuine examples become in the art-market of the day. The carvers of false gems largely devoted themselves to well-known subjects which were old in their day, and to this may be ascribed the numerous examples of gems more or less exactly alike.

The passion for gem collecting revived during the Renaissance and continued well into the 19th century. The practice of imitating them started once more and reached considerable proportions by the end of the 18th century. Many of these imitations were legitimate and were sold without any attempt to disguise their nature at a cost related to that of production. Belonging to this category were Wedgwood's cameos and intaglios and Tassie's* glass paste gems: these were not intended to deceive anyone into thinking them antique. It is worthy of note that the earliest of all cameos, pre-dating those carved from stone, were made from glass paste, or

were impressed into terracotta and then gilded to resemble gold medallions, but it is improbable that this was known to either Wedgwood or Tassie. 18th century forgeries were carved from semi-precious stones with lapidary* techniques, given some of the signs of age, and sold at enhanced prices as Greek or Roman work.

During the 4th century B.C. the gem was usually a thin slice of stone with a design carved in the face (intaglio) and set in a ring as a seal. Usually the stone selected was sard, varying in colour from golden to blood red. Other fairly common stones are onyx, sardonyx, agate, chalcedony, and jasper, and from the latter is derived the name of Wedgwood's stoneware. The introduction of cameo carving on a fairly large scale belongs to the 3rd century B.C., when advantage was taken of laminated stones with variously coloured layers, such as onyx and the sardonyx, to produce carvings in relief of a different colour from the background, similar in appearance to Wedgwood's jasper. According to Pliny, the first Roman to possess a carved gem of sardonyx was Scipio Africanus (234-c.183), and from this time sardonyx was much in favour. Cameo portraits appear to date from Alexander the Great (356-323), who forbade the engraving of his portrait by other than Pyrgoteles. Portraits of those living earlier than this date (e.g. Plato, Socrates, etc.) were made in Graeco-Roman times and taken from sources now unknown. The Greek tendency was always to idealise the person portrayed; the Romans in their portraiture, particularly in their bronzes, were realists preoccupied with presenting their subject "warts and all."

Wedgwood collected antique gems, and in 1772 he found himself hampered by the difficulty of identifying the subjects. He wrote: "we are continually asked...the names of gems, seals, &c...imagine how foolish we look when we can scarcely tell them a single head or subject." The Ornamental Catalogue of 1773 lists 285 intaglios and cameos, and although this number was augmented later, the greatest single increase took place between 1773 and 1774. At this time (1773) gems were being made in black basaltes and the white biscuit* body. The latter could be either polished or enamelled. Originally the seals had been set in London, but after December 1772, they were sent in increasing quantities to Birmingham for mounting, and it was at this time that Wedgwood was experimenting with a new white body for gems. By 1779 the number had risen to 1700, each marked with a catalogue reference number and greater variety had been achieved by the introduction of jasper.

Ancient gems had always been collected into cabinets, and Wedgwood supposed that those who bought his gems would follow this custom. They were, he wrote: "exactly taken from the finests Antique gems...by the favour of the Nobility &c. who are in Possession of original gems, or fine impressions of those in foreign Collections. We have been able to make our list pretty numerous, [and] by the same means it is perpetually increasing." To encourage collectors the heads of the Popes, a Christian equivalent of the pagan gem, were sold at "six-pence a piece, single, or three-pence a piece to those who take the set, which is nearly compleat." A set actually comprised 256 cameos after medals by Dassier*.

Some remarks in the 1779 catalogue on the subject of intaglios are illuminating: "We have found that many of the Intaglios take a good Polish, and when polished have nearly the effect of fine Black Jasper, but this work must be performed with great care, or the Work will essentially suffer by it. Heads may be polished safely, but figures scarcely admit of polishing without Injury unless there be such a Degree of Delicacy and Care observed as would greatly increase the price. We have also found out another Method of adding very considerably to the Beauty of these Intaglios by polishing the Bezels and giving a ground of pale blue to the surface of the Stone, which make them greatly resemble the black and blue onyxes, and equally ornamental for Rings and Seals.

"They are also now made in a fine blue Jasper that takes as good a Polish as Turquoise Stone or Lapis Lazuli.

"Though the superior Hardness, Sharpness, and Correctness of these Intaglios place them far above all other Imitations or copies of antique Gems, yet no Article in the whole extent of the fine Arts has ever been offered to the public at so reasonable a Price."

Wedgwood made extremely varied use of the sources from which he took his subjects. The Marlborough gem (now in the Boston Museum of Fine Arts) depicting *The Marriage of Cupid and Psyche** was one of his most popular subjects, made in basaltes, terracotta, and jasper, and in all sizes, from that of the original to large rectangular tablets* for chimney pieces*.

Edward Burch*, who modelled for Wedgwood, was also one of the best known gem engravers of the period.

See: Medallions; Sulphurs.

General Chamber of Manufacturers

An organisation of Chambers (or Committees) of Commerce founded in 1785, partly at the suggestion of Josiah Wedgwood who was a leading spirit. It owed its formation to a desire to combine to protect the interests of English manufacturers during the negotiation of the Irish Trade Treaty of 1785, which the Chamber opposed. Despite strenuous efforts by Wedgwood (who was President from November 1784 to March 1787) to promote the affairs of the Chamber, support from other manufacturers was lukewarm. A much-amended Bill passed through Parliament, but its majority in the Irish Parliament was so small that it was eventually abandoned.

In October 1785 we find Wedgwood suggesting to William

Nicholson, Secretary to the Chamber, that joint action be taken to deal with the nuisance of industrial spies*, and in December 1785, William Eden (see: Auckland*), who had opposed the Irish Trade Treaty, was appointed to negotiate a Commercial Treaty with France. The Chamber was divided in its attitude to the French Commercial Treaty*, the manufacturers of the Midlands and the North in the newer industries welcoming the attempt to free the trade with France from restrictions and imposts, and the older industries, fearful of competition, opposing the negotiations at every turn. Members from the Midlands and the North seceded from the Chamber, although Wedgwood's interest continued. On June 12th, 1787, he wrote to Eden: "The Chamber of Manufacturers sleepeth for the present, but may be waked at any time when its services are called for."

Genius

A protecting spirit, which was a matter of belief among both Romans and Greeks. The latter called them Daemons, and the best known Daemon was the one which guided Socrates*. It was believed that every man acquired a tutelary genius at birth, who accompanied him throughout life and guided him to the underworld after death. Genii are usually represented as winged beings.

Wedgwood subject:
Genii, by Lady Templetown*. Various sizes from 1¾ ins. by 3¾ ins. to 3ins. by 7ins.

Gentleman, David, RDI (b.1930)

English graphic designer and painter; studied at the Royal College of Art, 1950-53; Tutor, Royal College of Art, 1953-55; designer of murals and posters for the National Trust and London Transport, and of a number of important sets of British postage stamps; member of the Design Council, 1974; awarded the Gold Medal for stamp design, 1969, and Design Council Poster award 1973, 1976, 1977.

David Gentleman has designed a series of views of British castles for reproduction on bone china* plates in a limited edition of 5,000 sets. The first two views, Harlech Castle and Woburn Abbey*, were issued in 1977.

Gentleman, David. *Bone china plate decorated with a view of Harlech Castle in the British castles series issued in a limited edition of 5,000. Designed by David Gentleman, 1977.* Wedgwood.

George II. *Rosso antico bust of George II in parade armour after the ivory carving by Rysbrack. This bust is often incorrectly described as the Duke of Marlborough. Height 8ins.* Christie's.

George II (1683-1760)
King of Great Britain and Ireland and Elector of Hanover; grandfather of George III*. A bust, 10ins. high, of George II is listed in the 1773 Catalogue* "from an Ivory in the possession of Mr Ranby, carved by Mr Rysbrack." This bust, which exists in basaltes*, jasper*, and *rosso antico** is almost invariably described as the Duke of Marlborough*, but there can be no doubt of its true identity. Two portrait medallions, attributed to Matthew and Isaac Gosset*, were also issued by Wedgwood and they are listed in the 1779 Catalogue.

See: John Michael Rysbrack.

George III (1738-1820)
King of Great Britain and Ireland and Elector of Hanover; grandson of George II*; married, 1761, Charlotte Sophia of Mecklenburg-Strelitz. He seems to have approved of Queen Charlotte's* patronage of Wedgwood for, soon after the production of Queen's shape*, he ordered a new shape for himself. This, originally known as 'Royal shape' and closely resembling that used for the Frog* service made for Catherine II, Empress of Russia, followed the form of Queen's shape but

the rims of the plates were left plain.

Josiah's brother, John, was frequently at Court during the 1760s, and in 1770 Josiah and Bentley* were granted an audience of the King and Queen, to present, as Bentley proudly told his partner, Boardman, "some *bas-reliefs* her majesty had ordered; and to show some new improvements with which they were well pleased. They expressed in the most obliging and condescending manner, their attention to our manufacture; and entered very freely into conversation on the further improvement of it, and on many other subjects. The King is well acquainted with business, and with the characters of the principal manufacturers, merchants, and artists; and seems to have the success of all our manufactures much at heart, and to understand the importance of them."

Josiah was a staunch Whig, and can have had little regard for a king who had prosecuted a war against the American colonists, and who was later to dismiss Lord North and Charles James Fox in favour of the younger Pitt, but royal patronage took precedence over politics, and Wedgwood's business instinct was sure. In spite of an order for a life-size bust of the King in 1777, Wedgwood was too doubtful of its popularity to produce one, but no less than ten portrait medallions* were made, and three medallions were modelled specially to celebrate the King's return to health after his illness in 1789. Since the King's health was insecure (he suffered from porphyria), and the Opposition in Parliament was supported by the heir to the throne, Wedgwood secured his future by issuing six portrait medallions of George, Prince of Wales.

George II. *Jasper portrait medallion of George II from a wax portrait attributed to Isaac Gosset. First listed in the 1779 Catalogue.* Wedgwood.

George III. *Medallion commemorating the restoration of George III to health, 1789. A figure of Fame holding a trumpet, also holds an oval tablet with the inscription 'Health is Restored'. A bust of the King surmounts a pedestal in the background.* Wedgwood.

George III. *Jasper portrait medallion of George III, remodelled by Hackwood from a wax portrait by Isaac Gosset in 1776.* Wedgwood.

George III. *George III's Golden Jubilee in 1810 was celebrated by a number of special commemorative pieces. This bough pot is decorated with an orange print and famille rose type flowers.* Wedgwood.

Germaine, Pierre (b.1716)

Goldsmith; member of a family of goldsmiths of Avignon and Marseille, the latter his birthplace. He was apprenticed to Nicolas Besnier, and was received *maître* of the Guild in 1744. He published two books of designs in the rococo style, in 1748 and 1751. The edition of 1751, entitled *Élements d'Orfevrerie*, contains seven plates contributed by the goldsmith, Jacques Roettiers. This book appears to have been in Wedgwood's library. Plate 5 with alterations in pencil survives in the Wedgwood Archives, and seems to have influenced some of Coward's* carved wood block moulds now in the Museum.

See: Rococo Style; Silver Pattern.

German Cameos

Bas-reliefs designed specially to commemorate the coronation of Leopold II* as Holy Roman Emperor in 1790. These cameos are readily identifiable by the appearance in the design of the double-headed eagle or the Imperial crown.

Germanicus (15B.C.-A.D.19)

The son of Nero Claudius Drusus and Antonia, daughter of Marc Antony, Germanicus was adopted by his uncle, Tiberius, during the lifetime of Augustus. He had nine children by his wife, Agrippina, one of whom became the Emperor Caligula, and another the mother of Nero. Germanicus was successful in subduing the German tribes, but Tiberius was jealous of his influence and withdrew him before his work was completed, giving him command of the eastern provinces. There Germanicus died, probably poisoned. A bust of Germanicus, supplied by Hoskins & Oliver* in 1774, was finished by Hackwood*.

Gerverot, Louis-Victor (1747-1829)

Painter, colour chemist, potter and arcanist. Painter at Sèvres*, 1764-65; at Niderviller, Fulda, Ludwigsburg, Ansbach-Brückberg, Höchst, Frankenthal, Offenbach, Weesp (c.1771), Schrezheim (1773-75) and Oude Loosdrecht (1777-78). Gerverot came to England in 1786 prepared to barter his knowledge of the secret of porcelain for the secrets of English creamware and stoneware manufacture. He advertised his intention in the newspapers and was approached by Wedgwood with an offer of employment, which he is said to have refused. The detailed information about the Etruria* factory which he later retailed to the directors of Fürstenberg indicate that he must, at least, have paid a visit of several days' duration to the Wedgwood factory. Shortly afterwards he came to an agreement with John Turner* to build a porcelain factory at Lane End. He failed to fulfil the clauses of his agreement and was sued by Turner's sons. Returning to the Continent in 1788, he set up a factory in Cologne to manufacture black and white stonewares. In 1797 he became manager of the Fürstenberg factory, where he supervised the production of busts and medallions in imitation of Wedgwood's and Turner's.

Josiah Wedgwood rightly regarded Gerverot as a dangerous industrial spy, but it is nevertheless clear that Gerverot learned much about Wedgwood's methods, some of which he subsequently introduced at Fürstenberg. A porcelain beaker, now the property of the Antique Porcelain Company, was made by the Gerverot-Turner factory in 1787. It is decorated in reddish-brown enamel with two scenes, one signed by Fidele Duvivier, showing the interior of a pottery. These designs were reproduced on a jug, and possibly on other pieces, by Wedgwood in 1887.

Gessner, Solomon (1720-1788)

Swiss poet, who was born and died in Zürich, where he was a bookseller. His poetry, written in German, was exceedingly popular. He painted landscapes in a romantic* neo-classical* style, and did excellent engraving. He was one of the founders of the Zürich porcelain factory, and supplied subjects for the decoration of the ware. He also painted occasional landscapes on the porcelain of this factory.

His portrait medallion in jasper was issued in 1790, but the source of the original wax is not known. Wedgwood also produced a medallion about the same date which shows a classical tomb or monument surmounted by an urn with the Muses* of Poetry and Painting weeping over Gessner's profile. Flanking the monument, which stands above a rushing stream and rockwork, are two palm trees. This medallion was designed by Brandoin*. A second version of this memorial medallion uses only the figure of the two Muses weeping over the medallion profile of Gessner.

Gilbert and Sullivan Centenary Mug

Mug first issued in 1961 commemorating the fiftieth anniversary of the death of W.S. Gilbert. It bears portraits of A.S. Sullivan and W.S. Gilbert, with that of Richard D'Oyly Carte under the handle. The backstamp lists the following operas, with the date of the first performance: *Trial by Jury, HMS Pinafore, Patience, Princess Ida, Ruddigore, The Sorcerer, The Pirates of Penzance, Iolanthe, The Mikado, The Yeoman of the Guard,* and *Utopia, Ltd.* The mug is decorated with twelve transfer prints of characters from these operas with bands of blue and pink enamel. The mark is 'WEDGWOOD' impressed, and a circular printed mark reading 'Etruria Wedgwood Barlaston'. It was designed by Victor Skellern*.

Gilding

Josiah Wedgwood did not generally gild his wares, but for certain purposes gilding was essential; for instance, in executing Queen Charlotte's order of 1765. Writing to John Wedgwood on the 15th June of that year he asked for: "some gold powder such as is burnt in upon china. It is made by one Mr Shenton (only) and sold by him at 7 guineas an ounce. Mr Giles*, Enameller in Berwick Street, Soho [London], can tell you where Mr Shenton lives. [He] may perhaps give you instructions about the best way of using it." After signing this letter Wedgwood realised how much more he needed to know, for he sent his brother to Court to see Miss Chetwynd* with a

Gilding. *A Queen's ware teaset of c.1775 and a teapot enamelled with Chinese figures, c.1770, bearing traces of oil gilding.* Wedgwood.

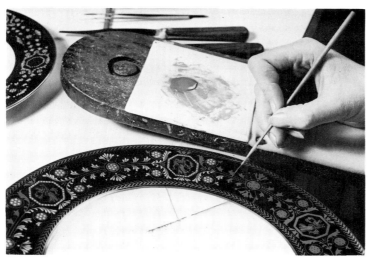

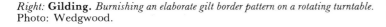

Above: **Gilding.** *Applying gold to the already enamelled border of a Black Astbury pattern plate to produce raised gilding.* Wedgwood.

Right: **Gilding.** *Burnishing an elaborate gilt border pattern on a rotating turntable.* Photo: Wedgwood.

long list of inquiries, among them, ''whether she expects the gold to be burnt in as it is upon Chelsea china, or secured with a varnish only, like Birmingham waiters and other japan work.''

Gold powder was made by grinding gold leaf in honey until it had attained the required degree of fineness, after which the honey was dissolved in water, leaving the powder behind. Gold generally is exceedingly malleable, and can be hammered into leaves of about 1/200,000th inch in thickness. It was supplied interleaved in books, and could be used directly by pressing on to a surface made tacky with gold size or japanner's varnish. This kind of gilding, however, if applied to pottery, was impermanent and subject to damage by wear and abrasion.

From Wedgwood's letter quoted above it seems that he was, at this time, unaccustomed to the use of gilding, but a letter of August 1765, reports the progress made: ''I have succeeded the first tryal in makeing the powder gold which I have always been told only one man in England could make [this was probably honey-gold], and desire you'l send me an ounce of *pure* Gold, either in Ducat or grain or some other form: send the powder too.'' In September 1767 a letter refers to an order for a Queen's ware service printed and gilt to be dispatched to the East Indies. In February 1769 we learn that vases marbled with gold were no longer popular, and in September of the same year Bentley in London raised the question of gilding vases, from which it seems evident that hitherto gilding had been done by laying gold leaf or powder on to varnish or gold size, because Wedgwood replied: ''Burning the gold in upon the vases would no doubt be a capital improvement, and I think the sooner you begin upon it the better... to cover the ornaments over thick enough to bear a polish [i.e. burnishing] will take an immense quantity of Gold, and be extremely tedious to polish [burnish]...I will make some tryals of Gilding here and let you know the result.''

The attachment of gold to the glaze proved troublesome,

and even as late as 1771 we find Wedgwood writing: ''I have some fear that the old Gilt pebble vases and gilt Dessert ware will want some repair before it is fit to send on so long a voyage [to Russia]. When the gold becomes in a loose state... we have found bakeing over again to secure it very well... I think you should get an oven built in the kitchen and James Bakewell* could show Nanny [the housekeeper at Newport Street] how to manage it for the Gilt ware...when an oven is the proper heat for bakeing household bread it is right for our gilt ware.''

Early ware exists, such as some pebble* vases, from which the gilding has almost completely worn away, although a few specks of gold remain. Generally, it is clear that Wedgwood avoided the use of gilding as much as possible, although long before his death the technical difficulties had been overcome, and mercuric gilding had been introduced at Derby*. A letter written in 1772 throws some light on contemporary opinion: ''The same noble contempt for Gold reigns...at Dublin as in London — They cannot bear anything Gilt beyond a picture frame, and their stomachs are a little squeamish even about the frames!...Gold, the most precious of all metals, is absolutely kicked out of doors, and our gilders must, I believe, follow it.''

See: Bronzed Basaltes.

Giles, James (1718-after 1776)

Independent decorator. According to Mortimer's *Directory* for 1763 James Giles of Berwick Street, Soho, London, was described as a ''china and enamel painter.'' He bought porcelain and painted it for sale, and his style has been identified on the porcelain of China, Chelsea, Worcester, and Bow, and on Bristol blue glass. In 1763 he claimed to copy ''patterns of any china with the utmost exactness, both with respect to the design and the colours, either in European or Chinese taste.'' Among the best known of his decorations are the so-called 'dishevelled birds' inspired by earlier bird

Colour Plate XII

Top: Four-colour jasper can cup and saucer with matching covered cream jug, c.1790. The white jasper body is ornamented with applied dark blue jasper cameos suspended from lilac ribbons, and green vine leaves. These examples are translucent, a quality which easily distinguishes them from later white ware or the earlier opaque 'waxen' jasper. Nottingham Castle Museum. Photo: Reilly/Charles Letts.

Centre left: Can cup and saucer in lilac dip jasper with applied lilac squares and green quatrefoils. c.1790. Centre right: Lilac jasper dip tea-cup and saucer with applied reliefs and engine-turned decoration, the interior lapidary polished. Translucent. c.1785. Nottingham Castle Museum. Photo: Reilly/Charles Letts.

Right: Green jasper dip tea bowl and saucer with applied reliefs and engine-turned decoration. Lapidary-polished rim and interior. Translucent. c.1785. Nottingham Castle Museum. Photo: Reilly/Charles Letts.

Giles, James. *Plate in the late Chelsea style on Wedgwood creamware probably painted by James Giles.* Wedgwood.

Giles, James. *Simulated Chelsea gold anchor mark on the reverse of the Wedgwood creamware plate illustrated.* Wedgwood.

Glacier. *Queen's ware glacier (ice pail or refrigerator) decorated with an enamelled armorial crest. Height 7½ ins. c.1803.* Liverpool City Museums. Photo: Wedgwood.

Glassware

Wedgwood have recently added the manufacture of glassware to their range of production. They acquired King's Lynn Glass Ltd. (now Wedgwood Glass) in 1969, and the Galway Crystal Company of Galway, Eire, in 1974. The first chief designer was Ronald Stenett-Willson. Lead crystal drinking glasses, decanters, candlesticks, and ornamental objects, including paperweights, are among the items produced.

painting at Sèvres, and some excellent painting of sliced fruit. Giles's kiln in Kentish Town was probably taken over by him in 1756 when the Kentish Town China Manufactory went out of business. In 1765 Wedgwood referred his brother, John, to Giles for information about where to buy gold powder (see: Gilding). In October 1770, when Wedgwood was contemplating an action against Neale* and Palmer* for the infringement of his patent relative to encaustic colours, he wrote to Bentley speculating that the offending wares might have been painted by James Giles. This was not improbable. Giles was having great difficulties at the time in obtaining supplies of white porcelain to paint, and was later financially embarrassed in consequence.

Glacier

An ice pail or refrigerator; illustrated in the first Queen's ware Catalogue, 1774. The 'glacier' is bucket shaped, with a cover and two side handles. The word is Wedgwood's own; the French term for this utensil is *rafraichissoir;* the secondary meaning of *glacier* is a dealer in ices.

Gladstone, Rt. Hon. William Ewart (1809-1898)

English Liberal politician and Prime Minister; collector of English and Continental pottery and porcelain, especially Wedgwood wares. His eulogy of Josiah Wedgwood, delivered in 1863, is often quoted. His collection was dispersed at auction in London on June 23rd to 26th, 1875.

Glassware. Madonna and Child, *the first Christmas plaque to be made by Wedgwood Glass. The figures are etched on a free-standing glass plaque. 1973.* Wedgwood.

Left: **Glassware.** *Cut-glass lead crystal decanter, engraved with coat-of-arms and commemorative inscription. Made by Wedgwood Glass.* Wedgwood.

Right: **Glaze.** *A spill vase in white stoneware with blue reliefs, covered with smear glaze, c.1830-40. Right: a turned jasper dip pillar candlestick, c.1820-30.* Wedgwood.

Glaze

A form of glass applied to the surface of biscuit* and other porous ware to render it impermeable (as in the case of earthenware) and to prevent surface staining (vitrified wares). Wedgwood's earliest glaze was a distinctive yellow-green and, contrary to the pronouncements of Wedgwood's eulogists, was sometimes disfigured by crazing*. This fault was almost eliminated by about 1763, when a refined creamware body was accompanied by a finer glaze which shows a paler green tinge and was applied more evenly. This green tint is particularly noticeable on the inside of foot rims and the interior of teapots and coffee pots. By the end of the 18th century the glaze had become almost colourless, except on pearl* ware, the 'blue-bag' tint of which is, unlike that of Leeds*, also greenish. Glaze may be coloured (usually by the addition of metallic oxides) or almost colourless; transparent or opaque. It is applied by spraying or dipping (see: Processes of Manufacture).

During the 18th century the poisonous effect on the workers in the pottery industry of lead used in glazes was widely recognised. Wedgwood's early creamware was finished with a lead glaze. For later Queen's ware he developed a glaze made from white clay and flint, using smaller quantities of lead, but he failed in his attempts to produce a satisfactory leadless glaze. In 1898 the Home Office ordered an official inquiry into the incidence of lead poisoning in the pottery industry, and, a year later, manufacturers were instructed to discontinue the use of raw lead.

The following are the principal Wedgwood glazes:

DYSART GLAZE

A deep creamy-yellow glaze used on Queen's ware, introduced for, and named after, the Earl of Dysart (see: Dysart Green) who required an ivory-coloured ware. Its introduction is a comment on the progress of Wedgwood's creamware from the early yellow-buff to the near-white of the 19th century.

GREEN GLAZE

A coloured glaze in various shades of green (derived from copper) developed by Wedgwood during his partnership with Whieldon*. The copper scales were bought from Robinson & Rhodes* of Leeds. Green glazes, particularly as decoration for leaf shapes, have been in use ever since. The colour has been copied, with varying success, by other manufacturers, notably Spode*. (See also separate entry.)

LEAD GLAZE

Transparent glaze containing lead, called Galena glaze in the 18th century, and employed to cover cream-coloured ware, Queen's ware, and pearl ware. It has been replaced, since the turn of this century, by leadless glazes.

MAJOLICA GLAZES

Transparent glazes, stained with colouring oxides of metal, were introduced at Wedgwood in 1860 for the decoration of dessert services and ornamental wares. The name, majolica, for this type of ware (also made by Minton* and others) is a misnomer. It is derived from the Italian *maiolica,* which was decorated with opaque glazes containing tin oxide; but the technique was based on that of Bernard Palissy*. Similar techniques were used during the last twenty years of the 19th century for the 'Etruscan Majolica' made at Phoenixville, Pennsylvania.

MATT GLAZES

Glazes with an 'egg-shell' sheen, somewhat resembling marble in appearance. Introduced in 1933, the Wedgwood matt glazes include moonstone* (which has been compared to driven snow), ravenstone (black), straw, and matt green. All (except ravenstone, which was not introduced until the 1950s) were extensively used by Keith Murray*, and moonstone has been continuously in production until the present day.

SALT GLAZE

Transparent glaze with a pitted surface ('orange-skin') produced by throwing salt into the kiln at maximum heat (see: Salt-glazed ware).

SMEAR GLAZE

This deposit of glaze by volatilisation on the surface of pottery is produced by smearing the inside of the saggar* with a glaze preparation. It is quite distinct from (though often mistaken for) salt glaze.

Glisson (Glesson), Miss (fl.1769-1774)

Painter at the Chelsea Decorating Studio* who worked on the Frog* service topographical views for payment of 12s.6d. a week.

Glost Oven

Glazing oven (see: Processes of Manufacture — Firing).

Glover, Thomas (fl.1769-1774)

Painter at the Chelsea Decorating Studio* who worked on the teaware of the Frog* service.

Godet

Small cup, in which a wick was suspended or floated in oil, used in the lower part of a *veilleuse** or food warmer*.

Gold Lustre Ware

Pottery decorated with lustre derived from gold. When applied by the English method of firing the metallic salts, gold yields a variety of colours. On a brown ground the colour ranges from coppery to golden yellow. On a white, pink, or light buff ground it varies from pale pink to ruby or purple, depending on the thickness of the coating and the firing temperature. Gold lustre of this type was first produced commercially in England between 1805 and 1806.

See: Lustre Decoration.

Goode, William James (fl.1850-1892)

The son of Thomas Goode, founder of the noted firm of china dealers, Thomas Goode & Co. Ltd., South Audley Street, London, of which he became a partner in 1857. William Goode was also a talented artist and designer. He painted porcelain and earthenware for Minton*, and devised a method of etching on porcelain which was praised at the Paris Exposition of 1878. His collection of Sèvres* porcelain was exhibited at Thomas Goode's premises until his death in 1892, when it was sold. A small Queen's ware dish, painted with caricature figures and sub-titled '1742' is in the Wedgwood Museum*. It is inscribed on the reverse: 'Oh! What a charming Cup & Saucer', followed by Goode's monogram and the words 'painted by W.J. Goode, 1864'. The figures were copied from Hogarth's *Taste in High Life; or dress in 1742*.

Goodwin, John Edward (1867-1949)

English ceramic designer; Wedgwood art-director in succession to Thomas Allen*, 1902-34. He was succeeded by Victor Skellern*. Goodwin designed Queen's ware shapes, some adapted from 18th-century originals, some of which are still in production. He particularly drew inspiration from the old relief-decorated jasper and basaltes wares for the American market, where early Wedgwood continues to be much admired because it expresses what is generally regarded as the best period of American taste, especially in architecture — the Federal (i.e. the neo-classical*) style. In 1908 the powder blue* ground on bone china was introduced, and the Fairyland* and Dragon* lustres of Daisy Makeig-Jones* also belong to the period of his art-directorship.

Goodwin's designs include the following:

Annular service (with Tom Wedgwood*), 1930.
*Apollo** vase, 1930.
Colonial shape (with Kennard L. Wedgwood*), 1928.
Edme shape (with Pannier Frères), 1908.
Montreal pattern, 1930.
Osier shape, 1906.
*Patrician** shape, 1926.
Ruby Tonquin pattern, 1930.
Ulander pattern, 1912.
*Wellesley** shape, 1932.
White House Service (for Theodore Roosevelt), 1903. Later reintroduced, without the Great Seal of the United States of America, under the name *Colonnade*.

Gosset, Isaac (1713-1777)

Member of a family of Huguenots who invented his own wax composition for modelling portraits. He exhibited at the Society of Arts and the Free Society from 1740-78. Gosset modelled many portraits of famous people during his lifetime, including members of the Royal family. Wedgwood portrait medallions adapted from this source include Frederick Lewis, Prince of Wales, William, Duke of Cumberland, and George III* and Queen Charlotte*.

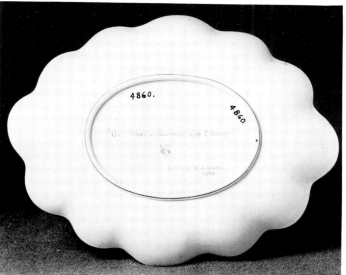

Goode, William James. *Creamware plate painted by Goode, and signed and dated 1864 on the reverse. The subject is taken from Hogarth's painting 'Taste in High Life'.* Wedgwood.

Gosset, Matthew (1683-1744)

Uncle of Isaac Gosset* and member of a Huguenot family which came to England at the time of the Revocation of the Edict of Nantes in 1685. Matthew Gosset, like his nephew, modelled portrait waxes, some of which were copied by Wedgwood. They include portraits of George I and George II.

Gothic Revival. Jug with arcaded moulding in the revived Gothic style with figures in niches. Shape No.958 in the 1817 Catalogue, and made in one colour (drab, cane, or white) or in two colours (cane and blue, or drab and white). Photo: Wedgwood.

Gothic Revival

The Gothic style proper, of which the pointed arch is a particular feature, prevailed in England from the end of the 12th to the end of the 16th century. It was revived briefly in the middle of the 18th century, when Horace Walpole converted his villa at Strawberry Hill, but it did not attract the potter at the time, and in consequence of the rising tide of neo-classicism* it almost disappeared until the early years of the 19th century, surviving only in the popular 'Gothick' novel. Josiah Wedgwood knew little about Gothic, and cared less. Even had it been sufficiently fashionable, it would have been a difficult style to translate into terms of pottery. Gothic began to return to favour in architecture early in the 19th century, when William Beckford commissioned Fonthill Abbey (a country house based on Salisbury Cathedral) from James Wyatt, and a limited use of Gothic motifs appeared on pottery soon afterwards.

Wedgwood's Gothic jug, illustrated in the 1817 Catalogue*, appears to have been the first of such pieces in a style which achieved great popularity in the 1840s. Produced at first in dry bodies*, "In one color as drab or cane or white, and in two colors as cane & blue or drab & white," and in three sizes, it was later reproduced in the same colours glazed. It is

ornamented with applied figures as well as cast decoration and was probably derived in part from a Rhineland stoneware jug of the end of the 16th century when the moulded arcade, each niche containing a figure (usually one of the Apostles), was a favourite form of decoration. Early German stoneware became popular among collectors at the beginning of the nineteenth century, and German influence gained strength with the arrival of Albert of Saxe-Coburg-Gotha, the Prince Consort.

Other English factories made more use of the style than Wedgwood. Minton started tentatively by putting a classical vase on a Gothic arcaded pedestal, and A.W.N. Pugin, a very influential Gothic designer, later worked for them. The Gothic style is most noticeable in the series of jugs produced by Charles Meigh & Son, T., J. & J. Mayer, T. & R. Boote, and W. Ridgway, Son & Co. between 1840 and 1860.

Goupy, Mme. Apolline (fl.1880-1915)

French sculptor; societaire des Artistes Français from 1898. Wedgwood portrait medallions of Albert I, King of Belgium, Marshal Ferdinand Foch, Marshall Joseph Joffre, Field-Marshal Horatio Herbert, 1st Earl Kitchener, and Victor Emmanuel III, King of Italy, were produced in 1915-16 from models by Mme. Goupy.

Gower, Granville Leveson-Gower, 2nd Earl

See: Stafford, 1st Marquis.

Graces, The Three

The three Charites; Aglaea (Brilliance), Euphrosyne (Mirth) and Thalia (Bloom), daughters of Zeus, and goddesses of beauty and grace. They attended Aphrodite*, and presided over physical exercise and dancing, and were the patrons of poetry and art. They were closely associated with the Muses*, and are usually represented naked, holding hands. Wedgwood produced two cameos of this subject: the first, which also

Graces, The Three. Jasper medallion. The three goddesses, Hera, Aphrodite and Athene, are clothed. When Paris also appears in the composition, the subject is called The Judgement of Paris. Probably from a gem by Tassie, c.1777. Wedgwood.

appears on early black basaltes* vases, shows the central figure nude and appears to have been copied from the print of a vase in the Hamilton* collection (from d'Hancarville*), or from the vase itself; the second, showing all three figures draped, is probably from a Tassie* gem.

Three Dancing Graces, a medallion of three chastely covered female dancers has its source in a wall painting which was reproduced in Bartoli, Bellori and La Chausse, *Picturae Antiquae,* published in 1750.

The 1787 Catalogue includes *The Graces erecting the statue of Cupid,* a tablet measuring 10¾ins. by 9ins. by Webber*. This appears to be a somewhat euphemistic title for the tablet properly described as *The Raising of Priapus*.*

Granby, John Manners, Marquis of (1721-1770)
Lieutenant-General; eldest son of the 3rd Duke of Rutland; commanded the Royal Horse Guards ('the Blues') at the battle of Minden, 1759, and distinguished himself in many battles during the Seven Years' War. He became a public hero after Minden, and has been immortalised in pottery and porcelain, and upon the signs of numerous public houses throughout Britain. A transfer-printed portrait occurs on Wedgwood creamware c.1763, the print by Sadler* probably taken from an engraving by Richard Houston after the painting by Sir Joshua Reynolds*. It is accompanied by a cartouche of cavalrymen with military trophies.

Grand Plat Ménage. *Centrepiece or épergne surmounted by an eagle. Similarly impressive creamware centrepieces were made also by Leeds. c.1790.* Wedgwood.

Grand Plat Ménage. *Table centrepiece or épergne of Queen's ware, surmounted by a pineapple. Plate 10, No.52 from the 1790 Catalogue.* Wedgwood.

Grand Plat Ménage
The term, *grand plat ménage,* is applied to a large centrepiece in the Leeds catalogue of creamware. Wedgwood described such pieces as *plats de ménage* or *épergnes,* although the latter term was more often applied at the time to glass centrepieces. The *plat de ménage* stood in the centre of the dining table. A very elaborate example illustrated in the 1774 Catalogue of Queen's ware is about two feet high, terminating in a large pineapple*. It has two tiers of hanging pierced sweetmeat baskets and sugar containers, all of obvious silver patterns. Objects of this kind are a very rare survival. In the 1780s and 1790s, Leeds produced even more elaborate examples than the one described, quite possibly in emulation.

Granite Ware
Earthenware with a greyish mottled glaze made by Josiah Wedgwood in imitation of granite.

See: Variegated Ware.

Granulated Jasper
A surface finish, consisting of small 'dimples', found only on fine examples of blue jasper produced during the lifetime of Josiah I*. It provides a textured background in contrast to the smooth finish of bas-relief* decoration.

Gravy Warmer
See: Argyll.

Great Newport Street, St. Martin's Lane, London
See: Showrooms.

Greatbatch, William. *Hexagonal teapot, modelled by Greatbatch and enamelled with Chinese figures, c.1765.* Zeitlin Collection.

Greatbatch (Greatbach), William (1735-1813)

Potter, engraver, modeller and blockcutter, apprenticed to Whieldon* during the Whieldon-Wedgwood partnership. In 1762 he set up on his own at Lower Lane, moving in 1764 to Lane Delph, where he made biscuit ware which was sent to Wedgwood's Ivy House* works for glazing. The wares he produced were chiefly cauliflower* and pineapple* shapes, leaf plates, and cornucopiae*, but other rococo* wares included melon, lemon and cucumber shapes, all of which seem to have been made in complete sets for tableware. Little of this ware has survived, although it was popular at the time and must have been made in considerable quantity. Wedgwood kept to himself the secret of colouring and glazing these wares, but they were widely imitated. More important to the collector are the teapots wholly or partly designed or modelled by Greatbatch. His patterns included 'China' teapots and caddies (usually hexagonal with Chinese decoration in relief), teapots in the shape of various fruits, a teapot moulded in relief with scrollwork framing a central landscape, shell-shaped spouts, and spouts and handles moulded with overlapping leaves.

The arrangement between Wedgwood and Greatbatch appears to have ended about 1770. He achieved some success later on his own account with such creamware items as teapots decorated with transfer prints illustrating the story of the *Prodigal Son**, *Aurora**, and *Captain Cook being directed by Britannia,* but he was ruined by a bad debt and secured employment with Turner* until the latter's death in 1787. In 1788 Greatbatch joined Wedgwood at Etruria* at a wage (according to Simeon Shaw) of 5s. a day and a free house. It seems that this arrangement was made to prevent his working for anyone else, and he was largely employed on administrative work until his retirement in 1807, when he was given a pension for life. A number of his original block moulds are preserved in the Wedgwood Museum*.

Greek Fret

A border pattern in which the lines, vertical and horizontal, are at right angles to each other. A meander* border.

Greek Street, Soho, London

See: Showrooms.

Greek Wave Pattern

See: Vitruvian Scroll.

Green Glaze

No.7 in Josiah Wedgwood's Experiment Book*, green glaze was perfected during his partnership with Whieldon*. The formula is dated March 23rd, 1759, and described as ''A Green glaze, to be laid on Common white biscuit ware. Very good.'' Later he added the note: ''This No. is the result of many Expts. which I made in order to introduce a new species of ware. . . to be of an even self colour, and laid upon the ware in the form of a coloured glaze. This No. has been used for several years very successfully, in a great variety of articles both for home and foreign consumption.'' Green glazed ware had been produced in England from early times, and the use of copper scales (which Josiah obtained from Robinson & Rhodes* from 1760 to 1766) was well known in Staffordshire and Yorkshire. Wedgwood's particular achievement was in the quality of the glaze, which was of a brilliance and depth of colour previously unrivalled. It was eminently suitable for the production of the rococo* style cauliflower, melon and pineapple shapes already made popular by the porcelain factories, but a whole new range of plates and dishes was soon added, moulded in low relief with leaf, vine and strawberry patterns. It was used, too, for some large hooped plant pots, comports, and candlesticks, and by 1790 it was being employed, with contrasting enamel colouring, to decorate turned vases, bough pots and twig baskets. Some rare green glazed hedgehog* crocus pots are also known.

Reintroduced in the 1860s, after an interval of about fifty years, green-glazed ware has remained popular until the present day.

Green, Guy (fl.1750-1799)

Partner in Sadler & Green (see: John Sadler); possibly co-inventor of the transfer-printing process in Liverpool. His signature, 'Green, Liverpool', appears on some subjects decorating Wedgwood creamware. He continued to operate the firm of Sadler & Green for ten years after Sadler's death, retiring in 1799.

Green, Thomas (fl.1760-1780)

Painter employed by Wedgwood in 1770, and believed to be responsible, with Thomas Dimcock*, for the decoration of dessert services painted with naturalistic flowers in purple monochrome, some of which are marked underneath with the letter 'G'.

Greenaway, Kate (1846-1901)

English illustrator, and writer of children's books. She specialised in coloured drawings of children, especially girls in pseudo-Regency bonnets and frilly dresses and ribbons, and small boys in frilled shirts and pantaloons. Kate Greenaway's work was popular in her day, and it has become somewhat of a cult in modern times. She was much praised by Ruskin. Sentimental lithographs by her, or after her drawings, were disseminated in large numbers. Her children are found as pottery figures and decorating nursery china. Wedgwood produced plates and nursery tiles decorated with Kate Greenaway designs, and the latter are occasionally to be found mounted in metal as teapot stands and jardinières.

Green Glaze. *On the right a cauliflower teapot in yellow and green glazes. Extreme left, an artichoke custard cup lacking its cover.*

Green Glaze. *Block mould showing decoration of overlapping vine leaves, popularly used for green-glazed ware.* Wedgwood.

Greenaway, Kate. *Tile representing December, from a set of the months by Kate Greenaway.* Wedgwood.

Griffin (Griffon, Gryphon)

Fabulous animal having the head of an eagle and the body and hindquarters of a lion. It was believed by the Greeks to inhabit the region of Scythia and to guard its gold. The figure of a griffin, 13¼ ins. high, was produced as a candlestick* in black basaltes*. The modelling is of extremely fine quality and may have been the work of Josiah I* with the assistance of Thomas Boot*. Wedgwood is known to have modelled a chimaera*. Meteyard* illustrates the griffin candlestick (*Life of Wedgwood*, Vol. II, Pl.42) but describes it as a chimaera. It is, perhaps, possible that the same confusion existed at Etruria* in Josiah's time.

Griffiths, Ralph (1720-1803)

LL.D. Philadelphia. Founder, proprietor, and publisher of the *Monthly Review;* member of the Wednesday Club*, brother of Thomas Griffiths (see: Cherokee Clay) who undertook the journey to South Carolina for Wedgwood in search of Cherokee clay; a friend of both Wedgwood and Bentley, who wrote to Wedgwood in 1780 breaking the news of Bentley's death. Ralph Griffiths had spent many years in South Carolina, and returned to live near Turnham Green, London. He is the subject of a jasper portrait medallion made about 1790, which was also made in Tassie's* glass paste.

Grotesques. *Modern teapot decorated with opposing grotesque animals terminating in foliage. Columbia pattern.* Wedgwood.

Griffiths, Ralph. *Portrait medallion in jasper of Ralph Griffiths (1720-1803), probably modelled about 1790.* Wedgwood.

Grotesques

French term for form of ornament characterised by fantastic shapes based on a combination of human, plant (acanthus), and animal forms. Grotesques are Roman in origin, and first came to light when the Golden House of Nero was excavated at the end of the 15th century, where they occurred in the form of frescoes. In this form they were employed by Raphael to decorate the *loggie* of the Vatican in 1509. These motifs were extremely popular during the 16th century with the *maiolica* potters, especially those of Urbino whose grotesques are characteristic, and were much copied elsewhere. The fashion continued unabated during the 17th century, and influenced the work of the designer Jean I. Bérain. During the 18th and 19th centuries grotesques were still employed occasionally, especially in the 19th century during Renaissance revivals, and the popular 20th century *Florentine* table ware pattern is based on 16th century grotesques. Grotesques were, of course, originally discovered below ground in what seemed to be a cave (*grotte*), hence the name, which, in Italian, is *Grotteschi.*

Ground Laying

See: Processes of Manufacture; Powder Colours.

Gubbio Lustre

A brilliant iridescent lustre developed by Maestro Giorgio Andreoli and applied from c.1498 to *maiolica* made at Deruta, Faenza, Castel Durante, and (later) Gubbio. Best known is a ruby colour, but lighter varieties were also employed, all probably from gold. Wedgwood attempted to reproduce this lustre in 1862-64 with the aid of Pietro Gaj* of Carocchi*, Fabbri & Co., but without success.

Guyatt, Richard Talbot, CBE (b.1914)

Artist and designer; co-designer of the Lion and Unicorn Pavilion, Festival of Britain, 1951; consultant designer to Wedgwood 1952-55 and 1967-70; principal of the School of Graphic Design, Royal College of Art. He designed the prize-winning commemorative mug for the Coronation of Queen Elizabeth II, 1953, the Prince of Wales Investiture mug, 1969, the Royal Silver Wedding mug, 1973, the Silver Jubilee mug, 1977, and a sporting mug in black and white jasper in 1968.

The latter, which was issued in a limited edition of 500, features views of British sporting centres and received a special award from the Council of Industrial Design.

Guyatt, Richard. *Award-winning mug designed by Richard Guyatt to celebrate the coronation of H.M. Queen Elizabeth II in 1953. The brown print is heightened with pink lustre and gold.* Wedgwood.

Guyatt, Richard. *Queen's ware mug with bicentennial design of the American eagle and flag in polychrome. Limited edition of 5,000. Designed by Richard Guyatt in 1976.* Wedgwood.

Hackwood, Louis (Lewis)

Engraver who worked for Wedgwood, 1799. Principally he engraved borders and ornaments for useful wares.

Hackwood Vine

An embossed vine persistent* pattern on bone china*, designed by William Hackwood* in 1812, and produced during the short first period of bone china manufacture (1812-c.1822). It is to be found outlined in gold.

Hackwood, William. *Portrait medallion in jasper of Mark Antony, attributed to Hackwood, 1775 (cf. Cleopatra).* Dwight and Lucille Beeson Collection.

Hackwood, William (c.1757-1839)

Modeller for Wedgwood, 1769-1832; chief modeller of ornamental work. Hackwood was the "ingenious boy," hired in 1769, who was doubtfully permitted two years later to attempt a portrait medallion* of Master Crewe. Later he was to become indispensable, particularly in the work of adapting busts*, reliefs, and designs bought in London. Many portrait medallions are by his hand, including portraits of Josiah Wedgwood, George III* and Queen Charlotte*. A few signed works exist: the portraits of Garrick and Shakespeare were signed on the truncation, but Wedgwood disapproved and Hackwood was instructed not to repeat this practice.

Wedgwood wrote in 1774: "Hackwood is of the greatest value and consequence in finishing fine small work, and of this kind we have and shall have enough to employ him constantly." Two years later he was wishing he had "half a dozen more Hackwoods." Hackwood seems, indeed, to have been capable of fine modelling on almost any scale. Besides his work in remodelling and finishing casts of large busts supplied by Hoskins & Grant*, he did much restoration and remodelling to gems* and figures* taken from borrowed models which became the foundation of jasper cameo* work. He was also probably responsible for modelling much of the work of Lady Templetown* and Lady Diana Beauclerk*. In 1776, while still only nineteen years old, Hackwood modelled the *Birth of Bacchus,* the largest jasper tablet made by that date. His own estimate of his worth was rising, and Wedgwood wrote in July of that year that Hackwood was "growing very extravagant in his prices, and I do not find it possible to keep him reasonable on that subject." In November 1778, he wrote to Bentley*: "Some of the tablets lately sent are finished very high by Hackwood at considerable expence...you will percieve [*sic*] the difference in the hair, faces, fingers, &c. and more palpably by all the parts capable of it being undercut*, which gives them the appearance, and nearly the reality of models." In 1802, seven years after Josiah I's death, Byerley* wrote to Josiah II* expressing his fears that Josiah Spode II might be trying to entice Hackwood to work for him. Hackwood was not to be tempted: he remained with the Wedgwood firm, retiring at last after an astonishing sixty-three years of service. His work for Wedgwood displays both vigour and fine detail. He was not in the true sense an artist, for very little of his work was original, but the best of his modelling — particularly evident in his portraits of Bourne* and Willet* — is unsurpassed by any of the artists employed by Wedgwood.

Hackwood, William (*c.1757-1839*). *From an engraving.* Photo: Wedgwood.

An exhaustive catalogue of Hackwood's work is not possible. The list below includes all the authenticated work, and much that is reliably attributed:

BUSTS (supplied by Hoskins, and believed to have been remodelled or finished by Hackwood).
Aggripina, 1774.
Antinous, 1774.
Antoninus Pius (2), 1774.
Augustus Caesar, 1774.
Brutus, Lucius Junius, 1774.
Brutus, Marcus Junius, 1774.
Cato, 1774.
Epicurus, 1774.
Faustina, 1774.
Germanicus, 1774.
Homer (2), 1775.
Horace, 1775.
Jones, Inigo, 1774.
Marcus Aurelius, 1774.
Minerva, 1774.
Palladio, 1774.
Pindar, 1774.
Plato, 1774.
Seneca, 1774.
Solon, 1774.
Venus de Medici, 1774.
Zeno, 1774.

BUSTS (from medals supplied by Veldhuysen*, 1779).
Boerhaave, Hermann.
Grotius, Hugo.
de Ruyter, Michel.
de Witt, Cornelis.
de Witt, Jan.

PORTRAIT MEDALLIONS
Anglesey, Henry Paget, 1st Marquis, c.1821.
Bentley, Thomas* (3), 1778-80.
Bourne, Edward*, 1778.
Queen Charlotte* (3), 1775-76.
Cleopatra (attributed), 1775.
Master Crewe, 1771.
Darwin, Erasmus* (attributed), 1780.
Elers, J.P.*, 1777.
Franklin, Benjamin (2), 1779 and (attributed) 1780.
Garrick, David (2), 1777.
George III* (4), 1775-76.
Louis XVI (after Renaud), 1778.
Mark Antony (attributed), 1775.
Priestley*, Joseph (attributed), 1779.
Shakespeare, 1777.
Stafford*, Granville Leveson-Gower, 1st Marquis (attributed), 1781.
Voltaire*, c.1777.
Wedgwood, Josiah*, 1782 and (attributed) 1778.
Willet*, William, 1776.
Woodward, Dr. John (attributed) c.1780.

BAS-RELIEFS
Aescalapius and Hygeia.
Antonia with urn (attributed), 1773.
Aurora, cameo, 1773.
Birth of Bacchus ('Bacchus and Mercury'), 1776-77.
Bacchus and Panther (attributed) 1772; remodelled 1776.
Bellerophon watering Pegasus, cameo, 1773.
Choice (Judgement) of Hercules, 1777.
Cupid and Psyche, 1796.

Cupid Market (Sale of Erotes), 1773.
Cupids as Four Seasons, 1777.
Dancing Hours (by Flaxman*), redraped 1808.
Diana the Huntress, cameo, 1774.
Erato (attributed), 1778.
Indian Bacchus, 1776.
Infant Academy, c.1785.
Marriage of Cupid and Psyche (see separate entry under this heading).
Muses watering Pegasus, cameo, 1775.
Music, 1782.
Night shedding Poppies, 1778.
Piping Faun.
Sacrifice to Flora, 1777.
Sacrifice to Hymen (attributed also to Flaxman), companion to *Marriage of Cupid and Psyche.*
Satyr head.
Slave medallion, 1786.
Sophonisba.
Sydney Cove Medallion (designed by Webber*), 1789.
Triumph of Bacchus, 1776.
Ulysses staying the chariot of Victory, 1773.
Venus and Cupid, 1778.
Venus chiding Cupid, 1774.
Venus Victrix, cameo, 1773.

Hackwood also modelled a bulb pot with arched top, 1796; the Rustic candlesticks (figures of Autumn and Winter), 1784; and worked, with Josiah I, Josiah II*, Webber*, and William Wood* on the Portland vase.

Hades
God of the underworld.
See: Pluto.

Hales, William (fl.1790-1815)
Engraver. He was responsible for the 12ins. and 14ins. oval dishes for the *Water Lily** pattern in 1807-8, part of the *Bamboo* (1808), *Blue Hibiscus* (1806-8) and *Blue Peony* (1808) patterns, and the engravings for underglaze red-printed *Water Lily,* c.1807-8.
See: Underglaze Blue Prints.

Half Figures and Busts
Figures and busts modelled in front and flat at the back to enable them to be fixed to a wall or a flat surface. Made in cream-coloured ware and white jasper for the use of architects, they were intended as an inexpensive substitute for carved marble ornament (Wedgwood to Bentley, October 27th, 1778). Specimens are very rare, and are notable for sharply detailed modelling. To Wedgwood's surprise and chagrin architects gave a cool reception to jasper as a material for interior decoration.

Half Palmette
A palmette* divided in half. It occurs both on classical pottery and as part of some neo-classical* decoration. In Wedgwood it occurs chiefly on encaustic* painted vases and as relief ornament on the square plinths of jasper vases.

Hamilton, Sir William (1730-1803)
Grandson of the third Duke of Hamilton; Knight of the Bath, 1772; Ambassador to the Court of Naples, 1764-1800; husband of Emma, Lady Hamilton, Nelson's mistress. Sir William took great interest in the excavations at Herculaneum and Pompeii, and made a notable collection of Greek and Italian vases which he later sold to the British Museum. The publication of his collection in 1766-67 in a work compiled by

Half Figures. *Pair of half figures for placing flat against a wall. Herculaneum subjects.* Wedgwood.

D'Hancarville* entitled *Antiquités étrusques, grecques, et romaines* greatly influenced a number of manufacturers. Wedgwood was presented with a copy of Sir William's catalogue by Sir Watkin Williams Wynn*.

Sir William also purchased the Barberini (or Portland*) vase from James Byres* and sold it to the Duchess of Portland. A number of letters written on various subjects to Sir William by Josiah Wedgwood are in the Wedgwood archives. Portrait medallions of Hamilton are listed in every Wedgwood catalogue, from 1773 to 1789. The first portrait, probably the work of Joachim Smith*, may have been made for presentation to Sir William at the time of the accession to the British Museum, on the 20th March, 1772, of the first part of the Hamilton collections. A superb and unique example of this portrait, of black basaltes with an encaustic* painted ground, is in the Beeson* Collection, Birmingham Museum, Alabama. The diameter of the long axis of the third portrait, produced in 1779, was 10½ ins.

Hammersley, James Astbury (1815-1869)
Born in Burslem, Hammersley studied painting under James Baker Pyne (1800-70). In 1844-45 he was either employed at Etruria* or supplied models or designs for Wedgwood. Four years later he was appointed head of the Manchester School of Design, becoming first President of the Manchester School of Fine Arts, 1857-61.

Hampton, Herbert (1862-1929)
Sculptor and painter; studied at Lambeth, Westminster and Slade Schools of Art and at the Académie Julien in Paris; exhibited at many London galleries from 1886 and at the Royal Academy. Hampton modelled two portrait medallions of Edward VII which were reproduced in jasper* in 1910 and 1911.

Hamilton, Sir William. *Jasper portrait medallion, modelled c.1772 by Joachim Smith.* Eugene D. Buchanan Collection.

Hancock, John (1757-1847)
Ceramic decorator, born at Nottingham. He claimed to have invented gold (pink) lustre, and silver (platinum, steel) lustre, which were used at Spode's* factory in Stoke-on-Trent. He worked for Wedgwood from 1816, and died in Etruria in 1847.

See also: Lustre Decoration.

Hancock, Robert (1730-1817)
English engraver, probably a pupil of John Brookes at Battersea. Hancock, who worked at Battersea, Bow, Worcester, and Caughley, pioneered transfer printing on porcelain. His two most widely known prints are probably the portrait of Frederick the Great of 1757, and *The Tea Party,* a version of which appears on Wedgwood creamware.

See: Guy Green; The Ladies' Amusement; John Sadler; Transfer Printing.

Handleing
When Josiah Wedgwood attained the age of fourteen years he was apprentice to his brother, Thomas, to learn the "Art Mistery Occupation or Imployment of Thrower and Handleing." The latter term refers to the process of putting handles on cups, jugs, teapots, and similar wares. The handles are made separately, and are attached to the unglazed vessel by luting them into position, using slip as an adhesive.

Handmaid to the Arts, The
A treatise, published by Robert Dossie in 1758 (reprinted 1764), containing many valuable instructions and recipes for

the making and decoration of a variety of objects, including soft-paste porcelain and papier mâché. A 110-page section dealt with enamel painting and the preparation of colours. In August 1765, while he was still trying to perfect the gilding of Queen Charlotte's* teaset, Josiah wrote to his brother, John*, instructing him to buy a copy of ''Vol 1st of the Handmaid of [sic] the Arts'' and to send it at once by coach.

Hardstones
See: Cameos; Variegated Wares.

Harrache, Thomas (fl.1750-1775)
Jeweller, china seller, and art dealer of Pall Mall, London. Wedgwood wrote from London to Bentley in Staffordshire, November 1768: ''...at Harrach's [sic] this afternoon, where we have amongst us spent near twenty pounds. Do you remember what Harrach asked for the Raphael* bottles? I think it was 10 guineas. They now ask twenty-five! Harrach has just returned from Paris and has brought a great many fine things with him. I bid £30 for three pair of vases; they asked £32 and would not abate a penny. There's spirit for you! Must we not act in the same way?''
See: J. Morgan.

Harrison, John (1716-1798)
Tradesman of Newcastle-under-Lyme, and partner with Thomas Alders* and Josiah Wedgwood in a potworks at Cliff Bank, Stoke-on-Trent, which made agate and marbled knife-handles, tortoiseshell and black wares, 'scratch blue' and salt-glazed ware, 1752-54.

Heath, John (fl.1830-1877)
Engraver of Hanley who worked for Wedgwood, 1840-77.

Hebe
The goddess of youth, daughter of Zeus and Hera. She filled the cups of the gods before Ganymede* arrived on Olympus. Hebe married Hercules* when he became immortal. She was reputed to be able to renew the youth of the aged.
Wedgwood subjects:
Hebe, medallion by Webber*, c.1785.
Hebe and the Eagle, medallion by Flaxman*, c.1777.
Hebe, statuette 7ins., attributed to Webber, c.1787.

Hector
Eldest son of Priam* and Hecuba, husband of Andromache*, and hero of the Trojans in their war with the Greeks. During the long siege of Troy, Hector fought with the bravest of the Greeks and slew Patroclus, the friend of Achilles*. Pursued by Achilles, Hector fled three times round the city walls before he was killed. At the command of Zeus*, Achilles surrendered Hector's body to Priam.

Wedgwood produced two versions of the subject *Achilles dragging the body of Hector around the walls of Troy*: the first, a bas-relief* by Pacetti*, was adapted from the Luna marble disc in the Capitoline Museum; the second, much smaller, medallion, shows the figures reversed and an Achilles figure of truly heroic proportions that dwarfs the horses, probably copied from a cast from Tassie* after a gem by Pichler*. Also attributed to Pacetti is the tablet, *Priam begging for the body of Hector from Achilles*, copied from a relief on the so-called sarcophagus of Alexander Severus.

Hector. *Green and lilac dip three-colour jasper medallion of* Achilles dragging the body of Hector around the walls of Troy, *3ins. by 4½ins. c.1785.* Wedgwood.

Handleing. *Jack Dawes piercing the strainer of a parapet teapot. Lying on the table are the handle, spout, teapot lid and finial, the handle and spout waiting to be fitted. In the background, the plaster mould.* Wedgwood.

Hedgehog Crocus Pot. *Jack Dawes putting the finishing touches to a black basaltes hedgehog crocus pot or bulb holder, a model which has remained popular since the 18th century.* Photo: Wedgwood.

Hedgehog Crocus Pot

A hollow receptacle realistically modelled in the form of a hedgehog, its bristly body pierced with holes which are large enough to admit a crocus bulb. It was accompanied by a tray to hold water. Moss or soil was placed inside the hedgehog, which was then placed on the tray and planted with bulbs. Made by Wedgwood in black basaltes and green glazed* creamware.

Heels

Heels for women's shoes were first made in blue and white jasper in 1959. They occur in both low and high styles, and in other jasper colours, marketed in both England and America.

Henning, John (1771-1851)

Modeller of portraits in wax and plaster, born at Paisley, Scotland. He moved to Glasgow in 1800 and made his reputation by modelling the portraits of many of the most celebrated inhabitants of the city. From 1811 he lived in London, where he completed models of the Parthenon and Phigaleian friezes from the Elgin Marbles and a series of small copies in plaster of the Raphael cartoons, as well as portraits and larger friezes for architectural decoration. Many of his portraits were modelled from pencil drawings of his sitters, and a number were reproduced in Tassie's* glass paste. It may have been through the Tassies that he first made contact with Wedgwood. Letters from Henning to Josiah II, starting in 1811, are preserved in the Wedgwood archives, and he sent Wedgwood a list of his ''medallion portraits done from life.'' The following were reproduced in jasper*: James Grahame (1813); Sir Samuel Romilly (1813); Sir Walter Scott (1813); Dugald Stewart (1811); and the Duke of Wellington (1813).

Henri Deux Ware

Properly, Saint-Porchaire ware. A very rare type of pottery made in France during the 16th century, principally during the reign of Henri II, decorated with grotesques, arabesques and strapwork, by inlaying with coloured clays. Fewer than one hundred specimens are known to have survived, and these were much sought by wealthy collectors during the 19th century and were copied at that time by a number of factories.

Some of the best copies were made by Charles Toft* for Minton*. Toft was also chief modeller at Etruria* 1872-89, and there is a record in the Wedgwood archives of a chess board decorated in the Henri Deux manner as an exhibition piece. This is generally attributed to Charles Toft. The border was designed by Walter Crane*, and the chessmen (after Flaxman originals) are signed by Thomas Mellor*, who was evidently responsible for the inlaying of the creamware bases of the figures. It is unlikely that Toft's ability and experience in ceramic inlaying would have been allowed to remain neglected, and there may be other Wedgwood examples of his work which remain to be identified.

See: Inlaid Ware.

Henshaw, William (fl.1769-1774)
(also Henshall and Henscholl)

Painter at Chelsea who worked on the Frog* service. Possibly the painter and engraver of that name, a pupil of Bartolozzi, listed as an exhibitor at the Royal Academy from 1775.

Hera

See: Juno.

Herculaneum

An ancient city of Campania in the shadow of Vesuvius, situated between Neapolis (Naples) and Pompeii. It was captured by the Romans in 88B.C. and partially destroyed by the earthquake of A.D.63. With Stabiae and Pompeii, it was buried by ashes and lava in A.D.79. The site was afterwards partially built over and the old city is now about seventy feet below ground-level. It was discovered in 1738 as the result of the sinking of a well. Many buildings have now been excavated and important works of art have been discovered there. Sir William Hamilton* collected vases and other works recovered from this site. A Liverpool* creamware factory was named after it at the end of the 18th century. The design of Wedgwood's ornamental wares was strongly influenced by Herculaneum. Early in the 1770s Lord Lansdowne gave Wedgwood permission to copy some bas-reliefs which had been made to his order from wall-paintings in the Villa dei Papyri. Discovered in the middle of the 18th century, these wall-paintings were much copied. The Wedgwood reliefs were at first issued in basaltes and terracotta, and later in jasper (see: Herculaneum Subjects).

For painted Herculaneum figures and pictures, see: Encaustic Painting.

Herculaneum Subjects

A series of fourteen oval or circular plaques, thirteen of which were inspired by Roman wall-paintings at Pompeii* (illustrated in *Le Antichita di Ercolano Esposte,* Vol.I, Naples 1757) but moulded directly from a set of casts in the possession of the Marquess of Lansdowne c.1772. They are listed as nos. 51-65 of Class II in all Wedgwood's Ornamental Catalogues from 1773, and were made in a pale terracotta or basaltes, sometimes with painted grounds and usually with moulded frames* of the same composition which might be painted or gilded. From 1778 they were also available in jasper. The full list is as follows (measurements include frames):

Dancing Nymph (holding tambourine), 15ins. by 12ins.
Dancing Nymph (holding cymbals), 15ins. by 12ins.
Dancing Nymph (with tray of figs), 15ins. by 12ins.
Dancing Nymph (with branch and sceptre), 15ins. by 12ins.
Dancing Nymph (holding veil), 15ins. by 12ins.
Dancing Nymph (with tray), 15ins. by 12ins.
Centaur (with Bacchante on his back), 16ins. diameter.
Female Centaur (with child on her back), 16ins. diameter.
Centaur (teaching Achilles), 16ins. diameter.
Polyphemus, 16ins. diameter.
Marsyas and young Olympus, 16ins. diameter.
Papyrius and his Mother (from a different unidentified source), 16ins. diameter.
Bacchanalian Figure (male dancer), 15½ ins. diameter.
Bacchanalian Figure (male dancer), 15½ ins. diameter.

These plaques were intended 'for the decoration of large Halls and Staircases', and the frames were described by Wedgwood as "rich compartments of the same material, modelled and burnt together with the Bas-reliefs."

Hercules

Greek Heracles. Hercules was the son of Zeus* by Alcmena, the wife of Amphitryon. Hera*, always jealous of her husband's *amours* with mortal women, sent serpents to destroy Hercules in his cradle, but he slew them by crushing them in

Herculaneum Subjects. *Girandole (wall-sconce), 15ins. by 8ins., of blue and white jasper with ormolu mounts, depicting a female dancer holding a veil in relief. Adapted from a Pompeian wall painting. 1785. Wedgwood.*

Hercules. *Jasper medallion of Hercules, modelled by Flaxman in 1776 and produced in two heights: 4ins. or 7ins. The figure is derived from the Greco-Roman statue in the Louvre, said to be a faithful copy of* Heracles at Rest *by Lysippus.* Wedgwood.

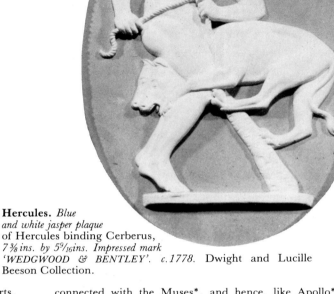

Hercules. *Blue and white jasper plaque* of Hercules binding Cerberus, *7⅜ins. by 5⁹/₁₆ins. Impressed mark* 'WEDGWOOD & BENTLEY'. *c.1778.* Dwight and Lucille Beeson Collection.

his hands. In his youth he was instructed in the martial arts, and became renowned for his great physical strength. He killed a huge lion which had created havoc among the flocks and herds of Mount Cithaeron, and from this time he wore its skin, and sometimes a helmet in the form of its upper jaw and head. Driven mad by Hera he slew his own children by Megara, as well as the two children of his half-brother, and in his grief he consulted the oracle at Delphi, who told him to serve Eurystheus for twelve years, after which he was to become immortal. The twelve Labours of Hercules, undertaken at the behest of Eurystheus, have often been depicted in art. The most frequently represented is his fight with the Nemean lion, which he killed by tearing its jaws apart. The Erymanthean Boar, which he had to capture alive, he exhausted by chasing it through the snow, and then carrying it off in a net. A popular subject has been his seizure of the Golden Apples of the Hesperides, which had been given to Hera at her wedding, and entrusted to the care of the Hesperides and the dragon, Ladon, on Mount Atlas. It was during his journey to find the Golden Apples that Hercules, to persuade Atlas* to fetch them for him, shouldered the heavens in his place. Another Labour depicted is the one in which he brought Cerberus, the fearsome tripled-headed guardian dog of the portals of Hades, to the upper world. When these Labours were finished Hercules became ill, and again consulted the Delphic oracle, which prophesied that he would be restored to health if he would serve for three years. He became a servant to Omphale, Queen of Lydia, and legend tells of a life of intimacy with her in the course of which Hercules became soft and effeminate, and Omphale wore his lion-skin and carried his club. When he died a cloud carried him to Mount Olympus amid peals of thunder, where he became reconciled to Hera, and married to her daughter, Hebe*. In works of art Hercules is usually represented with a lion's skin and a large club. In Rome he was sometimes

connected with the Muses*, and hence, like Apollo*, was called Musagetes (leader of the Muses).

Wedgwood subjects:

Hercules, bust, obtained from Flaxman Senior*, 1784.

Hercules and the Erymanthean Boar, medallion by Flaxman*, 1775.

Hercules binding Cerberus, medallion 9ins. by 6ins. by Flaxman, 1775.

Hercules strangling the Nemean Lion, medallion by Flaxman, 1775.

Young Hercules killing the Lion of Mount Cithaera, medallion by Flaxman, 1775.

Infant Hercules, cameo from a Tassie* gem.

Young Hercules, medallion, attributed to Flaxman, c.1777.

Hercules in the Garden of the Hesperides, painted by Rhodes* or Craft* (after the lower frieze design of a hydria* in the Hamilton collection of vases) on the First Day's Vases*, 1769. Flaxman used the same source for the tablet 5½ins. by 7ins., produced in 1787.

Hercules overcome by Love, cameo by Hackwood*, 1774.

Hercules and Theseus supporting the world [sic], or *The Power of Union,* medallion, 1773, after an engraved gem by Rossi.

The Farnese Hercules (Farnesian Hercules), medallion 4ins. by 3ins., and 7¼ins. (long axis), by Flaxman 1776.

Choice (Judgement) of Hercules, large oval medallion and rectangular tablet in various sizes, modelled by Hackwood, 1777.

Omphale with the club of Hercules, cameo by Flaxman, c.1777.

Omphale in Lion's skin, cameo by Flaxman, c.1777.

Among the medallions supplied to the Empress Catherine II* is one listed as *Hercules and Thetis.* This was presumably either *Hercules and Theseus,* or *The Birth of Achilles** (Achilles and Thetis).

Colour Plate XIII

Extremely fine solid blue jasper teapot with white jasper handle, laurel-leaf spout and cupid finial. The bas-relief figures by Lady Templetown are applied over a 'dimpled' or 'granulated' ground, providing an interesting contrast of texture. 'Cabinet' pieces of such quality are rare. c.1790. Wedgwood. Photo: Reilly/Charles Letts.

Hercules, Choice of

Bas-relief* modelled by Hackwood*, listed in Wedgwood's Catalogue* of ornamental ware of 1787 as no.60 "modelled according to the idea of Lord Salisbury." The subject was originally modelled in 1777, and was first mentioned in Wedgwood's list of tablets being made in the summer of 1778 as available in "3 or 4 sizes." It shows Hercules choosing Fame rather than Pleasure, both personified by young women. The bas-relief appears on oval medallions and rectangular tablets, both of which were used as ornament for chimney pieces*. It is known also as *Judgement of Hercules*.

Hermes

See: Mercury.

Hero and Leander

Hero was a priestess of Aphrodite in Sestus, Leander a youth of Abydos who was in love with her. Every night Leander swam across the Hellespont to visit his beloved until he was overwhelmed by a sudden storm and drowned. Next day his body was washed ashore and was found by Hero, who took her own life by throwing herself into the sea. Two large tablets* of this subject (17ins. by 8ins. and 20ins. by 9ins.) are listed in the 1779 Ornamental Catalogue*.

Herring Dish

A Queen's ware dish of rectangular form decorated with a moulded centre design of a herring and sometimes a simple hand-painted border. Length about 11ins.; first made in the last quarter of the 18th century.

Hesiod

One of the earliest of the Greek poets, whose name is frequently associated with that of Homer*, although he lived about a century later. His *Theogony* gives an account of the origin of the world and the birth of the gods. The mention in Wedgwood's letters of 'Homer and Hesiod', a name he gave originally to the bas-relief* now known as *The Apotheosis of Homer** or *The Crowning of a Citharist*, has given rise to the misapprehension that a separate bas-relief depicting *The Crowning of Hesiod* exists.

Hinks & Son, J.

Birmingham metal manufacturer who was associated with Wedgwood in the late 1870s in the making of oil lamps for domestic illumination. Wedgwood made the oil reservoir in jasper or Queen's ware on a pedestal foot, the Queen's ware usually transfer printed and painted with flowers and figures in the aesthetic* style of the period. Hinks made the metal parts, the wick holder, and shade and chimney carrier.

See also: Argand Lamp; Lamps.

Hippocampi

Sea horses, usually depicted in conjunction with Poseidon (Neptune), Nereids, Tritons, etc. Under the influence of the Renaissance grotesque* the hippocampus was sometimes given a dolphin's tail to replace its hindquarters, and fish-like paddles instead of fore hoofs. Hippocampi exist as figures in Chelsea porcelain and appear in painted form on Wedgwood.

Hercules, Choice of. Also known as Judgement of Hercules; *modelled by William Hackwood, 1777. Blue and white jasper plaque, 9⅞ins. by 13ins. The figure of Hercules is 7ins. high and the relief ½in. deep at the shoulder. Wedgwood.*

Colour Plate XIV

Solid blue and white jasper candlestick in the form of a tree trunk entwined with white vines. Beside it, the figure of Cupid with a basket of fruit symbolises autumn. One of a pair modelled by William Hackwood. c.1785. Wedgwood. Photo: Reilly/Charles Letts.

Hippocrates (460-357 B.C.)

The most celebrated physician of antiquity, born on the island of Cos. He died at the age of 104. His best known work is the *Aphorisms*, which was widely disseminated in both ancient and medieval times.

Wedgwood subjects:
Hippocrates, bust supplied by Hoskins & Grant, 1775.
Hippocrates, medallion by Flaxman, c.1782.

HN Monogram

This is found on one of two applied medallions on a cylindrical jasper beaker made about 1798. The second medallion bears a figure of Neptune. The beaker is otherwise decorated with swags of oak leaves, the base with Egyptian motifs, and round the rim is an inscription: 'The Navy of Britain'. The ornament is in white relief over dark blue dip, with the medallions of lilac jasper. The monogram is that of Horatio Nelson, and the beaker was undoubtedly made to commemorate the Victory of the Nile in 1798, probably at a time when souvenirs of this kind were urgently wanted and before there was a suitable medallion portrait of Nelson to put on it.

See: Britannia Triumphant.

Hoadley, Thomas (1793-1888)

Engraver of 40, Charles Street, Hanley (1834), who worked for Wedgwood, 1824-47. He also supplied designs to Ridgways.

Hodgkiss, James (fl.1900-1925)

Artist and designer at Etruria*, chief designer under the art direction of John Goodwin*, 1910, and closely associated with Daisy Makeig-Jones* in the production of lustre wares. With Goodwin and George Adams, successor to William Burton* as resident chemist, Hodgkiss was responsible for the development of powder colours*, and he designed a number of patterns for the decoration of ornamental bone china* pieces. These included a long line of bowls and vases, the exterior decorated with gold-printed Oriental designs over a powder blue ground, and patterns of flowers, animals, and birds in white reserves against powder blue. He also painted a series of bone china dessert sets with scenes of birds in natural landscapes. His work is often signed.

See: Fairyland Lustre; Ordinary Lustres.

Hollow Ware

The collective name given in the Potteries to cups, bowls, teapots, coffee pots, vegetable dishes, soup tureens and similar wares for holding liquids.

See: Flatware.

Holmes-Wedgwood Lampshade

Queen's ware pendant lampshades, lavender in colour, were made in 1937 to fit a patent fixture and marked: 'The Holmes-Wedgwood shade Patent No 362610 Wedgwood Made in England' (printed).

Holy-Door Marble

One of the crystalline* or variegated* bodies of mixed coloured clay or slip* to imitate natural stones. It is first mentioned in a letter from Wedgwood to Bentley dated June 1768: "Tomorrow the Liverpool coach goes through Newcastle [-under-Lyme] and takes up there two antique Vases, one is of the *Holy Door* Marble, and the other *Jaune Antique*..." Holy-door marble has been frequently misused to describe a variegated lustre introduced in 1806.

HN Monogram. *Dark blue jasper dip beaker, ornamented with Egyptian motifs and swags of oak, with two lilac and white applied cameos of Neptune and the monogram HN, around the rim the inscription impressed 'THE NAVY OF BRITAIN'. c.1798.* Wedgwood.

Homer

Greek epic poet, whose dates and birthplace are both disputed. He is generally regarded as the author of the *Iliad*, which recounts the exploits of Greek warriors during the Trojan war, and the *Odyssey*, concerned with the adventures of Odysseus (Ulysses*) during the course of his erratic journey homewards to Ithaca after the fall of Troy. Nothing is certainly known of Homer's life and antecedents, but tradition places him at about 950 B.C., and regards him as both blind and poor in his old age. Most representations of Homer seem to be based on a bust in the Naples Museum, but this, itself, is conjectural.

Wedgwood obtained a cast of this bust from Hoskins & Grant* in 1774, and it was produced in black basaltes*, after Hackwood* had worked on it, in two sizes (height 25ins. and 15ins.). A small bust, probably from the same model, was listed in the 1799 Catalogue*.

Flaxman's* *Apotheosis of Homer*, first produced as a bas-relief* for a tablet* in 1778, and subsequently adapted as ornament for a Pegasus* vase, was inspired by a calyx krater (see: Krater) in the British Museum.

Homeric Vase

A vase with ornament modelled by John Flaxman*, c.1777, and made in jasper, and later also in black basaltes. It depicts the Crowning of a Citharist, and the relief design was copied faithfully from a bell krater* in the Hamilton* collection. It is generally better known by Wedgwood's name, *The Apotheosis* *of Homer**. The vase has a handsome cover surmounted by a figure of Pegasus*. The same subject appears on Wedgwood tablets, and the Pegasus finial was used on the companion vase, *The Apotheosis of Virgil**, and on other important vases.

Homeric Vase. *Jasper vase with Pegasus finial, ornamented with the* Apotheosis of Homer, *18ins. high. c.1786.* Wedgwood.

Honey-Buff

Cane-coloured tableware made in 1920 for Heal & Son, Tottenham Court Road, London. It was reintroduced in 1956 in a slightly paler shade under the name of *Cane,* and, with the other coloured* bodies, was produced in traditional* shapes.

Honeysuckle Border

1. The anthemion border.
2. A border of alternating palmettes* and honeysuckle flowers. The anthemion is a stylised form of honeysuckle commonly employed as part of neo-classical* decoration in the last quarter of the 18th century.

Hooker, Sir Joseph Dalton (1817-1911)

English botanist; son of Sir William Jackson Hooker; director of Kew Gardens, in succession to his father; intimate of Charles Darwin*. Sir Joseph made many journeys of exploration, and his published works are numerous. He received many honours from English and foreign scientific societies and universities. He is buried at Kew. Dr. Hooker (as he was generally known) began to collect Wedgwood wares about 1860, and a catalogue of his collection was prepared by his second wife in 1877. It is now in the possession of the Wedgwood Society of London. Many of the entries give information about the source of the object and its price.

Sir Joseph was responsible for placing a memorial to his father, Sir William Jackson Hooker*, on the North Wall of Kew Parish Church. This is a combination of marble and

jasper which was suggested by a chimney piece he saw at Alton Towers. The central portrait was modelled by Thomas Woolner*, and the memorial was designed by Hooker's cousin, Sir Reginald Palgrave*. The portrait is in blue and white jasper, and it is surrounded by four shaped plaques of green and white jasper ornamented with ferns. Above is a narrow frieze of grasses. The memorial to Sir Joseph Hooker, erected after his death in 1911, took the form of a portrait by Frank Bowcher* surrounded by green and white jasper plaques depicting plants in which Sir Joseph had taken a special interest. They were designed and modelled by Matilda Smith, a cousin, who helped to illustrate the *Botanical Magazine,* of which he was editor.

Hooker, Sir William Jackson, FRS (1785-1865)

Director of the Royal Botanic Gardens at Kew, who was responsible for greatly extending and opening what was formerly a royal garden to the public. He also assisted in the foundation of a museum of economic botany. Sir William's memorial in Kew Parish Church, erected by his son, Sir Joseph Hooker*, is a combination of marble and Wedgwood jasper.

See: Sir Joseph Hooker.

Horace (65-8B.C.)

Quintus Horatius Flaccus, Roman poet; celebrated for his *Odes, Satires, Epodes,* and *Epistles,* the last being considered the most perfect of Horatian poetry.

Wedgwood produced two basaltes busts of Horace: the first 20ins. high, appears in the 1773 Catalogue*; the second, 15ins. high, was supplied by Hoskins & Grant* in 1775 and was refinished by Hackwood*.

Horne, Matthew

Josiah Wedgwood frequently received applications for employment from workmen who had been at other factories, but these were rarely in writing, which makes the following application from Matthew Horne of Lambeth, South London, the more interesting. The date of the letter is uncertain, but it can reasonably be placed to c.1775. Matthew Horne is otherwise unknown. Little is known about porcelain manufacture in Lambeth, and there are no known specimens. There is no doubt that Horne's claims were exaggerated but probably not entirely without foundation.

"Sir, I hear they are all going to make China in Staffordshire which I am afraid will be of hurt to some. I at last by long practice, have found out the best body in this kingdom it will make figures or ornaments four or five feet high without supports or props. It will make dishes any... it workes allmost as well as your cream colour clay it burns quite Transparent [*sic*] and will be maid very cheap. I have three Glazes that sute it very well. But have no where to [burn] them but in a house fire — I saw your man Gorge he promised to come to Lambeth — I tould him I had something to send to you as he Did *not* come I could not tell how to send them to you — This again I whall [will] to you and no One Else if you will avail me with a little Monney. — So you may understand that when my Brother John and Taylor Broke [i.e. became insolvent] I was bound for some Monney for him which I must pay soon. I am certain that if you would set the Troyals [trials] you would approve of it. I Don't want to make any Troyal but make a whole Kiln which I can as easy and certain as a Kiln of Staffordshire ware if you please I will take some things and show them to Mr Bentley and you will have is [*sic*] opinion of it — If you have a mind to Do Anything in it I will come down as soon as possible and worke for you half a year without wages and then if you find it to answer I shall leave it to you what I

Deserve yearly, and hope I shall be with you for Life   Your answer to this by return of you [sic] will greatly oblige, Sir,
    Your humble servant to command, Matthew Horne.''

Wedgwood's reply has not survived, but, by 1775, he was fully occupied in the production of his first jasper and was no longer interested in the production of porcelain.

Hors d'Oeuvre Dish

A dish, similar to a sweetmeat dish, divided by partitions into several compartments for serving *hors d'oeuvres*. It usually has a domed cover. The type was first made of Queen's ware in the 18th century.

Hoskins, James (d.1791)
Hoskins & Grant (from 1774)
Hoskins & Oliver

Not much is known of Hoskins' antecedents, but he held the position of moulder and caster in plaster to the Royal Academy from the inception of that institution in 1768 until his own death in 1791. He was, until 1774, in partnership with Samuel Euclid Oliver. The style of the partnership is a little uncertain, and was either Oliver & Hoskins or Hoskins & Oliver. Oliver exhibited the portrait of a nobleman in wax at the Royal Academy in 1769. He may have died in 1774, because in that year Hoskins took Benjamin Grant into partnership. Grant (fl.1775-1809) was a plaster figure-maker to the Royal Academy. Towards the end of his life Grant was in financial difficulties, and applied to the Academy for relief three times. He was granted the sum of ten guineas on each occasion.

Hoskins & Oliver and Hoskins & Grant supplied Wedgwood with both moulds and casts of figures and busts until 1779. Casts or moulds of the following subjects were supplied to Wedgwood by Hoskins and his partners:

Addison, bust, 1775.
Agrippina (Agrepina), bust, 1774. Worked on by Hackwood*.
Air, see: *The Elements* (below).
Alexander, bust, 1779.
Antinous (Antenos), bust, 1774. Worked on by Hackwood. This bust has been attributed to Hackwood.
Antoninus Pius, bust, 1774. Worked on by Hackwood.
Marc Antony, figure, 1775.
Ariadne, bust, 1779.
Augustus Caesar, bust, 1774. Worked on by Hackwood.
Aurora, cast, 1779.
Autumn, also called *Somnus.*
Bacchus, bust, 1779.
Bacon, Sir Francis, bust, 1779. Worked on by Keeling*.
Beaumont, Francis, bust, 1775.
Bentley, Thomas, 1773, portrait medallion from a wax model.
Boyle, Hon. Robert, bust, 1775.
Cato, bust, 1774. Worked on by Hackwood.
Charles III (King of Spain), mould from copper medal, 1775.
Chaucer, Geoffrey, bust, 1775.
Chrispagnia, figure, 1779.
Cicero (ascribed to Bacon*), bust, 1775.
Cleopatra, figure, 1775.
Congreve, William, bust, 1775.
Cupid & Hymen, medallion, 5ins. by 3½ ins., 1774.
Cupid inflaming the Mind, 1774.
Cupid and Psyche, cast from oval medallion, 1779.
Democritus (Democrates), bust, 1775. Worked on by Keeling.
Demosthenes, bust, 1775.
Dryden, John, bust, 1775.
Earth, see: *The Elements* (below).
Elements, The, four ovals: *Earth, Fire, Air* and *Water,* 1774.
Epicurus, bust, 1774. Worked on by Hackwood.

Faustina, bust, 1774. Worked on by Hackwood.
Fire, see: *The Elements* (above). Remodelled, 1778.
Fletcher, John, bust, 1774.
Galen, bust, 1775.
Ganymede and Bacchus, relief, 1770.
Garrick, David, portrait medallion, mould, 1773.
Garrick, David, bust, 1779.
Germanicus, bust, 1774. Worked on by Hackwood.
Harvey, William, bust, 1775.
Hippocrates, bust, 1775.
Homer, bust, 1775. Worked on by Hackwood.
Horace, bust, 1775. Worked on by Hackwood.
Johnson, Dr. Samuel, bust, 1775.
Jones, Inigo, bust, 1774. Worked on by Hackwood.
Jonson, Ben, bust. Worked on by Keeling.
Julia, bust, 1775.
Julius Caesar, bust, 1779.
Junius Brutus (Lucius), bust, 1774. Worked on by Hackwood, Flaxman*.
Locke, John, bust, 1774.
Madonna, The, bust, 1775.
Marcus Aurelius, bust, 1774. Two versions. Worked on by Hackwood.
Marcus (Junius) Brutus, bust, 1774. Worked on by Hackwood.
Mercury, bust, 1779. Two versions. Worked on by Hackwood.
Mercury (seated and tying sandal), 1779. From a figure by Pigalle*.
Milton, John, bust, 1775.
Minerva, bust, 1774. Worked on by Hackwood.
Morpheus, statuette, 1770. Worked on by Coward*.
Newton, Sir Isaac, bust, 1774. Second version 1775.
Newton, Sir Isaac, portrait medallion, probably cast from an ivory by David Le Marchand*.
Paiske, M., 1774. Two versions.
Palladio (Italian architect), bust, 1774. Worked on by Hackwood.
Pindar, bust, 1774. Worked on by Hackwood.
Plato, bust, 1774. Worked on by Hackwood.
Pope, Alexander, bust, 1775.
Prior, Matthew, bust, 1775.
Raleigh (Reighley), Sir Walter (William), bust, 1775.
Sappho, bust, 1775.
Seneca, bust, 1774. Worked on by Hackwood. Second version 1775.
Shakespeare, bust.
Socrates, bust, 1775.
Solon, bust, 1774. Worked on by Hackwood.
Somnus (also known as Autumn).
Spenser, Edmund, 1775. Worked on by Keeling.
Sphinx and Lyre, 1774.
St. Peter, 1774. Two moulds from medal.
Sterne, Lawrence, bust, 1779.
Swift, Jonathan, bust, 1774.
Venus and Adonis, medallion, 1775.
Venus de Medici, bust, 1774. Worked on by Hackwood.
Venus seated, figure, 1779. From a model by Pigalle*.
Vestal, bust, 1774. Worked on by Richard Parker*.
Virgil, bust.
Walpole, Sir Robert, portrait medallion, taken from a sulphur* cast supplied in 1774; probably modelled after the portrait by John Vanderbank in 1723.
Water, see: *The Elements* (above).
Zeno, bust, 1774.
Zeus (Jupiter), bust, 1774. Worked on by Hackwood.
Zingara,* figure, 1779.

Generally, the modellers of most of the originals are unknown, but it is reasonable to assume that Hoskins, Oliver, or Grant may have been responsible for some, and that others may have been cast 'from the antique' or from more recent work in another medium (marble, bronze or occasionally ivory). Reasons have been advanced elsewhere (see: Figures) for assuming that some may have been modelled by John Bacon* and cast by Hoskins.

Hoskins & Oliver were very expensive in comparison with some other suppliers of casts, but one of the reasons seems to be that they supplied moulds ready for use by pressing. Mould making was, in fact, a much more highly skilled operation than casting. It must also be remembered that Wedgwood's ceramic versions, much more durable than Hoskins's plaster, competed directly with plaster in the market for library busts, etc. Nevertheless, spurred on by the expense, Wedgwood started to make his own moulds, probably in 1774.

See: Casting; John Cheere; John Flaxman Senior; Processes of Manufacture; Repairers; Slip Casting.

Hot Lane, Burslem
The site of the first enamelling kiln in Staffordshire, established about 1750. The art of enamelling is traditionally said to have been introduced by two Dutchmen, and the Widow Warburton*, who lived there, supplied creamware to Wedgwood, 1760-70.

Hot-Water Plate
Hot-water plates were made with double walls in one piece, with a hole for filling the intervening space with hot water; or an ordinary plate was inset into a hot-water container of pewter. Generally they were made of porcelain in China, but Wedgwood was making them in creamware and pearl ware* about 1790. They were popular for keeping food warm during the 18th and the first half of the 19th centuries.

Hot-Water Plate. *Double-walled Queen's ware plate with two gravy pockets, made to contain hot water and filled at the left-hand end. Length 22ins. c.1790.* Buten Museum.

Houdon, Jean-Antoine (1741-1828)
French sculptor, who was born at Versailles and studied under Slodtz. He won the Premier Prix in 1761, was in Rome from 1764-74, and became an Academician in 1777. Houdon made busts in marble, bronze, and terracotta of many celebrated persons of his time, and he visited America from 1787-92. He exhibited in the *Salon* from 1777 to 1812. His well known seated figure of Voltaire* is dated 1781, and it was exhibited in the *Salon* of that year. The equally well known bust in the Victoria and Albert Museum (acquired in 1948) is the head and neck of the seated version, and it is said to be the only portrait which ever pleased its distinguished sitter. Wedgwood produced busts of Voltaire and Washington after Houdon.

Howell & James
Regent Street, London. Retail store established in 1820 to sell millinery, silks, and all kinds of 'art' products, especially pottery and porcelain. Beginning in 1876 Howell & James organised exhibitions to encourage amateur porcelain painting, and they had their own backstamp which was added to wares ordered from commercial factories and 'art' potteries of the day. The Wedgwood Tercentenary bust of Shakespeare, modelled by F.M. Miller*, bore an inscription 'Published under the special patronage of the National Shakespeare Committee by Howell, James & Co., London, April 24th, 1864'. The unusual impressed mark, 'Wedgwood & Son', also appears. The firm made a donation of £50 to the Committee as a token of gratitude for its support of the project.

Hubertusburg, Saxony
A *faience* factory founded in 1770 by J.S.F. Tännich. It came under the directorship of Count Marcolini of Meissen*, who made *Steingut* (creamware) in the Wedgwood manner. Styles were copied from Queen's ware, and some pieces were even marked 'Wedgwood', impressed (1815-35). Pierced borders in the so-called Leeds* style were also favoured. The factory closed in 1848.

Hulme & Walmsley
Merchants of Manchester and Cadiz (Spain) who exported Wedgwood wares. Copies of Wedgwood's catalogue in French were sent to Mr. Walmsley in Cadiz in 1774. In November 1774, Wedgwood refers to the demand there for crucifixes and portraits of saints, the latter to be inserted into bracelets, lockets, snuff boxes, etc. The small medallion portraits of the Popes, listed in the first Ornamental Catalogue, were eminently suitable for export to Catholic countries, but sales of them were disappointingly small.

Hulme, Jesse (1789-1852)
Engraver, designer, portrait artist; worked for Wedgwood, 1842-44.

Hulme, Paul (fl.1913-1951)
Engraver at Etruria* and Barlaston*, 1913-51; worked on the Barlaston mug of 1940.

Hunt Pattern
Wedgwood have used two moulded relief Hunt patterns for the decoration of jugs. The first, produced by Spode*, New Hall*, Davenport* and Turner* is well known: it appears on stoneware jugs with blue, black or brown glazed backgrounds to the white relief, or with the collars of the jugs enamelled in one of those colours. The Wedgwood version is not decorated with a coloured glaze, but sometimes has a coloured band of jasper slip at the rim. The relief decoration appears to be identical, and it shows two dismounted huntsmen with their horses close to a gate, with hounds in at the kill on the reverse. The second version, which appears to be Wedgwood's alone, shows two huntsmen, one mounted and one dismounted, in conversation, with hounds at their side. First produced c.1800 on a jug with a pinched spout, this relief was later transferred to a collared shape with hound handle which was produced until the 1960s in green glaze*, in Dysart glaze*, and in cream colour with enamelled figures or with silver lustre* ground to the relief. A similar relief pattern was produced c.1900 with a printed backstamp showing a portrait of John Peel (1776-1824), the Cumberland huntsman, surrounded by the inscription 'D'ye ken John Peel, 1829'.

Husk Service. *An example of the Husk pattern on Queen's ware.* Wedgwood.

Husk Border

A border pattern of continuous wheat husks. This was a motif employed by the Adam brothers, and should not be confused with the Husk* service made for the Empress Catherine II of Russia.

Husk Service

A service made by Wedgwood for Catherine II* of Russia in 1770 and decorated with the Husk pattern. The main part of the service is now on view in the Hermitage, Leningrad, but some pieces were sold in the State-controlled antique shop in Moscow and bought by Mr. and Mrs. Solanko in 1931. These were acquired from them in 1956 by Wedgwood. Some dishes are marked with an impressed 'Wedgwood', and some 'C II' for Catherine II. The plates of this service have a lobed rim (Queen's shape*) and they were decorated with flowers in the well and a husk border in purple. The decoration was executed at Wedgwood's Chelsea Decorating Studio*. Fragments of plates with this pattern have also been found at Williamsburg, Virginia and the Husk pattern is still being made as part of the Williamsburg Restoration.

See also: Frog Service; Poskotchin; Williamsburg Husk Service.

Hutchins, Thomas (fl.1769-1774)

Painter for Wedgwood, 1769-70; formerly of Soho. Worked on the Frog* service.

Hyacinth Border

A border pattern consisting of hyacinth flowers placed horizontally, end to end, all pointing in the same direction. It is found on jasper ware.

Hydria

A Greek term for a vase used for storing and carrying water. It is large, urn*-shaped, and has two or three loop handles for lifting. The shape was made by Wedgwood in plain basaltes, and basaltes with encaustic* painting.

Hygeia

Goddess of Health; wife (or daughter) of Aesculapius*. She is usually represented as a virgin in a long robe feeding a serpent from a cup.

Wedgwood subjects:

Hygeia, medallion 4ins. by 3¼ ins. Modelled by Flaxman* c.1775.

The Simulacrum of Hygeia, medallion, uncatalogued, attributed to Pacetti*, c.1788.

See: Aesculapius.

Hymen

God of marriage, personified by a handsome youth, taller than Eros (Cupid*) and carrying a torch. He was thought to be the son of Apollo* and one of the Muses*.

A medallion*, *Cupid and Hymen,* 3¼ ins. by 5ins., was reproduced in 1774 from a cast supplied by Hoskins & Grant*. At least two versions of *Sacrifice to Hymen* were produced: one by Flaxman* in 1778 as a companion to *The Marriage of Cupid and Psyche** (versions of both medallions are attributed to Hackwood*); and a second 10ins. high, by Webber* in 1782 as a companion to his *Sacrifice to Concordia.*

I

Ice-Cream Cup
See: Chocolate Cup.

Ice Pail
See: Glacier.

Illustrious Moderns
A series of portrait medallions*, produced in black basaltes* and jasper*, the first 122 of which were listed in Wedgwood's first catalogue of ornamental* wares in 1773. By 1788 the number had risen to 233 and included royalty, statesmen, military heroes, artists, scientists, and judges. The choice of subjects was carefully made to embrace not only the eminent, but also those whose popularity or notoriety would assist sales both at home and abroad, and there was thus a liberal sprinkling of American and European portraits.

Ilmenau, Thuringia
This factory, founded in 1777, produced from 1792-1808, or later, medallion reliefs in white biscuit porcelain which have a dull gloss and a pale blue ground in imitation of Wedgwood jasper. Subjects include classical and mythological figures and contemporary portraits. They are usually in a glazed porcelain frame decorated with beading.

Ilmenau. An oval plaque decorated in relief in Wedgwood style, the subject after Clodion. 6ins. Last quarter of the 18th century. Kestnermuseum, Hanover.

Imperial Queen's Ware
Delicately pierced Queen's ware vases and other ornamental pieces produced c.1860-1920.

Impressed
Indented, as distinct from incised or cut in. Impressed marks were made with a stamp while the clay was still soft.
See: Appendix II: Trade Marks.

Incense Burner
See: Pastille Burner.

Infant Academy, The
This subject of one *putto* painting the portrait of another was originally modelled by Hackwood* in 1789 after a painting by Sir Joshua Reynolds* of 1787. It appears on jasper medallions of various sizes, vases, circular plaques and dishes, and teapots. The bas-relief subject, *Music,* was modelled as a companion piece. *The Infant Academy* was used again in 1973 to decorate fluted plates in Portland blue jasper, and in black basaltes. The latter version of this plate is in a limited edition of 2,500 copies with a special inscription in gold.

Infant Reclining Figures
Figures of naked babies, lying down and holding apples, etc. They were modelled c.1785 by Hackwood* after Della Robbia*, and produced in white jasper with coloured jasper bases 5½ ins. long. They were reproduced in Majolica* glazes in the 19th century and are also known in basaltes*. These figures should not be confused with the *Somnus** series of five similar models.

Inkstandish (or Standish)
A receptacle which includes inkwells, a pounce pot or sand dredger, a taper stick for sealing and sometimes a spill vase, *en suite* with a pen tray as part of a stand containing all these utensils. Also known as a library set or a desk set, and made in silver, porcelain, and fine pottery. Wedgwood made these sets in jasper*, basaltes*, cane* ware, cream-coloured* ware, drab* ware, and *rosso antico**.

Inkstandish. Blue and white jasper inkwells with a taper holder in the form of a broken column. 3½ins. high. c.1790. Dwight and Lucille Beeson Collection.

Inkstandish. Boat-shaped basaltes inkstandish with a swan's head at prow and stern, a taper stick in the centre. Buten Museum.

Inlaid Ware. *Miniature tazza, 2½ ins. high, with inlaid decoration of arabesques. Signed by Thomas Mellor. c.1885.* Wedgwood.

Inlaid Ware. *Brown glazed teapot with inlaid decoration, a Greek key fret ornamenting the shoulder, c.1875.* Wedgwood.

Ivy House Works. *An old line engraving of the Ivy House Works, showing two bottle-kilns in the background.* Photo: Wedgwood.

Inlaid Ware

Ware decorated by impressing the unfired clay body with an intaglio* design which is then filled with slip* of a contrasting colour in the manner of Henri Deux* ware. Inlaid wares were made by a number of English factories during the nineteenth century, notably at Minton* by Charles Toft*. The Wedgwood Inlaid Pattern Book for 1859 lists eight separate bodies and glazes for inlaid decoration: lavender, sage, and red bodies; brown glaze; black; white stone; 'orange porous'; and 'white porous'. The inlaid patterns, often two-colour, were floral, chequered, or key designs, sometimes with simple lines inlaid in a contrasting colour. The range of pieces included candlesticks*, ale jugs, spill vases, tobacco jars, vases, porous water bottles with stoppers and saucer dishes, teapots, and inkstandish*. In the 1880s Thomas Mellor* produced inlaid chessmen* after the Flaxman* models and other ornamental Queen's ware* decorated in this style.

Intaglio

An Italian term meaning a design created by incising and carving below the surface, which is flat and even, and the opposite of a cameo* where the design is in relief. Wedgwood made intaglios in basaltes and variously coloured dry bodies* for use as seals, either mounted in holders or in signet rings. Those intended for mounting in holders could be purchased with shanks for the purpose. Early intaglios were polished. They were impressed with the catalogue number, as well as the initials 'W&B' or (after Bentley's death in 1780) 'Wedgwood'. About 1,700 different subjects were available, most of them also to be had in cameo form. They could be obtained in double form, mounted back-to-back, or mounted similarly in conjunction with a cameo of the same size. As in the case of cameos production seems to have started in 1771, and to have been well established by the Spring of 1772.

See: Cameos.

Intaglio China

See: Lithophanes

Iphigenia

By common tradition the daughter of Agamemnon and Clytemnestra, but, according to some, daughter of Theseus and Helena. Agamemnon, having killed a hart in the grove of Artemis, was punished by the goddess by a calm which prevented the fleet from sailing against Troy. To appease her, he sacrificed Iphigenia, who was rescued by Artemis and taken to Tauris, where she became the priestess of the goddess. There she later saved her brother Orestes* and fled with him to Greece. She appears twice in the tablet *Orestes and Pylades,* modelled by De Vaere*. The bas-relief erroneously described as *Sacrifice of Iphigenia* is Pacetti's* *Achilles in Scyros.*

See: Achilles.

Irish Trade Treaty, 1785

See: General Chamber of Manufacturers.

Isaacs, Miss (fl.1769-1774)

Painter at the Chelsea Decorating Studio*, said to have worked on the Frog* service.

Isis

Egyptian deity; the wife of Osiris and mother of Horus. Isis was worshipped as the goddess of the earth, and later as goddess of the moon. She was identified by the Greeks with Demeter*.

Wedgwood subjects:

Isis, bas-relief head for a medallion, 3ins. by 2½ins., modelled by Flaxman*, 1776.

Procession to Isis, encaustic-painted tablet, said to be after the decoration of an Egyptian vase, but taken from a Hadrianic relief in the collection of Paolo Alessandro Maffei and now in the Vatican.

Meteyard* (*Life of Wedgwood,* Vol.II, p.363) mentions Flaxman's medallion of *Iris,* a misprint for *Isis.*

Ivy House Works, Burslem (1759-1764)

Josiah Wedgwood's first premises as an independent manufacturer, dating from the 1st May, 1759. He began by producing salt-glazed and coloured-glazed wares which had been made during the course of his previous partnership with Whieldon* at Fenton Low. At Ivy House Wedgwood added improved green and yellow glazes and began the production of pineapple and cauliflower ware, much of which was produced in biscuit form by William Greatbatch*. Also made at this time were red wares, and block moulds for salt-glazed wares survive in the Museum at Barlaston. It is probable that Wedgwood perfected cream-coloured ware about 1762. The factory was moved to the Brick House* (Bell Works) in 1764.

Ivy Leaf

A border pattern of ivy leaves; sometimes of double ivy leaves. Originally Greek, it was employed by Wedgwood in the 18th century. Wedgwood's London Ledger for 1793-1806 has an entry dated 1795 for "green ivy plates" supplied to Queen Charlotte.

See: Napoleon Ivy.

Jackfield Ware

Red earthenware covered with a lustrous black glaze made at Jackfield (Shropshire) at a factory started c.1750 by Maurice Thursfield. Similar ware was made in Staffordshire, and it was included among Wedgwood's early productions.

Janeway, Carol

Designer of two Wedgwood patterns, 1948:

Crowned Seal, Queen's ware decorated in purple, yellow and brown.

Quilting Bird, Queen's ware decorated in green and yellow.

Janus

Ancient Italian deity with two faces, one looking forwards and the other backwards. The month of January was sacred to him. The doors of his Temple in the Roman Forum were shut during times of peace and open in times of war. The symbolism of the jasper tablet modelled by John Flaxman* in 1787, *Peace preventing Mars [the god of war] from bursting open the Gates of the Temple of Janus,* is thus explained.

Japanese Influence

Japanese influence became increasingly evident in the decorative arts after the London International Exhibition of 1862, but it was not very noticeable at Wedgwood until the 1870s. A transfer-printed and painted pattern of a central wood-block print, surrounded by vignettes of motifs taken from other prints, was produced on Queen's ware in 1873. The *Sparrow and Bamboo* pattern, a moulded shape, transfer printed, is also a good example of Japanese influence in design. It was first made, also in Queen's ware, in 1879. The Satsuma* shape is another instance of the trend, but Japanese-inspired Wedgwood is fairly rare, since the style never became so popular at Etruria as it did, for example, at Worcester.

These wares belong to a different category from those patterns (e.g. *Cryxa*) issued between 1805 and 1820 and known as 'Japans', of which there were several variations. These were made in competition with the Japan patterns of other factories, notably Derby, and were based originally on porcelain imported from Japan by the East India Companies by way of the port of Imari (Hizen Province), and known generally as Imari ware.

Japanese Influence. *An example of a Wedgwood 'Japan' pattern, c.1815. Patterns of this style, very popular at the beginning of the 19th century, were more or less distantly derived from porcelain shipped through the port of Imari (Hizen Province) and often called 'Imari ware'.* Wedgwood.

Janus. *Blue and white jasper plaque,* Peace preventing Mars from breaking open the Gates of the Temple of Janus, *modelled by Flaxman in 1787. 9ins. by 10½ ins.* Christie's.

Jasper

Wedgwood's most important contribution to the ceramic art, and the triumphant outcome of more than ten thousand recorded experiments, jasper is a dense white stoneware which, when thinly potted and fired at a slightly higher temperature than usual, may become translucent like porcelain. It was analysed by William Burton*, who found it to contain flint 10%, barium sulphate 59%, barium carbonate 2%, and clay (silica and alumina) 29%. The clay was refractory (i.e. it would fuse only at a very high temperature). Barium sulphate supplied the principal fusible substance, the clay holding the object in shape while fusion took place. The general principles, therefore, were those of porcelain manufacture, and Wedgwood recognised this when he referred to jasper as his "porcelain bisket."

Wedgwood described his jasper body in the 1787 Catalogue*: "Jasper, a white porcelain biscuit of exquisite beauty and delicacy, possessing the general properties of the basaltes, together with that of receiving colours through its whole surface in a manner which no other body, ancient or modern, has been known to do. This renders it peculiarly fit for cameos, portraits, and all subjects in bas-relief, as the ground may be made of any colour throughout, without paint or enamel, and the raised figures of a pure white."

Also mentioned in the Catalogue is a "white porcelain biscuit, with a smooth wax-like surface, of the same properties as the basaltes, except in what depends on colour." This body, similar in appearance to white jasper, is a coarser product, and was ultimately withdrawn from manufacture. It was probably introduced in the first place to compete with the highly successful biscuit porcelain of Derby* which, in turn, was copied from that of Sèvres*, but it was used principally for flower holders and bough pots, turned and slip-decorated in hooped or vertically ribbed patterns.

The jasper body was not one which lent itself to rapid development. Wedgwood first mentioned his experiments to Bentley* in January 1771: "I am making new Experiments with several different objects in view...first to make a white body, susceptible of being coloured & which shall polish itself in burning Bisket," but three and a half years later he was complaining: "If I had more *time,* more *hands,* & more *heads* I could do something...A Man who is in the midst of a course of experiments *should not be at home* to anything, or anybody else but that cannot be my case. Farewell — I am almost crazy." He was conscious of the urgency of his task: the rapidly expanding market for seals and cameos in imitation of Graeco-Roman gems, and the popularity of his basaltes copies, spurred him on in his search for a ceramic body which could be polished and laminated in colours to simulate gem stones. The sciences which, today, would reduce his research to an exercise in logical elimination, dealing with purified substances the behaviour of which could be predicted from analysis, were then in their infancy. Wedgwood was dealing with materials which were full of unrecognised impurities, and it is no surprise to find him writing in July 1774: "M[oor] stone and Spath* [a code word meaning spar] are the two articles I want, and several samples I have of the latter are so different in their properties that no dependence can be had upon them. They have plagued me sadly of late." Not only was the colour variable, but the behaviour under heat was unpredictable. Much of Wedgwood's frustration arose from a simple confusion between two forms of barium: sulphate of barium, known locally as 'cawk' and later to be used in the preparation of the pigment called 'permanent white', and carbonate of barium, which was to be found locally in small quantities in its native form of witherite.

Jasper. *Tobacco jar, diced pattern. Black jasper dip, engine turned to reveal the white body beneath, with applied yellow quatrefoils and running laurel borders. 8ins. high. c.1880.* Wedgwood.

In August 1774, he described himself as "almost crazy," but a month later he was able to write: "I believe I shall make an excellent white body, and with absolute certainty, without the fusible Sparr." In December he had "no doubt of being able to give a fine white Composition any tint of fine blue." At the same time he sent Bentley a few seals of the new composition. Bentley must have written approvingly in reply because, on New Year's Day 1775, Wedgwood expressed his satisfaction that the "white body" was of sufficient fineness, and his confidence in his ability to maintain its quality. He continued: "The blue body I am likewise absolute in of almost any shade, and have likewise a beautiful Sea Green and several other colours...and shall be able to make almost any of our Cameos...from the Herculaneum size to the least Marriage of Cupid* of the blue and other coloured grounds with the Figures and Heads in our fine white Composition."

Jasper was therefore in limited production early in 1775, but it was not until November that Wedgwood first used the name 'Jasper' for his new composition. The body continued to be fugitive and capricious, and a new obstacle was encountered when it was found that the coloured grounds of the cameos 'bled' into the white reliefs when they were fired together. Experiments were made in firing them separately and fixing

Left: **Jasper.** *Three-colour jasper vase, the upper part ornamented with blind basket work, the lower with a floral and foliate frieze and pendant swags of flowers.* Wedgwood.

Below: **Jasper.** *Jasper dip fluted spill vases richly ornamented with rams' heads, ribbon ties and festoons. c.1785.* Photo: Wedgwood.

Jasper. *Centrepiece in blue and white jasper with applied yellow and white intertwined strapwork and applied flowers inside the bowl. Vitruvian scroll border at the foot. Diameter 9½ ins. c.1790.* Wedgwood.

the reliefs to the ground afterwards, but this was laborious and unsatisfactory and Wedgwood reverted to the original method. By 1777 the cost of cobalt oxide*, used to produce the blue colouring throughout the body (solid jasper), had risen so steeply that jasper dip* (coloured jasper slip* used over white jasper) was introduced. This was found to produce less bleeding and also to increase the range and subtlety of colouring. Solid jasper was soon discontinued in favour of jasper dip, and the solid colour was not reintroduced until 1854. Jasper dip was not always applied over white grounds: rich effects could be obtained by dipping a dark blue ground in a paler shade and lapidary polishing* the edges to reveal the laminated appearance, or stamping an intaglio* through the dip to the colour beneath. A beautiful and extremely rare violet shade was achieved by dipping white jasper in lilac and then in pale blue.

The earliest jasper objects were on flat grounds — seals, cameos, and medallions — because reliefs applied to curved surfaces tended to lift and buckle in firing, but Wedgwood was quick to understand the potential of his new ceramic body as a material for fine vases, and he worked towards them by way of smaller objects with curved surfaces such as candlesticks, lamps, and small bowls with simple relief ornaments. No jasper vases were made during the Wedgwood & Bentley

partnership, and those white jasper plinths which bear Wedgwood & Bentley marks were made for marbled (see: Marbling) and variegated* vases. Some of these have since been translated to become bases for jasper vases of a later date.

From the outset Wedgwood was able to make jasper in several colours, though blue was always the most popular. His colours conformed closely with those used in interior decoration by the brothers Adam*. These were light blue, dark blue, sage green, grey, lilac, brown and yellow. In addition, there was a blue-black, used for the Portland* vase, and an intense black (which has a brownish tint) which is quite distinct from basaltes. All colours varied considerably in shade, leading to such later descriptions as 'pink', 'peach' and 'lavender'. In the 1780s they were used in combination to provide ornament in two, three and four colours, principally on cameos, but also on 'cabinet' cups and saucers and small vases. Extremely beautiful effects were obtained by using jasper ornament in simple trellis and strapwork patterns which required great delicacy and skill in application. Wedgwood's greatest achievement in jasper was undoubtedly the Portland Vase, but he personally considered the Homeric* vase to be his finest, and he presented a copy of it to the British Museum. At the time of his death in 1795 about two hundred and fifty models for vases had been produced, many differing in little more than the

200

Jasper. *Fine quality jasper plaque,* Sacrifice to Hymen, *pair to the* Marriage of Cupid and Psyche, *and variously attributed to Flaxman and Hackwood, c.1777.* Wedgwood.

Jasper. *Teapot of solid blue and white jasper with dimpled (granulated) ground ornamented with reliefs by Lady Templetown, with Cupid finial, split handle and laurel spout. 8ins. high. c.1790.* Wedgwood.

Jasper. *Cigar holder, 3¼ ins. long, shaped to hold both the cigar and its ash. c.1890.* Constance Chiswell.

decoration, and some important models were added during the time of Josiah II*. The work of many outside designers was used, but the three principal artists and modellers of the 18th century were Flaxman*, Hackwood* and Webber*. With rare exceptions (Hackwood's portraits of Edward Bourne* and David Garrick, for example) their work was unsigned and attribution depends on the surviving invoices, references in Wedgwood's letters, and the evidence of individual style. The best of the bas-reliefs designed by them were used on medallions and tablets and adapted for vases, and the composition of the subjects (particularly Sacrifices and Processions) may vary according to the size and shape of the grounds they ornament.

The quantity and diversity of Wedgwood's jasper wares is extraordinary. Seals, for example, number more than 1,700. Vases, tablets, and medallions for chimney pieces* and furniture, portrait medallions, small figures in the style of Sèvres* and Derby* (see: Clock Cases), flower holders of various kinds (jardinières, bough pots, root pots, bulb pots), ewers, and 'cabinet' teawares were among the most important types of ware manufactured, and jasper was also much in demand for mounting as snuff boxes, patch boxes, opera glasses, jewellery and scent bottles. Medallions and cameos were mounted in cut-steel by Boulton & Watt* and others. Beads, buttons and

buckles were also made.

Jasper has been made from 1775 to the present day, and much of the production has continued to be in the classical style. Attempts have been made, from time to time, to adapt jasper to prevailing fashion and contemporary styles of design, but these have seldom been successful. Jasper has remained essentially, and obstinately, neo-classical. The worst excesses of Victorian decoration left Wedgwood's jasper mercifully unscathed, though a hideous purplish-blue supplanted the rich dark blue of the 18th century, and the quality of the ornaments declined. Some pleasing fern and leaf ornaments were introduced in the 1850s (exhibited in the Great Exhibition of 1851 and in Paris in 1855), and towards the end of the century similar but elongated reliefs, tentatively art nouveau in style, appeared. Among the most satisfying of modern reliefs have been those designed by Anna Zinkeisen* and Richard Guyatt*.

New colours have also been attempted (see: Jasper Colours and Variations). Turquoise dip, made for about ten years from 1875 did not prove popular. The quality was not high, but examples have some rarity value. Crimson dip, on the other hand, is collected both for its rarity and, at its best, for its excellence. Introduced experimentally in 1910, it was attempted again in 1925-32, when Harry Barnard* and Bert

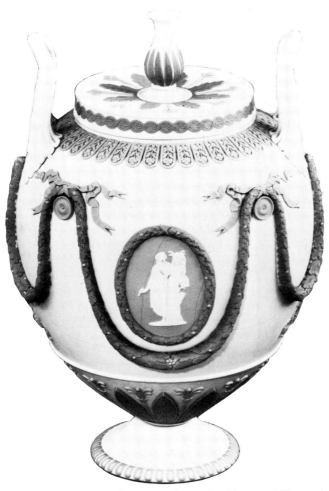

Jasper. *Three-colour jasper urn decorated with a medallion and festoons. The medallion shows a fine firecrack caused by fitting it to the curved surface. c.1790. Wedgwood.*

Bentley* produced some pieces of fine quality. Unfortunately, the colour bled into the white reliefs to such an extent that it had to be withdrawn from production. Dark olive green, made from 1920 to 1930 was also ruined by staining, but the colour was lifeless and unattractive, and the general quality poor. Yellow-buff with black ornaments was produced in small quantities from 1929 and 1933 and some attractive vases were made. More recent additions have included Royal blue, Portland blue, terracotta, and primrose, and solid lilac was introduced in 1960. It is perhaps of interest to the social historian that jasper, reckoned by value of sales, was twenty-seven times more popular after the Second World War than it was before it.

Undoubtedly the finest quality jasper belongs to the 18th century. The body is of a smooth and uniform grain, the reliefs are neither dry and chalky nor fused to the point of glassy vitrification. The ornaments are sharp and well-defined, and on the more important specimens they have been undercut* to accentuate details and the contrast between relief and ground. Later productions usually fell short of this standard because skilled labour was neither plentiful nor cheap, demand outstripped production, and competition from rivals became a factor in marketing.

The immediate and widespread popularity of Wedgwood's jasper inspired imitations throughout Europe. The best was

Adams* of Greengates, whose jasper closely resembled Wedgwood's in all but colour. Turner's* jasper, excellent as it was, came nearer to a form of porcelain. Palmer*, Neale*, Wilson and Samuel Hollins all made ware which more or less resembled jasper. Sèvres copied jasper in a body devised by Josse of the Fauborg Saint-Denis; other factories used biscuit porcelain. Meissen's* *Wedgwoodarbeit** was a porcelain with blue ground and integrally cast white reliefs. Doccia (Florence) made some blue and white porcelain portrait medallions in the Wedgwood style. Ilmenau* (Thuringia) made biscuit portrait medallions with white reliefs on a blue ground from 1792 to about 1808. The Vienna State factory attempted to produce imitations of jasper at the turn of the 18th century. The Poskotchin* factory at Morje (St. Petersburg) attempted to make a blue stoneware with white reliefs in the jasper style c.1835. None of these is deceptively close to Wedgwood's jasper in appearance, and the technical difficulties inherent in manufacture appear, on the whole, to have discouraged forgeries.

Jasper Colours and Variations

Black. Dip* 1778-1854, with reduced quantities until present day (prestige and limited editions). Solid for ornament and in the present century for Machin* chessmen* and some ornamental pieces.

Blue. Solid, 1775-78 and 1854 to present day. Pale blue solid and dip reintroduced 1949. Dark blue discontinued 1939. Royal blue (solid) introduced to commemorate the Coronation, 1953. Portland blue (solid) introduced 1972.

Brown. Trial pieces, dip, c.1778 and small quantities (dip) medallions early 19th century. Solid for ornament, late 18th century and early 19th century.

Crimson. Dip only 1910 and 1925-32.

Green. Sage green solid 1775-78; reintroduced 1957. Dip 1778-1854. Dysart green*, dip, c.1882. Dark olive green (dip) 1910-28.

Grey. Dip 1778-1854, but very small quantities. Trials of solid grey, 1960. Occasionally used for ornament (solid) after c.1785.

Lilac. Dip 1778 to 1854 (solid for ornament) but very small quantities. Solid: three examples, c.1785, known. Full production 1960-62.

Primrose. Solid, with white or terracotta reliefs, introduced 1976.

Terracotta. Solid, with white or black reliefs, 1957-59. Ornament and slip decoration from c.1775.

Turquoise. Dip only, 1875-c.1885.

White. Solid 1775 onwards. With coloured reliefs (up to three colours) from 1785 and reintroduced, after a gap of some forty years, in 1885. Trials of white with white reliefs, 1961. Used for ornament since 1775 and as the base for coloured dip since 1778.

Yellow/Buff. With black ornament 1929-33. Yellow dip from 1778 but very small quantities. Some dip portrait medallions, c.1878-90.

See: Granulated (dimpled) Jasper; Waxen Jasper.

Jasper Teaware

Although teapots, tea cups, chocolate cups*, coffee pots and coffee cans* were made from jasper no complete services of the kind available in Queen's ware* or pearl ware* were produced in the 18th century. The *cabaret,* popular with the Continental porcelain factories, was probably the commonest set. This was an early morning tea set comprising a teapot (or chocolate pot), two cups and saucers, a sugar box, a cream jug, and a tray. There were variations on this arrangement at the porcelain

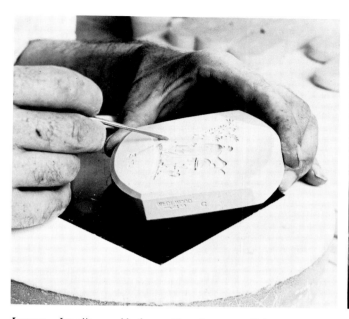

Jasper. *Intaglio mould for making jasper applied ornaments.* Wedgwood.

Jasper. *Intaglio mould for applied jasper ornament, filled with jasper body, being smoothed off with a spatula.* Photo: Wedgwood.

factories, but this composition seems to have been more or less standard with Wedgwood. Generally, cups and saucers were made in great variety, sometimes in three or more colours. They were often engine turned, or the decoration was under-cut, and lapidary* polishing of the rims or interior was not uncommon. Cups and saucers of this type were of high quality, elaborately decorated, and were not intended for general domestic use. The porcelain factories made a speciality of fine quality painting for similar wares, which were intended, as were the *cabarets* and specimen cups and saucers, to be kept in cabinets. The interior of these 'cabinet pieces' was unglazed.

See: Cabinet Pieces.

Jasper. *At work on a modern version of the* Apotheosis of Homer *vase.* Photo. Wedgwood.

Jasper Colours. *Primrose jasper teapot, creamer and sugar box in bamboo form with terracotta ornaments, 1976.* Wedgwood.

203

Jelly Mould. *Interior and exterior parts of a Queen's ware jelly mould, c.1790. Very rare complete.* Wedgwood.

Jelly Mould

A vessel for making gelatinous desserts. There are two parts: 1. A hollow mould to be filled with gelatine, and 2. a hollow cone, pyramid, or wedge-shaped piece with enamel decoration to fit inside the mould until the jelly is set, and thereafter to support it on the serving dish. Floral painting on the wedge is to be seen through the jelly. These were made by Wedgwood in cream-ware and pearl ware, but complete sets are now very rare.

See: Blancmange Mould.

Jewitt, Llewellyn Frederick William (1816-1886)

Largely educated by his father, Llewellyn Jewitt became a wood engraver before he was twenty-one, and subsequently went from Derbyshire to London to join F.W. Fairholt as an illustrator and engraver. In 1849 he was appointed Chief Librarian of the Plymouth Public Library and Curator of the Museum, but in 1853 he returned to Derby, where he became Vice-President of the Archaeological Society, Curator of the Museum, and founder of the *Derby Telegraph,* which he edited until 1869.

During this period he founded an illustrated magazine, called *The Reliquary,* principally devoted to historical and biographical subjects. He died in the village of Duffield, where he was brought up. His eldest son, Edwin (b.1847), who married the daughter of W.H. Goss the potter, survived him.

Jewitt's best known work, *The Ceramic Art of Great Britain,* was published in a two-volume edition in 1878. A one-volume edition, revised and omitting the colour plates, followed in 1883. That part of the book which concerned the 19th century was revised and expanded by Geoffrey Godden in an edition of 1972. Jewitt's *Life of Josiah Wedgwood* was published in 1865. This book, with a fulsome dedication to Gladstone*, preceded Eliza Meteyard's* biography by several months.

Jigger

A revolving mould which shapes the front of a plate from a bat of clay placed on it. It is used in conjunction with a stationary tool called a profile which is brought into contact with the back of the revolving plate, removing excess clay and forming the footring. The method is a very old one, and the jigger was certainly in use during the 18th century.

See: Jolley; Spreader.

Jolley

A revolving mould used in the quantity production of cups: the mould forms the outside, the profile is pressed into the mould to form the inside.

See: Jigger.

Jones, McDuffee & Stratton Company

Wholesalers and importers of pottery, porcelain and glassware. This Boston, Massachusetts firm traces its history back to 1810 when Otis Norcross founded a crockery business on Fish Street. The present company dates from 1871, and by the turn of the century was established as one of the largest importers of pottery and glass in the United States. In 1881 Wedgwood produced the first Calendar Tile* for Jones, McDuffee & Stratton, and these were designed annually until 1929. In 1899, thirty-five 'Wedgwood Old Blue Historical Plates' were copyrighted. They proved to be popular, and the quantity of views rapidly increased until, when the association was ended in the 1950s, more than 1,000 had been produced. They were, as one of the firm's advertisements stated, "excellent for the plate rail effect," but it would be a mistake to dismiss them as mere souvenirs, to be discarded with the ending of a Victorian fashion in decoration. The quality of the engraving was almost uniformly excellent, and the many sets comprise a remarkable and unique series of "named views," which will not be without historical significance.

See: Commemorative Ware.

Joseph, Felix (1840-1892)

Son of a Bond Street antique dealer and collector; educated at Ghent, with the intention of becoming an Admiralty clerk, but joined his father's firm, inheriting, in 1870, a large fortune. Felix Joseph amassed a formidable collection of ceramics, enamels, and drawings, and his collection of Wedgwood was one of the finest among the great hoards accumulated towards the end of the 19th century. On the opening of the Castle Museum, Nottingham, in 1878, Joseph offered the whole of the Wedgwood collection on indefinite loan, and there it remained (though there is some evidence that it was barely appreciated) until his death, when it was bequeathed to the Museum. The collection contains many important pieces, and at least two — an elaborate George, Prince of Wales vase, and a pale sage green *Apotheosis of Homer** vase — which appear to be unique. An exhibition entitled 'Mr. Wedgwood' was held at Nottingham Castle in 1975 at which the Felix Joseph collection was shown, probably for the first time, to its full advantage.

Judgement of Paris, The
See: Paris.

Julia (39 B.C.-A.D.14)
Daughter of Augustus* by Scribonia. She was thrice-married: to M. Marcellus, to Marcus Agrippa, and to the future Emperor Tiberius. In consequence of her profligate life Augustus banished her to the island of Pandataria. A bust of Julia, 15ins. high, was supplied by Hoskins & Grant* in 1775 and is listed in the 1777 Catalogue*.

Juno
The Roman name for Hera, wife of Zeus (Roman, Jupiter*). In Rome Juno was the queen of heaven, and the female counterpart of Jupiter. She was regarded as the Genius* of Womanhood. As Hera she occupies the same position in Greek mythology, and is the only married goddess, if we except the *mésalliance* between Hephaestus and Aphrodite. Nevertheless, her married life did not always run smoothly, and she was notable for the way in which she pursued and harried her husband's illegitimate offspring by mortal women. She greatly resented the judgement of Paris*, and became hostile to the Trojans in consequence. Hera usually wears a crown, a veil hangs down the back of her head, she may carry a sceptre, and she was often accompanied by a peacock.

Wedgwood subjects:
Juno standing with sceptre, medallion 8ins. by 6ins. from casts obtained in 1775 from John Flaxman Senior (probably from reliefs on the base of a candelabrum now in the Vatican collection). See: Jupiter.
Juno, statuette. Supplied by Theodore Parker*, 1769.

Jupiter. *Blue and white jasper plaque, 7⁷/₁₆ins. by 5½ins. Impressed mark 'WEDGWOOD & BENTLEY'. Dwight and Lucille Beeson Collection.*

Jupiter
The Roman name for Zeus, son of Cronos and Rhea, who married his sister, Hera (Juno*). When Zeus and his brothers shared the world between them, Poseidon* obtained the sea, Hades the Underworld, and Zeus the heavens, the earth being common to all. Zeus, called the father of gods and men, is the supreme ruler, who dwells on Mount Olympus. He is often described as the 'cloud-gatherer' or the 'thunderer'. He frequently carries a conventionally represented bolt of lightning as a symbol of his power. He had many *amours* with mortal women as well as with other goddesses, of whom Hera, his wife, was extremely jealous. By his wife he had two sons, Ares (Mars*) and Hephaestos (Vulcan*), and one daughter, Hebe*. The eagle and the oak were sacred to Zeus, and he carried a sceptre, a lightning bolt, or a statuette of Victory in his hand.

Wedgwood subjects:
Jupiter (holding a thunderbolt), medallion 8ins. by 6ins. from casts obtained in 1775 from John Flaxman Senior (probably from reliefs on the base of a candelabrum now part of the Vatican collection). See: Juno.
Jupiter and Ganymede,* tablet 3ins. by 6ins. Modelled before 1773.
Jupiter and Semele, medallion 3ins. by 2ins. Modelled before 1773.

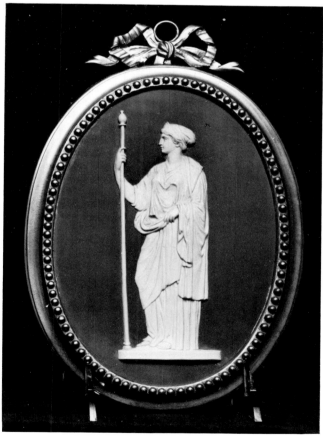

Juno. *Blue and white jasper plaque, 7⁷/₁₆ins. by 5½ins. Impressed mark 'WEDGWOOD & BENTLEY'. Dwight and Lucille Beeson Collection.*

Kantharos

Greek. A drinking cup, commonly associated with Bacchus*, having a tall, footed stem and two loop handles extending from the bottom of the bowl to the rim, or with long looped handles. Variants of this classical shape were used by Wedgwood in the 18th and early 19th centuries, particularly in basaltes with encaustic* painting.

Kauffmann, Angelica (1741-1807)

Swiss painter; the daughter of a painter. During the course of a visit to Italy in 1763-66 she painted Winckelmann's* portrait and became an enthusiast for the neo-classical* style. A founder member of the English Royal Academy, she numbered Sir Joshua Reynolds* among her friends. Her popular classical and allegorical subjects were sentimental, and through the medium of Bartolozzi's stipple engravings her works were widely disseminated. They were popular as decoration for interiors (wall and ceiling panels), porcelain figures and enamelled decoration, and painted furniture. She exhibited with the Royal Academy from 1768 to 1797.

Wedgwood subjects:

Cleopatra before Augustus (taken from a print by Burke).
Nymphs decorating a statue of Priapus, modelled by Webber*.
   This subject was also employed by other factories, notably a figure group at Derby*.

Keeling, Isaac (1789-1869)

Designer and engraver at Etruria*. A Wesleyan minister, he was the author of pamphlets, verses and sermons.

Keeling, William (fl.1763-1790)

Modeller and repairer* of large busts from 1769 onwards, who sometimes added a scratched K to his work. A bust of John de Witt and a figure of Voltaire have been noted with this mark. He also worked on the following models from Hoskins & Grant*: Francis Bacon, Democritus, Ben Jonson, and Spenser, and on the Shakespeare after John Cheere*.

Other work variously attributed to him is listed below:

Aristophanes, bust.
Figure candlesticks (pair).
Fletcher, John, bust.
Pedestal (square, with curved corners), 1767.
Pope, Alexander, bust.
Reading Lamp ('Vestal' lamp).
Ruined Pillar vase, 1786.
Tripod, vase with monopod figure supports.
Triton standing upon rocks, after Michelangelo.

Key Fret

Repetitive border pattern of short lines meeting at right angles (occasionally at an oblique angle) in a continuous design reminiscent of the wards of a key. Sometimes called a Greek* or Chinese fret.

See: Fret; Meander Border.

Keys, Edward (b.1798)

Modeller of figures and flowers, trained at Derby*, which he left in 1826 to work for Henry and Richard Daniel at Stoke-on-Trent. From 1831-42 he was employed by Minton*, and in the latter year he attempted to establish his own porcelain factory.

In this he failed, and in 1845 went to work for Wedgwood, where he remained until 1853. At Etruria* he was almost certainly employed in modelling Carrara* figures, but no record of his work has so far come to light.

Kiev-Mezhegorsky

The State factory of Kiev-Mezhegorsky was set up in 1798. It quickly became the largest Russian ceramics factory, producing *faience* that was advertised as the best in the country. The wares manufactured there included marbled*, red and chocolate coloured bodies*, and cream-coloured earthenware, often covered with coloured glazes. The quality was high and an unusually wide variety of goods was made, including barrel-shaped garden seats, picture and mirror frames, icons, and Easter eggs. The cream-coloured tablewares with simple border patterns, and the later green-glazed* moulded leaf-pattern plates and dishes, were evidently copied from Wedgwood styles. The factory closed down in 1875.

Kilns

A ceramic body is the product not only of the degree of heat attained, but of the length of time over which it is applied, in the kiln or oven.

In Josiah Wedgwood's day all firing was done in intermittent kilns, usually bottle shaped and made of brick. The kiln was packed when cold with the ware to be fired. The fire was then started and, when it had reached maximum temperature, was maintained at that heat for several hours, after which it was cooled slowly to a point where it was cold enough for the ware to be removed. Although some kilns of this type were converted from coal to oil firing early in the 1960s, even small manufacturers, who might have continued to use them, were forced to abandon them by the Clean Air Act. What will probably be the last firing of a bottle kiln took place in 1978 as a museum demonstration in the Potteries, and this particular kiln is being preserved as an industrial archaeological specimen.

The modern kiln is fired by gas, oil, or electricity. All Wedgwood's firing is now electrical. The ware is closely stacked on shelves mounted on wheeled trucks which are fire-proof, and these move extremely slowly through a tunnel about a hundred yards long, the truck taking seventy hours to traverse its length. The temperature of the tunnel, cool at the entrance, increases slowly as the centre is approached, after which point it falls, until it is normal at the exit. Wares which do not distort (i.e. those which are refractory) may be packed on the trucks without supports, and many can be placed one upon the other. Those wares which soften at high temperatures, like stonewares and porcelain compounded of clay and fusible materials which are liable to distortion, are supported with props made of highly refractory material.

In the old bottle-kilns wares likely to be damaged by contact with the flames were packed in fireclay boxes known as saggers*, the lids of which were sometimes sealed with plastic clay to prevent the entry of unwanted gases which, in the case of enamelled wares or coloured glazes, could spoil the decoration by reacting with the colouring oxide.

The glazing ('glost') kiln is also a tunnel kiln, but the temperature is lower, being sufficient only to melt the glaze particles and spread them over the surface. Care has to be taken that none of the objects touch one another in the glazing kiln; otherwise they would be irretrievably stuck together.

Muffle kilns are low-temperature kilns used for firing enamel painting and other forms of overglaze decoration. The heat is sufficient slightly to soften the surface of the glaze, and to convert the enamel into a kind of glass akin to glaze in its composition, but firing at a lower temperature. Some colours need a higher temperature to develop them than others, and these are fired first, the other colours being fired-on subsequently at a lower temperature. Enamels fired in the old muffle kilns were invariably enclosed in saggers to protect them. Muffle kilns vary in size, and some are hardly bigger than a domestic oven. Writing to Bentley, Wedgwood recommended using the bread oven at Greek Street for the purpose on one occasion, and gave directions for doing so, saying that the normal temperature for baking bread would suffice. It is not uncommon for enamel colours to be referred to as 'muffle' colours, as distinct from the high-temperature colours like cobalt and manganese, which are capable of bearing the full heat of the kiln used to fire the ware itself.

See: Pyrometer.

Knife Hafts (Handles)

Marbled* and variegated* hafts for knives and forks were excavated from the Whieldon* site in 1925, and early marked examples of Wedgwood hafts of this type are known. By c.1800 Wedgwood was producing jasper knife handles with relief decoration. These were reintroduced in 1959 in solid pale blue and white, and sage green and white, jasper. Queen's ware knife hafts with early painted decoration to match tableware patterns of the 1770-85 period also exist (e.g. in the Victoria and Albert Museum), but these are extremely rare.

Krater

A Greek pottery vase for mixing wine and water. It has a wide mouth and body, a small circular foot, and two handles. One of the most common of South Italian vase shapes, it is well known in four forms — the bell-krater, calyx-krater, columnar-krater, and volute*-krater. Wedgwood favoured particularly the bell-krater and volute-krater, both of which were produced in plain basaltes and in basaltes decorated with encaustic* painting.

Krater. *Black basaltes krater with encaustic painting and knot handles. 12 ¾ ins. high. c.1785.* Zeitlin Collection.

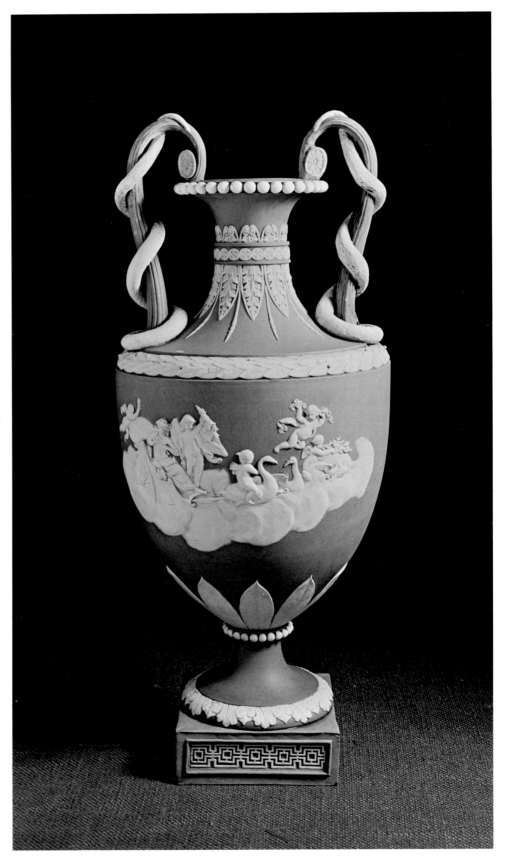

Colour Plate XV

Pale grey-blue jasper vase with white snake handles and applied ornament of Venus in her Chariot *after Charles Le Brun, and laurel and acanthus borders. Height 16½ ins. c.1785.* Wedgwood. Photo: Reilly/ Charles Letts.

L

La Charité-sur-Loire (Nièvre)

A factory founded by Francis Warburton (grandson of Anne Warburton*) in 1802 which made white earthenware (*faience-fine*), black basaltes*, and other English style wares. It was taken over in 1803 by Le Boult. The manager was Michael Willis.

Ladies' Amusement, The

Subtitled *The Whole Art of Japanning Made Easy,* this design book, compiled by Robert Sayer*, was published in London in 1762. The designs, including those after Pillement* and many by Robert Hancock*, were reversed so that they could be directly copied on to a copper plate. They include genre subjects, flowers, insects, and *chinoiseries*. They are known to occur on transfer-printed pottery and porcelain and enamels, and some were adapted for use on Wedgwood cream-coloured ware.

See: Robert Hancock.

Ladles

Large ladles for use with soup tureens, and a smaller size for gravy, were made by Wedgwood *en suite* with many of the early Queen's ware patterns. They were sometimes unmarked.

See: Cream Skimmer; Strainers.

Lag and Feather Pattern

Also known as *Flute and Wreath*. A painted pattern consisting of a fluted ribbon decorated with a continuous feathery motif. Developed by Wedgwood, c.1785. It was also employed on creamwares by the Leeds* and Spode* factories.

'L'Amours Pastorales'

'Rural Loves' — scenes of a shepherd and shepherdess engraved by Duclos after Boucher. Found as decoration in transfer-printed form on Wedgwood creamware.

Lamp Bases

Wedgwood jasper, basaltes and Queen's ware components were used in the 19th century for the manufacture of oil lamps and brackets, as jasper was used in the eighteenth century for the components of candelabra and girandoles, but shapes made specifically for use as lamp bases were not introduced until after 1878, following the invention of the electric filament lamp. Earlier bases were adapted from pedestals and bough pots.

Wedgwood lamp bases exist in jasper and basaltes (though the majority are vases converted after production), and in bone china, but only Queen's ware lamp bases were ever made in large quantities. These have been produced in various shapes in plain.cream colour, coloured bodies*, embossed Queen's ware*, and Queen's ware decorated with patterns which include *Napoleon Ivy*, *Peter Rabbit*, *Circus*, *Charnwood* and *Liverpool Birds*.

See: Lamps.

Lamps

Wedgwood made pottery lamps similar to those commonly used in the classical world, excavated specimens of which were fairly numerous in 18th century collections of antiquities. These were of flattened oval shape, covered, and contained colza oil. The wick protruded through a small spout at one end, and a small handle was provided at the other. Eighteen brown earthenware lamps in this Roman style were invoiced in July 1774, at 1s.6d. each. More elaborate lamps of black basaltes or jasper were sold at 31s.6d. (1776) and two guineas (1787). The 1779 Catalogue* refers to ''Lamps...both of the variegated Pebble and black composition. They bear the Flame perfectly well, and are fit for Chambers, Halls, Stair-cases, &c. The Tripod Lamps with several Lights are highly enriched, and will be suitable Ornaments for the finest Apartments.''

Probably the most elaborate was the Michelangelo* lamp, with three lights, borne upon the shoulders of three stooping figures. Among the most popular were certainly the 'Vestal' and 'Reading' lamps — boat shaped, turned or ornamented, on stands and plinths, the handles formed by finely modelled figures of seated women — and the rather similar oval footed lamps with lights at either end. The Michelangelo, Vestal and Reading lamps were originally made in black basaltes in the

Lag and Feather Pattern. *Examples of this popular pattern introduced c.1785.* Wedgwood.

Lamps. *Black basaltes oil lamps and covers known as the Vestal, left, and Reading, right, lamps. This pair of lamps exists in at least two different shapes and the cast ornament varies. The female figures were probably modelled by William Keeling, c.1773, but these popular models continued to be made as late as the 1920s.* Christie's.

Wedgwood & Bentley period, but all were reproduced in majolica* in the 1860s, and the latter pair were also known in 18th century jasper and in bone china* of the second period. All were continued in production in basaltes until about 1930.

See: Argand Lamp; J. Hinks & Son; Lamp Bases.

Lampshades

Bone china lithophane* shades were made for conventional light fixtures, candelabra, and girandoles c.1880, and lavender* body lampshades were produced for a light fixture patented by Holmes in 1937 (see: Holmes-Wedgwood lampshade). Wedgwood's most important production in this form, however, came with the introduction of in-glaze lustres and the designs of Daisy Makeig-Jones* between 1914 and 1931. At least two of these designs — *Willow Fairyland* and *Dogs and Deer* — were applied to lampshades. Examples are extremely rare.

See: Fairyland Lustre; Ordinary Lustres.

Lampshades. *Drawing showing the adaptation of the* Dancing Hours *to the decoration of a 13-inch electric light shade in lithophane style (intaglio china).* Wedgwood.

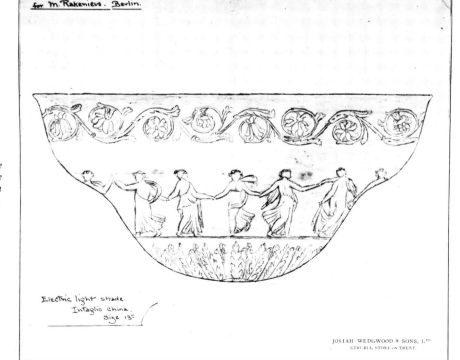

210

Landré, Mrs. Mary (fl.1769-1774)

Mrs. Landré supplied Wedgwood with casts in 1769 and 1774, and invoices from her are preserved in the Wedgwood archives. Little more is known about her, but her charges were moderate and it seems clear that none of the pieces obtained from Mary Landré was her original work.

The subjects listed on her invoices are as follows:

History of Apollo, a set of three bas-reliefs, each 3ins. by 6ins., comprising:

Apollo and Daphne, Apollo and Marsyas, and *Apollo and the Python,* 1769.

Bacchanalian Boys, a set of six rectangular medallions, 6ins. by 8ins., after Duquesnoy*, 1769.

Bacchanalian figures, five single figures from an antique vase, 1796.

Battle piece, 1796.

Caesars, set of twelve with six Empresses, from antique heads, 1769.

Christ and the Virgin, 1774(?).

Female Virtues, set of three bas-reliefs* representing *Faith, Hope* and *Charity,* 1769.

Four Quarters of the Earth.

Six Friars.

Horse, figure (bas-relief for medallion, 4½ins. by 5⅜ins.), 1774.

Horse, large, 1769.

Jesus dead, with Virgin and boys, 1774(?).

Joseph, 1769.

The Last Supper, bas-relief for plaque, 1769.

Magdalen, 1769.

Moses and the Serpent (Aesculapius?), 1769.

Naiad (Water-nymph), figure for a pair of candelabra, c.1769.

Neptune, large figure, c.1769.

Six Passions (Vices), 1769.

Philosopher reading on the immortality of the Soul, by 1779.

The English Poets.

Set of portrait heads, 1769.

Scripture pieces, set of four, 1769.

Shepherd, 1769.

Signs of the Zodiac, 1774.

Sphinxes (attributed).

Tritons (attributed).

Vintage, set of three, 1769.

It is probable that Mrs. Landré also supplied the five figures of Sleeping Boys* (erroneously called *Somnus**) after Duquesnoy.

Lapidary

A carver of hardstones, semi-precious stones, and gemstones, who makes use of the principle that a substance will always be cut by one which is harder, and will cut one which is softer. The chief decorative hardstones are agate, amethyst, lapis lazuli, turquoise, rock crystal, sardonyx, chalcedony, and cornelian, but other stones, such as granite, also reveal a decorative surface when cut and polished. All these stones exhibit a hardness of between 5·5 and 7 on Mohs's scale. A substance which is hard enough to cut these stones easily is emery (carborundum), well known to the Egyptians, which is 9 on Mohs's scale. Industrial diamonds, hardest of all, have a factor of 10. Steel, unless of a specially hardened variety, falls into a position of 5 on Mohs's scale, so it will not cut any of the hardstones here mentioned. Wedgwood's jasper and basaltes vary in hardness between 6 and 7 (i.e. between turquoise and agate), and Wedgwood employed lapidary techniques for a variety of processes, including the polishing of seals and cameos, the interiors of jasper cups, and so on. The usual method of working is to remove the unwanted material rapidly with a coarse abrasive, and then polish with a fine abrasive. Emery cloth, used in the engineering trades for a variety of purposes, cuts basaltes and jasper without trouble, and polish can be added by using the finest grade obtainable.

In 1877 the lapidary and glassworker, John Northwood*, was employed to finish the edition of the Portland* vase issued in that year. How often in the past the same methods may have been employed to improve a specimen can only be judged from a careful inspection under a glass.

Lapidary Polished

Tea ware, and other jasper and basaltes vessels intended to hold liquids were, at a later date, glazed inside to prevent staining, but early specimens were polished inside by lapidaries for the same purpose. As fine-grained vitreous bodies these, of course, are non-porous, and do not require a glaze, but polishing helped to obviate any tendency to surface staining. Cameos, seals, and the edge of 18th century portrait medallions were often polished in this manner, and rare examples exist of medallions with polished fields.

Lapis Lazuli

Natural lapis lazuli is an azure-coloured stone. Highly prized since ancient times, it was originally the source, in powdered form, of the artist's pigment, ultramarine. The term was used by Wedgwood for a type of variegated* earthenware which was blue and pebbled, with gold veining.

Last Day's Vases

See: First Day's Vases.

Lathe. *Turning the base of a vase.* Wedgwood.

Lathe

A machine tool in which the ware is held between rotating centres on a horizontal axis, and various stationary cutting tools are brought into contact with it as it turns for the purpose of uniformly paring down the surface, or incising simple ornament such as stepped rings. There are two kinds of lathe in use in the pottery industry, the simple lathe described above, and the engine-turning* lathe.

The lathe has been employed for wood-turning since the Bronze Age, when the pole lathe was in use, and for metal turning for many centuries. It was reputedly introduced into Staffordshire by the Elers Brothers shortly after 1700. Writing to Bentley in July 1777, about the improvements introduced into Staffordshire by John Philip and David Elers*, Wedgwood states: "The next improvement introduced by Mr. E. was refining our common red clay. . .and turning it on the outside upon Lathes."

Lathes for the pottery industry were made in the early part of the 18th century by Randle of Congleton. Improvements were devised by William Baddeley* in 1764, and by Wedgwood himself a little later. Wedgwood attempted to prevent the improved lathe from becoming generally available by offering Baddeley a high price, but with little success. He used the lathe extensively in the manufacture of cream-coloured ware, red ware and basaltes. The more highly skilled engine-turning*, sometimes employed in the decoration of other bodies, was largely confined to jasper and basaltes.

In May 1764, Wedgwood wrote to Bentley: "I have an excellent book on this subject [turning] in French and Latin; I have inclosed one chapter which if you can get translated for me will oblige me much and will thankfully pay any expense attending it." This book was the illustrated *L'Art de Tourner* by Plumier, published in Paris in 1701. Later, in February 1767, the book was sent to Bentley, and in May of the same year Wedgwood writes of seeing a lathe equipped to perform rosette turning (i.e. to incise curved ornament) which he tried to buy from Matthew Boulton. In November 1769, he writes: "We have got a third lathe up, and I have committed a sad robbery upon my works at Burslem to furnish it. I have taken James Bourn* to Etruria."

Lattice Work. *Jasper custard cup and cover ornamented with lattice work in white on a yellow ground, c.1786.* Wedgwood.

Le Brun, Charles. *Jasper vase, c.1786, with volute handles, ornamented with* Cupid watering Swans, *after a design by Le Brun.* Wedgwood.

Lattice Work

Applied lattice or trellis work was used as jasper ornament in the last quarter of the 18th century. Such intricate and delicate ornament, usually in white jasper over a ground of contrasting colour, required exceptional skill and examples are rare.

Laurel Border

A border pattern consisting of a series of laurel leaves placed horizontally, and separated by flowers and berries. It was used quite commonly on creamware and jasper during the period of the neo-classical* style.

Lavender

A grey-blue coloured body introduced in 1850.

See: Coloured Bodies.

Le Brun, Charles (1629-1690)

Principal French decorative artist of the reign of Louis XIV, and founder-member of the Académie. His output was prodigious and included numerous decorative designs of all kinds. The following, formerly attributed to Mme. Vigée Le Brun by a number of sources, are now much more credibly regarded as having been derived from the designs of Charles Le Brun:

Cupid Watering Swans.

Venus in her Car drawn by Swans (c.1776).

The snake-handled vase, often attributed to Le Brun is more likely to have been based on late 16th century Italian *maiolica* from Urbino (the type known as Raphaelesque — see: Raphael Ware) the design for which Wedgwood could easily have obtained from other sources.

Le Brun, Marie Louise Elizabeth (1755-1842) née Vigée

French painter, principally of portraits, previously credited with designs, now attributed to Charles Le Brun, which served as sources for Wedgwood bas-reliefs*.

See: Charles Le Brun.

Le Marchand, David (1674-1726)

Ivory carver of Dieppe, who produced, according to George Vertue, "a vast number of heads from ye life in basso relievo." The earliest dated English portrait in ivory by Le Marchand appears to be that of Sir Isaac Newton, 1718, but there is reason to believe that he was in England some years earlier. Wedgwood portrait medallions taken from his work include those of Boileau-Despreaux (the French critic), Anne Dacier, Matthew Raper II (Huguenot banker) and his wife, Sir Isaac Newton, and Sir Christopher Wren. A Wedgwood basaltes bust of Newton is also copied from the ivory bust by Le Marchand.

Leaf Dish

A dish naturalistically moulded in the form of a leaf, or of over-lapping leaves, usually with the veins in slight relief. This was a popular Wedgwood product in the 18th and 19th centuries, being made in large quantities in cream colour with the green glaze, and for a short period in majolica* glazes. Leaf dishes belong to the rococo* style.

Le Marchand, David. *Carved ivory portrait of Sir Christopher Wren by David Le Marchand, c.1723. This was later copied in black basaltes and jasper for the series of* Illustrious Moderns *portrait medallions and is listed in the 1773 Catalogue.* National Portrait Gallery.

Leda. *Jasper vase, the cover surmounted by a group of* Leda and the Swan, *with swan handles. This vase exists also in black basaltes of the Wedgwood & Bentley period.* Dwight and Lucille Beeson Collection.

Leafage Ware

Pearl* ware jugs moulded with overlapping leaves and decorated with enamel lines and washes, c.1810-30.

Leather Hard (Cheese Hard)

The state of an unfired pottery vessel after the evaporation of some of the moisture content. It is not unlike leather in firm-ness and pliability, and in this condition it can be turned on a lathe*, or ornament can be incised by engine turning*. It is also when the ware is in this state that slip is applied to the surface in the making of marbled* ware.

Leda

Wife of Tyndareus, King of Sparta. She was visited by Zeus* in the guise of a swan and subsequently laid two eggs. From one of these eggs came the twins, Castor and Pollux, and from the other, Helen of Troy. Leda also became the mother of Clytemnestra in a more conventional way. The story of Leda and the swan has always been a favourite among painters and sculptors, the Wedgwood version, modelled on the cover of a vase, being less explicit than most.

Leeds Pottery

The Old Pottery was founded in the 1750s (the precise date is uncertain). In 1774 its style was Humble, Green & Co., and in 1781 it became Hartley Greens & Co. The factory flourished until 1820, and subsequently changed hands several times before closing in 1878. The Hunslett Old Pottery, founded before 1792, made similar wares, and Slee's Modern Pottery (founded 1888) has used old moulds and patterns for wares with the old mark. Old Leeds is rarely marked, except for those pieces illustrated in the Pattern Books, but after 1790 a fair proportion of pearlware, blue-printed wares and figures were impressed* 'LEEDS POTTERY'. The greater part of the Leeds output was creamware of excellent quality. Great use was made of pierced* work in imitation of contemporary silver, and elaborate centre-pieces were a speciality. Like Wedgwood, Leeds issued a number of catalogues, the earliest in 1783 which was also printed in French, German, and Spanish versions. Transfer printing was largely done at the factory. Some painted wares are decorated in a style which also occurs on Wedgwood's creamware, and these are the work of Jasper Robinson and David Rhodes* or enamellers employed by Robinson & Rhodes at Briggate, Leeds.

Some gilded creamware of outstanding quality was probably done by James Giles'* studio, but much of the gilding at Leeds (attributed to Robinson & Rhodes) was applied gold leaf and has now worn away (see: Gilding). Early Leeds creamware was, like Wedgwood's, a deep cream or buff-colour, but after 1775, when Champion's* patent was withdrawn, it became paler, closely resembling Queen's ware*.

Among other wares made by Leeds may be included an agate* ware body, variegated* ware imitating marbling, red stoneware, black basaltes*, salt-glazed* stoneware, green-glazed* creamware, pearl ware*, lustre*, and slip*-decorated creamware with engine-turned* and dice pattern* decoration. The quality is generally excellent and seldom inferior to Wedgwood's.

Leg Pan

See: Foot Bath.

Leigh, Charles and James (fl.1775-1820)

A factory making *faience-fine* in imitation of English creamware was opened by the brothers Leigh at Douai (Nord) in 1781 with the assistance of a French merchant, Georges Bris. Their commonest productions imitate Leeds rather than Wedgwood, and they specialised in pierced ware. They also made variegated* ware, biscuit wares decorated with bas-reliefs, and unglazed red and black wares derived from English wares. Workmen were engaged from England who instructed pupils. These later worked at other French factories making similar wares. The factory closed about 1820. The letter which follows was addressed to the Leigh Brothers by a painter at Etruria, one Samuel Jones, but it was intercepted and is now in the Wedgwood Archives:

Staffordshire Pottery March ye 8th 1784

Sir: I take this opportunity of offering my service to you if you think it will be of any service to you I understand that you want some workmen in the Different Branches of the poting and I have it in my power to serve you if we can agree upon terms I can bring a turner a presser and handler a modeller and a man that can make as good a China glaze and enamel couleurs as any man in the country and both he and me are painters either in blue or enamel likewise his wife and I can prepare the coulers for either or bring some of it with me if you will answer this letter to let us know how you like my proposals and

what terms you wants us to come upon and you are willing for us to come we shall want some money which we should be glad if we could receive some in London to bair our expenses over, or if you chuse I will come my self first and settle for every one of us and come back a gain to England for all the rest of us are married except my self and I will run the hazard of anything happening from the masters in this country you must excuse my not dating my letter from any particular part of the pottery for I Do it for fear it should be broke open please answer this letter with all expedition and you will oblige yours at command

Samuel Jones.

Please direct for me to be left at Mr. Tho. Alsop.

Alsop's Bricklayer Ashbourn Derbyshire

Verso Emigrations the 8th March 1784. Samuel Jones Painter.

Leighton, Claire Veronica Hope (b.1900)

Painter and wood engraver; born in London, and studied at Brighton School of Art and the Slade School. Exhibitor at the Royal Academy. Designer, in 1952, of a series of twelve plates illustrating New England Industries. The plates were engraved in black on Queen's ware. The twelve subjects illustrated were Whaling, Marble Quarrying, Lobstering, Cranberrying, Ice Cutting, Logging, Farming, Gristmilling, Shipbuilding, Sugaring, Codfishing, and Tobacco Growing.

Leighton, Claire. *Plate from the New England Industries series.* Wedgwood.

Leopold II, Holy Roman Emperor (1747-1792)

In June 1790, Josiah II* and Tom Byerley* set out on a tour of the Continent in search of business, taking with them one of the copies of the Portland* vase. An invoice sent to Byerley at Frankfurt-am-Main lists a number of items commemorating the accession of Leopold II as Holy Roman Emperor in February 1790. Seven of the cameos listed were specially created to commemorate his coronation, but Wedgwood wrote to Byerley in September 1790: ''One of our papers gives us reason to suppose there will not be any coronation at Frankfurt this year. What do you think of this matter?''

Leopold exercised his influence among European powers in favour of the restoration of Louis XVI to the throne of France, but died in 1792, predeceasing his sister, Marie-Antoinette, who was guillotined in the following year.

The 'German cameos' include:

Fame Inscribing a Vase to the Memory of Elizabeth, upright oval cameo. Diameter of long axis 1⅞ ins.

The Genius of Empire holding the Bust of Leopold while a priestess is officiating at an altar, round cameo. Diameter 2⅛ ins.

Germany in the character of Minerva presenting Leopold with a Civic band as a reward for his code of laws, round cameo. Diameter 2⅛ ins.

Leopold the Lawgiver supported by Wisdom and Benevolence, upright oval cameo. Diameter of long axis 1⅞ ins.

Mars presenting a Crown to the Genius of Germany to be placed upon the bust of Leopold which stands on an altar, round cameo. Diameter 2⅛ ins.

Turkey and Russia, the two belligerent powers, consulting upon Peace, and Germany the mediator between them, round cameo. Diameter 2⅛ ins.

Coronation of Leopold, oval cameo. Diameter of long axis 2ins. The portrait medallion of Leopold which commemorated the coronation was for many years mistakenly thought to be of Prince Charles Edward (the Young Pretender).

Leslie, Sir John (1766-1832)

Scottish mathematician and physicist; private tutor to Josiah Wedgwood's family, 1790-92; elected Professor of Mathematics, Edinburgh, 1805; member of the Institute of France, 1820: knighted 1832.

Lessore, Emile (1805-1876)

Painter on pottery and porcelain at Bourg-la-Reine and Sèvres*, 1851-58; painted on Queen's ware* and Majolica* for Wedgwood, 1858-63; worked as a freelance for Wedgwood's, 1863-75, and on his own account on *faience-fine* made in France. Lessore is thought to have studied in the studio of Ingres, and his style is highly individual and easy to recognise. His drawing is free and attractive, in a manner much praised at the time, and his colouring, at first experimental, is muted; his treatment of landscape and his favourite rustic scenes owes something to the Barbizon school. He was driven to leave Sèvres because of the jealousy of other painters — proof, if any were needed, that the cult of mediocrity is not a modern phenomenon. After a brief period at Minton* he achieved a great reputation as a painter at Wedgwood, and his work, often signed, was exhibited by the firm in the London International Exhibition of 1862, the Paris Exposition Universelle of 1867, and the Vienna Exposition of 1873. Lessore's relations with Wedgwood were extremely amicable, but he could not stand the English climate, and he returned to France in 1868, settling at Marlotte, near Fontainebleau. From there he continued to supply Wedgwood with painted ware until his death. Lessore's talents were recognised during his lifetime, and his work was bought by Victorian collectors as an investment. He was a designer and craftsman at a time when these two functions had drifted apart. Francis Wedgwood* employed him in 1858, three years before William Morris founded his company of artist-craftsmen which is usually regarded as marking the beginning of modern theories of applied design. Lessore wrote his own tribute to Wedgwood's attitude: ''I was engaged by Mr. Wedgwood, free to name my own conditions, to choose my own workmen, my own materials. Mr. Wedgwood reposed confidence in me.

I did not abuse it. I have drawn and coloured 4,000 pieces in two years.'' His granddaughters, Thérèse Lessore* and Louise Powell* also worked for Wedgwood. Lessore signed his work 'Emile Lessore', 'E. Lessore', and 'ES'. Edouard Rischgitz*, a French painter of earthenware at Minton, was strongly influenced by Lessore's style in some of his work.

The following brief selection of subjects painted for Wedgwood by Lessore is intended to act as a guide to typical work:

Boy and Hens, painting.

Children Reading, decorated plate. 1866. Signed.

Climbing a Tree, decorated plate. Signed.

Crowning of Christ, decorated plate. Signed.

Cupids with Goat, painting. Two versions. Signed.

Domestic Scenes, 1868.

Europa, painted platter.

Ewer in the Renaissance style modelled by Hugues Protât* and painted by Emile Lessore.

The Free Companions, decorated platter. 1862. Signed.

Girl and Cat, saucer decoration. 1871. Signed.

Girl Crossing a Stream, plate decoration. 1871. Signed.

Ladies and Gentlemen outdoors, plate decoration. 1861. Signed.

The Last Supper.

Mother and Children, cup decoration. 1868.

Nymphs Bathing.

Perseus and Andromeda, vase.

Putti examining an evolutionary tree) decoration painted at Etruria
Putti playing with a Dolphin) on a Minton *cache-pot.*

Six Children having a picnic in a woodland glade, plaque, 17ins. by 12¼ ins., c.1870.

Soldiers drinking and playing dice, dish 21½ ins. diameter.

The Stork and the Wolf (from La Fontaine), oval dish 4¼ ins. by 6¼ ins. 1866.

Women and Children in Landscape, 1874.

After Lessore's death in 1876 Wedgwood sold their remaining stock of ware decorated by him to Mortlock*.

Lessore, Thérèse (1884-1945)

Granddaughter of Emile Lessore; sister of Louise Powell*. Thérèse did some excellent painting for Wedgwood in the 1920s working independently, either at home or at the factory. Her style differs markedly from contemporary factory work being distinctively French, and not infrequently reminiscent of the work of Lautrec. She married, as his third wife, the artist Walter Richard Sickert, RA, in 1926.

Letter Weight

A rectangular slab, generally of basaltes*, surmounted by a reclining figure or other suitable ornament. Early letter weights were sufficiently decorative to be regarded as ornamental figures and are now often so described. Fine examples of the 1780s, surmounted by one of several versions of the crouching sphinx*, demonstrate the handsome results to be obtained by the use of *rosso antico** with basaltes.

Liberty Bell

See: Paperweights.

Lily Border

A pattern of a series of stylised lilies with four petals and pairs of side leaves, the flowers set in adjacent pointed arches. It is to be seen on Wedgwood jasper.

Lindsay Ware

See: Lindsay Phillip Butterfield.

ÉMILE LESSORE
PEINTRE
1805 — 1876

Lessore, Emile. *Portrait of Emile Lessore by his son. Signed 'E. Lessore fils', 1878.* Photo: Wedgwood.

Lessore, Emile. *Original sketch for a Wedgwood creamware plaque,* Youthful Architects studying a Plan. Wedgwood.

Lessore, Emile. *Creamware plaque of Venus in her car drawn by dolphins and hippocampi and attended by Tritons and Cupids. Signed by Emile Lessore.* Wedgwood.

Lessore, Emile. *Creamware dessert service painted with scenes in the 18th century French style by Emile Lessore. Stands by Protât. c.1872.* Christie's.

Linley, Joseph (fl.1769-1774)

Painter at Chelsea Decorating Studio*, who worked on the oak borders, and later painted the fruit and flower baskets for the Frog* service.

Lithography

This method of decorating pottery and porcelain is now the most widely employed. It was first used experimentally in Staffordshire in the 1840s in conjunction with engraving. Wedgwood's first used lithographic transfers in 1863, and they were among a number of firms who worked to develop the process. It did not, however, come into general use until fairly recent times. Photolithographic* processes, first used by Wedgwood in 1878, were the subject of experiment at the same time.

The term 'lithograph' implies drawing on a stone, and the stone employed was absorbent limestone. Ceramic colour is attracted by grease and repelled by water in the same way as printer's ink, so the picture to be reproduced is drawn in greasy crayon on the surface of the stone. The stone is then moistened with water and inked. The oily ink adheres to the greasy crayon, but is rejected by the moisture, and impressions are then taken on paper from the stone. Later developments include the substitution of metal plates for stones since these can be made in cylindrical form to act as rollers, and more recently still the use of rubber has led to vastly improved methods of colour printing. In the case of photolithography zinc and aluminium surfaces can be given a light-sensitised coating.

Lithographs for ceramic printing are made with a backing of special paper, using pigments that can be fired in the enamelling kiln. The glaze is coated with varnish, and when this is tacky the picture is pressed on to it, causing it to adhere to the glazed surface. The backing paper is then peeled off and the ware fired again.

The earliest lithographs were monochrome, but multi-coloured designs applied in one operation were developed as a cheaper method of producing polychrome wares than outline transfers used in conjunction with hand enamelling. From 1945 Wedgwood developed the lithograph to provide designers with an even greater range of gradations and tones. Modern patterns decorated by lithography are often described as 'Decals' (from Decalcomania*).

See: Bat Printing; Silk-Screen Printing; Photolithography; Victor Skellern; Transfer Printing.

Lithophane. *Light bowl in the form of a lithophane, seen from below.* Buten Museum.

Lithophane. *Lampshades in the form of lithophanes, c.1920.* Buten Museum.

Lithophane (Berlin Transparency)

A translucent panel of unglazed porcelain with moulded intaglio decoration which becomes visible only by transmitted light. The process was patented in Paris in 1827 and the manufacturing rights were purchased by Meissen*. After the expiry of the French patent, lithophanes were made by several factories in Germany, at Sèvres*, at the Royal Copenhagen Porcelain Company, and in England by Minton*, Copeland (Spode*) and W.H. Goss. Wedgwood made some so-called lithophanes c.1920 from bone china. Although the decoration was in intaglio, they were not true lithophanes since they were cast from relief models and not from carved wax intaglios. A few examples exist in the form of bone china lampshades.

See: Email Ombrant.

Lochée, John Charles (b.1751)

Lochée enrolled at the Academy Schools and first exhibited in 1776. When he next exhibited, nine years later, he was becoming well known as a portrait modeller in wax, and between 1786 and 1790 he modelled the portraits of many of the Royal family. His connection with Wedgwood lasted from 1774-88, and his early work was not entirely satisfactory. It was heavily undercut and his plaster surfaces were full of pin holes. In 1791 he was declared bankrupt. The following Wedgwood portraits are from wax originals by Lochée:

Ferdinand, Duke of Brunswick. 1787.
Marchioness of Buckingham. 1788.
Marquis of Buckingham. 1788.
Princesse de Lamballe. 1787.
Prince Adolphus, Duke of Cambridge. 1787.
Prince Augustus, Duke of Sussex. 1787.
Prince Ernest, Duke of Cumberland. 1787.
Prince Charles of Mecklenburg. 1787.
Prince Charles von Ligne. 1787.
Prince William Henry, Duke of Clarence (later King William IV). 1787.
Prince Edward Augustus, Duke of Kent. 1787.

Lochée, John Charles. *Relief portrait in pink wax of Prince Charles von Ligne, modelled by John Charles Lochée in 1787. It was reproduced in jasper in the same year.* Formerly in the Reilly Collection.

London Jug, The
A black-printed Queen's ware jug, designed by Victor Skellern* and made for Liberty & Co. of Regent Street, London, in 1959. On one side is Wordsworth's poem, *On Westminster Bridge,* and the other is inscribed with the words of Dr. Samuel Johnson, 'When a man is tired of London, he is tired of life.' The base of the jug, in addition to the factory mark and the name of the firm for whom it was produced, bears the Wedgwood bicentenary symbol. It has since been repeated without the special backstamp

Longmore, Thomas (fl.1795-1810)
Engraver, who supplied Wedgwood with engravings for on-glaze red-printed *Botanical Flowers** and *Chrysanthemum** patterns, 1810.

Lotus Border
A border of heart-shaped lotus petals, all pointing up or down.

Lotus-Bud Border
A border of continuous interlacing circles with lotus buds covering interlaced segments, and a dot between each bud.

Lucretia (Lucrecia)
Wife of Tarquinius Collatinus. The outrage of her rape by Sextus Tarquinius led to the deposition of Tarquinius Superbus and the establishment of the Roman republic. (See: Lucius Junius Brutus.)

A bust of Lucretia was modelled by Arnold Machin* in 1944. A terracotta, 22ins. high, it was also known, somewhat unkindly, as *The Harlot.*

Lunar Society, The
A learned society, mainly centred on Birmingham, the members of which met monthly at each other's houses when the moon was full, so that they would not have to return home in total darkness. Membership included such men as Dr. Erasmus Darwin*, Dr. Joseph Priestley*, Matthew Boulton*, Samuel Galton and James Watt*. Wedgwood was not a member, but he was an occasional guest at meetings when his travels took him to Birmingham. The members were sometimes known as 'The Lunaticks'.

Lustre Decoration
The term applied to the deposition of a thin film of metal on the surface of the glaze, using an oxide or sulphide of the metal fired in a reducing kiln (a kiln from which the oxygen is removed at a certain point in firing, thus 'reducing' the metal oxide to free metal). The technique is at least 1,100 years old, and some of the most beautiful surviving examples come from 13th century Persia. In 16th century Italy, the potteries at Deruta and Gubbio (the latter presided over by Maestro Giorgio Andreoli, a pupil of Luca Della Robbia*) were, for a brief period, celebrated for the perfection of their lustred *faience*. Interest in this type of decoration declined for three hundred years, but was revived in the middle of the 19th century by the Castan family of Manises in Spain, by Ginori's Doccia factory in Florence, and by Carocchi, Fabbri & Co.* of Gubbio. Important developments in the form of in-glaze lustres were the work of the brothers Clément and Jérôme Massier of Vallauris and the French ceramist, Louis Franchet.

Early types of lustre fall into two groups: the iridescent

Lustre Decoration. *Part of a dessert service in nautilus and pecten shell shapes decorated with pink and purple 'splashed' lustre (an effect achieved by applying gold with a feather), later known by the unsuitable name of 'Moonlight Lustre'. c.1810-20.* Christie's.

lustres, fired in a reducing kiln, which showed a metallic or prismatic sheen; and the early 19th century metallised lustres, imitating solid metal and always fired in an oxydising atmosphere. The former were based on silver and copper; and the latter on gold and platinum. A third, modern group, the commercial (liquid) lustres, make use of many different metals, and are capable of producing the iridescent or metallised effects of the earlier groups.

Two inventions were fundamental to the early development of lustre decoration in England. The first was the discovery by Johann Friedrich Böttger at the Meissen* factory in 1716 that a lavender or puple lustre could be produced by the use of gold. The second, by John Hancock* in 1805, during the period of his employment at the Spode* factory, was the invention of the so-called 'steel' lustre based on the use of platinum. 'Silver' lustre, produced by adding a second coat of platinum, was introduced c.1812, some six years after gold or 'copper' lustre.

The first record of Wedgwood's interest in lustre occurs in 1776, when Bentley* made several experiments which he recorded in the London Experiment Book. The first, "Gold coloured glazing on Earthen ware by fumigation", produced "true copper glaze, looking like that metal, or betwixt that and Gold." No use appears to have been made of this. Two others, "to produce prismatic Colours on the surface of glazed vessels — by a partial reduction of the metals in the glaze", also succeeded, producing "an agreeable variety of changeable colours with perfect smoothness" and "some beautiful prismatic colours." From these descriptions it appears that Bentley came close to the successful production of both metallic and iridescent lustres, but there is no record that either was developed at that period.

There is no further documentary evidence of lustre made at Etruria* until 1806. However, on 2 February, 1805, an event of some importance occurred which merited commemoration, and a number of pieces of jasper*, basaltes* and lustred ware bear the mark, impressed or painted, 'Josiah Wedgwood Feby 2d 1805' (see: Marks). The appearance of this mark on pieces decorated with gold lustre has caused considerable confusion since it is generally accepted that gold or 'copper' was first made in 1806. It has been suggested (Una des Fontaines: *Wedgwood Fairyland Lustre*) that these pieces may have been deliberately antedated, and in the light of the evidence it is difficult to find any other convincing explanation. It seems certain, however, that Wedgwood's platinum ('steel') and gold (or 'copper') lustres were among the first to be made, and a letter dated December 1806 to Josiah II* from Professor John Leslie* confirms that both metallic lustres were in production by that date. These were used principally for teaware and coffeeware pieces, but several examples of tripod pastille* burners exist, and there are also a few very rare specimens of 'silver' or 'copper' lustred sphinx* figures.

Within a few years, probably by 1810, Wedgwood had developed the pink or purple 'splashed' lustre, with a copper-gold metallic reflection, produced by applying gold over Queen's* ware or pearl* ware. The splashed or mottled effect, produced by applying the gold with a feather, came later (perhaps not until the 20th century) to be known by the attractive but deceptive name, Moonlight Lustre. Marbled lustre, known as early as 1812 as 'Variegated lustre', was probably produced by a similar technique, but using gold, platinum, and iron separately to yield veined or marbled patterns in shades of orange, rose and grey which varied considerably. These two types of lustre were applied to pecten shell shapes, tripod pastille burners, and inkstands, candlesticks*, bell pulls*, jugs (one as large as 21ins. high, with a capacity of ten gallons), teaware, and vases. In spite of their popularity, the quantity of ware seems to have been comparatively small, and the period of production short. Similar wares were made by other Staffordshire manufacturers, notably Spode*, where some of the same shell shapes were produced.

In 1837 Dr. Heinrich Gottlob Kühn, Director of Meissen* from 1849-70, invented a technique for the production of a new range of background colours that were iridescent, based on the use of different metals, including uranium, lead and bismuth, as well as copper, silver and gold. A few years later, the French chemist, Jules Joseph Henri Brianchon patented his formula for "imparting to ceramic substances the colour of gold, white and coloured mother-of-pearl, the variegated and changing reflections of shells, of all kinds of minerals, and of the optical prism." These two developments led, by the end of the century, to the widespread use of liquid lustres in a wide palette of colours.

Resist lustre, is a technique, generally using 'silver' or gold lustre, by which a decorative pattern of the same colour as the body is contrasted against lustre of a different colour. The pattern, or the background, was painted over the glaze with a water-resistant or viscous substance (wax, gum and honey were all used) before the article was dipped in lustre. The 'resist' was subsequently washed off before firing, or burnt away in the kiln, leaving the pattern or ground free of lustre. Resist patterns both silver and gold, were used by Wedgwood for the decoration of jugs, candlesticks, and flower pots in particular. Jugs of the *Fallow Deer, Hunt,* and relief *Vine* patterns were produced during the 19th century, and were reintroduced in the 1950s.

In about 1850 Italian *maiolica* of the 16th century became popular among collectors of pottery, and a number of English factories began to produce decoratively enamelled wares inspired by this source. In 1862, Carocchi*, Fabbri & Co. exhibited red and yellow iridescent lustre ware at the London International Exhibition, where it was much praised. Francis Wedgwood* received an offer from Pietro Gaj*, who also made contact with Minton*, to supply the necessary details of production, and on 2 August Gaj signed an agreement to sell to Wedgwood "all his receipts, together with drawings of the kiln, method of manipulation &c. for making his Maestro Giorgio and Cinquecenti [*sic*] lustres" for twenty pounds down, twenty pounds when trials had been successfully completed, and ten pounds if, at the end of the year, they were the sole makers in England. The information supplied by Gaj was misleading and the trials failed.

Towards the end of the century William De Morgan* rediscovered the secret of smoke-reduced reflective lustres, and produced new colours, including a distinctive red. De Morgan and his partner, Fred Passenger*, both decorated ware produced by Wedgwood, but their techniques were too unreliable for modern production and examples of their work are rare. The great, and individual, development in Wedgwood's lustre wares was to be the work of Daisy Makeig-Jones*, who joined the firm as a trainee designer in 1909.

See: Fairyland Lustre; Ordinary Lustres, Charles Passenger.

Lustres

Candleholders with pendant drops of prismatically-cut glass similar to those employed for making chandeliers. The lustre is based on a jasper drum mounted in ormolu, the stem is of ormolu, and the drip pan and nozzle which surmount it of glass. The drops are suspended from the edge of the drip pan and the candleholder. The jasper drums may be white on blue,

Lustre Decoration. *Group of variegated and steel lustre wares of c.1820. In the foreground, right, a copy of a Gubbio or Deruta lustred maiolica portrait tazza of c.1510 inscribed Cintia Bella, probably inspired by Pietro Gaj and made c.1862.* Wedgwood.

Lustre Decoration. *Pair of moonlight lustre wall pockets in the form of nautilus shells. c.1810.* Buten Museum.

Lustre Decoration. *Covered soup cup (ecuelle) and stand in moonlight lustre. c.1810.* Buten Museum.

or white on black. The glass, occasionally amber-tinted, from Waterford, dates these lustres to around 1790.

The assembler of the complete object does not seem to be known, but the mounts almost certainly came from Boulton, and since the glass came from Waterford, and the jasper from Staffordshire, while London was the obvious market for something of this kind, it seems likely that they were assembled by one of the larger London china dealers.

Lustres, Ordinary
See: Ordinary Lustres.

Lysimachus
One of Alexander's generals who, when the provinces were divided after Alexander's death, obtained Thrace. In 286B.C. he became King of Macedonia, and died in battle in 281 at the age of eighty. A medallion portrait of Lysimachus, 4ins. by 3ins., described as 'a fine head', is listed in the 1774, 1777, 1779 and 1787 Catalogues, but this appears to be a copy of the portrait of Alexander* by Tassie* and the identification is therefore uncertain.

Lyth, Thomas (1892-1965)
Curator of the Wedgwood Museum at Etruria and later at Barlaston, 1944-60. Tom Lyth was born in Fenton, and joined Wedgwood in 1913. Wounded and gassed at Arras, while serving with the Duke of Wellington's Regiment in the First World War, he rejoined Wedgwood in 1919 as assistant to John Cook, succeeding him as Museum Curator in 1944. Although not in any formal sense a scholar, Tom Lyth acquired an unrivalled knowledge of Wedgwood wares, and of the firm to which he devoted his working life. He was not himself a collector, but he gave unstintingly generous help to researchers and collectors, and the debt owed to him by writers on the subject, and by the collections formed since 1945, is often underrated. In 1960, to mark the occasion of his retirement, he was elected the first Honorary Member of the Wedgwood Society*, London. His portrait medallion was modelled by his lifelong friend, Jesse Wilbraham*.

Lustres. *Candleholder with a jasper drum, ormolu fittings, and Waterford glass prismatically-cut drops, drip pan and candle nozzle. 11ins. high. c.1790. Wedgwood.*

Machin, Arnold, OBE, RA (b.1911)

Sculptor, modeller and designer, born in Stoke-on-Trent; studied at Stoke and Derby Schools of Art, and at the Royal College of Art, 1937-40; exhibited at the Royal Academy from 1940, and was elected Member of the Royal Academy 1956. He designed the new coin effigies in 1964 and 1967 (decimal coinage), the definitive issue postage stamp in 1967, and the commemorative crown pieces for the Silver Wedding, 1972, and the Silver Jubilee, 1977. Although some of his work has been criticised for its conventionality, Machin's Queen's ware figures for Wedgwood must be considered as among the most important of the twentieth century. His best work, of which the figure of Taurus is the outstanding example, shows strength, earthy humour, and a genuine understanding of Staffordshire pottery.

In 1968 he modelled a set of four hard-paste porcelain figures allegorical of the *Four Seasons* for the Worcester* Royal Porcelain Co. These were mounted in ormolu and produced in a limited edition of 1,500 sets.

Machin's work for Wedgwood includes:

Aphrodite, Queen's ware figure.

Beatrice, terracotta figure, 30ins. high, 1944.

Bridal Group, Queen's ware group enamelled, 10½ ins. high (also Windsor Grey body), 1941.

Cherub, terracotta head with salt glaze*, 5ins. high, 1944.

Chessmen, set. Produced in basaltes, white jasper, blue jasper, black jasper, and Queen's ware (cream colour and lavender), 1939.

Churchill, Winston, Queen's ware or basaltes bust, 8ins. high.

Country Lovers, Queen's ware group, enamelled.

Elizabeth II, portrait medallion (2 versions), 1971 and 1977.

Ferdinand, figure of a bull. Queen's ware, enamelled.

Helen, terracotta figure.

Lucretia, terracotta bust, 22ins. high, 1944.

Paintress, Queen's ware figure, enamelled.

Penelope, Queen's ware figure with slip decoration (also Windsor Grey body), 11ins. high, 1944.

Philip, Duke of Edinburgh, portrait medallion (2 versions), 1971 and 1977.

Roosevelt, Franklin D., Queen's ware or basaltes bust, 7¼ ins. high. Portrait medallion, jasper.

Saggar-maker, Queen's ware figure, enamelled.

Sea Nymph, terracotta figure.

Sylvia, Queen's ware figure.

Taurus, Queen's ware figure, 14¾ ins. by 6ins., 1945. Decorated with Ravilious* *Zodiac* pattern. A second version is decorated with the *Avon* pattern. Other, rarer, versions were made in plain basaltes, glazed and gold-printed basaltes, and gold-printed porphyry*.

Thrower, Queen's ware figure, enamelled.

Machin, Arnold. Bridal Group *by Arnold Machin, 1941. A model which admirably illustrates the artist's irreverent sense of humour.* Authors.

Machin, Arnold. Taurus, *decorated with Avon pattern, 1945.* Reilly.

Majolica. *Pair of wall brackets, c.1865. 9½ ins. high.* Sotheby's Belgravia.

Majolica. *Unusually large jardinière and stand decorated with grotesques. 37ins. high. 1891.* Sotheby's Belgravia.

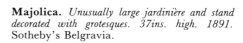

Majolica. *A covered jug or stein decorated with majolica glazes, 11⅛ ins. high, of 1870 based on a German stoneware tankard. The verse reads: "What tho' my gates be poor/Take them in good part/Better cheer you may have/But not with better heart."* Wedgwood.

Majolica. *Jug of overlapping vine leaves and grapes, and a dolphin candlestick decorated with coloured glazes. c.1870.* Wedgwood.

Majolica (1860-1910)

The term is a trade name for a type of ware made in the second half of the 19th century by a number of factories, beginning with Minton*. It was made in Germany under the name of 'Majolika'. The word is obviously derived from the Italian, *maiolica,* which is a kind of reddish earthenware covered with a glaze made white and opaque by the addition of tin oxide, and usually noted for the quality of its painted decoration. 'Majolica' is nothing like this; it is what was termed an art pottery, decorated with coloured glazes, usually transparent but sometimes opaque. It was the idea of Léon Arnoux of Minton, and it seems to have been inspired by the 16th century pottery of Bernard Palissy, who spent many years searching for the secret of Italian *maiolica,* and developed a coloured glaze ware instead. This was similar in many respects to the type of ware made by the Whieldon-Wedgwood partnership, and later by Wedgwood himself. Whieldon tortoiseshell ware resembles the mottled coloured glazes which Palissy used on the reverse side of his dishes. When Arnoux first introduced this type of decoration the pottery of Palissy was in great demand among antique collectors of the day.

Wedgwood 'Majolica' was the product of covering with coloured glazes a white body moulded with high quality relief ornament. Among wares of this kind were vases, umbrella stands, wall brackets, plaques, candlesticks, comports, and plates and dishes. The largest piece so far identified is the 'Swan' vase displayed by Harrods in 1973, which, including its 16-inch plinth, stood 54ins. high. The vase, of a conventional ovoid shape, is supported by the wings of three swans which stand on a triangular base of three waterlily leaves. The lid, 15ins. high, is topped by the figure of a swan with wings outstretched.

By strict definition green glazes* of the period may be included under this heading, and many new designs for leaf dishes thus glazed were introduced during the second half of the 19th century. Also in this category are the plates decorated in the so-called *email ombrant** technique.

Major, Thomas (fl.1770-1780)

Well-known engraver, from whom Wedgwood obtained six views of the river Thames for the Frog* service. It has frequently been stated that Major was employed at Chelsea* as a painter, but no evidence has been found to substantiate this, and it appears that his sole connection with Wedgwood was as a supplier of prints.

Majolica. *Ewer designed by Hugues Protât and painted by Emile Lessore. 16ins. high. c.1865-70.* Zeitlin Collection.

Makeig-Jones, Susannah Margaretta (1881-1945) 'Daisy'

Artist and designer at Etruria*, 1909-31; daughter of Dr. William Makeig Jones (the hyphen was added by Deed Poll in 1913); educated privately and studied at the Torquay (now Torbay) School of Art. In 1909, as the result of her own characteristically direct application to Cecil Wedgwood*, she joined the firm as an apprentice hand-paintress. After two years she was accepted on to the staff, and in January she was recognised as a designer in the Art Department directed by John Goodwin*. Her first designs were insignificant: toy tea sets and nursery ware decorated with rather woodenly drawn animals, aeroplanes, toy-soldiers etc., which gave no hint of any particular talent or invention. In 1912 she produced some dessert plates and salad bowls decorated with designs from illustrations of Hans Andersen's story of *Thumbelina,* and in the following year the first of her designs using Oriental dragons appeared.

In 1909 Messrs. Ashworth & Co. of Hanley had exhibited in London the first of their 'Lustrosa Ware', an impressive range of lustred pottery developed by their director, J.V. Goddard. Commercial painted-on lustres were commonly in use in Staffordshire, but Goddard relied for his effects upon reduction

Majolica. *Tazza, 8½ins. high, decorated with green, blue, ochre and brown glazes, 1869.* Sotheby's Belgravia.

Makeig-Jones, S.M. *'Daisy' Makeig-Jones (1881-1945) worked as a designer for Wedgwood for twenty years. Her Fairyland Lustre designs were not original, but her adaptations of the work of better artists for use as ceramic decoration, and her bold exploitation of colour and lustre, enabled Wedgwood to compete, for the first time, with the foremost manufacturers of ornamental china.* Photo: Una des Fontaines.

lustres, described by the *Connoisseur* four years later as "jewel-like in their brilliance and lustre." Powder blue, the first of the powder colours*, had been produced successfully in 1912, and it was these two techniques which inspired the use by Daisy Makeig-Jones of powder colours in combination with commercial lustres in the autumn of 1914. Her first ten 'Ordinary Lustres'* — pieces decorated with dragons, birds, butterflies, fish, fruit, or small animals — were followed less than two years later by the first of the Fairyland Lustre* designs. For the next thirteen years designs for Fairyland Lustre, Ordinary Lustre, and tableware decoration flowed from Daisy Makeig-Jones' studio. Their success, in a country tired of wartime austerity, was considerable, and by 1920 the lustres had lifted Wedgwood for the first time into the forefront of manufacturers of ornamental china. After the Wall Street crash of 1929 the popularity of lustres declined, and by the time the demand for them had revived in the mid-1930s, Daisy Makeig-Jones had left the firm.

In 1930, following the death of Major Frank Wedgwood*, Josiah V* became Managing Director. Adverse economic conditions dictated radical changes in production and organisation. Under such conditions it was probably inevitable that Daisy Makeig-Jones should have been among those invited to retire; but there were other reasons why Josiah wished her to leave. Her behaviour, never conventional, had become increasingly — and often embarrassingly — eccentric;

she had become dictatorial and over-demanding, treating the production departments as tiresome but necessary extensions of her studio; and she created designs for which the new generation of directors had little regard. In April 1931, she was asked to retire. Predictably, she refused. After an acrimonious interview with Josiah she left, having ordered the destruction of every piece of lustre in her studio. She retired to a life of stormy domesticity with her mother and two sisters, and died on 21st July, 1945.

Daisy Makeig-Jones does not merit serious consideration as an artist. Her draughtsmanship was no better than competent, and she appears to have been altogether lacking in invention. Her designs were thinly disguised adaptations of the work of others. She was not, legitimately, influenced by better artists: she deliberately plundered their work, hiding it beneath brilliant ceramic colours and glazes. There is nothing new, nor particularly disreputable, in the use by designers of the work of artists or illustrators, and such use is seldom acknowledged. It is, however, necessary to recognise the difference between adaptation and invention. Daisy Makeig-Jones' contribution as a ceramic designer is admirably summed up by Una des Fontaines (*Wedgwood Fairyland Lustre*): "Daisy was in fact a creative synthesist with a gift for massing colour and form in striking juxtaposition which was attractive to the popular taste of the period."

In addition to the Celtic Ornaments, Fairyland Lustre, and Ordinary Lustre designs described separately under those headings, Daisy Makeig-Jones was responsible for the following:

QUEEN'S WARE TABLEWARE PATTERNS
Blue Willow, plate 10ins. (Wedgwood's *Willow* with *Coq du Bois* figures superimposed, enamelled in colour.)
Cobble Bead and Zoo, nursery ware.
Coq du Bois, nursery ware.
Cretan, teaware.
Moa, nursery ware.
Yellowstone Zoo, nursery ware.

ORNAMENTAL QUEEN'S WARE
Istria, bowls and plates.
Leaping Chamois, Imperial bowls.
Silenus, bowl.
Sphinx, bowls, mugs and jugs.
Chick, pepper and salt.
Emily, sugar caster.
Dawg, salt.

BONE CHINA TABLEWARE DESIGNS
Hawk, teaware and coffeeware.
Magpie, teaware and coffeeware.
Nizami, coffeeware.
The Street that ran away, teaware.

BONE CHINA ORNAMENTAL WARES (Lustre Decorations)
Amherst Pheasant, bowls, melba cups, and lily trays.
Argus Pheasant, vases, bowls, *Lincoln* plates 10¾ins.
Crane and Rock, bowls.
Daventry, vases, bowls, cups.
Dogs and Deer, vase, lampshade.
Endymion, bowls.
Flame Daventry, vases, bowls, cups.
Hares, Dogs and Birds, bowl.
Hindu-Persian, Persian cup.
Lahore, bowls and vases.
Nizami, bowls, *Lincoln* plates 10¾ins., melba cups.
Rhages, bowls.
Silenus, dessert sets, bowls.

See: Lustre Decoration.

Early morning set or 'solitaire' in cane ware. The hollow ware pieces are moulded in bamboo shapes, with bamboo-style handles and knops, and all pieces are painted in 'encaustic' colours of blue and red. c.1792. Wedgwood.

Above: Solid blue jasper covered chocolate cup and saucer, often described as a trembleuse because the cup is set in a well with raised rim, making it suitable for carrying with a trembling hand. The applied relief of inverted grasses on the cup was one of Wedgwood's most attractive ornaments. The cup is engine-turned. Height 5¾ins. c.1785. Nottingham Castle Museum. Photo: Reilly/Charles Letts.

Right: Covered solid blue jasper vase on tripod supports of goats'-head monopodia, the domed cover with white lotus flower knop. Height 9ins. c.1789. Wedgwood. Photo: Reilly/Charles Letts.

Malachite

A decorative stone which, when polished, is a fine dark copper green with darker veins. It is one of the ores of copper, and was among the natural stones which Wedgwood attempted to copy in his variegated* or crystalline* wares.

Manganese Oxide

A substance employed to decorate pottery and porcelain. It yields a variable colour, from purple-brown to rich brown, similar in shade to the colour obtained by adding permanganate of potash crystals to water. In combination with iron and cobalt oxides, manganese yielded the black of basaltes* ware.

See: Drab Ware.

Mangiarotti, Michelangelo

Modeller in Rome* in 1787 under Flaxman* and Webber*.

Manzolini

Modeller in Rome in 1787 under the supervision of Flaxman* and Webber*. None of his work can be identified with certainty, but the model of *Three Warriors with a Horse* has been doubtfully attributed to him.

Marbled Lustre

See: Lustre Decoration.

Marbling (Marbled Ware)

The mingling of coloured slips on the surface of a piece or of wedging variously coloured clays. The effect imitates the marbled end-papers of books, or the surface marking of some decorative stones. The technique was developed about 1760 by Josiah Wedgwood and is sometimes known as combed ware. The same technique was used by Norman Wilson* in the 1950s for bowls and plates made in small quantities for the range of pieces known as unique* ware.

See: Variegated Ware.

Marchant, Nathaniel, RA (1739-1816)

Gem engraver and medallist who studied under Edward Burch* and at Rome; exhibited at the Royal Academy; elected RA, 1809; Fellow of the Royal Society of Arts; assistant engraver at the Mint, 1797; published Catalogue, 1792. He was especially noted for fine intaglios. Two cameos, *Garrick looking into the face of Shakespeare,* and *Priam and Achilles* were reproduced by Wedgwood from signed gems by Marchant.

Marcus Aurelius Antoninus (121-180)

Roman Emperor, adopted by the Emperor Antoninus Pius*, whose daughter, Faustina*, he married. Marcus Aurelius is best known for his devotion to the Stoic Philosophy, and his *Meditations* on the subject have survived. Wedgwood produced two busts of Marcus Aurelius: *The Young Marcus Aurelius,* 16½ins. high, and *Marcus Aurelius,* 25ins. high. Both were from casts supplied by Hoskins & Grant* in 1774 and are listed in the 1777 Catalogue*.

Marcus Aurelius. *Jasper portrait medallion of the Emperor Marcus Aurelius Antoninus. First listed in the 1779 Catalogue.* Wedgwood.

Maria Feodorowna, Empress of Russia (1759-1826)

Daughter of Duke Eugen of Württemberg; married, 1776, Paul, son and heir of Catherine II* (the Great), who succeeded as Tsar in 1796. She modelled a number of portraits of the Russian royal family, including one of the Empress Catherine as Minerva, and a double portrait of her sons, Alexander and Constantine, which were reproduced in Wedgwood's jasper in 1791. These, and other portraits of her sons and of the Empress Elizabeth, were also produced by James Tassie* in his glass paste, and it is possible that Wedgwood obtained his models from him. Maria Feodorowna's drawing of her six children, three of whom became Tsar, was engraved by J. Walker in 1790.

Marks

A mark on a piece of pottery or porcelain is, if genuine, a statement about its origin. In the 18th century marks were few and far between. They were used by a few exceptionally powerful and influential manufacturers, whose products were bought because they came from that particular source. The first 18th century manufacturers of porcelain in Europe, the Meissen* factory, employed a mark consistently from a very early stage, while many of their competitors, especially the smaller enterprises, either used no mark at all, or one calculated to be mistaken for the Meissen crossed swords mark (e.g. the crossed hayforks of Rudolstadt, or the crossed Ls of Limbach). Even the powerful royal factory of Sèvres*, in its first year or two at Vincennes, imitated Meissen, and a bowl of this period with the crossed swords mark exists.

In England the first porcelain factory at Chelsea* was, for a good many years, the only factory to mark its wares. The Bow* porcelain factory, started a few years afterwards, never marked its wares. The few marked specimens known were painted by a decorator like James Giles*, and it is noteworthy that even this mark contains the Chelsea anchor, as well as the dagger which came from the arms of the city of London. Worcester* marked its early wares with pseudo-Chinese ideograms because this is the ware they were copying. No Derby* porcelain was ever marked until after its proprietor had bought the Chelsea factory in 1770, although, when it was founded, it called itself 'the second Dresden' (i.e. Meissen). About the same time Champion's Bristol factory, as well as Worcester, was putting the Meissen mark on the base of English vases.

Apart from a mere handful of very exceptional pieces, no mark appeared on Staffordshire pottery until Wedgwood started to stamp his name on his product. With a few very rare exceptions, no one in Europe put their name, or that of the factory, on their wares, only some kind of device, and Wedgwood's action was a new departure which marks the beginning of modern marketing methods. It is, however, noteworthy that he adopted this policy only when he began to break away from improvements on the standard wares of the Staffordshire district, such as those he had made while in partnership with Whieldon*. From 1759-64 a mark seems to have been used rarely. From 1764-68 marks become more numerous. From 1769 virtually everything is marked, and ornamental wares especially are marked 'Wedgwood & Bentley' for the duration of the partnership, although in the case of a vase divided into several parts held together with a nut and bolt only the lowest part was marked, and if this was a square base now missing, then no mark will appear on that piece.

Wedgwood was doing at this time what had never been done before in Staffordshire — he was signing the products of his factory, and selling them, not only on their appearance and quality, but on the name attached to them. When Wedgwood began to mark his wares he was asserting his intention of becoming the leader of the industry in Staffordshire, and this cannot have been popular. It was only later that those, like Turner*, who followed his leadership, and were able to make wares of good quality using his techniques and styles, felt sufficiently certain of their position to add their own names.

It is noteworthy that, at this time, Wedgwood felt it important to make certain that no other name but his own appeared on his wares. Unlike the porcelain factories, which allowed occasional works to be signed, Wedgwood would not allow the name of the artist to appear, and the few pieces clandestinely signed by Hackwood* were a source of acrimony. For this reason, attributions to artists in the present work, and most others, are made from the surviving records, and not from signed examples. In the 19th century one or two of the more important artists, such as Lessore*, were permitted to sign their work, and in modern times the individual artist has assumed much more importance in the industry generally. For lists of marks see Appendix II.

Marks. *An example of the unusual and so far unexplained date mark which reads 'Josiah Wedgwood Feb 2 1805.' This particularly rare version is enamelled on the base of a pearl ware pedestal. Wedgwood.*

Marlborough, 1st Duke of (1650-1722)
John Churchill

English soldier; victor of the battles of Blenheim (1704), Ramillies (1706) and Oudenarde (1708); created Duke of Marlborough, 1702.

A Wedgwood bust, 10ins. high, which exists in basaltes*, jasper* and *rosso antico**, is generally identified as the Duke of Marlborough, but it is, in fact, a copy of a bust of George II* by Rysbrack*. A portrait medallion* of Marlborough was issued prior to 1773 after a medal by Jean Dassier* dated 1722.

Marlborough, Duke of. *Jasper portrait medallion of John Churchill, 1st Duke of Marlborough, from a medal by Jean Dassier dated 1722. First listed in the 1773 Catalogue. This version produced by Bert Bentley, 1920.* British Museum.

Marriage of Cupid and Psyche, The

One of the most famous and popular of all Wedgwood's relief subjects, it was produced in all sizes, from the largest tablet to the smallest cameo for setting in a ring. The subject was taken originally from a Renaissance gem*, a sardonyx, then in the Marlborough collection and now in the Museum of Fine Arts, Boston. Wedgwood produced three distinct versions of the subject, two of which show significant variations from the original. Dr. Lloyd Hawes (*The American Wedgwoodian*, Vol.1, No.2) points out that an engraving after Theodorus Netscher, published in 1724 in *Pierres Antiques Gravées,* served as the source for one revised version. The version closest to the original was probably taken from a sulphur* cast of the gem by Tassie*, who reproduced it in his glass paste, or from a direct study of the Marlborough gem. Wedgwood was acquainted with the 4th Duke. He visited the factory, and Wedgwood journeyed to Blenheim in 1770. The third version, attributed to Flaxman*, gives more space to the figures and incorporates details from the other two versions. In the sixth edition of Wedgwood's Catalogue he expresses "grateful acknowledgements. . .to the Duke of Marlborough for a cast of the exquisite gem in his grace's collection, the marriage of Cupid and Psyche." Bartolozzi* engraved the subject, either from the Marlborough gem or a Tassie copy, and no doubt this print was in Wedgwood's possession. Hackwood* worked on the subject in 1774 from a cast supplied by Tassie. Lochée* is reputed to have remodelled the subject in 1787 after Tassie. Webber* is also said to have worked on it. Flaxman's version seems to have been comparatively late, about 1787.

The small sizes were the first to be made, to be followed by the larger, and although the latter were copies, they were necessarily *measured* copies, although the enlargement inevitably gave rise to variations, however small.

Marriage of Cupid and Psyche. *Jasper medallion ornamented with the* Marriage of Cupid and Psyche, *the version attributed to Flaxman, 8ins. by 11¾ins.* Wedgwood.

Marryat, Joseph (1790-1870)

MP for Sandwich; brother to Captain Frederick Marryat, RN, author of *Mr. Midshipman Easy*. Joseph Marryat retired to Swansea in 1850 and published his *History of Pottery and Porcelain,* which was followed by revised editions in 1857 and 1868. This was the first book of its kind, and it contains information about 18th century Wedgwood wares. Marryat's own collection, which was extensive and included good examples of Wedgwood production, was sold by Christie's in a ten-day sale lasting from the 9th-19th February, 1867. Marryat was also a friend of Sir Joseph Hooker*. His book may still be read with profit.

Mars

Roman name for Ares, the god of war. The son of Zeus and Hera, Ares carried on an adulterous liaison with Aphrodite* (Venus*). He delighted in battle, slaughter, and the

Marsyas. Marsyas and the Young Olympus, *one of the Herculaneum subjects in blue and white jasper, 11 ¼ ins. diameter. Mark 'WEDGWOOD' impressed, c.1795.* Dwight and Lucille Beeson Collection.

Mars. *Solid white jasper statuette of Mars, 6ins. high, clad in armour, with a seated hound. c.1785.* Liverpool City Museums. Photo: Wedgwood.

destruction of cities, but was conquered by Hercules* and forced to retire to Mount Olympus. He is usually depicted as a warrior in armour. *Mars* is the subject of one of Wedgwood's rare small statuettes which appears for the first time in the 1787 Catalogue*. Made in white jasper, with a coloured jasper pedestal, as a pair to one of Venus, this was probably reduced from a figure by Bacon* supplied in 1769. The tablet, *Peace preventing Mars from bursting open the Gates of the Temple of Janus* * was modelled by Flaxman* in 1787. Flaxman was also responsible for the medallion, *Vulcan with Mars and Venus in a Net,* modelled c.1778. Webber* modelled the tablet, *Triumph of Mars* in 1782.

Marsyas

A satyr* of Phrygia, who found a flute discarded by Athene* which played beautiful melodies of its own accord. He challenged Apollo* to a musical contest, the victor to do as he pleased with the vanquished. The Muses* decided the contest in favour of Apollo, who tied Marsyas to a tree and flayed him alive.

Wedgwood subjects:

Marsyas and the young Olympus (Olympus was the surname applied to the Muses and all gods believed to live on Mount Olympus, and thus to Apollo Musagetes), circular tablet, 16ins. diameter, in the series of Herculaneum subjects*. Possibly the work of Bacon*.

Apollo and Marsyas, one of the set of three bas-reliefs depicting the History of Apollo, supplied by Mrs. Landré in 1769.

Masonic Ware

Pottery or porcelain decorated with Masonic insignia. On Wedgwood Queen's* ware, and other English earthenware, the decoration is usually transfer-printed* and consists of the arms of the Freemasons supported by two Masons, and pyramids surmounted by celestial and terrestrial globes.

entertaining "half a doz young Bloods." An illness for which he had received a good deal of sympathy had, according to the informant, been what Wedgwood referred to as "the foul Disease." He was said to work little at the books of account, but ordered everyone else to help him, and he overawed everyone by his violent and haughty temper, as well as by the high regard in which they thought he was held. Wedgwood considered it too risky to discharge him, since he might then, with his knowledge of the business, collect money from partnership debtors. So Mather was sent temporarily to Bath, and Peter Swift* went to London to examine the books, when Mather's defalcations were uncovered. A month later, in October 1772, Wedgwood had so far relented as to discuss Mather's future, suggesting that he should be retained on promising to amend, provided he was willing to give security for the eventual repayment of the missing cash. He was then sent to Chelsea to check the ware for painting, and eventually, after the death of David Rhodes*, he succeeded to the important post of colour-maker. In 1776, when the partnership was having trouble with Du Burk*, Mather was sent to Amsterdam to check the stock there, but in the following year, after five years of honesty, Mather relapsed into his old ways. Investigation revealed that "he is not only bad...but is making all the house as bad as himself." Once more he was given a chance to amend. Attempts to reform him were finally given up in August 1780, when Wedgwood wrote to Bentley: "We have both of us suffered sufficiently...for such an abandoned worthless wretch..." We are left to conclude that Mather must have been more than usually capable to have warranted so many attempts to reclaim him.

Matt Glaze

The smooth, velvety appearance of matt glazed ware is due to the partial crystallisation of the glaze during cooling, which is much slower than usual. Matt glazes are opaque.

Matt glazes produced by Wedgwood in the 20th century include Moonstone*, Ravenstone, Matt Green and Straw.

See: Keith Murray.

Mayer, Elijah (fl.1770-1813)

Potter, of Hanley, who made fine quality black basaltes*, and cane ware*. Unmarked pieces are often mistaken for Wedgwood, though the modelling generally lacks the sharpness of Wedgwood wares of the period. Mayer's basaltes appears to have been almost entirely teaware and coffeeware, but he made a small quantity of excellent vases in caneware. The mark, 'E. Mayer', impressed appears either on the extreme edge of the base or on the projecting rim around it, and it is consequently difficult to find.

Mayer, Joseph (1803-1886)

19th century antiquary and collector of coins, antiquities, manuscripts, Liverpool pottery and porcelain and Wedgwood wares. The collection of antiquities and ceramics was bequeathed to the City of Liverpool to be housed in a Museum bearing his name. The Wedgwood ware was described by C.T. Gatty in a *Catalogue of a loan collection of the works of Josiah Wedgwood*, Liverpool, 1879. The greater part of the Mayer collection of Wedgwood ware was destroyed by bombing during the Second World War, but his manuscript collection was fortunately preserved at the Wedgwood Museum*.

Meander Border

A type of Greek fret in which one or two continuous lines turning at right angles at equidistant intervals make a repetitive labyrinthine pattern.

See: Fret.

Masonic Ware. *Creamware tankard, 6¼ ins. high, decorated with Sadler & Green print in black of a Masonic coat of arms. Danish silver mounts. c.1781. Christie's.*

Mather, Ben (fl.1769-1780)

Head clerk in London; later colour-maker. Ben Mather came to live in Great Newport Street in September 1769, and apparently he took over the duties of head clerk from William Cox*, who about this time returned to Burslem. In 1771, when Bentley visited Etruria, Mather was left in charge of the Newport Street rooms to the entire satisfaction of the partners, but soon after this both of them began to question his trustworthiness. In 1772 Wedgwood received a confidential letter from London which confirmed his suspicions and prompted him to investigate. According to this letter Mather was pursuing a style of living beyond his means, and he was

Medallions. *Jasper medallion ornamented with* Music, *modelled by Hackwood, c.1785.* Wedgwood.

Medallions

Originally medallions were large medals issued by the Roman Emperors to mark special occasions, and when of gold or silver their weight was usually a multiple of the standard coin. Wedgwood medallions, thin and flat, of cream-coloured ware, jasper, or basaltes, bear a portrait or some other design in low relief. They are intermediate in size between the cameo* and the plaque* (tablet). Some of the very large portrait medallions could, perhaps, more accurately be called portrait plaques, but they fall under the general heading of medallions. Medallions were principally used for cabinet display. Plaques were made to ornament furniture and such architectural features as chimney pieces*, but medallions were often used as ancillary decoration. Portrait medallions*, usually in basaltes or jasper, were often framed in metal. Creamware medallions were frequently used as factory pattern models.

Medea

Daughter of the King of Colchis, the city to which Jason came to steal the Golden Fleece. In this undertaking he was abetted by Medea, who fled with him to Greece as his wife. There Jason deserted her. In revenge she murdered their two children and destroyed Jason's new wife with a poisoned garment.

Wedgwood subjects:

Medea, medallion by Hackwood*.

Medea rejuvenating Jason's father (Aeson), medallion, 4ins. by 3¼ins., by Flaxman*, c.1776.

Medical Spoon

A spoon having a loop handle, the terminal of which curves under the bowl and serves as a foot on which it will stand. Made of creamware throughout the 19th century by Wedgwood, Leeds, and others. Some examples, subsequent to 1875, have graduated markings in the interior.

Medusa

The hair of the young and beautiful Medusa was changed into hissing serpents by Athene* who objected to Medusa's copulation with Poseidon in one of her temples. Medusa's appearance became so terrible that anyone who saw her was turned to stone. Perseus slew her by using his polished shield as

a mirror, an event depicted in Guglielmo della Porta's* *Marriage of Perseus and Andromeda,* reproduced by Wedgwood c.1768. Athene placed the image of the head of Medusa in the centre of her shield and breastplate. Flaxman* modelled a superb bas-relief head of Medusa "from an exquisite marble in the possession of Sir W. Hamilton*," diameter 5ins., in 1776. A smaller, and inferior oval medallion also exists, 3ins. in diameter; and two profiles 1½ins. by 2ins. are of the same date.

Medusa. *Circular jasper plaque of the head of Medusa, 5¼ins. diameter. Modelled by John Flaxman in 1776.* Christie's.

Meissen (Saxony)

The oldest European porcelain factory, dating from 1710. A true porcelain body on the same principle as the Chinese was made there from the first. The formula was discovered after many years of experiment and research by E.W. von Tschirnhaus and J.F. Böttger, the latter an alchemist originally employed by the factory's patron, Augustus the Strong (Elector of Saxony and King of Poland), to make gold. Augustus was a notable patron of the arts, and of the factory artists, J.F. Höroldt, the *Obermaler* (Chief Painter), was also Court Painter, and J.J. Kändler, the *Modellmeister* (Chief Modeller) was Court Sculptor. Augustus was a porcelain collector who bought a palace (*Japanische Palais*) to house his collection of Oriental porcelain, and a representative selection of the products of his new factory. The factory itself was established at Meissen, some twelve miles from the City of Dresden.

The early factory style was predominantly Oriental, which rapidly gave place to a well-marked baroque. The artists enjoyed access to all kinds of sources of inspiration, from the designs of the Court Goldsmith, Dinglinger, to the exotic birds of the Moritzburg aviaries. Especially admired products of these early years are the figures of Kändler and his assistants, and the series of superb table services, of which the Swan Service, made for the factory's Director, the Count von Brühl, is the most generally known.

In the first half of the 18th century Meissen had little competition, but factories were gradually established elsewhere, usually under royal or aristocratic patronage, and they took their styles from Meissen which, until 1756, the opening of the Seven Years' War, almost completely dominated the European scene. The Chelsea* factory, which was founded in England in 1745 by a Huguenot silversmith, Nicolas Sprimont, started by using French silver shapes, but soon went on to copy Meissen with a series of distinguished figures and some of its service ware, turning in 1756 to Sèvres* instead as that factory's reputation grew and Meissen was occupied by the troops of Frederick the Great.

After the end of the War in 1763 Meissen recovered with great difficulty, and the next sixty years or so were a period of mounting troubles which culminated in the Napoleonic Wars and the bombardment of Dresden. The factory adopted a neo-classical style, and employed a French modeller, Michel-Victor Acier, who brought with him the current Sèvres styles. They introduced a number of novelties in an attempt to revive flagging trade, including *Wedgwoodarbeit* (Wedgwood work) which was an imitation of blue and white jasper in porcelain. After Waterloo the factory's fortunes began gradually to recover, and during the 19th century it became increasingly prosperous. It survived both world wars, and is now in East Germany.

According to the Meissen Jubilee Catalogue published in 1910, the Direktor Oppel obtained, in 1814, "cases of ornaments in the classical style from Etruria" to help with new designs. Few in Germany could then afford the high quality hand-painted porcelain which had been a Meissen speciality, and most of the wares selling at the time were either stonewares (*Steinzeug*), some being of the jasper and basaltes type, or creamware (*Steingut*). These were not necessarily imported from Staffordshire directly, since many of the former German *faience** and stoneware factories had to change to making wares in the Wedgwood manner in order to stay in business. Later, when the German States had recovered from the devastation of the Napoleonic Wars, these factories reverted for the most part to porcelain, and created a thriving export trade in wares based on their early styles, although these did not become so fashionable in the luxury trade as reproductions of earlier Sèvres porcelain produced by Minton*, Coalport*, and many others.

Wedgwood's own period of prosperity came when Meissen had passed its 18th century zenith, and it had little direct effect on his later wares; but some of his early wares, such as the cauliflower and pineapple tureens, certainly came originally from Meissen, probably at secondhand by way of the English porcelain factories (Chelsea, for instance) who copied the German factory's rococo wares. It is possible that Wedgwood's cauliflower ware may have been inspired by the local porcelain of Longton Hall, which must have been known to him.

There are not many references to Meissen in Wedgwood's letters, where he refers to the factory as either 'Dresden' or 'Saxon', but there is enough to be certain that he well understood the nature of the product, classifying it with Chinese porcelain.

According to Marryat (*History of Porcelain*) writing soon after 1850, Josiah Wedgwood II, when travelling in Germany in 1790, offered a rental of £3,000 per annum to take over the factory, an offer apparently refused. This was a fortunate escape, since the area was to be overrun by Napoleon within fifteen years, and the Continent generally was, at that time, heading for a difficult trade recession.

Mellor, Thomas. *Queen's ware chessman copied from Flaxman's design, the base inlaid in black by Thomas Mellor. 3ins. high. c.1880.* Wedgwood.

Mellor, Thomas. *Vase decorated by Mellor with inlaying and enamelling, the ornament based on 16th century arabesques. Signed. c.1885. Wedgwood.*

Meleager

Son of the Calydonian King, Oeneus, and leader of the Argonauts. He slew the boar which ravaged the woods of Calydon, an animal 'Scotticised' by Wedgwood as the 'Caledonian boar'. A medallion, 8ins. by 6ins., the figure modelled by Flaxman* in 1775, is listed in the 1777 Catalogue*.

See: Death of a Roman Warrior; Guglielmo Della Porta.

Mellor, Thomas (fl.1870-1890)

Pâte-sur-pâte artist at Minton*, where he was, with Charles Toft* and Frederick Rhead*, an apprentice of M.L. Solon's. In the 1880s he moved to Wedgwood, where he made inlaid* ware. A chess board, made as an exhibition piece in the manner of Henri Deux Ware*, was furnished with inlaid Queen's ware* chessmen* after the original models by Flaxman*, and one of the surviving examples is signed by Mellor. In the Wedgwood Museum* there is also a signed inlaid Queen's ware vase. It is probable that other examples of this artist's work remain to be identified.

Melon

Tureens, teapots and covered bowls moulded in the form of a melon were popular during the second half of the 18th century, and were made in creamware by Wedgwood, at Leeds*, and possibly by others. A porcelain version was made at Chelsea*.

Menai Suspension Bridge

The bridge, one of Thomas Telford's most important works with a span of 580 feet, was opened in 1826. It is the only road link between the Isle of Anglesey and the Welsh mainland. To commemorate the 150th anniversary in 1976 Wedgwood produced 2,000 special commemorative plates in Queen's ware designed by Islwyn Williams, graphic art student at Liverpool Polytechnic. The design bears a view of the bridge printed in green, with the inscription 'Pont Menai, 1826-1976.' The commemorative back stamp is in both Welsh and English.

Mence, William (fl.1769-1774)

Painter at the Chelsea Decorating Studio* who worked on the Frog* service border designs.

Mercury

The Greek Hermes; god of commerce, gain, and good luck; the messenger of the gods, who usually carries the caduceus* and wears wings on his helmet and sandals. The helmet is probably better described as a travelling hat. As Hermes he was the son of Zeus and Maia. He invented the lyre, and many of the useful arts.

Wedgwood subjects:

Mercury, large bust, from the antique, supplied by Hoskins & Grant*, 1779, and re-finished by Hackwood*.

Mercury. Bust, height 18½ ins., by Flaxman*, 1782.

Mercury joining the hands of Britain and France, tablet commemmorating the commercial treaty with France. Designed by Webber* and modelled by Flaxman, 1787.

Mercury on a Rock (tying his sandal), supplied by Hoskins & Grant, 1779, after the original by Pigalle*. Height 18ins.

Mercury presenting Bacchus to Juno* (properly, *The Birth of Bacchus*), medallion by Hackwood, 1777.

Mercury with caduceus, cameo attributed to Flaxman.

Victory and Mercury, medallion by Angelini*, c.1787.

Cupid and the Infant Mercury, medallion after a relief on a sarcophagus in the Capitoline Museum, c.1787.

Mercury. *Black basaltes figure, 18ins. high of Mercury on a Rock, tying his sandal, supplied as a cast by Hoskins & Grant in 1779 after the original by Pigalle. Wedgwood.*

Mercury. *Large black basaltes bust from the antique, probably modelled by Flaxman in 1782.* Wedgwood.

Meredith, Sir William (d.1809)

Politician, Privy Councillor and Comptroller of the Royal Household (1774). One of Wedgwood's earliest and most influential patrons. As MP for Liverpool he was certainly acquainted with Bentley*, to whom Wedgwood may have owed the introduction. In 1765 Wedgwood completed a large creamware dinner service for Sir William, who exerted his considerable influence to obtain for him the loan of antique gems, prints and pottery. Prior to 1770 he was among those who urged Wedgwood to introduce a whiter earthenware, and it was this desire for a colour more nearly approximating to that of porcelain that led Wedgwood to experiment with a 'white bisket' which developed into the invention of jasper*, and also to produce, in 1779, the first pearl* body and glaze.

Metallic Oxides

The oxides of certain metals are employed as pigments in pottery decoration, either underglaze (when they are applied to the surface of the ware before glazing), or overglaze (when they are applied to the already fired glaze in the form of enamels). These oxides are suspended in an oily medium to make them suitable for application with a brush, the medium burning away in the kiln, the actual colour being developed by subsequent firing. In modern times ceramic colours usually have a vegetable dye added as a guide to the developed shade, but in the 18th century a system of numbered palettes was often used, together with a similarly numbered guide to the appearance of the colours *after* firing. The oxides most widely used for the purpose were cobalt*, copper, iron, manganese*, and antimony, and variations of colour and shade could be obtained by simple mixing. The colours obtainable were somewhat variable depending on firing temperature, kiln atmosphere, and the composition of the glaze on which they were used. Copper, for instance, normally yielded a bluish green in the presence of a plentiful supply of oxygen, and a reddish purple in the presence of carbon monoxide (reducing* atmosphere). In the 19th century new colouring oxides, such as chromium, came into use, and in 1870 Wedgwood first used uranium oxide (see: Dysart Ware). Today the chemist has added a large number of new colouring agents. White glazes and enamels are usually the result of opacifying a transparent glaze with tin oxide.

Colouring oxides are also added to glazes for coloured glaze wares, and mixed with bodies for solid colours, such as solid jasper*. Mixed with slip* they are employed as a surface application.

See: Dip.

Meteyard, Eliza (1816-1879)

Author; born in Liverpool, the daughter of a doctor, who was appointed, in 1818, surgeon to the Shrewsbury militia. There, she later visited the home of Dr. Robert Waring Darwin*, who had formed an important collection of Wedgwood ware, including a first issue copy of the Portland* vase. From the age of nineteen Eliza Meteyard helped to support herself by writing, but from about 1850 she seems to have devoted an increasing amount of her time to the study of Josiah Wedgwood and his work. She made the acquaintance of Joseph Mayer*, who allowed her free use of his unrivalled manuscript collection relating to Wedgwood, and gave her introductions to collectors. After fifteen years of tireless research, she published her two-volume biography of Josiah Wedgwood. Sales of the book were adversely affected by the almost simultaneous appearance of Llewellynn Jewitt's *The Wedgwoods: Being a Life of Josiah Wedgwood,* and Miss Meteyard had spent a considerable sum on illustrations. Her biography was a financial loss. Undeterred, she published six further studies of Wedgwood before her death in 1879 (see: Bibliography).

During her life she had also written seven novels (three of them aggregating nine volumes) and six volumes of children's stories.

Eliza Meteyard's *The Life of Josiah Wedgwood* has been a standard work for more than a century. It contains statements that have been contradicted by modern research, and opinions that are now known to be erroneous, but it remains a monumental work of pioneer inquiry, which compels admiration and continues to be indispensable to Wedgwood collectors and to all writers on the subject.

Michelangelo (Buonarotti) (1474-1564)

Possibly the foremost sculptor of the Renaissance (at least, to modern taste), although he, himself, awarded the honour to Cellini*, a judgement with which the 19th century was largely in agreement. Nothing by Michelangelo in bronze survives, but a number of marbles still exist, including the *tondo* belonging to the Royal Academy. Casts of his best known works are in the Gallery of Casts, Victoria and Albert Museum. Michelangelo's work was used by some of Wedgwood's artists as a source of inspiration, particularly a Bacchus* figure modelled by Flaxman* in 1773, a Triton* figure standing upon rocks modelled by Keeling*, a large basaltes lamp, the figure of a lion, and one of a sphinx.

See: Michelangelo Vase.

Michelangelo Vase (Lamp)

Sometimes described as the 'Michelangelo Lamp', this vase is in the form of a large covered bowl with three burners, ornamented with acanthus* scrolls, upon a pedestal and column support. The cover is surmounted by three Sibyl*, or 'Widow', figures seated beneath a palm tree. Around the column, and supporting the bowl, are three stooping male figures. It was made in black basaltes*, c.1783. Two similar vases of Blue John* and ormolu* on a marble base were made by Boulton* & Fothergill for Sir Thomas Dundas in 1772. These were described as 'Persian candle vases', but there is nothing Persian about the figures. 'Persian figures' was an architectural description of any male figures used for the support of an entablature and was thus synonymous with Atlantes (see: Atlas). The vase is a fine example of 18th century eclecticism in design: the bowl is copied from a Hellenistic bronze of c.400B.C.; the figures derive from a silver-gilt crucifix by Antonio Gentile da Faenza (1531-1609), presented to St. Peter's, Rome by Alessandro Farnese in 1582; and the Sibyl finial figures were Wedgwood's (three Sibyls were similarly used for some of the largest pieces of the Frog* service). Sir William Chambers* stated that Gentile's 'Persian' figures were "cast from models of Michel Angelo Buonarotti, and repaired either by himself, or doubtless under his directions," and it is possible that Gentile may have copied the figures from models by Michelangelo in his workshop.

Wedgwood's source of these figures, which appears to have been the same as Boulton's, is uncertain, but there is reason to believe that they may have come as casts from John Flaxman Senior*.

This vase exists in two slightly different versions of about the same date. It was reproduced in the 19th century in basaltes, and also, with somewhat bizarre effect, in majolica* and in enamelled and gilt bone china*.

Miller, Alec (b.1879)

Sculptor. Born in Glasgow, Miller studied at the Glasgow School of Art and in Florence. He taught at the Cambridge School of Arts and Crafts 1902-14 and at Oxford City School of Art 1919-23. He lived for some years in Monterey, California. His Wedgwood plaque, *Diana and Actaeon,* 1906, is in the Buten Museum* of Wedgwood.

Miller, Felix Martin (1820-after 1880)

Miller, who was brought up in an Orphan School, joined the Royal Academy Schools in 1842, and exhibited at the Academy from 1842 to 1880. He specialised in bas-reliefs, and his work was favourably discussed on several occasions in the *Art Journal. Emily and the White Doe of Rylstone* is one of his works (of which he made three versions) which appeared in Parian porcelain. For Wedgwood Miller modelled a bust of Shakespeare*, 11½ ins. in height, to mark the tercentenary of

the latter's birth in 1564. It is impressed 'F.M. Miller Sc' in addition to the factory mark.

See: Howell & James.

Mills, Anne (fl.1769-1774)

Painter at the Chelsea Decorating Studio* who worked on the borders of the Frog* service.

Mills, Thomas (fl.1773-1774)

Painter at the Chelsea Decorating Studio* for the inside borders of the Frog* service.

Michelangelo Vase. *The vase or lamp has three burners, and is carried on the backs of three bowed figures. The body is ornamented with arabesques in relief.* Wedgwood.

Colour Plate XVII

Above left: Portland Vase in blue-black jasper from the original edition of 1790. Above right: Portland Vase in Portland Blue jasper, 1973. Wedgwood.

Below: Jasper chessmen, some on jasper dip bases, designed by John Flaxman in 1785. Height of Queen 3½ ins. c.1790. Another set of chessmen was designed by Arnold Machin, RA, in 1938. Wedgwood.

Minerva

Roman goddess of wisdom; patroness of the arts, professions, and trades. She represents prudence, courage and perseverance, and is usually clad in armour, with helmet and shield, looking a little like Britannia, whose representations are no doubt based on those of Minerva. She was identified by the Romans with Athene (Pallas Athene), the daughter of Zeus*, in whom power and wisdom were harmoniously blended. She is also the patroness of agriculture. The Palladium* was an image of the goddess, preserved at Troy, on which the safety of the city depended. It was stolen by Ulysses* and Diomedes* and taken by the latter to Greece.

Wedgwood subjects:

Minerva, bas-relief (figure) for a medallion, 7ins. by 5½ins., by Flaxman*, 1775.

Minerva, bust, 22ins. high, from a cast supplied by Hoskins & Grant*, 1774, and re-finished by Hackwood*. Originally produced in basaltes*, it was reproduced in enamelled and gilt Queen's ware* in 1900.

Minerva, seated figure, 13¾ins. high, for a candelabrum, modelled by Webber*, c.1790, as a pair to Diana*.

Minerva. *Bronzed basaltes bust of Minerva, 14ins. high, on a wood socle, c.1885. A fine example of Wedgwood 19th century reproduction of 18th century models.* Christie's.

Minerva. *Figure of Minerva in the form of a candlestick. The resemblance to Britannia is plain, but Minerva bears a Medusa's head on her breastplate and shield. Modelled by Webber, c.1790.* Wedgwood.

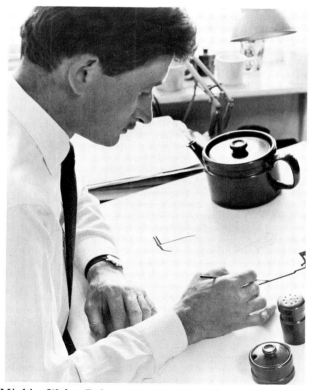

Minkin, Walter Robert. *Design Director of Wedgwood from 1979.* Photo: Wedgwood.

Minkin, Walter Robert, Des. RCA, FSIAD (b.1928)

Designer at Barlaston* from 1955; Chief Designer; Group Design Manager; and, from July 1979, Design Director.

Bob Minkin's most important designs include the cylindrical coffee set (1963), produced originally in black basaltes* and later in Ravenstone matt glaze*, *Sterling* oven-to-table ware*, *Ice Rose* pattern on bone china* (1959), and *Mayfield* pattern (two versions, 1958) on Barlaston shape* Queen's ware*. Recently he was responsible for the adaptation of the Egyptian Collection* gilded plaques from originals in the Tutankhamun treasure.

Minton, Stoke-on-Trent, Staffs.

The firm was founded by Thomas Minton in 1793 (operating from 1796) with the aid of William Pownall, who financed the enterprise, Joseph Poulson (master potter), and Samuel Poulson (modeller and mould maker). Thomas Minton's brother acted as London agent. When Thomas Minton died in 1836 his place was taken by his son, Herbert Minton. At first the principal products were blue-printed earthenware and bone china, but plain and enamelled creamware was made, and there is a record of Minton's purchasing "50 tons of Mr. Wedgwood's blue [lavender body] clay @ 10/6" in August 1817 for the manufacture of coloured bodies*. Wedgwood had bought considerable quantities of blue-printed ware from Minton between 1801 and 1806, including *Tulip, Willow, Pine* and *Nankeen Temple* patterns. The firm became more adventurous after it employed J.-L.-F. Arnoux from France as art director. He introduced, among other wares, one which he called majolica*, which became one of the successes of the Great Exhibition of 1851, where the Medieval Court contained objects designed by Pugin and made by Minton. Artists of importance came from France in 1848 (the July Revolution) and 1870 (the Franco-Prussian War). Marc-Louis Solon, who arrived from Sèvres in 1870, brought the *pâte-sur-pâte* technique with him. Parian* was successfully adopted by Minton in the 1840s, and models by John Bell and Hiram Powers (e.g. *The Greek Slave*) enjoyed great popularity. Carrier de Belleuse* also provided models. Some very good figure work was done by Minton, both free-standing figures and as part of ornamental dessert services. Hugues Protât*, Charles Toft*, and Eric Owen* all came to Wedgwood from Minton's, as did John Boyle*, Herbert Minton's partner 1836-41, and equal partner with Francis Wedgwood* at Etruria 1843-45. The firm still makes fine china and is now part of the Royal Doulton Group.

Monocular. *Monocular (opera glass) fitted with dark blue and white jasper outer case, and ormolu and ivory mounts. The bas-relief subject is the* Marriage of Cupid and Psyche. Wedgwood.

Miss Pit

A half-length portrait of a young lady, over a scroll inscribed 'Miss Pit', occurs on a Leeds* salt-glaze* teapot, and the same young lady is depicted taking tea in a garden on both salt-glaze and creamware teapots from Leeds. The reverse of these teapots is decorated with stylised buildings. A similar figure appears, painted in iron red, on a Wedgwood teapot with almost identical buildings on the reverse. These are all clearly the work of a Leeds enameller and may be attributed to David Rhodes*.

Mollart, J. (fl.1806-1811)

Engraver, who supplied Wedgwood with engravings of 'Minton's Willow' (see: Willow Pattern) in 1806, though it does not seem to have been produced until 1818. He was also partly responsible (with Hales* and Brookes*) for the *Blue Bamboo* pattern.

See: Underglaze Blue Prints.

Mongenot, Joseph (1769-1814)

Swiss modeller and designer who came to England in 1788, and also worked here as an engraver. He designed bas-reliefs* for Adams* of Greengates, including *A Sacrifice to Apollo*, to *Diana, Pomona,* and *Aphrodite*, which are Wedgwood-type subjects.

'Miss Pit'. *'Miss Pit' type teapot painted in enamel colours, probably by David Rhodes, c.1765.* Zeitlin Collection.

Monocular

An opera glass with a single eye piece. The ornamental jasper outer case was used in conjunction with brass tubes and lens carriers and an ivory eye piece. Made about 1785-90. Opera glasses in the form of binoculars with twin eye pieces were also made.

Monopodia

Figures having only one foot, supporting a vase or entablature. Wedgwood's early vases and candlesticks were sometimes supported in this manner, and sphinx*-head monpodia appear on objects in the revived Egyptian taste* of 1800-10.

Monteith

An oval bowl with an elaborately scalloped rim which is turned slightly inwards. Its purpose was to cool the bowls of wine glasses, which were suspended from the rim by the foot, the bowl resting in very cold water. Monteiths are rare, but they are to be found in silver, pewter, glass, and porcelain, and were also made by Wedgwood in cream-coloured ware and jasper. The type has also been reproduced in Queen's ware and glazed black basaltes as a decorative item in recent times. The name is derived from a Scotsman named Monteith who, at Oxford during the reign of Charles II, wore a cloak thus scalloped.

Montfaucon, Bernard de (1655-1741)

Montfaucon served in Germany under Marshall Turenne, but entered the Congregation of Saint-Maur in 1675 and devoted the rest of his life to scholarship. His best known work is the somewhat inaccurate *L'Antiquité Expliquée et Representée en Figures*

published in 1719 in five volumes. A five-volume supplement followed in 1724. An English version by D. Humphreys, London, appeared between 1721 and 1725. This work was in Wedgwood's library. He refers in 1786 to an early attempt to copy the Portland vase, using Montfaucon's illustrations. These comprised four engravings — the vase itself (a little too slender), the decoration on either side, and the base. A reference in a letter to Flaxman of December 1786, suggests that Wedgwood was in the habit of consulting Montfaucon's work. It was probably from this source that the sphinxes of 1769, and some of his comparatively rare excursions into objects in the Egyptian taste were derived. These need not necessarily be as late as Napoleon's Egyptian campaign or Nelson's victory of the Nile, though many of Wedgwood's productions in this style date from that period.

Monti, Raffaelle (1818-1881)

Italian sculptor, who visited England in 1846 and lived permanently in London from 1848 until his death. He executed some architectural sculpture, including the *relievo* over the proscenium arch of the Covent Garden Opera House in 1858, and was responsible for the interior decoration of Mentmore, Buckinghamshire, but he is best known for a form of sculpture, probably originated by Antonio Corradini, which gave solid marble statues and busts the appearance of being covered by a diaphanous veil. An example of this work is *A Veiled Woman* in the Wallace Collection, London. He also executed more conventional marble busts and statues, and his bust of Thomas Henry Huxley (1825-95) was reproduced in Wedgwood's Carrara* and in basaltes* c.1865.

Monteith. *Queen's ware Monteith with double foliate handles, painted in brown enamel with a Sacrifice to Priapus and, on the reverse, with an altar, the details picked out in pastel-coloured enamels, the fluted rim and foot and handles lined in brown. 12¾ ins. long. c.1775-80. It is hard to imagine that Josiah I could have approved of this subject, but it is possible that he failed to appreciate its significance. The shape is No.16 in the first Cream Colour Catalogue. Sotheby's.*

Monopodia. *Covered jasper vase ornamented with a Sacrifice subject on tripod support in the form of goats' head and leg monopodia.* Photo: Wedgwood.

Moonstone Glaze. *Fluted vase covered with Moonstone glaze.*
Wedgwood.

Moonlight Lustre
See: Lustre Decoration.

Moonstone Glaze
A matt white glaze developed by Wedgwood in 1953. It has
been extensively used since that date for shell-handled vases,
Nautilus* ware, shell dessert plates, a small number of
Norman Wilson* unique ware pieces, animal figures by John
Skeaping*, and a wide range of Keith Murray's* designs.

More, Samuel (fl.1769-1799)
Secretary of the Society of Arts, Adelphi, London, a friend of
both Wedgwood and Bentley, with whom they co-operated
during the years in matters of mutual interest. Wedgwood
wrote to Bentley in 1772: "I have a very friendly letter from
our good friend Mr. More with advice of the China Earth
being sent. I beg you will make my thanks and affectionate
regards known to him."

In the late summer of 1774 More and his wife visited
Etruria, and More influenced Wedgwood to begin a collection
of Wedgwood & Bentley's products for posterity. In 1774 the
Society of Arts moved to the Adelphi where it maintained
laboratories for the purpose of assaying specimens of ore. It
was to More that Wedgwood suggested turning when he
needed supplies of ground glass (see: Codes and Formulae.) In
the Autumn of 1777, when the price of cobalt* oxide had
doubled in less than six months to three guineas a pound,
Wedgwood experimented with zaffre* sent him by Mr. More.
In 1787 More, on behalf of the Society of Arts, sent enamels to
Etruria to be tested.

Morgan, J.
China dealer; occupied premises at the corner of Arlington
Street and Piccadilly, London. In November 1769, Wedgwood
wrote to Bentley asking whether Mr. Craft* had taken a
drawing of "The Seve [*sic*] vases" at Morgans. "I think them
composed in a very masterly stile. . . . I should like very much
to have drawings of those Seve vases." This is evidence not
only that the Manufacture royale de Sèvres was exporting to
England commercially, but also that the neo-classical*
Wedgwood was taking an interest in rococo* vases.

Morpheus
The son of Sleep and the god of Dreams, who was responsible
for the shape and content of dreams experienced by the sleeper.
See: Somnus.

Mortar Ware
A very hard vitreous stoneware* body introduced by
Wedgwood in 1779 for the manufacture of mortars, pestles,
and other chemical ware. It is non-absorbent and acid-resistant
(a fact which Veldhuyson* from Amsterdam reported as
"incredible history to several physicians"), and mortars made
from this body are probably still the best available. There are
letters from Dr. Joseph Priestley* asking for chemical
apparatus, including retorts of a 'porcelain nature', and
Wedgwood was at first prepared to supply such items as
retorts, crucibles, evaporating pans, and mortars and pestles
free to his scientific friends in the cause of chemical research. It
was not long, however, before the widespread demand for
these products, and most particularly for mortars used by
apothecaries and druggists, made it necessary for him to fix a
proper price for them. "Mortars," Wedgwood reported to
Bentley shortly before the latter's death, "go everywhere."

More, Samuel. *Jasper portrait medallion of Samuel More, Secretary of
the Royal Society of Arts. First listed in the 1773 Catalogue.*
Wedgwood.

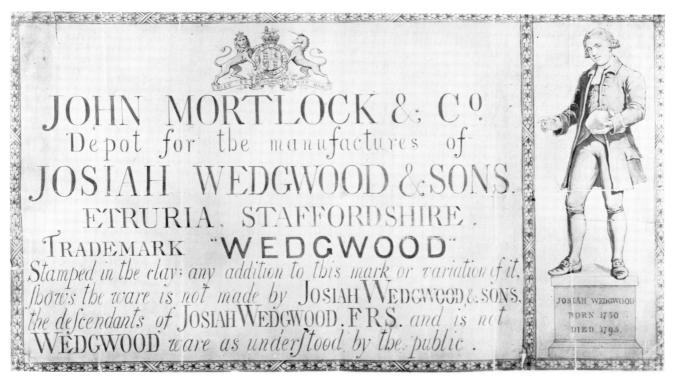

Mortlock, John. *Trade card of John Mortlock & Co.* Wedgwood.

Mortlock, John, Oxford Street, London

China dealer and merchant who ordered wares from various factories marked with his own back stamp. His transfer-printed mark added to the Wedgwood jug commemorating the death of Thomas Carlyle is in the form of a globe with radiating lines on which is an inscription consisting of the words 'John Mortlock, Oxford Street, London, W.' From a point a little south of the north pole projects a flagstaff carrying a flag with the figures '1748', suggesting that the business may originally have been started in that year. The jug also bears the Wedgwood impressed mark.

Morye, St. Petersburg

See: Poskotchin.

Mould

A matrix, usually of plaster of Paris or fireclay, used for the casting of figures and other ceramic wares which cannot be made on the potter's wheel. Moulds can be taken from a variety of sources — an original model in clay, wax, or carved wood, from another piece of ceramic ware, or even from a natural object.

There are three stages in the making of a pottery mould:
1. A hollow case mould is formed over the original model made in as many parts as may be necessary (see: Casting).
2. The case mould is used to make a block mould (patrix), which is a replica of the original object.
3. The block mould is used to make a working mould, and it is in the latter that the work is cast. New working moulds can be made from the block mould as necessary.

Intaglio moulds have sometimes been made by carving or modelling, and block moulds of wood or alabaster were often employed in the 18th century, made by men known as block-cutters. Coward* carved wooden block moulds for Wedgwood which are in the Museum at Barlaston. The plaster of Paris mould very commonly employed was introduced into Staffordshire about 1745, reputedly by Ralph Daniels of Cobridge.

Moulds from Silver

Apart from silver-pattern* wares, some Wedgwood creamware objects give the impression of being made from moulds taken from actual pieces of silver. There is little definite physical evidence for this practice beyond the shapes themselves, but in a letter to Bentley of February 1769, Wedgwood refers to the gift of a silver inkstand from Ralph Griffiths which he had been asked to transmit to their mutual friend, Bentley, and concludes: ''...but I have a notion of moulding from it first.'' It would not, of course, be difficult to take moulds in plaster or wax, not only from silver, but from any other reasonably uncomplicated object, especially cameos, gems, and bas-reliefs.

Moulds, Queen's Ware

Moulds of Queen's ware were made in the 18th century in many shapes and sizes, such as the fish-shaped mould for fish pastes, and appropriate shapes for butter, etc.

See: Jelly Moulds.

Mounts, Metal. *Miniature three-colour diced jasper jug mounted with Sheffield plate. 3½ ins. high. c.1790.* Wedgwood.

Mounts, Metal

Mounting porcelain in gilt-bronze or ormolu was fashionable during much of the 18th century, and vase mounts were made by Boulton* of Soho, Birmingham, although it does not appear that Wedgwood vases were ever mounted by, or with the knowledge of, the factory. Nevertheless, Wedgwood sent plaques, cameos, and seals to Birmingham for this purpose in increasing quantities after December 1772, and at a later date jasper was mounted as table lustres, opera glasses, etc.

See: Boden & Smith; Drum; Lustres; Monocular.

Mountstephen, Eley George (fl.1781-1791)

Born in County Meath, Ireland, Mountstephen moved to England in 1781, and exhibited wax portraits at the Royal Academy between 1782 and 1791. Among his works is a miniature painting of Josiah Wedgwood. The following Wedgwood portrait medallions are from wax originals by Mountstephen:

Lord and Lady Auckland*, two portraits, 1790.

Sir Eyre Coote (for many years catalogued as Ferdinand of the Two Sicilies), 1788.

Duc d'Orléans, 1788.

Christopher Wyvill, 1776.

Moustache Cup

A china cup with a pierced ledge immediately below the rim for the purpose of protecting the fashionable bushy moustaches from contact with the liquid in the cup. The type, introduced as a novelty about 1880, was made by most porcelain manufacturers of the day, including Wedgwood. Specimens bear the mark of the Portland vase in addition to the name.

Muffin Dish (Muffineer)

Round dish with a domed cover for the service of warm muffins. Made by Wedgwood in creamware and, after 1878, in bone china.

Murray, Keith, MC, RDI, FRIBA (b.1892)

Architect, and designer of pottery, glass, and furniture; born in New Zealand and educated at King's College, Auckland, and Mill Hill School, London. During the First World War, Keith Murray served with the Royal Flying Corps, being five times mentioned in dispatches and awarded the Military Cross and Croix de Guerre Belge. After the war he studied architecture, and during the depression of the early 1930s he produced many successful designs for glass manufactured by Stevens and Williams of Brierley Hill. In 1933 he began to design for Wedgwood, where he was attracted by the semi-matt moonstone* glaze which was produced, two years later, in green and straw colours. The emphasis in Murray's designs was on form rather than decoration, and he made extensive use

Mountstephen, Eley George. *Jasper portrait medallion of Sir Eyre Coote (1726-83), modelled by Mountstephen in 1788 from a bust by Nollekens dated 1779.* British Museum.

246

Murray, Keith. *Queen's ware 1-pint turned mugs and matching jug designed by Keith Murray, 1935. These pieces were also made in Celadon and cream colour.* Wedgwood.

of the traditional skills of throwing and turning. His work was characterised by strong shapes and sharply defined outline, perfectly in keeping with the art deco style of the period, and he won a Gold Medal at the 5th Triennale in Milan in 1933. Examples of his pottery were shown at the Victoria and Albert Museum and at the Royal Academy as early as 1935, and were well received two years later in Paris. In 1936 Murray formed an architectural firm in partnership with C.S. White, and, with Louis de Soissons, they were given the task of designing the Barlaston* factory, the building of which was begun in 1940, when Murray was once more in the RAF. A travelling exhibition of his work was shown at the Victoria and Albert Museum in 1976.

Keith Murray's work for Wedgwood includes the following shapes and designs:

Ash Tray, fluted shape 4117 (Moonstone or Matt Green).

Ash Tray, fluted shape 4107 (Moonstone, Moonstone with platinum, or Matt Green).

Ash Tray, ribbed shape 3881 (Moonstone, Matt Green, or Straw).

Bath Salts Holder, fluted shape 4125 (Moonstone, Moonstone with platinum, or Matt Green).

Banquet Candlestick, shape 4108 (Moonstone, Moonstone with platinum, or Matt Green).

Beaker, turned shape 3884, height 4ins. Basaltes.

Beaker, turned shape 3885, height 4ins. Basaltes.

Beaker, turned shape 3888, height 4ins. Basaltes.

Bowl, fluted shape 4129, diam. 10ins. (Moonstone or Matt Green).

Bowl, fluted shape 4119, diam. 10½ins. (Moonstone or Matt Green).

Bowl, fluted shape 4126, diam. 9ins. (Moonstone or Matt Green).

Bowl, fluted shape 4116, diam. 9ins. (Moonstone or Matt Green.

Bowl, fluted shape 4118, diam. 10ins. (Moonstone or Matt Green).

Bowl, fluted shape 3819, height 5ins. (Moonstone, Matt Green, or Straw).

Bowl, turned shape 3806, height 4½ ins. (Moonstone, Matt Green, or Straw).

Bowl, turned shape 3807, height 5ins. (Moonstone, Matt Green, or Celadon and Cream colour).

Bowl, turned shape 3813, height 4ins. (Basaltes or Celadon and Cream colour).

Bowl, ribbed and turned shape 3815, height 3½ ins. (Basaltes, Moonstone, Matt Green, or Straw).

Cigarette Box, shape 4112 (Moonstone, Matt Green, or Moonstone with platinum).

Cigarette Box, shape 3872, 2½ins. deep (Moonstone or Matt Green).

Cigarette Box, shape 3871, 2½ins. deep (Moonstone or Matt Green).

Comport, footed, shape 4120, diam. 9ins. (Moonstone or Matt Green).

Compôtier, round, shape 4121, diam. 10¼ins. (Moonstone or Matt Green).

Coffee set, shape 3901 (Moonstone with platinum handles).

Denture Box, fluted shape 4114 (Moonstone, Moonstone with platinum, or Matt Green).

Denture Tumbler, fluted shape 4115 (Moonstone, Moonstone with platinum, or Matt Green).

Dessert Plate, shape 4122, diam. 8ins. (Moonstone or Matt Green).

Inkstand, half-circular fluted stand, shape 4110 (Moonstone, Moonstone with platinum, or Matt Green).

Inkstand, rectangular with concave facets, shape 4131 (Moonstone or Matt Green).

Inkstand, rectangular ribbed shape 4122, diam. 8ins. (Moonstone or Matt Green).

Jug, shape 3974, 3-pint (Champagne glaze).

Jug, shape 3822, 3¼-pint or 6-pint (Moonstone, Matt Green, Straw, Champagne Glaze, or Celadon and Cream colour).

Jug, shape 3844, 3½-pint (Straw).

Mug, faceted foot, shape 3974, ½-pint (Cream colour or Champagne glaze; also produced in cream colour with lavender embossed relief decoration for the 1937 and 1953 Coronations).

Mug, fluted shape 3971, 1-pint (Cream colour or Champagne glaze).

Mug, fluted barrel shape 3970, 1-pint (Cream colour or Champagne glaze).

Mug, turned shape 3811, 1-pint (Matt Green).

Mug, turned foot, shape 3810 (Cream colour, Celadon and Cream colour, Moonstone, Matt Green, or Straw).

Mug, turned shape 3821 (Straw).

Powder Bowl, fluted shape 4113 (Moonstone, Moonstone with platinum or Matt Green).

Tobacco Jar, turned shape 3865 (Basaltes).

Tobacco Jar, fluted shape 4111 (Moonstone, Matt Green or Straw).

Tray, shape 3812, height 3ins. (Moonstone, Matt Green or Straw).

Vase, fluted shape 4127, height 4ins. (Moonstone or Matt Green).

Vase, fluted shape 4130, height 10ins. (Moonstone or Matt Green).

Vase, fluted shape 4124, height 8¼ins. (Moonstone or Matt Green).

Vase, fluted shape 4128, height 7¾ins. (Moonstone or Matt Green).

Vase, turned shape 3820, height 6¼ins. (Moonstone or Matt Green).

Vase, turned shape 3998, height 6ins. (Moonstone or Matt Green).

Vase, turned shape 3765, height 7½ins. (Moonstone, Matt Green or Straw).

Vase, turned shape 3805, height 11ins. (Moonstone, Matt Green or Straw).

Vase, fluted shape 3808, height 7½ins. (Moonstone, Matt Green or Straw).

Vase, turned shape 3842, height 9½ins. (Moonstone, Matt Green or Straw).

Vase, turned shape 3801, height 6ins. (Moonstone, Matt Green or Straw).

Vase, turned shape 3816, height 8ins. (Basaltes).

Vase, turned shape 3818, height 8ins. (Basaltes).

Vase, fluted shape 3991, height 8¾ins. (Moonstone, Matt Green, Basaltes).

Vase, turned shape 3868, height 6¼ins. (Moonstone, Matt Green, Basaltes).

Vase, turned shape 3869, height 7¾ins. (Basaltes).

Vase, turned shape 3870, height 5½ins. (Moonstone, Matt Green or Basaltes).

Vase, turned shape 3877, height 8ins. (Basaltes).

Vase, turned shape 3882, height 8ins. (Basaltes).

Vase, turned shape 3890, height 9½ins. (Basaltes).

Vase, turned shape 3891, height 9ins. (Basaltes).

The pieces listed as Celadon and Cream colour are turned two-colour slip* wares.

Many Keith Murray pieces are signed on the base.

Muses. *Oval medallion ornamented with the figure of Euterpe, the Muse of lyric poetry, carrying a flute.* Wedgwood.

Muses. *Erato, Muse of erotic poetry, with her lyre. c.1778.* Wedgwood.

Muses. *Pair of Wedgwood & Bentley period blue and white jasper dip plaques, each 6¼ ins. by 15¾ ins., ornamented with the figures of Apollo and the nine Muses. The figures are finely undercut and are probably the work of Flaxman.* Christie's.

Muses

The nine female divinities presiding over the arts and sciences; daughters of Zeus and Mnemosyne. They are: Clio, the Muse of history, represented with a roll of parchment or a chest of books; Euterpe, the Muse of lyric poetry, with a flute; Thalia, the Muse of comedy, with a mask, or an ivy wreath, or as the Muse of idyllic poetry with a shepherd's staff; Melpomene, the Muse of tragedy, with the tragic mask and cothurnus (a kind of high shoe to increase the height of the tragic actor); Terpsichore, the Muse of dance and song, with a lyre and plectrum; Erato, the Muse of erotic poetry and mimicry, sometimes with a lyre; Polyhymnia (Polymnia), the Muse of the sublime hymn, usually seated in a pensive attitude: Urania, the Muse of astronomy, standing pointing with a staff at a globe; and Calliope, the Muse of eloquence and epic poetry, with a tablet and stylus. Mount Parnassus was sacred to the Muses, who are often found accompanied by Apollo* Musagetes. Figures of the Muses were made in sets at several porcelain factories, and they are also found as painted or relief decoration.

The principal Wedgwood bas-relief ornaments depicting the Muses were modelled by Flaxman*. He supplied Wedgwood with four bas-relief figures (possibly casts made by his father) — Melpomene, Thalia, Terpsichore and Euterpe — with an accompanying figure of Apollo, in March 1775, and three months later Wedgwood commissioned the remainder of the set. Too late, he realised that they could be made up at less cost from existing models, and the group was completed by Flaxman. They appear on tablets and vases in groups of varying numbers, sometimes accompanied by Apollo, and also singly on oval medallions. The nine Muses were also modelled by Pacetti*. Hackwood* modelled a cameo of the *Muses watering Pegasus* in 1775, and a beautiful small bas-relief of the same subject is attributed to Flaxman. Angelini* modelled a bas-relief of *Apollo and Erato,* c.1787. *The Muses of Art and Poetry Mourning over a portrait of Solomon Gessner** was modelled after a design by Brandoin*.

The sources of Wedgwood's Muses are variously the Sarcophagus of the Muses (then in the Capitoline Museum, now in the Louvre), and gems by Pichler* and Tassie*.

Myrtle Pans

Large tubs, usually in hooped creamware, and made in several sizes for planting with evergreen plants and shrubs. A large number of these, in plain creamware or with coloured hoops, appear in the 1781 Auction* catalogue, and they continued in production until the latter part of the 19th century. Very few undamaged examples have survived the activities of enthusiastic gardeners.

Naked Boy, The

Decorative subject in relief depicting a naked Chinese boy in a tree amid foliage. It occurs on red stoneware, salt-glazed stoneware, and Whieldon-Wedgwood ware, especially on the spouts of teapots. Also called *The Boy in a Tree* pattern, it is of Chinese origin.

Napoleon Ivy

Persistent* border pattern of large ivy leaves, enamelled in naturalistic green and brown, originally ordered by the British government for Napoleon when he was exiled to St. Helena in 1815. One of the most distinguished and timeless of all Wedgwood Queen's Ware patterns, it is still in production as a print and enamel tableware service. It has been produced in more limited quantities on bone china*, and the grey print has also been used (from 1947) with a yellow groundlay (see: Processes of Manufacture) for the bone china pattern *Josephine*.

Nautilus Service

A Wedgwood table service made in Queen's ware in which all the pieces were in the shape of shells, faithfully copied from nature, the centrepiece being a large nautilus shell. A rococo* subject, the design dates from about 1790, often being decorated with hand painted border patterns.

Wedgwood was an amateur conchologist and, in a lettèr of September 1778 to Bentley, on holiday in Margate, he asks for specimens of shells for his collection.

Neale, James (1740-1814)

Humphrey Palmer's London agent who took over Palmer's business in 1778 when Palmer failed. Robert Wilson became a partner in 1786 and eventually succeeded Neale. Other partners were admitted, and the style changed from Neale & Wilson to Neale & Co. The factory was noted for many close imitations of Wedgwood's productions, not infrequently exact copies. They produced creamware, marbled vases, jasper, and basaltes of excellent quality.

Neo-Classical Style

The style of most of Wedgwood's production from 1769 onwards.

The term was not employed to describe this style before the middle of the 19th century; in the 18th century it was referred to as 'the true style' or 'the revival of the arts'. It was looked upon as a new, or revived, Renaissance classicism* supplanting the rococo* style, which had developed from the baroque under the influence of imported Far Eastern art. The discoveries at Herculaneum* and Pompeii* were a peg on which was hung not only what was tantamount to a revolution in the arts, but also great intellectual, social, and political changes, of which the French Revolution eventually became a part. Neo-classicism in its early stages was as much an expression of opposition to Louis XV and his Court as it was a new fashion in the arts. In the 1750s the beginning of the new style in France was almost an underground movement. Influenced by the King, the Court remained faithful to rococo and antagonistic to the new classicism, and those who sought to promote it, almost until Louis' death in 1774. It is reasonable to say that, at first, neo-classicism was a deliberately contrived style which was one of the overt signs of political opposition. It appealed to intellectuals, financiers, tax-farmers, and the affluent *bourgeoisie*, whose capital was in cash, and it was directed against the ruling aristocracy whose capital was in land, and whose efforts were directed towards keeping the *bourgeoisie* from positions of influence at Court. The objection to Mme. de Pompadour as the King's mistress was not a matter of morals: even the Queen gave her qualified approval. Her offence was that she came from the financial class and not the

Nautilus Service. *Queen's ware dessert service, the shapes based on the Nautilus and pecten (scallop) shells, hand-painted with pattern No.384 from the first Pattern Book. c.1798.* Wedgwood.

Neale, James. *Left and right: Pair of marbled vases, ornamented with medallions, floral and foliate friezes, and floral swags dependent from bird's head handles. Impressed mark 'NEALE'. Centre: an agate vase of the Wedgwood & Bentley period.* Zeitlin Collection.

aristocracy. To attack rococo was a relatively safe way of attacking those who favoured it without making the acquaintance of the Bastille, a fate which overtook several of the bolder leading spirits, like Voltaire*.

Neo-classicism, therefore, came to comprehend a variety of ideas, not all of them classical in origin, held by the loosely knit group opposed to the *régime* which they aspired to see become *ancien*. In particular it had to find room for the emerging Romantics. At first sight, this seems hardly possible, but, as the century wore on, Romantic Classicism became well-marked in almost every department of art: in painting (Greuze, Hubert Robert, *et al*.), in literature (Goethe, *The Sorrows of Young Werther**; Horace Walpole, *The Castle of Otranto;* Beckford's *Vathek;* and the 'Graveyard Poets'), and pottery and porcelain (Acier's groups at Meissen*, Lady Templetown's* designs for Wedgwood, etc.). Although the intense interest in Greece and Rome can hardly be called a manifestation of the familiar Romantic obsession with other times and exotic places, since it was the very root and foundation of European art, the early 19th century interest in Gothic (Beckford's Fonthill Abbey) and in Egyptian art was certainly Romantic in origin.

Rococo* never gained a very firm hold in England. Chippendale's furniture, silver (mainly by silversmiths of Huguenot descent who used French design books), and the work of the early porcelain factories who largely copied the designs of Meissen* and Sèvres*, were its principal manifestations. Most examples of pottery in this style were derived from porcelain in one way or another. Wedgwood's cauliflower* teapots and melon* tureens were a purely rococo theme which came to England by way of Meissen and Chelsea* around 1753. Architecturally, the principal English style was Palladianism, based on the work of Palladio who took his basic ideas directly from Vitruvius (see: Vitruvian Scroll). The first English exponent of the style was Inigo Jones (Queen's House, Greenwich; Banqueting Hall, Whitehall, London). Wedgwood produced two portrait medallions* and a basaltes bust of Jones. Under the influence of the Earl of Burlington some superb houses were built in this style in the

18th century by Colen Campbell, William Kent, and others. Neo-classicism, usually termed the Adam style, was regarded as little more than a passing fashion by those who took architecture seriously. Sir William Chambers* (Somerset House, London) thought it trivial; so did the knowledgeable George III ("The Adams have introduced too much of neatness and prettiness"). Horace Walpole, who spent a good deal of his long life Gothicising his villa at Stawberry Hill, Twickenham, thought Palladianism the only conceivable style for important buildings, and remarked "from Kent's mahogany we are dwindled to Adam's filigree," and later complained of "Mr. Adam's gingerbread and sippets of embroidery." To redress the balance one may quote Elizabeth 'Blue-stocking' Montague who wrote, in a letter to Lord Kames: "Mr Adam...has made me a cieling [*sic*] and Chimney-piece and doors which are pretty enough to make me a thousand enemies."

In England, as in France, the period from about 1760 was one of reaction against rococo, which hardly survived the decade. But the English did not adopt the luxurious French Louis Seize style in its stead. In the forefront of the new movement were the Adam brothers* and James 'Athenian' Stuart*, both of whom published books which were employed by contemporary architects, designers, and manufacturers, who also used the catalogue of Sir William Hamilton's* Collection and the works of the Comte de Caylus*, among others. The illustrations to these works were sometimes directly copied, but more often than not they were employed for the purpose of making *pastiches,* new objects combining parts of old ones. Wedgwood's Etruscan* vases, for instance, are usually copies of ancient vases in form and decoration, even though the decoration of one shape might appear on another; but most of Wedgwood's later wares are not referable in any exact sense to an ancient prototype, although one can always name a type which resembles it, often fairly closely, and trace the course of the modifications.

One of the features of the neo-classical style was the employment of new sources of inspiration, mainly from Herculaneum and Pompeii. These were small towns, affluent but provincial.

One of the new discoveries was a type of wall painting, not hitherto known, which aroused a good deal of controversy, because it did not entirely accord with the notion of ancient painting derived from literary sources. Wedgwood used the wall paintings of Herculaneum as a subject for reliefs.

These discoveries brought in their train a new outlook on ancient history, and one not always justified by the facts. As André Malraux pointed out, these excavations uncovered large quantities of white marble statues which, it was thought, was how they had appeared in antiquity, so white biscuit porcelain became popular for figures at Sèvres and Meissen, and Wedgwood made occasional figures in white jasper to imitate marble, as well as in black basaltes to simulate bronze. In the 19th century Carrara* or Parian* porcelain served the same purpose. In the north white marble is relatively uncommon and expensive. It occurred to no one that it was not in the least unusual in Italy, and that the Romans painted both structural marble and statues. This fact had not been lost sight of during the Renaissance, and the Victorian sculptor, John Gibson, caused a sensation at the London Exhibition of 1862 by showing his *Tinted Venus,* a carefully coloured, realistically carved, marble nude. The 'white world' of the neo-classicist was purely an 18th century invention. So, too, were the pastel colours of a good deal of 18th century interior decoration. The Romans, for the most part, liked strong colour.

There is much to be said for the proposition that the Rome of the 18th century neo-classicist was his own invention. Certainly Piranesi* provided a new view of Rome which was entirely his own, and had little to do with historical verisimilitude. In 1761 he published a work which stated that the Etruscans had brought the arts, particularly architecture, sculpture, and painting, to a perfection which the Romans maintained, but which was debased by the Greeks. A few years later he attacked the Vitruvian rule (see: Proportion) and, in effect, the Palladians. It is probable that here we have one of the origins of that confusion which led to Greek vases recovered from Etruscan tombs being assigned to Italian makers, and ultimately to the naming of Wedgwood's factory.

Throughout the 18th century classical learning was a great and essential part of education. The Latin and Greek languages were either fed into one end of the schoolboy, or beaten into the other. Not surprisingly, most of the literate population were as familiar (perhaps more familiar) with ancient literature, art, and history as with those arts of their own day based on contemporary subjects. Most of the subjects of Wedgwood's bas-reliefs* were recognisable, and the story attached to them well known, to his customers. Parliamentary sessions of the time were enlivened by speakers who employed classical allusions and quotations from Latin and Greek authors sonorously delivered in the original language. Classical institutions were used as a basis for 18th century political organisation, particularly to be seen during the aftermath of the French Revolution. When Wedgwood wished to commemorate the French Commercial Treaty of 1787 he commissioned two medallions from Flaxman* — *Mercury Joining the Hands of France and England* and *Peace Preventing Mars from Opening the Gates of War.* These gates were the doors of the Roman Temple of Janus, closed during times of peace, open when Rome was at war.

Putting aside such obviously contemporary subjects as portraits belonging to the *Illustrious Moderns** series, more than three-quarters of 18th century Wedgwood reliefs and figure subjects were classical in derivation. Most of the forms of jasper and basaltes objects were classically based and can be traced to ancient marble, pottery or metalwork prototypes. The commonest Greek pottery shape to inspire Wedgwood's painted basaltes vases was the krater*. Other shapes include the amphora, the hydria, the kylix (rare), and the oenechoe. But many such shapes were adapted and given applied relief decoration in techniques which were never employed by the potters of antiquity. For example, relief decoration was never applied, and the reliefs on the finer kinds of Samian ware are moulded integrally. Both *rosso antico* and basaltes may be said to resemble types of ancient pottery, but jasper bears no resemblance to any kind of pottery from classical sources, and it is more closely related in appearance, if not in technique, to cased glass (e.g. the Portland* vase). It is, perhaps, a little difficult to understand why Wedgwood did not make greater use of *rosso antico.* The name was obviously given to it by someone who had Samian ware in mind, and Samian ware was recovered in fairly large quantities from the ruins of Pompeii. At least one example is known of an unopened case which must have been delivered immediately before the eruption of Vesuvius. Possibly the resemblance Wedgwood saw to red teapots could not be overcome.

Many Queen's ware shapes were classically based, but Queen's ware never entirely lost sight of its rococo origins. The shell shapes, so often attributed to Josiah's interest in conchology*, were common rococo themes, going back at least to the silver shapes of Meissonnier and the porcelain crayfish salts of Chelsea, and as late as 1768 shell salts were made at Plymouth in the early Bow style. Most Queen's ware border patterns are derived from classical sources, and the acanthus is the most widespread of the ancient foliate ornaments, often occurring on jasper and basaltes. The fashion for striped grounds popular with such porcelain factories as Derby*, and painted on in enamel colours, was repeated by Wedgwood in an incised form done with the aid of the engine-turning lathe.

The neo-classical style employed the classical vocabulary of ornament which had persisted for millennia. The difference was largely in the type of ornament selected. This makes it relatively easy in some cases to pick out designs which are purely 18th century, and those like the Wine and Water* ewers or the so-called Michelangelo* lamp which were derived originally from Renaissance metalwork. 18th century designs are relatively plain and simple, making use of such ornamental details as swags (see: Festoons) and garlands, repetitive acanthus leaf borders, and the goat's head, often found at the base of handles, which is an old Roman motif with its origin in metalwork. Human masks, sometimes employed for similar purposes, are based on the ancient theatrical mask, and are descended from Roman mural painting and metalwork by way of the grotesques* popularised by Raphael*.

At the end of the 18th century the neo-classical style began to change in the direction of a greater interest in Greece rather than Rome, even though Rome retained its pre-eminence in the political sphere, and the Romantic movement also grew stronger. When Bonaparte, then First Consul, became Emperor of France neo-classicisim gave place to the Empire style, which, in England, became the Regency style. The Empire style was an extension of neo-classicism, florid and elaborate, with, at the larger porcelain factories, the emphasis on meticulously detailed topographical painting, and large areas of solid gilding. By this time Josiah Wedgwood was dead, and his place had been taken by Josiah II. Jasper and basaltes vases became larger and more elaborate, lustre* was introduced, and bone china* made its appearance. The greater use of Egyptian motifs was another Wedgwood concession to the Empire style (see: Egyptian Taste). Generally, Empire Egyptian motifs are much more accurate than those of the 18th century, when there was an obvious confusion, no doubt arising from the sources used, between Egyptian and

'Orientalised' Greek designs (see: Sphinxes).

The Empire style survived until about 1830, but the accession of Louis-Philippe, the Bourgeois King, marked its end in France. By this time a notion had grown up, referred to as eclecticism, which held that one style was as good as another, and all were equally valid. Logically, therefore, there could be no conceivable objection to mixing them together. About 1830 revived rococo* and neo-Gothic made their appearance. Designs of wares partly in one style and partly in another became more common, and Minton* produced a classical vase on a Gothic pedestal. During this period Wedgwood, apart from a few works in a low-key rococo, like jasper jugs with all-over floral and foliate ornament, remained faithful to their classical traditions, which, without doubt, have been largely responsible for the many distinguished designs produced in modern times.

Neptune

Roman name for Poseidon, god of the Mediterranean. He was the brother of Zeus and Hades, and was given dominion over the sea. In collaboration with Apollo* he built the walls of Troy, but the Trojans cheated him of his promised reward, thus incurring his enmity. He was also hostile to Ulysses after the blinding of his son, Polyphemus. He was the creator of the horse, and patron of horse races. He was married to Amphitrite, and Triton* was one of his children. Poseidon's symbol of power was the trident, and the dolphin*, the pine tree, and the horse were all sacred to him. In art he is usually represented with Amphitrite, Tritons, Nereids*, dolphins or hippocampi*.

Neptune was one of the very large figures first catalogued by Wedgwood in 1773. A basaltes figure, standing two feet high, it was a pair to a large Triton and was probably modelled by Bacon* or from a cast supplied by Mrs. Landré c.1769. This figure has been attributed to Flaxman* but its early date makes this unlikely, though it may have been taken from a cast supplied by John Flaxman Senior*.

Nereids

The fifty daughters of Nereus and Doris, of whom Thetis, mother of Achilles* was among the most celebrated. *Nereids,* a tablet 6ins. by 21⁷/₁₆ins. is attributed to Webber*, c.1780, but is possibly by either Pacetti* or Dalmazzoni*. It is a faithful copy of the relief on a Pentelic marble sarcophagus then in the Capitoline Museum and now in The Louvre. A plaque, 7⅞ ins. by 13½ ins., of nereids and a triton* with fantastic sea creatures, probably after Clodion*, was produced in majolica* glazes in the 1880s, and it is likely that this also existed in earlier basaltes and jasper versions though no example has been located.

See: Nymphs.

Nereids. *Creamware fruit dish formed from a net held by two nereids, with waves below. Late 19th century.* Wedgwood.

Nereids. *A rectangular jasper tablet (Wedgwood's 'long square') ornamented with nereids, c.1785-90. Tablets of this type were commonly used for chimney pieces, but this subject is extremely rare.* Zeitlin Collection.

Neunberg, G.V.

An 18th century china dealer at 75, Cornhill, London, who, to judge from the extent of his purchases (he spent about £4,000 with Wedgwood in the first half of 1784) was the principal stockist of Wedgwood in London, outside the firm's own show-rooms. A Wedgwood bill head of 1787 directs inquiries to the Greek Street showrooms, or to Mr. Neunberg's premises, as the only places in London where Wedgwood wares could be obtained.

New Hall Factory, Shelton, Staffs.

Josiah Wedgwood was approached by Richard Champion*, owner of the Bristol porcelain factory, for help in disposing of his patent for the manufacture of true (i.e. hard paste) porcelain in 1781. This patent he had inherited from William Cookworthy of Plymouth, and it gave Champion exclusive rights to the use of Cornish china clay and china stone. In 1775 he applied to Parliament for an extension of his patent rights, but he was strongly opposed by Wedgwood and other Staffordshire potters who wanted to use the Cornish materials for their own products. Faced with the delay to, and probable rejection of, his Bill in the House of Lords, Champion agreed with Wedgwood that his monopoly should reside only in the proportions in which the substances were employed. By 1781 Wedgwood was no longer interested in Champion's patent, but he appears to have helped him to the extent of an introduction to a number of master potters in Staffordshire who, between them, founded the New Hall Company, using Champion's patent. Unlike Champion, however, the new enterprise made only unambitious domestic wares, for the most part sparsely finished, and they abandoned the hard paste body altogether in favour of bone china in the early years of the 19th century.

Newdigate, Sir Roger (1719-1806)

Fifth baronet; antiquary, collector of ancient vases, marbles, and books; founder of the Newdigate Prize for English verse at Oxford. In 1777 Wedgwood was given permission to take casts from marbles and plaster casts at Arbury Hall, Sir Roger's Gothicised Warwickshire residence, the work being carried out by the factory modeller, Bedson*, who obtained nearly thirty casts which were used for pieces included in the 1779 Catalogue.

The *Triumph of Ariadne* probably came from this source. Arbury Hall contains a chimney piece* decorated with jasper plaques designed by Lady Templetown, including *Maternal Affection, Sportive Love,* and *Poor Maria!* Sir Roger also ordered forty dozen tiles ("as white as possible") for the dairy at Arbury in 1784.

See: Dairy Ware.

Night Lamp

See: Food Warmer.

Northwood, John (1837-1902)

Glass worker who revived the art of carving glass in the style of the Roman cameo carvers and *diatretarii,* and made the first copy of the Portland vase using a blank of dark blue glass cased with white opal glass, provided by Philip Pargeter, and the methods of the Roman craftsmen. This task took him three years and was finished in 1876. In 1877 Northwood was engaged by Wedgwood to finish the reliefs of a jasper edition of the vase, using lapidary methods. Northwood's monogram 'W' is incised above the impressed Wedgwood mark. Fifteen copies of this vase were sold by W.P. & G. Philips of Oxford Street, London. In 1877 Northwood also decorated a small number of Wedgwood's Rockingham* ware pieces by wheel engraving.

Nymphs

Minor female deities who peopled all parts of nature. The nymphs of the ocean (daughters of Oceanus) were called Oceanides; those of the Mediterranean were Nereids*; the Naiades were the nymphs of fresh water; and the Dryades and Hamadryades were nymphs of the trees. The Oreades were assocated with the mountains. Nymphs were believed to have prophetic powers and to be able to inspire men.

Wedgwood subjects:

Dancing Nymph (Terpsichore). See: Muses.

Dancing Nymphs, six separate figures. See: Herculaneum Subjects.

Nymphs Bathing, painted decoration by Lessore*.

Nymphs decorating a Statue of Priapus,* modelled by Webber* after Kauffmann.

Observatory, The Royal

A bone china plate in a limited edition of 1,000 issued in 1975 to mark the Tercentenary of the founding of the Greenwich Observatory by Charles II. The centre of the plate is a 17th century star map of the Northern Hemisphere, superimposed on which are portraits of the first eleven Astronomers-Royal, beginning with John Flamsteed (1675-1719). The border illustrates the old Royal Observatory at Greenwich, and the later establishment at Herstmonceux, with astronomical instruments and star motifs between. The diameter of the plate is 10¾ ins., and it is accompanied by a numbered certificate and an illuminated folder. The back stamp incorporates the names of the Astronomers-Royal.

Odysseus

See: Ulysses.

Oenochoe

Greek term for a wine jug with a vertical loop handle and a trefoil (pinched) lip. The shape was used by Wedgwood in the 18th century. It was also fairly commonly employed for decorative ware in the 19th century by Wedgwood and others, when it often had an elongated neck.

Oil and Vinegar Set

See: Cruet Set.

Old Wedgwood

The term is strictly used for Wedgwood ware of any kind made at the Ivy House* works, the Brick House* works, or at Etruria* during the lifetime of the first Josiah, but it might reasonably be extended to take in the wares of Josiah II*, some of which were inventive and original.

Oliver & Hoskins

See: James Hoskins.

Omphale

Queen of Lydia, to whom Hercules* was in bondage for three years.

Wedgwood subjects:
Omphale in the Lion's skin, cameo by Flaxman*, c.1775.
Omphale with the club of Hercules, cameo by Flaxman, c.1775.

O'Neale, Jeffryes Hamett (1734-1801)

Irish miniaturist, who was also a porcelain painter at the Chelsea* factory about 1752. He later executed an impressive series of plates and vases for Worcester*, working as an independent decorator. He was especially noted for his amusing depiction of animals. In 1765 he was a member of the Incorporated Society of Artists. About 1770 he was working for Wedgwood, receiving the relatively large sum of three guineas a week. Wedgwood considered this excessive, but admitted in a letter to Bentley (1771) that ''O'Neale works quick.'' His other work is often signed 'O'Neal pinxt' or 'ONP'.

Onion Pattern

The *Zwiebelmuster,* a very popular Meissen* underglaze blue* pattern derived from Chinese sources, and introduced in 1731 for the cheaper trade. The 'onions' are actually peaches. This pattern was widely copied elsewhere, including by Wedgwood, who used it to decorate stone china* in the 19th century. A simplified onion pattern appears, in underglaze blue enamel on both cream ware and pearl ware* from c.1779.

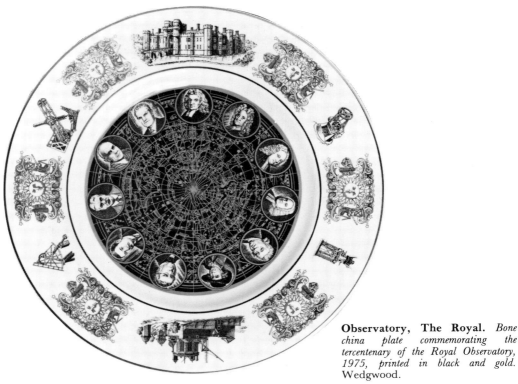

Observatory, The Royal. *Bone china plate commemorating the tercentenary of the Royal Observatory, 1975, printed in black and gold.* Wedgwood.

Ordinary Lustres. *A pair of Butterfly lustre vases of flared trumpet shape, 11¼ ins. high, the interiors decorated with an apricot lustre, the exteriors with blue, yellow and gilt butterflies on a mottled pale blue lustre ground. Pattern No.Z4832, c.1925, designed by Daisy Makeig-Jones.* Christie's.

Ordinary Lustres

Lustre decorations consisting of underglaze stainings (powder colours*, stippled or mottled) covered by modern commercial lustre and finally printed in gold with designs of dragons, butterflies, birds, fish, fruit, Oriental motifs or diaper patterns. The first ten of the lustre patterns were produced in October, 1914, and twenty-seven were designed between 1914 and 1928, some continuing in production until 1931. These designs, now generally known as 'Dragon Lustre', 'Butterfly Lustre' etc., are often wrongly described as part of the Fairyland Lustre* range of ornamental bone china. They were the work of the same designer, Daisy Makeig-Jones*, and many of the same shapes were used, but the style of decoration is quite distinct from that of Fairyland Lustre and should not be confused with it.

The lustre colours included mother-of-pearl, orange, purple, dark green, yellow, bronze, drab, ruby, pink, and black; and on bowls, vases and mugs they were often used in pairs, the interior lustre contrasting with the lustre colour of the exterior. A wide range of vases and bowls was made, and there were also mugs, buttons, brooches, and a miniature (and somewhat incongruous) Portland* vase. Technically brilliant, the so-called 'Ordinary Lustres' usually lack the startling juxtaposition of colour, the crowding of decoration, and the bizarre designs of Fairyland Lustre. For this reason they are, perhaps, less representative of their period. They are certainly less highly valued by collectors.

See: Lustre Decoration.

Orestes

The son of Agamemnon and Clytemnestra, and brother of Iphigenia*. After the murder of his father by Clytemnestra and Aegisthus, Orestes was saved by his sister and taken in secret to Strophius, King of Phocis, who was married to Agamenon's sister. There he formed a close friendship with his cousin, Pylades, with whom he journeyed to Argos, where he slew Clytemnestra and Aegisthus. Following the murder of his mother he went mad and fled from land to land harassed by the Eumenides (Furies or Avenging Deities). Finally, he took refuge in the temple of Athena, where he was acquitted of guilt by the court appointed by the goddess to try him.

Wedgwood's tablet *Orestes and Pylades,* modelled by John De Vaere* in Rome, is adapted from the bas-reliefs of a sarcophagus then in the Palazzo Accoramboni and now in Munich.

Oriental Patterns

Oriental influences, hardly to be seen in the 18th century, made an appearance during the first half of the 19th century, and they occur in such patterns as *Eastern Flowers** (designed by G. Allen*, 1845), *Palm Willows* (engraved by J. Mollart*, c.1806), and the Horticultural and Nankin patterns.

See: Chrysanthemum Pattern.

Ormolu

A term dating from the middle of the 18th century used to denote a light yellow alloy, very similar in composition to brass, used in England as a mount or an embellishment for a variety of materials, including Wedgwood's jasper (see: Lustres). It served the same purpose as gilt-bronze in France, where the gilding of bronze by the mercuric process was referred to as *dorure d'or moulu* (gilding with gold paste: i.e. an amalgam), and it is from this that the English term 'ormolu' is derived. That the term was current in England in 1776 is proved by a letter from Wedgwood to Bentley in which he refers to the vast quantity of 'D'Or Moulu' being made by Matthew Boulton*.

Ornamental Ware

Wedgwood divided ornamental wares into twenty different categories, as follows:

1. Intaglios and medallions or cameos.
2. Bas-reliefs, medallions, tablets, etc.
3. Medallions etc., of Kings, Queens, and illustrious persons of Asia, Egypt, and Greece (100).
4. Ancient Roman History subjects (60 medallions).
5. Heads of Illustrious Romans (40).
6. The Twelve Caesars and their Empresses.
7. Series of emperors — Nerva to Constantine the Great (52).
8. Heads of the Popes (253).
9. Kings and Queens of England and France (100).
10. Heads of Illustrious Moderns (230).
11. Busts and statuettes of boys, animals, and distinguished persons (142).
12. Lamps and candelabra.
13. Tea and coffee services.
14. Flower pots and root pots.
15. Ornamental vases in terracotta.
16. Antique vases of black basaltes with relief ornament.
17. Vases, tablets, etc., with encaustic painting.
18. Vases and tripods in jasper.
19. Inkstands, paint chests, eye cups, mortars, etc.
20. Thermometers for measuring strong fire (see: Pyrometer.)

See: Thomas Bentley; Useful Wares.

Ornamenting

A process also known as sprigging (see: Sprigged Ware). The process of applying small figures and other kinds of relief ornament made in 'pitcher' moulds* to a background, such as the surface of a jasper vase or plaque. The ornaments are applied to a slightly moistened surface and are affixed with gentle pressure, a task requiring considerable skill.

Jasper is noted for the fine quality and detail of its white relief ornament which is pressed in hard earthenware moulds, smoothed on the back, lifted from the mould, and fixed to the coloured ground.

The finely detailed relief ornament is the result of using hard-fired earthenware moulds instead of plaster moulds. They were once made from a model of comparatively large size, which shrank by about one-sixth after firing. Another mould was made from this reduced model which was still smaller in size and fired; and a fresh model was taken from the new mould. This, when fired, again shrank by one-sixth. The process was repeated until the desired size was attained. The clay employed for the moulds was very refractory, i.e. it had no tendency to fuse at the temperatures necessary to fire it, and the model in its reduced size retained its sharpness and clarity of detail. This is a point which should be borne in mind when making assessments of quality. This lengthy process is now seldom employed.

See: Pantograph; Processes of Manufacture.

Osier

German: *Ozier*. Literally, a willow twig of the kind used in basketry. The basket work, or *ozier*, border in moulded form decorating tableware was first produced at Meissen*, where there were a number of variations. It dates from about 1730 and was widely copied at other factories. Wedgwood's Osier shape was introduced in 1906 as one of John Goodwin's* tableware designs but it was certainly not original.

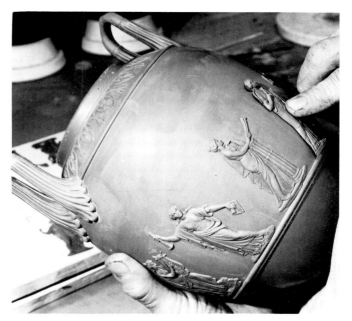

Ornamenting. *Placing in position a figure made in a pitcher mould.* Photo: Wedgwood.

Otto Factory

Founded by Karl Otto in 1801, at Perovo, near Moscow, the Otto factory was one of the earliest to produce Russian *faience*. It was sold to Ivan Krause in 1812 and shortly afterwards ceased production. The wares were finely potted and glazed, and a good cream-coloured ware was made. During the short existence of the factory, some faithful reproductions of the Wedgwood Husk* Service were produced, presumably as replacements for breakages.

Osier. *Engine-turned cane ware mug and jug, and a plate with pierced border, the surface imitating basket work.* Photo: Wedgwood.

Oven Books

Day-to-day manuscript records, preserved at the Wedgwood Museum*, of ware fired at the Wedgwood factory at Etruria*.

Oven-To-Table Ware

Wedgwood's first oven-to-table ware was produced in 1850 as a complement to the popular Game Pie* dishes. A dish or 'liner' of glazed vitrified stoneware, impervious to normal domestic oven heat, was used for cooking meat or game in the oven. When the content was cooked, the liner was placed inside an ornamental pie dish to be brought to the table. Surprisingly, no further development of oven-ware appears to have taken place until the introduction of the *Pennine* range of oven-to-table ware in 1965. Designed and modelled by Eric Owen*, this ware was immediately popular and it has been followed by many patterns, notably *Sterling* and *Wild Strawberry*, which are either available in a full range of tableware or to match existing patterns in Queen's ware* or bone china*.

Overton-Jones, Edward

Designer of two plates for Wedgwood, New York, in 1939:

Laurentia, 10ins. bone china plate, the design inspired by a brocade once worn by Martha Washington.

Richborough, 8ins. celadon coloured body* plate, printed and enamelled.

Ovolo

Classical (Roman) motif of decoration in the form of a quarter-round oval moulding. It occurs as relief decoration to the edges of vases and other decorative vessels in the neo-classical style. The somewhat flattened Greek version is termed an echinus.

Owen, Eric (1903-1975)

Chief modeller and sculptor for Wedgwood from 1946-67, and freelance modeller with facilities at Barlaston from 1967 until his death. Born in the Potteries, Eric Owen was apprenticed to a tile factory before joining Minton*, where he was chief modeller for twenty-five years. During his time with Wedgwood, Owen was responsible for modelling many tableware shapes, including *Barlaston* shape*, and designed and modelled the first oven-to-tableware, *Pennine,* introduced in 1965. He also modelled a number of portrait medallions, some of unusually large size. He travelled and lectured widely, teaching for a short period at the Royal College of Art, and was elected a member of the Society of Industrial Artists in 1957.

Eric Owen's work for Wedgwood includes:

PORTRAIT MEDALLIONS:

H.M. Queen Elizabeth II, 1953.

H.R.H. Prince Philip, Duke of Edinburgh, 1953.

Ludwig van Beethoven.

Thomas Jefferson.

John F. Kennedy, 1962.

Jacqueline Kennedy, 1962.

Richard Nixon.

Hon. Josiah Wedgwood.

Tom Wedgwood (large bas-relief set in wall facing Etruria Park, inscribed 'To commemorate the work of THOMAS WEDGWOOD of Etruria Hall, PIONEER OF PHOTOGRAPHY.' Unveiled 11th June, 1953, by the President of the Royal Photographic Society).

TABLEWARE, BAS-RELIEFS AND FIGURES:

Bull in chains, bas-relief for mug presented by Queen Elizabeth and Prince Philip to the Cider Makers' Association.

Barlaston shape, tableware designed by Norman Wilson*.

Pennine, oven-to-tableware created by Eric Owen.

Two 'Queen's Beasts' for the Queen's* Vase.

Pacetti, Camillo (1758-1826)

Son of a Roman gem engraver, and younger brother of the sculptor Vincenzo Pacetti (1746-1820), to whom he acted as assistant. One of the group of artists employed by Wedgwood in Rome from 1787, Camillo Pacetti modelled copies of antique reliefs under the supervision of the younger Flaxman* and Angelo Dalmazzoni*. Records of his work are not complete, but the following bas-reliefs* have been attributed to him:

Set of six tablets illustrating scenes from the life of Achilles* (*Birth of Achilles; Dipping of Achilles; Thetis delivering Achilles to Centaur; Centaur with Achilles on his back, hunting the Lion; Achilles in Scyros, among the daughters of Lycomedes; Achilles dragging the body of Hector around the walls of Troy*), all copied from the antique Luna marble disc presented to the Capitoline Museum by Pope Benedict XIV.

Achilles in Scyros, a second version of this subject, copied from the erroneously named sarcophagus of Alexander Severus in the Capitoline Museum. This bas-relief is frequently misnamed 'Sacrifice of Iphigenia'.

Aesculapius and Hygeia, bas-relief, modelled in wax in 1788 for a tablet 8¼ ins. by 6⅞ ins., copied from a Greek marble relief in the Capitoline Museum.

Apotheosis of Faustina, bas-relief, modelled c.1789.

Death of a Roman Warrior*, sometimes attributed to Pacetti, but without evidence.

Endymion on Mount Latmos, believed to have been copied by Pacetti in 1789 from the bas-relief in the Capitoline Museum.

Fable of Prometheus, bas-relief, modelled c.1788.

Nereids, bas-relief, sometimes attributed to Pacetti, but more convincingly assigned to Webber* or Dalmazzoni.

Priam begging for the body of Hector from Achilles, bas-relief copied from the back of the so-called 'Alexander Severus' sarcophagus.

Roman Procession*, modelled by Pacetti or Dalmazzoni, c.1787.

Simulacrum of Hygeia, attributed to Pacetti, c.1788.

Three Warriors and a Horse, bas-relief adapted from one side of the 'Alexander Severus' sarcophagus, usually found in circular form.

Triform Goddess*, medallion, c.1789.

Triumph of Achilles over Hector, bas-relief, c.1788.

Two Warriors and a Horse, circular bas-relief adapted from a side of the 'Alexander Severus' sarcophagus. It has been wrongly identified with the cast from a fragment by Phidias* invoiced by Flaxman in 1782.

Pacetti's bas-reliefs, first produced on jasper tablets and medallions, are also to be found used as ornament for vases.

Paint Chest

A paint box for the water colourist. From the Catalogue of 1779: "The paint-chest contains sets of large and small vessels and neat palats [*sic*] for the use of those who paint in water-colour." Wedgwood paint chests, oval, lidded boxes fitted with palettes and dishes for colours made in white stoneware, were produced in finely ornamented jasper and, very rarely, black basaltes.

Painted Etruscan

Black basaltes* ware painted in Wedgwood's encaustic* enamels in imitation of the red-figure* style of Greek and Italian pottery.

Palgrave, Sir Reginald Francis Douce (1829-1904)

Clerk of the House of Commons from 1886-1902; edited *Rules of the Procedure of the House of Commons*, 1886-96; a proficient water colourist Palgrave designed the memorial to Sir William Hooker in Kew Parish Church for Sir Joseph Hooker*, and modelled the floral ornament.

A Wedgwood portrait medallion* of his father the historian Sir Francis Palgrave, was modelled by Woolner* in 1899.

Palissy Ware

Ware decorated with coloured lead glazes, made in France in the 16th century by Bernard Palissy, who attempted to imitate Italian *maiolica* but did not actually succeed in discovering the tin-enamel glaze. The reverse of Palissy's dishes are mottled in blue, brown, and manganese, and are similar in appearance to Whieldon* tortoiseshell and mottled glazes, also made by Wedgwood in his early years at the Ivy House* works. In the 19th century the popularity of Palissy's pottery among collectors was responsible for the introduction by Wedgwood, Minton*, and others of the coloured glaze ware known as 'majolica'*. This was probably inspired by the vogue for exact copies of Palissy's rustic ware at Continental factories, for which they had gained a number of awards at Exhibitions.

Pacetti, Camillo. *Large blue and white jasper tablet, 7¾ ins. by 17¾ ins.,* Achilles in Scyros among the Daughters of Lycomedes *(usually described erroneously as* Sacrifice of Iphigenia*) modelled by Pacetti, c.1790. Christie's.*

Paint Chest. *Covered jasper paint box with small interior containers for pigments, and a palette. c.1785.* Buten Museum.

Palladium, The

Properly, any image of the goddess Pallas Athene*, but the term is used specifically to refer to one of the sacred images of Troy stolen by Ulysses* and Diomedes*. According to another story, only an imitation was stolen from Troy, and Aeneas bore the genuine image to Italy, where it was lodged in the Temple of Vesta in Rome.

Wedgwood subjects:

Cassandra grasping the Palladium, medallion, 1788. From an antique bas-relief* in The Louvre.

Diomedes carrying away the Palladium, medallion 3ins. by 3ins., attributed to Bacon, c.1769. Remodelled at least once for a new version in 1790.

Diomedes gazing at the Palladium, tablet, length 8ins., c.1778.

Pallas Athene

See: Athene; Minerva.

Palmer, Humphrey (fl.1760-1778)

Potter at the Church Works, Hanley, from 1760, who became bankrupt in 1778, when the business was continued by the London agent, James Neale* (of Neale & Bailey, Staffordshire and Glass-warehousemen), first as Neale & Palmer, and then as Neale & Co. Robert Wilson, Neale's manager, became a partner in 1786. In the 19th century the firm was absorbed by Ridgway. Enoch Wood* of Burslem was apprenticed to Humphrey Palmer. Here he made use of calcined bone in earthenware, and in a letter dated 26th September, 1826, claimed to be the first to do so, writing: "I was the first person to make use of bone in earthenware, when in my apprenticeship at Mr Palmer's of Hanley Green."

Josiah Wedgwood's production was imitated by Palmer, and as early as 1769 he was producing basaltes* vases with relief decoration. On the 31st August, 1768, Wedgwood wrote to William Cox* in London: "...the Bronze [see: Bronzed Basaltes] Vases sent you last [week] will be down here in a fortnight.... Caravella supplies Mr Palmer with all my patterns as they arrive at my rooms in London." In October 1771, it was discovered that Neale was selling vases decorated with encaustic painting thus infringing Wedgwood's patent, and the advantages of proceeding against Neale rather than Palmer were discussed in a letter dated 13th October. An injunction was obtained to prevent Neale from continuing to sell the offending wares, and on the 3rd November in the same year Wedgwood set out for London to discuss matters with his

Palmer, Humphrey. *Black basaltes vase modelled with nude figure handles by Jean Voyez for Palmer in 1769. 21ins. high. Marked: 'H. PALMER, HANDLEY, STAFFORDSHIRE,' impressed, and 'J. Voyez Sculpt 1769' incised.* Dwight and Lucille Beeson Collection.

partner and to consult a lawyer. On the 20th December, after his return to Etruria, Wedgwood wrote to Bentley: "I am informed that Mr P. will stand Tryal with us and says that his Vases are not made in imitation of ours but from a book published abroad [i.e. the book on the Hamilton* collection also used as a source book by Wedgwood] which they have bought, and this I suppose will be one of their strongest pleas against us." Later, Palmer added that Wedgwood's colours were not an invention but an improvement, and he contended that the patent was detrimental to trade. On the 11th May, 1771, Wedgwood wrote to Bentley that he had had a friendly discussion with Palmer about matters of mutual interest, and in the same month a meeting of Staffordshire master potters took place with the object of forming an association to deal with matters of general concern. On the 13th June Wedgwood and Palmer came to a provisional settlement in which it was agreed that each side should pay its own costs, and that Palmer should be given a share in the patent in consideration of a sum of money, conditional on the agreement of Neale and Bentley as the respective partners of Palmer and Wedgwood. Both men set out for London soon afterwards, where it was decided to refer the whole affair to arbitration. The matter was eventually settled in the early autumn of 1771.

Voyez* was first employed by Palmer in 1769. A black basaltes vase decorated with reliefs, signed by Voyez, dated 1769, and marked 'Palmer', is in the British Museum. Palmer also imitated creamware and agate vases, as well as seals and cameos, using the mark 'H. Palmer, Hanley' in circular form, similar to the Wedgwood & Bentley circular mark, obviously for purposes of deception.

In November 1773, Wedgwood reported to Bentley that he had found seals (presumably of basaltes ware) on sale in Birmingham which had come from Voyez and Palmer, those from Palmer being the better of the two kinds. These seals were supplied to mounters, such as Pemberton and Boden* & Smith, who professed to find difficulty in obtaining Wedgwood seals. Palmer had an agent in Birmingham to solicit orders for these things, which were being supplied in large quantities. Seals are known with 'HP' impressed.

After 1778 Neale continued to produce ware in the Wedgwood style, including some good black basaltes vases, and some rare oval portrait medallions* of very large size. He also made blue jasper*, green-glazed* ware with gilding, and marbled* or blue sprinkled vases in creamware*, which were marked 'J. Neale' impressed.

Palmette

Decorative ornament in the form of a stylised palm resembling a spread fan. In appearance it is not unlike the Greek anthemion. When divided in half it is termed a half palmette. A palmette border is a pattern consisting of a series of palmettes. This motif frequently occurs on copies of old red-figure* vases.

See: Half Palmette.

Pan

The god of flocks and shepherds, the son of Hermes, who wandered among the mountains and valleys of Arcadia. Pan is usually depicted with goat's horns and feet, in the act of dancing or playing the syrinx* (the shepherd's flute, now usually called pan pipes) which he is supposed to have invented. His sudden appearance before mortals induced feelings of terror, described as Panic fear. The Romans identified him with their god, Faunus (see: Faun).

Wedgwood subjects:

Pan, bas-relief head 3ins. by 2⅜ins. by Flaxman* (after Michelangelo*), 1776. Pair to *Syrinx*.

The Infant Pan, bas-relief after design by Beauclerk.

Sacrifice to Pan, bas-relief by Flaxman, 1778.

Pan reposing with young Satyrs, tablet 6ins. by 8ins. Previously attributed to Pacetti*, but probably by Landré after Duquesnoy*.

Pantograph

An instrument used for making precise copies of an object, usually a plan or drawing, on a larger or smaller scale. A more sophisticated version of the instrument used to reproduce drawings known as a pointing machine may be employed to copy statuettes or relief decoration, and this is used to enlarge or reduce bas-reliefs. In the past, reduction of bas-reliefs was achieved by progressive shrinkage in firing.

See: Bas-relief; Cameo; Ornamenting.

Palmette. *Cane ware vase with encaustic painting of a conventional design based on the palmette. c.1795.* Dwight and Lucille Beeson Collection.

Pair of blue and white jasper dip cassolettes, or incense burners, on dolphin tripod supports, with finely pierced lids, foliate swags and applied rosettes. This model exists in various sizes in jasper, black basaltes and rosso antico. Height 5 ¼ ins. c.1800. Wedgwood. Photo: Reilly/Charles Letts.

Black and white jasper dip square pedestal, and blue and white jasper square bulb pot, height 7ins. c.1796. Some of Wedgwood's early pieces were designed for more than one purpose. The square pedestal, might be used as a plinth for suitable vases; with a flat perforated flower-holder as a vase; or, with a shaped holder as a bulb pot. Wedgwood. Photo: Reilly/Charles Letts.

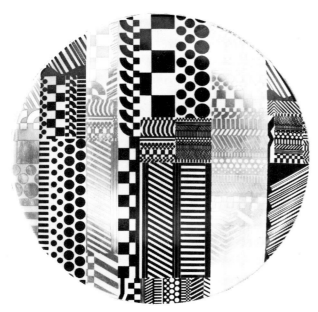

Paolozzi, Eduardo Luigi. *Bone china plate, coupe shape, one of a set of six entitled* Variations on a Geometric Theme, 1970. Wedgwood.

Paolozzi, Eduardo Luigi, CBE, ARA (b.1928)

British sculptor, born in Edinburgh; studied at Edinburgh College of Art, and at the Slade School of Fine Art, Oxford and London; Lecturer in sculpture at the St. Martin's School of Art, 1955-58; Visiting professor at Hochschule für Bildende Künste, Hamburg, 1960-62; Visiting Lecturer, University of California, Berkeley, 1968; Lecturer in Ceramics at the Royal College of Art from 1968. Paolozzi's many awards include First Prize for sculpture at the Carnegie International Exhibition, Pittsburg, 1967. He was elected Associate of the Royal Academy in 1972.

In 1970 Eduardo Paolozzi designed for Wedgwood *Variations On a Geometric Theme,* a set of six silk-screen designs reproduced, in a limited edition of 200 sets, on bone china*. Each set was accompanied by a numbered certificate.

Papera, Benjamin (fl.1800-1802)

Figure maker. Little is known of this man, who appears in the Soane Archives as the supplier of busts to Lord Bridport in 1802. In the Wedgwood Archives he is recorded as supplying busts of Mrs. Siddons*, Lord Nelson, and Mrs. Deamour (perhaps Mrs. Dawson Damer), and "one vase with lamp," all in 1802. J.P. Papera, probably a son, exhibited busts at the Royal Academy in 1829, and Louise Papera is listed in the London Directory of 1818 as a "figure-maker."

Paperweights

The 18th century house was a draughty place in winter and summer, as its numerous draught-screens testify, and the odours arising from inadequate sanitary facilities led to windows being opened whenever possible. The effect of this was to make it difficult to leave papers on a desk or table safely, and paperweights were devised to hold them down. Popular in France as *presse-papiers,* they were made in bronze, and in porcelain from Sèvres*. In England Wedgwood made basaltes sphinxes*, and some of the small groups of figures of boys after Duquesnoy* were probably intended as paperweights, because

similar groups in Sèvres porcelain were certainly intended for this purpose. During the 19th century glass paperweights became popular, and some of them, circular in shape with a transfer-printed scene on the bottom which could be seen from the top, were heavy enough, and very cheap. Since the 18th century the tendency has been for the paperweight to be a purely decorative item, like the 'Liberty Bell' paperweight here illustrated.

Papier Mâché

The commonest method of preparation for making decorative articles was to paste sheets of coarse paper together, one on the other, with a paste of flour, water, and size. The object could then be formed while still pliant by pressing into moulds, or sawn, cut, and joined when dry. The completed object, which was both light and strong, was then sized and japanned. Henry Clay* of Birmingham, Japanner in Ordinary to the King and the Prince of Wales, patented a new process of this type in 1772, the finished product being stoved, japanned black, crimson, or green, and finally varnished. Soon after Clay began to market his new product he was making tea caddies, small writing desks, dressing cases, etc., inset with Wedgwood cameos. Wedgwood wrote to Bentley on 14th July, 1776: "Mr. Clay has made three sets of Dressing-boxes very fully set with our cameos, and wants his assortment made up complete again."

Parapet Teapot

Teapot, usually oval, with the lid deeply recessed inside a parapet, the rim of which curves slightly outwards towards the spout. It was popular in the early decades of the 19th century, but was introduced in the 1770s and occurs in Wedgwood dry bodies*, Queen's ware*, and bone china*.

Paperweights. *The Liberty Bell paperweight in blue or black jasper with commemorative ornament in white jasper, and the inscription 'Proclaim Liberty throughout all the Land' in gold. Special edition No. 5 for the Wedgwood Collectors' Society. The Liberty Bell was cast at London's Whitechapel Bell Foundry in 1751, damaged in transit, recast in Philadelphia, and hung in 1753. It has been rung on many historic occasions, including the invasion of Normandy in 1944.* Wedgwood.

263

Parapet Teapot. *Bone china parapet teapot edged in gold, c.1812. The same shape with gold edge was made also in creamware.* Wedgwood.

Pargeter, Philip (1826-1906)

Stourbridge glassmaker. His uncle was Benjamin Richardson who offered a reward of £1,000 for anyone making an accurate replica of the Portland* vase. Pargeter persuaded his cousin, John Northwood*, to work with him on the production of a copy, he providing the blanks for Northwood to carve. Subsequently they made three *tazze,* signed by Northwood, emblematic of Science, Art, and Literature. These were provided with portraits of Newton, Flaxman*, and Shakespeare respectively which were taken from Wedgwood portrait medallions.

Parian

An unglazed porcellaneous body, slightly translucent, employed principally for the making of figures, but later also for tableware services and decorative pieces. Credit for the invention was variously claimed by John Mountford (who had joined Copeland & Garrett after working for some years for Derby*), by Thomas Battam, artistic director of Copeland, by Minton*, and by Thomas Boote, among others. Copeland were certainly the first to market the new body successfully under the name 'Statuary Porcelain' in 1846, but it was Minton who gave it the name 'Parian', after the particularly fine white marble quarried near the summit of Mount St. Elias on the island of Paros.

Some fine examples from the leading manufacturers were shown at the Great Exhibition of 1851, and Parian was widely manufactured in Staffordshire for the next fifty years. Two distinct forms of Parian were made: the soft-paste body (see: Porcelain), employed for all early work and for the production of leading manufacturers; and the hard-paste body, first introduced about 1860, which was coarser, cheaper to produce, and generally used for inferior imitations. Parian could be tinted, though the results are seldom entirely satisfying. Richer in appearance, and more successful, are the rare figures and tablewares made by Minton which combined unglazed or tinted Parian with fine enamelled decoration.

Wedgwood introduced Parian, under the name 'Carrara'* in 1848 or 1849. Glazed Parian vases, heavily ornamented and enamelled, were produced from c.1866-80 to compete with the decorative porcelain vases of Minton and Worcester* (see: Victoria Ware).

Parian. *A pair of glazed Parian vases, shape No.1316, enamelled in colour with chocolate-coloured ground. c.1868. Wedgwood's Victoria ware and glazed Parian (which is often mistaken for it) were conscious attempts to use jasper techniques and shapes to produce creamware and Parian vases in competition with the porcelain vases of Minton and Worcester.* Sotheby's Belgravia.

Paris

The second son of Priam and Hecuba; married to Oenone. Commanded by Zeus, through the agency of Hermes (Mercury*), to adjudicate between Hera, who promised him the sovereignty of Asia, Athena, who promised him renown in war, and Aphrodite, who promised him the fairest of women for his wife, Paris awarded the golden apple for beauty to Aphrodite. Under her protection he sailed to Sparta, whence he abducted Helen, the wife of Menelaus and the most beautiful woman in the world. This gave rise to the Trojan war in which Paris is said to have killed Achilles*. Wounded, Paris returned to Oenone, who refused to heal his wound. Paris died, and Oenone, overcome with remorse, killed herself. Paris is represented as a beautiful beardless youth, usually wearing a Phrygian cap.

Wedgwood's large tablet *The Judgement of Paris* was modelled by De Vaere in Rome c.1790 after a bas-relief on a sarcophagus from the Villa Pamphili, Rome. Two earlier and smaller versions, the second modelled by Flaxman* c.1775-77, are recorded. *Paris and Helen Ill-advised,* a group used frequently on modern jasper, was modelled in Rome from the Greek marble relief now in the museum at Naples. A fine basaltes bust of Paris (sometimes mistaken for that of Mercury) was produced c.1788, and was later reproduced in the Carrara* body.

Parker, Richard (fl.1769-1774)

Richard Parker may have been the son or brother of Theodore Parker*. He had a studio in The Strand, London, and worked for Wedgwood from about 1769. Parker was apparently a specialist in the making of plaster casts as well as a modeller, and he had the sole right to take casts from the work of the sculptor, Joseph Wilton, RA, 'statuary to His Majesty'. Wilton had studied in Rome with Roubiliac* in 1752, and afterwards travelled in search of antiquities. Settling in Florence, he spent several years making copies of antique marbles before returning to England, and he achieved a considerable reputation for this kind of work. It is evident, therefore, that someone able to provide casts of his work would be very useful to Josiah Wedgwood. In 1769 William Cox* reported from London that Mr. Parker had made an excellent job of casting some medallions, and in 1774 he is reported as modelling a Zingara*, a Vestal*, and a pug dog*. Parker is also known for his sets of plaster library busts after such sculptors as Roubiliac and Rysbrack*. It is not known whether any of them were used by Wedgwood.

Parker, Theodore (fl.1769-1774)

Very little is known of this man. He was probably the father or brother of Richard Parker*, and according to the Wedgwood Archives he modelled "statues of Flora, Seres [*sic*], Spencer [*sic*], Hercules, Juno, Prudence, Milton, Shakespeare, a boy [on] a couch [Somnus], and three doggs."

Pars, Miss (fl.1769-1774)

Employed at the Chelsea* Decorating Studios to paint ruins and landscapes for the Frog* service. She is thought to have been the sister of William Pars (1742-82), one of the leading artists in watercolour of his day, whose Greek drawings were used to illustrate the second and third volumes of Stuart* and Revett's *Antiquities of Athens* (1789 and 1795). Another brother, Henry, also an artist, conducted an art school (founded by William Shipley) in The Strand.

Passenger, Charles (fl.1875-1907)

Artist. Engaged, with his brother, Fred, by William De Morgan* c.1875 to decorate lustre* wares. The Passenger

Paris. *Black basaltes bust of Paris, 19½ins. high, first produced c.1788. This bust was reproduced in Carrara c.1850. Christie's.*

brothers became partners in the business in 1898, when Halsey Ricardo (see: Dysart Green) withdrew, and continued until 1907, two years after De Morgan himself had severed his connection with it. Charles Passenger's initials, 'CP,' appear on rare examples of Wedgwood Queen's ware decorated at the De Morgan factory.

Pastille Burner

A vase, or more rarely a dish or *tazza,* popular during the 18th and 19th centuries for burning cassolette* perfumes (powdered willow wood charcoal mixed with fragrant oils and gum arabic, in the form of cone-shaped pastilles) to counteract the smells of stuffy rooms and inadequate drains. Wedgwood's elegant tripod pastille burners (in imitation of the Roman form of incense burner) with their finely perforated covers were usually of jasper*, basaltes*, or basaltes and *rosso antico*, but very rare examples of Queen's ware with moonlight* lustre are known. They are the aristocratic counterpart of the gaily enamelled earthenware cottages and churches made by the Staffordshire potteries during the 19th century. The mysterious commemorative mark, 'Josiah Wedgwood 2d February 1805,' appears most frequently on tripod vases and tripod pastille burners.

See: Marks; Pot-Pourri Vase.

Pastry Ware

See: Game Pie Dish; Pie-Crust Ware.

Patera

Latin. A shallow vessel, similar in form to a deep saucer, with or without a handle, originally intended for wine to be drunk in a libation. *Paterae* were made in gold, silver, bronze or earthenware, the interior often ornamented with a type of rosette. Wedgwood made *paterae* in various bodies, including encaustic*-painted basaltes*, but he also used the term to describe circular or oval rosettes or palmettes* which resembled the interior ornament of the Roman *patera*.

Pâte-sur-Pâte

Pâte-sur-pâte is the French name given to the technique of painting on porcelain in white slip*, using successive layers to build up a semi-transparent relief on a coloured or tinted ground. The details are then carved or undercut* before firing. This expensive style of decoration was used in China during the 18th century, and introduced at Sèvres* about 1851. It was perfected at Meissen* in 1880, and the technique was brought to England by Marc-Louis Solon, who moved to Minton* from Sèvres during the Franco-Prussian war of 1870. Among Solon's apprentices at Minton were Thomas Mellor*, Frederick Rhead* and Charles Toft*, all of whom later worked for Wedgwood. Rhead and Toft both produced work in this style, but applied to earthenware, while they were working at Etruria*.

Patrician Shape

A wide moulded border designed by John Goodwin* in 1926. It is only slightly altered from the Arabesque* scroll modelled c.1775 and found on basaltes* vases of the Wedgwood & Bentley period, and also on jasper* coffee cans* and saucers and smear glaze* teapots and mugs made between 1785 and 1830.

Pattern Books

The pattern books, hand-painted factory records which have never been published (although extracts from some of them have been used as illustrations in several books dealing with Wedgwood wares), are of particular value in the identification of Wedgwood tableware decoration.

The first pattern book, preserved in the Wedgwood Museum*, was probably started in 1769 (the exact date is uncertain) and records borders used for Queen's ware. It was continued until c.1814, principally for border patterns, and it also includes some bone china patterns used up to 1816. There are 55 unnumbered pages, and 663 numbered patterns, described on the facing page. This book is not the original, but a copy made about 1810 of an earlier book which had, no doubt, become too dilapidated to use. Some of the earliest patterns are not included, so the record cannot be regarded as complete. The early patterns are in a restrained neo-classical* style, while towards the end of the period Chinese motifs reveal the reviving interest in Oriental design.

There are eight pattern books covering the period from 1770-1870. It is difficult to date these precisely, but J.K. des Fontaines (*The Wedgwood 1880 Catalogue of Shapes*) has estimated the dates from the watermarks on the paper. Details are given hereunder. The books themselves are in the possession of the Wedgwood Museum.

Book No.	Pattern Nos.	Watermark for year
1.	1-663	1810
2.	672-1284	1811-1814
Duplicates	709-1042	1823
3.	1298-1950	1831
4.	1403-1930	1831
	(apparently duplicates)	

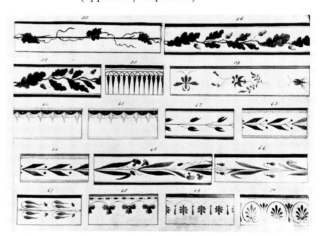

Pattern Books. *Enlargement of border patterns from the pattern book of 1770.* Wedgwood.

Pattern Books. *The first pattern book, beginning in 1770, which shows the pattern, drawn in watercolour, on the right hand page and a verbal description on the left.* Wedgwood.

Book No.	Pattern Nos.	Watermark for year
5.	1939-3285	1844
6.	3289-4329	1851
7.	4330-7054	1855
8.	7055-9998	1864

It is interesting to note that approximately 2,000 different patterns had been recorded by 1844, and another 8,000 were added to this total in the following twenty years — testimony to the enormous increase in demand for wares thus decorated.

Peace and Prosperity Jug

The 'Peace and Prosperity' jug, a special edition commissioned by the Wedgwood Collectors Society, is taken from a Staffordshire creamware jug of c.1800 now in the

Peace and Prosperity Jug. *The Peace and Prosperity Jug commissioned by the Wedgwood Collectors' Society, transfer-printed on Queen's ware. 6½ ins. high.* Wedgwood.

Victoria and Albert Museum, London. The centre panel contains the population statistics of the States of the Union, Virginia being the most populous.

Peace Destroying the Implements of War

Peace, holding a burning torch in her right hand, setting fire to the accoutrements of war is a rare subject by Flaxman which probably dates back to 1786. Writing to Flaxman in that year Wedgwood remarked: ''The burning of the implements of war and the figure of peace, then must form another group.'' There appears to be no example of the use of this subject before 1802, when it decorated a Louis Seize style clock case commemorating the Peace of Amiens between Britain and France.

Peace Plaques

A companion set of three majolica plaques made by Wedgwood for Soane & Smith of Oxford Street, London, W.1, in a limited edition of 250 sets and issued in 1919. The larger (17-inch) plaque is painted with the head of Bellona, Goddess of War, with the inscription '1919 Peace'. One of the smaller (14½-inch) plaques shows a bust of Britannia, and the other a bust of France, both in front of their respective national flags, the borders with the inscriptions 'Honi Soit Qui Mal Y Pense' and 'Liberté, Egalité, Fraternité' respectively. The marks are printed and impressed.

Pearl Ware

A white body containing a larger proportion of white clay and flint than creamware. The glaze had a small quantity of cobalt oxide added further to whiten the appearance of the body. A cream-coloured earthenware with a bluish glaze was produced in Staffordshire in the 1740s, but the name 'Pearl ware' was Wedgwood's, and the body and glaze he introduced in 1779 was very different from anything that had been made earlier. Wedgwood did not like pearl ware, but thought of it as meeting the competition of white porcelain. It did not, of course, have the disadvantages of creamware when employed in conjunction

Peace Destroying the Implements of War. *Jasper clock case (dark blue dip) in the Louis Seize style, Peace Destroying the Implements of War. Made to accommodate the French circular clock movement. Possibly modelled by John Flaxman. First discussed in 1786, and made in 1802 to commemorate the Peace of Amiens. This piece appears to be unique.* Liverpool City Museums. Photo: Wedgwood.

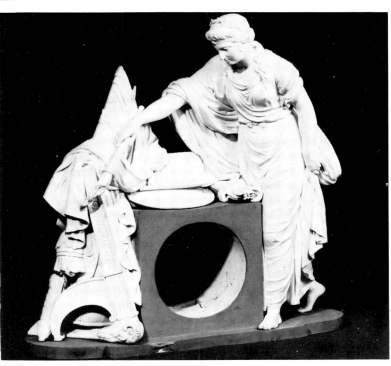

Peace Plaques. *Plaque commemorating the peace of 1919. The head of Britannia is printed and enamelled. 14½ ins. in diameter. Sotheby's Belgravia.*

with underglaze blue decoration, but no underglaze blue printing* was done at Wedgwood until ten years after Josiah's death.

Pearl ware was made by many other manufacturers, including Spode*, and the name was also used by Cheatham & Woolley of Lane End for dry bodies* used for ornamental wares, such as busts and figures, from about 1795.

'New Pearl Ware' was introduced by Wedgwood in 1809, and was used for many armorial services, including the Royal Golden Jubilee service made in that year.

See: Sir William Meredith.

Peart, Charles (1759-1798)
Charles Peart entered the Royal Academy Schools in 1781, and in the following year was awarded a Gold Medal for a group entitled *Hercules and Omphale*. He later worked as assistant to Lochée*, and he modelled portraits for Wedgwood from 1788 to 1794, including those of Sir William Chambers* (1787), Viscount Hillsborough (1786), and probably that of Princess Charlotte Augusta. Peart is sometimes credited with the portrait of Warren Hastings, but Flaxman's* invoice for January 1784 contradicts this attribution.

Pebble Vases
Vases of cream-coloured ware decorated with coloured glazes to resemble the cut and polished surface of natural stones. Introduced in 1769. Marbled, agate, and onyx wares had been introduced by 1764.

See: Variegated Ware.

Pecten Shell
The scallop shell; a rococo decoration popular in the 18th century, and much used by Wedgwood as enamelled decoration for tableware and relief ornament for jasper and black basaltes.

Pegasus
The winged horse which sprang from the blood of Medusa* when Perseus cut off her head. Pegasus was caught by

Bellerophon, and with his aid Bellerophon conquered the Chimaera*. Riding Pegasus towards the heavens, Bellerophon fell to earth. Pegasus continued upwards to dwell among the stars, and is associated with the Muses*.

Two small bas-reliefs — *Muses watering Pegasus on Helicon (Pegasus cared for by Nymphs)* and *Muses watering Pegasus* — were modelled by Flaxman* and Hackwood* respectively. The Pegasus finial* was also modelled by Flaxman.

See: Homeric Vase; Pegasus Vase.

Pegasus Vase
Several jasper vases with the figure of Pegasus* as a finial are thus loosely called. A glass vase of this name was also made by John Northwood*, who worked on the 1877 edition of Wedgwood's Portland* vase. This Pegasus vase was commissioned by Thomas Wilkes Webb and stands 21ins. in height. The subject is Venus* and Adonis*, and the general treatment is very similar to a jasper vase. The Pegasus finial to the cover is obviously derived from the finial of Wedgwood*s Homeric* vase.

Pemberton & Son, Samuel
Silversmiths of Soho, Birmingham, who bought seals for mounting from Wedgwood, and also from Palmer* and Voyez*.

Pen Tray
Shaped rectangular tray, often separated into two compartments and with a shallow raised ledge to protect pen nibs from damage. Ornamental pen trays were made in black basaltes* as early as 1769, and appear in various bodies including Queen's ware (enamelled and printed) and dry bodies*. Tooth brush trays, which are of similar shape, but were originally provided with lids, are often mistaken for pen trays.

Pearl Ware. *Oyster barrel and stand, 11¼ ins. high, decorated with Majolica glazes, c.1860. Impressed mark 'WEDGWOOD PEARL'.* Photo: Wedgwood.

Pegasus. *Blue and lilac dip three-colour jasper medallion of Muses watering Pegasus on Helicon, 2½ ins. by 4ins., modelled by Flaxman. c.1785.* Manchester City Art Gallery.

Pendant Ribbon Swag

A decorative motif in the form of a swag* of ribbons, or of ribbons suspended from a floral swag.

Penelope

Wife of Ulysses*, King of Ithaca, by whom she had one son, Telemachus. During the long absence of Ulysses she was beset by suitors for her hand, who assumed that Ulysses was dead. She deceived them by declaring that she would not yield to their importunities until she had finished the piece of cloth she was weaving. Every night, however, she unravelled her day's work. At length the suitors perceived the stratagem and began to press for an answer, but Ulysses returned in disguise and slew them all with arrows from the bow which only he could string. Another tradition makes Penelope the mother of Pan*, either by Hermes* or by all the suitors, and records that Ulysses repudiated her when he returned.

Wedgwood models:
Penelope, figure, modelled by Arnold Machin*, 1944.
Penelope and her Maidens, the name erroneously given to *Volumnia, wife of Coriolanus*, modelled by Flaxman* after d'Hancarville* II pl.26.
The painting, *Penelope unravelling her Web,* by Joseph Wright* (of Derby) was purchased by Josiah Wedgwood in 1784/5.

Pennine Glaze

A rich chestnut coloured semi-matt glaze developed by Wedgwood and introduced in 1964 for oven-to-table ware.

Pennington, Joseph

Painter, apprenticed at Etruria*, who went to work at Worcester* towards the end of the 18th century. He may have been related to John and James Pennington and Seth Pennington, potters of Liverpool.

Pepper, Elisha (fl.1839-after 1865)

Engraver of Slack Lane, Hanley, 1851-65; worked for Wedgwood, 1839-65; partner in the engraving firms of Green, Sergeant & Pepper, Green & Pepper, and E. Pepper & Son.

Percival, Dr. Thomas (1740-1804)

Manchester physician, and one of the pioneers of public health administration, who wrote a pamphlet on lead poisoning which referred to Queen's ware*. This was a cause of considerable concern to Wedgwood. Dr. Percival later wrote an article published in London in 1774 in which he stated that there was

"no objection to the common use of this beautiful pottery, but... vessels of it are improper for the preserving of acid fruits and pickles." All reference to Queen's ware was deleted in later reprints. In 1773 a Dr. Goulson followed Percival's pamphlet with one on the same subject. Wedgwood remarked that "quieting one of these Gentlemen was only lopping off one of the Hydra's heads." Wedgwood began experimenting with a leadless glaze which he was not successful in achieving. The Society of Arts offered a premium for a leadless glaze in 1793 which was claimed by Coalport* in 1820. The danger of the lead glaze was not to the user of the finished product, but to the workmen handling the raw glaze before firing.

Perfume bottles

See: Scent Bottles.

Persephone Pattern

Transfer-printed pattern in black, with linear scroll border and centre motif representing fruit and fish enamelled in blue, yellow or green. It was designed in 1937 by Eric Ravilious*, when it was a commercial failure, and reintroduced in 1951, when it soon became one of Wedgwood's most popular

Pegasus. *Finial to the cover of a blue and white jasper vase, ornamented with relief figures of Apollo and the Muses on a dimpled ground. c.1785.* Dwight and Lucille Beeson Collection.

Queen's ware patterns. It provides a fine modern example of Wedgwood's traditional policy of employing, and putting faith in, young contemporary designers. This pattern, printed in gold on bone china*, and with the Royal Arms substituted for the central motif, was chosen for the dinner service to be used at the Foreign Secretary's Coronation banquet in June 1953.

See: Proserpine.

Perseus

Son of Zeus and Danae, the daughter of Acrisius, King of Argos. Polydectes, King of Seriphos, who was in love with Danae, sent Perseus on a quest for the head of Medusa*, one of the Gorgons, the sight of whom turned men to stone. Perseus cut off the head of Medusa, looking at the reflection of her figure in a mirror, and, on his way home, married Andromeda*, whom he had rescued from a sea monster. Attacked by Andromeda's uncle, Phineus, at his wedding feast, he used the head of Medusa to turn him to stone. He later gave the head to Athena, who placed it in the middle of her shield or breastplate. At the games at Larissa, he accidentally slew his grandfather, Acrisius, with the discus, thus fulfilling a prophecy made before his birth.

Two Wedgwood bas-reliefs* illustrate parts of the story:

Perseus and Andromeda, probably remodelled by Flaxman* after a copy, supplied by Tassie*, of a Roman gem now in the Capitoline Museum. The subject was produced in two sizes: a cameo*; and a medallion, 6ins. by 5ins.

The Marriage of Perseus and Andromeda, plaque or tablet, 6ins. by 9ins., c.1768, probably after della Porta*.

Persian Figures

See: Michelangelo Vase.

Persistent Patterns

Name given to patterns and shapes which have persisted more or less unmodified from the 18th and early 19th century to the present day (e.g. Napoleon Ivy*).

Pesez

Medallist of Amsterdam, whose medals depicting portrait heads were 'picked up' by Bentley during a visit to Paris in 1776. Wedgwood wrote: "I observe Pesez... is a strong mannerist, and has given a family likeness to them all in the thickness of their Lips, and a peculiar bold opening of the Nostril. However, he has a free bold touch Slight and Masterly, and superior to the common run of Head-makers. I sorted out his Heads as the production of the same Artist before I saw he had put his name to them." Nothing otherwise appears to be known of him.

The following portraits are from medals by Pesez:

Barry, Comtesse du, c.1780.

Boccage, Anne Marie Fiquet de, c.1776.

Boerhaave, Dr. Herman (modelled by Flaxman after Pesez), 1782.

Boileau-Despreaux, Nicolas, c.1776.

Burlamaqui, Jean Jacques, c.1776 (attributed).

Châtelet-Lomont, Gabrielle Emilie, Marquise du, c.1776.

Clairon de la Tudi, Josepha Hippolyte Léris, c.1776.

Corneille, Pierre, c.1776.

Crébillon, Prosper Jolyot de, c.1776 (attributed).

Dacier, Anne, c.1776 (attributed).

D'Alembert, Jean Le Rond, 1776.

Descartes, René, c.1776.

Deshoulières, Antoinette, c.1776.

D'Estrées, Gabrielle, Duchesse de Beaufort, c.1776.

Grignan, Françoise Marguerite, Comtesse de, c.1776.

Hein, Pieter (modelled by Flaxman, probably after Pesez), c.1782.

La Fontaine, Jean de, c.1776.

L'Enclos, Anne (Ninon de L'Enclos), c.1776.

Le Sueur, Eustache, c.1776.

Molière, c.1776.

Montaigne, Michel Eyquem, Seigneur de, c.1776.

Pascal, Blaise, c.1776.

Racine. Jean-Baptiste, c.1776.

Ruyter, Michel Adriaanszoon de (modelled by Flaxman after Pesez), 1782.

Scudéry, Madeleine de, c.1776.

Sévigné, Marquise de, c.1776.

Sorel, Agnes, c.1776.

Suze, Henriette de Coligny, Comtesse de la, c.1776.

Peter Rabbit Set

Since 1949 Wedgwood have had exclusive rights to the production of Peter Rabbit nursery ware, the patterns reproduced from Beatrix Potter's* original paintings. A four-piece set in a gift box includes a plate, mug, porringer, and egg cup. There have been many additions to the range, including a hexagonal money box.

Phaeton

Son of Helios, the sun god, who importuned his father for permission to drive the chariot of the Sun. Helios yielded reluctantly, but Phaeton was not strong enough to hold the horses in their correct course, and, coming too close to the earth, the heat from the chariot began to consume it. Zeus saved the earth from destruction by killing Phaeton with a thunderbolt, hurling him into the river Eridanus.

Wedgwood subject:

The Fall of Phaeton, tablet 10½ins. by 19⅜ins. Modelled by George Stubbs*, c.1785.

Phidias (c.490-417B.C.)

One of the greatest of Greek sculptors, born at Athens. He superintended the erection of the Parthenon, and the sculptures from this source now in the British Museum were carved under his supervision.

The cast of a 'Fragment by Phidias' was invoiced to Wedgwood by Flaxman* in September 1782, but it is not known whether any use was made of it. The bas-relief* known as *Two Warriors and a Horse,* attributed to Pacetti*, has been erroneously identified with this cast.

Phillips & Greaves

Independent enamellers of Stoke-on-Trent, responsible for some painting in blue enamel on Wedgwood creamware c.1764.

Photographic Ware

See: Photolithography; Satsuma Shape.

Photolithography

It is not inappropriate that Wedgwood's should have been among the earliest users of photographic decorative techniques, since Tom Wedgwood* had been one of the pioneers of photography at the end of the 18th century. The first photographic process to be used in the decoration of porcelain and enamels was the invention of a Paris manufacturer, Lafon de Canarsac*, in 1854. He exhibited a cup and saucer decorated with a photographic portrait at the London Exhibition of 1862, where he was awarded a Gold Medal. In the 1860s a technique of transferring photographs on prepared backing paper to the surface of pottery and porcelain glazes was devised, and several methods of applying photographs to enamel and wooden surfaces were patented during the 1870s. Wedgwood made limited use of the technique around 1878 (see: Satsuma Shape), but it never

Phaeton. The Fall of Phaeton. *Jasper tablet 19⅜ ins. by 10½ ins., modelled by Stubbs, c.1785.* Wedgwood.

achieved great popularity. The discriminating public apparently prefers its pottery decorated by traditional methods, or those which resemble them, and photographic processes usually seem out of place when used for these purposes. W.E. Henry and H.S. Wood published a book entitled *Photoceramics* in 1896.

See: Henry Hope Crealock.

Physic Cup
Made of Queen's ware, and so called by Wedgwood. It is a type of spouted feeding cup with two side handles, and a third handle in the form of a dog's head opposite the spout. The type is sometimes called a pap boat.

Pichler, Johann or Giovanni (1734-1791)
Gem engraver; born in Rome into an Austrian family of engravers. His gems were highly esteemed, and it is said that his own copies of ancient gems were brought to him for copying by collectors, who had bought them believing them to be antique. Pichler lived in England c.1764-76 and engraved gems, many of which were reproduced in Tassie's* glass pastes. After the purchase of the Portland* vase by James Byres*, and before it was sold to Sir William Hamilton*, Pichler was commissioned to take a mould from it. This was subsequently used by Tassie for sixty copies cast in plaster. Gems by Pichler are thought to have provided the source for Wedgwood's jasper bas-relief*, *Achilles dragging the body of Hector around the walls of Troy* and the Muse* *Euterpe*, and there are no doubt others, supplied by Tassie, so far unidentified. Pichler also engraved a gem with the popular subject *Nymphs* decorating the Statue of Priapus.* The composition is almost identical with Angelica Kauffmann's*, but Pichler's nymphs are naked.

Piece Mould
A plaster mould made of several interlocking parts so arranged that each will draw from the surface of a cast without damaging it, leaving the mould to be reassembled and used again.

Piecrust Ware
Shallow pie dishes of buff stoneware simulating pastry were made during the period of the Flour Tax after 1800. Dishes of this kind were made by Wedgwood in cane ware*, and in a similar ware by Turner*, who found a vein of clay in 1780 especially suitable for this purpose.

See: Game-Pie Dish

Pierced Decoration
Type of decoration found principally on cream-coloured ware from Wedgwood and Leeds* during the last quarter of the 18th century which consists of piercings similar to those ornamenting contemporary silver. The clay was pierced when in a state of leather-hardness* with punches in a variety of shapes. Cruet stands, punch glass stands, the covers of chestnut baskets, fish trowels, food warmers, and other wares capable of being thus treated can all be recognised as having a silver prototype.

Pigalle, Jean-Baptiste (1714-1785)
French sculptor; a pupil of Robert le Lorrain and Lemoyne, he worked at the Academy in Rome, returning to Paris in 1744, exhibiting two plaster statues in the Salon in the same year. He was a regular exhibitor until 1753, and executed several commissions for Louis XV, including the statues of Mercury* and Venus*, and the figure of Mercury tying his sandals, copied by Wedgwood. He was among the 'outside' sculptors (who included Caffiéri, and Houdon*) employed by the Sèvres* factory after 1766 to model reduced versions of their most celebrated work for reproduction in biscuit porcelain. Pigalle became an Academician in 1744, and was elected Chancellor of the Academy in 1785.

See: Carrara; Figures.

Piggin
A small, pail-like receptacle with a single handle, used as a dipper for milk or cream. Made in engine-turned red ware, c.1765, and also in cream-coloured ware. The type was made in porcelain at Bow, c.1755.

271

Pierced Decoration. *Silver pattern dessert basket in Queen's ware with pierced gallery.* Wedgwood.

Pill Slab

A flat rectangular slab for rolling pills, a feature of apothecary ware in one form or another in England from the 17th century. Wedgwood made pill slabs but few have survived. A specimen in the Buten Museum* is of Queen's ware*, marked with a painted scale for cutting a long cylinder of the mixture into equal parts before rolling them into spheres.

Pillement, Jean (1728-1808)

French landscape painter and designer, born in Lyon, the son of an *ornemaniste*. His own work consisted principally of fantastic rococo* *chinoiseries** and *singeries**, many of which were published in Paris and London. Designs after Pillement are to be found in *The Ladies' Amusement**, a design book compiled by Robert Sayer*, where they were engraved by Robert Hancock*. Pillement had, successively, two wives, and a son, Victor, all of whom helped him with his work. Designs after Pillement are to be found on English silver and porcelain, especially transfer-printed Worcester, and some Wedgwood prints were derived from this source.

A Wedgwood creamware monteith* in a private collection is decorated with a black transfer-print of a river scene applied by Sadler & Green. This is plate 96 in *The Ladies' Amusement* and is inscribed 'Pillement invt.'

Pinchbeck

An alloy of copper and zinc simulating gold introduced by Christopher Pinchbeck (1670-1732) and employed for the manufacture of jewellery and small objects of vertu. The best were mercurically gilded to increase their deceptive appearance.

Pindar (518-438B.C.)

Greek lyric poet, born near Thebes. The only poems of his which have survived are in commemoration of victories in the games. A bust 25ins. high was supplied by Hoskins & Grant* in 1774 and re-finished by Hackwood*. A miniature bust, 4½ins; high, was produced c.1778.

Pineapple

The pineapple, a tropical fruit, was grown under glass in a hot bed during the 18th century. It was introduced into England early in the 1660s, and the first pineapple was grown by the King's gardener. Charles II had it served at dinner and gave a slice to John Evelyn, the diarist, who did not like the flavour. A painting of the gardener presenting the first fruit to the King is in Ham House, South West London.

In addition to Wedgwood's early pineapple* ware the fruit was employed as a knop to the cover of tureens and similar vessels by Wedgwood and others during the currency of the neo-classical* style, and it formed part of the decoration of a large Queen's ware centrepiece in the 1770s.

Pineapple Ware

Creamware naturally modelled and decorated with coloured glazes to represent the pineapple, usually in the form of a teapot, coffee pot, or covered bowl, made by Wedgwood, c.1760 onwards, and covered with his improved green and yellow glazes. Pineapple finials occur during the currency of the neo-classical* style.

Pingo, Thomas (1692-1776)

Medallist, born in Italy, who came to England c.1743 and became assistant engraver at the Mint. The Wedgwood portrait medallions of David Garrick and Lord Camden were modelled from Pingo's medals, the former by Hackwood*. He was also probably responsible for the copper plaques of the battles of Pondicherry and Plassey and *Birth of the Prince* invoiced in 1769 by John Ireland on behalf of 'Mr Pingo'. Some confusion has been caused in the identification of Pingo by the existence of a letter from Mrs. Theodosia Pingo, dated 1800, drawing Wedgwood's attention to her husband's illness and inability to attend to business. As Thomas Pingo died twenty-four years earlier, it has been assumed that he could not have worked for Wedgwood. The medals of Garrick (1772) and Camden (1766) are signed by him, and there is no reason to suppose that the copper tablets are not by him. The letter probably refers to his son, Lewis (1743-1830). There is no evidence that either Thomas or Lewis was employed by Wedgwood, but Thomas's work was certainly copied at Etruria*.

Pink Lustre

Metallic lustre on a glazed body of white, cream, or buff. The pink colour is due to the use of gold. Pink splashed lustre was made by Wedgwood from about 1806; wares of this kind were also made elsewhere in Staffordshire, and in Sunderland.

See: Lustre Decoration.

Pipe Clay

A fine white clay used to make tobacco pipes and good quality earthenwares.

Pipes, Tobacco

Pipe bowls, in basaltes*, sometimes ornamented with reliefs in *rosso antico*, and in jasper* with classical or leaf ornament, were made during the Wedgwood & Bentley* partnership. The Christie* sale catalogue of 1781 lists a number of them and several varieties were in the Mayer collection in Liverpool, the greater part of which was destroyed by bombing during the Second World War. A blue and white jasper pipe of unusual shape is in the Buten Museum*. The lipped ovoid bowl is extended downwards into a spherical trap to collect moisture and nicotine. It is impressed 'Staite's Patent' and was made in 1875.

Pipkin

A small pot, usually circular, with a straight, horizontally-disposed, handle principally used for warming brandy. The term was also employed for small earthenware cooking vessels. Writing to Bentley in February, 1780, Wedgwood refers to ''pots and pipkins.''

Piranesi, Giovanni Battista (1720-1778)

Italian engraver who specialised in recording the architectural aspects of the city. His engravings were very popular, and were often reprinted and imitated. Piranesi is noted for fantastic interiors and dramatic effects of shadow and perspective. Much of his work exhibits a Romantic distortion which leads to highly imaginative views of Rome, to many of which the term *capriccio* could properly be applied. He also published some highly original and inaccurate interpretations of history, alleging that the Greeks debased classical art, and attacking Vitruvius. His engravings were used by Wedgwood in 1958 for a set of scenes of Rome. These were printed in black on Edmé* shape.

See: Neo-Classical Style.

Pitcher Mould

Small mould of fireclay into which clay is pressed in the making of such small ornaments as leaves, scrolls, swags, figures, and other kinds of relief decoration for application to the surface of a variety of wares, particularly jasper.

See: Ornamenting.

Plant, J.H. (fl.1870-1900)

Painter of landscape and animal subjects employed at Coalport* c.1880-90, and subsequently at Wedgwood and Doulton.

Plant Labels

Plant labels in matt mortar* ware were made specially for Kew Gardens c.1830. These were produced in various sizes, in a pointed 'T' shape, and stamped 'KEW'. They were also made for general sale in a variety of shapes, including one with a moulded snowdrop pattern, priced at 2d.-3½d. per dozen.

Plaque

Flat, thin tablet* of ceramic ware (creamware*, jasper*, basaltes*, *rosso antico*, etc.), decorated in relief, or painted with enamels. Plaques or tablets were principally used as wall decoration, for insertion into chimney pieces and furniture, and for the ornamenting of such objects as clock cases. Some plaques were made with a raised surround simulating a picture frame, others were decoratively framed in metal, probably by Boulton* & Fothergill. Although it would be desirable to confine the term to oval or circular examples, using 'tablets' for those which are square or rectangular, the word actually refers to any of these shapes. 'Cameo'* is generally used of an oval, circular, or rectangular bas-relief, similar to a plaque,

but smaller, and generally mounted as jewellery or inset in such objects as patch-boxes, toothpick cases, combs or chatelaines.

Platinum Lustre

Decoration in a platinum lustre* pigment which is like silver or steel in colour. For this reason it is often called 'silver' or 'steel' lustre. Objects inspired by contemporary silver and Sheffield plate, and wholly covered with lustre, were often known as 'poor man's silver'. Platinum was first isolated in 1750; it was first used as a lustre pigment at the end of 1805.

See: Lustre.

Plato (c.428-347B.C.)

Greek philosopher, born in Athens; perhaps a descendant, on his mother's side, from Solon*. Plato was a pupil of Socrates*, and after travels in Egypt and Italy returned to teach in the Academy. Many of his philosophical writings have survived, and to him we owe the account of the death of Socrates and the story of Atlantis.

Three busts were produced by Wedgwood: the first, 25ins. high, from a cast supplied by Hoskins & Grant* in 1774 and remodelled by Hackwood*, and a second, 15ins. high, possibly from the same model, in the same year; the third was obtained from Cheere* in 1779. A portrait medallion was issued c.1778.

Plato. *Portrait medallion in jasper of Plato. First listed in the 1779 Catalogue.* British Museum.

Platter

A large shallow dish, usually oval, for serving food, known in Scotland as an 'ashet'. Large meat platters of the 18th and 19th centuries were often made with feet, so arranged to tilt the dish towards one end, where the juices collected in a shallow well. Platters were sometimes also provided with drainers*.

See: Platter Tilter.

Platter Tilter

A rectangular wedge-shaped slab placed under one end of a platter* so that the gravy flows to the opposite end. Examples in cream-coloured ware were made by Wedgwood in the 18th and 19th centuries, sometimes decorated to match particular tableware patterns.

Pluto (Hades)

Hades was God of the Underworld, brother of Zeus and Poseidon, and husband of Persephone*. Since he was King of the Underworld he was supposed to provide men with metals, which came from under the earth, hence with riches. The name Hades was hated and feared, and Pluto was commonly used instead.

Wedgwood subject:

Pluto carrying off Proserpine, preceded by Hercules, medallion attributed to Angelini*.

Pollard, Robert (1755-1838)

Painter and engraver employed by Wedgwood to polish seals and gems in the 1770s. His friend, Thomas Bewick*, was probably responsible for introducing him to Wedgwood. Pollard painted landscapes and seascapes, exhibiting his work at the Free Society in 1783 and becoming a member of the Society of Artists. Later he concentrated on engraving, mostly from his own work.

Polyphemus

A son of Poseidon (Neptune*); one of the Cyclopes. Polyphemus was a giant with one eye in the centre of his forehead, who lived in a cave near Mount Aetna. When Odysseus (Ulysses*) was shipwrecked on the coast of Sicily and seized by Polyphemus he escaped by putting out the monster's single eye. The figure of Polyphemus appears as one of the Herculaneum Subject* plaques. It has been attributed to Flaxman*, but the date makes this extremely unlikely unless it was from a cast supplied by Flaxman Senior*, and it is more convincingly assigned to Bacon*.

Pomona

Roman divinity of fruit trees. This title has been given to one of the so-called 'Dancing Nymphs' in the series of Herculaneum Subjects*.

Pompeii

A city of Campania in the shadow of Mount Vesuvius. It was once on the coast, but is now about two miles from the sea. It was overwhelmed by an eruption of the volcano in A.D.79, at the same time as the neighbouring towns of Herculaneum* and Stabiae. Pompeii was buried in a fall of ashes and cinders. The lava flow did not reach it. Consequently it is in an excellent state of preservation. About half the city has been excavated since the discovery of the site shortly before the middle of the 18th century. The best contemporary account of the destruction of Pompeii is to be found in the letters of Pliny the Younger, whose Uncle, the elder Pliny, was killed while attempting to evacuate some of the inhabitants.

See: Sir William Hamilton; Neo-classical Style.

Pompeii Jasper Compôtier

A limited edition of 1,000 pairs of *compôtiers* of pale blue and white jasper in presentation boxes was made for sale by the Royal Academy of Arts, Burlington House, London, during the exhibition, *Pompeii A.D.79,* which ended in February 1977. The figures in relief in white jasper are of a type modelled before 1783 from models in the collection of Lord Lansdowne after wall-paintings discovered in the ruins of Herculaneum*,

not far from Pompeii, which was buried by ash and cinders at the same time.

Pont-aux-Choux, Paris

A factory founded in 1740 which started by making tin-glazed earthenware (*faience*), but from 1765 it produced a cream-coloured ware for which it became widely known. In 1772 the factory was advertised as the 'Manufacture royale de terres de France à l'imitation de celles d'Angleterre' (earthenwares of France in imitation of those of England). The quality is excellent. The wares are moulded in relief with flowers, foliage, etc., inspired by contemporary (rococo*) silver. The colour is pale cream; the glaze is soft and easily rubbed. Exact imitations of Staffordshire salt-glazed wares are known.

Porcelain

Porcelain manufacture was a matter of serious interest to most 18th century potters, including Josiah Wedgwood. Properly defined, it is a compound of a refractory refined clay and a fusible rock, with the addition of a small quantity of flux to assist fusion of the rock. This is fired to the point of vitrification, when it becomes translucent if it is about 5mm or less in thickness. The type of porcelain usually termed true porcelain was first made in China during the Yüan dynasty (1280-1366), although translucent wares had been made for some centuries before this. Because of the difficulty in finding a suitable clay and a fusible rock possessing the necessary properties, Chinese porcelain was known in Europe for several centuries before the secret of its manufacture was discovered. The first European true porcelain was produced as the result of the experiments of von Tschirnhaus and J.F. Böttger at Meissen* about 1709. The most admired property of Chinese porcelain, which arrived in Europe in the 14th century, was translucency, and it was imitated late in the 16th century in Italy (at Florence) and late in the 17th century in France (at Saint-Cloud) in a body prepared from white-burning clay and what was, in principle, ground glass, the latter replacing the fusible rock. This artificial porcelain was brought to its highest point of development in France at Vincennes shortly before 1752, at a factory purchased by Louis XV and removed to Sèvres* in 1756. This is still the Manufacture nationale de Sèvres of France, with an important museum of ceramics attached to it. In England the first factory making artificial porcelain was located at Chelsea*, where a body was produced which was admired by the Vincennes directors. Chelsea was founded in 1745, to be followed by Bow before 1750. At Bow cálcined cattle bones (bone ash) were added to the body, which reduced kiln wastage at the expense of quality, and this substance was later employed in the manufacture of bone china*. The Worcester* factory made a type of porcelain from 1752 onwards which employed soaprock as a fusible rock, and were therefore using the same principle as the Chinese, even though the rock employed fused at a lower temperature.

In 1768 William Cookworthy, Quaker, apothecary and chemist of Plymouth, who had been experimenting with Cornish materials similar to those of China, took out a patent for the use of china clay and feldspathic rock (Cornish- or growan-stone) in the manufacture of true porcelain. The Plymouth factory was transferred to Bristol, where the manager was Richard Champion*, who bought both factory and patent in 1775.

Every manufacturer on a reasonably large scale was interested in adding porcelain to his range. Almost throughout the 18th century it was the most fashionable material among the wealthier classes, although Wedgwood's creamware supplanted it to some extent. It is, however, at least arguable whether some of Wedgwood's success was not due to the greater suitability of his bodies to the neo-classical* style, since porcelain rarely translated well into classical forms. Derby*, for instance, eventually came to terms with the style by emphasising fine painting, and Worcester did much the same.

It would be a mistake, however, to assume that Wedgwood was uninterested in porcelain. Apart from claiming basaltes as his 'black porcelaine' and jasper as his 'biscuit porcelain' (which considering their nature was not unreasonable) he was experimenting before 1773 with Chinese kaolin (china clay) and petuntse (feldspathic rock) sent to him by John Bradby Blake*, who died in that year. On the 14th January, 1776 in a letter in which he tells Bentley* that it was then possible to fire jasper with as much certainty as basaltes, he begs Bentley to wait a little longer for white china. "I have been too much engaged hitherto to have brought porcelain making to such forwardness as to admit of having any ready for sale this season." From the paragraph which follows this statement it seems that, although he was perfectly able to make porcelain, he considered it would have the effect of ruining the trade for cream-coloured ware, then very profitable, and he was not prepared to take the chance until he could be assured of making porcelain in sufficient quantity to replace it.

It is difficult to believe that Wedgwood was very apprehensive of the consequences of infringing Champion's patent. He had already seen how easily his own patent for encaustic colours had been evaded by others, and Champion was not financially in a position to pursue expensive lawsuits. Nevertheless, Bentley did, on several occasions, urge him to avoid firing jasper to the point of translucency (to be noticed with some early examples) to avoid infringements of Champion's patent.

Josiah Wedgwood did not refrain from making porcelain because he did not know how to do it. On the contrary, he understood the manufacture of both true and artificial porcelain very well, and in 1776 was suggesting to Bentley the possibility of making an artificial frit to replace Champion's 'felt spar' or 'Moor stone', and a reference to 'Bone Ashes' shows that he was well acquainted with what had gone into the porcelain of the (by then) defunct Bow factory, and which was then being employed at Derby. In the same letter there is a reference to a frit of sand, salt, and glass which suggests that he was probably acquainted with the methods used at Sèvres. A frit is a mixture of a number of substances fused together and subsequently ground to powder for mixing with the clay. It takes the place of fusible rock.

Undoubtedly the risks, and particularly the kiln-wastage factor, of establishing a porcelain manufactory were very high, but when Wedgwood first established his own enterprise it was an extremely fashionable material, and during the currency of the rococo* style it was an important art form. By 1770 it was beginning to decline in favour, and by 1778, when Champion was abandoning his factory and attempting to sell his patent, Wedgwood was 'absolute' both in basaltes and jasper, and porcelain no longer attracted him. He was leading the market, not following it.

Porcelain in the form of bone china* was introduced by Josiah II in 1812 and is said to have been abandoned by 1822. Actually it appears from the records that manufacture went on, and that small batches were made, probably to special order, for some years afterwards. The manufacture of bone china was revived in 1878 and has been a staple product of the factory ever since. The most recent research reveals that late in the 19th century (probably between 1870 and 1878) Wedgwood produced small experimental quantities of true porcelain, but this appears to have been abandoned in favour of bone china*.

Porphyry. *Creamware vase coloured to resemble porphyry.* Wedgwood.

Porphyry
A decorative stone of purplish or reddish-brown or mottled green colour imitated on creamware vases by means of coloured glazes.
See: Variegated Ware.

Porta, Guglielmo Della (d.1577)
Italian Renaissance artist, sculptor and designer whose work was copied or adapted for reproduction by Wedgwood. The following subjects are associated with della Porta and were first produced c.1768:
The Calydonian Boar Hunt.
Downfall of the Giants (also sometimes attributed to Cellini*).
Destruction of Niobe's Children.
Feast of the Gods.
Marriage of Perseus and Andromeda.

All appear in black basaltes as oval plaques, often with basaltes frames and occasionally with traces of bronze or gilding. *The Boar Hunt* and *Feast of the Gods* seem to have been particularly well known in the 18th century, and the latter was probably copied by Wedgwood from an intermediate source, a bronze relief by Jakob Cornelisz Cobaert (d.1615). Some of della Porta's reliefs were also copied by the Doccia factory for reproduction in porcelain.

Portland, 3rd Duke of (1738-1809)
William Henry Cavendish Bentinck; Whig statesman; educated at Eton and Christ Church, Oxford. He succeeded to the Dukedom in 1762 and married Lady Dorothy Cavendish, daughter of the Duke of Devonshire, in 1766. He was Prime Minister in 1786 and again in 1807. He lent the Portland vase to Wedgwood to copy. This had been bought privately from Sir

William Hamilton* by the Duchess, and put up for auction after her death. Until this time it had always been known as the Barberini vase, and it has been suggested that Wedgwood agreed with the Duke not to bid for it at auction in consideration of the loan which enabled him to copy it.

Wedgwood's showrooms* at Portland House, Greek Street, were rented from James Cullen, but the Duke, who owned a great deal of property in the vicinity, was the head landlord. In April 1790, an exhibition of the Portland vase was held in Portland House, admission being by ticket only. This was the last function of importance to be held there. The expiry of the twenty-one-year lease almost exactly coincided with the death of Wedgwood, and Josiah II found it difficult to renew the lease because the Duke was proposing to sell the estate on which it stood. The showrooms were, therefore, moved to York Street, St. James's Square.

Portland Vase, The

Now in the British Museum this vase, once thought to be of onyx or chalcedony and now known to be of cased glass, is probably the best known of all surviving Roman works of art. Possibly made in Alexandria, centre of glass making in the ancient world, it is most likely to have been made by Alexandrians in Italy c.27B.C.-A.D.14. The vase itself is a combination of two layers, a foundation of dark blue (almost black) glass covered with a layer of white glass. The decoration was carved out of the white layer by gem engravers or *diatretarii* at the beginning of the present era. The shape is a little curious. Originally it was an amphora similar in shape to the large terracotta amphorae used for the storage of oil or wine, but the base was broken off or removed, and the present base in the form of a carved medallion let in to the remainder. The subject of the decoration has been a matter of controversy for centuries, but the suggestion that it represents the marriage of Peleus and Thetis* (the mother of Achilles*) is widely accepted. At one time it was believed that the vase was a cinerary urn, that the decoration portrayed the Emperor Alexander Severus and his mother, Mamae, and that it had been found in 1582 in a marble sarcophagus. None of these beliefs is true, and its origin and early history are unknown. It is first recorded in the winter of 1600-1 when it was seen in the possession of Cardinal Francesco Maria del Monte (1549-1627).

The Portland vase was also known as the Barberini vase because it was sold to Cardinal Francesco Barberini, nephew of Pope Urban VIII (1623-44). It was in the Palazzo Barberini in Rome, and was sold by the Princess of Palestrina, the last of the Barberini line, about 1780 to a Scottish antiquary, James Byres*, who sold it to Sir William Hamilton* before 1783. The latter brought it to London in 1784, apparently in want of money, and sold it to the Dowager Duchess of Portland. After her death in 1785 it was sold to a buyer named Tomlinson, who was presumably acting for the third Duke of Portland*, the Duchess's son. In 1786 he lent it to Josiah Wedgwood (it is thought under an agreement by which Wedgwood refrained from bidding at the auction in consideration of the loan) for the purpose of reproducing it in jasper. Plaster of Paris replicas had been made before 1783 for Byres by James Tassie*. Byres sold sixty of these replicas, one of which is in the British Museum with the vase itself and Wedgwood's version. The Wedgwood replicas were issued in 1790, and are a *tour de force* of the potter's art. Those who worked on the prototype include Josiah I*, Josiah II*, Henry Webber*, William Hackwood*, and William Wood*. Sir Joshua Reynolds* inspected the finished work and gave it the seal of his approval. Fifty copies

are reputed to have been made, but the exact number is uncertain. Of this first edition, sixteen are known to survive. A few copies with a slate-blue background instead of the very dark blue were made from this period onwards.

There have been several editions subsequent to the first. One of 1839, two years after Victoria's accession, is remarkable for the draping of the figures. The later editions, which include vases in all sizes and colours, are inferior in quality to the 1790 edition, except for an edition of fifteen copies issued in 1877. These were taken from the original moulds and finished by the glass engraver, John Northwood*, using lapidary* techniques. A short while earlier Northwood had produced the first known copy of the vase in glass using the ancient techniques and tools of the gem engravers. The work had occupied him for three years. This edition was sold by Phillips of Oxford Street, London.

The cheap edition of 1839 was the first in which the relief ornament was cast integrally, the background being painted with enamel colour. This method of production has only been employed for cheap editions of a quality much inferior to that of the jasper versions.

All the later editions, except the limited edition of 1877, and the Barnard* edition of 1923-30, lack the medallion at the base, which was a later addition to the original glass vase, and may have been inserted when it was in the possession of the Barberinis, possibly to remedy the result of an accidental breakage.

Four engravings of the vase were executed by William Blake in 1791 for Dr. Erasmus Darwin's *Botanic Garden*.

The original Portland Vase was smashed in February 1845 by an Irish scene painter, while it was displayed, on loan, in the British Museum. It has since been restored twice at intervals of more than a century, and now belongs to the nation.

Portland Vase Mark

A mark depicting the Portland vase, printed in various colours on bone china* since its reintroduction in 1878.

Portrait Medallions

The last quarter of the 18th century was a period in which the British passion for portraiture amounted almost to frenzy. A number of disparate influences — which included the classical revival following the excavations at Herculaneum* and Pompeii*, the improvement in communications and consequent recognition of public heroes, and the desire of the prosperous middle class to equip their house in the manner of the aristocracy — combined to create a feeling for the importance of the individual, a celebration of the family, and a reverence for history. Likenesses of the great, of family and friends, were demanded and provided in a bewildering variety of media. Portraits in oils; miniatures in watercolour on ivory; figures and busts in marble and bronze; small busts in relief, carved, modelled or cast in ivory, wax, glass paste, jasper* and black basaltes*; profiles cut out or painted in silhouette; bronze medallions; even needlework portraits worked in the sitters' own hair; all illustrate a fashion never equalled in any country.

Josiah Wedgwood was not slow to take advantage of this fashion. In 1771 he wrote to Bentley* of his proposal to produce portrait medallions of George III* and Queen Charlotte*, "fully perswaded [sic] a good deal may be done in that way with many of Their Majesty's subjects." Two years later he published the first of his Catalogues* of Ornamental Ware. This listed 609 portrait medals and medallions which included 254 Popes and the first 122 of the important medallions known as 'Heads of the Illustrious Moderns'*. In

Portland Vase. *The Portland Vase of 1790.* Wedgwood.

Portland Vase. *The 'Erasmus Darwin' copy, tilted forward to show the original number 12 inside the mouth of the vase.* Dwight and Lucille Beeson Collection.

WEDGWOOD®
Bone China
MADE IN ENGLAND
FLORENTINE
W2714

Portland Vase Mark. Wedgwood.

Portland Vase. *One of the original wax models for the relief decoration.* Wedgwood.

Portland Vase. *List of subscribers.* Wedgwood.

List of Subscribers
to the Portland Vase

from Thomas Byerley's notebook
1789.

Portrait Medallions. *Modern portraiture. The Presidents Plate, 10ins. in diameter, depicting the thirty-seven Presidents of the United States to Gerald Ford. The reverse is shown on the right. Limited edition of 3,000. Modelled by the American artist Karen Worth. Similar multiple-portrait medallions were produced in bronze in Austria in the 17th and 18th centuries. Two examples are in the Kunsthistorisches Museum, Vienna.*

his introduction, he advertised his ability to supply portraits, in cameo* or intaglio*, in sizes from those "proper for a ring, seal or bracelet" to six inches in diameter. The original wax portrait* cost from three to six guineas; copies in black basaltes or "polished biscuit with cameo grounds" were 10s.6d. each for not less than ten. Portrait medallions from the 'Illustrious Moderns' series could be had, according to size and body, for between 2s. to 7s.6d. each.

The invention of Jasper in 1775 gave Wedgwood the variety of colours that he sought. By 1788 he had catalogued 857 portrait medals and medallions, of which 233 were 'Illustrious Moderns', and this list did not include portraits of his family or friends, or those private commissions which were thought to lack public appeal.

The majority of Wedgwood's portrait medallions were not original. They were copied or adapted from existing medals, reliefs cast in glass paste, carvings in ivory, wax portraits, or horn medallions. The rest were modelled in wax, either *ad vivum* or from engravings, drawings, portraits in oils, or sculpture, by artists employed or commissioned by Wedgwood. The largest source was the medallists, and many of the classical and French portraits were copied from medals by the Dassier* family and Pesez*. Glass paste portraits were obtained from James Tassie*. Among the principal modellers whose work was reproduced by Wedgwood were John Flaxman*, William Hackwood*, John Charles Lochée*, Eley George Mountstephen*, Joachim Smith*, and John De Vaere*.

Portrait medallions have continued to be produced by Wedgwood, though generally in small quantities, to the present day, and recent additions to the list include portraits of HM The Queen and the Duke of Edinburgh, Princess Anne, Prince Charles, and Earl Mountbatten of Burma.

Poseidon
See: Neptune.

Poskotchin
Sergei Poskotchin's factory in Morye (Shlisselburg district of the Province of St. Petersburg) manufactured high quality *faience* and heat-resistant wares for the kitchen and for technical use. The factory was founded early in the 19th century by E. Friedrichs, but its reputation rests on the ware produced after it passed into the hands of Poskotchin (1817-42). These included various coloured bodies*, black ware, and cream-coloured ware. Many of Poskotchin's products were in conscious imitation of Wedgwood, and an attempt was made to manufacture a blue stoneware body with white ornaments in the jasper style. In about 1810, Poskotchin made some well potted and decorated replacements for the Husk* service.

Pot Bank
A term which has come to mean any pottery factory, though it is generally used to describe smaller factories. The word 'bank' was, however, used by Josiah Wedgwood to denote his stock of ware, made by other potters, from which he completed orders for creamware which he could not supply from his own manufacture. Among those who supplied him with creamware was Anne Warburton*. Josiah I expressed extreme irritation when Byerley* was unable, on one occasion, to distinguish between Wedgwood creamware and that of the 'bank'.

Pot-Pourri Vase
A vase, sometimes mounted in ormolu, which is characterised by piercing on the shoulders and in the cover. It was used for holding pot-pourri, a liquid deriving its odour from decomposing flower petals and herbs, as the word *pourri* (rotten) suggests. In England dry mixtures of flowers and herbs

Colour Plate XIX

Above: Large majolica jardinière, based on a Sèvres shape, designed by Hugues Protât, with panel designs painted by Emile Lessore. One of Wedgwood's less harmonious blends of different styles. Wedgwood.

Right: Majolica sphinx candlestick, decorated in dark blue, green and brown semi-transparent glazes and gold. c.1865. Zeitlin Collection.

Below: Circular dish, diameter 9ins., decorated in crimson lustre and gold by William de Morgan and Charles Passenger, whose monogram appears in the circular cartouche on the base. c.1898. Zeitlin Collection.

Poskotchin. *Dish painted with the Husk pattern from the Poskotchin factory. Probably a replacement for a broken dish from the service supplied to the Empress Catherine II of Russia in 1770. c.1809-10.* Wedgwood.

Pot-Pourri Vase. *Small blue jasper dip pot-pourri vase ornamented with white reliefs, c.1880.* Reilly.

were placed in open bowls as well as vases, and received the same name of pot-pourri, although it is strictly incorrect. Josiah Wedgwood made pot-pourri vases in Queen's ware, and the dry bodies*.

See: Cassolette; Pastille Burner.

Potter, Beatrix (1866-1943)

Writer and illustrator of childrens' books, born in South Kensington, London. Her first books, *The Story of Peter Rabbit* and *The Tailor of Gloucester* failed to attract a publisher and were privately printed in 1900 and 1902. Soon afterwards she began a personal and professional association with Frederick Warne & Co., who published twenty-four of her books during the following thirty years. In 1902 she became engaged to Norman Warne, but he died a few months later. She married a solicitor, William Heelis, in 1913. Her portrait by Delmar Banner is in the National Portrait Gallery, London. Wedgwood's Peter Rabbit* nursery sets, decorated with precise reproductions of Beatrix Potter's illustrations, are produced under licence from Frederick Warne & Co.

Pounce Pot

A small box with a pierced top for containing pounce, powdered gum sandarac, employed to prepare the surface of parchment for writing, or to restore it after erasures. The pounce pot usually forms part of the early inkstandish* or the library set.

Powder Colours

Colours imitating in appearance the powder-blue ground of the Chinese, made at several of the porcelain factories during the 18th century, and revived by Wedgwood in 1912. The Chinese applied the colour in powder form by blowing it through a silk screen at the bottom of a bamboo tube on to a surface prepared by a light application of oil, hence the French term for this ground, *bleu soufflé*. It was imitated in England by first laying a ground of solid colour and then stippling it with a fine-grained sponge. Wedgwood's have used this technique to produce 'powder' colours for bone china tableware border patterns (e.g. *Whitehall, Ulander*) in blue, turquoise, 'shagreen', ruby, pink, lilac and grey; and the ruby and blue grounds have also been used for 20th century bone china vases and bowls decorated with Chinese dragons printed in gold.

See: 'Daisy' Makeig-Jones; Ordinary Lustres.

Powell, Alfred H. and Louise (fl.1904-1949)

English potters and ceramic designers. Louise was the granddaughter of Emile Lessore*. The Powells joined Wedgwood in 1905 and founded a new school of freehand painting at Etruria*. Their patterns were of two distinct types: simple sprigs of flower and foliage derived from the formal early Wedgwood borders, and rich foliate designs, sometimes with central figures of animals or birds, which owed their inspiration to the work of William Morris and his followers. In addition to brilliantly coloured enamels, the Powells made free use of platinum (steel) lustre*. Some of their work was painted in their own studios. The designs of the Powells, though recognisably in the tradition of English pottery, are a clear departure from Wedgwood's modern factory production and mark the determination of the directors to reinvigorate the Wedgwood tradition.

The Powells also painted furniture for Ernest Gimson and Sydney Barnsley. Some of their work for Wedgwood was signed with their personal monograms (see: Appendix II).

Alfred Powell designed and painted a number of important plaques, bowls and vases (some of which were private commissions) of which the following are examples:

Barlaston Hall, circular plaque, diameter 24ins. Purple lustre. 1942.

Sailing Ships, circular plaque, diameter 16ins. Matt platinum, Moonstone* and silver. 1940.

White Stag, circular plaque, diameter 16ins. Underglaze blue, grey and green. 1938.

Owl and *Peacock,* pair of Queen's ware plaques or chargers, diameter 18½ ins. Polychrome enamel decoration of forest animals and semi-formalised oak leaves radiating from central roundels of an owl and a peacock. The underside decorated with slender wreaths of leaves and Powell's monogram in black.

Press Moulding

A process in which a body is pressed by hand into a mould of plaster of Paris or fired clay, and used in the making of small ornaments, such as the reliefs employed to ornament jasper. The absorbent mould removes some of the moisture from the body, which shrinks slightly in consequence, facilitating removal from the mould. In former years quite large objects were made by pressing, but this has now been replaced to a great extent by slip casting*.

See: Casting; Sprigged Ware.

Powell, Alfred and Louise. *Vase, the shape based on a Chinese ginger jar, decorated with fish by Louise Powell, c.1925.* Wedgwood.

Powell, Alfred and Louise. *Superb creamware charger (one of a pair) decorated with animals, plants and flowers in polychrome enamel. c.1920. 18½ ins. in diameter.* Zeitlin Collection.

Powell, Alfred and Louise. *Charger decorated with a sailing ship, the border pattern apparently derived from Italian maiolica.* Buten Museum.

Powell, Alfred and Louise. *Queen's ware charger, 18⅛ ins. in diameter, painted and gilded, the border apparently derived from Italian maiolica. 1923.* Buten Museum.

Powell, Alfred and Louise. *Base of vase decorated by Louise Powell, showing artists' and workmen's marks.* Constance Chiswell.

Priapus. *Two nymphs assisted by a satyr raising a statue (actually a term) of Priapus. Jasper tablet, almost certainly after Clodion.* Photo: Wedgwood.

Pretty Mantua Maker, The

From an engraving by Grignion after Brandoin*, this transfer print by Sadler* occurs on early creamware in two versions, the later of the two having added bushes and a girl in a full length skirt.

Priam

King of Troy during the Trojan war. According to Homer* he had fifty sons, nineteen of whom were by his second wife, Hecuba. His eldest son, Hector*, was slain by Achilles*. When Troy was captured Priam was killed by Pyrrhus, son of Achilles.

The tablet, *Priam begging the body of Hector from Achilles,* after a relief on the sarcophagus once believed to be that of Alexander Severus (Capitoline Museum), is attributed to Pacetti*, c.1787.

Priapus

Son of Dionysus and Aphrodite. Regarded as the god of fruitfulness, he was worshipped as the guardian of flocks of sheep, goats, bees, the vine and all garden produce. In carved images he was usually represented as a phallic figure or as a garden deity with tumescent genitalia. Wedgwood's medallion *Nymphs decorating the statue of Priapus,* modelled by Webber* after a design by Angelica Kauffmann*, engraved by Bartolozzi, shows chastely draped female figures garlanding a benign-looking truncated statue on a pedestal, and could have offended no one. A tablet of about the same period, *The Raising of Priapus,* probably after Clodion*, is very much more suggestive. Priapus is sometimes depicted holding a sickle or cornucopia.

Price, Alan, Des. RCA (b.1926)

Artist and designer, who joined Wedgwood at Barlaston* in 1953. His designs for Wedgwood include the *Federal City* series, the *Boston Bowl,* after Paul Revere's silver bowl of this name, the *Washington Presidential Bowl,* and the *St. Lawrence Seaway* plate among many original drawings for modern commemorative ware, engraved by the Design Studio at Barlaston. Alan Price has lived for more than twenty years in America, where he has established a fine reputation as an artist.

Priestley, Dr. Joseph (1733-1808)

Born a cloth dresser's son at Fieldhead, near Leeds, Joseph Priestley was educated at a Dissenting Academy, and became a Dissenting Minister at Needham Market, Suffolk, in 1755. In 1758 he was appointed Minister at Nantwich, and later tutor in languages and *belles-lettres* at Warrington Academy. He was elected Fellow of the Royal Society in 1766, and published his *History of Electricity* in the following year. In 1774 he isolated oxygen without realising the significance of his discovery. He was elected to the French Académie des Sciences in 1772 and to the St. Petersburg Academy in 1789. His reply to Burke's *Reflections on the French Revolution* incited a Birmingham mob to plunder and destroy his home, and in 1794 he emigrated to America, settling in Pennsylvania. His numerous scientific works have never been published in a collected edition, but his *Theological Works,* in twenty-six volumes, were published in London between 1817 and 1832.

Josiah Wedgwood's friendship with Priestley was of long standing, and they corresponded over many years. Wedgwood made laboratory apparatus to his requirements. While in Birmingham Priestley was a member of the Lunar Society*. The first portrait medallion was modelled by Giuseppe Ceracchi about 1779. A large portrait medallion measuring 10¼ins. by 13ins. was remodelled by Hackwood* after Ceracchi, also in 1779. Wedgwood wrote to Bentley: "Dr Priestley is arriv'd and we are with great reverence taking off his presbyterian parson's wig and preparing a Sr I. Newton as a companion to him."

Prime Movers

Until the 18th century prime movers were limited to the human being, horses and oxen, the water mill, and the windmill. Human beings provided motive power by working a treadle or turning a wheel. The horse or ox trudged in a circle, harnessed to a bar turning a central mechanism which could be geared either up or down. The longer the bar (within reason), and the nearer to the end the point of attachment of the animal, the greater the power which could be exerted. More sophisticated were windmills and water mills, and Staffordshire, which had numerous rivers with strong currents, made great use of water power for grinding materials for the pottery industry.

The project for a windmill at Etruria* was first discussed in 1768 when Erasmus Darwin* sent Wedgwood a drawing for a mill with horizontal sails instead of vertical. Wedgwood doubted the efficiency of the design, and eleven years later he went to Lichfield to consult with R.L. Edgeworth*, James Watt*, and the Doctor about the project. There is no evidence that this mill was built, or even started, and in 1782 Wedgwood ordered his first rotary steam engine from James Watt, thus becoming a pioneer of the use of steam power in the industry. A watercolour of Etruria by Stebbing Shaw dated 1794, seen from a point near the bridge over the canal, shows the top and sail of a vertical windmill appearing over the roof of the building fronting the water. This seems to have been in existence since 1774, and before this time Wedgwood used a mill owned by John and Thomas Wedgwood*. It appears to have been used principally for grinding glaze material and enamel colours, but Wedgwood utilised subsidiary belt drives off the main shaft for other purposes. The mill was demolished at the end of the 18th century, perhaps in or about 1796, when Boulton & Watt supplied a new 10h.p. rotary steam engine. Watermills have continued in use in Staffordshire for grinding pottery colours and similar materials until modern times.

Priestley, Dr. Joseph. *Jasper portrait medallion of Dr. Joseph Priestley, by Giuseppe Ceracchi. c.1779.* Wedgwood.

Prince of Wales Vase

An important centrepiece of three-coloured jasper (white, blue and olive-green) in a restrained rococo* style. The form is unusual for a piece made at so late a date, and it was probably designed in deference to the taste of the recipient. The base is octagonal, figures of a lion and unicorn flanking the central vase. On the front an oval medallion portrait of the Prince is surrounded by a wreath and surmounted by the Prince of Wales's feathers; on the reverse side is a bas-relief* of Flora* holding a cornucopia*. Surmounting the domed cover is a seated figure of Britannia, which, like other figures of Britannia, is modified from a Minerva*. This unique centrepiece is in the Nottingham Castle Museum. Traditionally supposed to have been presented to the Prince of Wales (later King George IV) on the occasion of his twenty-first birthday, 1783, this piece is now believed to have been made no earlier than 1790, and may have been presented to the Prince on his marriage to Princess Caroline of Brunswick in 1795. It is attributed, on the evidence of style alone, to Webber*.

Processes of Manufacture

The various processes of manufacture are summarised below. The more important are discussed at greater length under an appropriate heading elsewhere. These are marked with an asterisk.

Casting* The process of formation by pouring slip* into plaster of Paris moulds*. When the cast is dry enough it is removed for further processing, and the parts of the mould reassembled for further use. Casts in plaster of Paris instead of slip are used for a variety of purposes, including the making of fresh working moulds to replace those which have become worn.

Dipping The process of glazing by submerging the article in liquid glaze* material (see: Dip).

Enamelling Adding colours over the glaze, either by painting or printing. They are fixed by a low-temperature firing in the enamelling or 'muffle' kiln. Several firings may be required for elaborately decorated articles. Enamel colours may be applied free hand or to fill in printed designs (print and enamel decoration).

Engraving The cutting of designs on a copper plate with the aid of a tool known as a scorper. It leaves a line of variable depth and width according to the pressure exerted on it, which governs the amount of ink the line will hold. Prints from the engraved plate inked with ceramic colour are used for making transfer prints.

Fettling Finishing an article after removal from the mould by trimming off seams, mould marks, etc., and touching up blemishes.

Firing The process of subjecting the object to heat of varying intensity according to the purpose and body. Earthenware bodies are fired at a lower temperature than vitreous bodies. Glazes are fired at a lower temperature than the body, and enamel colours receive the lightest firing of all. Stonewares and porcelain are referred to as 'hard' fired wares; earthenware receives a 'soft' firing.

Glazing The application of glaze (a kind of glass) to the surface of the ware. Wedgwood give the ware a preliminary firing to biscuit, and it is then covered with glaze and fired in the glost or glazing kiln (see: Glaze).

Ground-laying The process of giving the ware a coloured ground. A coating of oil is applied to the surface of glazed ware in places where the ground colour is required. Powder colour is then dusted on to the oil until it will absorb no more. Firing burns off the oil, leaving the colour fixed firmly to the glaze (see: Aerograph).

Casting. *Liquid slip being piped into plaster of Paris moulds.* Wedgwood.

Dipping. *Dipping plates decorated with underglaze colour into liquid glaze.* Wedgwood.

284

Enamelling. *Adding colour with a brush to the printed Florentine pattern.* Wedgwood.

Engraving *the Florentine border pattern. The tool is the lozenge-shaped scorper used to incise ink-retaining lines in the copper surface.* Wedgwood.

Fettling. *Cleaning off mould marks and blemishes after casting. Seams as yet unremoved may be seen above and below the spout and around the handle.* Wedgwood.

Firing. *Entrance to an electric tunnel kiln showing laden trolley entering the kiln.* Wedgwood.

285

Glazing. *Modern semi-automatic glazing machine at the Adams factory (one of the Wedgwood Group).* Wedgwood.

Ground-laying. *Sponging on a powder-blue ground.* Wedgwood.

Jiggering. *The lower turntable is a mould which forms the upper surface of the plate. The lower surface (here uppermost) is formed by the profile suitably shaped, shown removing surplus clay.* Wedgwood.

Jolleying. *The cup is shown inside the white plaster mould. The round part of the machine moves down while the mould is rotating to form the interior.* Wedgwood.

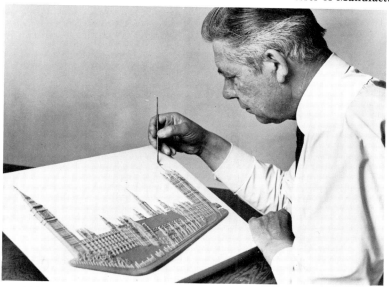

Modelling. *Tom Harper preparing a clay model of the Houses of Parliament for the Christmas Plate.* Wedgwood.

Mould-making. *Lifting a slip-cast coffeepot from a plaster mould.* Wedgwood.

Mould-making. *Mould sections being removed.* Wedgwood.

Ornamenting. *Putting the finishing touches to a modern plate commemorating the first moon landing, 1969.* Wedgwood.

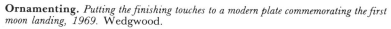

Ornamenting. *Applying acanthus leaf ornament to a black basaltes bowl.* Wedgwood.

Overglaze (Onglaze) decoration. *Adding a gold line overglaze to a Florentine plate which is carried on a light turntable moved by the operative.* Wedgwood.

Printing, *left. Peeling a lithograph transfer from the surface of a coffee pot.* Wedgwood.

Throwing, *left. Forming a vase on the potter's wheel by manipulating the clay as it turns. Objects thus formed must necessarily be of circular section.* Wedgwood.

Turning. *The consistency of the clay may be judged from the appearance of the waste material.* Wedgwood.

Processes of Manufacture *continued*

Jiggering The process of making plates by placing a bat of clay on a revolving disc in the form of a plaster mould, which forms the front of the plate. A profile having the shape of the back is then brought into contact with the clay as it revolves, and this, by removing surplus clay, shapes the back. The technique dates back at least to the 18th century.

Jolleying A process for forming cups which is on the same principle as jiggering for plates (see above). The mould forms the exterior of the cup, the profile the interior.

Modelling The making in a plastic material, such as clay or wax, of the original pattern or design from which the master mould is taken. The original model is usually taken from a design which has been drawn or sketched, and it is important that the model be made larger than the size required for the finished object, since clay shrinks by about one-sixth during firing.

Mould-making The replication of objects in the course of manufacture requires the making of moulds from an original model. The making of a working mould from the wax or clay model is usually done in three stages. The first mould to be made is a hollow mould (matrix) which is used to reproduce the object (patrix) in plaster. The patrix is used to make a series of working moulds, which can be replaced when worn out by casting fresh moulds as required. In this way the standard of reproduction is maintained. Instead of wax or clay, the original model from which the matrix was taken was sometimes of carved wood. The Wedgwood Museum at Barlaston has examples of carved wood models by John Coward* which were used for this purpose. Aaron Wood was a notable 18th century block cutter who supplied almost everyone of note in the Potteries, and no doubt Wedgwood also.

Ornamenting* The process of applying relief decoration to the ware. The reliefs are made in pitcher* moulds and applied to the moistened surface of the background by skilful pressure of the craftman's fingers. Although the most usual example of ornamenting is blue jasper decorated with white, there are many other colour schemes, such as *rosso antico** decorated with black reliefs, or cane ware* ornamented with blue.

Overglaze (Onglaze) decoration Painting or transfer-printing on the surface of the glaze which has been fixed by a light firing in the 'muffle' or enamelling kilns. (See below: Underglaze decoration.)

Painting The application of ceramic colours with brushes, either on biscuit ware subsequently glazed (underglaze painting), or on the surface of the glaze (overglaze or enamel painting). The smallest brushes are known as pencils — hence the occasional use of the term 'pencilled ware' for hand-drawn linear decoration.

Photographic decoration Decoration based on photographic processes, first used by Wedgwood c.1878. (see: Photolithography.)

Printing The art of transferring engraved patterns to the ware by means of tissue paper and ceramic colour instead of printer's ink. Ceramic printing was invented by John Brooks, and developed independently by Sadler & Green* of Liverpool about 1757. Wedgwood bought the right to do his own printing in 1763, but for many years he continued to send cream coloured ware to Sadler & Green for printing (see: Lithography; Silk Screen Printing).

Throwing Process of making ware on the potter's wheel. A ball of soft clay is thrown on to the revolving wheel, centred, and worked into shape with the hands. All wares thus made have a circular section; oval or square section wares are slip cast*. The jigger*, the jolley*, and the lathe* are all developments of the potter's wheel.

Turning The process of shaping (or turning) on a horizontal lathe*. The ware in a leather-hard* or green hard state is placed on the 'chum', a hollow drum which holds it in place, the surface is then shaved as it turns with stationary tools (see: Engine-Turning Lathe; Lathe; Rose Engine-Turning).

Underglaze decoration Decoration which is painted or printed on biscuit ware before the glaze is applied. The most common colours are cobalt blue and the less popular manganese-purple, but many new underglaze colours were added in the 19th century (see: Underglaze Blue Prints).

Procession of Deities

A large bas-relief*, evidently modelled under the direction of Flaxman* and Webber* in Rome, after the *Puteal of the Twelve Gods,* formerly in the collection of Cardinal Albani and now in the Capitoline Museum. It appears on jasper*, basaltes* and *rosso antico** vases from c.1790.

Procession of Deities. *Pair of ovoid vases with double foliate handles in dark blue jasper dip, 15ins. high. The principal relief ornament,* Procession of Deities, *was modelled under the direction of Flaxman and Webber in Rome after the* Puteal of the Twelve Gods. *The necks of the vases are ornamented with musical trophies. c.1800.* Sotheby's.

Prodigal Son, The

A series of transfer prints made by William Greatbatch* illustrating the New Testament parable and set in 18th century England. The following are known:

The Prodigal Son receives his Patrimony (two versions).
The Prodigal Son taking his leave (two versions).
The Prodigal Son in Excess (with three prostitutes).
The Prodigal Son in Misery (feeding swine).
The Prodigal Son returns reclaim'd.
The Prodigal Son feasted on his return.

The prints are coloured with enamels and signed 'Greatbatch', or 'W. Greatbatch, Lane Delf, Staffordshire.' The engraver of these plates was undoubtedly Greatbatch, but after his bankruptcy of 1782, or his later bankruptcy of 1788, his plates may well have fallen into other hands. These prints are to be found on teapots or coffee pots made by Wedgwood or at Leeds, c.1780-90, probably bought by Greatbatch for the purpose. Some of the teapots may have been made by him. A complete set of these prints occurs on teapots in the Castle Museum, Norwich (Bulwer Collection, 100, 223, 447).

Prometheus

Son of Iapetus and Clymene, and brother of Atlas*. He is the great benefactor of men, stealing fire from heaven to give to them. He also taught them the useful arts. In retribution Zeus chained him to a rock on Mount Caucasus where, every day, an eagle came and fed on his liver, which regenerated itself during the night. Hercules* killed the eagle and released Prometheus.

Wedgwood subject:
The Fable of Prometheus, modelled by Pacetti*, c.1788.

Proportion

Classical architecture was based on a fairly rigid system of proportion which has survived in the works of Vitruvius, a Roman military engineer (1st century B.C.), who wrote the *Ten Books of Architecture* (now lost) based on Greek authorities. The same system was employed by Renaissance classical architects, and especially by the Palladians, who regarded the works of Vitruvius as a kind of Holy Writ. The system was still employed, with minor modifications, by such neo-classical architects as the Adam* Brothers, with the result that chimney pieces*, for instance, followed more or less the same proportional rules, whatever their size. For this reason Wedgwood's chimney piece tablets* were of standard proportions. During the Renaissance representation of the human figure was subject to these mathematically-based rules until the development of the Mannerist school after the middle of the 16th century, and a good deal of later classical sculpture, including Wedgwood's derivations from classical sources, still followed the proportional tradition. Vitruvius laid down that a man standing with his legs apart, and his arms raised and extended to form an X, should be contained within a circle of which the navel was the centre. The unit of measurement was the 'head', and the body was divided in halves at the pubic bone, and subdivided into 'heads'. For instance, two 'heads' were allowed from the pubic bone to the knee, and two from the knee to the sole of the foot. Certain special cases, like the muscular Hercules, were permissible exceptions to some of the rules.

Proprietors of Wedgwood

1759	Josiah Wedgwood I.
1766-89	Josiah I and Thomas Wedgwood* (one-eighth share for useful* wares only).
1769-80	Josiah I and Thomas Bentley* (equal shares for ornamental* wares only).
1790	Josiah I, his sons John* and Josiah II*, Thomas Wedgwood, and Thomas Byerley*.
1793	Josiah I, Josiah II and Thomas Byerley.
1795	Josiah II and Thomas Byerley (quarter share).
1800	Josiah II (half share), John (quarter share) and Thomas Byerley (quarter share).
1811	Josiah II.
1823	Josiah II and Josiah III*.
1827	Josiah II with his sons Josiah III and Francis*.
1841	Josiah III and Francis.
1842	Francis.
1843	Francis and John Boyle* (equal shares).
1845	Francis.
1846	Francis (60 per cent) and Robert Brown (40 per cent).
1850	Francis and Robert Brown (equal shares).
1859	Francis (80 per cent) with his son Godfrey* (20 per cent later increased to 25 per cent).
1863	Francis with his sons Godfrey and Clement Francis*.
1868	Francis with his sons Godfrey, Clement Francis and Lawrence*
1870	Godfrey with his brothers Clement Francis and Lawrence (equal shares).
1891	Lawrence, with his nephews Cecil* and Francis Hamilton*.
1895	Incorporation as Josiah Wedgwood & Sons Ltd.
1919-55	Overseas companies formed in America (Josiah Wedgwood & Sons Inc.) 1919; in Canada (Josiah Wedgwood & Sons, Canada, Ltd.) 1948; and in Australia (Josiah Wedgwood & Sons, Australia, Pty.) 1955.
1967	Registration as a Public Company, and the shares offered on the London Stock Exchange. Formation of the Wedgwood Group*.

Proserpine

Roman name for Persephone, the daughter of Zeus and Demeter. She was the wife of Hades (Pluto*), and Queen of the Underworld. With her husband, she ruled over the souls of the dead. A bas-relief* of *Proserpine* was modelled by De Vaere*, while he was in Rome in 1788. A larger bas-relief for a tablet, 9ins. by 26½ ins., *Pluto carrying off Proserpine, preceded by Hercules,* is attributed to Angelini*, though apparently without evidence. The title (sometimes altered to *The Rape of Persephone* or *The Procession of Persephone into the Underworld*) appears to have become confused at some stage since the procession is led by Mercury*.

See: Persephone Pattern.

Protât, Hugues (fl.1835-1871)

French sculptor, modeller, and designer who, during his sojourn in England, executed some of the stone carvings adorning the India Office, London, and worked for Jackson & Graham, makers of elaborately decorated furniture said to be in the style of "all the Louis's." Protât then went to Staffordshire and worked for Minton* as a modeller before going on to Wedgwood in 1858. His work for Wedgwood includes the Protât vase, a *jardinière,* and ornamental pieces. From 1843-50 he exhibited in the Paris Salon, and from 1850-64 he acted as Modelling Instructor at the Hanley and Stoke Schools of Design. He settled in London in 1864/5 but continued to design for Wedgwood until his return to France in about 1871.

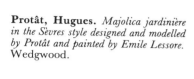

Protât, Hugues. *Majolica jardinière in the Sèvres style designed and modelled by Protât and painted by Emile Lessore.* Wedgwood.

Protât, Hugues. *The 'Protât ewer and stand' in black basaltes, the design based on Renaissance metalwork. A similar, but less heavily ornamented, ewer was also made in majolica and painted by Lessore. 22ins. high.* From an old photograph in the Wedgwood archives.

Prunus Blossom

Raised flowering sprigs of prunus and the tea plant were first used in England about 1690 by the Elers Brothers to decorate their red stoneware teapots, and then, in the 1750s, by the porcelain factories, especially Chelsea* and Bow*. They were copied from similar decoration on the *blanc de Chine* imported from Tê Hua (Fukien Province, China), and from the red teapots of Yi Hsing. Wedgwood refers to the Elers use of the tea branch ''in imitation of the Chinese method of ornamenting this ware'' in a letter to Bentley of July 1777. By the 1760s this kind of decoration was becoming unfashionable, but some rare objects of creamware are thus decorated. Although Josiah Wedgwood made little use of this pattern, it is more than probable that it was as responsible as silver for inspiring some of his embossed floral patterns of the 1760s. The prunus blossom was used at Etruria* during the period of popularity of Oriental patterns at the end of the 18th century and the early years of the 19th, although there are distinct divergences from the Tê Hua types.

Raised prunus blossom was again employed in 1977 as decoration of the newly-introduced primrose jasper*. A variety of shapes owing little to the Orient include a small square section vase — a shape dating back to the late 17th century, when it was copied from vases made at Arita (Hizen Province, Japan).

Psyche

Psyche is the personification of the human soul. She excited the jealousy of Aphrodite (Venus*) by her beauty. In revenge Cupid* was ordered to inspire her with love for the meanest of men, but fell in love with her himself. Unseen, and unknown, he visited her every night, but one of her sisters, curious about the mysterious lover, brought a light to see him asleep. A drop of hot oil fell on Cupid's shoulder and, waking, he fled. After many wanderings in search of him, Psyche was made immortal and was united with her lover.

Wedgwood subjects:

Cupid and Psyche, basaltes group on oval base, height 12ins.
Source unidentified. c.1820.

Prunus Blossom. *White prunus blossom ornaments on primrose jasper, introduced in 1977.* Wedgwood.

Below: **Punch Pot.** *Punch pot, transfer-printed with a hunting scene. Creamware, c.1775.* Buten Museum.

Marriage of Cupid and Psyche, see separate entry under this heading.

Psyche, figure, height 8ins., after the marble (1757) by Falconet*. This figure was reproduced in Sèvres* biscuit porcelain in 1758, and was supplied to Wedgwood, probably in the form of a cast (with the matching figure of Cupid), by Flaxman Senior*, in 1781.

Pug Dog

See: Trump.

Pug Mill

A cylindrical mill fitted with knives which ensures the homogeneity of plastic clay by slicing and compressing it, forcing it through a tapered outlet.

Punch Pot (Punch Kettle)

A large vessel resembling an outsize teapot in shape, but usually lacking the interior strainer at the base of the spout. Punch pots were used for brewing and serving hot punch (a blend of spirits, and milk or water, flavoured with oranges, lemons, sugar and spices). Some examples have bail handles* of the type associated with rum kettles*, but the latter are smaller in size and usually have beak-shaped pouring lips instead of curved spouts. Whieldon-Wedgwood* and Wedgwood punch pots were made in earthenware decorated with coloured glazes, in creamware (often decorated with Sadler & Green* transfer prints or enamelled flowers), *rosso antico** and black basaltes*.

Pye, John (1745-after 1775)

Engraver who worked for Sadler & Green* in Liverpool. A pupil of Thomas Major*, he engraved nine plates for the Wedgwood Queen's ware Catalogue of 1774, which he prepared and printed. Pye engraved landscapes for the print seller, Boydell*, and supplied views and drawings for the Frog* service.

Pyrometer

The word 'thermoscope' is often used as an alternative term for an instrument used for measuring those extremely high temperatures which are beyond the range of the ordinary mercury thermometer. Although modern conditions demand an ability to measure temperatures in excess of 3000°C, when Josiah Wedgwood began his career as an independent manufacturer the only way in which the kiln master could judge the temperature of a kiln was by observing the colour of the interior fire, which he did by withdrawing a small plug set in the kiln wall. Success or failure depended to a great extent on this man's skill and experience.

Naturally, someone with Josiah Wedgwood's logical mind and talent for experiment could not remain content with a state of affairs in which so much was left to chance, and he began by placing trial pieces in different parts of the kiln to observe the effect of variations in temperature arising from position inside the oven itself. These wares were marked 'GO', 'BO', and 'WO', meaning Gloss Oven, Biscuit Oven, and White Oven respectively. Of the three, the gloss (or glost) oven was used to fuse the glaze, the biscuit oven to fire ware to the biscuit or unglazed state, and the white oven for hard-fired stonewares or porcelain. Of these, the glost oven had the lowest temperature, and the white oven the highest. The letters 'B' or 'M' prefaced to the letters quoted meant bottom or middle of the oven. The letter 'T' referred to the top, and 'TT' to the highest point of all. The letters 'TBO', which have in the past been mistaken for the sign manual of Mr. Tebo*, actually meant 'Top of the biscuit oven'. These letters are normally seen only on trial pieces.

In 1780 Wedgwood experimented with a red burning clay by withdrawing trial pieces from the kiln at two-hourly intervals while the temperature was still rising, and the colour changes in these trials suggested to him the possibility of constructing a thermoscope which would enable clay cylinders of a standard composition to be matched against a set of cylinders fired at known temperatures and ranging in colour from buff (low temperature) to red (high temperature). This instrument has recently been reconstructed at Barlaston* and the temperature range found to be from 950° to 1250°C. In 1782 Sir Joseph Banks*, then President of the Royal Society*, advanced the objection that few people were very good at matching colours. Wedgwood then turned to the possibility of using the shrinkage of clay during firing as a method of temperature measurement. No doubt he had noticed that the cylinders of his thermoscope became uniformly smaller as the firing temperature increased.

His first sketch for his pyrometer (which he always referred to as a thermometer) was dated 1st January, 1782. This consisted of two straight-edged wooden rulers mounted on a baseboard. They were ½ in. apart at the top and ⅓ in. apart at the bottom. One of the rulers was marked with a graduated scale. He then prepared small clay cylinders which were ⅖ in. high and ½ in. in diameter. The clay cylinder was fired and allowed to cool, shrinking as it did so by an amount proportionate to the temperature to which it had been subjected. It was then placed between the rulers and pushed along until it would go no further, and the temperature at this point was read off the scale graduated in degrees Wedgwood, which ran from 0 to 240. This pyrometer soon became widely known, and since it was the first instrument to provide anything like an accurate estimate of temperature it was in great demand for many scientific purposes, apart from potters' kilns. Wedgwood started by having the pyrometers made in brass, but this was an expensive metal in the 18th century, and by the Autumn of 1783 he was experimenting with pyrometers made from stoneware and porcelain. From 1786 pyrometer sets were being made in buff stoneware, and boxed. Two gauges were provided, one reading from 0 to 120, and one from 120 to 240; 60° on the pyrometer scale being equivalent to 1100°C. A set presented to George III* for his collection of scientific instruments is now in the Science Museum, South Kensington. Additional clay cylinders were obtainable ready packed from the factory, and an instruction booklet, probably included with the boxed sets, was available from 1784. One thousand copies of a French translation were printed in 1785, and 500 copies in German in the following year.

Buller's rings are a development of Wedgwood's pyrometer which are in use today. After firing the ring is put into a brass gauge engraved with a temperature scale and fitted with a pointer. Temperature is judged by the amount of shrinkage.

Until recent times temperatures were commonly measured by cones invented by Seger at the Berlin porcelain factory. They are usually termed Seger cones in Europe, and a similar device in use in America is termed the Orton cone. Seger cones are in the form of a small three sided pyramid, and there are about sixty different compositions, ranging from low-temperature glaze material to pure alumina, with a temperature range of 500° to 2000°C. The attainment of the temperature for which a particular cone is designed is indicated by the tip of the pyramid, which softens and curves over. Usually three cones are set, the middle one indicating the desired temperature. The collapse of the first at a lower temperature allows time for the rise in temperature to be controlled, so that when the middle cone bends over, the third should remain untouched. They are observed by removing a small observation plug. In the modern tunnel kiln temperatures are maintained at the correct level by thermo-couples which adjust the gas or electricity supply as necessary. Thermo-couples generate an electric current which is proportional in strength to the heat of the kiln, and a number are provided along the length of the tunnel so that the temperature is everywhere maintained at optimum level.
See: Kilns.

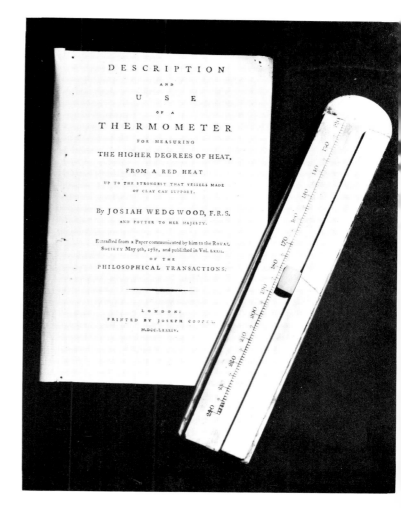

Pyrometer. *Wedgwood's pyrometer and title page of the instructions of 1784, printed by Joseph Cooper.* Wedgwood.

Queen's Shape

A Wedgwood tableware shape with a hexafoil lobed rim. The name refers to Queen Charlotte*, for whom the original dinner service of this shape was made.

Queen's Shape. *Dinner plate, Queen's shape, Queen's ware. Modern.* Wedgwood.

Queen's Vase, The

Bone china vase with heraldic figures of the 'Queen's Beasts' co-operatively made to commemorate the Coronation of Queen Elizabeth II, and presented to her by the British Pottery Manufacturers' Federation. The decoration and moulding of this vase were shared by Wedgwood, Worcester*, Minton*, Derby*, and Copeland*. A replica of the vase was sent to each Commonwealth country.

Queen's Ware

Cream-coloured ware*, or creamware, was renamed Queen's ware by Wedgwood after it had received the patronage of Queen Charlotte* in 1765. Wedgwood also referred to it as 'Ivory' ware, but the term does not seem to have come into general use. Wedgwood creamware, and coloured bodies* are still known as Queen's ware, and the name has come to be used, erroneously, as a generic term for creamware of other factories.

Quintal Flower Horn

See: Finger Vase.

Quirk, William (fl.1769-1774)

Painter at the Chelsea Decorating Studio* who worked on the Frog* service.

Queen's Shape. *A very early example of the Queen's shape decorated with a mottled glaze in the Whieldon-Wedgwood manner, c.1762.* Wedgwood.

Quiver Vase

Jasper vase, 6¾ins. high, in the shape of a quiver, the feathered arrow shafts protruding from the top. The four sides are ornamented with panels of horizontal fluting. These vases were made in two- and three-colour jasper c.1790. A pair in the Beeson* Collection is complete with swan-finial lids. A similar but not identical shape, 6ins. high, was made in Queen's ware and decorated in panels with figures of children by Emile Lessore*, 1869-71.

Quiver Vase. *Jasper vase in the form of a quiver, the arrow flights projecting above the rim. 6½ins. high.* Wedgwood.

Radix Amethyst

Josiah Wedgwood's name for a mineral with which he experimented during his researches which culminated in the discovery of jasper*. It was not generally known by this name, but there is little doubt that he meant what was usually termed 'Blue John' or 'Derbyshire Spar', a fluorspar with dark purple veinings which Boulton* used for making vases mounted in ormolu*. 'Blue John' is found only at Treak Cliff, near Castleton, Derbyshire, and deposits are now almost exhausted.

Radix Jasperini

Cawk* or barium sulphate* (No. 74 in Wedgwood's code), the principal ingredient of jasper*. 'Radix jasperini' was a code word employed by Wedgwood in his letters to Bentley* (e.g. 15th December, 1777).

See: Spies, Industrial; Spath.

Raphael (Rafaëlle) Ware

Raffaello Sanzio da Urbino (1483-1520), the great Renaissance painter, employed motifs decorating the then newly-discovered Golden House of Nero to ornament the walls of the *loggie* of the Vatican. These motifs, now known as grotesques*, became popular with the painters of *maiolica*, especially those of Urbino, where Raphael's paintings were also copied with the aid of engravings by Marcantonio Raimondi. For this reason Urbino *maiolica* became widely and inaccurately known as Raffaelle ware, and he was believed to have painted some of it himself. In England it seems probable that certain types of Italian *maiolica*, notably that decorated with grotesques and *istoriato* painting, were known as 'Raphael ware' whatever the factory of origin, and this term lingered well into the 19th century. In November 1768, Wedgwood wrote from London to Bentley* in Staffordshire: "Do you remember what Harrach [Thomas Harrache*] asked for the Raphael bottles? I think it was 10 guineas. They now want twenty-five." An Urbino vase of c.1590 in what was called, in England, the Raphaelesque style — ovoid in shape, with masks at the base of handles in the form of serpents — was popular. Wedgwood used the basic form in the 18th century, and the vase itself, with grotesque painting similar to that which appeared on the late 16th century original, was much reproduced in the 19th century by several factories. In the 1860s, 'Raphaelesque porcelain', an ivory-toned body sometimes decorated with coloured reliefs in the style of 18th century Doccia, was made by Worcester*.

Rattlesnake Seal

Basaltes seal by Wedgwood and Bentley showing a coiled rattlesnake. It bears the motto 'Don't tread on me.' Made in 1777, and adapted from the first American flag, it was distributed privately to friends of the American cause who supported the colonists in the War of Independence.

Ravilious, Eric, ARCA (1903-1942)

Artist, designer and book illustrator. Studied at Eastbourne and Brighton Schools of Art, and the Royal College of Art, where his tutor was Paul Nash. As an artist in watercolour (he described oils as 'like toothpaste'), his work shows splendid draughtsmanship in a distinctive linear style, a sure sense of design, and a dry use of colour that gives full value to the texture and light provided by the paper. As a book illustrator, Eric Ravilious worked for the Golden Cockerel Press, the Cresset Press, and the Golden Hours Press. His engravings were of outstanding quality, and their simplicity and wit is reminiscent of the work of Bewick*.

Designs commissioned by Wedgwood include the *Garden Implements* design on a 'Liverpool' jug (1938), the children's *Alphabet* set (1937), *Garden* pattern (printed tableware enamelled in yellow or green, 1937), *Persephone* pattern (printed tableware enamelled in yellow, green, or blue, 1938), the *Boat Race* goblet and bowl (1938), and *Travel* pattern (printed in black, with turquoise enamel), which was not produced until after his death. Ravilious also designed the Coronation mugs for Edward VIII (never issued) and George VI (1937), and his design was re-issued in different colours for the Coronation of Elizabeth II in 1953. In the same year the border of the *Persephone* pattern was chosen as a gold print on bone china with the Royal Arms as the centre decoration, for the Foreign Secretary's Coronation banquet service. Ravilious' last design for Wedgwood was the mug commemorating the firm's removal to Barlaston* (1940).

In 1941, Eric Ravilious was appointed an official war artist. He was killed a year later while taking part in an air-sea rescue off the coast of Iceland.

Ravilious, Eric. *Part of a Travel pattern tea service printed in black and onglaze turquoise enamel.* Wedgwood.

Ravilious, Eric. *Coronation mug by Eric Ravilious designed for the Coronation of Edward VIII in 1937 and adapted, in different colours, for the Coronation of George VI and, in 1953, for Queen Elizabeth II.* Wedgwood.

Ravilious, Eric. *Persephone pattern, designed for Queen's ware by Eric Ravilious in 1938, and reproduced as a gold print on bone china (the Royal Arms replacing the centre design) for the Foreign Secretary's Coronation banquet service in 1953.* Wedgwood.

Red China (Red Porcelain)

Fine red stoneware usually imitating that of Yi-Hsing which, in the 17th century, was especially popular for teapots. It was made in Germany at Meissen* by J.F. Böttger, in Holland by Arij de Milde, and in Staffordshire by the Elers* Brothers, who had originally come from the Cologne region, home of German stonewares. The Elers made red stoneware into the early years of the 18th century, and it continued to be produced as a more or less standard ware by various manufacturers, and especially by Wedgwood, who refined it still further and termed it *rosso antico*. It was never very popular with him (he referred, in a letter to Bentley in 1776, to "the extreme vulgarity of red wares"). The firm, however, continued to make it after his death until well into the 19th century.

Red Figure Style

The decorative style of Greek Pottery, c.530-400B.C., the distinctive feature of which is red figures and ornaments reserved on a black ground. The black is a kind of slip mixed with wine lees or urine to promote an even flow over the surface. The type was imitated more or less contemporarily in Southern Italy, although the style of decoration differs to a sufficiently marked degree to make it fairly easy to separate Italian from Greek work. The style also inspired Wedgwood's black basaltes* ware painted with encaustic* enamels.

Red Stoneware

See: Rosso Antico.

Reda Von Redern, Baron (1719-1789) Sigismund Ehrenreich

Born in Brandenburg, director of the Berlin Academy of Sciences and a Curator of Berlin University. He retired to France, receiving letters of naturalisation from Louis XV in 1769. He studied physics and chemistry, and visited England in 1782, when he accompanied Josiah Wedgwood to Cornwall in search of china clay, and pottery materials generally. A

jasper portrait medallion* is listed in the 1788 Ornamental Catalogue. The name appears below the truncation.

Reda Von Redern, Baron Sigismund Ehrenreich. *Jasper portrait medallion of the Baron Sigismund Ehrenreich Reda von Redern (1719-89), chemist and physicist, who accompanied Josiah I on his Cornish journey. c.1787.* Mrs. Stanley B. Rose Collection.

Reducing Kiln

A kiln the atmosphere of which is heavily charged with carbon monoxide instead of oxygen. It is employed for firing wares coloured with metallic oxides* which yield different colours according to the prevailing kiln atmosphere. For instance, copper oxide used as a glaze colouring will, in the presence of oxygen, yield a variable colour from bluish-green to turquoise according to the constituents of the glaze itself, and in the presence of carbon monoxide it will give crimson-purple or bluish-red.

Reeding

Also called ribbing. Moulded or turned relief ornament in the form of parallel convex reeds. The converse of fluting.

Refrigerator

See: Glacier.

Regency Style

The English version of the French Empire style. It is a continuation of the neo-classical* style, and is generally accepted as extending from 1805-37, although the Regency itself lasted from 1810-20. The vocabulary of neo-classical ornament continued to be used, with the addition of Egyptian motifs (see: Egyptian Taste) resulting from interest in Napoleon's Egyptian campaign and renewed interest in Egyptian archaeology. Marine motifs, anchors, twisted rope, etc., were inspired by Nelson's naval victories. Egyptian motifs, such as the canopic jar and the sphinx* employed during the lifetime of the first Josiah, were derived from illustrations to Montfaucon's* *Antiquité Expliqué* and similar works included in Josiah's library.

Registry Mark

A Patent Office mark on British manufactured goods using registered designs. The scheme started in 1842 and was discontinued in 1883, when its place was taken by a system of registered numbers. The mark shows the year, day, and month of manufacture, and places the object in one of several categories.

See: Appendix III.

Repairers (Repairing)

Those skilled in the art of making figures, and certain vases, candlesticks, lamps, etc., from moulded components. The original model was made of clay or wax, and this was dissected by the moulder into convenient parts. Each part was moulded and cast separately and luted together with slip by a workman known as a repairer, who rebuilt the original model from the moulded parts. Those features of the model which might sag under their own weight during firing, such as arms unsupported at one end, were propped with clay strips dusted with a refractory powder (alumina is used today) to prevent adhesion to the model while lending support.

The design of a figure is very important if it is to be successfully produced in quantity. The designer has to bear in mind the necessity for adapting his figure so that it can be moulded in the fewest possible number of pieces, and to see that, wherever possible, supports are incorporated into the design so that temporary supports are not required during firing. For this reason many figures either have drapery from the waist downwards, or are leaning against a tree trunk. Parts which are unduly thick, and might for this reason lead to fire-cracks*, also have to be avoided. If Wedgwood's figures of Voltaire* and Rousseau* are examined it will be seen that if they had been posed on their legs alone there would have been considerable danger of the legs bending or collapsing during firing, so Voltaire was given a long cloak and Rousseau a short tree trunk. A figure of Jupiter* has one hand attached to his head and the other to his body, thus supporting both arms, and his legs are supported to the ankles. In the case of candle-holders, we find the figures closely clasping the shaft on which the candleholder rests. Good designing makes repairing easier, and ensures the minimum of kiln wastage.

Slight variations in the pose of figures can arise during the repairing process, but in more recent times they have been kept to a minimum by rigid adherence to a standard, to which the repairer works, and a system of inspection of the finished product. Variations due to this cause are more likely to occur in 18th century wares.

Wedgwood demanded very high quality in figure-work not only because it was the policy of the firm, but because his figures were unglazed. Jasper and the white body are strictly analogous to the biscuit porcelain of Derby*, a contemporary factory specialising in porcelain biscuit figures, whose price list survives. There, only perfect figures were sold in biscuit form. Those with minor imperfections were glazed and painted to disguise them, and sold more cheaply than the biscuit versions. This is sufficient proof of the market requirements which were being supplied both by Wedgwood and Derby.

See: Mr. Tebo.

Resist Lustre

An overglaze decorative process ordinarily used in conjunction with 'silver' (platinum) lustre.

Designs are painted or printed on ware by using 'resist' material, such as china clay mixed with honey or treacle, wax, varnish, or even paper stencils. The lustre, a metallic oxide suspended in an oily medium, is brushed over the surface of the ware, which is then fired. The lustre, of course, does not adhere to the parts treated with the 'resist' material, which burns away in the kiln leaving behind its simulacrum in the colour of the body or the underlying glaze — usually white, but sometimes yellow, the remainder of the glaze being covered with lustre.

See: Lustre Decoration.

Revere, Paul (1735-1818)

American silversmith of Huguenot descent who worked at Boston and took part in the Boston Tea Party in 1773. In 1775 he rode from Charleston to Lexington, rousing the Minute Men on the way, and in so doing became the hero of Longfellow's poem — *The Midnight Ride of Paul Revere.* Two Wedgwood bowls are based on engravings of his silverwork — the *Boston Bowl* designed by Alan Price*, and the Harvard Old Buildings bowl (see: American Independence Series).

Reynolds, Sir Joshua (1723-1792)

Founder member of the Royal Academy (1768) and first President. He was also one of the earliest members of the Incorporated Society of Artists. Reynolds was born near Plymouth, came to London to study in 1740, and was in Rome from 1749-52, where he studied Raphael and Michelangelo. Returning to London in 1752 he rapidly achieved a high reputation, especially as a portrait painter. He was knighted in 1769, and became painter to the King in 1784. He ceased to paint in 1789 when his sight became affected, and died two years later. His distinguished portrait of Josiah Wedgwood*, painted in 1782, was engraved in mezzotint by John Taylor Wedgwood* and Samuel W. Reynolds in 1841. The portrait of Mrs. Wedgwood* was painted in 1783. Reynolds and Wedgwood were friends. Reynolds introduced the modeller Henry Webber* to him, and gave a testimonial to the quality of Wedgwood's copy of the Portland* vase in 1791. Subjects inspired by Reynolds are listed hereunder:

Edward Gibbon, portrait medallion. Probably modelled by Hackwood after the Reynolds portrait of 1779, or the engraving by B. Reading in the *European Magazine* of 1st April, 1788.

The Infant Academy, modelled by Hackwood after a painting, 1787.

The Infant Hercules slaying a Serpent, after a painting.

Music Lesson, after a painting (pair to *Infant Academy*).

Venus chiding Cupid, after a painting.

Sir Joshua Reynolds, portrait medallion c.1787 attributed to Flaxman.

The engraved portrait of Josiah Wedgwood printed on the Bicentenary jug and plate of 1930 were based on the Joshua Reynolds portrait.

Reynolds, Sir Joshua. *Jasper portrait medallion of Sir Joshua Reynolds, PRA, attributed to Flaxman, c.1787.* Nottingham Castle Museum.

Rhead, Frederick A. (1856-1929)

Ceramic designer and craftsman. After studying at the Newcastle School of Art he joined Minton*, where he was apprenticed to M.L. Solon. Rhead moved to Wedgwood in 1877, and a *pâte-sur-pâte** vase made by him was shown in the Wedgwood exhibit at the Paris Exposition in the following year. He was later Art Director at Brownfields (for whom he produced the 'Gladstone Vase' in 1888), and Wood & Sons, Burslem. His work for Wedgwood included a platter with sgraffito* decoration, signed and dated 'Wedgwood's '78' (Buten Museum*), a Majolica* pilgrim bottle 11½ ins. high, and a Majolica charger or platter, diameter 14½ ins., with slip* decoration, the reverse incised 'F. Rhead Wedgwood's '78.'

Rhead was co-author with his brother, G. Woolliscroft Rhead, of *Staffordshire Pots and Potters,* 1906.

Rhodes, David (d.1777)

Independent enameller and partner in the firm of Robinson & Rhodes of Leeds. Between 1760 and 1766 Wedgwood obtained copper scales, the colouring material for his Green Glaze*, from Robinson & Rhodes, and he also sold cream-coloured ware to them for enamelling. This led to the imitation of some of Wedgwood's wares in Yorkshire, of which the production of cauliflower ware at Leeds* is an example. In 1763 Jasper Robinson retired from the partnership which then became D. Rhodes & Co., but he continued to work for the firm until Rhodes left for London five years later. In 1768 Rhodes became Wedgwood's tenant in the new premises at Newport Street, and until his death nine years later he appears to have worked exclusively for Wedgwood. During 1769-70 he was in partnership with William Hopkins Craft*. Rhodes was Wedgwood's principal enameller at Newport Street and the Chelsea Decorating Studio*. In 1768 Josiah described Rhodes as ''A Master Enameller and China piercer (perhaps an indication that Rhodes was responsible for some pierced or reticulated wares at Leeds)...who is sober and steady...he paints flowers and landskips very prettily, prepares a pretty good powder gold, and has a tolerable notion of Colours.'' Records in the Wedgwood archives show that he also painted figures, tableware borders, Etruscan* vases, and the veining (marbling) of creamware vases.

During the years immediately following 1768, Wedgwood and Leeds shared certain types of enamel decoration which are particularly associated with Rhodes, for example the figure and landscape painting in black and iron-red, and a distinctive mixture of stripes, chevrons and other motifs known as 'Chintz'. The palette used by Rhodes includes red, black, blue, green, yellow and rose-pink. Rhodes painted the First Day's Vases*, possibly in association with Craft, and was responsible for the master decoration of the Frog* service, but he is most widely known for his teapots. He is also recorded as having painted some 'Hopped' (hooped) garden pots.

Rhyton
See: Stirrup Cup.

Ribbon and Leaf Border
Neo-classical border pattern consisting of a continuous twisting ribbon with a leaf in each curve.

Ricardo, Halsey
See: Dysart Green.

Ridgehouse Estate
See: Etruria.

Riding, Jessie M. (fl.1919)
Modeller who executed a portrait medallion* of Georges Clemenceau (signed on the truncation) in 1919. A specimen in the Buten Museum* is white on green jasper dip with a narrow integral black frame.

Rischgitz, Edouard (1828-1909)
Porcelain painter of French origin employed by Minton*, c.1864-70. His figure subjects and landscapes appear on both porcelain and earthenware, and his style is often remarkably similar to that of Lessore*, although his subjects usually differ.

Roberts, Ann (fl.1769-1774)
Painter at the Chelsea Decorating Studio* who worked on the border decoration of the Frog* service.

Roberts, Grace (fl.1769-1774)
Painter at the Chelsea Decorating Studio* who worked on the borders of the Frog* service.

Roberts, John (fl.1769-1774)

Painter at the Chelsea Decorating Studio* who worked on the Frog* service.

Robinson, Jasper (fl.1750-1765)

Partner, until 1763, in the independent enamelling firm of Robinson & Rhodes of Leeds, which continued until 1768 as D. Rhodes & Co.

See: David Rhodes.

Robinson, John (fl.1793-1819)

Engraver, printer and print seller of London, who supplied Wedgwood with engravings of the on-glaze red-printed *Water Lily** pattern in 1807, the underglaze blue-printed *Water Lily* with cut reed border in 1809, and a large part of the *Corinth* pattern in 1811.

See: Underglaze Blue Prints.

Rockingham Ware

Ware made in England and America (Bennington Ware), and particularly popular in the latter country. It is distinguished by a thick, lustrous, often treacly brown glaze, the colour of which was due principally to manganese*. It was originally developed at the Rockingham factory, Swinton, Yorkshire c.1796. Wedgwood used it to a limited extent from 1865 to 1940 over creamware. It was employed for teapots, and minor ornamental wares, occasionally with acid-etched and wheel-engraved decoration by John Northwood*. The Wedgwood mark is sometimes accompanied by the word 'ROCKINGHAM' impressed.

The practice of engraving ornament through a dark brown glaze to a light-coloured body beneath was started early in the 18th century by Continental glass engravers who used Chinese porcelain of this kind. This was known as 'Batavian' ware from the port of transhipment.

Rococo Style, The

The mainstream of European art is classical*, which is also to say that for the most part it adheres strictly to a system of symmetry and proportion* that altered remarkably little in two thousand years. There was, however, an interregnum provided by the Gothic style, beginning at the end of the 12th century, which had its roots in the architecture of Islam, and another is to be found in the short-lived rococo style which begins to be apparent at the end of the 17th century, and for most practical purposes can be regarded as over before the accession of Louis XVI in 1774. This, too, owed much of its original inspiration to the Orient, but in this instance to Japan and China. The Gothic style manifested itself mainly in architecture; the rococo style in the decorative arts, and especially porcelain and silver. Both Gothic and rococo abandoned the strict principle of symmetry, and it is not entirely unrelated that a revival of the Gothic style took place around 1750, when rococo was at its most fashionable. The rococo style was followed by the neo-classical*, sometimes known as the Adam* style in England and the Louis Seize style in France.

The impact of rococo in England was not so great as it was on the Continent. It is chiefly to be seen in the furniture of Chippendale, the silver of those of Huguenot descent, or more recent arrivals, like Paul de Lamerie or Nicolas Sprimont (the latter one of the founders of the Chelsea Porcelain Factory*), and in the work of the early porcelain factories generally.

It is often said that Wedgwood did not work in the rococo style, but this is a misapprehension. His early wares are definitely rococo, and he adopted the neo-classical style very slowly in the years between 1760 and 1769, for the most part

Rockingham Ware. *Jug covered with a Rockingham brown glaze with a design of parrots wheel-engraved through it. c.1877.* Wedgwood.

under the influence of that convinced classicist, Thomas Bentley*. After Bentley entered into partnership with Wedgwood we find fewer traces of rococo remaining, apart from one or two vase shapes which were copied from Sèvres*, the greatest European exponent of the rococo style in porcelain, as Wedgwood was to become the leading manufacturer in the neo-classical style (see: J. Morgan).

Wedgwood's rococo works include those early examples with crabstock* handles and spouts, and those with rococo silver-pattern handles. *Chinoiseries* in relief under green and yellow glazes; cauliflower and pineapple ware; salt-glazed* wares with fruit and flowers in relief; landscapes in relief; cornucopiae* (flower holders with the tip twisted to one side in typical rococo style) in earthenware covered with coloured glazes, and in salt glaze; unglazed red stoneware imitating the stoneware of Yi-Hsing; creamware enamelled with rococo subjects, including the red and black scale ground; twisted double strap handles starting or terminating in moulded leaves; floral knops twisted to one side; and shell-shaped dishes, are all rococo concepts. The Fitzwilliam Museum, Cambridge (Glaisher Collection) has a circular moulded tureen covered with green, yellow and purple glazes which has what seems to be a fish finial to the cover similar to one employed on French faience tureens. In the same Museum there is a four-sided dish with cruciform rococo surface

Rococo Style. *Coffee pot, 8¾ ins. high, with shell moulding (sometimes described as rocaille) round the body, spout, neck and rim of domed cover, entwined strap handle and flower knop. The details of the moulding are picked out in turquoise enamel, and there are traces of original gilding. A late example of Wedgwood rococo, c.1777, illustrating Josiah's slow conversion to neo-classicism. Sotheby's.*

moulding covered with green, blue, and purple-brown glazes. Both of these belong to the 1760-65 period. W.B. Honey (*Wedgwood Ware*) refers to a painted pattern of shells and fishes which has considerable affinities with Marseilles *faience,* and in the Wedgwood Museum* there is a vase decorated with coloured glazes, marked Wedgwood & Bentley, based on a Sèvres vase which is essentially rococo. Transfer prints of exotic birds are not very distantly derived from Sèvres bird painting in the rococo style by Evans and Aloncle.

During the 19th century in spite of the eclecticism of the time, the revival of rococo in the 1830s, and the application of revived Gothic to pottery design by A.W.N. Pugin and others, Wedgwood remained remarkably faithful to the neo-classical style. Even during the Dark Ages of the Great Exhibition of 1851 the classical style did not entirely disappear, and Wedgwood developed a contemporary version as individual in its own way as that of their 18th century predecessors. In the case of some of the more ornate wares of the 1860s the style might well be termed neo-baroque, but hardly rococo, a particular example being the ewer designed by Hugues Protât* and painted by Emile Lessore*, which is remarkable for scrolling acanthus, a female figure seated precariously on the shoulder, and an infant clutching the foliate entwined handles. This is obviously based on 17th century metalwork, and Protât probably took it from a design book of the period, of which there were many in existence. In the 20th century the factory continues to develop its own individual style which is soundly based on tradition inherited from the 18th century.

Roman Procession

Also known as *Procession of Senators,* this important basaltes tablet was modelled either by Pacetti* or by Dalmazzoni*, c.1787, after part of the relief decoration on the monument celebrating the victories of Augustus in Spain and Gaul. This monument was, however, fragmented and incomplete, and the figures were augmented and restored by the modeller, two of the additional figures being either copied from the earlier tablet, *Death of a Roman Warrior*,* or reproduced from the same source. *A Roman Procession* is listed in the French edition of the Catalogue, 1788, but not in the last English edition published in the previous year.

Romantic Style

The word 'romantic' is very loosely used to denote a large number of vague concepts which vary from one writer to another, and it is not, therefore, easy to define.

The mainstream of European art is termed 'classical', and it has its roots in the distant past. Developed by the Greeks, it was the style of Etruscan and Roman art. Classical art and architecture were governed by fairly strict rules of mathematical proportion developed by the Greeks, and given concrete form by Vitruvius in the *Ten Books of Architecture,* written during the reign of Augustus* and largely based on Greek sources. The first published edition appeared in Rome about 1490. It strongly influenced the work of Palladio, and such English architects as Inigo Jones, the Earl of Burlington, and Sir William Chambers*. Leonardo da Vinci and Albrecht Dürer both took up the problem of applying rules of proportion to the human figure, and Renaissance and neo-classical* sculpture usually observes these rules (see: Attributes).

Departures from these rules occurred at a comparatively early date, for instance in the case of Hellenistic art of the 2nd century B.C., and art of this kind may be regarded as romantic. Also romantic is Gothic art of the 12th century onwards. Decorative art based on Chinese and Japanese sources, and the rococo* of the 18th century, may also be regarded as romantic, and romantic tendencies occur during the neo-classical period, both in the 18th and 19th centuries. It may be seen in Wedgwood decoration, especially in the work of Lady Templetown*, and the other ladies who designed for him, in which there is a well marked sentimental flavour. The most important influence on the Romantic School of the 18th century was undoubtedly Goethe's novel, *The Sorrows of Werther,* from which Wedgwood produced the relief of *Charlotte Mourning at the tomb of Werther** — a very popular piece of neo-classical sentimentality.

Romantic art, therefore, is art which is concerned with the expression of emotion ungoverned by rules, to which may be added a love of the exotic. It was at its height during the early decades of the 19th century, but it survives today, usually in films and television shows made for mass-consumption, and in cheap literature intended to appeal to the emotionally immature. It often exhibits a very marked sentimentality, as distinct from sentiment, the former a vice to which much 19th century art was prone, but which Wedgwood was notable for being able, for the most part, to avoid.

Rome

Rome in the 18th century was not only the most important staging post on the Grand Tour, but also a place of pilgrimage for artists, and especially for sculptors. Despite the attention paid to Pompeii* and Herculaneum*, the importance of Rome to the neo-classical* artist and designer was undiminished. It is not surprising, therefore, that Wedgwood, following Matthew Boulton* before him, should employ a number of artists in

Rome under the general direction of John Flaxman* and Henry Webber*. Their work was either adapted on the spot to the needs of the factory by Flaxman or Webber, or sent to Etruria* to be worked on by Hackwood* and the factory modellers. Apart from De Vaere*, several Italian modellers were employed — Dalmazzoni*, Pacetti*, Angelini*, Manzolini*, Fratoddi*, Mangiarotti*, and Cades* — and they were principally engaged in making copies, adaptations, and reductions of the work of classical and Renaissance sculptors. De Vaere sent models "after the antique" to Etruria, but Wedgwood complained of the nakedness of the figures, pointing out the considerable additional cost of clothing them before they could be used. Scarcely any record exists of the work of the Italian modellers, and attributions are, for the most part, conjectural. A good deal of damage was sustained in transit, which necessitated repairs at the factory, and increased the cost of these models. It is difficult to avoid the conclusion that Wedgwood maintained these modellers largely for prestige reasons, since it does not seem to have been very profitable. After the return of Flaxman and Webber to England affairs in Rome were looked after by an English resident named Jenkins.

Root Dish
An early term for a covered vegetable dish or tureen.

Root Pot
A pot or vase, often with a flat back and a semi-circular front, and the top pierced with holes for cut flowers or for planting bulbs. Root pots were a popular product at Etruria*, and a type of bulb holder of this kind was made in the form of a hedgehog*. Root pots were termed bough pots at the porcelain factories, and Wedgwood also used this description for vases with pierced flower-holders inserted into the top.

Rose Engine-Turning
Curved, symmetrically-disposed, repetitive ornament of a geometric kind incised into the body of some stonewares with the aid of the engine-turning* lathe by using a guide tool known as a rosette*.

Rosette
1. A stylised rose with the petals equally disposed on a circular plan, sometimes with leaves in addition.
2. A special tool which, when fitted to the engine-turning lathe*, enables curved patterns to be cut.

Rosso Antico
Literally, antique red: an unglazed red stoneware commonly produced in Staffordshire, and originally made in a refined version by the Brothers Elers* at Bradwell Wood at the end of the 17th century, and the beginning of the 18th, when they used the red clay of the district mainly for teapots in the style of the red stoneware wine pots of Yi-Hsing. Wares of this kind, including (it is said) those manufactured by Wedgwood, occasionally bear a pseudo-Chinese seal mark impressed into the base, but this cannot be accepted as evidence of origin, and certainly very few such specimens were made by the Elers. John Astbury and Joshua Twyford were among other potters producing similar wares. In 1729 Samuel Bell of Newcastle-under-Lyme was granted a patent for a refined red stoneware containing calcined flint and capable of taking a polish. This 'red china' was decorated with sprigged* relief ornament.

For the most part Wedgwood used the red body for making ordinary objects — teapots, jugs, bowls, flower pots, etc., and later for some simple classical shapes ornamented with applied reliefs in black or white, or with some quite elaborate engine-turning. Early specimens of this kind, however, are rare, and *rosso antico* does not become at all common until about 1805.

Wedgwood wrote to Bentley* in July, 1777, discussing the matter of Paul Elers, son of John Philip Elers, who was, at that time, plaguing Wedgwood with letters seeking favours of one kind or another: "The...improvement introduced by Mr. [John Philip] E[lers] was the refining of our common red clay by sifting, and making it into Tea and Coffee ware in imitation of the Chinese Red Porcelaine [i.e. the red stoneware of Yi-Hsing, also imitated in Holland and at Meissen*] by casting it in Plaister [sic] moulds, and turning it upon the outside on Lathes*, and ornamenting it with the Tea branch in relief, in

Root Pot. *Creamware with surface agate decoration. 8¾ ins. high.* Wedgwood.

Root Pot. *Black basaltes stepped root pot with serpentine front and feet of acanthus scrolls based on ormolu. Integrally cast panels of cupids in low relief.* Dwight and Lucille Beeson Collection.

Rosso Antico. *Rosso antico parapet teapot with applied floral ornament and rustic handle and spout. c.1810.* Wedgwood.

Rosso Antico. *Bough pot, 7½ ins. high, of rosso antico, the lower part of the body of simulated basket work, ornamented with black reliefs. c.1783.* Wedgwood.

Rosso Antico. *Inkwell in rosso antico decorated with Egyptian motifs in black.* Wedgwood.

imitation of the Chinese manner of ornamenting this ware.'' To Wedgwood has been attributed an early red ware teapot (before 1764) the body shaped like the section of a tree trunk, the handle of crabstock* type, the straight spout copied from contemporary silver, and decorated with prunus blossom in relief. The treatment is very close to that of a Japanese porcelain teapot made at Arita about fifty years earlier, and the prunus blossom also occurs on the white porcelain of Tê Hua, as well as on the red ware of Yi-Hsing. Prunus sprays in particular were copied by the English porcelain factories in the 1750s, although the tea plant was occasionally substituted at Chelsea. Engine-turned red ware, unmarked as most of these early wares are, belongs to the period after 1763, and was made by Wedgwood. Fluting, reeding, dicing, and basket work are all examples of engine turning.

Writing to Bentley in January, 1776, Wedgwood gave his thoughts on the subject of red ware: ''You recommend red clay for Cabinet heads. My objection to it is the extreme vulgarity of red wares. If it had never been made in T. pots and the commonest wares my objections would not have existed.''

Bentley apparently insisted, and *rosso antico* was born. No doubt the partners were looking at the question from two distinct viewpoints — Wedgwood from that of the Staffordshire

potter accustomed to red ware as a staple of the industry, Bentley as a man well acquainted with collections of classical pottery, who had seen specimens of Roman red ware (the *terra Sigillata* or Samian ware). There is little doubt that Bentley was responsible for this innovation, for we find in a letter of 10th March, 1776: ''I will try to imitate the Antico Rosso from your description, but when I have done my best I am afraid where one spectator thinks of Antico Rosso an hundred will be put in mind of a Red teapot.''

The red body, however, was produced in 1776 under this name in colours varying from red to a deep chocolate according to firing conditions. Wares were made in greater variety than Wedgwood perhaps anticipated. The jasper technique was sometimes employed, *rosso antico* reliefs being used on a basaltes background, or black reliefs on a *rosso antico* ground. Nevertheless, the first Josiah made comparatively small use of this body, and it was a great deal more popular with Josiah II*, when effective use was also made of white on a red ground, and, very occasionally, red reliefs on cane ware. Much of the red ware with black reliefs in the Egyptian taste* belongs to the early years of the 19th century, inspired by Napoleon's Egyptian Campaign of 1798 and Nelson's victory at Aboukir Bay. Napoleon's invasion was also cultural, as well as military and political, and the real inspiration for Egyptian ornament came from one of his entourage, the Baron Vivant Denon, who accompanied the expedition and wrote a book entitled *A Journey to Upper and Lower Egypt* which was published in 1802. The illustrations were taken from drawings made on the spot, often at great personal hazard. After 1802 ornament of this kind tends to be a good deal more accurately rendered than earlier examples in the Egyptian taste which had been taken from sources such as Montfaucon*.

Later wares in *rosso antico* tended to deteriorate in quality. Terracotta*, an orange-red ware similar in its nature to *rosso antico,* belongs to the period beginning in 1805, and specimens decorated with flowers in opaque enamel colours in the style of the Chinese *famille rose** are not infrequent. Similar painting was done on black basaltes* ware.

Roubiliac, Louis-François (1695-1762)

French sculptor, born at Lyon, who became a pupil of Balthasar Permoser's at Dresden. He was later employed as assistant to Nicolas Coustou, and came to England in 1732, where he was fortunate enough to attract the attention of Edward Walpole (brother of Horace), who introduced him to Sir Henry Cheere, a well-known sculptor and brother to John Cheere*. Roubiliac's first independent commission was a statue of Handel (terracotta in the Fitzwilliam Museum, Cambridge). He settled in St. Martin's Lane, London, in 1737, and it has been suggested that he provided models for the Chelsea Porcelain Factory*, although this is uncertain. Certainly he was godfather to the daughter, Sophie, of the proprietor, Nicolas Sprimont, and one of his minor works, a terracotta of Hogarth's pug-dog Trump*, was made in porcelain about 1750. Roubiliac died in 1762.

Among the Wedgwood subjects which are regarded as originating with Roubiliac may be numbered the model of Trump in black basaltes, and the portrait medallion of Newton modelled by Hackwood* after Roubiliac, who executed a bust of Newton in 1751 and a statue in 1755, both now in Trinity College, Cambridge. The portrait medallion of John, Duke of Marlborough has been erroneously attributed to Roubiliac.
See: Richard Parker.

Rousseau, Jean-Jacques (1712-1778)

Born at Geneva of a Huguenot family, Rousseau, after many vicissitudes, arrived in Paris in 1741. Here he gained a precarious living by copying music. His *Discourse on Arts and Sciences,* in which he denounced culture as a cause of corruption, brought him notoriety, and in 1753 he published his *Discourse on the Origin of Inequality* in which he advocated the return to a primitive life, holding that wealth is criminal, government tyrannical, and social legislation unjust. He lived in a cottage lent to him by a rich *patronne,* but his uncouth behaviour caused bitter quarrels, and he left for Montlouis, in the south, where he was befriended by the Duke of Luxembourg. *The New Heloïse* was published in 1760, followed by *The Social Contract* in 1762. In the same year he published *Emile* containing his views on education, kings, and government, before fleeing to the protection of Frederick the Great* in Switzerland. A copy of *Emile* was bought by Josiah Wedgwood. In 1766 Rousseau came to England, and stayed for a year or more, but, suspecting the intentions of the British government, he returned to France under the protection of the Marquis de Mirabeau. He died in 1778, probably insane, and possibly by his own hand. His social and political ideas became widely known at the time, despite efforts to suppress them, and they contributed towards the unrest which culminated in the Revolution.

Small busts of Rousseau, who was very popular in England, were produced in both porcelain and earthenware, and were in great demand. Wedgwood produced a statuette in basaltes and in cane ware* as a pair to his statuette of Voltaire*. This was modelled in 1779 by Hackwood* who worked from a drawing supplied by Sir Brooke Boothby. Hackwood modelled a bust of Rousseau in 1776, and Flaxman* another in 1781. One bust of Rousseau was 20ins. high, but another was 4ins., to pair with a bust of Voltaire. These were probably both the work of Hackwood, since they appear in the 1777 Catalogue, but Josiah himself is believed to have worked on the larger bust. The figure of Voltaire appears in the 1779 Catalogue, but not its companion Rousseau. Voltaire is 12ins. high, Rousseau (holding a walking stick in his left hand, his hat under his left arm, and a bunch of flowers in his right hand) measures 11¾ins. A portrait medallion, of which the mould survives at Barlaston, is listed in both the 1773 and the 1779 Catalogues. It was copied in glass paste by Tassie* in 1790.

Rousseau, Jean-Jacques. *Rare black basaltes bust of Rousseau, 18ins. high, the base impressed 'WEDGWOOD & BENTLEY'. Since the socle appears to be original and Flaxman's bust of Rousseau was not modelled until 1781, this must be the bust modelled by Hackwood in 1776 upon which Josiah Wedgwood himself is believed to have worked.* Christie's.

Royal Academy of Arts, The (London)

George III* who acceded to the throne in 1760 encouraged the arts generally, and was himself especially interested in architecture. Before 1760 a number of unsuccessful attempts had been made to form an Academy which would help in the cultivation and improvement of the arts of painting, sculpture, and architecture. The first public exhibition of works of art was opened in 1760 with the help of the Royal Society for the Encouragement of Arts, Manufactures, and Commerce in Great Britain (see: Royal Society of Arts), and in 1765 the King granted a Charter whereby the Incorporated Society of Artists came into being. This was not entirely successful, and a group of the members petitioned the King for his help in establishing a national school of art. This, the Royal Academy of Arts, was founded with the King's approval on December 10th, 1768, with Sir Joshua Reynolds* as first president, G.M. Moser as Keeper, and William Chambers* as Treasurer. Professors of painting, architecture, perspective, and anatomy were appointed, and the school was opened to anyone capable of benefiting from its teaching. The Academy at this time was given accommodation in Somerset House which had been acquired by the nation. The first exhibition was held there in 1781.

Royal Shape

Lobed creamware tableware shape, similar in appearance to Catherine shape* and specially created for George III*.

Royal Society of Arts

Learned society, founded in 1754 as the Royal Society for the Encouragement of Arts, Manufactures and Commerce, to promote the study of the practical arts and sciences, and, by the award of prizes, to encourage invention in these fields. The Society was responsible for the first exhibition of contemporary art in England, the success of which led to the founding of the Royal Academy; the first industrial exhibition, 1761; and the first international exhibition, 1851.

During the present century the Society has been particularly concerned with industrial design. Membership is 6,200 Fellows of the Society. Her Majesty the Queen is Patron, and HRH Prince Philip, Duke of Edinburgh, President.

Josiah Wedgwood was elected Fellow of the Society in 1786.

See: Adelphi, The; Samuel More.

Ruins. *Vase modelled in imitation of an excavated classical vase with simulated damage which, nevertheless, does not disfigure the more important decorative features. Jasper, 6½ ins. high. Impressed mark 'WEDGWOOD'. Dwight and Lucille Beeson Collection.*

Ruins. *Blue and white jasper vase in the form of three broken columns. c.1785. Dwight and Lucille Beeson Collection.*

Ruins. *Transfer print by Sadler & Green on Queen's ware of a Mediterranean harbour scene with ruins in the foreground. c.1780.* Wedgwood.

Royal Society of London for Improving Natural Knowledge

Generally known as the Royal Society, it is one of the oldest of European societies devoted to scientific inquiry, being granted its first charter by Charles II in 1662. The King was one of the members. They met regularly to read scientific papers which were subsequently published in the *Philosophical Transactions*. Josiah Wedgwood was proposed for election as a Fellow in May, 1782, and his candidature was supported by no fewer than fourteen members, headed by 'Athenian' Stuart*. The Royal Society Club held meetings in less formal surroundings than those of the official meetings — usually at an inn. Non-members were invited as guests, especially those likely to be candidates for Fellowship of the Society. Wedgwood was the guest of 'Athenian' Stuart in 1780 and 1781.

Ruins

Classical ruins and obelisks were fashionable subjects of decoration from 1750 onwards. Artificial ruins were built as garden ornaments, and painters like Piranesi* and Hubert Robert found in them a source of inspiration, the latter to a point where he became known as 'Robert les Ruines'. Chelsea* porcelain was painted with ruins before 1760, probably by J.H. O'Neale*. Sadler* & Green printed ruins in black on Wedgwood's creamware, and Hancock's transfer prints of this subject occur on Worcester porcelain. Wedgwood also made somewhat bizarre jasper flower holders and inkstands imitating broken columns and damaged urns. The vogue was undoubtedly inspired by excavations at Herculaneum* and Pompeii*, and contemporary interest in these and other classical sites. Ruins are also indicative of the Romantic aspect of the neo-classical* style.

Rum Kettle

An 18th century vessel, somewhat smaller than a tea kettle, with a short beak-shaped pouring lip or spout and bail handle*. Kettles of 5ins. and 10-11ins. in height were made in black basaltes* during the Wedgwood & Bentley period, and the miniature version was reproduced in bone china* early in the 19th century. It is evident that some, at least, were intended as ornamental, rather than useful, wares since they bear the Wedgwood & Bentley impressed mark and have unglazed interiors.

See: Punch Pot.

Rum Kettle. *Black basaltes rum kettle or punch kettle decorated with classical figures in relief and satyr masks, with bail handle and 'widow' finial. c.1780.* Photo: Wedgwood.

Rustic Handle

See: Crabstock.

Ryles, Robert Daniel (fl.1816-1865)

Engraver of Lane End; married in 1817; worked for Wedgwood, 1816-54. He engraved the *Old Vine* pattern, 1854.

Rysbrack (Rijsbrack), John Michael (1694-1770)

Rysbrack was the son of a landscape painter of Antwerp who appears to have arrived in England in 1720 with a recommendation to the architect James Gibbs. He soon gained a considerable reputation for his portrait busts and was responsible for an enormous amount of statuary and carving of all kinds, from chimney pieces to monuments. There is no suggestion that he worked for Wedgwood directly, but the following busts were based on his work (probably through the intermediate stage of casts from Hoskins* or Cheere*): George II; Ben Jonson; John Locke (philosopher), adapted from an original in Kensington Palace.

S

Sacrifice

An offering to a deity: usually a prayer, or an act of thanksgiving, penitence, or propitiation. Wedgwood sacrifice groups are not always easy to identify with certainty because some of the figures composing them were apparently considered interchangeable and might be increased or reduced in number to suit the size and shape of the ground (tablet, medallion, or vase). The titles have also become confused and duplicated. Wedgwood bas-reliefs of *Sacrifice* subjects are as follows:

Abraham sacrificing his son, Isaac, Carrara* group by Beattie*, c.1860.

Bacchanalian Sacrifice (see: Bacchus).

Fauns sacrificing, tablet by Flaxman* 8½ins. by 15ins., 1777.

Sacrifice to Aesculapius, medallion 4ins. by 3½ins., c.1772.

Sacrifice to Bacchus, also known as *Sacrifice to Pan,* tablet 8¼ins. by 19ins. and 9½ins. by 22ins., c.1778.

Sacrifice to Ceres, tablet attributed to Flaxman, c.1779.

Sacrifice to Concordia, tablet modelled by Webber*, 1787. Height 10ins.

Sacrifice to Cupid, tablet, probably misnamed, showing Cupid on a pedestal flanked by figures of Diana and other goddesses. Attributed to Flaxman, c.1780.

Sacrifice to Eros, tablet, similar in composition to *Sacrifice to Love,* but fewer figures, 11ins. by 22ins. Possibly the work of Webber, c.1787.

Sacrifice (Offering) to Flora, tablet, modelled by Hackwood*, 1777.

Sacrifice to Hymen, tablet; a pair to *The Marriage of Cupid and Psyche,* variously attributed to Flaxman and Hackwood, 1777.

Sacrifice to Hymen, tablet, height 10ins., as pair to *Sacrifice to Concordia,* modelled by Webber, 1787.

Sacrifice of Iphigenia, correctly *Achilles in Scyros* (see: Achilles).

Sacrifice to Love, tablet 9½ins. by 21ins. and 10½ins. by 25ins., attributed to Flaxman, c.1778.

Sacrifice to Peace, medallion 3¾ins. by 2¾ins., first catalogued, 1777.

Sadler & Green. *Transfer-printed landscape by Sadler & Green on Queen's shape. c.1775.* Wedgwood.

Sadler, John (1720-1789)
Sadler & Green

Transfer-printer; partner in the firm of Sadler & Green of Liverpool, who may also have been manufacturers of earthenware, although no specimens have been identified. Sadler is said to have invented transfer printing about 1750. It was also invented independently by John Brooks in London some time before 1753, and used by the Bow* Porcelain Factory and the Battersea Enamel Works. By 1756 it was also being employed at Worcester*. Sadler & Green decorated large quantities of cream-coloured ware for Wedgwood which was sent to Liverpool for that purpose, and some of their accounts survive. They decorated tiles* with scenes from Aesop's Fables* or subjects from the contemporary theatre which are much prized. Sadler retired in 1770, but Guy Green* continued the business until 1799.

See: Transfer Printing.

Sacrifice. *Brown and white jasper tablet, 23¾ins. long, ornamented with* Sacrifice to Love, *attributed to Flaxman, c.1778.* Sotheby's.

Saggar

A protective box of highly refractory fire clay used to enclose objects during firing to prevent direct contact with the flame. Some are pierced at irregular intervals with triangular holes through which saggar pins are inserted to support ware during firing.

Saint-Amans, Pierre-Honoré-Boudon de (1774-1858)

Chemist and pottery technician; in England from 1798 to the Restoration of the French Monarchy in 1815, studying the pottery industry in this country. From 1816-22 he experimented at Sèvres*, and again from 1829-36. He particularly interested himself in white earthenware with a transparent glaze (*faience-fine*), and the process of slip casting (see: Processes of Manufacture), as well as introducing transfer printing*. In 1836 he was adviser to the Creil* factory which made and decorated creamware in the manner of Wedgwood, and Saint-Amans was probably responsible for the production of black basaltes there.

See: Spies, Industrial.

St. Lawrence Seaway Plates

Two designs were commissioned in 1959 to commemorate the opening of the St. Lawrence Seaway — one, a sepia print by Peter Wall* for Manchester Lines Ltd., whose ships use the seaway, and the other by Alan Price* for the *Toronto Evening Telegram.*

Salpion (fl.A.D.100)

Greek sculptor. Hackwood's* tablet, *Birth of Bacchus*, was modelled from Montfaucon's* engraving of Salpion's original bas-relief now in the Naples Museum.

Salt-Glazed Ware

Stoneware covered with a thin, hard glaze having a minutely pitted surface reminiscent of the appearance of orange peel. It is produced by throwing a shovelful of salt (sodium chloride) into the kiln when the fire is at its hottest. The salt splits into its components — sodium and chlorine. The sodium combines with the silica on the surface of the ware to form the characteristic glaze; the chlorine passes out of the kiln chimney. Wedgwood produced wares thus glazed during his first partnership with John Harrison*, and it was, seemingly, the principal manufacture during his association with Whieldon*, although at this time it was becoming unfashionable, and was being sold for very low prices. With his removal to the Ivy House Works* Wedgwood continued to make good quality salt-glazed ware for a few years, side by side with the other wares which had been produced at Fenton. There is no record of the date on which its manufacture was discontinued.

Saltram

Saltram, near Plympton, Devon, was purchased by George Parker, ancestor of the Earls of Morley, in 1712, and his son John began to enlarge it after 1743. The grandson, also John, succeeded in 1766, and employed Robert Adam* to make extensive alterations to the east wing. John Parker was created Baron Boringdon in 1784. The second Lord Boringdon, also named John, succeeded his father in 1788. Sir Joshua Reynolds*, born not far away and a frequent visitor to the house, advised Lord Boringdon on the acquisition of pictures, and painted the family portraits.

There are some early Wedgwood vases at Saltram made more interesting by invoices and documents relating to them. The vases of cream-coloured ware of a pronounced ivory tone are unmarked, and belong to the period 1764-68. Decorative grooving in the body was done with the engine-turning lathe*, and the gilding* with a granular appearance is unfired. The

Salt-Glazed Ware. *Block mould for Wedgwood's salt-glazed cornucopia moulded with a bust of Flora. A typically rococo subject, probably modelled by W. Greatbatch.* Wedgwood.

Salt-Glazed Ware. *Block moulds for a rococo teapot and creamer, with two rustic spouts. The teapot shape is known in both salt-glazed ware and early creamware.* Wedgwood.

form of these vases is not entirely neo-classical*, and some of them exhibit baroque and rococo* elements. They belong to the group which Wedgwood later called "my first vases." The Blue Pebble vases, made to imitate Boulton's ormolu-mounted Blue John* vases, are almost certainly early products of Etruria, made in 1769 or soon afterwards, because two of them bear the Wedgwood & Bentley mark. Matt encaustic* enamels were employed on basaltes* vases to imitate ancient classical red-figure* vases, and bell kraters* at Saltram are decorated with subjects taken from Sir William Hamilton's* Catalogue, a work which we know Wedgwood was consulting in 1767.

Saltram is now administered by the National Trust.

Sand Box
A box with a pierced top for sprinkling fine sand or pumice powder on to paper for the purpose of drying the ink; used until c.1820, when its place was taken by blotting paper. It should not be confused with a pounce pot*.

Sandby, Paul (1730-1809)
Painter. A founding member of the Royal Academy, Sandby was one of the most celebrated and influential artists in watercolour of the 18th century. His work included landscape, architecture, portraits and even caricature. His *Gate of Coverham Abbey* (British Museum), or a print from it, was copied by Wedgwood in 1773 on a trial plate for the Frog* service.

Sappho
One of the leaders of the Aeolian School of Lyric Poetry, fl. c.600B.C., who was born in the Island of Lesbos, where she was the centre of a female literary coterie, most of the members of which were her pupils. Only fragments of her works survive.

Wedgwood subjects:

Sappho, bust, 15ins. high. Supplied by Hoskins & Grant*, 1775.

Sappho, bas-relief figure supplied by Flaxman*, 1775.

Left: **Sappho.** *Jasper portrait medallion of the Greek poetess, Sappho, taken from a cast obtained by Wedgwood from Astle in 1776.* City Museum and Art Gallery, Stoke-on-Trent.

Right: **Satsuma Shape.** *Satsuma shape teapot introduced in 1878, the form based on Japanese pewter, decorated in the manner of Lessore.* Wedgwood.

Satsuma Shape
As the name suggests, Japanese in inspiration (but taken from lacquer or pewter, not from ceramics), the Satsuma shape was introduced in 1878, sixteen years after the London Exhibition which gave rise to a fashion for Japanese decoration. The tea-pot is flat-sided, the mouth of the vessel being rectangular with a stepped cover and a curved handle. The flat sides were easily decorated, and lent themselves particularly to the new photolithographic* process. The Wedgwood Museum* contains examples decorated with typical Highland scenes by Crealock* and painting in the style of Lessore*.

Satyr
See: Faun; Pan; Silenus.

Sayer, Robert (1725-1794)
One of the principal print and map sellers in England, trading from the Golden Buck, 53 Fleet Street, London. In business on his own account for twenty-four years, Sayer was in partnership with J. Bennet from 1775-84. Thereafter, he again traded alone until his death. His publications include *The Complete Drawing Book,* 1758; *The Dramatic Characters* or *Different Portraits of the English Stage,* 1770; *The Artist's Vade Mecum;* and *The Draughtman's Assistant,* 1777. *The Ladies Amusement*,* issued in at least two editions between 1758 and 1762, is described on the title page as "extremely useful to the PORCELAINE and other Manufacturers depending on Design." The illustrations by Pillement*, Hancock*, and others were certainly used by Wedgwood, Sadler* & Green, and the Bow*, Chelsea* and Worcester* porcelain factories.

Scent Bottle
In former times scent bottles were usually notable for qualities of design and workmanship, and were often made in a variety of precious materials. In the 1750s and the early 1760s the Chelsea Porcelain Factory* made a notable series of scent bottles in porcelain which are now keenly sought. Wedgwood's jasper scent bottles are less elaborate because they had to be in a form which permitted decoration in the jasper technique of applying reliefs, and like the porcelain bottles the mouth was formed to accept a mount of silver, gold, or pinchbeck, together with a small mounted stopper attached to the neck by a chain. Most scent bottles have, by now, lost their original mounts. In addition to the customary scent bottle Wedgwood used some general purpose moulds for making jasper bell pulls to make scent bottles. The double-ended scent bottle, for holding two kinds of perfume, is a considerable rarity. Allied to scent bottles in size and shape are Chinese snuff bottles. Wedgwood made a snuff bottle of this kind in pearl* ware glazed in red with a Dog of Fo in black. This, marked *Wedgwood Etruria England,* was made about 1900, probably to contain scent.

Sayer, Robert. *Queen's ware 'Liverpool shape' jug, decorated with onglaze transfer prints of a fashionable woman walking in the countryside and* An Opera girl of Paris in the Character of Flora *(illustrated), printed for Robert Sayer, 1771. 7¾ ins. high.* Wedgwood.

Scheemakers, Peter (1691-1781)

Sculptor born in Antwerp, who came to London. He paid a short visit to Rome before his arrival in England, and then left for a protracted stay in Rome in 1728. He was back in London before 1741, in which year he had a studio in Vine Street. Scheemakers became even better known and more successful than Rysbrack*, and the Shakespeare Monument in Westminster Abbey is among his many works. Lord Radnor bought a head of Zingara* from him, and a statue of the same subject by his hand was among the lots in the sale of Dr. Richard Mead in 1755. He also carved a relief, *Et in Arcadia Ego,* for Shugborough, Staffs., seat of Thomas Anson, M.P., for whom Wedgwood and Boulton* together made ''an immense large Tripod'' to the design of 'Athenian' Stuart* in 1771.

Scheemakers left England for Antwerp in 1771, and there is no record that he ever worked for Wedgwood, but suppliers of casts, such as Hoskins* and Parker*, may well have supplied casts based on his work, and it is possible that future research may reveal a more direct connection.

His brother, Henry Scheemakers, also came to London and was in partnership with Henry Cheere, brother to John Cheere*.

Schenck, Frederick (fl.1870-1890)

Modeller at Etruria* in 1872-73. He later worked for George Jones & Sons of Stoke-on-Trent, modelling *pâte-sur-pâte* wares, which he signed with his monogram.

Scent Bottle. *Blue and white jasper perfume bottle ornamented with a portrait of Queen Charlotte. 2½ ins. in diameter.* Wedgwood.

Scent Bottle. *Dark blue jasper dip perfume bottle ornamented with* Mars contemplating his armour. *Metal mount. 3½ ins. high. c.1785-90.* Wedgwood.

Schreiber, Lady Charlotte Elizabeth (1812-1895)

Welsh scholar and collector. Daughter of Albemarle Bertie, 9th Earl of Lindsay, Lady Charlotte married, in 1833, Sir Josiah John Guest, whose iron works in Wales she managed after his death in 1852. Three years later she married Dr. Charles Schreiber.

Her large and important collection of English porcelain, earthenware, and enamels (including some rare examples of early Wedgwood), was given to the South Kensington Museum (now the Victoria and Albert Museum) in 1884. A three-volume *Catalogue*, compiled by Bernard Rackham, was issued by the Museum in 1928 and 1930. Her *Journals* (edited by M.J. Grant), which contain many interesting references to purchases of Wedgwood, were published in London in 1911.

Seals

Intaglio seals were made at the Chelsea Porcelain Factory* from about 1755, and Wedgwood's black basaltes* seals were marketed from December 1772. By the following year he was already in need of a catalogue to describe his subjects, and the 1779 Catalogue* lists 379 numbered intaglios of subjects from mythology and ancient history, and classical and modern portraits. In his introduction to the 1779 Catalogue Wedgwood wrote: "The Improvements made in the Intaglios, since the publication of the First Edition of our Catalogue [1773], require some Notice. We have found that many of them take a good Polish, and when polished, have exactly the Effect of fine black Jasper; but this operation must be performed with great Care, or the Work will essentially suffer by it. . . . We have also found out another Method of adding very considerably to the Beauty of these Intaglios, by polishing the Bezels, and giving a Ground of pale blue to the flat Surface of the Stone, which makes them greatly resemble the black and blue Onyxes, and equally ornamental for Rings or Seals. . . . They are also now made in fine blue Jasper, that takes as good a Polish as Turquois [sic] Stone or Lapis Luzuli." He added that portraits suitable for seals might be obtained at "moderate Expence," a model for a portrait in wax costing about three guineas and any number of copies ("not fewer than ten") in black and blue onyxes for seals or rings at 5s. each.

Many of the original gems copied by Wedgwood were lent to him by such friends as Sir Watkin Williams Wynn* and Sir Roger Newdigate*, but the greater number were supplied to him by James Tassie*.

Seder Set

Gold-printed bone china* set, made in 1959 for Blancol Ltd., consisting of a tray, 15½ ins. diameter, illustrating the order of the Passover ceremony, with six footed cups to hold the ceremonial foods.

Seigmund, George (fl.1769-1774)

Painter at the Chelsea Decorating Studio* who worked on the Frog* service.

Semper, Gottfried (1803-1879)

German architect and designer; member of the Prince Consort's circle in Britain. He designed an ebony cabinet on stand with gilt metal mounts which had a painted porcelain panel in the door surrounded by Wedgwood plaques. The panel was painted by George Gray with a copy of William Mulready's *Crossing the Ford* (Exhibited RA 1842); the cabinet was made by Holland & Sons, and shown in the Paris Exposition of 1855. It is now in the Victoria and Albert Museum, but commercial copies exist.

Seneca, L. Annaeus (?5B.C.—A.D.65)

Roman Stoic philosopher, who wrote largely on moral and philosophical subjects, but was also the author of ten tragedies. In his early years he gained a reputation as a pleader of causes. His most important surviving work is *De Beneficiis,* in seven volumes. He killed himself on the orders of Nero, to whom he had been tutor and later a chief counsellor.

Wedgwood subjects:

Seneca, bust, 20ins. by 15ins. Cast supplied by Hoskins & Grant*, 1774, refinished by Hackwood*.

Seneca carried dead from the bath, a tablet with this title is mentioned in Wedgwood's letter to Bentley* dated 13th January, 1771. It does not appear in any of the Catalogues* and it seems probable that this title is wrong.

Settling Pan

Dairy ware; a large oval pan of Queen's ware, about 17ins. long by 12ins. wide, with a pouring lip at one end. Milk was poured into it and allowed to stand until the cream or butter had risen to the surface, and this was taken off with a skimmer*. It was first made in the 18th century.

Sèvres, Manufacture Royale de

This porcelain factory, originally housed in the fortress of Vincennes to the south-east of Paris, was removed to Sèvres, to the south-west, in 1756. By this time Louis XV, persuaded by Mme. de Pompadour, had become the principal shareholder, as well as being the factory's principal customer for its finest quality wares. The King was a powerful patron and protector, who issued edicts preventing the manufacture of porcelain elsewhere in France, and limiting the colours which might be employed to decorate *faience.* Despite this, a few small porcelain factories managed to operate clandestinely under the protection of the King's relations, a fact known to Wedgwood, and referred to obliquely in his letter to the Duc de Choiseul* when he was attempting to promote the sale of Queen's ware in France. After the death of Mme. de Pompadour in 1764 these edicts were progressively relaxed, although there were periods of more stringent application, and by the time the factory was inherited by Louis XVI they were hardly enforced at all. It is pertinent to note that the date of Wedgwood's first creamware Catalogue in French is 1774, the year in which Louis XV died. The situation was finally regularised by the Anglo-French Trade Treaty of 1786, in the negotiations for which Wedgwood advised Sir William Eden (later Lord Auckland*) on aspects affecting the export of English wares, a treaty more or less terminated by the Revolution of 1789. During the Revolution the factory became the Manufacture Nationale, and under Napoleon I the Manufacture Imperiale, reverting to the Manufacture Royale at the time of the Restoration of Louis XVIII.

From about 1750, and for about thirty years thereafter, Sèvres was the supreme arbiter of ceramic taste in Europe, taking the lead from Meissen* at the start of the Seven Years' War in 1756. They yielded this place to Wedgwood in the 1780s, at a time when a potter named Josse invented a special biscuit porcelain in which the jasper* of Wedgwood could be imitated. During this period Sèvres enjoyed the assistance of several distinguished painters and sculptors, who acted as designers and supplied models. Usually they were persuaded by Mme. de Pompadour, who had great influence in artistic circles, and they included such men as Boucher, Falconet*, and Pigalle*, whose occasional influence may be traced in some Wedgwood products.

From the first the Vincennes-Sèvres factory worked in the rococo* style, and only departed slightly from it until the death of Louis XV, who remained faithful to rococo until the last. They specialised in fine quality ground colours and miniature painting in reserves which ensured that many of the more important pieces made at this time are considerable works of art. Exotic* birds painted by artists such as Evans and Aloncle, shipping scenes by Morin, and cupids after Boucher were favourite subjects copied elsewhere. In 1752 the art director, J.-J. Bachelier, introduced the use of biscuit* (unglazed) porcelain for figure work. This became extremely fashionable, and many high quality figures were issued. They influenced both Derby* and Wedgwood in England to use a similar medium. Wedgwood certainly regarded his jasper as a kind of biscuit porcelain, and made other bodies using the same principle. Several of his vases* are closely based on porcelain vases from Sèvres, and there can be no doubt of his interest in

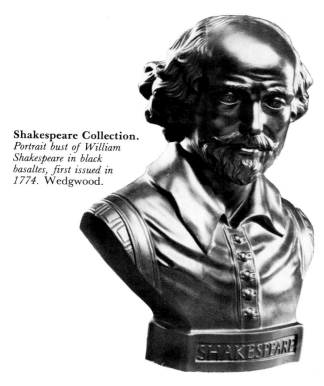

Shakespeare Collection. *Portrait bust of William Shakespeare in black basaltes, first issued in 1774. Wedgwood.*

The Sèvres factory, and artists and designers trained there, dominated Staffordshire quality production during the 19th century, some of them coming to England during the political disturbances of 1848 and the Franco-Prussian War of 1870. Wedgwood, with their own strong tradition of neo-classical styles, was probably least affected, since they left the copying of *vieux Sèvres* to others, but names which spring to mind are Emile Lessore* and Hugues Protât*, both influential in their own ways and both employed at Etruria*.

The Manufacture Nationale de Sèvres is still the major French porcelain factory.

Sgraffito

Decoration resulting from incising a design through slip of a contrasting colour to the body. This operation is carried out before glazing. It is a very ancient technique, and is almost universal. Wedgwood examples of the technique exist in some of the work of Harry Barnard*, Millicent Taplin* and Norman Wilson*.

Shakespeare Collection, The

Wedgwood have been making products of interest to lovers of Shakespeare for over two hundred years, beginning in 1774 with the first 11-inch black basaltes library bust. Three years later a portrait medallion in jasper modelled by Hackwood* was issued in varying sizes, the largest an oval medallion with a long axis of 4ins., down to a cameo of ⅞ in. To celebrate the Tercentenary of Shakespeare's birth in 1564 the factory made the Carrara* bust by F.M. Miller*, commissioned and sold by Howell & James*. In 1964, the four hundredth anniversary of Shakespeare's birth, several specially designed pieces were issued. These included the Shakespeare Mug* decorated with characters from twelve of the plays, based on prints illustrating Bell's 18th century edition, and a sage-green jasper plate, the white relief illustrating Shakespeare's birthplace. The basaltes bust of 1774 was reissued, as well as the Hackwood portrait medallion, 4¼ ins. by 3¼ ins., in a gilded wood frame. The bust also exists in Queen's ware. The decoration on the mug was adapted for use on a Queen's ware plate, the characters arranged round a central view of the Globe Theatre, Southwark.

the products of the royal factory. These he would have been able to see at some of the great houses he visited, like the Duke of Bedford's Woburn Abbey*, and in 1769 he was supplying vases to the Duchess of Bedford, who may well have influenced him in this direction. The fine quality of the Sèvres porcelain at Woburn is widely known today, and it is important to note a letter written by Josiah to Bentley in October, 1765: "I have been three days hard and close at work taking patterns from a set of French china at the Duke of Bedfords, worth at least £1,500, the most elegant things I ever saw."

As late as the Shape Book* of 1880 there are several forms which owe inspiration to 18th century Sèvres. This is hardly surprising, considering the wide popularity of the numerous porcelain copies and reproductions of early soft-paste Sèvres (referred to as *vieux Sèvres*) by Minton*, Copeland, and others.

When, in 1770, suitable materials for the manufacture of true porcelain, similar to that made by Champion in England, were found at Saint-Yrieix, near Limoges, the Sèvres factory started to abandon the soft-paste body and, at the same time, to adopt the neo-classical* style more widely. One result of the change was that the wares lost a great deal of their former artistry, and Wedgwood began to assume the leadership of European fashion in consequence, factories all over the Continent imitating Queen's ware, jasper, and basaltes.

With the onset of the Revolution, and the period of maladministration and bad trade which followed for the former royal factory, Wedgwood became supreme, but he was hardly able to reap the full benefit of his achievement because the Revolution brought a general disturbance of European trade in its train. The great *bureau du roi,* made for Louis XV by Oeben and Riesener and now in the Louvre, had the two Sèvres plaques bearing the royal monogram, which were inset at either end, removed and replaced by plaques which are either of Wedgwood's blue and white jasper, or excellent contemporary copies. No one has yet removed them to make a certain identification.

Shakespeare Mug. *Queen's ware mug commemorating the tercentenary of the birth of Shakespeare, 1964. Wedgwood.*

Shakespeare Mug

This Queen's ware mug, issued in 1964, commemorates the tercentenary of Shakespeare's birth. It was designed by the Wedgwood Design Studio and sponsored by the 1964 Shakespeare Anniversary Council, Stratford-on-Avon. The backstamp gives details of the figures which make up the principal design. These are as follows:

Mr. Garrick as King Lear
Mr. Grist as Othello
Mr. Smith as Richard III
Mr. Garrick as Macbeth
Mr. Kean as Hamlet
Mr. Shuter as Falstaff
Miss P. Hopkins as Lavinia
Miss Lessingham as Ophelia
Mrs. Buckley [sic: Bulkley] as Mistress Ford
Mrs. Hartley as Hermione
Miss Baddeley as Joan de Pucelle
Miss Hopkins as Volumnia.

Shakespeare Tercentenary Bust

This bust was produced under the patronage of the National Shakespeare Committee in 1864. The project apparently emanated from Howell & James*, London retailers, who subscribed £50 towards the Committee's funds in exchange for their participation. The model, by F.M. Miller*, was made by Wedgwood in 1864 in an 11½-inch version and suitably inscribed. The inscription reads as follows: ''Published under the special patronage of the Shakespeare National Committee by Howell, James & Co., London, April 24th, 1864.'' An 8-inch version in bronze was also issued about the same time with the same inscription, but not, of course, by Wedgwood.

There is a 17-inch basaltes version similarly inscribed in the Wedgwood Museum, and the bust was reissued in two sizes in 1867 — 11½ ins. and 17ins.

Shape Books

The hand-drawn factory records have never been published. The earliest surviving book probably dates from 1802, or shortly afterwards, and was copied from much earlier records. It also contains some border patterns and specimen lettering. Drawing books of this kind are still kept at the factory.

The first published Shape Book was the Queen's ware Catalogue* of 1774, with thirty-five designs by John Pye* engraved on nine plates and printed by Joseph Cooper*. This was the first Catalogue of its kind to be published, and it was not until 1783 that the Leeds* Pottery issued their much larger and more ambitious cream-coloured ware Catalogue. Wedgwood's next Queen's ware Catalogue was issued in 1790, and comprised ninety numbered shapes on thirteen plates. Like the 1774 Catalogue it was produced in both an English and French version. The so-called 'William Blake' Shape Catalogue is regarded as dating from 1817, but no copy exists which can certainly be dated before 1840-49. The earliest edition in the Wedgwood Museum has 18 plates engraved by Blake, two by John Taylor Wedgwood*, and nineteen by an unknown hand. The second edition has forty-four plates, and the third edition forty-six, with drawings of 386 shapes. The last two editions also have an index. The 1873 *Illustrated Catalogue of Shapes* contains fifty-five plates with 369 subjects. The next Catalogue is generally regarded as having been published in 1880. This contains forty-four pages with 319 designs, from which it is evident that some of the less popular shapes had been dropped, although some had survived the test of time from the 18th century. A facsimile of this Catalogue of Shapes was published in 1971 by the Wedgwood Society of London with an introduction by J.K. des Fontaines. The most recent Shape Book, published in 1950, still includes shapes, now regarded as timeless, from the 18th century (e.g. 129 and 146 shapes).

Sharp, William (1749-1824)

Engraver. Early in life he specialised in heraldic engraving, but later became well known for his reproductions of the work of such classical painters as Guido Reni, and Carracci as well as portraits by Reynolds*, Benjamin West, J.S. Copley and others. He supplied Wedgwood with engravings c.1795-1805.

Shell Edge

A moulded border, based on the edge of the pecten shell, to be found on creamware and pearlware plates. Introduced in 1770, it was especially popular with Wedgwood during the period 1779-1830. The moulding was often enhanced with bright blue or green enamel. The type of decoration in question originated at Vincennes (later Sèvres*) early in the 1750s, and was also occasionally employed at the English Bow* porcelain factory. The shape has continued in production until the present day, being employed for such popular patterns as *Cornflower* (engraved by Henry Sherwin*, 1860) and *Bramble* (1862).

See also: Embossed Queen's Ware.

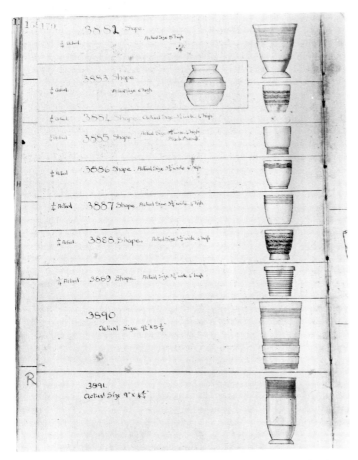

Shape Books. *A page from a factory Shape Drawing Book showing Keith Murray shapes for turned vases.* Wedgwood.

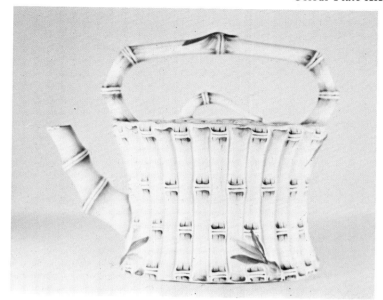

Glazed and enamelled bamboo-form teapot, reproduced from a late 18th century shape originally made in cane ware. Registry mark for 1872. Zeitlin Collection.

Circular wall plaque painted by Thomas Allen with a portrait of Sir John Falstaff on a richly gilt ground. c.1880. Wedgwood.

Majolica dolphin candlestick and lidded beer stein, height 11ins. 1870. Wedgwood.

Sherwin, Henry (fl.1839-1864)

Engraver and decorator; worked for Wedgwood, 1860-64; engraved *Cornflower* pattern, 1860; exhibited a series of designs for plates at the International Exhibition, 1862, based on the parsley leaf, etc. He engraved a number of local topographical views in 1839.

Shout, Robert (fl.1778-1810)

Sculptor and maker of plaster casts, in partnership at Holborn with his father, Benjamin Shout, with whom he was responsible for busts and a large number of monuments. Their work included casts of Canova's* figures of Hebe, Venus, Paris and Perseus, and in 1798 Wedgwood issued a black basaltes bust of Nelson, 11ins. high, copied from the model by Robert Shout.

Showrooms

Wedgwood always recognised the importance of a London address, and for some years his affairs were looked after by his brother John*, of Wedgwood & Bliss, London general warehousemen, with premises at 3, Cateaton Street (now Gresham Street), near the Guildhall. He is listed in the Directories for 1763 and 1765, but not for 1766. In October of that year John Wedgwood went to live in Liverpool. While his brother was looking after his affairs in London, Josiah Wedgwood had two rooms for display purposes at the sign of the Artichoke, Cateaton Street. After his brother's death, and until the partnership with Thomas Bentley*, Wedgwood's affairs in London were looked after by his Burslem book keeper, William Cox*, who was dispatched to London for the purpose.

Wedgwood's next London showrooms were opened in November 1766, at the Queen's Arms, Charles Street (now Carlos Place), Grosvenor Square. There again, he had two rooms. Wedgwood did not regard this as more than temporary accommodation, and was soon looking for new premises. By April 1768, he had settled on a house on the corner of Great Newport Street and St. Martin's Lane. The rent was 100 guineas a year. There was good access for carriages, and a showroom sixty feet long. The Royal Arms, which proclaimed

Shout, Robert. *Bust in black basaltes of Admiral Sir Horatio Nelson, KB (later Viscount Nelson), 11ins. high, issued in 1798. In addition to the 'WEDGWOOD' mark impressed, early examples of this bust bear the inscription: 'Pubd. July 22nd 1798. R. Shout sculp. Holborn.'* Christie's.

him potter to Her Majesty, were taken down at Charles Street, regilded, and resited at Newport Street. Joseph Pickford, architect of Etruria*, was sent to London to oversee the necessary alterations, and by August 1768, the showrooms were open for business.

At the close of 1769 Wedgwood & Bentley acquired a house in Cheyne Row, Chelsea, for use as a painting studio. When Bentley first arrived in London to take charge of partnership affairs in the capital he lived first at Great Newport Street, but later, in 1770, he moved to Chelsea, the more effectively to oversee work there. When this project was first mooted in December 1769, Wedgwood had written that removal from Newport Street to Chelsea would make it more difficult to keep a proper check on the handling of money at Newport Street, and these fears eventually proved to be well-founded when the chief clerk, Ben Mather*, was discovered misappropriating funds. At Newport Street James Tassie* and Hoskins & Grant* were neighbours.

In December 1770, Wedgwood wrote to Bentley reporting a conversation between himself and Matthew Boulton*, from which it is evident that Wedgwood & Bentley were negotiating for showrooms in The Adelphi*, then in little more than the advanced planning stage, and that Boulton proposed to do the same. Two years later the plan to acquire showrooms there was quietly shelved, and then abandoned. It seems that the partners failed to agree on the terms of a lease with the Adam* brothers, who by that time were in financial difficulties. We

Shell Edge. *Moulded edge based on the edge of the scallop shell. The interior border is termed the 'mared' pattern, a form of onion, not to be confused with the Meissen onion pattern.* Zeitlin Collection.

know from an earlier letter that Wedgwood did not view The Strand itself with favour. It was then a very congested road much used by heavy goods drays.

The partners then began to look for suitable premises elsewhere. By this time Wedgwood's showrooms had become a place of fashionable resort, where people foregathered to view the display and to gossip, leaving their servants to wait in the hall. Circumstances also made it extremely desirable to house Mr. and Mrs. Bentley, the showrooms, the painting studios, and the packing warehouse under one roof. New showrooms were acquired at 12 Greek Street, near Soho Square, in 1774. These premises, called Portland House after the Duke of Portland, who owned the estate on which they stood, were rented on a twenty-one year lease at two hundred guineas a year from James Cullen of 59 Greek Street. The main galleries were on the first floor, and the ground floor included a spacious entrance hall, a large room for display purposes, and a counting house. The outbuildings in the large courtyard at the rear included a painting shop, a laboratory, a retort room (no doubt a muffle kiln for firing-on decoration), printing and pattern room, and a packing and unpacking house. Mr. and Mrs. Bentley moved to 11, Greek Street, next door. In July 1974, J.K. des Fontaines, Chairman of the Wedgwood Society*, London, unveiled a plaque on the wall of a Greek Street restaurant to mark the site of Portland House.

The Greek Street premises were ready for occupation in May 1774, and opened with an extremely well-attended display of the Frog* service. A closing down sale was advertised at Newport Street, where the nobility and gentry had to apply for tickets to the Greek Street exhibition. It says a great deal for the strength of Wedgwood's position in fashionable London that he could make such a condition. According to Mrs. Delany's diary the service occupied three rooms below and two above, and many of those who came to see it owned houses depicted on the plates and dishes.

Bentley's health was affected by living in Soho, and in 1777 he decided, despite the risk of highwaymen, to move to more rural surroundings at Turnham Green, where his friend, Ralph Griffiths*, was already living. The last special exhibition at Portland House was staged in April 1790, admission by ticket only, when the Portland* vase was first shown. The lease of Greek Street terminated in 1795, within a month of Josiah's death. There were difficulties in the way of renewing it because the Duke wished to sell the whole of the estate, and the search for new premises began.

New showrooms were found in St. James's Square, on the corner of Duke Street. They were on the north side of the Square, where it is joined by what is now Duke of York Street. The house was bought for £8,500, and a further £7,000 was spent on restoration and furnishing. The building has now been demolished to make way for the invasion of the Square by government offices, but a view of the interior of the showrooms is provided by plate 7 of Ackermann's *Repository of the Arts* of February 1809. The neighbourhood at this time was exclusively residential, and Byerley* was in charge from 1804 until his death in 1810. He was followed by his son, Josiah Byerley, who stayed until 1814, when he resigned to occupy himself with the stock exchange. From 1814 to 1829, when the house was sold, the manager in charge was John Howorth. The location of these showrooms has been criticised as being in too exclusive a residential area, but trading difficulties at this time were due to many other factors largely beyond the control of the partners. The movement of fashionable London westwards had begun long before, and York Street was not in an isolated position. It was only a minute or two's walk from Jermyn Street and Piccadilly, and in another direction, no

great distance from Buckingham House (as it then was) which George III* had bought for Queen Charlotte*. This was, perhaps, a not inappropriate position for the potter to Her Majesty. By 1828 trading conditions were so bad that retrenchment had become essential. A clearance sale took place during the winter of 1828 and the spring of the following year, which included trial pieces, moulds, and 'seconds' which had accumulated over the years.

In 1875 Wedgwood returned to London with the acquisition of new showrooms at 4-6 St. Andrew's Buildings, Holborn Circus, thus moving back towards the City. In 1890 the showrooms were moved to 108, Hatton Garden, on the other side of the Circus. In 1902 Harry Barnard* became manager and remained until 1918. Nine years later the showrooms were moved again to 24-27, Hatton Garden. They were closed in 1941, and in 1948 the firm moved to its present showrooms at 34, Wigmore Street. In 1951 an exhibition was held principally devoted to the wares made by the first Josiah. This included important pieces from the collection of Eustace Calland, recently purchased by the Wedgwood Museum* and shown to the public for the first time. The Catalogue*, *Early Wedgwood Pottery,* is a valuable record.

There are also showrooms today in New York, Toronto, Sydney and Melbourne, and the retail organisation, the Wedgwood Rooms*, provides smaller but more widespread displays of tableware and ornamental wares based on the ideas originally formulated by Josiah I for his London Showroom.

Wedgwood's example in establishing showrooms in London was followed in the 18th century by the larger among his Staffordshire competitors, although none enjoyed his success in the fashionable world. Most potters in the provinces had to be content with the services of one or other of the china dealers.

Showrooms. *Ticket of admission to view the Portland Vase, 1790, at the Greek Street Showrooms.* Wedgwood.

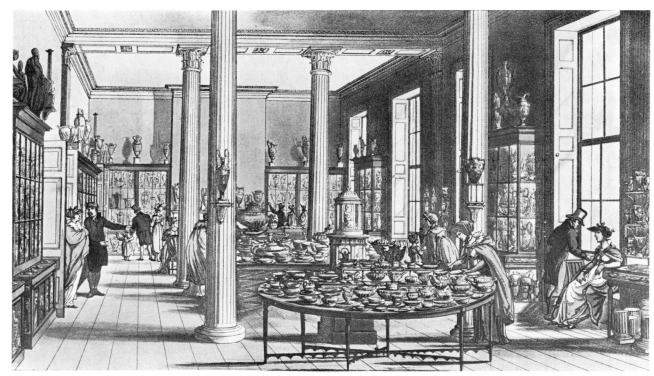

Showrooms. *View of the showrooms of Wedgwood & Byerley, York Street, 1810. Ackermann's Repository of the Arts.* Photo: Wedgwood.

There are many testimonies to the cachet possessed by Wedgwood's showrooms. Of 'Squire Hanger', a celebrated beau, Lord Townshend wrote:

At Tattersall's, Wedgwood's, and eke the Rehearsal,
Then straightway at Betty's he's sure to converse all;

and in one of Wedgwood's letters he writes: "Mrs. Byerley is just returned from London and brings a strange acct. of their goings on in Newport Street. No getting to the door for Coaches, nor into the Rooms for Ladies and Gen^ts."

The management of the London Showrooms was, from the first, of exceptional importance to the firm, and the appointment of London Manager (later Director) became one of increasing seniority and prestige in the pottery industry. The list of Wedgwood's London Directors is as follows:

John Wedgwood*	1765-67
William Cox*	1767-69
Thomas Bentley*	1769-80
William Brock	1780
James Jennings	1781
Thomas Byerley*	1781-1810
Thomas Howship	1810
Josiah Byerley	1810-14
John Howarth	1814-29
Charles Bachhoffner	1875-85
James Buttle	1885-97
S.H. Dyer	1897-1902
Harry Barnard*	1902-18
Felton Wreford	1918-53
Arthur Bryan*	1953-60
Robin Reilly	1960-64
Charles Dean	1964-66
Fred de Costobadie	1966-74
Roy Wadland	1974-

Shuter, William (fl.1770-1791)

Painter at the Chelsea Decorating Studio* who was responsible for the view of Fortescue House and landscapes for the Frog* service. Principally a painter of portraits and flowers, he exhibited six landscapes in the exhibitions of the Incorporated Society of Artists and the Free Society of Artists.

Sibyl Finial

See: Widow Finial.

Sick Pot

Term applied in the 18th century to the invalid's feeding cup*.

Siddons, Mrs. Sarah (1755-1831)

English tragic actress; daughter of Roger Kemble; married William Siddons, 1773. In 1775 she was engaged by David Garrick for Drury Lane. Mrs. Siddons achieved success in both London and the provinces in many roles, one of the best known being Lady Macbeth, in which she made her farewell appearance at Covent Garden, London, in 1812. Her portrait by Reynolds* as the *Tragic Muse* hangs in the Dulwich Gallery, London.

Wedgwood's first bust of Mrs. Siddons was taken from a mould by John Flaxman*. In a letter to Flaxman in February 1784, Wedgwood wrote: "...you have my free consent, as it will so much oblige your friend Mr Burgess [probably James Bland Burges, the politician and friend of Pitt and Wilberforce] to let him have the bust of Mrs Siddons; the mould will serve my purposes..." Flaxman's chessmen are referred to in the same letter. These, in the medieval style, include Mrs. Siddons as the Queen in the role of Lady Macbeth. There are two portrait medallions: the first, of 1782, has been traditionally ascribed to Flaxman; the second may be based on an engraving of 1795 by T. Burke after J. Bateman. Another bust of Mrs. Siddons was made for Wedgwood by Benjamin Papera* in 1802.

Silenus

The satyr who accompanied Bacchus* on his travels, and by whom he is said to have been brought up and instructed. Silenus was a son either of Mercury* or of Pan*. He is usually represented as a fat, jovial old man with a bald head, carrying a wine skin. Since he was drunk for most of the time he is depicted asleep, or supported by other satyrs, or riding on an ass. Flaxman* modelled a bas-relief, *Triumph of Silenus*, produced as a medallion, 4½ ins. by 7½ ins., first catalogued in 1779; Angelini* modelled a *Silenus* bas-relief c.1787; and *Silenus and Boys* was among the six rectangular medallions of *Bacchanalian Boys* after Duquesnoy* supplied by Mrs. Landré* in 1769.

Silk-Screen Printing

A modern process employed by Wedgwood for fine quality multi-colour printing in which colour is sifted through the interstices of an appropriately woven silk screen. The early colour range was somewhat limited, but in recent years wide ranges of colour and subtle gradations of tone have been achieved. The most recent innovation (1960) was the development of printing in gold by this method, producing a perfection and clarity seldom achieved by earlier methods.

See: Transfer-Printing.

Silver Pattern

Pottery the design of which has been adapted from a silver prototype, or is decorated with ornament first used on silverware. 'Silver-shape' means pottery which is a more or less direct copy of a silver prototype. Silversmiths were often employed as designers. Many of Wedgwood's earliest shapes in creamware* and basaltes* appear to be directly related to contemporary silver, but it is not always possible to determine whether the prototype was silver or ceramic.

See: Pierced Work.

Right: **Siddons, Mrs. Sarah.** *Portrait of Sarah Siddons attributed to John Flaxman. First listed in the 1787 Ornamental Catalogue.* Wedgwood.

Below: **Siddons, Mrs. Sarah.** *Figure of a Queen from Flaxman's chess set modelled in 1784, reputed to be a portrait of Mrs. Siddons as Lady Macbeth.* Wedgwood.

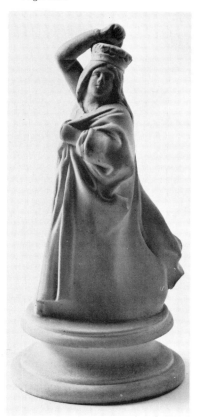

Silenus. *Cameo depicting Silenus with a grape vine and a panther.* Wedgwood.

Silver Pattern. *Pierced dessert basket, the surface simulating basket work of a contemporary silver pattern.* Wedgwood.

Silver-Plated Ware. *Wedgwood stoneware creamer silver-plated (electroplate).* Buten Museum.

Silver-Plated Ware

In the 1890s a small quantity of white stoneware ornamented with bas-reliefs in the manner of jasper* was plated (possibly by Elkington & Sons*) in silver over a thin coating of copper. The appearance is heavy, the relief ornament is blurred by the metal coating, and the process was expensive. The experiment was both commercially and aesthetically a failure, and examples are mercifully rare.

The method employed was to coat the ceramic surface with plumbago (black lead) and connect it by a wire to one pole of an electric battery. At the other pole was a bar of the metal to be deposited, copper or silver. The object was then placed in a bath of suitable electrolyte, and when the current began to flow metal was taken from the bar and deposited, particle by particle, onto the plumbago-coated surface until the necessary thickness had been built up. The preliminary deposition of copper was essential to form a good base for the silver. This, of course, is the standard method of electro-plating, but in its application to a ceramic body it can never have been more than experimental.

See: Batteries, Electric; Electricity and Pottery Decoration.

Silver Resist

A popular term for platinum resist lustre, so-called from its silvery colour.

See: Lustre Decoration; Resist Lustre.

Sim(p)cock, Thomas (fl.1769-1774)

Painter at the Chelsea Decorating Studio* who worked on the Frog* service. He was sent to London in May 1770, as "a new made flower hand."

Simon, Joseph (fl.1767-1774)

Enameller employed by Wedgwood from 1767, and later at the Chelsea Decorating Studio*, who worked on the Frog* service.

Simons, George (fl.1769-1774)

Painter at the Chelsea Decorating Studio*, employed on the Frog* service.

Singeries

From *Singe*, a monkey. Anthropomorphic rococo* decoration consisting of monkeys dressed in human attire. Not often employed in England, the subject was popular in France, where a notable series of wall decorations in this style by Christoph Huet are to be found at Chantilly. Perhaps the most popular of all *singeries*, is the Meissen* 'Monkey Band'.

See: Jean Pillement.

Skeaping, John Rattenbury, RA (b.1901)

Sculptor, draughtsman and engraver; born at South Woodford, Essex, the son of the painter, Kenneth Mathieson Skeaping; studied at Goldsmith's College, at the Central School of Arts and Crafts 1917-19, and at the Royal Academy Schools 1919-20. In 1924 he was awarded the Prix de Rome, and in the same year married Barbara Hepworth. The marriage was dissolved in 1933. He first exhibited at the Royal Academy in 1922. In 1926 he produced the first of many animal figures for Wedgwood, and these were reproduced in cream colour, basaltes, and moonstone*. During the Second World War he served with Intelligence and in the SAS. In 1953 he became Professor of Sculpture at the Royal College of Art, and seven years later was elected a member of the Royal Academy.

John Skeaping was a prize winner in the Wedgwood International competition of 1930 for a vase to commemorate the birth of Josiah Wedgwood, and his original drawing is preserved in the Wedgwood Museum*. His animal figures for Wedgwood include:

Bison, 9ins. by 9¾ins.
Buffalo, 7½ins. by 8¼ins.
Duiker, 5ins. by 7ins.
Duiker (standing), 8ins. by 5⅞ins.
Fallow Deer, 7½ins. by 7ins.
Kangaroo, 8¾ins. by 9ins.
Monkeys, 7¼ins. by 7ins.
Polar Bear, 7ins. by 7½ins.
Sea Lion, 8ins. by 8½ins.
Tiger and Buck, 7¾ins. by 13ins.

All these figures were available in moonstone, plain Queen's ware, or black basaltes, with optional wooden bases. Small quantities were also made in matt straw glaze and, when they were reintroduced after the war, in Windsor grey body, and grey body with rust glaze.

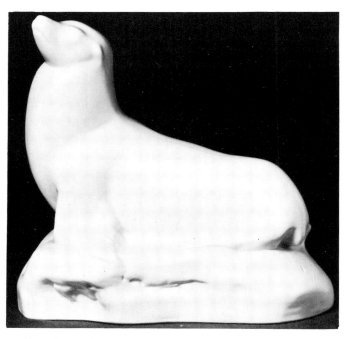

Skeaping, John. *Sea lion. Moonstone glaze figure.* Wedgwood.

Skellern, Victor, ARCA, FSIA, NRD (1909-1966)

Born in Fenton, in the Potteries, Victor Skellern began work in the Design Department at Etruria in 1923. He left to study at the Royal College of Art, graduating in 1933, when he returned to Wedgwood. In the following year he succeeded John Goodwin* as Art Director, an appointment that he held for thirty-one years. Victor Skellern's designs reveal his instinctive understanding of clay, his devotion to the Wedgwood tradition of quality, and his lifelong loyalty to two fundamental principles of design which he stated with his customary directness: "Decoration must be designed for the shape, and must add something relevant to it"; and "there is no such thing as 'Traditional' or 'Contemporary' design. These are merely convenient labels. Design is either good or bad: if good, it lasts; if bad, it doesn't." His influence over Wedgwood design was paramount for thirty years, and he was largely responsible for the crucial but controversial decision to introduce lithograph* decoration on Queen's ware* and bone china*. He retired in 1965. The long list of his important contributions to Wedgwood tableware design includes the following:

Ashford, 1951, bone china, lithograph.
Asia, 1956, bone china, silk screen.
Avocado, 1959, Queen's ware, *Queen's* * shape.
Corinthian shape, in collaboration with Kennard L. Wedgwood*, 1935.
Evenlode, 1947, Queen's ware, *Corinthian* shape.
Fairford, 1941, bone china.
Forest Folk, 1934, Celadon* body.
Green Leaf, 1949, Queen's ware, *Queen's* shape.
Greyfriars, 1937, bone china.
Hampton Court, 1937, Queen's ware, *Corinthian* shape.
Lichfield, 1953, bone china, lithograph.
Mandarin, 1949, Queen's ware, *Queen's* shape.
Meadow, 1940, Queen's ware, *Edme* * shape.

Slave Emancipation Society Seal. *Medallion modelled by Hackwood in 1787 for the Slave Emancipation Society. Black on white jasper, 1 ⅜ ins. in diameter. Wedgwood.*

Morning Glory, 1936, Queen's ware, *Patrician* * shape.
Moselle, 1957, bone china.
Persian Pony, 1936, bone china.
Pimpernel, 1947, bone china.
Runnymede, 1940, bone china.
St. James, 1936, bone china.
Sandringham, 1947, bone china.
Seasons, 1935, Queen's ware, *Catherine* * shape.
Strawberry Hill, with Millicent Taplin*, 1957, bone china lithograph.
Wild Oats, 1954, bone china, *Coupe* shape.
Wildflower, 1945, bone china.
Winchester, 1947, Queen's ware, *Patrician* shape.
Woodstock, 1939, bone china.

Skellern also designed engine-turned jasper vases for presentation to H.M. Queen Mary in 1936 and 1939, and the mug commemorating the Wedgwood bicentenary in 1959.

Slave Emancipation Society Seal

Medallion by Hackwood* of 1787 produced by Josiah Wedgwood for the Slave Emancipation Society. It shows a chained negro slave kneeling in a suppliant posture, and it bears the inscription: "Am I not a man and a brother?" Wedgwood played an active part in the affairs of the Society and became a member of the Committee. The medallion was taken from the Seal of the Committee, and many hundreds were made. Some were mounted in gold in the lids of snuff boxes, ladies wore them mounted as bracelets, or as hair ornaments, and the wearing of these cameos became very fashionable. Many were executed in black on white jasper, but the medallion exists also in other bodies. A quantity of black on white jasper medallions was reproduced in 1959.

Skellern, Victor. Forest Folk, *designed by Victor Skellern in 1934.* Wedgwood.

Sleeping Boys

Five figures of *Sleeping Boys*, naked infants lying in characteristic poses, were produced by Wedgwood by 1773 in basaltes*, and subsequently they were made in white jasper on rectangular coloured jasper bases (4½ ins.—5½ ins. long). These were reproduced from casts, probably supplied by Mrs. Landré*, after the originals by Duquesnoy* (Il Fiammingo). They are almost identical to the five *Enfants du Roi* produced by Sèvres* from the same source. Considerable confusion has been caused by the common practice of calling these figures *Somnus*, a name which properly belongs to a similar but much larger figure after a marble by Alessandro Algardi. The *Sleeping Boys* were reproduced during the nineteenth century in both basaltes and majolica*. The same figures also occur in pearl ware*, but are considered to be the work of Ralph or Enoch Wood* (see: Figures).

See: Infant Reclining Figures.

Sleeping Boys. *One of the series of five models of* Sleeping Boys, *first produced in basaltes in 1773 and later in jasper, probably supplied by Mrs. Landré in the form of casts after originals by Duquesnoy.* Christie's.

Slip

Clay, or a ceramic body, diluted with water to the consistency of thin cream. As decoration it is washed over the entire body in a contrasting colour, often with a design incised through it (*sgraffito**), or applied in a trailing pattern of lines and dots. Slips of several colours are sometimes applied and combed together to give an effect of marbling*. Slip-cast ware is produced by pouring slip into plaster of Paris moulds. This process was introduced into Staffordshire about 1745, reputedly by Ralph Daniels of Cobridge. Wedgwood thought that plaster of Paris was first used by J.P. Elers*. The process of decorating ware with two different coloured and contrasting slips — 'two-colour slip' — is a modern development (1936) of an old technique.

See: Slip Casting; Slip Decoration.

Slip Casting

Casting with slip in plaster of Paris moulds. The plaster absorbs water from the slip, leaving a layer of firm clay adhering to the walls of the mould. Surplus slip is poured off when the layer is thick enough, and the cast allowed to become leather hard*. In so doing it shrinks away from the walls of the mould, which facilitates extraction. Slip casting is now employed to make a good deal of hollow ware, and it is used for anything that does not have a circular section.

Slip Decoration

The process of decorating pottery by applying slip* to the surface by a technique similar to that employed in decorating a cake with icing, by trailing it in lines and dots (trailed slip), or by applying differently coloured slips which are combed* to produce marbled* or variegated* wares. Speckled* ware is produced by spraying slip onto the surface of the ware.

Slipper

A term sometimes used by Wedgwood for a *bourdalou**, also known as a crinoline slipper and, more formally, as a coach pot. Correctly, the term 'slipper' refers to the normal wedge-shaped bed pan. Sanitary ware of this kind was made by most potters during the 18th century, and for a greater part of the 19th.

Smalt

A deep blue pigment made by fusing together zaffre*, potassium carbonate, and a form of silica (eg. sand) to produce a coloured glass. This was ground to a fine powder, and could be used as the pigment for cobalt blue painting (either as an enamel or under the glaze), transfer-printing, and ground-laying. It was also employed to make coloured bodies*, such as jasper dip. Smalt in the 18th century was imported from Saxony until native deposits of cobalt were found in Cornwall.

See: Cornish Journey.

Smear Glaze

See: Glaze.

Smear Glaze White Ware

White ware very thinly glazed as the result of the volatilisation of glaze material present inside the saggar* during firing. This effect should not be confused with the 'waxen biscuit' body*. Where unglazed this ware is porous, and it is therefore a type of earthenware.

See: Glaze.

Smiles, Samuel (1812-1904)

Born in Haddington, East Lothian, Smiles was the third of fourteen children. He was apprenticed to a local doctor, and in 1829 he moved with his employer to Leith, which enabled him to qualify at Edinburgh University. As a doctor he made no very great headway, and in 1838 he became the editor of the *Leeds Times*. In 1845 he was employed by the new Leeds and Thirsk Railway in an executive capacity, which led him to become interested in George Stephenson, whose biography he published in 1857. This was followed by what is, perhaps, his best known book, *Self Help,* which became a best-seller in Victorian England, and was translated into several languages. Smiles could not find a publisher for the first edition and published it himself, making a considerable profit thereby. The book was a series of homilies illustrated by anecdotes from the lives of famous men, mainly on the subject of Failure conquered by Perseverance and Hard Work. It was principally addressed to young men, and some of the biographical material, which included a number of references to Josiah Wedgwood, was inaccurate. The lives of several of the more illustrious potters were glanced at in brief, including Palissy and Böttger, in addition to Wedgwood, and various improving lessons were drawn.

Smiles' *Life of Josiah Wedgwood* came much later, in 1894, and was the last of a number of books. It was commissioned by Godfrey Wedgwood*, whose first choice was Charles Tindall Gatty (1851-1921), Curator of the Liverpool Museum, but Gatty was unable to undertake it, and Smiles was substituted. His book failed to add anything of importance to the earlier works of Jewitt* and Eliza Meteyard*.

Smith, Joachim (fl.1758-1803)

Portrait modeller. In 1758 he received a Premium of ten guineas from the Society of Arts for a wax portrait. He had, apparently, devised a method of colouring wax so as to make it suitable for modelling portrait miniatures. In 1773 Wedgwood began to reproduce Smith's portraits in his white biscuit body, and later in the white terracotta*. To some extent the relationship between Wedgwood and Smith was unusual, since Smith was employing Wedgwood to give permanent form to the portraits of some of his sitters. In July 1774, Wedgwood wrote to Bentley: ''...I must beg of you to bespeak a little of Mr Smith's patience for us, and his Ladies shall be the better for it for ever;'' and later: ''Please to make my best compliments to Mr Smith and tell him I do not forget him, but bear him in rememberance every day, and almost every hour, and employ both my head and hands in his service continually.'' In some irritation he wrote: ''I wish Mr Smith would be quiet a little. I do all I can for him.'' No doubt, however, some of Mr Smith's medallions were to Wedgwood's order. Chief among these must be those of Thomas Bentley* 1773, Sir William Hamilton* of the same year, Wedgwood's own portrait, and that of his wife (1774). Also by or attributed to Smith are the portraits of Mrs. Anna Letitia Barbauld (sent to Etruria in January, 1775, and produced by July, 1775); John Bradby Blake*; Matilda Fielding; Lady Charlotte Finch ('Lady Cha') and Henrietta Finch, her daughter, both 1774; John Reinhold Forster, 1776; and Mrs. Elizabeth ('Blue Stocking') Montague, 1775.

Smith, Joachim. *Portrait medallion of Thomas Bentley modelled, as a pair to one of Josiah I, by Joachim Smith. 1773.* Manchester City Art Gallery.

In a letter of 18th December, 1774, Wedgwood writes of having a polisher in the rooms in London to work on a variety of objects, including ''Mr Smith's portraits.'' He goes on to mention recent experiments from which he does not doubt being able to give his new white composition any tint of a fine blue. ''I propose making the heads of this composition, and sometimes the grounds, but each separate. By this means we shall be able to undercut the heads a little.'' This is an indication of the experimental nature of the portraits being made for Joachim Smith, and his clients did not find them entirely satisfactory. For this reason Smith and Wedgwood parted company, and the latter sought fresh modellers. Wedgwood, however, was incensed to hear that Smith had been in touch with William Duesbury*, owner of the Derby* and Chelsea* porcelain factories, presumably with the object of obtaining a new source of supply. Wedgwood feared that Smith might pass on what he had learned during their own business connection.

Smith, John (fl.1773-1774)

Painter at the Chelsea Decorating Studio*, who worked on the Frog* service. He is sometimes listed as John 'Warwick' Smith (1749-1831), the noted painter of landscapes in watercolour. The latter appears to have been in London, studying with Sawrey Gilpin, at the time when the Frog service was being decorated, so it is possible that he worked for a short period at the Chelsea studios.

Smith & Co., William

Earthenware manufacturers of Stockton-on-Tees, founded in 1824. They were principally imitators of Wedgwood, employing the impressed mark 'WEDGEWOOD'. Presumably they hoped that the misspelling would enable them to avoid the consequences of plagiarism, but Wedgwood's applied for an injunction in 1848 to restrain Smith's from continuing to copy the products of Etruria*, and in this they were successful. The firm made a considerable variety of ware, including cream-coloured ware and white ware, and their marks include 'W. S. & Co's WEDGEWOOD' and 'W. S. & Co's. QUEEN'S WARE.'

Sneyd, T. Hanley

Name found on crude imitations of the Portland* vase dating probably from the early years of the 19th century.

Snuff Bottles

A snuff bottle, the form inspired by Chinese snuff bottles made during the reign of Chia Ch'ing (1796-1820), was made of pearl ware* by Wedgwood about 1900. A specimen in the Buten Museum* is about 2½ins. high, decorated with a Staffordshire version of the Chinese Dog (or, more correctly, Lion) of Fo (Buddha), and marked 'Wedgwood, Etruria, England.'

Society of Antiquaries, The

London Society, founded c.1572 and incorporated in 1751. It was devoted to the study of antiquities. Wedgwood was elected a member in May 1786, proposed by seven members, all of whom were also members of the Royal Society*. Sir Joseph Banks* was among their number.

Society of Bucks

A transfer print of the Arms of the Honourable Society of Bucks occasionally appears on Wedgwood creamware mugs. It is signed 'Sadler, Liverpool' at the bottom, among the scroll-work. The design, rococo in style, has a central cartouche containing a buck with two huntsmen standing on either side. The same print is also found on contemporary porcelain mugs.

Sock Boot

A hollow utensil in the form of a boot made in creamware c.1890. It was filled with hot water, and was used for drying and warming a sock drawn over it.

Socrates (469-349 B.C.)

The celebrated philosopher, born in Athens, was the son of a sculptor, and was trained in that profession. As a teacher he appears to have achieved fame by middle age, but he never officially opened a school, nor delivered public lectures. His method of teaching was to bring his hearer to an understanding of what he wanted to impart by a series of carefully framed questions. His influence became so great that he was eventually charged with corrupting the youth of Athens, and of trying to replace the divinities of the State with his own. Plato* who was one of his followers, records all that is known of his defence, and of his enforced death by drinking a cup of hemlock.

A cast of a bust of Socrates, 20ins. high, was supplied by Hoskins & Grant* in 1775. *Teletes and Socrates,* a medallion by Hackwood*, was produced after 1787.

Solander, Dr. Daniel (1736-1782)

Swedish naturalist, educated at the University of Uppsala. He was a pupil of the naturalist, Linnaeus, and travelled to London in 1760 to obtain employment at the British Museum. In 1767 he accompanied Sir Joseph Banks* and Captain Cook to Otaheite to observe the transit of Venus. Solander was a visitor to the meetings of the Lunar Society* in Birmingham. His London house in Soho Square was near Wedgwood's Greek Street showrooms*. A portrait medallion was modelled by Flaxman in 1775, the name being impressed below the truncation. A large portrait (13ins. by 10ins.) was possibly adapted from an unsigned medallion in the British Museum.

Solid Agate

Coloured clays (usually white, blue, and brown) wedged (i.e. mingled by slicing and kneading) either at random or in a predetermined sequence, used by Wedgwood for vases in imitation of agate and other natural stones. Wedgwood made other wares of this kind in his early years, including teapots and knife handles. Solid agate ware was also made at Apt (Vaucluse), and at Kassel and Königsberg in Germany.

See: Variegated Ware.

Solon (c.639-?559 B.C.)

Athenian legislator. In his youth Solon became a merchant and travelled abroad. He also acquired a reputation for amatory verse, and later for philosophical and moral wisdom in verse form. He was chosen archon (head of State) in 594, and instituted many reforms, introducing a new system of weights and measures, rectifying the calendar, and promulgating new laws.

In a letter to Bentley* dated 7th May, 1777, Wedgwood writes: ''We are at a loss about the Solon Bust order'd, having no other Solon than what we have called Demosthenes...Mr Cox says it was called Solon when it first came here in Plaister, & continues under that name in our Catalogue — We shall send you one or two of these.'' It is certainly comforting to find that confusion in the naming of Wedgwood subjects is not confined to the 19th and 20th centuries.

Hoskins & Grant* supplied casts of busts described as Solon and Demosthenes on 21st March, 1774, and 1st January, 1775, respectively.

Solander, Dr. Daniel. *Jasper portrait medallion of Dr. Daniel Solander, 13ins. by 10ins., perhaps adapted from an unsigned medal in the British Museum. Modelled in September 1779 for the series of large portraits.* Lawrence Pucci Collection.

Somnus

God of Sleep, the son of Night, and the brother of Death. Wedgwood produced a large figure, 25ins. long, of a sleeping boy, after a black marble (or basalt) by Alessandro Algardi (1602-54) now in the Galleria Borghese, Rome. The original figure was illustrated in an engraving published in 1704 (Maffei and Rossi, *Raccolta di Statue Antiche e Moderne,* Pl. 151). The Wedgwood copy is illustrated in Meteyard* (*Life of Wedgwood,* Vol. II, facing p.230, with the correct title). Wedgwood, however, called this figure, *Morpheus* or *Autumn.* This confusion, which has persisted, arises from a Hoskins & Oliver* invoice dated May 1770, for a ''Mould for the Morpheus for Pressing, cutting the model in pieces and joining it together again after it was moulded.'' This then became 'Morpheus, reclining figure' listed in the 1773 Catalogue*. This rare figure is known only in basaltes*, and an example is in the Buten Museum*.

See: Infant Reclining Figures; Sleeping Boys.

Sophonisba

The daughter of the Carthaginian general, Hasdrubal. She married a King of Numidia. Scipio Africanus insisted on her becoming a Roman captive because of her Carthaginian origin, but her husband sent her a poisoned draught which she drank.

Wedgwood subject:
Sophonisba, medallion by Hackwood*.

Sorrows of Young Werther, The

This was one of two works of contemporary fiction employed as inspiration for the decoration of jasper in the 18th century. The other was Sterne's* *Sentimental Journey*. Goethe wrote his sentimental best-selling romance in 1774. It was suggested by the suicide of a fellow student at Leipzig University, who shot himself while possessed of a hopeless passion for the wife of another man. The work was an instantaneous success and was soon translated into several languages. Young men and women gave way to imaginary sorrows to emulate Werther, and men even committed suicide holding a copy of the book. Werther and Charlotte were widely used as porcelain decoration, Meissen* producing tea services decorated with different scenes from the book around 1780. A favourite subject at a number of factories was Charlotte weeping at the tomb of Werther, the Wedgwood jasper* version of which was designed by Lady Templetown* about 1787.

Southwell, Mrs. (fl.1750-1775)

Visitor to Etruria* in July 1772, and, according to Josiah Wedgwood, "adapt [*sic*] in the Art of disposing the most beautiful productions of Nature in the most agreeable, picturesque and striking manner to the eyes of the beholder." She examined every flowerpot then in production and advised Wedgwood how they might be improved. He wrote to Bentley*: "Mrs. Southwell is a charming woman... and having such a Mistress in the science of flower dressing, I hope our future productions will show that I have profited accordingly." Wedgwood constantly consulted his wife, and other ladies of his acquaintance, to gain "experience in Female tastes, without which I should have made but a poor figure among my Potts."

Sparks, Thomas (1773-1848)

Engraver of Hanley, who supplied engravings for tableware patterns to Ridgway, Spode*, Stevenson's of Cobridge and Wedgwood, among others. He was responsible, in 1810, for a number of engravings for the *Peony*, *Bamboo*, and *Hibiscus* patterns. In 1818 he wrote from London to Josiah II* soliciting work, and suggesting "designs after the manner of the antique, printed, coloured and gilt in imitation of Bronze" for Wedgwood's Stone China*.

See: Underglaze Blue Prints.

Spath (Spaith)

An 18th century term, equivalent to the modern *spar,* for kinds of crystalline or non-lustrous minerals which can easily be cleaved, such as fluorspar, calcite, etc. The description *spathic* is used today of a mineral resembling a spar, particularly in the property of cleavage, as in *feldspathic.* The word *spath* is of German origin, and is still used in France to mean *spar.* Wedgwood used the term *'Spath fusible'* to denote the fusible part of his fine stonewares, as distinct from the refractory clay.

Speckled Agate (Speckled Ware)

Coloured slips sprayed on to the surface of the ware to produce a speckled effect. This technique was employed by both Wedgwood and the Woods* of Burslem.

See: Variegated Ware.

Spence, Benjamin Edward (1822-1866)

Sculptor who studied under R.J. Wyatt and John Gibson, and exhibited at the Royal Academy on five occasions between 1849 and 1866. His *Joseph Interpreting Pharaoh's Dream* was modelled by William Beattie* for Wedgwood in 1867 and produced in Carrara* ware.

Sphinx

A combination of the human form with that of the lion. There are two types: the Greek and the Egyptian. The Greek sphinx derived originally from Egypt, but was said to be the daughter of Hades and the Chimaera*. She is represented as seated in a typically feline position, and has the head and breasts of a woman, the body of a lion, and a pair of wings. The Egyptian sphinx, originally male, is represented as reclining, the upper part human, and the remainder of the body that of a lion. In 18th century England the Greek sphinx was known from black-figure vases in particular, the Egyptian from illustrations in such works as Montfaucon's* *Antiquité Expliquée*. Wedgwood produced both varieties from c.1769 in basaltes, and later in jasper and *rosso antico**. Some fine reproductions have been included in the Egyptian Collection introduced in 1978. The modelling of these figures is of excellent quality and has been variously assigned to several artists. It would appear from Wedgwood's correspondence that the majority were the work of Boot* and of Josiah himself.

Wedgwood models include the following:

Lyre and two Sphinxes, tablet 10ins. by 22ins., supplied by Hoskins & Grant*, 1774.

Egyptian Sphinxes, pair of figures, 6ins. long (1779 Catalogue*).

Grecian Sphinxes, pair of figures, 12ins. long (1773 Catalogue).

Grecian Sphinxes, pair of figures, 5ins. (1773 Catalogue).

Egyptian Sphinxes with lotus to hold candles, 6ins. long (1773 Catalogue).

Sitting Sphinxes with nozzles to hold candles, 10¼ins. (1773 Catalogue).

Seated sphinxes also appear as supports for basaltes vases, and sphinx monopodia* as tripod supports. Sphinx heads were also popular as handles for vases, and for the lids of inkwells and vases.

See: Canopic Jars; Egyptian Collection; Egyptian Taste.

Sphinx. *One of a pair of exceptionally rare black basaltes sphinxes, first catalogued in 1773, of which examples were sent to Du Burk in 1770. This type of sphinx first appears c.1700 in sheets of designs by the dessinateur du roi, Jean I Bérain, and by 1715 it begins to appear in the form of bronze chenets as portraits of fashionable beauties. It occurs in early German porcelain, and c.1750 in the porcelain of Bow and Chelsea. These English versions are portraits of the popular actresses Peg Woffington and Kitty Clive, and may have been inspired by an engraved plate in Montfaucon. Wedgwood's versions are clearly copied from the Chelsea or Bow models, of which there are several. Zeitlin Collection.*

Sphinx. *Early black basaltes version of the Greek sphinx, derived from Egypt by way of Mesopotamia, and originating in this form in Corinth, c.800 B.C.* Wedgwood.

Spies, Industrial

Wherever secret industrial processes exist, information about which could be turned to profit, there will also be industrial spies. No one knew this better than Josiah Wedgwood who, in matters of business, was always a realist. As far back as the Whieldon-Wedgwood partnership he recorded the results of his experiments in code. In February 1776, Wedgwood wrote to Bentley*: "...as jasper is one of 17, six of 74, three of 22, and ¼ of 20, you can hardly conceive the difficulty and trouble I have had in mixing two tons of this composition and leaving everybody as wise as they were." In 1768 he wrote to Cox* in London regarding patterns and designs reaching his competitors: "The person from whom I have the information assures me of his own knowledge that Caravalla [a china dealer] supplies Palmer* of Hanley with all my patterns as they arrive at my rooms in London, and Fogg [another china dealer] does the same for Bagnall & Baker, and the last let any of the other potters have them, they paying a share of the expenses. You must try if you can recollect any particular person repeatedly buying a few pairs or single articles of your new patterns as they arrive."

A number of Continental potters endeavoured to gain employment with Wedgwood. The most notorious spy was Louis-Victor Gerverot*. The Royal owner of the Ludwigsburg porcelain factory (near Stuttgart), the Duke Karl Eugen, visited Staffordshire, including Wedgwood's factory, in 1776. In the same year Ludwigsburg started to make creamware, and a little later the modellers, Scheffauer and Dannecker, produced reliefs inspired by jasper in biscuit porcelain.

In 1785 Wedgwood wrote to William Nicholson, Secretary of the General Chamber of Trade, on this subject: "The

foreign gentry...have, some of them, exhibited the greatest share of impudence... For having been refused admittance by one clerk, they have come again when he has been absent, and almost forced their way to the machines they wanted to see. In another instance, having been turned out of one door, they have waited an opportunity of entering in under different pretences by another. Sometimes they pretend to be possessed of improvements to the machines they want to take drawings or models of. At other times they procure recommendations from gentleman who are not aware of their intentions...and therefore no time should be lost nor any Diligence spared on our part to prevent them."

Apart from this clandestine trade in industrial secrets, attempts were frequently made to recruit workmen for other factories, home and foreign, and Wedgwood himself was not above poaching skilled operatives from elsewhere, as some of his letters prove.

The growth of the industry in England and on the Continent during the 18th century was marked by frequent instances of this kind, and the spread of porcelain manufacture on the Continent was largely made possible by migratory workmen who acquired manufacturing secrets at one factory to sell at another. They even acquired a special name — 'arcanists'; those who had acquired the arcanum or secret.

With this in mind Wedgwood wrote a pamphlet in 1784 for circulation among the factory's workpeople. It was entitled *An Address to Workmen in the Pottery on the Subject of Entering the Service of Foreign Manufacturers.* On the title page are the words "A rolling stone gathers no moss. Old Prov."

See: Codes and Formulae.

Spill Vase

A small cylindrical vase to contain folded slips of paper or thin strips of wood known as spills. They were used for lighting candles and tobacco pipes from the grate. Spill vases were made by Wedgwood in Queen's ware and the dry bodies* from c.1775.

Spirit Barrel

Large containers for spirits — for rum and whisky — were made by several manufacturers, the earliest being of salt-glazed* stoneware. They were used for bulk storage in public houses and bars. Wedgwood made spirit barrels of pearl* ware with printed and hand-painted decoration, with the name of the spirit lettered prominently, and fitted with a pewter spigot for drawing off the contents. These were produced c.1890-1915.

Spode

Josiah Spode was apprenticed to Whieldon* in 1749, and by the time of Wedgwood's partnership with Whieldon (1754) he appears to have graduated to journeyman. Shortly thereafter he joined William Banks and John Turner* at Stoke. Between 1764 and 1779 he was a partner in factories at Shelton and Stoke. After that date he was in business on his own account. At first his production was probably confined to Black Egyptian*, creamware*, and a form of Pearl* ware painted in blue, and it was left to Josiah II (1754-1827), who assumed the direction of the firm after his father's death in 1797, to convert a successful business into a major force in the pottery industry. When he died twenty years later, Spode had taken the lead from Wedgwood.

He was succeeded by his son, Josiah III, who survived him by only two years. The firm was then bought by William Taylor Copeland, who was already a partner, and it became first 'Copeland late Spode', and then 'W.T. Copeland & Sons'. Josiah Spode II is generally credited with having introduced the manufacture of bone china* into Staffordshire in 1799, and stone china* about 1805, and he made many improvements in the art of transfer printing*. Outline transfers as an aid to the painters were employed on bone china.

Spode captured a large share of the porcelain market and made a speciality of Japan patterns. In the 1840s Copeland introduced Parian* ware, which was later manufactured by Wedgwood under the name of Carrara*. Under the Copelands the firm produced elaborately gilded wares with rich coloured grounds, drawing heavily on Sèvres* for inspiration.

The range of wares produced by Spode during the late 18th and early 19th centuries conformed closely to Wedgwood's. It included creamware, basaltes*, a form of jasper* body (in reality a white stoneware similar to Wedgwood's white body, decorated with coloured slip and sprigged ornament, but not a true Wedgwood jasper), red ware (similar to *rosso antico* *), cane ware*, drab body*, pearl ware, lustre* and bone china. Many of the shapes and ornaments are almost indistinguishable from Wedgwood's.

Sponged Ground

A ground colour applied underglaze by dabbing with a sponge. Examples are the so-called powder-blue ground introduced at the beginning of the 20th century, and the mottled and tortoiseshell grounds of the Ivy House Works* in which several colours were applied in much the same way. Modern sponged grounds include blue, turquoise, green, shagreen, ruby, pink and grey.

Spreader

A tool, nowadays operated automatically, for flattening a ball of clay into a circular bat for use with the jigger*.

Sprigged Ware (Sprigging)

Pottery decorated in low relief with ornament stamped or moulded separately and applied to the ware by sprigging, using slip* as an adhesive. The process was extensively used by Josiah Wedgwood, for instance in the decoration of jasper, but it was in use before his day, notably at some of the early porcelain factories, where sprays of prunus or tea blossom were applied in this way.

Spurs (Stilts)

Small pieces of fired clay used to separate ware stacked in the glost oven*. Three spur or stilt marks* are usually visible on the underside of earthenware plate rims.

Stafford, 1st Marquis (1721-1803)
Granville Leveson-Gower

Eldest son of the 1st Earl Gower, whom he succeeded in 1754. Member of Parliament for Westminster; Lord of the Admiralty, 1749; Lord Privy Seal, 1755 and 1784; Lord President of the Council, 1767-69 and 1783. Friend and patron of Josiah Wedgwood's, a frequent visitor at Etruria*, and host to Josiah at Trentham Hall, Lord Gower is frequently mentioned in Wedgwood's letters to Bentley*. He exercised his considerable influence on behalf of English potters in general and Josiah Wedgwood in particular, and was one of Wedgwood's most constant admirers and most liberal customers. He was created Marquis of Stafford in 1786. His portrait medallion*, attributed to Hackwood*, was issued c.1782.

Stafford, 1st Marquis. *Portrait medallion of Granville Leveson-Gower, 1st Marquis of Stafford, usually attributed to Hackwood, c.1782.* Wedgwood.

Stafford Pottery

An earthenware pottery at Stockton-on-Tees which, from 1826 to 1853, traded as William Smith & Co.* They used the name 'WEDGEWOOD' or 'WEDGEWOOD & CO.' until Wedgwood obtained an injunction to stop this infringement of their trade mark in 1848.

Staithes Patent Pipe

A patent pipe bowl made by Wedgwood in blue and white jasper. It has a detachable receptacle at the bottom to trap moisture and nicotine. Manufactured about 1875. Mark impressed 'STAITHES' PATENT WEDGWOOD.'

Stamped

1. Impressed with a stamp, as in the case of the mark impressed by Wedgwood from the 18th century onwards.
2. The process of making small ornaments from intaglio moulds for attachment by sprigging*.
3. Technique of decoration in which unfired clay is impressed with ornament with the aid of metal stamps.

Stella, Jacques de. *Black basaltes ewer with festoons, masks and fish-tail handle, known to Wedgwood as 'Stella's ewer'. Similar handles occur in French faience. c.1770.* Dwight and Lucille Beeson Collection.

Statuary Porcelain

A mid-19th century term for Parian* or Carrara* porcelain. It was originally intended that this body should be employed for the reproduction of statuary in miniature.

Steam Engines

See: Prime Movers; James Watt.

Steele, Aaron (fl.1780-1845)

Painter, at the Greek Street* decorating studios from April 1784. He appears to have specialised in the decoration of Etruscan* vases, and as late as 1807 Byerley* was suggesting that he should be put to work on these again. "He is," Byerley wrote in April of that year, "the only man in the country with much knowledge of that work, and as such very valuable." Aaron Steele is also known to have been responsible for the fine and detailed painting of birds on bone china* teaware c.1812, each bird being named on the reverse.

Steele, Daniel (fl.1762)

Painter, with Thomas Daniel(l)*, of the raised flowers decorating a caudle* and breakfast set presented by Wedgwood to Queen Charlotte* about 1762.

Stella, Jacques de (1596-1657)

French painter and etcher, born in Lyon and died in Paris, who belonged to a family of painters and engravers of Flemish origin. Jacques de Stella spent a number of years in Rome, where he met his friend, Poussin, who later greatly influenced him. In Paris he received royal patronage, and was responsible for some important decoration in churches. He is particularly noted today for his decorative work. The *Livres de Vases aux Galeries de Louvre* (Paris, 1667) contained illustrations of vases by Stella, engraved by his niece, Françoise Bouzonnet. Wedgwood's fish-tail* ewer appears to have been taken from this book (although the handle had earlier appeared on French *faience*), because Wedgwood referred to them as "Stella's ewers" in a letter of 1770 and was therefore acquainted with the source.

Stephan, Pierre (fl.1770-1795)

A French modeller who worked for Derby*, probably Chelsea*, and possibly Bristol. In 1774 he supplied Wedgwood with models and moulds. There seems to be no evidence that he was, as has been generally assumed, employed at Etruria*. Josiah did not think highly of Stephan's work, writing to Bentley on 22nd August, 1774: "I have received & examined Mr Steven's [*sic*] moulds of Hope & the Conquer'd province, & am glad to find the drawing & proportions so well preserved, but in everything else they are infinitely short of the exquisite originals. The Drapery is hard and unfinish'd." He added, in horror: "the characters of the Faces are those of common mortals *of the lower Class.*"

Stephan's splendid statuette of Lord Rodney, produced in black basaltes*, shows that he was capable of fine and vigorous figure modelling. He supplied models and moulds of Lion, Greyhound, and Lap Dog (probably Spaniel) knops (see: Finials) for teapots in September, 1774, and two wax models of *Hope* and a *Conquered Province* in August. The latter appear to have been remodelled by Flaxman* in 1775, perhaps from Stephan's originals. Stephan's son, Peter, worked as a modeller for Coalport*.

Sterne, Laurence (1713-1768)

English novelist, born at Clonmel in Ireland. Sterne was educated at a school in Halifax and then at Cambridge University. He entered the Church and procured a living at Sutton (Yorks.). The first two volumes of his most famous novel, *Tristram Shandy*, were published in 1760 and were an immediate success. The remaining volumes appeared over the next seven years. Sterne spent much time in London and in travelling on the Continent, and he led a life which was, perhaps, rather more dissolute than that of many 18th century members of the cloth. *The Sentimental Journey* was published in 1768, and in the same year he died of consumption. His body was exhumed and used at the Cambridge Anatomy School. Wedgwood produced a bust from an original model supplied by Hoskins & Grant*, but specimens are exceedingly rare.

The bas-relief figures of *Poor Maria* and *The Bourbonnais Shepherd* (from *The Sentimental Journey*) were modelled by Hackwood* in 1783 after designs by Lady Templetown*, the former adapted from a painting by Joseph Wright* of Derby.

Still

See: Whisky Still.

Stilt Marks

Also called 'spur' marks. Small defects in the surface, or the glaze where this is present, on the underside of flatware which is not supported on a footing during firing. These mark the places where the object stood on small pointed 'stilts' or 'cockspurs' in the kiln. They occur on Wedgwood earthenware but they are, on modern Queen's ware, ground out before being finally passed. They are so invariable on Chelsea and Japanese (Arita) porcelain as to be a reason for instant rejection when they are absent. They were very widely found on certain other wares.

Stirrup Cup

An English drinking vessel adapted from the ancient Greek rhyton. Usually it is in the form of the head of a fox or hound, but less often it is shaped like the head of a hare or some other animal, or even of a fish head. These cups had no handle or foot, and were made to be drained at one draught. Principally they were for huntsmen to drink a toast to the day's sport, or for the rider who wanted to drink without dismounting.

Wedgwood made a hare's head stirrup cup in basaltes ware, probably modelled by Tebo*, foxes' heads (often mounted in silver), and a classical head in the form of a handled and footed ewer copied from an antique bronze now in the Louvre. The last is not technically a rhyton, but is usually described as such.

Stone China

Dense, hard, porcellaneous ware generally composed of china stone, china clay, flint, blue clay and a bluish stain, first developed by Turner* of Lane End c.1800, and made in quantity by Spode* under the name of 'Stone China' or 'New China' from 1805. Wedgwood's Stone China was first produced in 1820 and continued in production until 1861. The patterns used on Stone China were underglaze blue printed* designs or Oriental-style prints with on-glaze enamelling and gilding. The 'WEDGWOOD' impressed mark does not usually appear on Stone China, which is printed with the words 'WEDGWOOD'S STONE CHINA' in underglaze blue or on-glaze black. On gilded patterns the pattern number is added in gold.

Although Wedgwood's Stone China was in production for more than forty years, it appears to have been made in comparatively small quantities and never achieved the popularity of Mason's so-called 'Ironstone', which was a similar, if not identical, body.

Stirrup Cup. *One of a pair of Wedgwood & Bentley black basaltes stirrup cups in the form of foxes' masks, mounted in contemporary silver. This pair is particularly rare since each head bears the impressed mark on the left ear. Most known examples are unmarked. 5¼ ins. long.* Christie's.

Stone China. *Stone china dish decorated with Oriental flowers, c.1830.* Wedgwood.

Stoneware

A type of pottery midway between earthenware and porcelain which is composed of clay and fusible rock. It is fired to a point where vitrification of the fusible part renders it impervious to liquids, but not sufficiently to make it translucent, except in the case of some of the thinnest and most refined of these hard-fired wares. Vitrification makes a glaze unnecessary, but a glaze of some kind is usually added to wares intended for domestic utility, usually a salt-glaze, since this can be added at the same time as the ware is fired. Lead glazes were employed occasionally, as they were on certain types of porcelain, but this was unusual, and mainly for decorative purposes. Vessels of domestic utility were always glazed *inside* for aesthetic reasons, although some of Wedgwood's finer stonewares, such as jasper and basaltes, were lapidary polished* rather than glazed in the 18th century. Wedgwood stonewares include jasper, basaltes, and caneware, as well as the salt-glazed ware of the early period.

Stothard, Thomas, RA (1755-1834)

Painter and book illustrator; studied at the Royal Academy Schools, 1777; exhibited at the Society of Artists, 1777, and at the Royal Academy, 1778; elected RA 1794. Stothard, a friend of Flaxman*, designed the Wellington Shield (silver, now at Apsley House, London). His three sons were all sculptors.

Several Wedgwood bas-reliefs* are said to have been designed by him, including *Blind Man's Buff* (certainly Flaxman's*), and a series of figures variously described as *Aerial Figures, Nymphs,* or *Zephyrs,* which appear to have been adapted from illustrations in Bartoli, Bellori and La Chasse (*Picturae Antiquae,* 1750).

Strainer

See: Drainer.

Strapwork, Applied

Decoration in the form of vertical strips interwoven with horizontal strips applied to the surface of, for instance, a jasper bowl. The vertical and horizontal strips may be different colours, such as yellow and white. This kind of decoration often occurs on wares which, because of the shape, could not easily be worked on the engine-turning lathe.*

See: Dice Pattern.

Stringer, Edward (fl.1770-1783)

Josiah Wedgwood's mother was a Stringer, and it is probable that the Knutsford family of artists of that name — who included Samuel (exhibited Liverpool Society of Artists 1774), James (architect), Daniel and Edward — were cousins. Edward, referred to by Josiah as "Young Stringer" and described as "a sad, untutor'd raw young fellow," was nevertheless employed to provide a number of views for the Frog* service, and a view of Etruria Hall*, enamelled on Wedgwood biscuit* earthenware (Wedgwood Museum), is attributed to him. This appears to be the original from which the Frog service view of Etruria Hall was taken. It is of particular interest as it pre-dates by at least two years the work of George Stubbs* on Wedgwood biscuit plaques*.

Stuart, James 'Athenian' (1713-1788)

Painter and architect, authority on classical art, and member of the Dilettanti Society. Stuart began life as a fan painter. He visited Rome in 1741, and ten years later went to Greece in company with Nicholas Revett. The product of this journey was the publication of the first volume of the *Antiquities of Athens* in 1762, which was acquired for Josiah Wedgwood's library. Wedgwood was enthusiastic enough to write to Bentley in 1773: "Please let Mr Stuart know that I am a subscriber to his

second volume." It eventually appeared in 1787, a year before Stuart's death. Stuart was both friendly and influential. He lent Wedgwood original works of art to copy, discussed with him the proposal to open showrooms* in The Adelphi*, and travelled with Wedgwood to visit Oxford, Blenheim, and Boulton's* works at Soho, Birmingham, in 1770. Two portrait medallions of Stuart were produced, the first being listed in the 1773 Catalogue.

Stubbs, George (1724-1806)

Painter, particularly of animals, and now considered to be the greatest of British painters of horses. His *Anatomy of the Horse,* for which he engraved his own detailed anatomical drawings, was published in 1766. Through his friend, the miniature painter Richard Cosway, he became interested in painting in enamel colours on copper, but soon found that limits of size and weight made copper plates unsuitable to his purpose and turned instead to ceramic plaques. He made enquiries with Coade*, and by 1775 his search for a ceramic support for his enamel painting had come to the attention of Thomas Bentley*. Josiah Wedgwood was enthusiastic about the proposal, and began experiments to produce earthenware plaques of a suitable size. He was not immediately successful. The first plaque was sent to Stubbs in December 1777, but Wedgwood's troubles were not over and he was obliged to make costly alterations to his kilns. In 1780 Stubbs visited Etruria* and, from that date until Wedgwood's death in 1795, he was supplied with biscuit plaques, the largest of which measured 30ins. by 41½ins. Wedgwood's object, it is clear, was not merely increased prestige. In May 1779, he wrote to Bentley: "If Mr Stubbs succeeds he will be followed by

Stuart, James 'Athenian'. *Jasper portrait medallion of the architect, James 'Athenian' Stuart.* Wedgwood.

others...etc. if the oil painters too should use them [ceramic plaques] they may become a considerable object.'' Stubbs did succeed, but the success was technical: others did not follow, and the experiment was a failure for both parties. The colours were considered garish and the technique (all obvious signs of brushwork being destroyed in firing) unworthy of an artist. Much of Stubbs' work in enamels remained unsold until his death when, at the sale of his effects, his plaques realised pathetically low prices.

In addition to his enamelled plaques, Stubbs painted an important portrait of the Wedgwood family, and one of Josiah's father-in-law, Richard Wedgwood, both on panels, and also modelled two fine bas-reliefs*: *The Frightened Horse* (1780) and *Fall of Phaeton* (c.1785). Nineteen relief studies of horses by Edward Burch* are also after Stubbs, probably modelled from the artist's original drawings. Some of Stubbs' paintings in enamel are untraced, and it is not certain from the descriptions whether they were on copper or earthenware biscuit supports.

The following work by Stubbs is associated with Wedgwood:

OIL PAINTINGS ON PANEL
The Wedgwood Family in the park of Etruria Hall, 1780, 47½ins. by 59½ins.
Richard Wedgwood, 1780, 28ins. by 23ins.

ENAMEL PAINTINGS ON QUEEN'S WARE BISCUIT PLAQUES
Darwin, Erasmus, portrait, 1783, 26ins. by 20½ins., oval.
Equestrian portrait of Warren Hastings, 1791, 34ins. by 25½ins., oval.
Farmer's wife and the Raven, 1782, 27½ins. by 37ins., oval.
Haycarting, 1795, 28½ins. by 39½ins., oval.
Haymakers, 1794, 28½ins. by 39½ins., oval.
Labourers, 1781, 27½ins. by 36ins., oval.
Lion attacking a Stag, 1778, 17ins. by 23½ins., oval.
Lion and dead Tiger, 1779, 17¼ins. by 24ins., rectangle.
Miss Isabella Saltonstall as *Una* in Spenser's *Faerie Queene*, 1782, 18⅞ins. by 25⅛ins., oval.
Panther, undated, 7½ins. by 11ins., rectangle.
Reapers, 1795, 30ins. by 41½ins., oval.
Self-portrait, 1781, 27ins. by 20ins., oval.
Self-portrait on a white hunter, 1782, 36½ins. by 27½ins., oval.
Stallions fighting, 1781, 22ins. by 37ins., oval.
Wedgwood, Josiah, portrait, 1780, 20ins. by 16ins., oval.
Wedgwood, Sarah, portrait, 1780, 20ins. by 16ins., oval.
Young Gentleman shooting, 1781, 18ins. by 24½ins., oval.

BAS-RELIEFS FOR BASALTES OR JASPER
Fall of Phaeton, 10½ins. by 19⅜ins., c.1785.
The Frightened Horse, 11¼ins. by 17½ins., c.1780.
19 Small bas-reliefs of horses, modelled by Edward Burch, c.1790.

Sugar Caster
A small container with the top pierced with holes for the purpose of sprinkling sugar. Also called a sugar dredger. Pierced ladle-shaped spoons were employed for the same purpose. Both types were made in creamware by Wedgwood and Leeds*.

Stubbs, George. *Portrait of Sarah, wife of Josiah Wedgwood I, painted in enamel on biscuit earthenware by George Stubbs, 1780. Oval 20ins. by 16ins.* Wedgwood.

Stubbs, George. *Oval black basaltes plaque,* The Frightened Horse, *modelled by George Stubbs in August 1780. The subject was adapted from an engraving after his painting* Horse Frightened by a Lion. Wedgwood.

Sulphurs

Casts or impressions of gems* made in a wax and sulphur composition were very popular during the 18th century. The mixture made sharp and accurate casts from ancient gems, and originals of all kinds, and sulphurs were collected into cabinets in the same way as antique* gems and Wedgwood's cameos*. Sulphurs were also used by Wedgwood in the process of making cameos, some of them procured from James Tassie*.

Sunflower, The

A favourite decorative motif of the Aesthetic Movement in the 1880s. Often used by the architect and designer Thomas Jeckyll, the Sunflower occurs as decoration on objects of art of all kinds. A dessert plate moulded in this form, with a pierced border, appears in the Catalogue of Shapes of 1880. It was made in green glaze*, and enamelled, and decorated in majolica glazes*.

Supper Set

A service for use on a sideboard or supper table consisting of several fan-shaped dishes which, when placed side by side, form a circle, often within a wooden tray especially made for the purpose. In the centre is space for a circular dish or tureen. These dishes were often provided with covers, which are now missing, and in this case the rims will have recesses into which the covers fitted. Supper sets were made of creamware by Wedgwood from the last quarter of the 18th century. They were first made in China in porcelain almost a century earlier.

Surface Agate

Coloured clay slips trailed on to the surface of the ware to be decorated, and combed to mingle them, with an effect similar to the marbled end-papers of some 19th century books. Random marbling with slips of several colours on creamware was also done at Leeds* and Swansea.

See: Variegated Wares; Slip.

Swag

See: Festoon

Sweetmeat Set

A set of dishes in the form of segments of a circle which surround a central dish or stand, similar to a supper set*. A sweetmeat dish is a dish with several compartments for holding sweetmeats, similar to an *hors d'oeuvre* dish. These were all made of creamware in the 18th century.

Swift, Peter (fl.1766 onwards)

Peter Swift, described by Wedgwood as ''Cashier, Paymaster-General, and Accountant'' was his most valuable and trusted servant. He was engaged in September 1772, at a salary of £25 per annum for two years, and £30 for the third. Swift was sent to London in 1772 to investigate the Ben Mather* embezzlement. Early in 1777 he bought the Leopard Inn in Burslem, and also, about the same time, went into partnership with one Cobb, formerly Wedgwood's warehouseman, to manufacture a brown salt-glazed ware known locally as 'critch' ware (probably similar to a ware made in Derbyshire and known as Crouch or Critch ware). After about a year Swift tired of his new responsibilities and offered to return. Wedgwood accepted, and wrote: ''I am not sorry he has made the trial.'' In 1779 we find Swift acting as tutor to the Wedgwood children in the art of writing.

Sword Hilts

The hilt of a sword said to have belonged to George 'Beau' Brummel (1770-1840) is inset with Wedgwood jasper cameos in cut steel. The sword was probably made by I. Dawson, Bloomsbury, London, but the suggestion that it was owned by 'Beau' Brummel is unlikely to be correct. It is in the Nottingham Castle Museum. Another example of a court sword thus ornamented is in the Buten* Museum.

Above: **Sunflower, The.** *Majolica dessert plate with moulded ornament in the form of a sunflower, c.1880.* Wedgwood.

Left: **Supper Set.** *Hand-painted Queen's ware supper set (also sometimes known as an hors d'oeuvre or breakfast set) in original circular mahogany tray. c.1785.* Wedgwood.

Sydney Cove Medallion

Circular medallion of jasper representing Peace, Art and Labour attending upon Hope, designed by Henry Webber* and modelled by William Hackwood* in 1789. The clay had been sent by Governor Arthur Phillip of New South Wales at the request of Wedgwood's friend, Sir Joseph Banks*, and the medallion was inscribed 'Made by Josiah Wedgwood of clay from Sydney Cove'. It inspired Dr. Erasmus Darwin* to poetic fervour in June 1789. When the Bastille* fell in the same year, and Wedgwood was faced with the task of supplying a commemorative medallion quickly, he took the figure of Peace from the Sydney Cove medallion, removed her olive branch, and added the Phrygian cap of the Revolutionaries, transforming her into a figure of Liberty. He completed the operation by placing her under a classical arch.

Sykes, Mr.

A merchant of Paris and Bordeaux supplied by Wedgwood under an agreement, initially for one year, concluded after the signing of the French Commercial Treaty* of 1786.

See also: Dominique Daguerre.

Syp Teapot

The 'Simple yet Perfect' teapot was introduced by Wedgwood in 1905. A horizontal perforated ledge separated the dry tea-leaves from the hot water. When the teapot was tilted backwards it rested on two short legs at the back and on the curved handle, permitting the hot water to pass through the perforations into the tea-leaves. When the tea was brewed, the pot was set down on its base and the tea was ready to be poured through the conventional spout at the front. The separation of the used tea-leaves from the prepared liquid tea prevented the tea from becoming 'stewed'.

These teapots were decorated with printed or print-and-enamel patterns, usually with the words 'THE CEYLON TEAPOT' printed on the front section of the lid. Height 7½ ins.

Syrinx

A nymph of Arcady who, pursued by Pan*, fled into the river and prayed to be changed into a reed. Of this reed Pan made his pipes, which became known as a syrinx.

Wedgwood subjects:

Children with Pan pipes, attributed to Beauclerk*.

Syrinx, medallion head, 3ins. by 2⅜ins., modelled by Flaxman* in 1776 as a pair to *Pan* and described by Wedgwood as "exquisitely fine."

Colour Plate XXI

Above left and right: Fairyland lustre bowl, the exterior decorated with Poplar Trees *the interior with* Woodland Bridge *and inscription 'YE WELLE OF LOVE AND LIFE WHEREIN LIES TRUTH'. Diameter 11ins.* Sotheby's Belgravia.

Left: Octagon bowl, outside diameter 8½ins., decorated with Fairyland lustre design Fiddler in Tree *(interior,* Ship and Mermaid*). Pattern Z4968, black Fairyland. Designed by Daisy Makeig-Jones.* Zeitlin Collection.

Below: Chalice bowl (introduced c.1924), the interior decorated with Fairy Gondola *and the exterior with* Twyford Garlands. *Pattern No. Z5360. Diameter 10½ins.* Wedgwood.

Table Lustre
See: Lustres.

Tablets

It would be desirable to define the term 'tablet' to mean a flat, tile-like object, rectangular in shape, and either painted or ornamented in bas-relief, reserving the term 'plaque' for those objects which are oval or circular, and larger, and of a different character, from those ordinarily defined as medallions*. Tablets, like plaques, were made principally for the decoration of furniture, walls, and chimney pieces. Unfortunately, this admirably logical arrangement is not always possible, since Wedgwood himself used the word 'tablets' indiscriminately. Wherever possible, however, the present authors make this distinction.

The first tablets preceded 1768. In November of that year Wedgwood wrote to Bentley: "I have lately had a vision by night of some new Vases, Tablets, &c. with which Article we shall certainly serve the *whole World.*" These early pieces included some large size Herculaneum* figures moulded in one piece in a cream, buff, or hard terracotta body. Basaltes tablets with figures applied by sprigging* came a little later. Described as being in a 'new vein', this technique was adopted in 1772, and was later developed as the principal method of decorating the jasper body. Technical troubles were frequent in these early years. On 15th November, 1772, Wedgwood complained to Bentley of the difficulty experienced in making long narrow tablets — "we cannot keep them straight." Difficulty was also experienced in making exact sizes to customers' requirements ("we shall make the black tablets for Lady Wynne as near to size as we can and the Glass grinders must do the rest" — Wedgwood to Bentley, 13th September, 1772). All these early pieces had the individual attention of Wedgwood himself, and hands had to be trained to do this kind of work. He wrote, for instance, "our fish-drain maker at the Usefull works has been trying his hand at long square [i.e. rectangular] tablets for two months past, and has made some tolerable good ones" (Wedgwood to Bentley, 6th November, 1774).

Plain black basaltes tablets were sent to London to have figure subjects painted on to them at the Chelsea Decorating Studio*. This type of encaustic* painting, in a more extensive palette than that employed for copies of the red-figure* vases, seems to have started in 1772. In the following year Wedgwood supplied basaltes tablets thus decorated to Robert Adam*, who was engaged on remodelling a house in Saint James's Square for Sir Watkin Williams Wynn*. These were used for chimney piece* decoration, and Wedgwood evidently regarded them as a kind of *chef d'oeuvre*, for, in September 1774, he wrote to Bentley reporting a visit from Lord Gower, the Duke of Bedford, Lord Trentham, and the great Mr. 'Capability' Brown*, adding, in reference to Mr. Brown, "I wish he could see Sir Watkin Williams Wynn's chimney-piece."

But success had to pay for failures, hence the larger tablets were proportionately more expensive. On the 2nd May, 1776, Wedgwood wrote to Bentley: "You will receive a tablet; the only one which has stood free of cracking out of four," — a kiln-wastage of seventy-five per cent!

Wastage in the making of jasper tablets created such difficult problems that at the end of 1776 chimney piece tablets were being made of red ware, red on black, or 'black bronz'd' (see: Bronzed basaltes), and all these were supplied to the customer with the information that the 'appendages', the small ovals, could be had in jasper. In 1775 Wedgwood wrote to Bentley telling him that Hackwood* was working on two tablets — the *Birth of Bacchus** and the *Triumph of Bacchus* — which could not possibly be made in a continuous frieze, and suggesting that they should be made in five separate pieces. In February 1776, he wrote: "Those with coloured grounds are difficult and expensive to make and should be charged accordingly. It is harder, finer, and better work'd than Marble, and what would it cost .in that Material?" The year 1777 saw considerable progress towards the successful manufacture of large jasper tablets. By the next summer success seems to have been assured, and Wedgwood was busy making tablets for a winter exhibition in London. Twelve large tablets were sent to London with his letter dated 19th August, 1778: "*The Marriage of Cupid and Psyche** (five sizes); *The Dancing Hours** (two tablets to make the twelve hours); *Etruscan, with Homer; Apollo and the Nine Muses* (in two friezes, or to be used as separate tablets); *Choice of Hercules* (three or four sizes); *Triumph of Bacchus* (largest, with attending Fauns); *Birth of Bacchus* (largest, with attending Fauns); *Boys and Goat,* largest, has only been made in red, but is a good thing; *Sacrifice to Flora,* new and large; *Sacrifice to Bacchus,* new, very large." Wedgwood proposed to make one

Tassie, James. *Portrait of James Tassie, modeller and inventor of glass pastes in imitation of gemstones, by David Allen.* National Portrait Gallery, Scotland.

tablet to add to this list at that time — the *Triumph of Ariadne,* and these were the first jasper tablets to appear in London after Wedgwood had overcome the technical difficulties. In another letter of the same month Wedgwood suggests that Bentley ought to sell his stock of black and red tablets before the new jasper tablets reached the London market. Jasper tablets were never produced in large quantities and fine specimens must be accounted among the rarest of surviving early Wedgwood specimens.

Tablets continued to be made during the 19th century but on a much smaller scale. A chimney piece in the old style was shown at the Paris Exposition of 1867. Halsey Ricardo* reconstructed Lord Dysart's Leicestershire house, Buckminster Park, in the 1880s, when jasper tablets were made at Etruria* for chimney pieces and a drawing room sideboard, some with a background of Dysart* green. Many of the bedrooms were equipped with a jasper-faced clock built into the overmantel, the dial appropriately decorated with Flaxman's* *Dancing Hours.* 19th century furniture decorated with Wedgwood jasper includes a cabinet designed by Gottfried Semper* and made by Holland, and a cabinet by Wright & Mansfield* (see: Furniture, Ornamental), both now in the Victoria and Albert Museum.

Taplin, Millicent, MSIA, NRD

Painter for Wedgwood, 1927; head of painting department, 1956. Her floral patterns, some of which incorporate the use of platinum ('steel') lustre are still popular. Some of her floral sprigs, stars, and floral motifs generally, are reminiscent of early New Hall* painting and the work of Louise Powell*. She designed the following patterns for bone china:

Autumn, 1938.
Buds and Bells.
Cynthia, 1942.
Falling Leaves, 1930.
Kingcup (lithograph), 1948.
Papyrus, 1934.
Sgraffiti coffee set, 1939.
Silver Buttercup.
Strawberry Hill (lithograph), 1957, with Victor Skellern*.
Westover.
Windrush, 1947.

In addition, Millicent Taplin decorated a number of vases and some platinum-painted Norman Wilson* unique ware.

Tassie, James (1735-1799)

Born at Pollokshaws near Glasgow, Tassie started life as a stonemason and went to Dublin in 1761 in the hope of becoming a sculptor. There he met Dr. Henry Quin who was engaged in reproducing gems and precious stones, and in copying antique cameos. Working with Quin, Tassie produced a white material resembling porcelain, but made from finely powdered glass, and it would seem that he anticipated the *pâte de verre* process of the latter end of the 19th century. The substance was formed in plaster of Paris moulds which had been taken from the original wax models or sulphurs*.

Tassie came to London about 1769 and obtained financial help from the Society for the Encouragement of the Arts. He took premises not far from Wedgwood's showrooms in Great Newport Street. He supplied Wedgwood with moulds of cameos and *intaglios* for reproduction, especially in basaltes, and he was commissioned to take plaster moulds of the Portland* vase. He produced above five hundred portraits, many of them modelled from life, some of which were supplied to Wedgwood. After his death Tassie's business was carried on by his nephew, William (d.1860).

Wedgwood's connexion with Tassie was mainly through Bentley, and dates from 1769. In a letter of 1776 Wedgwood wrote: "Mr. Tassie and Voyez* between them have made terrible depredations on our Seal Trade. The former by making them more beautifull, and the latter by selling them cheaper..." The relationship between the rivals was, however, friendly. Wedgwood reproduced Tassie's portraits complete with his signature on the truncation, and recent research has revealed that Tassie reproduced portraits obtained from Wedgwood. An important catalogue of Tassie's gems and cameos was compiled by R.E. Raspe and published in two volumes in 1791.

Taylor, Christopher (fl.1769-1775)

Painter at the Chelsea Decorating Studio* who worked on encaustic vases*.

Tea Caddy

The term 'caddy' is probably a corruption of the Malayan word 'kati', which is a quantity of about one pound and a third. Sheraton's *Catalogue* of 1803 mentions the word 'caddy' as being applied to a variety of tea chests of square, octagonal, and circular section. Decorative caddies occur in ivory and tortoiseshell ornamented with jasper* cameos*, most of them made towards the end of the 18th century. Queen's ware caddies, more properly described as tea jars, are to be found in very early versions, long antedating the introduction of the word 'caddy'. The earliest tea jars with embossed ornament probably belong to the Ivy House* period. Slightly later plain specimens are decorated with Sadler & Green* prints. They are also known in black basaltes*, jasper* and cane ware*, and were made in bone china* both in the early period and after its reintroduction in 1878.

See: Canisters.

Tassie, James. *Glass paste portrait of Charles Watson Wentworth, 2nd Marquis of Rockingham, modelled by James Tassie, c.1787. This portrait was reproduced in jasper and is listed in the 1787 Catalogue.* Scottish National Portrait Gallery.

Tea Jar
See: Tea Caddy.

Tea Party (Tea Drinkers)
One of the most popular transfer-printed designs of the 18th century, and to be found on Liverpool and Worcester* porcelains and the creamware produced at the Liverpool Herculaneum* pottery, at Cockpit Hill, Derby, and by Wedgwood. The print appears in several versions, usually upon teapots, and shows a man and woman seated at a typical tripod tea table. The man gestures with his right hand towards a black page boy. That this subject was in use by Wedgwood by 1763 is clear from Sadler's* letter dated 8th July apologising for the quality of an engraving: "The Tea Drinkers large teapot you'll see are [sic] very pale, tho' quite a new plate: but thee Engraver sent it down not half finished — he left it just as it was etch'd, without ever touching it with the Graver. . . but we shall mend that Matter very soon I hope."

Tea Party. *Creamware teapot decorated with a transfer-print of the Tea Party in black. The teapot has the overlapping leaf spout and pierced ball knop typical of the period. c.1777. Sotheby's.*

Tebo, Mr. (fl.1750-1780)
'Tebo' is probably an anglicisation of the Huguenot name, Thibaud or Thibault. There is strong stylistic evidence for thinking that he acted as a repairer (assembler) and modeller at the Bow, Chelsea, Plymouth, Bristol, and Worcester porcelain factories. He began to work for Wedgwood, who had a poor opinion of his abilities, in 1774. His models of heads of hares were described witheringly by Wedgwood as "like the head of a drown'd Puppy" and "full as like Pigs as Hares." It would seem, however, that it was not so much lack of talent as a modeller, but the inability of a rococo* modeller to adapt to the new style and to new disciplines. Wedgwood's own standards had been set by his early purchases of moulds from such suppliers as Hoskins & Grant*, and John Flaxman, Senior*, who were working from classical sculpture and the carvings of such sculptors as Rysbrack*, whereas Tebo, who had been working at the porcelain factories until well after 1770, was accustomed to seeking inspiration from porcelain figures made elsewhere, usually at Meissen*. Tebo often signed his work with an impressed 'Tᴼ', but signatures were not permitted at Etruria*, and an occasional 'TBO' found on Wedgwood experimental ware is believed to mean 'Top of the Biscuit Oven'.

The following may be regarded as the work of Tebo:
Ceres, figure (repair).
Lamps, pair. Not certainly identified.
Stirrup cup, Hare's Head.

By the middle of 1775 he was regarded as a useful hand for repairing large figures, but he was not as capable of original work. He left in the autumn of 1775 and travelled to Dublin, where he started to model portraits which he wanted Wedgwood to fire for him. In a letter of July 1776 to his Dublin agent, Wedgwood agreed to do this, but stated that Tebo was not to be considered his modeller.

Temple
Byerley* wrote from Etruria in January, 1798: "We have got our Temple put together, and the effect answers my expectations. The dome, the entablature, the columns, and the base are all to be thrown and turned'. Both Hackwood* and Theed* appear to have worked on this piece and it has, for many years, remained unidentified. The description and date, however, correspond well with the temple shown as a centre-piece to the engraving of the York Street showrooms*, 1809.

Temples in classical style as part of a table decoration originated at Meissen* in the 1740s, and several examples have survived, wholly or in part. They were made in several parts and erected on the table.

Temple. *A temple, probably a centrepiece for a table decoration. Enlarged from an engraving of the Wedgwood & Byerley showroom in York Street. No specimen appears to have survived.* Photo: Wedgwood.

Templetown, Elizabeth, Lady (1747-1823)

The daughter of Shuckburgh Boughton of Poston, Hereford, Elizabeth married, in 1769, Clotworthy Upton, who was raised to the peerage as Lord Templetown in 1776. An amateur artist and sculptor, her designs for Wedgwood were created between 1783 and 1789. These designs, mostly in the sentimental manner popular in the last quarter of the 18th century, and depicting figures of women and children engaged in domestic pursuits, were supplied to Wedgwood as drawings or as 'cut Indian paper' from which Hackwood* modelled the bas-reliefs*. Josiah wrote to her in June 1783, to express his pleasure at hearing that his first bas-relief copies of her work had received her approval, and, somewhat obsequiously, soliciting more. Two years later he sent bas-reliefs from Templetown designs to Charles James Fox to demonstrate to him the method he proposed to follow in copying Lady Diana Beauclerk's* drawings. Lady Templetown's name is often erroneously spelt Templeton.

The identification of Lady Templetown's work presents some problems. No bills survive, her style closely resembles those of Lady Diana Beauclerk and Emma Crewe*, and Hackwood's modelling of the work of all three has obscured stylistic differences. Two bas-reliefs only may be assigned to her with certainty, both being described as her work in Josiah's 1787 Catalogue*. These are: *Offering to Peace* (dated, evidently in error, 1777) for tablets 6½ ins. by 11½ ins. and smaller; and *Friendship consoling Affliction* for tablets 7ins. by 8¾ ins., and smaller sizes to 3ins. by 4ins. The latter was copied precisely from an antique bas-relief formerly in the Albani Collection, and now in the Louvre, and the design had been used c.1765 by the Adam* brothers at Syon House. Other designs reliably attributed to Lady Templetown are as follows:

Bourbonnais Shepherd, 1787, 3¾ ins. by 3ins.
Charlotte at the tomb of Werther, 1787, 5ins. by 4ins. reducing to 2¾ ins. by 2¼ ins.
Contemplation, 4ins. by 3¼ ins.
Domestic Employment, various sizes from 4½ ins. by 5¾ ins. to 2¼ ins. by 3ins.
Family School, and a companion piece, 4½ ins. by 5¾ ins. reducing to 2ins. by 3¼ ins.
Genii and a companion piece, 3ins. by 7ins. reducing to 1¾ ins. by 3¾ ins.
Maternal Affection, 4ins. by 3¼ ins.
Poor Maria, 1785, 3¾ ins. by 3ins. (see: Sterne).
Study and a companion piece, 3¾ ins. by 3ins. reducing to 2¼ ins. by 1¾ ins.
Sportive Love, 1783, 4ins. by 3¼ ins. reducing to 2¾ ins. by 2¼ ins.

Maternal Affection, Poor Maria, and *Sportive Love* were specially ordered by Sir Roger Newdigate* for a chimney piece* at Arbury Hall in 1788.

Term

A tall, quadrangular, tapering pedestal surmounted by a classical bust. The bust (sometimes a torso) is about half the height of the pedestal, and the two more or less merge into each other. The word is an abbreviation of 'terminal figure'.

Terracotta

A term meaning an unglazed earthenware made of a clay which burns to a brownish-red. It is ordinarily employed as a term in sculpture for models of clay fired to render them permanent. Terracotta of this kind is hardly ever glazed. Wedgwood's *rosso antico** (antique red) is unglazed, and more or less the right colour, but it cannot be regarded as a terracotta by strict definition because it is actually a stoneware, and it was used for quantity production. On the other hand, Wedgwood used the term 'terracotta' very loosely, sometimes referring to the white ware which preceded jasper* as a 'white terracotta', or even as 'terracotta' without qualification. An orange-red ware, a little coarser than *rosso antico,* made by Wedgwood early in the 19th century, can more accurately be described as a terracotta, but in general the word is better avoided in discussing factory-made wares.

Terre de Pipe Anglaise

A French term for ware similar to Wedgwood's creamware, such as that made by the brothers Leigh at Douai, c.1781-84.

Theatrical Awards

The Executive Committee of the Society of West End Theatre Awards chose a Wedgwood vase in Portland blue and white jasper for twelve awards to be made annually. The vases for 1977 were decorated with reliefs of the Muses* and Apollo* Musagetes, god of poetry and music. For 1978 they bore medallion portraits of David Garrick and Sarah Siddons*. There is an inscription in gold on the base of each vase. The design of these vases is unique.

Theed, William, RA (1764-1817)

Painter, sculptor and designer. Theed studied at the Royal Academy Schools in 1786, and exhibited portraits and paintings in the neo-classical* style from 1789-1805. He visited Rome in 1791, remaining there for three years, and it was there that he met Flaxman*. He began to work for Wedgwood in 1799, but left in 1804 to design for Rundell, Bridge and Rundell the London silversmiths. In 1810 he accepted a commission from Wedgwood to model a portrait medallion of Thomas Byerley*, and this was reproduced in jasper. Apart from the capital for a column (see: Temple), the Byerley portrait is the only work of Theed's for Wedgwood that has been certainly identified.

Thetis

A sea nymph, daughter of Nereus and Doris. Although both Zeus and Poseidon sued for her hand, a prophetic divinity, Themis, said that her son would be greater than his father, so she married Peleus and became the mother of Achilles*.

The marriage of Peleus and Thetis is thought to be the subject of the Portland* vase.

Tiles

Until Wedgwood started to make them, tiles were of tin-enamelled ware (delft) made in Liverpool, or in Holland whence they were exported in large quantities. Tiles in cream-coloured ware were introduced before 1767. We find the first Wedgwood reference to them in a letter written to Bentley in August of that year: "Cream colour Tyles are much wanted, and the consumption will be great for Dairys, Bath [*sic*], Summer Houses, Temples, etc., etc." In 1769 he wrote: "Lady Gower will build a Dairy on purpose to furnish it with cream colour, if I will engage to make Tiles for the walls," and by the Autumn of 1776 we find the demand for Tiles disrupting the beginning of trade with Russia, which had been discussed with Boulton & Fothergill* a few months earlier: "the rising fashion for furnishing Baths, Dairys, etc., with Tiles must stop their exportation to Russia for some time." He goes on to refer to four or five hundred dozen tiles as necessary to furnish a 'Bath', which suggests the scale on which manufacture was probably carried on. Black-printed tiles were sold by Guy Green* in 1776 at 5s. a dozen, less elaborately decorated tiles for 3s.6d., and half-tiles for borders for 2s.9d. Wedgwood quoted 1s. *each* for hand-painted tiles, and sold plain tiles for about 3s. a dozen. Sizes varied: seven inches square was customary, but the size could be varied to order, and six inches square was a not unpopular size. After Sadler's* retirement in 1770 his partner, Guy Green, continued to print tiles for Wedgwood, although by this time some other types of ware were being printed at Etruria.

In the 1780s orders for tiles and dairy* ware greatly increased. It is not always possible in the case of plain tiles to say, in the absence of records, whether they were made by Wedgwood or by some other factory. Wedgwood, however, was widely known for tiles and dairy equipment, and in 1788 the duc d'Orléans (later to become notorious as Philippe Egalité) ordered dairy ware for the Laiterie at the Château de Raincy.

Creamware tiles of interest to the collector bear some kind of decoration. Particularly sought are creamware tiles bearing transfer-printed decoration by Sadler & Green from Aesop's Fables, or a theatre subject, but these are on Liverpool delft, and a specimen of Wedgwood creamware plates bearing one of these prints is very rare. Less interesting, and probably only available as a result of demolition, are tiles with a variety of floral and foliate patterns, especially those which are part of a repetitive motif.

On the 26th June, 1776, we find Wedgwood writing to Bentley of ''Patterns of Bricks for a Jasper floor 9 squares long x 6 broad with a border of porphyry and black ones sufficient for one side and one end.'' It seems probable that a specimen pavement of this kind was laid in the Greek Street*, Soho, London showrooms, and that it consisted of jasper stoneware tiles (as thin as could be safely laid) with a marbled surface, not unlike some of today's popular plastic floor tiles. The 'porphyry' tiles seem to have been of red clay superficially spotted with black and white. These floors did not achieve any great popularity, and from a manufacturing viewpoint were probably more trouble than they were worth.

The manufacture of creamware tiles was discontinued soon after 1800, but it was again started in 1870, when decorated tiles were made in sets. Subjects included the *Months, Red Riding Hood, A Midsummer Night's Dream, Robin Hood,* animals, sailing ships, photographic American views, moral homilies, etc. The department was closed in 1902 as a measure of retrenchment during a period of bad trade caused largely by the Boer War and the Spanish-American War. The decorative tiles made between 1870 and 1902 are sometimes to be found mounted in metal to form stands for teapots and jardinières.

See: Harry Barnard; Calendar Tiles; Dairy Ware; William de Morgan; Kate Greenaway.

Tiles. *A set of the* Seasons, *the heads titled* Spring, Summer, Autumn, *and* Winter. *c.1875.* Zeitlin Collection.

Tiles. *Tile decorated with the figure of a Japanese girl, apparently adapted from a wood-block print. Pseudo-Japanese characters are printed upper right. Simulated bamboo frame. c.1880.* Zeitlin Collection.

Tiles. *Tile decorated with the head of a sporting dog by H.H. Crealock*, c.1875.* Zeitlin Collection.

Till, William (fl.1881-1883)

Modeller at Etruria*.

Titans

The sons and daughters of Uranus (heaven) and Gaea (Earth), the creators of the world, who were subdued by Jupiter* (Zeus) and shut up in the underworld. Among the descendants of the Titans were Prometheus*, Hecate, Latona, Helios (the Sun), Selene (the Moon), and Circe, all of whom were divine or semi-divine.

Wedgwood model:

The War of Jupiter and the Titans (also known as *The Fall of the Giants*), basaltes oval plaque after a design by Guglielmo della Porta*, c.1768.

Tithe Pig, The

A popular 18th century transfer print which exists in several versions. It depicts a parson, a farmer, and his wife. The farmer holds a pig, the wife a child. The couple are refusing to part with the tenth (or tithe) pig to the parson unless he agrees to take the tenth child. There are some lines of verse beneath the print. A version signed by Sadler is found occasionally on Wedgwood creamware. Derby made a group, and a set of three figures, of this subject.

Toby Jug

A pottery jug in the form of a seated man, holding a mug and usually also a pipe. He wears a tricorn hat, the brim of which provides a pouring lip. The removable crown was sometimes a small cup. Probably named after 'Toby Philpot', the nickname of Harry Elwes, whose fondness for alcohol was celebrated in a song, *The Brown Jug*, published in 1761. The first examples are thought to have been made by Ralph Wood I. They were later made by his son, Ralph Wood II and copied by many of the English potteries. Innumerable reproductions and forgeries exist, and the general form has been adapted to commemorate modern statesmen and military commanders. Wedgwood have produced only one model of this type, a jug 6ins. in height, covered in an amber glaze, representing Elihu Yale, benefactor of Yale University. The following inscription is impressed in the base: 'THE ELIHU YALE TOBY, Patent applied for, RGE Sculp. 1938, WEDGWOOD MADE IN ENGLAND.'

Toft, Alphonse (Alfonso)

Engraver for Wedgwood, 1842-43. There may have been two engravers of this name at different addresses in the district between 1829 and 1889.

Toft, Charles (1832-1909)

Ceramic decorator, modeller, and potter, who studied at the Stoke School of Design. At Minton* Toft was responsible for copies of Henri Deux* inlaid ware using a somewhat similar technique to that employed originally. He also modelled figures for Parian* ware. He went on to Elkington*, the silversmiths, in Birmingham, and became chief modeller to Wedgwood in 1872, remaining until 1889. In the latter year he started a small factory of his own in Stoke, where he produced rustic wares. His son, Albert Toft, was a well known sculptor, and author of a book on technical aspects of the art.

The work of Charles Toft for Wedgwood includes a medallion portrait of Gladstone*, the 'Peace and War' vase for the Paris Exposition, 1878, models after designs by Walter Crane*, and a self-closing jug lid on which Wedgwood paid him a royalty. Record of a chessboard decorated in the Henri Deux style suggests that Toft may have decorated other pieces in this way for Wedgwood.

Topographical Painting

Carefully detailed representations of an existing scene, usually landscapes with buildings, but sometimes of street scenes. This type of painting became extremely popular as ceramic decoration in the last quarter of the 18th century and the first decades of the 19th, and where the painting was of a scene which was named on the reverse it was referred to at the time as a 'Named View'. An important Wedgwood example of topographical painting is the Imperial Russian Service for Catherine II* (see: Frog Service), which played an important part in popularising in England a type of decoration which had hardly then become fashionable on the Continent.

Tortoiseshell Ware

Earthenware covered with a lead glaze which is mottled with blue, brown, and green, using the oxides of cobalt, manganese, and copper. The tortoiseshell glaze was in many ways similar to that employed by Bernard Palissy in the 16th century for the reverse side of his rustic dishes, and it was popular in mid-18th century Staffordshire, especially in the case of Whieldon* wares. Wedgwood continued to make tortoiseshell ware during the first years of production at Ivy House*.

Toby Jug. *Jug, covered with an amber glaze, representing Elihu Yale. 6ins. high. 1938.* Zeitlin Collection.

Tower of London

A pale blue and white jasper plate 6½ins. in diameter was introduced in 1978 to commemorate the 900th anniversary of the Tower of London (1078-1978). It is decorated with a white bas-relief of the Tower within an oak-leaf border. A dark blue back-stamp gives details of the Tower.

338

Traditional Shapes

The term used to describe a set of shapes comprising Paris or concave shape flatware, 146 shape teapots and cream jugs, 129 shape coffee pots and milk jugs, and round plume shape vegetable dishes and tureens. Cups were usually of pear or Bute shape. This set, assembled from among Josiah I's earliest and simplest shapes, has been in use for nearly two hundred years for creamware patterns, coloured bodies*, and, with slight alterations and some substitutions (e.g. Lincoln shape plates), for many bone china* patterns.

Transfer Printing

The making of a transfer print requires considerable skill. Its quality is dependent partly on the excellence of the engraved plate and partly on the dexterity of the operative taking the print from it. A heated mixture of colouring oxide and oil is applied to the plate and wiped off, leaving the engraved lines charged with colour. A sheet of wet tissue paper is then laid on the plate, and a thick pad of flannel placed on top of it. The sandwich is then put in a press, usually in modern times a pair of spring-loaded rollers, after which the tissue paper can be peeled off. It bears the engraved design in reverse. The paper is applied to the surface of the glaze, and the back rubbed with a flannel pad to transfer the design to the glaze. The paper can then be gently washed off with water, and the design fired in the muffle or enamelling kiln*. The commonest colour employed in the 18th century was black, but red was popular, and brown, purple, and green occur very occasionally. Since the 18th century a number of mechanical improvements have been made to this method, but it remains the same in principle.

The art of transfer printing was invented by the Irishman,

Transfer Printing. *Queen's ware coffee pot transfer-printed in red by Sadler & Green with* Rural Lovers *from an engraving by Francis Vivares after a painting by Thomas Gainsborough. Rococo spout. c.1775.* Wedgwood.

Transfer Printing. *Fred Farmer engraving a copper plate from the designer's drawing.* Wedgwood.

Transfer Printing. *Modern transfer printing by machine.* Wedgwood.

Transfer Printing. *Modern printing machine. Taking a print from between two rollers, one of which is an engraved copper cylinder.* Wedgwood.

Transfer Printing. *Fitting a new design to tableware.* Wedgwood.

John Brooks, in 1752, and was subsequently used at the Battersea Enamel Works, the Bow* porcelain factory and, from 1757, at the Worcester* porcelain factory. It is probable that the process was discovered independently by John Sadler* of Liverpool, who was in partnership (c.1756-70) with Guy Green*. Sadler & Green decorated Liverpool delft tiles made by Zachariah Barnes by printing them at their works in Harrington Street, Liverpool. These, five inches square, were decorated with portraits of actors and actresses, scenes from Aesop's Fables after Francis Barlow*, and a variety of other subjects. They are often signed 'J. Sadler, Liverpool', and could be supplied at an extremely low price in comparison with the painted Dutch tiles then being imported.

The first record of a connection between Sadler & Green and Josiah Wedgwood is an invoice dated September 1761, and in 1768 they were rendering their accounts weekly. After Sadler's retirement in 1770 Guy Green continued to print for Wedgwood until 1793. An invoice of April 1764, charges £64 for printing 1,760 pieces, specified as follows: "Teapots in three sizes; mugs in two sizes; bowls, all sizes; coffee-pots; sugars; cream-ewers; and cups and saucers." But the trade between Burslem and Liverpool was not limited to sending creamware for printing. Sadler & Green bought creamware from Wedgwood for transfer printing on their own account, and they sold these pieces from their Liverpool warehouse. Prints on creamware sold in Liverpool often bear the name of Sadler, but it is unlikely that the name ever appeared on ware returned to Burslem. This trade between Burslem and Liverpool became so large that Wedgwood's interest in turn-

pikes, and the Trent and Mersey Canal, is understandable. By 1771 invoices for printing were averaging about £650 a month, and the value of creamware supplied by Wedgwood to Sadler & Green for their own purposes amounted to almost as much. This arrangement was to the advantage of both. From Wedgwood's viewpoint, not only was his printing being done by highly skilled people, but he was also selling a great deal of plain creamware. It is also probable that Wedgwood was doing his best to prevent Sadler & Green from working for anyone else by absorbing as much as possible of their productive capacity. It is, however, by no means certain that the statement that Wedgwood did not at any time do his own transfer-printing is true. He certainly took a great deal of interest in the subject, buying prints for Sadler & Green to use, and as early as 1765 he wrote to his brother in London asking him to procure engraved plates from Samuel Wale* who also worked for Sadler.

The Bow porcelain factory had, about 1755, introduced a type of transfer printing in which the subject was delineated in outline only. This enabled semi-skilled painters to be used to fill in the outlines with colour. Very soon afterwards Worcester adopted the same practice for its cheaper enamelled wares. Wedgwood did not consider using this technique until April 1770, when he discussed the matter at length in a letter to Bentley. This letter leaves little doubt that transfer printing was being done at the Chelsea Decorating Studio*. In September 1776, writing on the subject of armorial* services, we find Wedgwood remarking: "Mr Green prints and then colours the Arms, and we must do the same in London, or transfer near half our business from thence to Liverpool.'' In a letter of December 1790, to Tom Byerley* he wrote: "In order to finish the two Etruscan services I believe it will be necessary for us to have our printer back again into the country.'' The fact that Wedgwood bought the right to do his own printing in 1765 does not mean that he exercised it. This was a normal business precaution. But it cannot be doubted that printing was being done at Chelsea in 1770, or that Wedgwood was employing his own engravers by 1780. When John Wedgwood died in 1767 an inventory was made which included engraved plates for decorating useful ware, but unfortunately this has not survived.

The early cream-coloured ware prints were similar in their subjects to those being employed elsewhere — George III*, Queen Charlotte*, Frederick the Great (a popular hero among the people of England during the Seven Years' War), the Marquis of Granby, John Wilkes, and John Wesley. An exceptional print depicts the death of General Wolfe*, adapted from an engraving by William Woollett, after the painting by Benjamin West, first published in 1776. The well-known *Tithe Pig** subject, signed 'Sadler, Liverpool', occurs on a Wedgwood mug. This was the subject of a popular Derby* porcelain group. The Society of Bucks* print, well known on Liverpool porcelain, also occurs on a Wedgwood mug signed by Sadler. In both examples we must assume that these were mugs sold by Sadler & Green at their Liverpool warehouse. *The Tea Party** is another popular print of the time engraved at Worcester by Robert Hancock*, which occurs on Wedgwood creamware in a version from Sadler & Green. Exotic* birds were a popular subject. They were a successful form of decoration started at Sèvres* some years before, and had been taken up by the English porcelain factories before 1760.

Although Sadler & Green supplied their own subjects, there is plenty of evidence that Wedgwood both suggested and demanded particular prints. Very few of the Liverpool firm's tile prints ever appeared on Wedgwood's creamware, although rare instances are known, and Wedgwood did not allow subjects employed on creamware printed for him to appear on the wares of other potters. A Wedgwood creamware plate of about 1775, printed in red with the *Fox and the Goat* from Aesop's Fables — a Sadler & Green tile engraving — is in the Schreiber* Collection (Victoria and Albert Museum).

Although underglaze blue printing* was being done at Worcester by 1759 it was not attempted on creamware during the 18th century, presumably because the cream colour would have tended to turn the blue to an unattractive green. No blue printing was done by Wedgwood until 1805. The *Water Lily** pattern of 1808 on pearl* ware is an example. Outline transfers were also used in the decoration of bone china, for instance the *Dragon* and the *Butterfly* patterns. Transfer printing continued to be used throughout the 19th century to a variable extent, and the names of engravers employed are recorded elsewhere in this volume. From 1870-1902 transfer-printed tiles* were made in sets, and limited editions of plates, dishes, and jugs commemorating places and events were made, principally for the American market. The Carlyle jug (see: Commemorative Ware) is an example. Transfer printing by itself was not much used during the early decades of the 20th century. Victor Skellern* revived it with his 'Forest Folk' series.

See also: Bat Printing; Lithography; Underglaze Blue Prints.

Translucency

If, when a ceramic body is held up to a source of light, it is seen that light is transmitted, then it is said to be translucent. Only sufficiently thin vitreous bodies of good quality which have been fired at a high temperature will be translucent, and

porcelain is the most translucent of all ware. Nevertheless, a thickness greater than 5mm will usually prevent light from passing. At one time the passage of light was regarded as an essential property of porcelain in Europe, and any translucent ware was so described. The Chinese definition of porcelain is any ware that gives a ringing tone when struck. The fact of translucency is the reason why we find Wedgwood sometimes describing jasper* as his "biscuit porcelain," because thinly potted examples are sometimes slightly translucent. It is for this reason that we find Bentley* urging Wedgwood not to fire jasper at too high a temperature so that it becomes translucent. By this time jasper contained Cornish materials in the form of china clay, and Bentley was afraid of infringing Champion's* patent which gave the latter a monopoly of the use of Cornish materials in porcelain manufacture. Bone china* was the first ware produced by Wedgwood which is normally translucent.

Trays

Trays of Queen's ware*, basaltes*, and jasper*, in oval and octagonal shapes, were made for sets of custard cups* and for *cabarets à deux** or early morning teasets as early as 1783. Similar trays were also produced in enamelled cane ware*. Trays for early morning teasets measured 13¾ins. by 11ins. Flat pieces of jasper of such a size were difficult to fire and they

Translucency. *Demonstrating the translucency of a modern bone china plate.* Photo: Wedgwood.

Fine blue and white jasper cabaret a deux with an unusually large circular tray, 15½ ins. in diameter. c.1790. Flat pieces of such a size were particularly difficult to fire without warping, and this example appears to be the largest circular jasper tray surviving. Christie's.

Triton Candlesticks. *Pair of Tritons carrying shells which act as candleholders. 11ins. high.* Wedgwood.

are now extremely rare.

During the 19th century some very large trays were made in Queen's ware and bone china. An eleven-sided Queen's ware tray in the Buten Museum*, c.1880, is 22¼ ins. wide, and a bone china 'dumb waiter'* of the same date measures 18¾ ins. in diameter.

Trembleuse
See: Chocolate Cup.

Triform Goddess
This is a reference to Hecate, one of the Titans whom Zeus allowed to retain her power. She was identified with Selene (Luna) in Heaven, Artemis (Diana*) on Earth, and Persephone* (Prosperpine) in the Underworld. She was thus a threefold goddess, with three bodies and three heads, and for this reason was called Triformis or Triceps. She was a sorceress, who dwelt at crossroads, or in tombs with spirits of the dead. Dogs howled when she approached.

Wedgwood subject:
Triform goddess, medallion by Pacetti*, c.1788.

Triton
Son of Poseidon (Neptune*) and Amphitrite. Later literary references mention Tritons in the plural, and they are depicted riding on sea horses (hippocampi*) or dolphins*. The upper part of the Triton's body is human, but it terminates in a fish tail. In art, the Triton is often represented blowing a conch shell as a trumpet to still the waves. Wedgwood's Triton figures modelled as candlesticks grasp whorled shells which are often erroneously described as cornucopiae*.

Wedgwood subjects:
Triton, figure, 24ins. high, attributed to Bacon* after Bernini, c.1769-70.
Triton candlesticks, pair of figures kneeling on rocks, and grasping whorled shells surmounted by candleholders. Height 11ins. Often attributed to Flaxman* but possibly by Keeling*. Catalogued by Wedgwood as "after Michelangelo."
Triton-handled vase, the pair to the Satyr-handled vase. These are better known as the *Wine and Water** ewers and were possibly made from casts supplied by John Flaxman Senior* in 1775, though they are usually credited to the younger Flaxman.

Triton Candlesticks
A pair of candlesticks in the form of bearded, naked Tritons with seaweed or fishing net clinging to their thighs. The Tritons are depicted kneeling, holding a large cone-shaped shell (often erroneously described as a cornucopia*). They are

generally believed to have been modelled by John Flaxman*
after antique originals and measure 11ins. in height. First
produced in basaltes and jasper (usually blue and white), they
were later produced in creamware decorated with silver lustre*
and, in the 1860s, in majolica*.

Triumph

Originally a grand military procession in which the victorious
general entered the city at the termination of a campaign.
Roman processions were led by the Senate, the members of
which went out to meet the army, and they terminated in the
Temple of Jupiter Capitolinus on the Capitoline Hill. Other
processions commemorating success or victory came to be
referred to as triumphs, and Wedgwood made a number of
reliefs representing such processions. These include:

Bacchanalian Triumph (see: Bacchus).

Triumph of Ariadne (with choral figures), tablet 10½ins. by
14¼ins., modelled by Flaxman*, 1778.

Triumph of Bacchanalian Boys, cameo, 1½ins. by 2ins., c.1775.

Triumph of Bacchus, tablet, 6½ins. by 14ins. and 7¼ins. by
10ins., modelled by Hackwood*.

Triumph of Bacchus and Ariadne, tablet, 9½ins. by 23ins. and
10¼ins. by 26ins., first catalogued 1773.

Triumph of Cupid, two bas-reliefs modelled in 1782 by Flaxman,
and intended as ornaments for teapots.

Triumph of Mars, tablet modelled by Webber*.

Triumph of Silenus, medallion 4½ins. by 7½ins. by Flaxman,
c.1778.

Triumph of Venus, attributed to Flaxman.

Trophies

Although trophies were a fashionable kind of decoration during
the 18th century they were not often employed by Wedgwood.
Originally trophies were the arms of a beaten enemy which
were hung up in a tree to celebrate a victory. Later, weapons
were grouped together as a form of modelled or painted ornament. The notion was extended to a variety of objects —

Trophy Plate. *Three-colour jasper trophy plate, rather less elaborately
over-ornamented than some examples. c.1865.* Sotheby's Belgravia.

musical instruments were emblematic of music, and a palette
and brushes of the visual arts. Trophy-like ornaments occur on
vertical tablets made by Wedgwood for the jambs of chimney
pieces*.

Trophy Plate

A jasper plate, diameter 8¾ins., the surface of which is almost
entirely covered by jasper designs and motifs, surrounding a
central bas-relief*, often in several colours. The number of
reliefs employed varies between one hundred and fifty and one
hundred and eighty, and the production of this piece, which
has continued intermittently for more than a century, requires
great technical expertise. The total effect is generally
pretentious and more nearly resembles the work of a
confectioner than an example of the potter's art.

Trump

William Hogarth's* pug-dog which appears in his self-portrait,
and, in a reclining pose, was also manufactured by Chelsea* in
porcelain about 1750. The Chelsea version was modelled after
a terracotta* by L.-F. Roubiliac*. A black basaltes* reclining

Trophies. *Pair of black basaltes amphora, 19¾ins. high, with cast
and applied ornaments of the Muses, anthemion border, and mask
terminals, with musical, martial and amatory trophies at the neck.*
Christie's.

Trump. *Black basaltes figure of Hogarth's pug-dog, Trump, the base
11¼ins. long. One of a pair modelled c.1774 after a terracotta by L-F.
Roubiliac. Models of Trump are extremely rare, and none has so far been
found with the Wedgwood & Bentley mark impressed.* Christie's.

Tureen. *Tureen of Queen's ware, hand painted, placed on an oval dish from the same service. Border decoration Green Water Leaf. c.1790.* Wedgwood.

pug, very similar in size and pose to the Chelsea model, was sold by Christie's* in 1973. This almost certainly belongs to the Wedgwood & Bentley period, and is, no doubt, the pug-dog bought in 1774 by Wedgwood from Richard Parker*, the seller of plaster casts, who may have bought the mould or a plaster cast at the sale of the contents of Roubiliac's studio after his death in 1762. In the Wedgwood & Bentley Auction* Sale of 1781 "two pug dogs from Hogarth" and "a pair of pug-dogs from a favourite dog of Hogarth's" were listed. They are listed only briefly in the Ornamental Catalogue of 1779 as "Two pug dogs," and it is evident that a mirror-image had been modelled since 1774 to make a pair. A small version on an oval base was sold at Sotheby's in the autumn of 1973. All these models are exceedingly rare, and all appear to be unmarked.

Tureen

A circular or oval bowl, often on a low foot, with a cover and handle and a conforming stand. It varies in size according to its purpose. Covers of soup and sauce tureens usually have a small recess in the rim at a convenient point to allow room for a ladle. Made in Queen's ware*, pearl* ware and bone china* as part of a dinner service. In comparison with other tableware pieces, soup tureens were always made in small quantities, and their size made them particularly vulnerable to breakage. Perfect and complete specimens made prior to 1900 are therefore rare.

Turkish Merchant

Print employed by Sadler & Green for decorating Liverpool delft tiles which also occurs on some rare Wedgwood cream-ware plates. It is derived from the popular series of Harbour Scenes introduced at Meissen* in the 1730s, which very occasionally appear on Chelsea* porcelain of c.1751.

Turner, John (1738-1787)

Potter at Lane End, 1762-1787. The factory was continued after his death by his two sons, John and William, until 1803, when it was enlarged and became Turner & Co. Turner manufactured creamware, stoneware, jasper, basaltes and dry bodies generally. The quality was excellent, and his wares were similar in style to those of Wedgwood. In 1775 he was involved

Turner, John. *Left and right: Cassolette and rum kettle with bail handle and lion finial in Turner's cane ware.* Zeitlin Collection. *Centre: a contemporary Wedgwood cane ware teapot with bamboo handle, finial and spout.* Laver Collection.

Turning. *Three vases of turned creamware with integrally cast relief ornament. c.1765.* Wedgwood.

with Wedgwood in an attempt by the Staffordshire potters to prevent an extension of Champion's* patent, and together they leased clay mines at Redruth and St. Austell. John Turner later became a member of the New Hall* porcelain company. Although Turner's sons continued to make high quality wares in the manner of their father, and the firm was even enlarged, it came to an abrupt end in 1806 with the bankruptcy of the Turners, which was due to the wartime blockade and the loss of their very considerable Continental trade. Like Wedgwood, they had a flourishing business with Holland, and like Leeds* they shipped creamware there for decoration. John Hancock*, who was employed by Turner's sons, introduced a technique of burnishing gold.

Turner's jasper closely resembles that of Wedgwood, but his blue differs in shade and is closer to a slate-blue. Also, the surface shows a perceptible sheen. Although he often copied Wedgwood's subjects, the style is less severely classical. Turner's cane ware*, a vitreous body containing china clay and china stone, is light buff in colour and of fine quality.

See: Cornish Journey.

Turner, Dr. Matthew (d.1788?)

Described by Meteyard* (*Life of Wedgwood*) as "A good surgeon, a skilful anatomist, a practised chemist, a draughtsman, a classical scholar, and a ready wit", Matthew Turner was called to attend Josiah Wedgwood in Liverpool in 1762. On one of his visits to his patient, he brought with him Thomas Bentley*, and was thus responsible for introducing the two men, who were to form one of the most important partnerships in ceramic history. Turner was also responsible for introducing Joseph Priestley* to the subject of chemistry through a series of lectures he delivered at the Warrington Academy in 1765. Turner was a founder member of the Liverpool Academy of Arts, and shared Wedgwood's sympathy with the American colonies. He prepared varnishes and colours for Wedgwood,

and it was his brown varnish that was first used as a ground for the bronze powder in the production of bronzed basaltes* vases.

Turner's Jaspe Ware

A terracotta* body covered with slips* of various colours (blue, green, chocolate, buff, etc.) and decorated with bas-reliefs*, many of which were believed by Jewitt* to be the work of Flaxman*. These wares were said to be made from moulds originally in the possession of John Turner* by Gildea & Walker of Duke Hall, near Burslem, in the third quarter of the 19th century. It is not, in fact, uncommon to find the moulds of one factory later being used by another.

Turning

A method of finishing ceramic ware after it has been thrown on the potter's wheel and has attained leather hardness*. Turning is done on a lathe. The vessel is rotated horizontally between two centres and, while it is turning, various stationary tools are brought into contact with the surface, either paring down the thickness of the walls, or incising rings, steps, etc. for ornamental purposes. Incised *discontinuous* geometric decoration is the product of the engine-turning lathe*. Much of Wedgwood's finest work in black basaltes*, jasper*, and cane ware* owes its particular quality to the skill of turners, and the distinctive decorative effects obtained by use of engine-turning.

See: Dice Pattern; Rose Engine-Turning.

Twig Basket

A circular or oval fruit dish made up of strips of clay woven together by hand to form an open basket shape. An example, with matching stand, appeared in Wedgwood's 1790 Catalogue* of creamware shapes, and twig baskets have been made intermittently ever since.

Two-Colour Clay Bodies

See: Coloured Bodies.

Twig Basket. *The modern twig basket is still made by hand in the same way as those of the 18th century. The photograph shows the method very clearly.* Photo: Wedgwood.

Ulfsunda, Sweden

A minor *faience* factory which began to make black basaltes* and red and white stoneware in the Wedgwood style at the end of the 18th century. In 1819 the factory was called the Wedgwood-Fabriket.

Ulysses

Roman name for the Greek hero of the Trojan war, Odysseus. Homer's *Odyssey* recounts the adventures of Ulysses after the war, when he set out for home. For some reason he was not popular with Wedgwood and only one bas-relief illustrating any of his exploits is recorded. This is a cameo by Hackwood*, *Ulysses staying the chariot of Victory*. Penelope*, the wife of Ulysses, is the subject of a painting by Joseph Wright* of Derby, *Penelope unravelling her Web*, bought from the artist by Josiah I* in 1784/5.

Unaker

See: Cherokee Clay.

Undercutting

The method of hand-finishing a bas-relief* after it is removed from the mould* and while it is in a cheese-hard or leather-hard* state, to accentuate the contrast between the relief and the ground, and to sharpen the modelling. It is particularly noticeable in features that are on a plane horizontal (or parallel) to that of the ground (e.g. the nostrils and ears of portraits), and provides an extra dimension which cannot be obtained from the mould. Undercutting is a feature of the finest 18th century jasper, and is also to be seen on the small quantity of portrait medallions finished by A.H. ('Bert') Bentley* in 1922. Josiah wrote to Thomas Bentley* on 4th November, 1778: "Some of the tablets lately sent are finish'd very high by Hackwood at a considerable expence... you will easily percieve the difference in the hair, faces, fingers &c, & more palpably by all the parts capable of it being undercut which gives them the appearance, & nearly the reality of models."

Underglaze Blue Prints

Underglaze blue printing was probably introduced into the Potteries c.1780, though some authorities credit William Adams* with having brought the technique to Staffordshire in 1775. Josiah Wedgwood, who was certainly conversant with it, made no attempt to use it at Etruria*. The most likely explanation for his refusal to do so is his conversion, by Bentley*, to neo-classicism. Creamware was an unsatisfactory background for blue prints, which tended to appear on it as a muddy green, but pearl* ware had been introduced in 1779, and it was not therefore the lack of a suitable body or glaze that prevented Josiah's adoption of a promising form of decoration. The majority of Wedgwood's tableware patterns had always been simple, elegant borders based on natural objects — foliage, flowers, fruit, seaweed, shells, etc. — or upon designs of respectable classical origins, and it is probable that he considered the all-over Oriental style of decoration offensive. It is also certain that he was aware of the technical difficulties of printing underglaze blues to the standards he demanded.

After his death, Byerley* was left in charge at Etruria. It soon became clear that he was unequal to the task. By the time Josiah II* and John Wedgwood* returned to Etruria the market for blue-printed wares was already established, and the lead had been taken by other manufacturers. Minton* had opened his factory in 1793, and the *Willow** pattern was the first in production. Spode* had already introduced a number of successful blue prints of Chinese origin, and the demand for tablewares of this style had become so great that Wedgwood were obliged to satisfy orders by buying them from competitors.

In 1805 with the approval of the absentee Josiah II, John Wedgwood and Byerley set the engravers to work, and by the end of the year substantial orders had been received from St. Petersburg. During the following forty years Wedgwood gradually established themselves as serious contenders for supremacy in the market. The quality of design and printing (and, after the return of John to active management, also of potting and glazing) was of such excellence that in 1813 Josiah II was able to state with some justification: "There are no blue printed plates like mine in Staffordshire." Some of these designs, notably *Willow, Landscape* and *Ferrara**, have survived in production until the present day, but unquestionably the finest were the bold floral designs of which *Water Lily**, *Peony*, *Hibiscus* and *Chrysanthemum* are examples. This style of pattern was unique to Wedgwood.

The manager of the blue-printing department at Etruria, from its inception to his death in 1835, was Abner Wedgwood*.

Wedgwood's underglaze printed patterns were, with few exceptions, Chinese in character. They varied considerably in colour, those made for the American market tending to be much darker in hue, but all appear to have a sparkling clarity of tone which is only partly due to the brilliance of the glaze. Some blue-speckling occurs on many pieces, but the all-over decoration employed masks these minor faults. Borders were generally of two types: narrow bead or reeded designs, or wide borders applied over the entire rim and falling over the shoulder of the plate or dish into the well. The latter were sometimes Oriental in inspiration but more often unashamedly floral and English. This curious mixture of styles is surprisingly satisfying, though the later centre patterns of views and landscapes are more obviously suitable.

Wedgwood's earliest underglaze patterns, some of which were reproduced on stone china* and bone china* include:

Bamboo, December 1805.
Basket, December 1805.
Basket of Flowers, 1820-22.
Blue Birdcage, embossed, 1829.
Blue Chinese Temples, 1828.
*Blue Ferrara**, 1832.
Blue Grotto, 1832.
Blue Group of Flowers, 1819. *Blue Rose*, 1823-24.
*Botanical Flowers**, 1809-10.
Brosely, 1817.
Cairo, 1834.
Chinese Bridge on a Scroll (Blue Bridge), 1811.
Chrysanthemum, 1808.
Claude, 1822.
Corinthian, 1811.
Goats, 1842.
Hibiscus, 1806-7.
Landscape, 1824.
Palisade, 1815.
Pavilion, 1822.
Peony, 1807.
*Water Lily**, 1808.
Zodiac, 1841.

Underglaze Blue Prints. *Pearl ware plate decorated with the Hibiscus pattern, c.1810.* Reilly.

Underglaze Blue Prints. *Pearl ware soup plate decorated with Blue Bamboo pattern, c.1806.* Reilly.

Underglaze Blue Prints. *Landscape pattern, first produced in 1824, printed underglaze in blue. The centre view is used in conjunction with a typical rose border.* Wedgwood.

Underglaze Colour

Decoration, either printed or painted, applied to the surface of the ware before the application of the glaze, and therefore lying under it. Until the 19th century was fairly well advanced the only two pigments which could be employed in this way were blue from cobalt oxide and purple or brownish-purple from manganese oxide. Josiah I employed glazes thus coloured, but painted or printed decoration underglaze is known only after 1805. The underglaze palette is still limited, and no satisfactory method has yet been devised for the application of gold underglaze.

See: Underglaze Blue Prints.

Unique Ware

A range of ornamental vases, bowls, and small trays, designed and produced under the direction of Norman Wilson* from 1932-39, and from 1954-63. Many decorating techniques were employed, including *sgraffito** and painted lustre*, but the majority of these wares rely for their effect on the sensitive use of brilliant glazes — sometimes as many as five of different colours superimposed and separately fired. Shapes of Chinese or Korean origin predominated, but vases and bowls with turned horizontal or vertical fluting were also popular. Since the patterns of glazes could not be precisely controlled, each finished piece was unique. Production of Norman Wilson Unique Ware was limited by cost, and the finest pieces, which are both beautiful and technically superb, are sure to attract the attention of collectors in the future.

Unique wares bear the initials 'NW', printed or impressed, in addition to the Wedgwood marks.

Unwin, Ralph (fl.1770-1812)

Miniaturist and enameller, who occasionally painted landscapes. He exhibited thirty-three works, mostly miniatures, at the Royal Academy. He was hired in May 1770, as a painter at the Chelsea Decorating Studios* and painted part of the *Husk* service for Catherine II*, and landscapes for the Frog* service. Unwin also painted 'Herculaneum* Pictures', and copied a painting of 'Dead Game' by P.P. Burdett*. A miniature portrait by him of Josiah Wedgwood has been lost.

Urn

This word had many meanings, although it is often believed that the Roman *urna* were used only for cinerary purposes. The name was primarily given by the Romans to a narrow-necked, full-bodied pitcher, on a base of relatively small diameter, used for carrying water from a fountain. The cinerary urn (*sepulcrum*) was less full-bodied, with a wide mouth, two upstanding handles on the shoulder, and a cover. The First Day's* vase is, in its shape, a Roman sepulcrum (or *Lebes gamikos*). The name, *urna*, was also applied to vases of slender form which were used for collecting votes or drawing lots. The term, therefore, need not be strictly confined to vases employed for funerary purposes. At the same time, the term is often employed very loosely. Most garden urns, for instance, are far closer to the krater*, and most tea urns, like those of Adam design in Sheffield plate, are based on the sepulcrum. A sepulchral shape in black basaltes was employed on a number of occasions as part of a monument. One such vase was ordered by Miss Deborah Chetwynd* when her father, Lord Chetwynd, died. It stood on a rectangular inscribed slab in Ashley Church, Staffordshire. The Wedgwood Museum* has examples of funerary urns in basaltes and creamware. Creamware urns with a slight decoration of relief festoons*, agate* surface, gilded handles, and a basaltes or white jasper* base (mark 'Wedgwood & Bentley') were made about 1775. Wedgwood also experimented about 1778 with sideboard ùrns in the style popularised by Robert Adam*, and used either for holding water for washing glasses, or for storing knives, but it proved difficult to arrive at an efficient design which would not topple over when the top was opened and allowed to fall back. The project seems to have been abandoned.

See: Vases.

Useful Wares

The difference between these and 'ornamental' wares was of considerable importance, since Wedgwood's partnership with Bentley* was limited to the production of the latter, and his partnership with his cousin, Thomas, to 'useful' wares. He defined these terms in a letter to Bentley of the 3rd September, 1770. In this letter he states that he considers table services, teapots, chamber pots, and such things, no matter how richly decorated, to be useful ware, and a flower pot, vase, or candlestick ''be it ever so plain'' to be 'ornamental'. Included under the heading of ornamental wares, of course, were figures*, busts*, plaques*, tablets*, cameos*, seals and medallions*. Wedgwood's purpose in drawing this distinction was to leave his cousin, Thomas, with an incentive to improve the quality of table services, etc. then being produced at the Brick House Works*.

See: Ornamental Wares.

Utzschneider, François Paul (1771-1844)

Partner, with Joseph Fabry, in the firm of Utzschneider & Cie, the largest manufacturers of fine earthenware in France during the 19th century. Founded at Sarreguemines (Moselle) in 1778 by Nicolas-Henri Jacobi, Paul Augustin Jacobi, and Joseph Fabry, the factory produced *faience* until 1799, when the Jacobi interests were transferred to Utzschneider in a new partnership for the manufacture of 'English' earthenware and stoneware. Price lists of 1810 advertised products ''in the English taste'', including Queen's ware, basaltes, agate and marbled wares. Known as the French Wedgwood', Utzschneider specialised in wares of this type, winning Gold Medals at Expositions in Paris in 1806, 1819, 1823, 1827 and 1834. In 1836 Utzschneider handed over direction of the factory to his son-in-law, Alexandre de Geiger (1808-91) in partnership with Fabry's heirs.

Variegated Ware. *Ewer and two vases, the surfaces decorated to imitate semi-precious hardstones. All of the Wedgwood & Bentley period, c.1775. The ewer, 11⅛ ins. high, is decorated in green, grey, brown, and black; the left hand vase, 8⅞ ins., in green, brown and cream; and the right hand vase, 8¾ ins. in blue, green, brown and black. Dwight and Lucille Beeson Collection.*

Variegated (or Marbled) Lustre
See: Lustre Decoration.

Variegated Ware
Earthenware in which the body comprises variously coloured clays wedged or partially mixed together (as in solid agate* ware), by mixing colours in the form of slip on the surface of the ware to give a similar effect, or by mixing or mingling colours in the glaze, usually by dusting the body with metallic colouring oxides before glazing (as in mottled and tortoise-shell* wares). These techniques have a variety of names including agate, onyx, mottled, pebble sprinkled, veined, and tortoiseshell. Most of them were intended to imitate the markings of decorative hardstones.

Hardstones of all kinds, the surface cut and polished, have always been sought and valued for their decorative colourings and veinings. Some of the stones popular in the middle years of the 18th century include porphyry, red jasper, chalcedony, lapis lazuli, malachite, amethyst, agate, onyx, granite (mainly for pedestals), a variety of coloured marbles, and what Boulton* called "root of amethyst" (Wedgwood's radix amethyst, otherwise 'Blue John', or Derbyshire Spar). The imitation of all these stones was the ambition of glass makers from early times, and Von Tschirnhaus and Böttger at Meissen* were experimenting with artificial hardstones before they made porcelain. In 1771 Boulton & Fothergill sent some of their ormolu-mounted 'Blue John' vases to Christie's for sale by auction at a time when Wedgwood was finding a ready sale for his 'Blue Pebble' vases.

Mottled, marbled, and agate wares were made by Whieldon* during the period of his partnership with Wedgwood, and Wedgwood made these wares from the beginning. He improved all these techniques, using them for vases which closely imitated hardstones. He also sprayed the colours in such a way as to produce a speckled effect — a type known as 'speckled agate' — and metallic oxides were dusted onto the surface before glazing in a manner similar to that used in making tortoiseshell ware. Porphyry was a sprinkled green glaze, and granite was a mottled greyish blue.

Vases made from hardstones were much the more expensive. In 1771 Boulton realised £52 10s. at auction for an ormolu-mounted 'Blue John' vase, while Wedgwood variegated creamware vases were sold for prices in the region of £1 10s.

Wedgwood solid agate wares were very well imitated by a number of Continental factories, notably Apt, in the Vaucluse, and Kassel and Königsberg in Germany. His variegated or crystalline* vases were also imitated in England, most notably by Neale*, whose vases were of excellent quality.

After the first few years this kind of decoration was largely limited to vases, and in November 1769, we find Wedgwood protesting against a request from Bentley* to make a 'pebble' tea-set for Sir George Young.

In 1961 Norman Wilson* made some experimental marbled plates in black and white and green and white, but these were not approved for production. A small number of beaded-edge bowls in black and white were among the varied range of his Unique Ware.

Vase Candlestick
An urn-shaped vase with a reversible cover, one side of which is provided with a candle nozzle. When the shoulders and cover are pierced it becomes a cassolette*. Vase candlesticks were made by Wedgwood in creamware, black basaltes* and, after 1780, in jasper*.

Vase Candlestick. *Creamware vase candlestick (the type sometimes called a cassolette) of surface agate, a meander on the base probably copied from a Chinese source, and a scrolling floral and foliate band at the shoulder.* Wedgwood.

Vases, Creamware
Creamware vases were, perhaps, Wedgwood's first strictly ornamental product. Made almost from the first, they were well established as one of the most important items of manufacture when the Wedgwood and Bentley* partnership was inaugurated in 1769. The body of the vase was generally affixed to the stem and base by a brass screw and nut, a practice which dates from 1771. In April of that year Wedgwood wrote to Bentley referring to difficulty experienced with vases fired in one piece, which warped in firing: "There is a way," he wrote, "in which I believe they may be made with slender and yet straight feet, and that is to make and fire them separate, and afterwards fix the vase, foot, and plinth together with a pin, screw, and nut, as I believe in this way they may be made to hold water by putting a piece of leather betwixt the screw head and the bottom of the inside of the vase." This suggestion was not only put into practice, but soon became widely used elsewhere.

Although vases had been produced for some years, and the

summer of 1767 saw a great increase in the demand for them, it was not until the summer of 1768 that the first basaltes* vase was made. A documentary source for early Wedgwood vases is Saltram House, South Devon, where the creamware vases date to 1764/5. These (unmarked, as with most wares at this time) are in a body of pronounced ivory tone, and Wedgwood once considered calling this ware 'Ivory'. Rococo* elements are not uncommon in the early designs, and these belong to the category which Wedgwood called ''my first vases.'' The debt owed by Wedgwood to Sèvres* in the shape of some of his creamware vases is considerable, and his request to Bentley in November, 1769, to send Mr. Craft to take drawings of the 'Seve' vases at Morgan's, the Arlington Street china dealer, is clear evidence of the interest he was taking in the products of the Royal factory.

In the early summer of 1767 Wedgwood was in London searching for new and more commodious rooms in which to display his wares. His old rooms had, by this time, come to be a fashionable meeting place, and Wedgwood proceeded to give his assistants a lesson in the art of display. This was so effective that, as he reports, vases which had remained unsold for several months, ''and wanted nothing but arrangement to sell them,'' were bought for two or three guineas a set. At this time Wedgwood was not entirely satisfied with his vases. In May 1767, he referred to the ''rude state'' in which vase production then was, and told Bentley: ''I am picking up every design and improvement for Vase work.'' When he engaged the boy apprentice, William Wood*, to learn to model in the autumn of 1767 he intended him to model free-hand festoons on vases, as ''they will look infinitely richer than anything made out of moulds.''

In August 1768, the first basaltes vases were sent to London, but they were in an early stage of development, and Wedgwood reported that only one in six emerged from the kiln in a saleable condition. Creamware vases at this time were so popular that any novel types sent to London were bought by the agents of Wedgwood's competitors and travelled straight back to Staffordshire, to be copied there. In November 1768, Wedgwood wrote from London: ''Mr Boulton* is picking up vases and is going to make [i.e. mount] them in bronze.'' Boulton's intention was to supply them with rococo mounts in gilt-bronze or ormolu* in imitation of the contemporary French style. He was staying in London at the same time, and proposed to Wedgwood that they should go into the mounted vase business together, Wedgwood supplying the vases and he the mounts. Wedgwood was undecided, and when Mr. Cox* called at the Soho Works (Birmingham) on his way to Etruria in September 1769, he found Boulton & Fothergill affronted because Wedgwood would not co-operate. They stressed that several potters were offering them vases, but they had determined to start their own factory.

Wedgwood was again in London in February 1769, where he met Lord Bessborough, ''who admires our Vases and manufacture prodigiously... He has given me four Guineas for three vases, one of them a large Blue... the other two Etruscans at a Guinea each... I hope he will set these large Blue ones agoing.'' This was the start of a run on vases which led to urgent letters to Staffordshire: ''Let all hands that can be spared and can work at Vases be employed in them,'' and to the remark, ''large ones, very large ones, are all the cry.'' John Coward* was set to work to 'tinker' defective vases, making new covers, feet, plinths, and snake handles from carved wood. On 9th April, 1769, we find Wedgwood writing to Bentley: ''I had a piteous letter from Mr Cox — not a Vase scarcely of any sort to sell, Blue Pebble & Marbled, all gone...

To assist him a little I have sent him this week-end Vases to amot. of £136, & they are not much more than a good Crate full!''

The 'Pebble' vases were perhaps his most important work at this time. In making them Wedgwood's experience at Ivy House* in the production of agate* ware stood him in good stead. 'Pebble' was less specialised in its meaning in the 18th century than it is today, and was used to refer to the commoner decorative hardstones, such as agate, onyx, etc., as well as loosely to 'marbled' ware. These were a natural development from the earlier vases of plain creamware, and were made with coloured slips or glazes. They were either marbled*, combed*, or speckled* in a way which gave a passable imitation of the markings of natural stones, and some were decorated by engine turning* or, especially after 1769, by gilding*, though only traces now remain. The use of medallions and bas-relief as decoration to vases of this kind was a comparatively recent innovation in 1769.

By the Autumn of 1769 we find Wedgwood concentrating on four kinds of vases — Blue Pebble, Variegated Pebble, Black Etruscan and Etruscan Encaustic (i.e. the imitation of red-figure* vases). The term 'basaltes' for the last two did not come into use until about 1774. ''These [he says] with the variations of sizes, forms, Ornaments, Gilding, Veining, Bass Reliefs, &c. will produce business enough for all the hands we can possibly get together, and, I think, variety enough for all our *reasonable* customers.'' In November 1769, he wrote that he had taken James Bourn*, the turner, from Burslem to work on vases: ''...we have not got one Engine Turner left there now. Poor Burslem — Poor Cream coloured. They tell me that I sacrifice all to Etruria and Vases!'' In December he wrote: ''We have some Medallion Vases in the oven, and are making plenty of them which you shall see in due time. I now give myself up allmost entirely to *Vasemaking* and find myself to improve in that Art and Mysterie pretty fast.'' In August 1770, Wedgwood wrote to Bentley recording a visit from Sir Charles Bingham from Ireland, who gave Wedgwood reason to think that ''there seemed to be a violent *Vase madness* breaking out'' among the Irish. Sir Charles was certain that had Wedgwood a room in Dublin a large quantity might be sold. When this was written, however, the 'Vase madness' in England was already starting to abate, and the volume of trade generally was falling. Wedgwood's answer to this recession was to attempt to extend the rationalisation of production already employed in making utility wares to those intended for ornament. In this way he expected to lower prices to bring the ornamental wares within reach of a new class of customer. This was achieved by building up a stock of moulds, and making them as inter-changeable as possible, so that a variety of wares could be made more expeditiously, more cheaply, and in greater quantities, without lowering the prices paid to the workmen, who had already complained about time wasted in making short runs of a particular article. In August 1772, Wedgwood wrote to Bentley: ''We now have upwards of 100 Good forms of Vases, for all of which we have moulds, handles, and orna-ments, and we could make them almost as currently as useful ware, and at one half the expence we have hitherto done, provided I durst set the men to make from 6 to 12 doz of a sort... The Great People have had these Vases in their Palaces long enough for them to be seen and admired by the Middling Class of people, which class we know are vastly, I had almost said infinitely, superior in number to the Great, and though a great price was, I believe, at first necessary to make the Vases esteemed *Ornaments for Palaces,* that reason no longer exists... The middling People would probably buy quantitys of them at a reduced price...''

Vases, Creamware.
*Three marked Wedgwood
& Bentley period cream-
ware vases decorated to
simulate porphyry. Two
are additionally
ornamented with applied
medallions, and all have
handles terminating in
masks. c.1770. Zeitlin
Collection.*

Among the more spectacular vases are those which have
been dipped into a slip of contrasting colour, usually black,
followed by its partial removal down to the original colour,
either with a special tool or with the engine-turning* lathe.
Reeding and fluting are done in this way, and a ribbed effect
has a similar appearance to the fashionable enamelled striped
grounds on porcelain. Vase forms thus decorated often owe a
good deal to Sèvres and hardly anything to classical sources,
and a striped ground in blue enamel with a painted oval
medallion was a popular decorative scheme both at Sèvres and
the Derby* factory in the porcelain version of neo-classical
vases.

Creamware vases painted with enamel colours, apart from
simple border motifs, are unusual from Wedgwood at this
time, but not unknown. (For more detailed information about
'pebbled' and marbled decoration see: Variegated ware.) The
earliest creamware vases are unmarked. Those marked
'Wedgwood' only may predate the Wedgwood and Bentley
partnership, but such early examples are uncommon. Those
bearing the circular Wedgwood and Bentley wafer mark are
much sought, and here consideration should always be given to
the possibility of a missing plinth having been replaced, or
added to a vase made outside this period. This, of course, is
only possible with vases made in parts and joined together with
a screw, unless there has been restoration. It should be borne
in mind that, on the evidence of Wedgwood's letter quoted, the
screw and nut method of assembling vases dates from 1771. No
jasper vases were made before Bentley's death in 1780, but
basaltes or jasper plinths were matched to variegated vases
during the Wedgwood & Bentley partnership.

During the lifetime of the first Josiah about 250 vase shapes

were made, some of course very much rarer than others, and
many of them are to be found in creamware, basaltes, and
jasper, since the moulds were interchangeable. This number
was greatly increased during the 19th century, and some
excellent painting on creamware vases came from both Emile
Lessore* and Thomas Allen*. Remembering Wedgwood's
remark quoted earlier about the demand for "very large
vases" it is interesting to note that among the vases sold in the
Auction Sale* of 1781, which followed Bentley's death, was
one five feet in height ornamented in bas-relief which was listed
among the 'pebble' wares. This was about twice the size of any
other Wedgwood vase of the 18th century in any material. It
has now been lost sight of, but may still exist somewhere
unrecognised.

The decorative vase, without any immediate practical
purpose, was very much a product of the 18th century, and
began with the collecting of Oriental porcelain earlier in the
century, and the subsequent copying of Chinese and Japanese
vases by European factories. The Oriental vase, of course,
often had either a practical purpose or had been made as an
altar vessel. The decorative vase in European style was
developed at Meissen, and then in a much more sophisticated
form at Sèvres, as a purely luxury product during the
currency of the rococo* style. Classical vases, such as those copied by
Wedgwood from Greek and Roman sources, were also made
for eminently practical purposes originally, and a definite use
attaches to each form. During the 18th century, however, their
greatest use was either to contain pot-pourri, or to act as
receptacles for small objects not immediately wanted, to which
the name of one Sèvres vase — *cache-pot* — is adequate
testimony.

Veilleuse

A ceramic utensil of several parts for keeping warm the contents of a teapot (or kettle), bowl or cup. The lower part consists of a pedestal, pierced to allow the circulation of air, with an arched aperture for a *godet** (a small cup containing a wick, floating or suspended in oil). A veilleuse is illustrated in the 1790 Catalogue, and is shown in more detail in the 1817 Catalogue (Plate 15 engraved by William Blake*). This is the form known as a *veilleuse-théière*, the upper part of which is a teapot or kettle. In France, this was also called a *veilleuse-tisanière* because it was used to make infusions (*tisanes*) of camomile or herbs.

See: Food Warmer.

Venus. *Venus seated on a rock, after Pigalle, 1779. 19ins. high.* Zeitlin Collection.

Veldhuyson (Velthuyson), L. van

Amsterdam merchant: Wedgwood's agent in succession to Du Burk*. Wedgwood wrote in 1778: ''We have a pretty good order this week from Mr Velthuyson... I am told his warehouse is fitted up very elegantly, and believe he is likely to do very well, both for himself and us.'' His successors still do business with Wedgwood after two centuries.

Venus

Formerly the Roman goddess of Spring, she became identified with the Greek Aphrodite*, goddess of love, in the 3rd century B.C. The worship of Venus was fostered by Julius Caesar*, who traced his ancestry back to Aeneas, son of Mars* and Venus. The goddess is often depicted with Cupid*, her son, or with the most famous of her human lovers, Adonis.

Wedgwood subjects:

Crouching Venus, Figure 12½ins., after the copy of the antique by Coysevox.

Shell Venus, model by Flaxman*, 1781.

Triumph of Venus, tablet* 8ins. by 17ins., and 9ins. by 20ins., by Flaxman, 1779.

Venus, seated figure on a rock, 19ins., after Pigalle*. Supplied by Hoskins & Grant*, 1779, (see also: Mercury.)

Venus, statuette, height 7ins., on a pedestal as companion to one of Mars*, c.1785.

Venus and Adonis, tablet. Bas-relief* supplied by Hoskins & Oliver, 1774.

Venus and Cupid (with emblem of Fire), medallion 5ins. by 4ins. The same figures appear on the tablet *Venus and Cupid* [Selene and Eros] *visiting Endymion**, 1777.

Venus and Cupid. (*Aphrodite carrying the flower of fertility preceded by an Eros*), from a print of an antique gem*, medallion, c.1777.

Venus and Cupid (Venus seated), medallion 13½ins., c.1775-78.

Venus Callipygous ('Collipyge'), bas-relief often attributed to Flaxman but too early for his work (perhaps supplied by Flaxman Senior), used for medallions 4ins. by 3ins. and 10½ins. by 7¾ins., and also for the decoration of porphyry* vases. First catalogued 1773.

Venus captive, medallion by Flaxman.

Venus bound by two Cupids, medallion by Flaxman.

Venus chiding Cupid, cameo attributed to Hackwood* after a painting by Reynolds*.

Venus de Medici ('de Medicus'), bust, 18ins. high, supplied by Hoskins & Oliver, 1774, and finished by Hackwood.

Venus de Medici, figure, height 10½ins., modelled by 1774.

Venus de Milo, figure, height 20½ins., probably 19th century.

Venus in her chariot drawn by Swans, bas-relief after Charles Le Brun*. Used for the decoration of jasper vases and also for tablets 4¼ins. by 9ins.

Venus reclining, medallion, 1787 or earlier, for a frieze.

Venus rising from the sea, figure, height 6¾ins., attributed to Flaxman, 1777, and listed as ''upon a pedestal richly ornamented with figures representing the seasons.''

Venus Victrix, cameo attributed to Hackwood, 1773.

Vulcan with Mars and Venus in a net, medallion attributed to Flaxman, 5½ins. by 6ins.

Verde Antique

Name given to a kind of green marble very much prized in France for the tops of *commodes* and *console* tables, and for pedestals. Josiah Wedgwood used the name to describe one of his 'crystalline' bodies in varying colours of dark green, grey and black.

See: Variegated Ware.

Venus. *Black basaltes plaque, diameter of long axis 14¾ ins., of Venus Callipygous (Collipyge) with integral basaltes frame. First catalogued in 1773. Christie's.*

Venus. *Medallion,* Venus and Cupid, *attributed to Hackwood. Solid blue jasper in an ormolu frame, possibly by Boulton & Fothergill. Diameter of long axis 6½ ins. 1778. Wedgwood.*

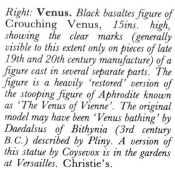

Left: **Venus.** *Solid white jasper statuette of Venus, height 7ins., robing herself after the judgement of Paris, whose apple she holds in her left hand. She is accompanied by Cupid and a dolphin. c.1785.* Liverpool City Museums. Photo: Wedgwood.

Right: **Venus.** *Black basaltes figure of* Crouching Venus, *15ins. high, showing the clear marks (generally visible to this extent only on pieces of late 19th and 20th century manufacture) of a figure cast in several separate parts. The figure is a heavily 'restored' version of the stooping figure of Aphrodite known as 'The Venus of Vienne'. The original model may have been 'Venus bathing' by Daedalsus of Bithynia (3rd century B.C.) described by Pliny. A version of this statue by Coysevox is in the gardens at Versailles.* Christie's.

Veronese Glazes

Coloured glazes used on earthenware ornamental pieces from 1930-40. The range included vases, lamps, and covered jars of Chinese shape, and the red, blue, and green glazes were decorated with simple art deco style designs in 'platinum' lustre*.

Vestal

A virgin priestess who helped to keep the eternal fire burning on the goddess Vesta's hearth or altar. Vesta was one of the great Roman divinities, goddess of the Hearth and therefore connected with the Penates (household gods). The temple of Vesta was situated in the Forum, between the Capitoline and Palatine hills.

Wedgwood subjects:

A Vestal, medallion, 5ins. by 4ins., by Flaxman*. First catalogued in 1777.

Vestal. Two busts of this title appear to have been supplied to Wedgwood. The first, 15ins. high, came from Richard Parker* in February 1774, and is listed in the Catalogue for that year. The second, uncatalogued, was supplied by Hoskins & Grant* in 1775.

Victoria Ware

Queen's ware vases, ornamented in relief with swags, medallions, etc., in the manner of jasper*, but decorated with enamel ground-lays, often in more than one colour, and lavishly gilt. These vases, introduced c.1875, were made to compete with the porcelain vases produced by other manufacturers, notably Coalport*, Derby* and Worcester*, and were, in the words of Tom Lyth*, "Earthenware made to look like porcelain." Vases almost identical in appearance were also made in enamelled, glazed, and gilt Parian*. The production of these evidently followed closely upon the experiments in glazed Parian (Carrara*) made in the 1860s, and they

Victoria Ware. *Creamware vase decorated in the classical style in the manner of jasper. c.1875.* Wedgwood.

therefore precede in date the similar vases in Queen's ware, though both versions were probably simultaneously in production for a short period.

At first sight it may be difficult to distinguish between the Queen's ware vases and those of glazed Parian, but a closer examination reveals that the Parian body is harder, whiter, and heavier than Queen's ware, and the modelling has a porcelain crispness which the relief ornament of the Queen's ware lacks.

See: Worcester Style.

Vignette

A picture or design which does not have a frame or well-defined border.

See: Thomas Bewick.

Viol da Gamba

Italian. A viol held between the legs, corresponding to the modern violoncello. Wedgwood produced a small jasper vase approximating to the shape of this instrument in 1801 as part of a set of ornaments. Byerley* wrote from Etruria* in February, 1801: "You will receive this week four new ornaments in form of Viol del Gamba [*sic*] or Violoncello for Musical Amateurs — to be used either as flowerpot, bulbous-root, or candlestick. They belong to a set intended to captivate musical people."

Violins in tin-enamelled ware were produced at Delft, Holland, during the 18th century

Viol da Gamba. *Jasper vase based on the shape of the viol da gamba, first produced in 1801.* Wedgwood.

Virgil, P. Vergilius Maro (70-19 B.C.)

The greatest of the Roman epic poets, and author of the *Aeneid*, the *Georgics, Eclogues, Bucolics,* and possibly of other, lesser works. The *Aeneid* was started about 27 B.C., probably under the patronage of Augustus Caesar*. Virgil died at Brundisium and was buried near the road from Puteoli to Naples, where a monument supposed to be his tomb still exists. A painting of it by Joseph Wright* of Derby is dated 1779. On 2nd August 1779, Josiah Wedgwood, dissatisfied with attempts to model a head of Virgil, sat down at the modellers bench. Later that day he wrote to Bentley*: "I this morning resumed by old employment, took the modelling tools into my hands, and made one side of the head pretty near like the gem. . . I have opened his mouth, and shall send him to you saying some of his own divine poems if I send him at all."

Wedgwood subjects:

Virgil, bust, 15ins. high. Cast supplied by Hoskins & Grant*, 1775, and refinished by Josiah Wedgwood with the aid of a gem (intaglio) portrait.

Apotheosis of Virgil, bas-relief by Flaxman, probably in 1785. At one time erroneously titled 'Alexander crowned by Victory', it was modelled as a pair to the *Apotheosis of Homer*, and first appeared as ornament for a large plaque. Later it was adapted to the Pegasus* vase as a companion to the Homeric* vase.

Vitalba (fl.1773-1774)

Painter at the Chelsea Decorating Studios*, who executed landscapes for the Frog* service. Also listed as Nitalba.

Voltaire, Jean-François-Marie Arouet de. *Portrait medallion of Voltaire (1694-1778), modelled by Hackwood. c.1778.* Wedgwood.

Vitreous Bodies

A term which embraces basaltes*, jasper*, stonewares* of all kinds, and porcelain, although it is rarely employed to include the last, which is regarded as a separate category. Ordinary earthenware is fired at a comparatively low temperature which results in a point-to-point attachment of the particles. For this reason it remains porous. Vitreous bodies are non-porous because they are fired at a temperature high enough to convert all but the clay into an amorphous mass which, in effect, is a kind of glass. Chips and fractures have much the same appearance as those in ordinary thick glass. The principle is the same, whether the material be common stoneware or the finest porcelain, the differences in quality largely being due to differences in the substances employed and the refinement of the processes. Basically, the formula is refractory clay, plus fusible rock, with a flux added. Clay is so refractory that most reasonably pure clays will only fuse or melt at temperatures in the region of 1600° centigrade. The rock employed will fuse into an amorphous mass (i.e. natural glass) at a much lower temperature, between 1100° and 1400° centigrade according to its nature. The flux is a substance added to promote fusion, and it induces it to take place at a somewhat lower temperature than would otherwise be possible. Clay is plastic, and when blended with the rock in powdered form, the flux, and a certain quantity of water, it yields a substance capable of being shaped in any of the ways commonly used by the potter. When firing is taking place the clay holds the object in shape during the vital period when the rock is at fusion point. Porcelain, jasper, and basaltes are all fired at a higher temperature than the commoner stonewares and ironstone china, and one result of this is that thinly potted examples of jasper, and certain other fine stonewares, are sometimes translucent. Porcelain of less than 5mm in thickness is invariably so. Stonewares, because the body is amorphous, do not ordinarily need a glaze, although they are sometimes given one for aesthetic reasons. Jasper teaware intended for domestic use is glazed on the inside because the surface might otherwise be stained. Porcelain is also glazed for these reasons.

Vitruvian Scroll

Classical ornament, a favourite with the brothers Adam*, consisting of a succession of convoluted scrolls resembling stylised waves. It is also known as the Greek wave pattern.

Voltaire, Jean-François-Marie Arouet de (1694-1778)

Educated by the Jesuits, Voltaire was banished in 1716 for a satire on the profligate Régent, the duc d'Orléans, and an even more scurrilous effort in 1717 earned him a spell in the Bastille. He arrived in England in 1726, where he became acquainted with many influential people, and later he was appointed Chamberlain to Frederick the Great of Prussia. He settled in Switzerland in 1755, and published the first of his anti-Christian writings in 1762. Voltaire enjoyed considerable success as a dramatist, and his philosophical writings were widely esteemed.

There are two Wedgwood portrait medallions of Voltaire, one by Hackwood* based on a portrait bust by J. A. Houdon*, and a 12ins. statuette which is a pair to that of Rousseau*. The statuette was made in basaltes, a material which Wedgwood thought might make its subject more attractive to the clergy! It was also made in cane ware*, and was first produced in 1778. Cane ware examples are very rare because it was found almost impossible at this time to fire examples without some degree of discoloration. Wedgwood suggested painting both the Voltaire and Rousseau figures sent to London in an attempt to disguise this fault. The modeller appears to have been Keeling*, working from drawings perfected by Thomas Bentley*, which were taken originally either from a statue by Houdon or a similar figure by the sculptor, Jean-Claude-Joseph Rosset du Pont (1703-86).

A small bust, 4-4½ins. in height, also after Houdon, was produced, with a companion bust of Rousseau in time for inclusion in the 1777 Catalogue.

Volumnia

Wife of Coriolanus*. There seems to have been some confusion at Etruria* about the story of Coriolanus and his relationships, and this has been further confused by the erroneous re-titling of bas-reliefs.

See: Penelope.

Volute

A spiral curve; a helix. A volute handle, to be found on some kraters*, terminates above the rim of the vessel in a helical scroll.

Voyez, Jean (1735-1800)

When Wedgwood engaged Voyez as a modeller in 1768 he wrote to Bentley telling his friend that reports described Voyez, who had been apprenticed to a silversmith, and had worked for a porcelain factory (?Bow* or Chelsea*), as well as carving in wood and marble for the Adam* Brothers, as the best modeller in London. "Voyez," wrote Wedgwood, "is a perfect master of the antique style in ornaments, vases &c., and works with

Voyez, Jean. *Portrait medallion in jasper of Jean Voyez, possibly a self-portrait. A creamware version is dated 'Sept. 20th, 1768'. A profile portrait in wax is in the Nottingham Castle Museum. Sotheby's.*

equal facility in wax, wood, or stone." Voyez had also worked for Coade* of Lambeth, and exhibited with the Free Society of Artists. He therefore seemed suitable in every way to model ornamental wares in the new basaltes body. Wedgwood paid his debts, and transported him and his wife to Burslem, entertaining him in his own house until accommodation had been prepared. In less than a year Voyez had been sentenced to three month's imprisonment at the Staffordshire Assizes for some unspecified offence. One detects almost a conspiracy of silence in the way in which Wedgwood and contemporary records avoid particularising his crime, which must have been trivial to have attracted so slight a sentence at a time when a man might be hanged for stealing a sheep. There is a legend to the effect that Wedgwood discovered Voyez modelling the naked daughter of the coachman, and it is not improbable. Wedgwood's attitude to Voyez subsequently would have been fully in keeping with his character if it were true. Voyez later considerably annoyed Wedgwood by marketing copies of seals and cameos as the genuine product of Etruria*. In 1769 he was working for Humphrey Palmer* of Hanley, and in 1772 he exhibited intaglios, etc. with the Free Society. He also worked for Hales of Cobridge and Ralph Wood* of Burslem, as well as working independently. A black basaltes vase in the British Museum with the mark of Palmer is signed and dated 1769. A creamware vase is marked 'Voyez and Hales fecit.' Jugs in the Ralph Wood style include the 'Fair Hebe' jug, some examples of which are signed 'I. VOYEZ 1788' impressed. A mould for a portrait medallion said to be of Voyez, and to have been modelled by him, is in the Wedgwood Museum*. A wax portrait, reputed to be of Voyez, is in the Nottingham Castle Museum.

Vulcan

Roman god of fire and furnaces, identified by the poets with Hephaestos. He was represented as a vigorous but lame man, bearded, and carrying a hammer or some other instrument of the smith. He wears an oval cap and the chiton, leaving the right shoulder and arm bare.

Wedgwood subjects:

Vulcan with Mars and Venus in the net, medallion, 5½ins. x 6ins., first catalogued in 1777.

Vulcan forging a suit of armour, watched by Juno in her Chariot, tablet, 6⅜ins. by 10ins., c.1789.

Vulliamy, Benjamin (1747-1812)

English clockmaker to George III; the son of Justin Vulliamy, a Swiss who came to England in 1730, and Mary, daughter of Benjamin Gray, clockmaker to George II. During the last quarter of the 18th century he produced mantel clocks in the Louis Seize style ornamented with biscuit figures from Derby* which were modelled by John Rossi and the Swiss, Jean-Jacques Spängler. At least one Vulliamy clock is known with figures in white jasper instead of biscuit porcelain, the name, Wedgwood, being impressed on the sole of the foot. It is probable that more such clocks remain to be discovered.

The Vulliamy Clockbook, preserved in the British Horological Institute Library (Ilbert Bequest), shows that twenty-six clocks made between 1797 and 1806 were decorated with Wedgwood plaques or cameos inset, and it is certain that Vulliamy clocks (probably the work of Justin, who died in 1797) were inset with Wedgwood jasper ornaments at least ten years earlier.

Wakral, H.

A basaltes figure of a maiden seated on a high conical rockwork base moulded with scrolling foliage was sold in the collection of the late Mrs. E.L.T. Hendry at Christie's in December 1976. The signature, 'H. Wakral', was incised into the base. No other example of this artist's work for Wedgwood has been identified.

Wale, Samuel (d.1786)

London painter, illustrator and engraver of 'landskips' (landscapes). After an apprenticeship as a silver engraver, he became a pupil of Francis Hayman, whose style he imitated in his paintings, but he was primarily an illustrator. A founder-member of the Royal Academy, he was later to be its first pensioner. He exhibited fourteen paintings at the Academy between 1760 and 1778. He worked for Sadler* & Green about 1763. His work occurs on Wedgwood's creamware transfer-printed in Liverpool. On the 6th July, 1765, Wedgwood wrote to his brother, John*, in London asking him to secure a copper plate from Wale suitable for decorating creamware vases.

Wakral, H. *Black basaltes figure of a naked maiden seated on a high rock. c.1890, 11½ ins. high.* Christie's.

Warburton, Mrs. Anne. *Creamware plate, 'WARBURTON' impressed mark, probably by Peter and Francis Warburton of Cobridge, grandsons of Anne Warburton, c.1785. A deep cream colour, the plate is enamelled in a style reminiscent of Chinese export ware.* Zeitlin Collection.

Wall, Peter, ARCA, Des. RCA, MSIA (b.1926)

Designer at Barlaston* from 1952; Deputy Art Director 1961-70. Peter Wall designed tableware patterns for bone china* and Queen's ware*, *Big Top* nurseryware (1958), the St. Lawrence Seaway* plate (1959), King and Queen wall plaques (1962), and original bas-relief ornaments for basaltes* and jasper* cylindrical cigarette box and lighter sets (also made in gold-printed bone china, 1962). The following were among his most successful tableware patterns:

Beaconsfield, lithograph on bone china, 1956.
Greenwood, lithograph centre and *Thames Green* slip border (two-colour clay technique) on bone china, 1955.
Hathaway Rose, lithograph on bone china, 1959.
Ivy House, lithograph on bone china, 1957.
Spring Morning, lithograph on bone china, 1959.
Starflower, lithograph on bone china (teaware and coffeeware only), 1953.
Woodbury, lithograph on Barlaston shape*, 1958.

In 1970 Peter Wall became Head of the School of Ceramics at the Birmingham (Warwickshire) Polytechnic.

Wall Pocket

Also termed a cornucopia. A flower vase, flat on one side, made to be hung on a wall, and pierced at the top for suspension. Made by Wedgwood, wall pockets occur in salt-glaze and cream-coloured ware in the early period. Later, in the 19th century, the wall pocket in the form of a nautilus shell in lustre* ware made an appearance, and it has since been produced in Moonstone* glaze.
See: Flora.

Wallace, Nathaniel (1769-1774)

Painter at the Chelsea Decorating Studio* who worked on the Frog* service.

Warburton, Mrs. Anne (1713-1798)

'The Widow Warburton' was a master potter, in partnership with her son, Thomas, as Anne Warburton & Son of Hot Lane, Burslem. She decorated wares manufactured elsewhere, but her cream-coloured wares were also bought by other

manufacturers, Bills of sale exist showing that Wedgwood bought cream-coloured ware from her during his early years at the Ivy House* and Brick House* works. According to Simeon Shaw, Wedgwood sent creamware to be enamelled by the Warburtons, but no evidence has been found to substantiate this. It is likely, on the other hand, that early cream-coloured ware attributed to Wedgwood is actually the work of the Warburtons. Anne's son, Jacob, became a founding partner of the New Hall* factory, and her grandsons, Peter and Francis, manufactured fine creamware. Francis founded the firm of La Charité-sur-Loire*.

Wareham (or Warham), William (fl.1860-1874)
Engraver, Newcastle-under-Lyme, 1865; worked for Wedgwood, 1860-74.

Watch Cases
Jasper cameos, convex and about 1½ ins. in diameter, were made to be fitted into the cases of verge watches, being mounted by the bezel in the same way as a glass. They are thinner than the normal cameo, and decorated with classical subjects in low relief. Because of their fragility few have survived.

Water Lily Pattern
The first Wedgwood printed pattern reproducing botanical engravings from identifiable sources, the Water Lily pattern was first printed in brown for the three years 1808-11. It is described in the first pattern book in two versions: the first 'shaded in red and cut up with gold, and gold outside edge'; the second, with 'orange outside edge.' The pattern is composed of three plants; a water lily (*Nymphaea stellata*) and two forms of the lotus (*Nelumbium speciosum* and *Nymphaea lotus*). This accounts for the name 'Lotus', sometimes given to the pattern.

Josiah Byerley, who had succeeded his father (Thomas Byerley*) as Manager of the London Showrooms* in 1810, had suggested that the Water Lily pattern should be made in blue, "a variety of pattern in blue being necessary, and the Lily being certainly novel;" and in 1811 Josiah II* yielded to persuasion and economics and wrote: "If you have any Brown Lily in the rooms, turn it all out that you may not take orders for it which we cannot execute but at a loss — we will print some in Blue." At the same time the border was changed from the 'botanical' interlacing rings to a 'cut reed' border. This proved to be extremely popular and is generally considered to be one of Wedgwood's finest underglaze blue prints*.

The early versions of the Water Lily pattern were:
Brown-printed (botanical border), 1808-11.
Red-printed (botanical border), 1810.
Blue-printed, underglaze (cut reed border), 1811.
Red-printed, underglaze, c.1827.

The pattern continued in production during the 19th century, and a series of plaques, 12ins. in diameter, was issued in 1907. These were decorated with green leaves and border, with the flowers in various colours, some (in red) with mother-of-pearl lustre*. An octagonal plate, printed in purple and enamelled in colours, was produced in 1928. In 1978 a tankard, printed in underglaze blue, was produced in a limited edition for the Wedgwood Collectors' Society*.

Watson, Edward (fl.1768-1769)
Modeller who has been credited with an inkstand, and with an engraving of Dr. Johnson of 1770 from which the later portrait medallion by Flaxman* may have been taken.

Watt, James (1739-1819)
Engineer; FRS, 1785; LL.D Glasgow, 1806; partner with Matthew Boulton* in the firm of Boulton & Watt, 1775-1800; member of the Lunar Society*. Watt began life as a scientific instrument maker, and, in 1764, while repairing a model of Newcomen's steam engine, he discovered the reason for its waste of power. He patented his own steam engine in 1769, and renewed the patent ten years later. He began to experiment to convert the reciprocating engine to rotary motion about 1780, and supplied a rotary engine to Wedgwood about two years later, subsequently making many improvements to

Water Lily Pattern. *Three pieces of the Water Lily pattern. c.1812.* Wedgwood.

this type of engine which was, of course, essential for driving factory machinery. In 1780 he invented copying ink, which enabled documents to be duplicated, and in 1784 he designed a screw propeller for ships. His son, also James, became a partner in Boulton & Watt in 1794. He specialised in marine engines.

E.W. Wyon* modelled a portrait bust of James Watt for Wedgwood which was reproduced in black basaltes* in the 1850s.

Wax Portraits

Wax is one of the earliest known media for portraiture, dating at least from 300B.C., and wax portraits were extremely popular from 1760 until well into the 19th century. Wedgwood bought wax models for cameos* and portrait medallions*, and he also supplied basaltes tablets and medallions to the modellers to serve as a background for their wax reliefs.

The original portrait was modelled and carved from wax, and an intaglio mould of plaster of Paris taken from it. Into the recesses of this mould the modeller pressed a thin sheet of wax, pushing it into all the mould crevices. The mould was then filled with molten wax, which was left to harden. The next step was to extract it from the mould, make any finishing touches, and mount it on a suitable background, which varied from a black basaltes medallion to a sheet of blue or painted glass, or a tablet of plaster of Paris covered with a thin layer of dark wax. Portraits were made in coloured waxes, and were often painted in addition. Finally they were framed and glazed, a flat glass

Wax Portraits. *Wax portrait by Flaxman of the Dutch physician. Hermann Boerhaave (1668-1738). Modelled in 1782 from a medal by Pesez. An example in jasper is in the Wedgwood Museum, Barlaston. Formerly Reilly Collection.*

before 1790, and often a convex glass thereafter. Several copies were made of most portraits, usually by the modeller's assistants, sometimes for distribution to the sitter's friends, and sometimes, in the case of a celebrity, for public sale. Around 1820 prices charged for the original model from life were seven guineas in the case of a gentleman, and two guineas for copies, and ten guineas for a lady, and three guineas for copies, partly because there was more work involved, and partly because ladies were more critical and demanded time-consuming alterations and improvements. Clergymen were charged at the same rate as ladies. The head of a gentleman would be made free of charge if he ordered twenty or more copies.

The best of the wax portraitists exhibited with the Royal Academy, and they also sold portraits of celebrities. Most portraits were profiles, but Samuel Percy (1750-1820) abandoned the profile in favour of the three-quarter or almost full-face portrait modelled in high relief. This, however, was not entirely new. A wax portrait of Cleopatra in the Victoria and Albert Museum attributed to William Hackwood* about 1775, and similar to the jasper medallion, is of this type, and Wedgwood's medallions include several full and three-quarter face portraits, of which that of Erasmus Darwin* is an example. Other full-face portraits in high relief include those of Sir Eyre Coote, modelled by Eley George Mountstephen* in 1788, and the Marquis of Anglesey by William Hackwood, c.1822.

There is an important distinction to be drawn between the wax portraits supplied to Wedgwood by professional modellers in wax, and those modelled by sculptors. The former were intended for reproduction in wax, and the models supplied were frequently from moulds. Wedgwood noticed that models from Lochée* were "full of pin holes," indicating that they were moulded copies of an original. Flaxman's waxes, on the contrary, were originals, intended for reproduction in basaltes or jasper, and not for duplication in wax. The portraits he supplied to Wedgwood were therefore unique. They were also modelled in a particularly hard white wax which was specially suitable for Wedgwood's purpose of taking an intaglio mould in plaster of Paris. Most professional modellers used their own wax compositions, and Isaac Gosset's* ivory wax composition, which shows no sign of discoloration with the years, is easily recognised. The majority of Wedgwood's series of portraits of *Illustrious Moderns** were taken from originals in wax, as were many of Tassie's* portraits of contemporaries, some of which were modelled from life.

Waxen Jasper

The earlier of Wedgwood's white jasper bodies, occasionally referred to as 'waxen terracotta', but accurately described by Josiah I in his 1787 Catalogue: "White porcelain biscuit, with a smooth wax-like surface, of the same properties as the basaltes except in what depends on colour." This is in contrast to "Jasper — a white porcelain biscuit of exquisite quality, possessing the general properties of basaltes, together with that of receiving colours through its whole surface..." The two bodies were in production concurrently: the first, hard and densely opaque; and the second, finer and often translucent.

A waxen finish is also sometimes to be seen on jasper fired in a saggar* in which remaining glaze material volatised and settled on the ware. Such jasper has the appearance of having a smear* glaze. Some restored jasper has a similar appearance as a result of light varnish sprayed on to disguise the repair. This undesirable finish may be removed with a cotton wool pad moistened with acetone.

Webber, Henry (1754-1826)

Modeller for Wedgwood; head of the ornamental department, 1785-1806. Webber was the son of a Swiss sculptor, and a pupil of John Bacon the Elder. He attended the Royal Academy Schools, where he won a Silver Medal in 1774. Webber was recommended to Wedgwood by Sir Joshua Reynolds* and Sir William Chambers* in 1784. In 1787 he was sent to Rome to collect material in the Capitoline Museum, and he travelled home by way of Switzerland and Paris with John Wedgwood*, who had also been in Rome. Upon his return Webber was not only engaged in translating his Italian drawings and models into jasper and basaltes, but he also played an important part in the production of the Wedgwood copies of the Portland* vase. Webber worked for Wedgwood until the latter's death in 1795, when he left to work on the monument to David Garrick in Westminster Abbey. It is probable that, after the expiry of the original seven-year contract with Wedgwood entered into in 1784, Webber gave only part of his time to the factory's affairs, since he was paid only twelve guineas a month. He appears to have been on very friendly terms with Josiah's eldest son, whom he appointed his executor. A clay model by Webber, *Hercules Holding Cerberus,* is preserved in the Soane Museum, Lincoln's Inn, London.

Much of Webber's work on vases and tableware must remain unrecognised, but the following are certainly recorded as his, or may be attributed to him with some confidence:

CAMEOS, MEDALLIONS AND TABLETS
Boy leaning on his quiver, with doves.
Cupid.*
Cupid drawing his dart.
The Graces erecting the statue of Cupid (probably *The raising of Priapus*), tablet 10¾ ins. by 9ins.
Hebe (bearing food to the Gods).
Hope addressing Peace, Labour and Plenty (Sydney Cove* medallion) design, 1789 (modelled by Hackwood*).
*The Marriage of Cupid and Psyche** (attributed).
Masque of Alexander.
Nereids,* tablet 21½ ins. by 6ins., c.1780.
Nymphs decorating the statue of Priapus.*
Sacrifice to Concordia, tablet 10ins. in diameter.
Sacrifice to Hymen, tablet 10ins. in diameter.
Triumph of Mars.
Portrait medallion of Mrs. Wedgwood (attributed) 1782.

FIGURES, VASES, ETC.
Apollo and Daphne as a beaupot (sic).
Britannia Triumphant.*
Diana) Seated figures holding two-branch candelabra,
*Minerva**) height 13¾ ins.
The Britannia and Minerva figures for all the above appear to have been adapted from the Britannia on Bacon's monument to Lord Chatham in Westminster Abbey.
*Prince of Wales** Vase.*

Webber's elder brother, John, an accomplished artist, accompanied Captain Cook on his third voyage in 1776-79.

Wedg Wood, John (1813-1857)

The son of John Wood of Brownhills and Mary Baddeley, the daughter of the potter John Baddeley of Shelton and niece to John Wedgwood of Bignal End. The great-grandson of John Wedgwood (1705-80), John Wedg Wood lived for some years in the Big House, Burslem and owned the Woodlands Pottery, Tunstall. It seems certain that he is responsible for the wares impressed 'WEDG WOOD' which are often mistaken for the products of the Etruria* factory. Careful examination is required to notice the gap between the first four letters of the mark and the last four, and it is difficult to escape the conclusion that the use of this mark was a deliberate attempt to deceive. The production of the Woodlands Pottery seems to have been confined to creamware, and some landscape decoration in pink lustre*, in the manner usually described as 'Sunderland', has been attributed to Wedg Wood. It is also possible that he was responsible for the yellow glazed* ware which bears the impressed mark.

Wedgwood & Co.

There were two manufacturers bearing this name. For the Burslem company, see: Ralph Wedgwood. An earthenware factory was established about 1840 with this name by Enoch Wedgwood (1813-79) and Jabez Charles Wedgwood. The style was E. Wedgwood & Co., and it became a limited company in 1900.

Webber, Henry. *Pair of blue and white jasper bough pots, 8¼ ins. long, with sarcophagus-shaped containers and solid white jasper reclining figures which are usually identified as Cupid and Psyche. Webber is recorded as having modelled figures of Apollo and Daphne as bough pots, c.1785, and these two figures are clearly also from his hand. c.1790. Sotheby's.*

Webber, Henry. *Britannia, her feet on the prostrate figure of France, who is about to provide nourishment for the British lion. Britannia holds an oval portrait of George III. Probably Webber's most important work for Wedgwood, c.1802. The figure, designed to celebrate British naval victories in the war with France, was adapted by Webber from his earlier Minerva, which he had, in turn, adapted from the figure of Britannia on the tomb of the Earl of Chatham in Westminster Abbey. 13ins. Wedgwood. (See Frontispiece.)*

Wedgwood, Abner (d.1835)

Son of Thomas Wedgwood*, Josiah I's partner in the production of useful* wares, and elder brother of John Taylor Wedgwood*. He was appointed by John Wedgwood* to be manager of the blue-printing department at Etruria* in 1805, and continued to direct it for thirty years.

Wedgwood, Cecil, DSO (1863-1916)

Only son of Godfrey Wedgwood*; educated at Clifton College; partner at Etruria* from 1884, at first with his uncle, Lawrence*, and later with his cousin, Francis Hamilton Wedgwood*. After the incorporation of the firm as Josiah Wedgwood & Sons Ltd. in 1895, it was controlled by representatives of three branches of the fifth generation: Cecil, Francis Hamilton (Frank), and Kennard Wedgwood*. The newly-formed company suffered severe reverses. The Spanish-American War had a depressing effect on American sales, and the Boer War took both Cecil and Frank away from their business. Cecil was awarded the DSO in 1902. After their return strenuous attempts were made to reinvigorate the company, and business improved. John Goodwin* became principal designer, the work of Alfred and Louise Powell*, who founded a school of freehand painting at Etruria, helped to update Wedgwood design, and powder-blue, first of the important powder colours*, was perfected in 1912. Daisy Makeig-Jones* joined the firm in 1909, but Cecil Wedgwood did not live to see the extraordinary effect that her employment was to have on the company's fortunes. Having rejoined his regiment at the outbreak of the First World War, he was killed leading his battalion in July, 1916.

Wedgwood, Cecily Stella 'Star' (b.1904)

The daughter of Francis Hamilton ('Major Frank') Wedgwood*, and sister to Clement Tom Wedgwood*, 'Star' designed two bone china* patterns: *Coronation* and *Lady Jane Grey.* The former, three white plumes outlined in platinum against a ground of ruby-red, was made in 1937 to celebrate the coronation of George VI and Queen Elizabeth.

'Star' Wedgwood married Frederick Maitland Wright, MBE in 1937. Eight years later he joined the Wedgwood board of directors as company secretary, becoming Joint Managing Director, with Norman Wilson*, in 1961. He retired in 1963.

Wedgwood, Dame Cicely Veronica (b.1910)
OM, DBE, FR. Hist. Soc., FBA

Celebrated historian; daughter of Sir Ralph Wedgwood, 1st Baronet, fourth son of Clement Francis Wedgwood*; educated privately and at Lady Margaret Hall, Oxford; sister to Sir John Hamilton Wedgwood*. Dame Veronica is the author of many distinguished works of history and biography. She has been a member of the Royal Commission on Historical Manuscripts since 1953 and was a Trustee of the National Gallery from 1962-68 and from 1969-76. Awarded numerous honorary degrees by both British and American universities, including Oxford and Harvard, she was made CBE in 1956, DBE in 1968, and a member of the Order of Merit in 1969. Her publications include: *Strafford* (1935); *The Thirty Years' War* (1938); *William the Silent* (1944); *The King's Peace* (1955); *The King's War* (1958); *Truth and Opinion* (1960); *The Trial of Charles I* (1964); and *The Political Career of Rubens* (1975). Dame Veronica's biography of her uncle, Josiah Clement, Lord Wedgwood of Barlaston*, *The Last of the Radicals,* was published in 1951.

Wedgwood, Clement Francis (1840-1889)

Second son of Francis (Frank) Wedgwood*; educated privately, and at Mannheim and Paris; partner at Etruria*

Wedgwood Collectors' Society. *The Josiah Wedgwood tea-poy, a modern creamware piece made in a special edition for the Wedgwood Collectors' Society of America. The decoration is adapted from the Sadler & Green print of* The Tea Party *and portrays Josiah I and his wife, Sally, taking tea in the garden of Etruria Hall. Pastoral scene on the reverse.* Wedgwood.

from 1863, at first with his father and later with his brothers, Godfrey* and Lawrence*. During the period of his partnership, cut short by his premature death at the age of forty-nine, the manufacture of bone china* and tiles* was reintroduced, and Victoria* ware, Worcester-style* wares, commemorative* ware, and white jasper* with multicoloured relief ornament were added to the factory's range of production.

Wedgwood, Clement Tom (1907-1960)

Son of Francis Hamilton ('Major Frank') Wedgwood; joined the firm in 1930, becoming director in charge of plant and building until his retirement to Rhodesia in 1950. During the period of the move from Etruria*, and the building of the new factory at Barlaston*, Tom bore the heaviest burden of planning and reorganisation, working closely with Norman Wilson*. In the war years he accepted the additional responsibility for production, and he is remembered with affection for his charm, energy, and inventiveness. He was never one to stand on his dignity as a director, and was often to be found, his overalls caked with clay, wrestling with recalcitrant machinery in the factory. His son, Dr. Alan Wedgwood, joined the firm as a non-executive director in 1966.

Wedgwood Collectors' Society

A Society, administered from the New York offices of Josiah Wedgwood & Sons Inc., whose members have exclusive rights to purchase special editions of Wedgwood pieces made in limited quantities for them. Some of the items are reproductions of earlier work, or colour variations on well-established jasper* pieces, but many have been specially designed. The first special edition, issued in 1969, was a Zodiac plate, 9ins. in diameter, in pale blue and white jasper. Since that date, many distinguished and unusual designs have been created for jasper, black basaltes*, Queen's ware and bone china* in editions as small as 250, and some of these have already become rarities.

Wedgwood, Doris Audrey (1894-1969)

Doris Audrey Wedgwood, second daughter of Cecil Wedgwood*. In his absence at the war, and after his death in action in 1916, she represented their branch of the family on the Board of Directors, becoming Company Secretary in 1918. In 1928 she married Geoffrey, youngest brother of her close friend, Daisy Makeig-Jones*. She retired in the same year. Her portrait medallion*, modelled to commemorate her marriage, was modelled in 1928 and produced in blue and white jasper* for limited distribution to friends and relations.

Wedgwood, Doris Audrey. *Portrait medallion produced on the occasion of her marriage to Geoffrey Makeig-Jones in 1928. It bears the inscription 'DAW 31.7.28 DAM-J' below the relief portrait.* Zeitlin Collection.

Wedgwood, Frances Julia (1833-1913)

Julia 'Snow' Wedgwood was the first child of Hensleigh (fourth son of Josiah II) and Frances, daughter of Sir James Mackintosh. For much of her life she suffered from a deafness which made general conversation difficult, and this influenced her to become a writer, initially under the *nom-de-plume* of

Florence Dawson. At first a novelist, she later turned to more serious work, and in 1883 she published *The Moral Ideal,* the product of twenty years' study of world ethical history. She began to write her biography of her great-grandfather when in her seventies. It was unfinished at her death, but before she died she asked Professor Charles Harold Herford to complete it. The book was published in 1915 with an Appendix by J.W. Mellor D.Sc. on Wedgwood as an industrial chemist. Her younger sister, Katherine, Lady Farrer, edited the *Letters of Josiah Wedgwood,* published in 1903.

Wedgwood, Francis (1800-1888)

Master Potter of Etruria*; third son of Josiah II* and Elizabeth 'Bessy' Allen. He was educated at Rugby School and Cambridge, and joined his eldest brother, Josiah, as a partner in the family firm in 1827. After the withdrawal of Josiah II and Josiah III*, Frank Wedgwood was in sole charge of the Etruria works, but in 1843 he entered into a partnership with John Boyle* which lasted for two years, and from 1846 to 1859 he was in partnership with Robert Brown. In the latter year he was joined in partnership by his eldest son, Godfrey*, and later by his younger sons, Clement Francis* (1863) and Lawrence* (1868). He was a firm Unitarian, and somewhat ascetic in his way of life, but he had a natural geniality which was in sharp contrast to the austere silences of his father and eldest brother, and established an enviable reputation for fair dealing with his customers and employees. He retired in 1876.

Frank Wedgwood presided over some important changes and developments at Etruria, including the introduction of Lavender (see: Coloured Bodies), Carrara*, inlaid* ware, and majolica*, and it was during this period that Emile Lessore* created a new style in Wedgwood decoration that gained much prestige for the firm at international exhibitions. Frank's will, dated 9th May, 1874, in which he left the Stubbs* painting of the Wedgwood family to his son Godfrey, contained the remarkable bequest to his youngest daughter of "his ass and the ivory screen which belonged to Lady Mackintosh."

Wedgwood, Francis Hamilton (1867-1930)

Eldest son of Clement Francis Wedgwood*; educated at Clifton College, at Mannheim, and at Trinity College, Cambridge; partner at Etruria* from 1889, following the early death of his father. After the incorporation of the firm as Josiah Wedgwood & Sons, Ltd. in 1895, Cecil*, Frank, and Lawrence*, all first cousins, represented the fifth generation of the family. The adverse effects of the Spanish-American War, which depressed American sales, and the Boer War, in which Frank served as Captain in the North Staffordshire Regiment, brought the company's fortunes to a low ebb. In 1906 Kennard went to America, where he subsequently founded the subsidiary company in New York. At Etruria Cecil and Frank undertook the difficult task of reviving business. Their efforts were interrupted by the outbreak of the First World War, in which Cecil was killed. Frank, who had rejoined his regiment, was luckily stationed at Lichfield Barracks organising recruitment, and from there he was able to maintain almost daily contact with the factory. In Cecil's absence, and after his death, his daughter, Doris Audrey Wedgwood* represented their branch of the family on the board of directors. After the Armistice 'Major Frank' became Chairman and Managing Director.

With his cousin, Cecil, Frank had presided over something of a transformation in the company's designs. John Goodwin* had become art director, the Powells* had introduced new styles, and Daisy Makeig-Jones* had created Fairyland Lustre*. The shortage of high-grade coal following the war adversely affected the quality of the factory's production, and, in 1928, Norman Wilson* installed the first gas-fired glost tunnel oven. This was the first of many technical improvements which were to put Wedgwood on the road to expansion, but it was left to Frank's successors — the new generation represented by Josiah*, Hensleigh*, Tom* and John* — to take the essential step of moving from Etruria. Frank died suddenly in October 1930, just five months after the celebration of the bicentenary of the firm's founder.

Wedgwood, Godfrey (1833-1905)

Eldest son of Francis (Frank) Wedgwood*; partner at Etruria* from 1859 to 1891, at first with his father, and later with his younger brothers, Clement Francis* and Lawrence*. With his brothers he was responsible for the reintroduction of bone china* in 1878, and the manufacture of tiles* in 1875, and also for the introduction of Victoria* ware, Worcester-style* wares, commemorative* ware, and white jasper* with multi-coloured relief ornament.

Wedgwood Group

Formed in 1966, the Wedgwood Group comprised, in 1979, the following companies (shown with their dates of acquisition):

Josiah Wedgwood & Sons Ltd.
William Adams*, 1966.
Royal Tuscan, 1966.
Susie Cooper*, 1966.
Coalport, 1967.
Johnson Brothers, 1968.

King's Lynn Glass (now Wedgwood Glass), 1969.
Merseyside Jewellers, 1969.
J. & G. Meakin, 1970.
Midwinter, 1970.
Crown Staffordshire, 1973.
Mason's Ironstone, 1973.
Precision Studios, 1973.
Galway Crystal, 1974.

Wedgwood, Hensleigh (b.1908)

Great-grandson of Hensleigh, youngest brother of Josiah II*; in America from 1931; later President of Josiah Wedgwood & Sons Inc. of America, retiring in 1960; co-author with John Meredith Graham II of *Wedgwood — A Living Tradition*, a short illustrated history of Wedgwood wares to accompany an important exhibition held in the Brooklyn Museum in 1948. Hensleigh Wedgwood joined the firm at Etruria in 1927 to learn the art and occupation of the potter, starting with the bulk handling of clay and gaining practical experience of the work of each department, finishing as a salesman. He was responsible for reviving the manufacture of crimson jasper*, abandoned after the earlier attempt in 1905 because the crimson 'bled' into the white reliefs. Despite fresh efforts to overcome this difficulty 'bleeding' remained troublesome, and manufacture again had to be discontinued.

Wedgwood in the Nineteenth Century

This entry provides an outline of production during the period with references to key entries elsewhere in the *Dictionary*.

After Josiah I's death in 1795 Tom Byerley*, who held a

Wedgwood in the Nineteenth Century. *Two typical teapot shapes of the first quarter of the 19th century. Background: a bone china teapot painted by John Cutts. Foreground: a parapet teapot decorated with a Japan pattern.* Wedgwood.

Wedgwood in the Nineteenth Century. *A decoration in brown of agricultural implements, c.1820, which is exceptionally simple and effective for its period, when excessive decoration was popular.* Wedgwood.

quarter interest, continued in partnership with Josiah II*, the style of the firm being Wedgwood & Byerley. Josiah I's eldest son, John*, had withdrawn from the firm in 1793, and neither he, nor his younger brother, Josiah II, showed much inclination to give up their lives as country gentlemen to return to the Potteries. The French Revolution and the Napoleonic wars had seriously damaged Continental trade, relations with the United States of America were deteriorating (prior to the War of 1812), and the general prospect was worse than at any time since the firm had been established. Josiah II thought it not worth continuing. Most of the large European factories were in an equally precarious condition, and for some years Meissen* was on the verge of closing down.

Under Byerley's direction the factory declined, discipline becoming slack, and the standard of production falling. John returned to the firm in 1800, and from 1804-12 took a leading part in restoring its fortunes. He was rejoined in active partnership by Josiah in 1806. Together they effected

considerable improvements, introducing lustre* in 1806, and bone china* in 1812. Queen's* ware, jasper* and basaltes* continued to be made, but new bodies were also introduced, the most significant being the Celadon coloured body* in 1805. During the same period the drab* body was being made, and a white porous biscuit, occasionally employed during the lifetime of Josiah I, was produced. This was usually given a smear* glaze, and vessels had to be glazed inside. It was used mainly for flower holders, bulb pots, and jugs, sometimes engine-turned* but more often ornamented with sprigged* decoration in blue, green, lilac or chocolate in the style of jasper. Basaltes and *rosso antico**, decorated with enamelled patterns in the *famille rose** style, were introduced c.1810 for teaware, coffee-ware, bulb pots, inkstands, and pot pourri jars of Chinese form.

Styles were changing elsewhere, but Wedgwood made fewer concessions to current fashion than most factories, and the designs and moulds of the 18th century by Flaxman*,

Webber* and others were still in use. Hackwood*, who had joined the firm in 1769, was to work on until 1832, dying four years later, but little can be safely attributed to him after Josiah's death. He re-draped the *Dancing Hours** in 1808.

At this time the fashionable style was Regency, the English version of French Empire. Wedgwood's vases became larger, more opulent, and often based on the silver shapes made popular by such silversmiths as Paul Storr. Oriental patterns began once more to be fashionable after several decades in which they had been employed for cheaper wares, no doubt under the influence of the Prince Regent, whose pleasure palace at Brighton clearly re-echoed Marco Polo's description of Kublai Khan's at Shang-tu, and Wedgwood produced a number of patterns of this kind. This period, too, saw the revival of interest in Egyptian patterns and decoration, and Wedgwood were not slow to introduce ornament of this type, with some added 'hieroglyphs', in jasper, basaltes, *rosso antico* and cane*.

In 1805 Wedgwood followed the lead given by Minton* and others and produced the first of a large number of underglaze blue printed* earthenware patterns, principally for export to America. The quality of these wares was excellent, but they were never manufactured by Wedgwood in the quantities made by their competitors.

Pastry* ware and game-pie dishes* of cane ware had been made from about 1796, but were in greatest demand during the flour shortages of the next two decades, when even the royal palaces used rice flour as a substitute.

Josiah III* became a partner in 1823, and was joined by his younger brother, Francis, four years later. In 1828 a severe trade depression caused the firm to give up their London show-rooms* and to sell off the stock and moulds. It is not known which moulds were sold, or who bought them, but no doubt this is the explanation of the fate of some of those now missing, and accounts also for the appearance of recognisable Wedgwood reliefs on the 19th century wares of other manufacturers. Stone china* was introduced in 1820 and made until 1861.

In 1842 Josiah III retired, and his father died in the following year. The firm was carried on by Francis, who entered into various partnerships with John Boyle* (1843-45), Robert Brown (1846-59), and his own sons, Godfrey*, Clement Francis* and Lawrence*. In November 1870 Francis retired, leaving his three sons to direct the business until 1891, when a new agreement was drawn up between Lawrence, Cecil* (Godfrey's son) and Francis Hamilton* (son of Clement Francis). Four years later the firm was incorporated as a limited company (see: Proprietors of Wedgwood).

The forty years following the retirement of Josiah III were a period of considerable technical advancement, coinciding with

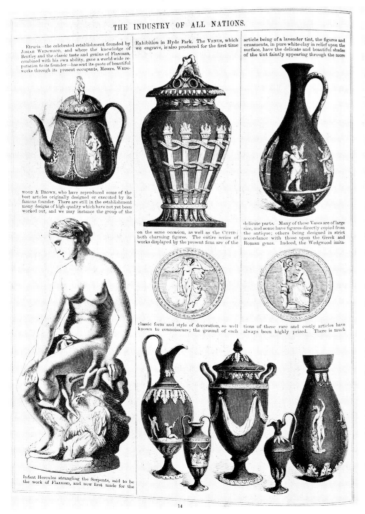

Wedgwood in the Nineteenth Century. *Wedgwood & Brown exhibits in the Great Exhibition, 1851. From* Art-Journal Illustrated Catalogue. Photo: Wedgwood.

Wedgwood in the Nineteenth Century. *Bright blue jasper vases, one decorated with flowers, butterflies, berries and a spray of mountain ash, c.1858, and the other with flowers in an unusual technique suggesting the inspiration of Sèvres pâte d'application.* Sotheby's Belgravia.

Wedgwood in the Nineteenth Century. *Two pages from the* Art-Journal Catalogue *of the 1862 Exhibition, including Wedgwood exhibits of vases by Lessore.* Photo: Wedgwood.

the use of the lozenge-shaped registry mark* (1842-83). Parian* porcelain (Carrara*) was produced from 1848, principally for portrait busts, and the Lavender coloured body was introduced in 1850.

In 1851 Wedgwood exhibited with some success in the Great Exhibition, where their jasper vases in particular were much admired. The fidelity of these wares to the neo-classical style in an exhibition in which medievalism and revived rococo* was so strong a feature caused much comment, not all of it favourable. The Portland* vase was again on view, and the

object of some interest since the original had been smashed by a drunken Irishman in 1845. Apart from jasper, the solid variety of which had been reintroduced in 1854, Wedgwood's exhibits included Queen's ware, much of it in 18th century shapes, green glazed* wares, then at the beginning of their revival in popularity, black basaltes, and the so-called Rockingham* brown glazed ware.

Green-glazed wares became very popular in the decade or so which followed. Leaf dishes and comports were specially in demand, and the fashion for Oriental motifs inspired such relief decoration as prunus blossom and bamboo leaves. The same moulded motifs appeared beneath glazes of pink or blue. The fashion for Japanese wood-block prints may be seen in a pattern produced in 1872, transfer printed* and painted on Queen's ware, which has a central representation of one of these prints surrounded by *vignettes* from the same source. The *Sparrow and Bamboo* pattern of 1879 is moulded in relief and transfer printed. A vase of square section, decorated with the Eight Trigrams (a series of broken and unbroken lines used in divination) copies an ancient jade astronomical instrument known as a *tsung,* no doubt in imitation of an 18th or 19th century Chinese porcelain vase of similar form. The subject is an unusual one for a European potter and it seems likely that the original was seen by one of Wedgwood's designers at an international exhibition.

Emile Lessore* began his career at Wedgwood in 1858. His 'natural' style, which became extremely popular, was then quite new in the field of ceramic painting. He was one of a number of important artists, including Protât* and Allen*, who joined Wedgwood from Minton.

The first majolica* was marketed in 1860. This continued to be made for fifty years and was used for such large and showy pieces as wall-brackets, plaques, umbrella stands and garden seats, as well as for comports, plates and dishes. Portrait busts,

Wedgwood in the Nineteenth Century.
Black basaltes krater, ornamented with embossed figures of putti and a pattern of intertwining vine leaves and grapes. A metalwork shape perhaps derived from an ancient or Renaissance bronze. 11¾ ins. high. c.1865. Sotheby's Belgravia.

Wedgwood in the Nineteenth Century.
Group of decorative Queen's ware painted by Emile Lessore, c.1868. Wedgwood.

Above: Open vase shape 2413 decorated with Fairyland lustre pattern Dragon King *designed by Daisy Makeig-Jones. Height 23¾ ins.* Photo: Una des Fontaines.

Pair of Fairyland lustre vases, 2409 shape, decorated with Pillar *pattern (known at the factory as 'Fire Escape'), with a vase 2046 in Flame Fairyland. Heights 14ins. and 11ins.* Sotheby's Belgravia.

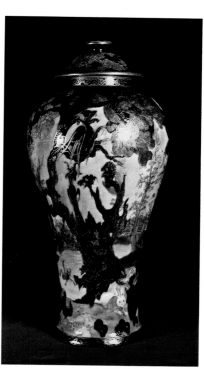

Left: Covered vase shape 2046, height 16ins., decorated with Fairyland lustre pattern Demon Tree *(part of* Ghostly Wood*) designed by Daisy Makeig-Jones.* Zeitlin Collection.

Right: Fairyland lustre plaque, Torches, *height 10ins., designed by Daisy Makeig-Jones.* D. Newbon. Photo: Una des Fontaines.

popular as Victorian library furniture, were reproduced in black basaltes from the earlier moulds, and new subjects were modelled by the sculptor E.W. Wyon* and others. *Email ombrant** was introduced about 1860 under licence from Rubelles, who held the patent.

Interest in lithography dates from the 1860s, and photo-lithography* was first used for decoration in the 1870s. Wedgwood exhibited at the London International Exhibition of 1862, in the Paris Exposition Universelle of 1867, the Vienna Exhibition of 1872, and other major exhibitions of the period. This was a period when exhibition successes played a considerable part in a company's international trade, and large and imposing pieces were specially made and decorated with the intention of outshining the work of rivals. It was also another period of shameless imitation. In 1875 Victoria* ware was introduced to compete with the porcelain vases of other English manufacturers, and an ivory-ground Queen's ware was produced in the wake of Worcester's* popular ivory porcelain. Thomas Allen, later art director, came to Wedgwood in 1876, and bone china* was reintroduced two years later after an interval of more than fifty years. The two

Wedgwood in the Nineteenth Century. *The Elizabeth Thompson Vase. 18th century creamware shape, painted by an amateur artist, Elizabeth Thompson, c.1880, with a scene of nude children on the seashore and a large crab. Nude children were a popular subject in art of this period.* Wedgwood.

three colours was introduced ten years later. Some new shapes were modelled, but the greater part of production continued to be copied from those of the 18th and early 19th centuries.

There were, throughout the century, many revivals of 18th century styles and fashions, and among them was the decoration of furniture with jasper medallions (see: Furniture, Ornamental). The architect, Gottfried Semper*, designed a cabinet using jasper medallions to surround a porcelain painting after Mulready; Wright & Mansfield*, among the best of Victorian cabinet makers, used jasper to ornament a large cabinet in the style of Adam*; Halsey Ricardo* designed chimney pieces inset with jasper tablets for Lord Dysart (see: Dysart Green); and the Victoria and Albert Museum acquired, in 1867, a dreadful chimney piece made specially for the Paris Exhibition.

The registry mark was replaced in 1883 by registry numbers, and in 1891 three new marks were brought into use: ENGLAND; IMPORTE D'ANGLETERRE; and WEDGWOOD, ETRURIA, ENGLAND. The mark, MADE IN ENGLAND, was first used in 1898. The country of origin was added to the trademark to comply with the McKinley Tariff Act for exports to the United States.

From 1895 trading conditions again deteriorated as a result of the Spanish-American War and the Boer War, two of Wedgwood's directors being engaged in the latter.

For a brief survey of events after 1900, see: Wedgwood in the Twentieth Century.

Wedgwood in the Nineteenth Century. *Glazed Parian vase, height 12½ ins., dark green enamelled ground and lavish gilding and ornament. c.1875.* Wedgwood.

events were probably connected since Allen had been a leading porcelain painter at Minton. The Portland vase printed mark on bone china was introduced in 1878, and soon after this date lithophanes* were made in the form of lampshades*.

The manufacture of tiles* was reintroduced in 1870. They were made until 1902, when production was again discontinued as a measure of economy during a period of trade recession. They were transfer printed in sets, sometimes with additional enamel colouring.

About 1880 basaltes vases and urns were made with gilded and bronze reliefs, and a new bronze body, also with gilt ornament, was introduced (see: Bronze and Gold). During the 18th century Josiah I had frequently issued transfer-printed Queen's ware and jasper cameos and medallions to commemorate people and events (e.g. Bastille* medallion and Slave Emancipation Society Seal*). In 1880 Wedgwood began to make commemorative ware in earnest. The greater part of this, which comprised plates, dishes and jugs, usually of printed Queen's ware, was designed specifically for the important American market. The first Calendar tile* was produced for Jones, McDuffee & Stratton Co.* in 1881, and during the following seventy years more than one thousand printed historical views were made for them as sole importers.

Turquoise jasper dip was made for about ten years from 1875, and white jasper with relief ornament in as many as

371

Wedgwood in the Twentieth Century. *Plate decorated with hand-painted fish and powder-green rim and gold edge. Diameter 9¼ ins. Pattern No. W1473. c.1910.* Sotheby's Belgravia.

Wedgwood in the Twentieth Century

This entry provides an outline of the firm's development from 1900-80, with reference to key entries elsewhere in this *Dictionary*.

The turn of the century found the Company, incorporated in 1895, once more in difficulties. The Spanish-American War had depressed business in America, and the Boer War had taken Cecil* (who won the DSO in 1902) and Frank* from Etruria*, leaving Kennard* in sole charge of the factory. In 1906 Kennard went to America, where he later formed the subsidiary company in New York (1919). Cecil and Frank set about the task of reviving the firm's fortunes. In this they were greatly assisted by the employment of John Goodwin* as Art Director, and the prestigious order from America for the White House Service*. Alfred and Louise Powell* created new styles of design, the best-selling Edme* shape was introduced, and a real technical advance was achieved when Powder Blue* was perfected in 1912. With the introduction of Ordinary Lustres* in 1914 and Fairyland Lustre* in November 1915, Wedgwood took the lead in the production of ornamental bone china*, and this lead was maintained in spite of the First World War in which Cecil was killed.

From about September 1915, orders had outstripped production, and absolute priority had been given to fulfilling orders from America. In 1920 sales reached the all-time record of £170,000 compared with £67,000 (itself a record figure at the time) for 1913; but much of the improvement was accounted for by inflation and the increase in volume sales was small. Orders, however, were running at double the figures for sales and the directors agreed upon a major programme of expansion to be carried out over a period of several years. This was subsequently modified to a programme costing £52,350, of which nearly £36,000 was to be laid out in 1921 and 1922. By the end of 1920, the company's deficit, which had amounted to

£25,000 in 1903, had been converted to a surplus of £14,000.

Little of significance was introduced between 1920 and 1927, though some interesting and inventive work was done by Harry Barnard*, unsuccessful attempts were made to produce crimson jasper* in quantity, and a particularly ugly new jasper colour, dark olive green, made a mercifully brief appearance. In 1927 Norman Wilson* and Hensleigh Wedgwood* joined the Company, and they were soon followed by three more members of the sixth generation — Josiah V* (1928), Clement Tom* (1930) and John Hamilton* (1931) — Frank having died suddenly in 1930.

The arrival of a younger generation (the eldest, Josiah, was thirty-one when he succeeded Frank Wedgwood as Managing Director, and all the rest under twenty-five) coincided with the beginning of the worst slump in the history of the pottery industry, following the Wall Street crash of 1929. During the next decade, while many other firms closed their factories, Wedgwood was saved by the resolute action of the young directors and the inventiveness of Norman Wilson. Stringent economies were made, new outside designers were commissioned, new glazes invented, and modern methods of production introduced. The designs of Victor Skellern*, as resident Art Director, and of outside artists John Skeaping*, Keith Murray*, Arnold Machin*, and Eric Ravilious*, in particular, created for Wedgwood a public image that was at once relevant to contemporary taste and, in quality of design and production, in accord with the firm's history and reputation. This was, indeed, evidence of the 'living tradition' that was later the declared policy of Wedgwood.

By 1935 the progressive subsidence of the Etruria buildings was causing serious concern. The company was once more making modest profits, and at an important exhibition at the Grafton Galleries, London, in 1936 the new Alpine Pink* bone china, and the work of John Skeaping, Keith Murray and Norman Wilson, created much favourable attention. The

Wedgwood in the Twentieth Century. *Allegorical circular plaque in blue and white jasper representing* Sun and Night, *by Anna Zinkeisen, 1924.* Wedgwood.

success of this exhibition was instrumental in persuading the directors that the factory must be moved to a new site where the most modern methods of production might be employed economically. In 1937 they bought an estate of 382 acres near Barlaston village, where the family of Francis Wedgwood* had lived for several generations. Keith Murray and his partner, Charles S. White, were appointed architects for the factory. The planning of a model village of one hundred houses for employees was to be the task of Louis de Soissons, the architect of Welwyn Garden City. Keith Murray and Norman Wilson had travelled in America and on the Continent inspecting factories abroad, and their ideas were translated into formal plans with the active participation of Tom Wedgwood. The foundation stone was laid on 10th September, 1938, and the earthenware factory for six hundred employees, with the first electric tunnel kiln in Britain, was completed shortly before the outbreak of the Second World War. The china factory was still at Etruria.

John and Hensleigh Wedgwood, and Norman Wilson joined the armed services for the duration of the war. Josiah and Tom were left to struggle with the teething troubles of the new factory, the perennial problems of the old one, and shortages of materials and manpower. Wedgwood's dollar-earning capacity was recognised as a national asset. More than eighty per cent of the factory's output during the war years was exported. The rest, confined to the purely functional and undecorated 'utility' earthenware permitted by the Government, was distributed at controlled prices in the home market. Jasper production was stopped.

So highly was Wedgwood's export performance regarded that building was permitted immediately after the war. The earthenware factory was extended and the new china factory completed by 1949. With the return of those who had served in the forces, labour shortages could be made up, and production increased to deal with the arrears of export orders. The manufacture of jasper was resumed with a new jasper body developed by Norman Wilson, new workshops were built, and figure makers and ornamenters trained. In 1950, having seen the factory he had helped to plan safely through the war years and in full production, Tom Wedgwood retired, for reasons of health, to Rhodesia, where he died ten years later.

Modern methods of production and new trends in design required the production of fresh shapes and patterns. Lithography was introduced for the decoration of Queen's ware and bone china, and Victor Skellern's designs were augmented by those of Peter Wall* (from 1951) and Robert Minkin* (from 1955) and of outside artists, notably Richard Guyatt*, Edward Bawden*, and Lawrence Whistler*. It was also necessary to recruit an efficient sales force, and among those who joined the company after war service was Arthur Bryan*. The London Showrooms* had been closed since 1940, but the lease of premises at 34 Wigmore Street had been acquired during the war, and showrooms and offices were opened there in 1948. In 1953 the first of the Wedgwood Rooms* was opened in London.

In 1947 Kennard Lawrence Wedgwood*, Chairman of the company, retired. He was succeeded by Josiah V, and the Presidency of the New York company was taken over by Hensleigh Wedgwood. In 1955 Ian Taylor was appointed Director of the newly-formed Australian company, and five years later, Arthur Bryan, who had been General Sales Manager in England, succeeded Hensleigh as President in New York. On the retirement of Norman Wilson and Maitland Wright in 1963, Arthur Bryan returned to England as Managing Director, being succeeded in New York by Ray

Smyth. Four years later Bryan succeeded Josiah V as Chairman. Earlier in the year the company's shares were introduced for the first time to the London Stock Exchange.

Since 1966 the company has been engaged in almost continuous planned expansion. During the first three months of that year the Wedgwood Group* was formed with the acquisition of the businesses of William Adams*, Royal Tuscan, and Susie Cooper*. Further acquisitions and diversification have more than doubled the Group's size in fourteen years, and in 1979 Wedgwood expanded in America by purchasing for $13 million the assets of the Franciscan dinnerware and architectural tile manufactory in Glendale, California. Plans had already been made to complete, by the end of 1980, a £9.5 million development programme to increase production capacity in England by more than twenty-five per cent and the number of employees to more than 10,000.

Throughout this latter period of expansion, planned by Sir Arthur Bryan (knighted for services to export in 1976) and the Deputy Chairman, Peter Williams, Wedgwood maintained and strengthened its international reputation for quality and inventiveness, reaffirming the belief of the directors that a living tradition is one which is continuously reborn.

Wedgwood in the Twentieth Century. *Pair of lustres in the 18th century style with cut glass and brass fittings on yellow and black jasper drums. c.1931. Sotheby's Belgravia.*

Wedgwood, John (1721-1767)

Josiah Wedgwood's elder brother who, from 1751, had been in business in the partnership of Wedgwood & Bliss, general warehousemen, at 3 Cateaton Street (now Gresham Street), London, not far from the Guildhall and the present Bank of England. His family nicknamed him 'the Alderman', although he never occupied this office. Apparently he retired from business at the end of 1764, but remained in London until 1766 executing commissions for Josiah. In October 1766, he went to live in Liverpool, according to one of Josiah's letters, but June 1767, found him back in London, possibly on holiday, because he visited Ranelagh Gardens to watch the fireworks one evening, and then dined at the Swan Inn, Westminster. There he asked for a bed for the night, but finding the inn to be full, he set off, after midnight, to find other accommodation. Sometime after this he either slipped, or was pushed, from the bank of the Thames into the river and was drowned.

Wedgwood, John (1766-1844)

Eldest son of Josiah I; partner at Etruria*, 1790-93, and 1800-12; married, 1794, Louisa Jane ('Jenny') Allen, younger sister of his brother Josiah's wife, Bessie.

John had worked in the factory as early as 1781 but he never cared for the business. He was sent to Paris in 1786 to improve his French, and in the following year he went to Italy, spending a year in Rome "to try," as Josiah told his friend Edgeworth*, "what he can glean from thence for the improvement of the manufacture of modern Etruria." From Rome, John informed his sadly disappointed father that he did not wish to make a career in the Potteries. Nevertheless, he became, soon after his

Wedgwood, John *(1766-1844) from a miniature.* Wedgwood.

return, a partner in the firm. In 1794 Josiah bought him a share in a newly-formed banking house, Alexander Davison & Co. In 1816 the bank, which had absorbed most of his considerable fortune, failed. Messrs. Coutts took over the assets and debts, and John was saved by a subscription of £12,000 raised by his brother Josiah, his sisters Kitty and Sarah, and Robert Darwin*.

In 1800 John rejoined the firm as a partner, and spent much of his time travelling between Westbury-on-Trym, near Bristol, where he lived, his office in London, and Etruria. In 1804 he moved to Seabridge, near Newcastle-under-Lyme, to be nearer to the factory, which he had come to understand required more active direction than Byerley* could give to it. His letters to his brother, Jos, in Dorset reveal a sorry state of affairs at Etruria. In February 1804, he wrote: ''There are many things that may be done... The whole system of the slip kilns and clay beating is gone to ruin... When I was at the works this last week I found the clay was in miserable order... The whole system of the ovens also requires a fresh arrangement.'' Next month he was reporting sixty dozen plates spoiled from one oven and forty dozen from another, ''and the men seemed inclined to consider that as a very fair sample of firing.'' He set about restoring discipline and standards of production. In this formidable task he was joined by Jos in 1806, and it is clear that their joint efforts saved the firm from final failure. It is also clear that John played the leading part in the firm's restoration, and it was he who was responsible for the introduction of the *Water Lily** and *Botanical Flowers** patterns, the most original of Wedgwood's underglaze blue prints*. Byerley wrote to Josiah II, ''Your brother is extremely active and intelligent, and is fast paving the way for a radical reform, and will greatly benefit the concern.''

In 1801, John, who was specially interested in botany and horticulture, suggested to William Forsyth, the King's gardener at St. James's and Kensington, the founding of the Horticultural Society, of which he became the first Treasurer three years later. He withdrew from his Wedgwood partnership in 1812, but continued to live in Staffordshire until 1825. None of his four sons was associated with the firm.

Wedgwood, Sir John Hamilton, Bt. (b.1907)

Son of Sir Ralph L. Wedgwood, CB, CMG, 1st Baronet, fourth son of Clement Francis Wedgwood*; succeeded to the baronetcy on the death of his father in 1956; educated at Winchester College and Trinity College, Cambridge; married Diana Mildred, daughter of Colonel Oliver Hawkshaw, and great-granddaughter of Francis Wedgwood*.

John Wedgwood joined the firm at Etruria* in 1931 and was therefore one of the 'new generation' of directors involved in the courageous decision to leave Etruria and move to a new Factory at Barlaston. He served as major in the army during the Second World War, and returned to the firm to become Sales Director. From 1955 until his retirement in 1966 he was Deputy Chairman of the Company with special responsibility for Public Relations.

Wedgwood, John Taylor (1783-1856)

Youngest son of Thomas Wedgwood*, Josiah I's partner in the production of useful* wares, and brother to Abner Wedgwood*, who managed the blue-printing department at Etruria*. He was well known for his portrait engravings, and was appointed official engraver to the Royal College of Surgeons and to the British Museum. He was responsible for the engravings of Plates 19 and 20 for the 1817 Catalogue*, and also for the engraving of the portrait of Josiah Wedgwood after the painting by Sir Joshua Reynolds*.

Wedgwood, Josiah I, FRS (1730-1795)

Josiah Wedgwood I was the last child of a family of twelve. He belonged to the fourth generation of a family of potters, whose traditional occupation has continued through another five generations. No other instance of a family business surviving in this way has been recorded.

From the age of six Josiah walked seven miles a day to school in Newcastle-under-Lyme. When he was nine years old (and, according to his master, "a fair arithmetician and master of a capital hand") his father died, and Josiah left school to work for his eldest brother, Thomas*, who had inherited the Churchyard Works*. Five years later, in 1744, he was apprenticed to Thomas to learn "the Art, Mistery, Occupation or Imployment of Throwing and Handleing." During this apprenticeship he suffered an attack of smallpox which permanently disabled his right leg, leading eventually, in 1768, to amputation. Since the potter's wheel was often turned by kicking his illness made it difficult for him to continue his work as a thrower.

Josiah's apprenticeship ended in 1749, but he seems to have continued to work for his brother, Thomas, until 1752, when he formed a partnership with Harrison & Alders* of Cliff Bank, Stoke. This venture lasted for only two years, and in 1754 he entered into a new partnership with Thomas Whieldon* of Fenton Hall, whose pottery had been established since 1740. It is evident, from the terms of the second agreement, that Josiah had already achieved a considerable reputation, for it was agreed that, while any discovery he might make was to be used for the benefit of both partners, Wedgwood should not be obliged to disclose his own secret formulae.

Wedgwood experimented to improve most of the wares then current in Staffordshire, especially agate* ware. His fine green and yellow glazes are sometimes said to have been used late in his partnership with Whieldon for rococo* wares in the form of the cauliflower* and the pineapple*, but from a note in the *Experiment Book* these glazes were not developed until the 23rd March, 1759, and Wedgwood left Whieldon to become an independent potter on the 1st May in the same year. It is also noteworthy that no shards of green glazed ware have been found on the Whieldon 'waster' tips. Wedgwood remained on very good terms with Whieldon, and the only reason for the dissolution appears to have been that Whieldon was not sufficiently enterprising at a time when the public was evincing dissatisfaction with most of the standard wares of the region. Wedgwood wrote in his *Experiment Book:* "I saw the field was spacious and the soil so good as to promise ample recompense to anyone who should labour in its cultivation." This appears to confirm the reason for his break with Whieldon.

Josiah rented the Ivy House* and Potworks from his uncles, Thomas* and John* of the Big House, Burslem, for £10 a year — a considerable sum at the time. His cousin, Thomas*, agreed to serve him as a journeyman (i.e. a skilled artisan working for wages) for six years from the 1st May, 1759. By 1765 Thomas was Josiah's principal assistant, and in 1766 he was taken into partnership with a one-eighth share of the profits. The partnership was limited to the manufacture of useful* wares, and it lasted until Thomas's death in 1788.

One of Josiah's greatest assets was his ability to turn his hand to almost anything, however skilled, from mixing clay to designing the wares. Therefore the organisation of factory operations came more easily to him than to most of the potters of his day. His crippled knee was in one sense an advantage, since he was unable to take an active part in the life of his contemporaries when young, and he turned to books instead.

Wedgwood, Josiah I. *From the portrait by George Stubbs.* Wedgwood.

He was largely self-taught; he could not have done more in his short years at the village school than learn the basic elements of reading, writing, and arithmetic. In his letters however, beginning in the 1760s, we find mention from time to time of books in his library, and most of these could not have been available in Staffordshire at the time, except, perhaps, in a few libraries in the great houses. These books included Du Halde's account of China, in which he describes the making of porcelain and the Chinese methods of quantity production.

Wedgwood speedily outgrew the Ivy House Works. In 1764 he transferred to the Brick House Works*, known locally as the Bell works from the method of summoning the workmen. At the Ivy House the early wares were no doubt similar to those being made at Fenton during the Wedgwood-Whieldon partnership, and Wedgwood's early production included salt-glazed stoneware. At this time he began to produce dessert plates of leaf-form moulded with the ribs in relief, or dishes in the form of overlapping leaves. The green and yellow glazes were used to cover wares moulded in cauliflower and pineapple form which William Greatbatch* modelled for Wedgwood. Wedgwood also introduced a much improved cream-coloured earthenware covered with a clear lead glaze, the body including both pipe clay and ground flint, which he referred to as "a species of earthenware for the table, quite new in appearance, covered with a rich and brilliant glaze, bearing sudden alterations in heat and cold, manufactured with ease and expedition, and consequently cheap, having every requisite for the purpose intended." At this time the delft ware industry was supplying most of the demand for cheap tableware, the largest potteries being located in London, Bristol, and Liverpool. Very little delft was ever made in Staffordshire. The new creamware was not only superior to delft in every way, except perhaps aesthetically, but it could be made more cheaply. Its glaze chipped less easily, and chips were not so unsightly as those to delft, the white opaque glaze of which covered a buff or reddish body. Creamware could be glazed in one operation; the finest delft required two, an additional transparent glaze being superimposed on the tin-enamel glaze. Creamware* was not so well adapted to painted decoration, but Wedgwood largely overcame this by having much of his decoration transfer printed by Sadler* & Green, and by confining his enamelled tableware patterns generally to simple border designs. Finally, creamware could easily be adapted to neo-classical* forms, which was difficult in the case of both delft and porcelain. Creamware, later to be named Queen's ware*, was the foundation of Wedgwood's success. It enabled him to establish a profitable export trade, and by the end of the 18th century the manufacture of delft had been virtually extinguished, not only in England, but also in Holland and Germany, while the manufacture of tin-enamelled ware (faience) in France had been greatly diminished.

From the first Wedgwood demonstrated an initiative unique among potters of his time, and he was always the first to adopt technical aids and improvements. For instance, he brought the engine-turning lathe*, primarily a metal-working tool, to Staffordshire in 1763, and it was so efficient for its purpose that when, in the 20th century, the demand for engine-turning

became too great for the 18th century machine to cope with it, another was created by copying the old one. To the purist, works decorated by engine-turning perhaps resemble metal-work too closely, but the bronzing of black basaltes* ware was also an attempt to imitate metalwork, and these were effects at which Wedgwood was aiming.

In 1764 Wedgwood married his cousin Sarah* (Sally), daughter of Richard Wedgwood, cheese merchant of Spen Green, Cheshire. Their first child, Susannah (Sukey), was born on the 3rd January, 1765, and married Robert Waring Darwin* (son of Erasmus Darwin*) in 1796. She became the mother of Charles Darwin*.

By 1765 the name of Wedgwood was becoming increasingly heard in London, and in November 1766, he opened his first London showrooms* in Charles Street, Grosvenor Square, London, W, although the earliest surviving record of this address appears to be the 9th January, 1768. In June 1765, Wedgwood received, through the medium of Miss Deborah Chetwynd*, an order to make a tea service for Queen Charlotte* which had to be decorated with raised flowers on a gold ground (see: Gilding). In 1766 Wedgwood was confirmed as 'Potter to Her Majesty', and creamware was renamed Queen's ware.

Wedgwood met Thomas Bentley* in 1762. Bentley, destined to have a profound influence on Wedgwood's subsequent

Wedgwood, Josiah I. *The Wedgwood family in the grounds of Etruria Hall, painted in the autumn of 1780 by George Stubbs. Josiah and his wife, Sarah, are seated beneath a tree; the children, mounted on horses, are, left to right, Thomas, Susannah, Josiah II and John; and the small children, left to right, Mary Ann, Sarah, and Catherine. Painted in oils on a wood panel, 47½ ins. by 59½ ins.* Wedgwood.

Wedgwood, Josiah I. *Engraving of the memorial by Flaxman in Stoke Church. After Jewitt.* Photo: Wedgwood.

career, was a cultivated man who had acquired both classical learning and a knowledge of languages. He was a convinced neo-classicist, and his guidance directed Wedgwood designs towards this style. About the same time as he met Wedgwood, Bentley entered into partnership with Samuel Boardman of Liverpool as general merchants, and Bentley & Boardman became Wedgwood's Liverpool agents.

In 1766 Wedgwood bought the Ridgehouse Estate of some three hundred and fifty acres, situated between Burslem, Hanley, and Newcastle, and there he built a factory which he named Etruria*. In 1767 Bentley agreed to become Wedgwood's partner in the production of ornamental* wares; the so-called useful wares continued to be made at Burslem until 1772.

The new factory was inaugurated on the 13th June, 1769, and the partnership deeds between Wedgwood and Bentley were signed on the 10th August in the same year. The event of June 13th was commemorated by six First Day's Vases*, which were thrown by Wedgwood on a wheel turned by Bentley. Much of the first production at Etruria was a black body, an improved version of Staffordshire Black Egyptian*, which Wedgwood hardened and refined into something which he later called 'basaltes'*.

The year 1769 was a very eventful one. The partnership

acquired a house in Chelsea* to be used as an enamelling studio, and Bentley began to reside there to oversee the work in 1770. In the previous August new showrooms had been opened in Great Newport Street, off St. Martin's Lane, which were rapidly becoming a fashionable meeting place. Lord Townshend, writing of 'Squire Hanger', a man of fashion, is quoted in *Johnson's England*:

> At Tattersall's, Wedgwood's, and eke the Rehearsal,
> Then straightway at Betty's he's sure to converse all.

In 1769 Wedgwood took out his first and only patent for the enamel which he referred to as 'encaustic'*. This patent was infringed by Humphrey Palmer* in 1770, and Wedgwood started a law suit against him which was settled amicably in 1771.

From 1772 virtually everything coming from Etruria was marked, and Wedgwood was the first earthenware potter to do this consistently. The porcelain of Meissen*, Sèvres*, and Chelsea* was marked fairly consistently, and marking became more popular with the porcelain factories as the century progressed, although many of the products of the lesser manufacturers were left unmarked in the hope that they might be mistaken for the wares of one of the more fashionable factories. The makers of earthenware, whose products resembled each others, did not, as a general rule, mark their wares until Wedgwood took the initiative, and it is evident that much goodwill was already attaching to his name. There is one interesting difference to be noted between the marking of pottery and that of porcelain, where the mark was usually some kind of device. The small porcelain factories tried to copy the device of the large ones, especially of Meissen. The Staffordshire potters stamped their wares with their own names. Wedgwood was the first to do so consistently, but others like Spode*, Turner* and Adams*, who copied Wedgwood's wares, soon followed his example. Wedgwood's regular marking was part of his sales policy, and in this aspect of his career he was many decades in advance of his time. He undertook market research, he developed the art of public relations, and he took pains to produce wares for specific markets.

Early in 1773 Wedgwood received an important order from Catherine II* of Russia for a dinner and dessert service of nearly a thousand pieces for the Chesman Palace near St. Petersburg, often known as La Grenouillère (the Froggery) which was built near a marsh of that name. This subsequently became known as the Frog* service. Three years earlier he had supplied a large Husk* service to the Empress, and at a later date jasper* plaques* were employed as ornament in her apartments at Tsarskoë Selo.

The completion of the Frog service marked the removal of the showrooms from Great Newport Street to Greek Street, Soho (see: Showrooms), and the new premises were opened to the public with an exhibition of the service before its dispatch to Russia. The enthusiastic reception accorded to this exhibition is ample evidence of the popularity of Wedgwood and Bentley in the metropolis. By this time they were already having some difficulty in satisfying the demand for their ornamental wares, and Wedgwood was nearing the successful completion of his experiments towards the jasper* body. This was employed for the most part in relief (usually white) on a background of a contrasting colour (usually blue). It derived its inspiration from classical hardstone cameos*, or cameo-cut glass, an example of the latter to be found in the Portland* vase.

Jasper was the first innovation of importance in ceramic history since the Chinese discovery of porcelain nearly a

Wedgwood, Josiah II. *Black basaltes bust modelled by Arnold Austin.* Wedgwood.

thousand years before, and it proved to be particularly well suited to the neo-classical style of decoration. John Flaxman Junior* was the first artist of note to design for this medium, and he was one of a number of artists later to distinguish themselves who provided designs in their youth for Wedgwood. Undoubtedly one of the secrets of Wedgwood's success was his commissioning of promising young artists — Flaxman*, John Bacon*, George Stubbs*, Joseph Wright* of Derby — and his ability to interest those who had already arrived, such as Sir Joshua Reynolds*, who were prepared to lend their influence. The list of his noble and aristocratic friends is a long one. They helped to promote sales, and lent him Roman and Greek antiquities to copy. Visits to the Etruria factory by some of the most eminent people of the day were frequent.

Wedgwood led the Staffordshire potters when they contested the renewal of Richard Champion's* patent for the manufacture of feldspathic porcelain from Cornish materials — china clay and feldspathic rock. It is doubtful whether any of the participants was very interested in making porcelain, which at best was a hazardous occupation, but they all wanted access to Cornish materials for making other kinds of ware. Since the Trent & Mersey Canal*, in the promotion of which Wedgwood had played a very active part, was nearing completion, the carriage of these raw materials from Cornwall to the Potteries no longer presented any great obstacle. The matter was settled by Champion's agreement to limit his patent to the quantities necessary to make porcelain, leaving the use of the materials open for any other purpose. Wedgwood knew quite well how to make porcelain from a variety of materials, and a long letter written to Bentley in January 1776, gives his considered views on the technicalities and difficulties of manufacture. In that year he made porcelain experimentally from materials sent to him from China, and there is no doubt that he could have added this type of ware to his production at any time had he wanted to do so.

Bentley died in 1780 at the age of fifty, and no one ever replaced him as a friend and colleague. Thereafter, perhaps Wedgwood's closest friend was Erasmus Darwin*. In business he made increasing use of his nephew, Tom Byerley, and his sons were reaching an age when they could help him. Alexander Chisholm* was engaged to assist him with experiments and correspondence, and to educate the children. Wedgwood's friendship with Erasmus Darwin seems to have dated from 1765, when they were jointly engaged on a pamphlet on the Trent & Mersey Canal. The Doctor may have belonged to Bentley's circle in Liverpool.

In January 1783, Wedgwood became a Fellow of the Royal Society. He contributed five papers to the *Transactions,* three (dated 1782, 1784, and 1786) on the measurement of high temperatures. He was also acquainted with the chemist, Joseph Priestley*, whom he helped with his researches. In 1783 Wedgwood represented the Staffordshire potters in the negotiation of a commercial treaty at the end of the American War of Independence, which had interrupted a flourishing export trade. Also in 1783 Wedgwood published a pamphlet entitled *An Address to the Workmen in the Pottery on the Subject of Entering into the Service of Foreign Manufacturers* By this time Wedgwood's reputation had spread widely on the Continent, and the factory's skilled workmen received tempting offers from abroad. No doubt language difficulties prevented many from accepting the proffered lure, although English potters had already established factories for the manufacture of creamware in Northern France, but after the War of Independence American potters provided far greater temptation. Wedgwood wrote: ''They had an agent amongst us hiring a number of our hands for establishing a new Pottworks in South Carolina [the source of Cherokee clay*] having got one of our insolvent Master Potters there to conduct them.'' This was a period of inflation, and Wedgwood remarked: ''As the necessities of life, and consequently the price of labour amongst us, are daily advancing, it is probable that more will follow them.'' Wedgwood had many visitors from the Continent, some of whom were industrial spies*, notable in this class being L.-V. Gerverot*. By now Wedgwood wares were the subject of numerous copies both in Staffordshire and on the Continent, even such factories as Meissen* and Sèvres* copying jasper, while creamware was being made from the shores of the Baltic (*flintporslin*) to the potteries of Italy (*terra inglese*).

Wedgwood was very active in promoting the General Chamber of Manufacturers of Great Britain, which was concerned with the drafting of the Irish Trade Treaty of 1785, and the French Commercial Treaty of 1786, when his advice was sought by William Eden (see: Lord Auckland). The Society for the Suppression of the Slave Trade, of which Wedgwood was an active committee member, was founded in 1787.

In 1790 Wedgwood took his three sons, John*, Josiah II*, and Thomas*, into partnership, and his nephew, Tom Byerley, became a partner at the same time. John and Thomas relinquished their partnerships in 1793. The firm was now known as Wedgwood, Sons, & Byerley, and in 1790, the year in which the copy of the Portland* vase was finally completed Wedgwood began progressively to retire from business.

Wedgwood's last years were spent in pursuing old interests and promoting new ones. In 1790 he received a request for assistance from the French chemist, Antoine Lavoisier, who wanted a pyrometer*. At the time Wedgwood was on holiday in Weymouth, a south coast resort, and it was there that he received a letter from Josiah II describing the attack of the Birmingham mob on Priestley's house. In January 1792, he sent Lord Auckland, a report on the current state of the Potteries. In December of the same year Josiah II married Elizabeth Allen and received a gift of £3,000 from his father. In 1793 we find Wedgwood working to promote friendly societies among the workmen, who paid 2d. or 3d. per week and received 3s. or 4s. per week when sick, and a smaller sum when superannuated. His son, John, disliked the pottery industry and became a junior partner in the London & Middlesex Bank (later taken over by Coutts). John ultimately retired to Dorset. He was the chairman of the meeting which founded the Royal Horticultural Society. Tom relinquished his partnership for reasons of health. He died young, in 1805, but not before he had laid the foundations of photography.

Wedgwood died on 3rd January 1795, surrounded by his family, after an illness of about three weeks. In 1863 William Ewart Gladstone, the Liberal politician who was a collector of Wedgwood wares, said of him that "he was the greatest man who ever, in any age or country, applied himself to the important work of uniting art with industry." Wedgwood himself would, no doubt, have preferred the less fulsome tribute which appears on his monument: "[He] converted a rude and inconsiderable Manufactory into an elegant Art and An important part of the National Commerce."

Wedgwood, Josiah I, Statues of

The suggestion that a statue should be erected to Josiah Wedgwood is thought to have originated with Joseph Mayer*. It was favourably received, a Statue Committee was formed, public subscriptions invited, and Edward Davis* selected to carry out the work. He provided a statue which showed Josiah with his most famous work — the Portland* vase, and, when completed, the bronze was sent to the International Exhibition of 1862, where it was put on view to the thousands who flocked to London for this event. At the end of the Exhibition the statue was taken to Stoke-on-Trent and set up in front of the railway station. It was unveiled on the 24th February, 1863, in the presence of the Earl of Harrowby and assorted municipal dignitaries. The large gathering included processions representing each of the Five Towns, a company of Volunteers with their band, and the First Staffordshire Artillery Volunteers (Etruria) with their cannon. After the unveiling, 'God Save the Queen', a speech of thanks to Lord Harrowby by Alderman Copeland, and a *feu de joie* from rifles and cannon, the party moved to the Railway Hotel for a banquet at which only champagne was served (a vintage felicitously named Crême de Bouzy).

For the next century or so the statue became part of the townscape of Stoke, not often noticed except by visitors. Then

a Corporation employee noticed a plaster statue of Josiah lying neglected in a store room. It was brought out, repaired by Eric Owen*, and placed outside the offices at Barlaston*. This was the plaster version of the bronze unveiled in 1863, and it was soon decided to send it to London to have it cast by the Corinthian Bronze Company of Peckham. This bronze was placed in its present position at Barlaston in 1957.

The statue of Wedgwood on the façade of the Victoria and Albert Museum, London, is by Albert H. Hodge (1875-1918). See: End papers of *Dictionary*.

Wedgwood, Josiah I, Statues of. *Bronze statue of Josiah Wedgwood, FRS, holding the Portland Vase, by Edward Davis, at the entrance to the Barlaston factory.* Wedgwood.

Crimson dip jasper teapot and spill vase, 1928. Wedgwood. Photo Reilly/Charles Letts.

Solid black jasper sporting mug, ornamented with white reliefs of famous British sporting centres. Designed by Richard Guyatt, 1966. Wedgwood. Photo: Reilly/Charles Letts.

Vase of Chinese form decorated by Louise Powell, c.1925. Wedgwood.

Boat Race *goblet or vase, designed by Eric Ravilious in 1938.* Wedgwood.

Wedgwood, Josiah II (1769-1843)

Second son of Josiah Wedgwood, and partner at Etruria* from 1790 to 1841. He was educated principally at home by his father and Alexander Chisholm*. Shortly after coming of age, and becoming a partner in the firm, he travelled with Byerley* on the Continent, showing the Portland* vase and other ware at the European Courts. According to Marryat* (*History of Porcelain*) he visited the Meissen* factory and offered £3,000 per annum to be allowed to take it over. Marryat, who collected Wedgwood ware, gives no authority for this statement, but his book was published in 1852, only nine years after the death of Josiah II, when there were many people living who might have contested the truth of it. In 1792 'Jos' married Elizabeth ('Bessie' Allen), whose younger sister was to marry his brother, John, two years later.

The earliest record of Josiah's interest in pottery is in March 1783, when he reported to his father by letter on trials of cane ware*, but this interest was not sustained long beyond his Continental tour. Shortly after his father's death he left Staffordshire and went to live at Cobham, Surrey. In 1800 he leased a house in Dorset from his brother, Tom*, and remained there until after Tom's death. From Surrey and Dorset he seldom visited the factory more than twice a year and seemed content to leave the management of the firm to Byerley, who had held a partner's share since 1790.

In 1800 John*, who had retired from the firm in 1793, returned as a partner and took to making frequent visits to the factory. In 1804 he went to live in Staffordshire to be nearer to Etruria, and more effectively to control the business which was failing. He wrote frequently to Jos, complaining that discipline and standards of production had deteriorated. Josiah postponed his own return until 1806, probably because of the declining health of Tom, who died in July, 1805. By then John had already done much to revive the firm. Celadon, the first of the coloured bodies*, had been introduced in 1805, and the first steps had been taken in the production of underglaze blue prints*, orders for which had previously been satisfied by buying them from other manufacturers. Illustrations of the first Wedgwood patterns of this type were distributed to dealers in December, 1805. During the next seven years some of the finest blue-printed patterns were produced, including the outstanding *Botanical Flowers** and *Water Lily**, and the brothers' strenuous efforts to save the firm began to show results. Nevertheless, in 1811 Jos wrote, "the business is not worth carrying on, and if I could take my capital from it, I would tomorrow."

Circumstances were certainly not favourable. The war with France had ruined Wedgwood's Continental trade. John again withdrew, this time finally, in 1812. Byerley had died in 1810, and Josiah was left with sole responsibility for the business. In 1812 bone china* was made for the first time. The quality was excellent, the shapes were satisfactory, and the styles of decoration generally suitable, but the venture did not succeed. Manufacture of bone china was progressively reduced after 1816, and after 1822 production was limited to special requests and orders for replacements. Smear-glazed* stoneware, jasper*, basaltes*, Queen's* and pearl* ware provided the factory with sufficient work to make the business profitable, and stone china* was introduced in 1820, but the period was not notable as one of inventiveness, and there was little evidence of the driving enthusiasm and energetic inquiry that had characterised the working life of Josiah I. Apart from Celadon and the best of the underglaze blue prints, little of lasting significance was introduced.

In 1823 Josiah III* was taken into partnership, and, four years later, his brother Francis* joined the firm. Josiah II

Wedgwood, Josiah II. *From the portrait by William Owen, RA.* Wedgwood.

became Member of Parliament for Stoke-on-Trent in 1832. In 1828 the London Showrooms* were given up, and the irreplaceable stock of moulds sold. With the 18th century ware disposed of at the time, this sale realised the sum of £16,000 — nearly twice the firm's recorded profits for 1810 — but there is little evidence of a pressing need for the money, and Josiah's decision to sell the moulds and dispose of original Flaxman* wax models has been as much condemned by his successors as it would have been by his father.

Josiah's nephew, Charles Darwin*, wrote of him: "He was silent and reserved, so as to be a rather awful [awe-inspiring] man; but he sometimes talked openly with me. He was the very type of an upright man, with the clearest judgment. I do not believe that any power on earth could have made him swerve one inch from what he considered the right course."

Wedgwood, Josiah III (1795-1880)

Eldest son of Josiah II*, and known to the family as 'Joe'. Josiah III joined his father at Etruria* as a partner in November 1823, but withdrew in March 1842, four months after his father's retirement, leaving his brother, Francis*, in sole charge. In 1837, Joe married his cousin, Caroline, daughter of Robert Waring Darwin*, and their second daughter, Margaret Susan, was the mother of the composer, Ralph Vaughan-Williams.

Joe Wedgwood was never much interested in the firm, and shortly after his marriage he bought a four hundred-acre estate on Leith Hill, Surrey, to which he retired for the last thirty-eight years of his life.

Wedgwood, Hon. Josiah V (1899-1968)

Chairman, Managing Director, and from 1967 first honorary Life President. The second son of Josiah Clement, 1st Baron Wedgwood*, Josiah V was the great-great-great grandson of the founder of the firm. Educated at Bedales School (from which, with his elder brother Charles, he ran away) and the London School of Economics, where he qualified as Bachelor of Science and Doctor of Philosophy, he joined Wedgwood at Etruria as Company Secretary in the winter of 1927. On the sudden death of Francis Hamilton ('Major Frank') Wedgwood* in 1930, Josiah succeeded him as Managing Director, becoming Chairman in 1947. His appointment as chief executive of the company was swiftly followed by the Wall Street crash and one of the worst periods of depression Britain had ever seen. This was felt particularly in the Potteries, and obliged Josiah V to make stringent economies. His swift and resolute action probably saved the firm from bankruptcy and was certainly responsible for keeping it in business when many others withdrew, dismissing all their employees, or failed. Only five years later he made the momentous decision to raise finance for the building of a new, electrically-fired, factory in rural surroundings at Barlaston*. The purchase of the estate and the move from Etruria was not completed when in 1939 war broke out, and it was not until 1947 that all manufacture at Etruria finally ceased.

During the thirties, Josiah V was concerned to maintain standards of production and quality control, and to improve standards of design. To this end he employed, as had Josiah I, outside designers who would reinvigorate the Wedgwood tradition. Among these were Eric Ravilious*, John Skeaping*, Keith Murray*, and Arnold Machin*. This policy was again pursued after the war, when the art department under the direction of Victor Skellern* was instrumental in re-establishing Wedgwood as the mainspring of commercial pottery design in Britain. During this period Richard Guyatt*, Edward Bawden*, and Laurence Whistler* were commissioned to design new patterns, and Norman Wilson* (then Production Director) created Barlaston shape* and his important range of Unique* ware.

In 1953 Josiah put into effect a plan, which he had nurtured for many years, to improve the standard of retail sales and display. The first Wedgwood Room* was opened in the autumn of that year.

Josiah V's brilliant administrative ability was widely recognised outside the Potteries. From 1942-46 he was a Director of the Bank of England, and he was a Director of the District Bank from 1948. He was a member of the Monopolies Commission, Chairman of the Advisory Council of the Royal College of Art (of which he became one of the six Senior Fellows), and a founder member of the Council of Industrial Design. In 1964 he was succeeded by Arthur Bryan* as Managing Director, continuing as Chairman until the autumn of 1967, when he retired. He was appointed first honorary Life President. He died suddenly in May 1968.

Josiah V possessed exceptional qualities of leadership, courage, and foresight, combined with business acumen and a total devotion to his family firm. He was a shrewd judge of character and ability, and gathered around him an outstanding team of designers, technicians, and salesmen. He was satisfied to delegate responsibility, but never relinquished control of policy, and he took a detailed interest in every aspect of the business. The extent of his achievement in reviving the fortunes of the firm after the slump of the 'thirties, and restoring Wedgwood to pre-eminence in the British pottery industry, has yet to be measured, but it must be ranked as second only to

Wedgwood, Hon. Josiah V. Photo: Wedgwood.

that of Josiah I. Josiah V's son, Dr. John Wedgwood, was appointed a non-executive director of the Company in 1968.

Wedgwood, Josiah Clement, PC, DSO (1872-1943) 1st Baron Wedgwood of Barlaston

Politician. Born at Barlaston, the second surviving son of Clement Francis Wedgwood*; naval architect; served in the South African War; Liberal MP for Newcastle-under-Lyme, 1906-19; served in the First World War, being awarded the DSO at Gallipoli. He joined the Labour party in 1919, continuing to represent the constituency of Newcastle-under-Lyme until a year before his death. Vice-Chairman of the Parliamentary Labour Party, 1921-24, he was Chancellor of the Duchy of Lancaster in the first Labour Cabinet. He was created a baron in 1942. His publications include *Staffordshire Pottery and its History* (1913) and *Memoirs of a Fighting Life* (Foreword by Winston Churchill, 1940). A radical idealist, Josiah was known for his vigorous, outspoken opinions, his sincerity, and his generosity (especially to refugees from Nazi Germany). His second son, Josiah V*, became Managing Director of Wedgwood in 1930.

Wedgwood, Kennard Lawrence (1873-1950)

Eldest son of Lawrence Wedgwood*; educated at Uppingham; a director, with his first cousins, Cecil* and Francis Hamilton*, at Etruria*, and, from 1906, in America, where he represented the firm and then founded the subsidiary company in New York.

Wedgwood, Lawrence (1844-1913)

Third son of Francis Wedgwood*; partner at Etruria* with his father and elder brothers from 1868-70, with his brothers, 1870-91, and with his nephews, Cecil* and Francis Hamilton*, 1891-95, when the firm was incorporated as Josiah Wedgwood & Sons Ltd. During his period of partnership the firm introduced the first of the distinguishing prefix letters for pattern numbers, reintroduced the manufacture of bone china* and tiles*, and employed Thomas Allen* as art director. Lawrence's son, Kennard Wedgwood*, founded the subsidiary company in America.

Wedgwood Museum

The first museum, at Etruria*, was housed in a small single storey building. It was opened in 1906. After the move to Barlaston* in 1939, no room was found for the display of the museum collection. A small part of it was arranged in show-cases in the 'Long Gallery', a corridor in the factory, and the rest was stacked in a Nissen hut, where the Curator also conducted his research and replied to correspondence from collectors. The Eustace Calland collection, which was acquired in 1951, was displayed for some years in the London Showrooms*. In 1965 the manuscript collection was transferred on loan to Keele University, where it is being professionally catalogued, and in 1969 the Wedgwood Museum Trust was established. On 30th September a new museum was officially opened by Lord Clark, former Director of the National Gallery.

The new Museum, with the picture gallery containing family portraits by Stubbs*, Reynolds* and Romney, shows a great part of the collection in a coherent sequence and in conditions worthy of its importance for the first time in the firm's history. Adjacent to the Museum is a lecture theatre and a large demonstration area where visitors (who number more than 100,000 a year) may see many of the most interesting production processes.

Curators of the Wedgwood Museum since its inception have been:

Isaac Cooke 1906-19.
Harry Barnard* 1919-31.
John Cook 1931-45.
Tom Lyth* 1945-60.
Bill Billington 1960-72.
Bruce Tattersall, MA 1972-78.
Gaye Blake-Roberts 1979-

Wedgwood Museum. *Photograph taken in the original Wedgwood Museum at Etruria on 7th May, 1906, showing Isaac Cook, first Curator of the Museum.* Photo: Wedgwood.

Wedgwood, Ralph

The eldest son of Thomas Wedgwood*, Josiah's partner and manager in the manufacture of useful* ware. Ralph Wedgwood made creamware in Burslem under the style of Wedgwood & Co. Suffering from the trade depression of 1793, he became bankrupt, and went to Ferrybridge, Yorkshire, where he was in partnership with others until 1797. The impressed mark 'Wedgwood & Co.' is his, and belongs to the Burslem period.

Wedgwood Rooms

An organisation of specialist 'shops-in-shops' (departments in multiple stores, stocked, staffed, and administered by Wedgwood) started in the autumn of 1953, when the first Room was opened at Marshall & Snelgrove, Oxford Street, London. From the first special emphasis was placed on staff training, a high standard of display (including table settings), and the 'open stock' system, enabling customers to buy small quantities and replacements of any pattern on display. The success of this organisation significantly influenced Wedgwood design, sales, and production, and transformed attitudes in department stores towards their own standards of china display and stock policy. After fifteen years of operation, Wedgwood Rooms existed in every city and most major towns in the British Isles, and the system had been extended, with some modification, to Canada and the United States.

See: Sir Arthur Bryan; Hon. Josiah Wedgwood.

Wedgwood, Sarah (1734-1815)

Wife, and cousin, of Josiah Wedgwood*; daughter of Richard Wedgwood of Spen Green, Cheshire, the youngest brother of Thomas and John Wedgwood* of the Big House, Burslem, where Josiah first met and courted her. They were married on 25th January, 1764, at Astbury, Cheshire, after prolonged delays while Sarah's father and Josiah negotiated a suitable marriage settlement. A year later, when Josiah was engaged in experiments for "a white body and glaze," he wrote: "Sally is my chief helpmate in this as well as other things." Later he was to pay tribute to her practical judgement in the design of useful* wares for the table: "I speak from experience in Female taste, without which I should have made but a poor figure among my pots, not one of which of any consequence is finished without the approbation of my Sally."

A shrewd, devoted and considerate woman, she bore him eight children, one of whom died in infancy. She suffered from severe rheumatism, and for this complaint and others she was attended by Dr. Erasmus Darwin*, whose son, Robert* was to marry her eldest daughter, Susannah ('Sukey'). After Josiah's death, Sarah left Etruria Hall and lived for some years in Somerset. A widow for twenty years, she died in 1815 at Parkfields Cottage, Tittensor, now the home of Wedgwood's Chairman, Sir Arthur Bryan*, and his family.

Wedgwood Society, London

The Society was formed in 1954 by a group of enthusiasts, following an exhibition of Wedgwood ware held at The Iveagh Bequest, Kenwood, to which many private collectors contributed. The first chairman was the late Sir George Barnes, then head of BBC television and later principal of the University of North Staffordshire, Keele. The present chairman is John K. des Fontaines, FRSA. The object of the Society is to encourage the study and appreciation of the wares and history of the Wedgwood factory, to publish the results, and to promote friendly social activity among members. Meetings are held about six times a year in London. Membership is open to all genuine students and collectors of ceramics by introduction or application to the Hon. Secretary and subsequent approval by the Committee. Publications: *Proceedings, of the Wedgwood Society* (periodically); *The Wedgwood 1880 Illustrated Catalogue of Shapes.*

Wedgwood, Sarah, *wife of Josiah I, and her husband, from the portraits by Sir Joshua Reynolds.* Wedgwood.

Wedgwood Society. *Creamware plate to commemorate the twenty-fifth anniversary of The Wedgwood Society, London, 1954-1979. Transfer printed in sepia with a view of Etruria Hall. Specially designed for a limited edition of 300. Mrs. Brixie Jarvis.*

Wedgwood, Thomas (1685-1739)
Master potter of the Churchyard Works*, which he had inherited from his father. Having failed to prosper in his craft, and sired twelve children, he died, leaving each of the seven who survived him the sum of £20. The youngest, then nine years old, was Josiah Wedgwood I*.

Wedgwood, Thomas (c.1717-1773)
Eldest son and heir of Thomas Wedgwood* (1685-1739) of the Churchyard Works*, Burslem, and brother of Josiah I*. After their father's death, Josiah worked for him, being officially apprenticed to him for five years from 1744. In 1749 Thomas declined to accept Josiah as his partner, giving early evidence of a lack of business judgement which became increasingly apparent with the passage of years. After his death, Josiah had the disagreeable task, as his brother's executor, of dealing with Thomas's second wife, who disliked her step-children. In 1780. Josiah bought the Churchyard Works from his nephew, who had inherited them seven years earlier.

Wedgwood, Thomas (fl.1759-1788)
Josiah Wedgwood's cousin, his partner, and manager at the Burslem works from 1759 to 1771-72, and subsequently at Etruria* until his death in 1788. He was in charge of the production of useful* wares. He was an excellent potter, who had experience at the Worcester* porcelain factory, and bore a great part of the responsibility for the production of the Frog* service. His eldest son was Ralph Wedgwood*.

Wedgwood, Thomas (1771-1805)
Third surviving son of Josiah I* and often described as 'the first photographer'. Tom was educated principally at home, though he spent a few terms at Edinburgh University in 1787-89. He became a partner in the firm in 1790, but withdrew three years later, transferring his shares to his elder

brother, Josiah II*. Tom evidently inherited his father's interest in chemistry and scientific experiment, and he read two papers before the Royal Society in 1791-92, when he was only twenty, which demonstrated precocious powers of research. In 1802 he published in the *Journal of the Royal Institution of Great Britain* 'An Account of a Method of copying Paintings upon Glass, and of making Profiles by the agency of Light upon Nitrate of Silver invented by T. Wedgwood Esq., with observations by H. Davy*'. In this paper he showed that copies of silhouettes were obtainable when their shadows were thrown on a piece of white paper or leather sensitised by moistening with nitrate of silver, but he was never able to fix the images thus obtained and was therefore obliged to keep his experiments in a dark room. He deserves the credit for being the first to understand and publish the concept that the chemical action of light might be utilised for the purpose of copying images, but the images he produced were photograms, not photographs.

The most brilliant of Josiah's sons, Tom suffered all his life from ill-health and a perpetual restlessness, which prevented his being able to take full advantage of his talents. He was generous and had many friends, including the poets Thomas Campbell, Samuel Taylor Coleridge, and William Wordsworth. After Tom's early death at the age of thirty-three, Wordsworth wrote of him: ''His calm and dignified manner, united with his tall person and beautiful face, produced in me an impression of sublimity beyond what I had ever experienced from the appearance of any other human being.''

Wedgwood, Thomas *(1771-1805). From the portrait formerly attributed to Flaxman. Wedgwood.*

Wedgwood, Thomas and John

The brothers, Thomas (1703-76) and John (1705-80), of the Big House, Burslem, were master potters who were distant cousins of Josiah I*, their common ancestor being Gilbert Wedgwood (1588-1678). They were fourth generation potters, and their father, Aaron, was said to have been an associate of the Elers* brothers. Thomas and John were makers of fine salt-glaze*, and builders of the first considerable brick residence (the Big House) in Burslem. A third brother, Richard, was the father of Sarah Wedgwood*, and it was at the Big House that Josiah I met and courted his 'Sal'. From 1759-62 Josiah rented the Ivy House* and pottery from Thomas and John for £10 per annum.

Wedgwood Ware

A term often applied specifically to the jasper ware developed by Josiah Wedgwood in the 1770s, but properly it includes all other wares made by the Wedgwood factory, including Queen's ware (creamware), tortoiseshell ware, cauliflower ware, pineapple ware, salt-glazed ware, agate ware, marbled ware, variegated ware, black basaltes, Etruscan ware, *rosso antico,* cane ware, pearl ware, bone china, Parian (Carrara) porcelain, lustre wares, majolica, coloured bodies, etc. All these are discussed elsewhere under the appropriate headings.

Wedgwoodarbeit

Literally, Wedgwood-work. The name used to describe wares in imitation of jasper made at Meissen* during the directorship of Count Marcolini, 1774-1814. The material used was porcelain decorated in low relief with an enamel blue ground.

Wedgwoodarbeit. *Solitaire in blue biscuit porcelain imitating jasper. Grosbreitenbach (Thuringia). c.1797.* Kestnermuseum, Hanover.

Wednesday Club

This London Club met at the Globe Tavern, Fleet Street, for convivial evenings. Wedgwood was an occasional visitor. One of the members, Sir Joseph Banks*, wrote to Wedgwood on 6th April, 1784: "We attend the [Wednesday] Club with tolerable regularity; Hodgson makes punch and talks of politics; [Ralph] Griffiths* drinks it and makes jokes, but we all look for your assistance."

Weisweiler, Adam (fl.1770-1810)

Ébéniste of German origin who assisted David Roentgen and arrived in Paris in 1777, becoming a *maître-ébéniste* in the following year. He was noted for small pieces of furniture made for royal palaces, especially the Château of Saint-Cloud. He employed Sèvres* porcelain plaques in the decoration of his furniture, and a *sécretaire à abbatant* in the Metropolitan Museum, New York, attributed to this maker, is inset with Wedgwood plaques*. A console table by Weisweiler in the Walker Art Gallery, Baltimore, is also mounted with a Wedgwood jasper plaque.

Wellesley Shape

A wide moulded border of fruit, enclosed at the rim by a narrow ovolo* border, designed by John Goodwin* in 1932. The ovolo border is based on an earlier design which appears on black basaltes* lamps c.1780.

Westmacott, Sir Richard (1775-1856)

English sculptor, who studied in Rome under Canova*, 1793-97. He exhibited at the Royal Academy from 1791-1839, was elected RA in 1811, was professor of sculpture at the Royal Academy from 1821-37, and was knighted in the latter year. Westmacott worked mainly on monuments, busts, and statues. He executed the Achilles statue in Hyde Park, cast from Waterloo cannon and dedicated to the Duke of Wellington by the women of England. The Vitruvian Scroll in the sixth (and last) edition of the Ornamental Catalogue (1787) is attributed to Westmacott.

Whieldon, Thomas (1719-1793)

Master potter, and one of the pioneers of English pottery manufacture, at Fenton Low and, after 1747, at Fenton Vivian. It seems certain that Whieldon made all types of ware generally produced in Staffordshire during the first half of the 18th century, including red wares, salt-glaze*, and cream-ware*, but his name is particularly associated with relief-moulded wares and figures decorated with beautiful semi-transparent coloured glazes. These were often applied to produce a mottled effect, and the word tortoiseshell* in ceramics has become almost synonymous with the name of Whieldon, although many other potters made similar wares. Excavations at the Fenton Low and Fenton Vivian sites (the latter as recently as 1969) have yielded much useful information about Whieldon's work, and it is evident that he used the same moulds for red, salt-glaze, and cream-coloured wares. Both Whieldon, in his notebook, and Wedgwood in his Experiment Book, refer to "white-ware" and "white stone-ware" as the staple of Whieldon's production, and this has been interpreted as a description of salt-glaze. There is now, however, good reason to suppose that both were referring to creamwares, which Whieldon is known to have produced as early as 1749. In the absence of evidence to connect them with another pot bank, tortoiseshell and other coloured glazed wares of the period are usually described under the generic term 'Whieldon-type'. Wares thought to belong to the period 1754-59 are known as Whieldon-Wedgwood*.

Whieldon was appointed High Sheriff of Staffordshire in 1787.

Whieldon, Thomas. *Teapot decorated with mottled coloured glazes. Whieldon-Wedgwood type, c.1760.* Wedgwood.

Whieldon, Thomas. *Rare punch pot, 7ins. high, moulded in relief and coloured, with fruit and vegetable forms arranged between columns. Inset cover and floral knop. Whieldon, c.1757.* Sotheby's.

Whieldon-Wedgwood Ware

Earthenware and salt-glazed stoneware made during the partnership of Thomas Whieldon* and Josiah Wedgwood at Fenton Vivian, near Stoke-on-Trent, 1754-59. Much of the production was experimental, and there Wedgwood developed an excellent green glaze and a good yellow later used in the production of cauliflower and pineapple ware. It is doubtful whether either of these was used during the period of the partnership, although some evidence has been found that cauliflower shapes were in production at Fenton Vivian.

Wedgwood's experiments, which led to great improvements in the wares manufactured, not only by Whieldon, but

commonly in Staffordshire at the time, probably did not begin in earnest until early in 1759, and apart from Wedgwood's notebook, we have little information about events of this period. The Experiment Book in the Wedgwood Museum* at Barlaston is very informative, but refers only to the period at the end of the partnership. It is possible to deduce from it that the staple wares of the partnership had been agate* and tortoiseshell* ware, white salt-glazed* stoneware, and cream-ware, and that the public were tiring of the first three. It may be that the partners failed to agree on the remedies for this state of affairs. The parting was amicable, and the two men remained on terms of friendship.

Whieldon-Wedgwood Ware. *Silver pattern tortoiseshell plate, c.1760.* Wedgwood.

Whieldon-Wedgwood Ware. *Punch pot and cover, 6½ins. high, of depressed globular shape with crabstock handle and spout. The sides are moulded with scrolling sprays of stylised flowers picked out in green, blueish-green and ochre on a streaked grey ground with green borders.* Sotheby's.

Whisky Still. *Cream colour whisky still and burner of cylindrical shape, the upper part with a condenser with pyramid-shaped lining, a spout, and protruding outlet for the cooler. 17½ ins. high. This shape appears in the first Cream Colour Catalogue. Examples are extremely rare. Sotheby's.*

Whisky Still
Creamware still, made in three pieces, the cylindrical top with lid, down-curved spout and bung hole, resting on a two-handled stand similar in form to the lower half of a food warmer* or veilleuse*. An example of this extremely rare object is in the Colonial Williamsburg Collection and may be dated c.1770. It may originally have been intended for laboratory use.

Whistler, Laurence, CBE (b.1912)
Artist, engraver on glass, poet and author; educated at Stowe and Balliol College, Oxford (Hon. Fellow, 1974); winner of the first King's Gold Medal for Poetry, 1935; first President of the Guild of Glass Engravers, 1975; younger brother of Rex Whistler*. The greatest British glass engraver of the 20th century, Whistler has engraved windows or panels for many buildings including Stowe School, Buckinghamshire, St. Hugh's College, Oxford, Sherborne Abbey, Dorset, and the Guards Chapel, London. His varied publications include *Sir John Vanbrugh*, 1938; *Rex Whistler, His Life and Drawings*, 1948; *The World's Room* (Collected Poems), 1949; *Engraved Glass*, 1952-58; *Pictures on Glass*, 1972; and *The Image of Glass*, 1975.
In 1955-56 he designed for Wedgwood a *Dolphin* Border, and

a series of six designs entitled *Outlines of Grandeur,* both for bone china* dinner plates. *Outlines of Grandeur* represented famous architecture characteristic of six periods of British history. The subjects include St. Paul's Cathedral, the Taj Mahal, and the Clifton Suspension Bridge.

Whistler, Rex John (1905-1944)
Painter, particularly of murals and portraits, stage designer and book illustrator; studied at the Slade School of Art, 1922-26, and in Rome; painted the murals for the refreshment room of the Tate Gallery, 1926-27. For Wedgwood he designed the *Clovelly* pattern in 1936. He was killed in action in Normandy in July 1944.
See: Laurence Whistler.

White Biscuit Ware
A white stoneware biscuit body, made to a limited extent during the lifetime of Josiah I, but used to a far greater extent during the period of Josiah II. During the first period it was used for plant pots, engine-turned in vertical stripes through slip* of contrasting colour (often black). In the 19th century it was usually given a smear glaze*. Coloured applied relief decoration in the style of jasper* was often employed, in blue, green, lilac or chocolate. This body is sometimes confused with white jasper, but it is softer and not so dense.

White House Service
A dinner service of bone china made for the White House, Washington, in 1903 during the Presidency of Theodore Roosevelt. It is decorated with the *Colonnade* border printed in gold and a polychrome enamel representation of the Great Seal of the United States. The service was the work of John Goodwin* and Herbert A. Cholerton*.

Whitehall Pattern
A bone china tableware pattern consisting of a narrow vine border printed in gold. It was designed in 1942, and has been produced in conjunction with a wide variety of coloured grounds including 'powder'* (sponged*) colours (blue, turquoise, green, ruby, pink and grey), ivory, Mazarine (underglaze) blue, and Arras (underglaze) green.

Whitehurst, John (1713-1788)
Horologer; maker of chronometers and scientific instruments; Fellow of the Royal Society, 1779. At Derby, 1736-75, removed to London, 1778. Whitehurst supplied a time recorder for use in the Etruria factory, and he was among those consulted by Wedgwood on the factory plans. In 1778 he published *An Inquiry into the Original State and Formation of the Earth* to which Wedgwood asked Bentley* to subscribe on his behalf to the extent of two copies.

Widow Finial
A finial in the form of a woman seated on the ground with a shawl drawn over her head (i.e. in widow's weeds). Introduced about 1774, it is said to represent a widow named Sneyd, a not uncommon name in the Potteries. There is a tradition that Wedgwood used the wife of his friend, Ralph Sneyd of Keele, as the model. This finial was described by Josiah Wedgwood as the Sibyl (in ancient times a mouthpiece of the gods endowed with prophetic or oracular powers), and it is possible that the figure was intended originally to represent a gipsy*. Sibyl finials appear on creamware vases, on the glaciers* of the Frog* service, and frequently upon black basaltes* teapots from the 18th century until the 1930s. They are also to be found, in various poses, on the productions of other factories including Caughley, Shorthose & Heath, Keeling & Toft*, Elijah Mayer*, Neale* and Turner*.

Wilbraham, Jesse (1891-1963)

Modeller and master-craftsman. Jesse Wilbraham joined Wedgwood at Etruria at the age of thirteen and served the firm for fifty-four years. One of his first jobs was to assist in setting up the Wedgwood Museum*, when he was responsible for finding some of Josiah I's trial pieces. In 1906 he became an apprentice figure-maker, and won a scholarship from night school to Newcastle Art School. During the First World War he served with the 6th Leicestershire Regiment, being wounded in the right hand. Returning to Wedgwood, he started the training school which earned him the nickname of 'The Schoolmaster'. After the Second World War he was responsible for training figure-makers in the ornamental department of which he became head. He modelled portrait medallions* of Josiah V*, Hensleigh Wedgwood*, Norman Wilson* and of his close friend Tom Lyth*. Of the latter portrait he said: "I have made him a great deal nicer looking than he really is just to please his wife." Jesse Wilbraham also modelled a self-portrait, a gold-inscribed copy of which was presented to him to commemorate his fifty years' service in 1953.

Willcox, Mrs. Catherine (fl.1769-1776)

Born Catherine Frye, daughter of Thomas Frye, one of the founders of the Bow* Porcelain Factory. She was a skilled painter, especially of figures, and came to Etruria* with her husband from Worcester*. She worked at the Chelsea studios from the autumn of 1769, painting encaustic vases*, Herculaneum Subjects*, and landscapes for the Frog* service.

Willcox, Ralph (fl.1769-1776)

Husband of Catherine Willcox*; apprenticed to a Liverpool porcelain factory, and later with Worcester*, before joining Wedgwood in 1769. Wedgwood wrote approvingly of him: "He seems a solid, sober man, and has nothing flighty or coxcomical in his dress or behaviour." Somewhat against their will, Willcox and his wife set out for London in the autumn of 1769 to work at the Chelsea Decorating Studios*, where Willcox painted encaustic vases* and the inside borders for the Frog* service.

Willet, William (c.1698-1778)

Unitarian minister at Newcastle-under-Lyme; married, c.1754, Josiah Wedgwood's sister, Catherine (b.1726). Through his friendship with Joseph Priestley* at Warrington Academy, Willet may have been responsible for introducing him to Josiah. He played an important part in directing Josiah's attention towards scientific studies, and the two men seem to have been on terms of warm friendship. Willet's portrait was modelled by Hackwood* in 1776 and signed on the truncation. Writing to Bentley* on 5 July, Wedgwood added a postscript: "I send you this head of Mr Willet as a specimen of Hackwood's modelling. A stronger likeness can scarcely be conceiv'd. You may keep it as the shadow of a good Man who is marching with hasty strides towards the Land of Forgetfulness." Produced for private circulation, early examples of this portrait are usually unmarked.

Williamsburg Husk Service

This service is similar in form and decoration to the one supplied to Catherine the Great. Shards have been excavated on the site of Colonial Williamsburg, Virginia, which was the political, social and cultural centre of the colony. The State Government was transferred to Richmond in 1780 and Williamsburg subsequently declined, but since 1926 it has been largely restored to its 18th century appearance under the sponsorship of John D. Rockefeller, Jr. The Husk Service is being produced for the Williamsburg restoration.

Whitehall Pattern. *Plate and cup and saucer of the Whitehall pattern, developed in 1942 to meet the demand for a formal pattern which is suitable for use with all styles of decoration. It has remained popular for more than thirty-five years.* Wedgwood.

Whitehall Pattern. *Tureen with powder colour border and gold vine Whitehall pattern on bone china.* Wedgwood.

Willow Pattern

A transfer-printed decorative subject originally engraved by Thomas Minton for Thomas Turner, and introduced at Caughley, c.1780. The more familiar versions of this well-known pattern were not engraved until the 19th century, and the 'Chinese' scene represented is purely an English invention. The pattern was used by Wedgwood in underglaze blue* printed form. J. Mollart* engraved 'Minton's Willow' for Wedgwood in 1806 but for some unexplained reason it does not appear to have been produced before 1818.

See: Underglaze Blue Prints.

Willow Pattern. *The Wedgwood version of the Willow Pattern, unknown to China, engraved in 1806 and first produced c.1818. The elaborate outer border was probably inspired by one of the borders found on Chinese export porcelain. Modern example.* Wedgwood.

Wilson, Norman (b.1902)

Master potter, designer and inventor; Works Manager at Etruria*, 1927; Production Director, 1946; Joint Managing Director, 1961.

The son and grandson of china and Parian* manufacturers, Norman Wilson was educated at Ellesmere College and graduated, as Silver Medallist, from the North Staffordshire Technical College, where he was later to serve for many years as examiner and Governor. After two years working for his father, he spent several months breaking in polo ponies in Canada. He was recalled from this diversion by Frank Wedgwood*, who appointed him Works Manager at Etruria in September 1927. After Frank's death in 1930, and the unprecedented slump which followed the Wall Street crash, the firm's success in its struggle for survival was largely due to the

single-minded determination and economic brilliance of Josiah V*, and the technical inventiveness and managerial skills of Norman Wilson.

In 1928 Norman Wilson had introduced the first gas-fired china glost tunnel-kiln. Three years later he installed the first oil-fired earthenware glost tunnel-kiln in Britain. He also introduced new bodies, two-colour earthenware and Alpine Pink*, and designed the best-selling Globe shape coffee pot, sugar box, and creamer, and lamp bases for decoration in Veronese glaze*. His matt glazes* — Moonstone*, Matt Straw, April Green, Dark Green, and Turquoise — sometimes decorated with platinum, were triumphantly successful and provided a purity of finish for the designs of Keith Murray* and John Skeaping* that was perfectly in accord with the art deco styles of the period.

By 1935 the firm was again making modest profits, and the decision was made to leave Etruria and build a new factory at Barlaston*. In the detailed planning of this enterprise Tom Wedgwood* took a leading part. The foundation stone was laid in 1938, and the earthenware factory was established, but due to the war, in which Norman Wilson served as a Lieutenant-Colonel in the Royal Artillery, the move of the china factory was postponed until 1947. In the absence of Norman Wilson, it was Tom Wedgwood who shouldered the burden of production when output was limited to goods for export and utility ware for the home market.

Appointed Production Director in 1946, Norman Wilson applied himself to the formidable task of reviving manufacture,

Wilson, Norman. Photo: Wedgwood.

expanding and training the work force, and reintroducing the production of jasper* (with a jasper body of his own invention) in a newly-built factory. This achieved, he found time during the following fifteen years to design Leigh shape hollow ware for bone china*, the Barlaston shape*, and the range of vases and bowls decorated with brilliant and original glazes known as Norman Wilson Unique* ware. From 1961 until his retirement in 1963 he was joint Managing Director with F. Maitland Wright.

Norman Wilson's achievement was threefold: with Victor Skellern* he exercised an influence on Wedgwood design unrivalled during the first sixty years of the century; as an inventor and technician, he raised Wedgwood to a preeminence in production unknown since the 18th century; and as Production Director he selected and trained a team of young and talented managers who would build upon the secure foundations that he had laid.

Winckelmann, Johann Joachim (1717-1768)

German art historian and, with the Comte de Caylus* and Sir William Hamilton*, one of the most important influences on the neo-classical* style. As Librarian to Cardinal Albani in Rome he took great interest in the excavations at Herculaneum*, Pompeii*, and Paestum. He was made Superintendent of Antiquities in Rome in 1763, and was murdered at an inn in 1768. His *Monumenti Antichi Ineditii*, published in 1766, was an inspiration to Wedgwood, a plaque erroneously entitled *Patroclus hearing of the Death of Achilles* (which, of course, should be *Achilles hearing of the death of Patroclus*) being adapted from one of the illustrations.

Windmills

See: Prime Movers.

Wine and Water Ewers

A pair of ewers, one of which (Water) has a Triton* seated on the shoulder, clasping the neck, and the other (Wine) has a satyr* in the same position. The Water vase is also decorated with a festoon of aquatic leaves and the head of a marine monster, the Wine vase with a festoon of vine leaves and a goat's head in high relief. These models were supplied by Flaxman* in 1775. They are to be found in black basaltes, and in this body they are not uncommon, since many were produced in the 19th century. Only 18th century jasper* versions are known, and these are exceedingly rare. They are unlikely to have been original models by Flaxman, but are probably models based on the antique*, or on Renaissance metalwork, probably the latter. They were reproduced, with somewhat bizarre effect, in majolica* in the 19th century, and bone china* examples were also made after 1880.

Wine and Water Ewers. *Majolica 'Water' ewer of Queen's ware decorated with coloured glazes. Second half of the 19th century.* Christie's.

Wine and Water Ewers. *Pair of wine and water ewers, based on metalwork prototypes from models supplied by Flaxman, 1775.* Wedgwood.

Wine Coolers

Ornamented wine coolers of almost ovoid shape, about 9½ ins. high were made in the *rosso antico** body with basaltes or black jasper reliefs c.1800. They were also produced in jasper ornamented with *art nouveau* style designs towards the end of the 19th century, the shape being similar to the inverted bell form of the Vase 43 in the Shape Book*.

Wine Label

A small creamware plaque with a suspensory chain made to be hung round the neck of a bottle, and lettered with the name of the bottle's contents. Wine labels were made by Wedgwood from the last quarter of the 19th century, sometimes in vine-leaf shape.

See: Bin Label.

Woburn Abbey

Woburn Abbey, Bedfordshire, is a classically designed house, built in 1744 on a site on which once stood a Cistercian Abbey. It is the seat of the Dukes of Bedford, now open to the public, and it contains a notable art collection. John Russell, fourth Duke of Bedford (1710-71), was prominent in public affairs, becoming Lord-Lieutenant of Ireland during the Duke of Devonshire's administration, 1756-57, and an Ambassador for

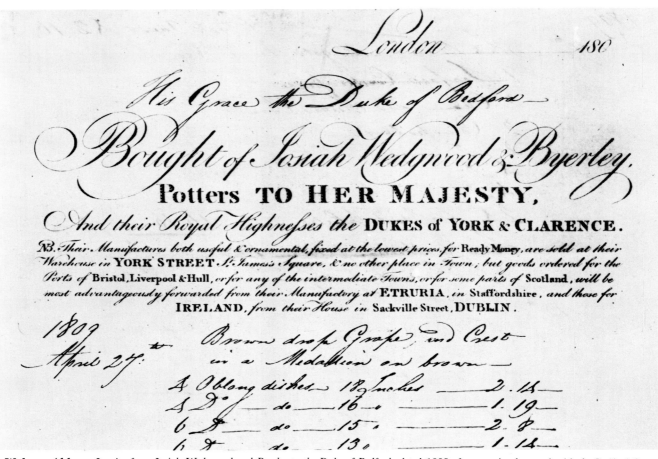

Woburn Abbey. *Invoice from Josiah Wedgwood and Byerley to the Duke of Bedford, dated 1809, for a service decorated with the Bedford Grape pattern for Woburn.* Wedgwood.

the Treaty of Peace with France, 1762-63. Wedgwood's association with the Duke and Duchess was fairly close, although we do not know when it started. In October 1765, he was at Woburn taking patterns from the Duke's French and Oriental china. In February 1769, we find the first mention of the hitherto unidentified Bedford* vase, which was universally admired, and from another reference in 1770 it is evident that the Duke and Duchess were valued clients awarded special treatment. Francis Russell, the fifth Duke, started to buy Wedgwood wares in 1786, and many invoices are preserved in the Wedgwood Archives. The first order was for a table and dessert service costing £9 9s. 6d. and a black basaltes coffee pot for 8s. Soon afterwards an order arrived for blue and white jasper and Etruscan painted ware. In February 1789, another order called for a large creamware armorial service which has now disappeared. This, like a service ordered in 1787, bore the Bedford Crest on each piece.

The 1789 service was decorated with a border pattern which has since become known as the Bedford Grape design, and in 1809 there was another large order for this, together with red and black Egyptian ornaments, lilac and white jasper, and gold-edged white ware. An order for eighty dozen tiles* in 1795 was for the Chinese Dairy designed by the architect, Henry Holland.

Much of the ware supplied to Woburn at this time has disappeared, but surviving pieces, and orders in the Archives, suggested a Loan Exhibition of early wares, which was held at Woburn in April and May 1973.

Wolfe, James (1727-1759)

English soldier; as major-general, killed at the siege of Quebec, 1759, the capture of which gained Canada for the British and, by destroying French power in North America, opened the way for the American Revolution. The victor of one of the three great battles of 1759, 'the year of victories', Wolfe became a national hero. Benjamin West's painting, *The Death of Wolfe* was exhibited in 1771, and the engraving by William Woollett (1776) achieved greater sales than any engraving of the period. Wedgwood reproduced this engraving on Queen's ware* teapots and jugs, c.1778. There was evidently an earlier representation of Wolfe, for Sadler* mentions this as 'in hand' in October 1763. A 'portrait', which bears little resemblance to Wolfe, signed 'J. Sadler', appears on a Liverpool delft bowl in the Victoria and Albert Museum, and it seems likely that this was also used by Wedgwood.

In 1959, to celebrate the bicentenary of the battle of Quebec, Wedgwood issued a Queen's ware jug printed in black with a reproduction of Houston's well-known full-length mezzotint superimposed over an engraving of the landing at Anse au Foulon, and, on the reverse, with a view of Quebec from the south-east. Both engravings were also used for rectangular Queen's ware trays.

Wolfe, James. *Jug transfer-printed with a composite portrait of Wolfe pointing across the St. Lawrence river towards Quebec (from two 18th century engravings) and (reverse) a view of Quebec from the south-east. Bicentenary issue, 1959.* Reilly.

Wood, Enoch (1759-1840)

Potter and modeller, sometimes styled 'Father of the Potteries'; second son of Aaron Wood, first cousin to Ralph Wood*, and younger brother of William Wood*. Aaron had been apprenticed to Thomas Wedgwood* (1703-76) of the Big House, Burslem, becoming the most sought-after-block-cutter in Staffordshire and employed by Whieldon*. William Wood worked for Wedgwood, modelling a large number of the tableware shapes which helped to establish Queen's ware* in a critical market that demanded elegance combined with utility. Enoch is believed to have been apprenticed to Josiah Wedgwood at Etruria* in the 1770s and later joined Humphrey Palmer* of Hanley. In 1784 he entered into partnership with Ralph Wood, making creamware*, cane ware*, black Egyptian*, and coloured bodies*. From 1790-1818 he was in partnership with James Caldwell, and from 1818 the style of the firm was Enoch Wood & Sons. He was a noted maker of figures and busts, two well known examples being the busts of Wesley and Whitfield. A life-size self-portrait bust, incised on the back with a long inscription, is in the British Museum.

Enoch Wood made jasper* and basaltes* in the Wedgwood style, and experimented with porcelain. A pair of bronzed basaltes* Triton* candlesticks* are recorded, which appear to be identical with the Wedgwood models, apart from the turned brass nozzles; and when the Wood & Caldwell factory at Fountain Place was closed after the expiry of Hope & Carter's lease in 1880, block moulds for jasper bas-reliefs* were found the subjects of which are precisely the same as Wedgwood's.

The creamware figures* bearing the impressed mark of Wedgwood (e.g. *Faith, Hope, Charity,* and *Fortitude*) are recognisably in the style of Enoch Wood, and indeed some of them are known with the mark of Wood & Caldwell. It seems probable that these were made to the order of Wedgwood rather than with any attempt to deceive.

Wood also made underglaze blue printed* wares of excellent quality, primarily for the American market.

In 1827 Enoch Wood & Sons issued a small booklet, *A Representation of the Manufacturing of Earthenware, with twenty-one quaint copper-plate engravings, and a short explanation of each showing the whole process of Pottery.* This book, published in London, measures 5½ ins. by 3½ ins. and consists entirely of illustrations of processes of manufacture, with a brief title to each. It is an invaluable social and historical record.

Enoch Wood is further distinguished as the first collector of English pottery. In 1816 he "exhibited various ancient specimens of earthenware descriptive of the progressive state of the manufacture during the last 150 years which he divided into epochs of fifty years from the Butter Pot... down to the time at which the excellent specimens of Queen's ware, Jasper, etc., left by the late Mr. Wedgwood were produced." Part of Wood's collection was bought in 1852 by the South Kensington (now Victoria and Albert) Museum; and another part, acquired by the Jermyn Street Museum (Museum of Practical Geology) was transferred to the Victoria and Albert Museum in 1901. Other pieces have been acquired by the Museums of Stoke-on-Trent and Edinburgh. An important part of the collection (182 pieces), however, was a personal gift from Enoch Wood to the King of Saxony in 1835.

Wood, Ralph

There were three generations of Staffordshire potters with this name. The elder Ralph Wood (1715-1772) made wares similar to those being made generally in Staffordshire at the time, but became noted for well-modelled figures and Toby jugs

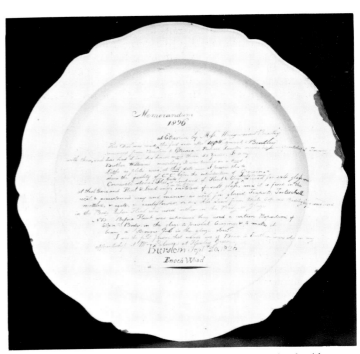

Wood, Enoch. *Creamware dish of Royal shape, painted with an inscription signed and dated by Enoch Wood, 'September 26, 1826'. Part of the inscription reads: 'This dish was made at Etruria by Messrs Wedgwood & Bentley the first year after Messrs Wedgwood & Bentley removed from Burslem to Etruria — Richard Lawton served his apprenticeship at Turning with them and has had it in his house more than 50 years. It is my brother William's modeling' [sic]. Wedgwood.*

decorated with coloured glazes. His son (1748-1795) decorated his figures with enamel colours, and made some figures in a black basaltes body. Voyez* is reputed to have worked for him. Falknor (*The Wood Family of Burslem*) cites evidence purporting to prove that Wood supplied Wedgwood with glazed and painted figures* bearing the Wedgwood mark. One of these, a bust entitled *Sadness,* certainly appears to be the work of Enoch Wood*, Ralph's cousin, with whom he was in partnership from 1783, and all the models so far discovered are fairly typical of the Wood family's work.

Wood, William (1746-1829)

Brother to Enoch Wood*; apprenticed to Wedgwood in 1762. In a letter of the 31st December 1767 to Bentley, Wedgwood wrote: "I have just taken a Boy apprentice for seven years to Model and am beginning to teach him to Draw; he has served three years to handling &c., has good fingers, and is a pretty active well-behaved Lad. We shall want many of this branch to work festoons upon Vases, free, without moulds, which Boys may be taught to do at moderate expence..." The 'Lad' was William Wood, who later assisted Flaxman*, Webber* and Josiah Wedgwood to produce the Portland* vase, and became chief modeller of useful wares*. Many of the fine shapes of the period were undoubtedly from his hand, but no record of them appears to have been preserved. His father, Aaron, worked for Whieldon* during the period of his partnership with Josiah I*. William Wood remained in the service of the Wedgwoods until his death at the age of eighty-three.

Woolner, Thomas, RA (1825-1892)

Poet, painter, sculptor of portrait busts, and one of the original pre-Raphaelites. He modelled the portrait medallion* of Sir William Hooker*, 10ins. in diameter, which forms part of the memorial to him in Kew Parish Church, designed by Sir Reginald Palgrave* for Sir Joseph Hooker*. He also modelled the portrait medallion of Sir Francis Palgrave (Sir Reginald's father) produced by Wedgwood in 1899.

Worcester Porcelain Factory
(Worcester Royal Porcelain Company)

This factory, established in 1751 by absorbing Lund's Bristol factory, was the largest and most productive maker of porcelain in England during the 18th century, using a body which contained soaprock instead of the Cornish stone employed in Champion's* porcelain. Among the founders at Worcester was Dr. John Wall. In 1783 the factory was bought by its London agent, Thomas Flight, for his sons, Joseph and John. In 1862 it was incorporated as the Worcester Royal Porcelain Company, and it is the oldest manufactory in England with unbroken continuity. Throughout this period it has continued to make porcelain, and has produced relatively little earthenware.

There are few references to the factory in Wedgwood's correspondence. It is evident that he knew about the part played by soaprock in their porcelain, but had probably acquired this knowledge from his Liverpool connections rather than from Worcester. Robert Willcox*, the painter, had been apprenticed at Liverpool, but came to Wedgwood from Worcester, together with his wife, Catherine Willcox* (née Frye), who became chief female painter of the Frog* service. From 1756 onwards transfer printing* by Robert Hancock* and others was extremely popular at Worcester, and the factory has some subjects in common with Sadler* & Green, for instance, *The Tea Party*. Mr. Tebo*, the Bow* repairer and modeller, also modelled figures for Worcester which usually bear his mark, and from there he entered the employment of Wedgwood.

Worcester Style

Bone china* ornamental pieces, the exterior covered with an ivory ground and decorated in enamel and gilding in imitation of the Worcester Porcelain Company's* popular ivory porcelain. Designs were varied and included birds, leaves, and traditional flower and swag patterns. Vases of the same shapes as 18th century basaltes* and jasper* models were sometimes used with heavy raised gilding, and these are often mistaken for Victoria* ware. Victoria ware vases were not made in bone china and are not marked with the Portland vase outline mark. Worcester style bone china was introduced c.1880.

Wright & Mansfield

London cabinet-makers, fl.1860-80. They were represented in the London International Exhibition of 1862, and in 1867 exhibited a satinwood cabinet ornamented with marquetry, ormolu mounts, and Wedgwood plaques at the Paris Exposition of that year. This was acquired by the Victoria and Albert Museum. Their copies of Adam satinwood furniture in particular have often been mistaken for 18th century work, but they also did fairly close copies of other 18th century types, including Chippendale.

Wright, Joseph, of Derby (1734-1797)

Also known as the 'Candlelight Painter' from his frequent choice of subject, Wright spent most of his life in his native Derby. He paid a visit to Italy in 1773-75, and in consequence painted the illumination of Vesuvius in eruption. Wright was not a member of the Lunar Society*, but many of his paintings, such as the well-known 'Experiment with an Air-pump' (Tate Gallery) of 1768, relate to the varied interests of some of its members and he painted portraits of several of them. Wright, of whom it has been said that he was the first painter to express the spirit of the Industrial Revolution, was specially interested in problems of light. He was elected to the Royal Academy in 1782, but later resigned. In April 1784, Wedgwood wrote to his friend, Joseph Wright, about his painting, 'The Corinthian Maid', in terms of excessive delicacy: "I could not speak with you when I was with the ladies at your house about the particular sort of drapery of the Corinthian Maid I liked the least, but finding afterwards that some of the ladies had seen that part of the drapery in the same light with myself, and not being able to wait upon you again, I begged Dr Darwin to mention it to you. The objections were the divisions of the posteriors appearing too plain through the drapery and its sticking so close, the truly Grecian, as you justly observe, gave that part a heavy hanging-like (if I may use a new term) appearance, as if it wanted a little shove up.'' Wedgwood later paid 100 guineas for the 'Maid' and also

Worcester Style. *Ewer in the so-called Worcester Style, the decoration on an ivory ground exhibiting pronounced Japanese influence. c.1890. Buten Museum.*

395

purchased 'Penelope unravelling her Web' and 'The Lady in Comus' in 1785. Wright's self-portrait, bought in 1784, has disappeared.

Wright painted a portrait of Bentley* in 1780, but this is not the portrait in the Wedgwood Museum Gallery. Nor is the portrait of Richard Arkwright, said to have been in Wedgwood's possession and later presented to the Manchester Royal Exchange, an original painting by Wright.

The Wedgwood portrait medallion of Erasmus Darwin* (1780) was copied from Wright's painting of 1770.

Wright of Derby has occasionally been confused with Patience Lovell Wright's* son, Joseph, of whom he was no connection.

Wright, Mrs. Patience Lovell (1725-1786)

Painter and modeller in wax, born in Bordentown, New Jersey. She came to London in 1772, and was described in the *London Magazine* of December 1775, as having been "reserved by the hand of nature to produce a new style of picturing superior to statuary and peculiar to herself and the honour of America, for her compositions, in likeness to the originals, surpass paint or any other method of delineation; they live with such a perfect animation, that we are more surprised than charmed, for we see art perfect as nature." Her wax portrait of Benjamin Franklin was reproduced by Wedgwood in jasper* and basaltes c.1775, and an engraving of George Washington by her son, Joseph (not to be confused with the painter, Joseph Wright of Derby*), was copied for a portrait medallion* in 1789.

Wynn, Sir Watkin Williams, 4th Baronet (1748-1789)

Member of parliament for Salop, 1772-74. The rich and youthful head of a respected Welsh family, Sir Watkin was an enthusiastic and generous patron of Wedgwood's. No less than 245 of the cameos and intaglios listed in Wedgwood's first catalogue are believed to have been copied from originals in Sir Watkin's collection, and he presented Josiah with a copy of Hamilton's and d'Hancarville's *Antiquités Etrusques*. The Wedgwood archives bear witness to the quantity and variety of Sir Watkin's purchases, which included tiles* for his dairy in 1783, but from the connoisseur's point of view the most important is the encaustic* painted tablet* made for the chimney piece* at 20, St. James's Square. This tablet, in black basaltes*, is painted and shaded in natural colours after a design in gouache by Zucchi*. Although there is evidence in the 1777 Catalogue that Wedgwood produced "many large Tablets, in a great Variety of Colours," no other example of multi-coloured encaustic painting appears to have survived.

Wyon, Edward William (1811-1885)

Sculptor; student at the Royal Academy Schools, 1829; exhibited at the Royal Academy 1831-76, showing nearly one hundred busts, medallions and wax portraits. At the Great Exhibition of 1851 he showed 'A Tazza Modelled from a Greek Design for the Art Union of London', and in the following year he made a bust of the Duke of Wellington for reproduction by Wedgwood. This began an association with the firm which appears to have lasted until at least 1859.

The list of Wyon's work reproduced by Wedgwood in black basaltes* or Carrara* includes the following:

Nubian Water Carrier.
Hope.
Oberon.
Titania.
Lord Byron, bust.
Thomas Moore, bust.
Sir Walter Scott, bust.
Robert Burns, bust.
John Milton, bust.
John Bunyan, bust.
The Duke of Wellington, bust.
General Sir Colin Campbell, bust.
General Sir Henry Havelock, bust.
George Stephenson, bust.
Robert Stephenson, bust.
James Watt, bust.
Lord Palmerston, bust.

Wyon, E.W. *Carrara bust of Robert Stephenson after a model by E.W. Wyon, 1856. Sotheby's Belgravia.*

Y

Yellow (Glazed) Ware
Creamware* or pearl ware* dipped in a yellow glaze. It is often, misleadingly, described as 'canary yellow' or 'canary lustre'. The colour varies considerably, and the decoration might be lustre*, transfer printed*, stencilled, enamelled, or sprigged*, or a combination of processes. Yellow wares were made in England and Wales c.1780-1835, and similar ware was produced for a short period at Creil*, France. Some examples of Yellow ware bear an impressed 'WEDGWOOD' mark, but no documentary evidence has been found to support the assumption that this ware was ever produced at Etruria*, and some of the shapes concerned bear little, if any, resemblance to Wedgwood shapes. A likely explanation is that they were made at the Woodlands Pottery operated by John Wedg Wood* at Tunstall.

Yi Hsing Stoneware
Chinese red stoneware which first arrived in Europe in the 17th century in the form of small spouted wine pots used for making the new drink of tea. These pots were extremely popular and much sought. They were imitated by Böttger at Meissen*, by Arij de Milde in Holland, by John Dwight* in London, and by the Elers* brothers in Staffordshire. The latter made the red ware from which Wedgwood developed his *rosso antico*.

Z

Zaffre
Or Zaffer. The word is of Arabic origin, and was in use during the 18th century. Zaffer was made by fusing cobalt oxide with sand, and it was the colouring agent employed in the manufacture of smalt*.

Zeno (335-263B.C.)
Founder of the Stoic philosophy, born in Cyprus. He began to study the Socratic philosophers comparatively early in life, and about the age of thirty he was shipwrecked in the neighbourhood of the Piraeus. After this experience he decided to stay on dry land and to study philosophy under the Cynic, Crates, and at the Academy. After many years of study he opened his own school, and his followers were called Stoics after the Stoa Poicile where it was situated.

Wedgwood subject:
Zeno, bust, 25ins. high, from a cast supplied by Hoskins & Grant*, 1774, and refinished by Hackwood*.
Zeno, large framed oval plaque, 10½ins. by 7¾ins., produced in black basaltes, c.1772.

Zeus
See: Jupiter.

Zingara
A bust with this title was supplied by Richard Parker* in 1774, and Hoskins & Grant* provided a figure in 1779. According to Eliza Meteyard*, Zingara was the heroine of a burletta produced at Marylebone Gardens in April, 1773. *Zingara* means gipsy girl, and may, in fact, have been the name of the piece, rather than that of an actress. The bust and the figure are both exceedingly rare, and it is very doubtful whether either was intended as a portrait. The subject seems to have been popular, and either the first stage production must have taken place several years before the one recorded above, or the figure is of classical origin and has no connection with the burletta, since John Flaxman Senior* made a bust with this title for James West of Alcot Park in 1767. A white marble copy of the bust was also made by Canova*.
See: Peter Scheemakers.

Zinkeisen, Anna (1901-1978)
Painter; studied at the Royal Academy Schools, where she won Bronze and Silver Medals. Exhibited at the Royal Academy. She modelled for Wedgwood in 1924 the plaques *Adam, Eve,* and *Sun and Night,* which were reproduced in blue and white jasper. These plaques, which are of excellent quality and satisfying design, are surprisingly rare. The first two have been reproduced for the Wedgwood Collectors' Society*.

Zinkeisen, Anna. Eve. *Original model on slate.* Wedgwood.

Zinkeisen, Anna. Adam *plaque by Anna Zinkeisen, 1924. Blue and white jasper.* Wedgwood.

Zodiac, Signs of the

The word is derived from the Greek *zodion,* meaning the sculptured figure of an animal, and seven out of the twelve divisions of the heavens are represented by animals of one kind or another. Wedgwood was originally supplied with the Signs of the Zodiac by Mrs. Mary Landré* in 1774. They were modelled by Hackwood*. They were used as a frieze on some fine black basaltes vases of the Wedgwood & Bentley period, and were then reduced in size for use as cameo borders, and for jasper pieces generally. In recent times they have been reproduced as separate figures for setting in cuff links and brooches. A rare, but not inappropriate, 18th century use for a circular cameo decorated with the Signs of the Zodiac was to mount it in brass as a clock pendulum. Other examples of the use of this motif include Arnold Machin's* *Taurus the Bull* of 1945 which is decorated with Zodiac symbols designed by Eric Ravilious*.

Zucchi, Antonio (1726-1795)

Painter and engraver; son of the painter Francesco Zucchi, and pupil of his uncle, the theatrical designer, Carlo Zucchi. With the brothers Adam* he travelled through Italy designing classical monuments and ruins*. Later he came to live in London, where he exhibited for fourteen years, being elected an Associate of the Royal Academy in 1770. He designed and painted the decorations of several great houses, notably the ceiling at Osterley Park. He was regularly employed by Adam, and was responsible for the original *gouache* designs for the 'encaustic' painted tablets* produced by Wedgwood for Sir Watkin Williams Wynn's* house at 20, St. James's Square.

In 1781 he married Angelica Kauffmann* and returned to Rome where he remained for the last years of his life.

Zodiac, Signs of the. *Three-colour jasper cameo, 1½ ins. diameter, ornamented with a central relief of a sacrifice subject and an outer border of the signs of the Zodiac, c.1790.* Wedgwood.

— Adieu

ever most affec^{ty} Jr your

Jos: Wedgwood

Appendix I

Wedgwood Chronology

1719-24	Publication of Bernard de Montfaucon's *Antiquité Expliquée.*
1730	Birth of Josiah Wedgwood. Birth of Thomas Bentley.
1734	Birth of Sarah Wedgwood.
1738	Discovery of Herculaneum.
1739-44	Josiah apprenticed to his brother, Thomas Wedgwood.
1747-1810	Thomas Byerley (Partner 1790-1810).
1748	Discovery of Pompeii.
1752-54	Josiah in partnership with John Harrison.
1754-59	Whieldon-Wedgwood partnership.
1756-70	Publication of Comte de Caylus's *Recueil d'Antiquités.*
1759-64	Ivy House Works: Wedgwood production including creamware, variegated wares, green glaze, fruit and vegetable shapes (cauliflower, apple, melon, pear, pineapple).
1759-95	Period of wares generally described in the past as 'Old Wedgwood.'
1761	Creamware tablewares introduced.
1761-99	Sadler & Green transfer-printed Wedgwood creamware.
1762	Josiah's first meeting with Bentley.
1762-1829	William Wood employed.
1763	Introduction of engine-turning lathe.
1763-81	Boulton & Fothergill partnership.
1764	Marriage of Josiah and Sarah Wedgwood.
1764-70	William Greatbatch supplying Wedgwood.
1764-73	Brick House (Bell) Works, Burslem.
1765	Queen's ware named. *Rosso antico* body introduced.
1766-67	Publication of Hamilton and d'Hancarville's *Antiquités Etrusques, Grecques et Romaines.*
1766-88	Thomas Wedgwood (cousin) in partnership with Josiah in production of 'useful wares.'
1768	Black basaltes introduced.
1768-69	Voyez employed.
1768-74	Newport Street, London Showrooms.
1768-77	David Rhodes employed in London.
1769	Etruria Works opened. First Day's Vases produced.
1769-74	Mrs. Landré supplying casts.
1769-74/5	Chelsea Decorating Studios.
1769-80	Wedgwood & Bentley partnership.
1769-1832	William Hackwood employed.
1770	First production of busts. Cane ware introduced. Shell edge shape introduced. Husk service for Catherine II of Russia.
1770-79	Hoskins & Grant supplying casts and models.
1771	First portrait medallions produced.
1772	Joachim Smith supplying portrait medallions. Herculaneum subjects produced.
1773	First Ornamental Ware Catalogue.
1774	First Creamware ('Useful ware') Catalogue. Frog service for Catherine II of Russia. Black basaltes with applied ornament introduced. George Stubbs working at Etruria. Goethe's *Sorrows of Werther* published.
1774-95	Greek Street, London Showrooms.
1775	Jasper perfected and introduced. John Flaxman's first work for Wedgwood.
1777	Jasper dip introduced. Homeric Vase produced.
1778	*Dancing Hours* modelled.
1779	Mortar ware introduced. Pearl ware introduced. Series of large portrait medallions (10½ ins. high) produced.
1780	Death of Thomas Bentley. End of Wedgwood & Bentley partnership.
1781	Auction sale of Wedgwood & Bentley partnership stock. Introduction of jasper vases.
1783-89	Lady Templetown supplying designs.
1784	Chessmen designed by Flaxman.
1784-c.1815	Aaron Steele employed.
1785-89	Lady Diana Beauclerk supplying designs.
1785-1806	Henry Webber employed.
1786	French Commercial Treaty medallions. Three-colour jasper introduced.
1787	Slave medallion produced. Lochée's portraits of the royal princes produced.
1787-95	Wedgwood's studio of modellers in Rome.
1787-1818	Miss Emma Crewe supplying designs.
1789	*Rosso antico* with black applied ornaments introduced.
1789-90	French Revolution medallions.
1790	John Wedgwood and Josiah II into partnership with Josiah. Portland Vase produced. German cameos produced.
1793	John Wedgwood withdraws from partnership.
1795	Death of Josiah I.
1795-1829	York Street, London Showrooms.
1796	Pastry ware introduced.
1798	John De Vaere's portrait medallions of British admirals produced.

1800	John Wedgwood returns to partnership. Drab ware introduced.
c.1800	*Britannia Triumphant* produced.
1805	Underglaze blue printing introduced. Celadon coloured body introduced. 'Josiah Wedgwood Feb 2nd 1805' mark. Egyptian 'hieroglyphic' relief ornament introduced.
1806	Lustre introduced.
1808	*Water Lily* pattern introduced.
1811-23	Josiah II sole proprietor.
1812	First printed mark.
1812-22	Bone china, first period.
1815	*Napoleon Ivy* pattern introduced. Smear glaze introduced.
1820-61	Stone china produced.
1823	Josiah III in partnership with Josiah II.
1827-41	Francis Wedgwood into partnership with Josiah II and Josiah III.
1828	Clearance sale of trial pieces and moulds.
1842-43	Francis Wedgwood sole proprietor.
1842-83	Registry marks used (not on all wares).
1843-45	John Boyle in partnership with Francis.
1845	Francis sole proprietor.
1846-59	Robert Brown in partnership with Francis.
1848-49	Carrara (Parian) ware introduced. Produced until 1880.
1850	Lavender coloured body introduced.
1858-71	Hugues Protât designing for Wedgwood.
1858-75	Emile Lessore decorating wares for Wedgwood at Etruria (some later work decorated in France).
1859	Godfrey Wedgwood in partnership with Francis.
1859-85	Inlaid ware produced.
1860	Majolica introduced. Three-letter impressed mark (dating code) introduced for earthenwares and (occasionally) for stonewares.
1863	Clement Francis Wedgwood in partnership with Francis and Godfrey.
1865	Rockingham glaze introduced.
1867-88	Walter Crane designing for Wedgwood.
1868	Lawrence Wedgwood in partnership with Francis, Godfrey and Clement Francis.
1871	Letter prefixes introduced for the designation of pattern numbers by type of body and decoration.
1875-85	Turquoise jasper produced.
1875-90	Holborn Circus, London Showrooms.
1875-1900	Victoria Ware produced.
1875-1902	Tiles produced.
1877	Northwood copies of Portland Vase.
1877-c.87	F. Rhead designing for Wedgwood.
1878	Bone china reintroduced. Portland Vase printed mark introduced for bone china. Satsuma shape introduced.
1879-1929	Calendar tiles.
1879-1953	Commemorative ware for Jones, McDuffee & Stratton.
1880-1900	Thomas Allen, Art Director. Worcester style produced.
1880-1910	Basaltes, bronzed and gilt produced. Bronze basaltes produced.
1885	White jasper with up to three colour ornament introduced. Horizontal acanthus relief ornament applied to plinths.
1890-1927	108 Hatton Garden, London Showrooms.
1891	'England' mark introduced.
1891-95	Lawrence Wedgwood in partnership with nephews Cecil and Francis Hamilton.
1895	Incorporation of firm as Josiah Wedgwood & Sons Ltd.
1898	'Made in England' mark introduced.
1900-20	Lithophane-type intaglio china produced.
1902-34	John E. Goodwin, Art Director.
1903	White House Service for Theodore Roosevelt.
1905-42	Alfred and Louise Powell working for Wedgwood.
1906	Wedgwood Museum, Etruria opened.
1908	Edme shape introduced.
1909-31	Daisy Makeig-Jones designing at Etruria.
1910-28	Crimson jasper, and dark olive-green jasper introduced.
1912	Powder blue decoration introduced.
1914	Ordinary Lustre wares introduced.
1915	Fairyland Lustre wares introduced.
1919	Josiah Wedgwood & Sons Inc., New York, founded.
1924	Anna Zinkeisen designs produced. Dysart glaze introduced.
1923-30	Barnard edition of Portland Vase.
1925	Cameograph Company portrait medallions issued.
1926	Patrician shape introduced.
1927	John Skeaping animal figures introduced.
1927-41	24-27 Hatton Garden, London Showrooms.
1927-63	Norman Wilson with Wedgwood (Works Manager, Production Director, Managing Director).
1929	Wedgwood sans serif mark introduced.
1929-33	Yellow-buff jasper with black relief ornament produced.
1930	Champagne coloured body introduced. Commemorative pieces to celebrate bicentenary of birth of Josiah I. Veronese glazes introduced.
1930-64	Josiah V, Managing Director (Chairman 1947-67).
1932-39	Norman Wilson Unique Ware produced.
1932-40	Keith Murray designing for Wedgwood.
1933	Coloured matt glazes introduced.
1934-66	Victor Skellern, Art Director.
1935	Corinthian shape introduced.
1936	Two-colour slip ware introduced. Alpine pink bone china introduced.
1937-39	Eric Ravilious designing for Wedgwood.
1939	Arnold Machin's first designs for Wedgwood.
1940	Barlaston factory started production.
1942	*Whitehall* pattern introduced.
1944	Underglaze lithograph decoration introduced.
1948	23 Wigmore Street, London Showrooms. Canadian company formed.
1949	Pale blue jasper reintroduced.
1952-55	Richard Guyatt as Consultant Designer (also 1967-70).

1953	Royal blue jasper introduced to celebrate the Coronation of Queen Elizabeth II.
1954	Norman Wilson Unique Ware re-introduced.
1955	Barlaston shape designed and introduced. Australian company formed.
1955-56	Laurence Whistler designs.
1957	Sage-green jasper reintroduced.
1957-59	Terracotta jasper with black or white relief ornament produced.
1960	Wedgwood Group formed. Gold silk-screen printing introduced.
1960-62	Lilac jasper reintroduced.
1963	Arthur Bryan appointed Managing Director. *Design '63* range introduced.
1967	Arthur Bryan appointed Chairman in succession to Josiah V. Oven-to-table ware introduced. Wedgwood registration as a public company: shares quoted on the Stock Exchange.
1968	Death of Josiah V.
1969	New Wedgwood Museum opened at Barlaston.
1971	Short reintroduction of terracotta jasper with black relief ornament.
1973	Portland blue jasper introduced. Three-colour jasper vases reintroduced.
1976	Primrose jasper with white or terracotta relief ornament introduced. American Bicentennial Editions produced.
1978	Egyptian Collection produced.
1979	Robert Minkin, Art Director. Acquisition of Wedgwood's first American factory by purchase of Franciscan, USA.
1980	250th Anniversary of Josiah I's birth, and 200th anniversary of the end of the Wedgwood & Bentley partnership (and Bentley's death).

Appendix II

Wedgwood Trade Marks

1. wedgwood / WEDCWOOD — Impressed: the letters being stamped individually and sometimes in a curve. The first marks, irregularly used c.1759-69. Much of the Wedgwood of this period was unmarked.

2. WEDGWOOD — Impressed, in varying sizes, on useful wares from 1769-80, and on all wares from 1780 onwards unless otherwise stated below.

3. WEDGWOOD & BENTLEY (circular) — Impressed. The earliest form of the Wedgwood & Bentley mark. Ornamental wares only, c.1769.

4. WEDGWOOD & BENTLEY : ETRURIA (circular) — Impressed or raised, sometimes lacking the word ETRURIA, this mark appears on the inside corner of plinths of early basaltes vases, and sometimes on the pedestals of busts and large figures, 1769-80.

5. WEDGWOOD & BENTLEY : ETRURIA (circular stamp) — Circular stamp, with an inner and outer line, always placed round the screw of basaltes, granite and Etruscan vases, 1769-80. Never on jasper vases, but sometimes found on white jasper plinths of granite vases.

6. Wedgwood & Bentley (script) — Extremely rare script mark, 1769-80, ornamental wares only.

7. Wedgwood & Bentley 356 — Impressed on very small cameos and intaglios, 1769-80, with the Catalogue number.

8. W. & B. — Impressed. Used on very small cameos and intaglios with the Catalogue number. Sometimes the Catalogue number only was used.

9. Wedgwood & Bentley (oval) — Rare oval impressed mark found only on chocolate and white seal intaglios, usually portraits made of two layers of jasper with polished edges.

10. WEDGWOOD & BENTLEY / WEDGWOOD & BENTLEY ETRURIA — Impressed mark on plaques, tablets, medallions and other ornamental wares. The addition of ETRURIA is uncommon.

| 11 | Wedgwood. | Impressed mark, varying in size, used for all types of ware from 1780 until c.1795. Known as the 'upper and lower case' mark (or simply 'lower case'). |

| 12 | WEDGWOOD & SONS | Impressed mark, c.1790. Very rare. |

| 13 | JOSIAH WEDGWOOD
Feb. 2nd 1805 | Rare mark found on some lustre wares, and basaltes and jasper pieces, usually tripods. |

| 14 | WEDGWOOD | Printed on bone china c.1812-22, in red, blue or gold. |

| 15 | WEDGWOOD'S
STONE CHINA | Printed on stone china, 1820-61. |

| 16 | WEDGWOOD
ETRURIA | Impressed mark in various sizes, c.1840-45. |

| 17 | PEARL
P | Impressed 'PEARL' on pearl body c.1840-68; initial 'P' only thereafter. |

18 JBS

Impressed three-letter marks were used to date earthenwares from 1860-1906. The first letter indicated the month, the second the potter, and the third the year. As may be seen from the table below, the third letter may indicate two possible dates for the years 1860-64 and 1886-90. After 1891 the word ENGLAND was added. The words MADE IN ENGLAND appear from c.1898 but were not in general use until about 1908 (see trade marks 21 and 24). The example shown, JBS, indicates a date of January 1864 or 1890.

Code (first) letters for months:

January	J			July	V	(1860-63)
February	F				L	(1864-1907)
March	M	(1860-63)		August	W	
	R	(1864-1907)		September	S	
April	A			October	O	
May	Y	(1860-63)		November	N	
	M	(1864-1907)		December	D	
June	T					

Code (third) letters for years:

A		1872	1898
B		1873	1899
C		1874	1900
D		1875	1901
E		1876	1902
F		1877	1903
G		1878	1904
H		1879	1905
I		1880	1906
J		1881	
K		1882	
L		1883	
M		1884	
N		1885	
O	1860	1886	
P	1861	1887	
Q	1862	1888	
R	1863	1889	
S	1864	1890	
T	1865	1891	
U	1866	1892	
V	1867	1893	
W	1868	1894	
X	1869	1895	
Y	1870	1896	
Z	1871	1897	

| 19 | 3BS | From 1907 the figure 3 was substituted for the first (month) letter. From 1924 the figure |
| | 4BD | 4 was used. The last letter continued to indicate the year as shown below: |

J (3)	1907
K	1908
L	1909
M	1910
N	1911
O	1912
P	1913
Q	1914
R	1915
S	1916
T	1917
U	1918
V	1919
W	1920
X	1921
Y	1922
Z	1923
A (4)	1924
B	1925
C	1926
D	1927
E	1928
F	1929

From 1930 the actual date was impressed, at first as the last two figures of a mark including the month numbered in sequence and a potter's mark (e.g. 3B35 = March 1935) and later simply as two figures (e.g. 57 = 1957).

Workmen's errors occur in the numbers and letters of marks 18 and 19, and the letters are not always legible.

20   *E. Lessore*   Signature of Emile Lessore c.1858-76.

21   ENGLAND   Impressed or printed from 1891 to conform with Mckinley Tariff Act. 'Made in England' added from c.1898, but not invariably used until c.1908.

22    WEDGWOOD   Printed on bone china (and occasionally, and probably in error, on Queen's ware) from 1878. 'England' added below from 1891. Some bone china bears the standard Wedgwood impressed mark.

23    WEDGWOOD ETRURIA. ENGLAND   Rarely found impressed on Queen's ware c.1891-1900.

24   MADE IN ENGLAND   Impressed or printed with standard WEDGWOOD mark from c.1898, but not in general use until c.1908.

25    WEDGWOOD   Printed on bone china from c.1900 with ENGLAND or MADE IN ENGLAND added below.

26    WEDGWOOD BONE CHINA MADE IN ENGLAND   Printed on bone china from c.1902 (BONE CHINA added).

27	a. Painted monogram of Alfred Powell.	b. Painted monogram of Louise Powell.

28   **WEDGWOOD**   Sans serif type impressed from 1929. The old type continued to be used for a short time after this date, but no sans serif marks were used before 1929.

29  Rejafix machine-printed mark used on bone china from c.1950-62.

30 Improved bone china mark introduced in 1962.

31 Queen's ware printed mark from c.1940.

32   **BARLASTON**   Address of the firm added to standard marks from 1940.

33   **N W** or **NORMAN WILSON**   Impressed or painted on Norman Wilson Unique Ware, added to standard mark for the period.

34   **ENGRAVED BY WEDGWOOD STUDIO**   Printed on engraved patterns from 1952.

35   **WEDGWOOD ETRURIA BARLASTON**   Extremely rare mark impressed on basaltes vases, replicas of those laid in the foundations of the factory at Barlaston in September 1938.

Appendix III

Registry Marks

Introduced in 1842 to protect designs from being pirated by other manufacturers, registry marks were widely used throughout England, but seldom on Wedgwood wares. The marks were printed or impressed.

1842-67

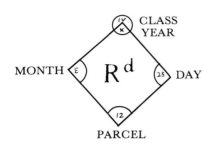

1842 X	1855 E
1843 H	1856 L
1844 C	1857 K
1845 A	1858 B
1846 I	1859 M
1847 F	1860 Z
1848 U	1861 R
1849 S	1862 O
1850 V	1863 G
1851 P	1864 N
1852 D	1865 W
1853 Y	1866 Q
1854 J	1867 T

1868-83

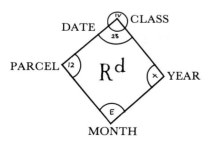

1868 X	1876 V
1869 H	1877 P
1870 C	1878 D
1871 A	1879 Y
1872 I	1880 J
1873 F	1881 E
1874 U	1882 L
1875 S	1883 K

Appendix IV

Pattern Number Prefixes

Pattern numbers prefixed by a code letter were introduced by Wedgwood in 1871. The prefixes were as follows:

A   Queen's ware, 1871-1932.
B   Queen's ware toilet-ware from 1872.
C   Queen's ware 'fancies' (ornamental pieces) from 1872.
F   Hand-painted designs from 1875-1927.
G   Queen's ware tableware gilt from 1875.
Z   Bone china 'fancies' (ornamental pieces) gilt from 1879.
W   Bone china tableware from 1879.
X   Bone china tableware from 1879-1915.
Y   Bone china teaware and coffeeware 1879-1921.
Q   Tiles from 1884-1902.
R   Marsden pattern tiles, 1888.
K   Majolica patterns, 1888.
O   Ornamental Majolica, 1888.
H   Hand-painted designs from 1928.
K   Underglaze decoration from 1928.
L   Underglaze print and onglaze enamel decoration from 1928.
M   Onglaze decoration from 1928.
P   Powder-blue patterns from 1929.
S   Bone china teaware patterns from 1931.
T   Queen's ware tableware patterns from 1932.
D   Bone china and Queen's ware lithograph decoration 1945-58.
N   Queen's ware lithograph decoration from 1958.
R   Bone china lithograph or silkscreen decoration.

(Example: TKD = Queen's ware underglaze lithograph)

Appendix V

The Wedgwoods of Etruria

I The Family of Josiah Wedgwood

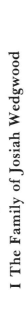
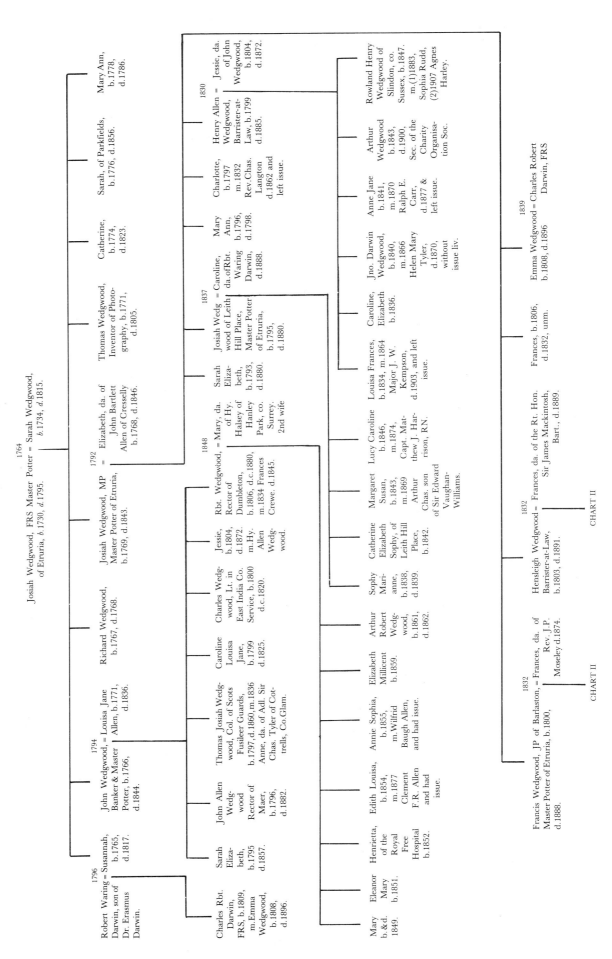

Josiah Wedgwood, FRS Master Potter = Sarah Wedgwood, of Etruria, *b.*1730, *d.*1795. | *b.*1734, *d.*1815.

1764

Mary Ann, b.1778, d.1786.

Sarah, of Parkfields, b.1776, d.1856.

Catherine, b.1774, d.1823.

Thomas Wedgwood, Inventor of Photography, b.1771, d.1805.

Josiah Wedgwood, MP Master Potter of Etruria, b.1769, d.1843.

1792 Elizabeth, da. of John Bartlett Allen of Cresselly b.1768, d.1846.

Richard Wedgwood, b.1767, d.1768.

John Wedgwood, = Louisa Jane Banker & Master Allen, b.1771, Potter, b.1766, d.1836. d.1844.

1794

Robert Waring = Susannah, Darwin, b.1765, son of d.1817. Dr. Erasmus Darwin.

1796

Henry Allen Wedgwood, Barrister-at-Law, b.1799 d.1885.

1830 Jessie, da. of John Wedgwood, b.1804, d.1872.

Charlotte, b.1797, m.1832 Rev.Chas. Langton d.1862 and left issue.

Mary Ann, b.1796, d.1798.

Caroline, da. of Rbt. Waring Darwin, d.1888.

1837

Josiah Wedgwood of Leith Hill Place, Master Potter of Etruria, b.1795, d.1880.

Sarah Elizabeth, b.1793, d.1880.

Rbt. Wedgwood, = Mary, da. of Hy. Rector of Halsey of Hanley Dumbleton, Park, co. b.1806, d.c.1880, Surrey. m.1834 Frances 2nd wife Crewe d.1845.

1848

Jessie, b.1804, d.1872. m.Hy. Allen Wedgwood.

Charles Wedgwood, Lt. in East India Co. Service, b.1800 d.c.1820.

Caroline Louisa Jane, b.1799 d.1825.

Thomas Josiah Wedgwood, Col. of Scots Fusileer Guards, b.1797, d.1860, m.1836 Anne, da. of Adl. Sir Chas. Tyler of Cottrells, Co. Glam.

John Allen Wedgwood Rector of Maer, b.1796, d.1882.

Sarah Elizabeth, b.1795, d.1857.

Charles Rbt. Darwin, FRS, b.1809, m.Emma Wedgwood, b.1808, d.1896.

Arthur Wedgwood b.1843, d.1900, Sec. of the Charity Organisation Soc.

Rowland Henry Wedgwood of Slindon, co. Sussex, b.1847. m.(1)1883, Sophia Rudd, (2)1907 Agnes Harley.

Anne Jane b.1841, m.1870 Ralph E. Carr, d.1877 & left issue.

Jno. Darwin Wedgwood, b.1840, m.1866 Helen Mary Tyler, d.1870, without issue liv.

Caroline, Elizabeth b.1836.

Louisa Frances, b.1834, m.1864 Major J. W. Kempson, d.1903, and left issue.

1839 Emma Wedgwood = Charles Robert Darwin, FRS b.1808, d.1896.

Frances, b.1806, d.1832, unm.

Lucy Caroline b.1846, m.1874, Capt. Matthew J. Harrison, R.N.

Margaret Susan, b.1843, m.1869 Arthur Chas. son of Sir Edward Vaughan-Williams.

Catherine Elizabeth Sophy, of Leith Hill Place, b.1842.

1832 Frances, da. of the Rt. Hon. Sir James Mackintosh, Bart., d.1889.

Hensleigh Wedgwood = Barrister-at-Law, b.1803, d.1891.

CHART II

Sophy Marianne, b.1838, d.1839.

Arthur Robert Wedgwood, b.1861, d.1862.

Elizabeth Millicent b.1859.

Annie Sophia, b.1855, m.Wilfrid Baugh Allen, and had issue.

Edith Louisa, b.1854, m.1877 Clement F.R. Allen and had issue.

Henrietta, of the Royal Free Hospital b.1852.

Eleanor Mary b.1851.

Mary b.&d. 1849.

1832 Frances, da. of Rev. J.P. Moseley d.1874.

Francis Wedgwood, JP of Barlaston, = Master Potter of Etruria, b.1800, d.1888.

CHART II

II The Families of Francis and Hensleigh Wedgwood

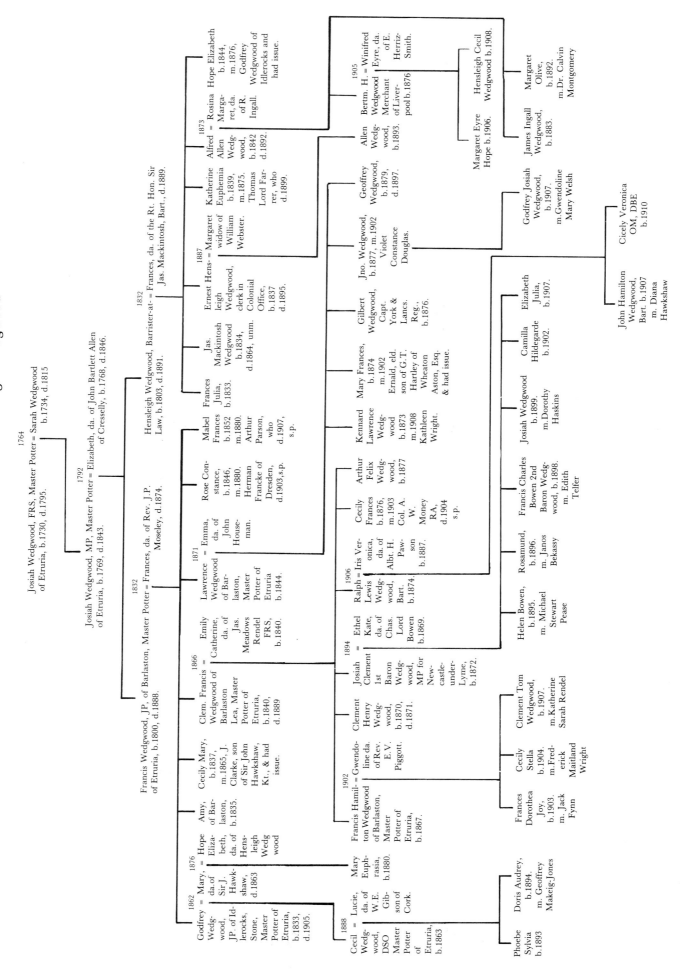

Josiah Wedgwood, FRS, Master Potter = Sarah Wedgwood
of Erruria, b.1730, d.1795.   b.1734, d.1815

1764

Josiah Wedgwood, MP, Master Potter = Elizabeth, da. of John Bartlett Allen
of Erruria, b.1769, d.1843.   of Cresselly, b.1768, d.1846.

1792

Francis Wedgwood, JP, of Barlaston, Master Potter = Frances, da. of Rev. J.P.
of Erruria, b.1800, d.1888.   Moseley, d.1874.

Hensleigh Wedgwood, Barrister-at-law = Frances, da. of the Rt. Hon. Sir
Law, b.1803, d.1891.   Jas. Mackintosh, Bart., d.1889.

1832

Bibliography

MANUSCRIPT MATERIAL

Letters, invoices, memoranda, shape and pattern books, and oven books in the Wedgwood Archives at Barlaston and Keele University.

PUBLISHED BOOKS AND SPECIALIST MAGAZINES

American Wedgwoodian.

Barnard, Harry, *Artes Etruriae renascuntur,* London 1920; *Chats on Wedgwood Ware,* London 1924.

Bartoli, Pietro Santi, F. Bartoli, G.P. Bellori, and M. de la Chausse, *Picturae Antiquae, Cryptarum Romanarum, et Sepulcri Nasonum,* 3 parts, Rome 1750.

Bénézit, E., *Dictionnaire des Peintres, Sculpteurs, Dessinateurs et Graveurs,* 8 vols., Paris 1960.

Bentley, Richard, *Thomas Bentley,* London 1927.

Boardman, James, *Bentleyana,* Liverpool 1851.

Bubovna, E., *Old Russian Faience, "Iskusstvo",* Moscow, 1973.

Burton, William, *History and Description of English Earthenware and Stoneware,* London 1904; *Josiah Wedgwood and His Pottery,* London 1922.

Buten, Harry M., *Wedgwood ABC but not middle E,* Buten Museum 1964; *Wedgwood Counterpoint,* Buten Museum 1962; *Wedgwood and Artists,* Buten Museum 1960; *Wedgwood Rarities,* Buten Museum 1968.

Caylus, Anne-Claude-Philippe, Comte de, *Recueil d'Antiquités Egyptiennes, Etrusques, Grecques et Romaines,* 8 vols., Paris 1756-70.

Church, Sir Arthur H., *English Earthenware,* London 1884; *Josiah Wedgwood, Master Potter,* London 1894.

Constable, W.G., *John Flaxman,* London 1927.

Delieb, Eric, and M. Roberts, *The Great Silver Manufactory. Matthew Boulton and the Birmingham Silversmiths, 1760-90,* London 1971.

Des Fontaines, Una, *Wedgwood Fairyland Lustre,* London and New York 1975.

Dictionary of National Biography.

Encyclopédie Photographique de l'Art. La Musée du Louvre, vol.III, Paris 1938.

Erskine, B.C., *Lady Diana Beauclerk,* London 1903.

Falkner, Frank, *The Wood Family of Burslem,* London 1912.

Farrer, Lady K.E., *Letters of Josiah Wedgwood,* 3 vols., London 1902-6.

Godden, Geoffrey, *British Pottery,* London 1974; *British Pottery and Porcelain, 1780-1850,* London 1964; *Encyclopedia of British Pottery and Porcelain Marks,* London 1964; *Jewitt's Ceramic Art of Great Britain* (revised and ed.), London 1972; *Minton Pottery and Porcelain of the First Period, 1793-1850,* London 1968.

Gorely, Jean, *Wedgwood,* New York 1950.

Grant, M.H., *The Makers of Black Basaltes,* London 1910.

Gray, J.M., *James and William Tassie,* Edinburgh 1894.

Gunnis, R., *Dictionary of British Sculptors 1650-1851,* London 1953.

Hamilton, Sir William, *Collection of Engravings from Ancient Vases of Greek Workmanship,* 3 vols., Naples 1791-95.

Hamilton, Sir William and d'Hancarville, P.H., *Antiquités Etrusques, Grecques et Romaines,* 4 vols., Naples 1766-67.

Hardie, Martin, *Watercolour Painting in Britain,* 3 vols., London 1966-69.

Haynes, D.E.L., *The Portland Vase,* London 1964.

Hillier, Bevis, *Master Potters of the Industrial Revolution. The Turners of Lane End,* London 1965; *Pottery and Porcelain 1700-1914,* London 1968.

Hobson, R.L., *Catalogue of English Pottery in the British Museum,* London 1903.

Honey, W.B., *English Pottery and Porcelain,* London 1933; *European Ceramic Art,* 2 vols., London 1949-52; *The Art of the Potter,* London 1946; *Wedgwood Ware,* London 1948.

Honour, Hugh, *Neo-Classicism,* London 1968.

Hughes, G.B., *Victorian Pottery and Porcelain,* London 1959.

Jewitt, Llewellyn F.W., *The Ceramic Art of Great Britain,* London 1878; *The Wedgwoods,* London 1865.

John, W.D. and Baker, W., *Old English Lustre Pottery,* Newport, Monmouth 1951.

John, W.D., and Simcox, Jacqueline, *Early Wedgwood Lustre Wares,* Newport, Monmouth 1963.

Jonas, Maurice, *Notes of an Art Collector,* 2nd (enlarged) edition, London 1907.

Jouveaux, Emile, *Histoire de trois potiers célèbres: B. Palissy, J. Wedgwood, F. Böttger,* Paris 1874.

Kelly, Alison, *Decorative Wedgwood,* London 1965; *Wedgwood Ware,* London 1970.

King-Hele, D., *Erasmus Darwin,* London 1963.

Litchfield, H.E., *Emma Darwin,* Cambridge 1904.

Litchfield, R.B., *Thomas Wedgwood,* London 1903.

Lockett, T.A., *Davenport Pottery and Porcelain,* Newton Abbot 1972.

Macht, Carol, *Classical Wedgwood Designs,* New York 1957.

Malet, Hugh, *The Canal Duke: A Biography of Francis 3rd Duke of Bridgewater,* Newton Abbot 1961.

Mankowitz, Wolf, *The Portland Vase and the Wedgwood Copies,* London 1952; *Wedgwood,* London 1953.

Mankowitz, Wolf, and Haggar, R., *The Concise Encyclopedia of English Pottery and Porcelain,* London 1957.

Manners, Lady Victoria, and Williamson, G.C., *Angelica Kauffmann,* London, nd.

Meteyard, Eliza, *A Group of Englishmen 1795-1815,* London 1871; *Choice Examples of Wedgwood's Art,* London 1879; *Memorials of Wedgwood,* London 1874; *The Life of Josiah Wedgwood,* 2 vols., London 1865-66; *The Wedgwood Handbook,* London 1875; *Wedgwood and his Works,* London 1873.

Montfaucon, Bernard de, *Antiquité Expliquée,* 5 vols. and supplement 5 vols., Paris 1719.

Moore, N. Hudson, *The Old China Book,* London 1903; *Wedgwood and his Imitators,* London 1906.

Mountford, Arnold, *The Illustrated Guide to Staffordshire Salt-Glazed Stoneware,* London 1971.

Pargeter, P., *Red House Glass Works,* Stourbridge, 1877.

Pearson, Hesketh, *Doctor Darwin,* London 1930.

Rackham, Bernard, *English Pottery,* London 1924.

Raspe, R.E., *Catalogue raisonné d'une Collection Générale de Pierres Gravées Antiques et Modernes,* London 1791.

Rathbone, Frederick, *Old Wedgwood,* London 1898.

Reilly, Robin, *Wedgwood Jasper,* London 1972; *Wedgwood Portrait Medallions. An Introduction,* London 1973.

Reilly, Robin, and Savage, George, *Wedgwood: The Portrait Medallions,* London 1973.

Rhead, G.W., and F.A., *Staffordshire Pots and Potters,* London 1906.

Savage, George, *Dictionary of 19th Century Antiques and later objets d'art,* London 1978.

Savage, George, and Finer, Ann, (ed.), *The Selected Letters of Josiah Wedgwood,* London 1965.

Savage, George, and Newman, H., *An Illustrated Dictionary of Ceramics,* London 1974.

Sayer, Robert, *The Ladies' Amusement,* London 1762.

Schofield, R.E., *The Lunar Society of Birmingham,* Oxford 1963.

Shaw, Simeon, *History of the Staffordshire Potteries,* Hanley 1829.

Shinn, C., and D., *The Illustrated Guide to Victorian Parian Porcelain,* London 1971.

Smiles, Samuel, *Josiah Wedgwood,* London 1894.

Smith, Alan, *The Illustrated Guide to Liverpool Herculaneum Pottery,* London 1970.

Solon, L.M.E., *Ceramic Literature,* London 1910.

Stuart, James, and Revett, Nicholas, *Die Alterthümer zu Athen,* Leipzig nd.

Tassie, James, *Catalogue of Impressions in Sulphur of Antique and Modern Gems,* London 1775.

Thomas, John, *The Rise of the Staffordshire Potteries,* London 1971.

Towner, Donald C., *Creamware,* London 1978; *English Cream Coloured Earthenware,* London 1957; *The Leeds Pottery,* London 1963.

Turner, William (ed.), *William Adams, An Old English Potter,* London 1904.

Wakefield, Hugh, *Victorian Pottery,* London 1962.

Warrilow, Ernest J.D., *History of Etruria, Staffordshire, 1760-1951,* Hanley 1952.

Waters, Grant M., *Dictionary of British Artists, 1900-50,* Eastbourne 1975.

Wedgwood, Dame C.V., *The Last of the Radicals,* London 1951.

Wedgwood International Seminar, *Minutes,* 1956-78.

Wedgwood, Josiah, see: Catalogues; Correspondence of, see: Farrer, and Savage and Finer.

Wedgwood, Josiah Clement, *History of the Wedgwood Family,* London 1908; *Staffordshire Pottery and its History,* London 1913; *Wedgwood Pedigrees,* 1925.

Wedgwood, Josiah Clement, and Ormsbee, T., *Staffordshire Pottery,* London 1947.

Wedgwood, Julia, *The Personal Life of Josiah Wedgwood,* London 1915.

Wedgwood Review, 1957-79.

Wedgwood Society, *Proceedings 1956-79,* London.

Whiter, Leonard, *Spode,* London 1970.

Williams, Iolo, *Early English Watercolours,* London 1952.

Williamson, G.C., *The Imperial Russian Dinner Service,* London 1909.

PUBLISHED CATALOGUES

1. Wedgwood's Catalogues of Queen's ware and Ornamental wares.

A catalogue of cameos, intaglios, medals, and bas-reliefs; with a general account of vases and other ornaments, after the antique, made by Wedgwood & Bentley, London 1773, 60pp.

A catalogue of cameos, intaglios, medals, busts, small statues, and bas-reliefs; with a general account of vases and other ornaments, after the antique, made by Wedgwood & Bentley, and sold at their rooms in Great Newport Street, London. 2nd. ed. with additions, London 1774,.73pp.
2nd edition, French translation, 1774, 82pp.
3rd edition, 1775 (reissue of 2nd edition with 6 additional pages and woodcut illustration of inkstand).
4th edition, 1777, 93pp.
4th edition, Dutch translation, Amsterdam 1778.
5th edition, 1779.
5th edition, French translation, 1779.
5th edition, German translation, 1779.

Catalogue of cameos, intaglios, medals, bas-reliefs, busts, and small statues; with a general account of tablets, vases, escritoires, and other ornamental and useful articles. The whole formed in different kinds of porcelain and terra-cotta, chiefly after the antique and the first models of modern artists. By Josiah Wedgwood FRS, potter to Her Majesty, and to His Royal Highness the Duke of York and Albany. Sold at his rooms in Greek Str., Soho, London, and at his manufactory in Staffordshire, 6th edition, 1787, 107pp.
6th edition, French translation, 1788.

A catalogue of different articles of Queen's ware, which may be either plain, gilt, or embellished with enamel paintings, manufactured by Josiah Wedgwood, potter to her Majesty, 1774 (contains 9 engraved plates and 35 numbered designs).

The 1790 Queen's ware Catalogue, published with English and French texts (contains 13 engraved plates and 80 numbered shapes).

The 1817 Catalogue, issued in three editions between c.1817 and 1849, and contains between 39 and 46 engraved plates of which William Blake drew and engraved Plates 1-18. Plates 19 and 20 are by John Taylor Wedgwood. The third edition illustrates 386 shapes.

Illustrated Catalogue of Shapes, March 1873, contains 55 engraved plates illustrating 369 shapes.

The 1880 Illustrated Catalogue of Shapes, contains 44 engraved plates illustrating 319 shapes. The precise date of this publication is not known, but it is certainly between 1878 and 1890. Reprinted by the Wedgwood Society, London, in 1971, when it was titled the *1880 Catalogue.*

Catalogue of bodies, glazes, and shapes, current for 1940-50, 218pp.

2. Catalogues of Collections and Exhibitions

Arts Council of Great Britain, *The Age of Neo-Classicism,* 1972.

Barnard, Harry, *Exhibition of replicas of eighteenth-century sculptured miniatures: Wedgwood's portrait medallions of illustrious moderns made and finished by Bert Bentley,* 1922.

Burnap, *The Frank P. and Harriet C. Burnap collection of English pottery in the William Rockhill Nelson Gallery of Art, Kansas City, Mo.,* 1953.

Chaffers, William, *Catalogue of an Exhibition of old Wedgwood at Philipp's Galleries, London,* 1877.

Des Fontaines, John, with Chaldecott, John, and Tindall, John, *Josiah Wedgwood: 'the Arts and Sciences United',* 1978.

Gatty, T., *Catalogue of a loan exhibition of the works of Josiah Wedgwood exhibited at the Liverpool Art Club,* 1879.

Gorely, Jean, and Schwartz, Marvin D., *The Emily Winthrop Collection: the work of Wedgwood and Tassie,* Brooklyn, 1965.

Gorely, Jean, and Wadsworth, Mary, *Old Wedgwood from the Bequest of Grenville Lindall Winthrop* (exhibition), Fogg Museum of Art, Harvard University, 1944.

Graham, John Meredith II, and Wedgwood, Hensleigh, *Wedgwood: A Living Tradition* (catalogue of the exhibition held at the Brooklyn Museum), 1948.

Gunsaulus, Frank W., *Old Wedgwood 1760-95: a collection acquired . . . by W. Gunsaulus, loaned to the Museum of the Art Institute of Chicago*, 1912.

Hayden, Arthur, *Catalogue of the Wedgwood Exhibition held in Conduit Street, London, December 1909*.

Hobson, R.L., *Catalogue of English Pottery and Porcelain in the Department of British and Mediaeval Antiquities and Ethnography*, British Museum, 1903.

Hobson, R.L., *Record of the collection in the Lady Lever Art Gallery, Port Sunlight*, 3 vols., Vol.II *Chinese porcelain & Wedgwood pottery*, London 1928.

Kansas University Museum of Art, *Wedgwood: an exhibition of Wedgwood pottery emphasizing the work of Josiah Wedgwood*, 1957.

Kenwood House, *Exhibition of Wedgwood at Kenwood House, Iveagh Bequest*, London County Council 1954.

Lessore, Emile, *A Catalogue of the works on Queen's ware painted for Messrs. Wedgwood by the late Emile Lessore. On exhibition at Messrs. Mortlock's Galleries*, London 1876.

Nottingham Castle Museum, *Catalogue of the Wedgwood in the Felix Joseph bequest*, 1930; *Josiah Wedgwood 1730-95. A guide to an exhibition of Wedgwood's works*, 1930; *Mr Wedgwood*, catalogue of an exhibition of Wedgwood organised for the Nottingham Festival, 1975.

Rackham, Bernard, *Catalogue of the Schreiber Collection*, 3 vols., Vol.II *Earthenware*, 1930.

Rathbone, Frederick, *A catalogue of the Wedgwood Museum, Etruria* 1909; *A catalogue of the collection . . . formed by Lord Tweedmouth*, London 1905; *Old Wedgwood and Old Wedgwood ware. Handbook to the collection formed by Richard and George Tangye* (Birmingham Museum and Art Gallery), London 1885; *Catalogue of a loan exhibition of selected pieces of old Wedgwood at the Wedgwood Institute, Burslem*, Burslem, 1895.

Sanderson, Arthur, *Catalogue of a collection . . . the property of Arthur Sanderson, exhibited at the Museum of Science and Art, Edinburgh*, 1901.

Scheidemantel, Vivian J., *Josiah Wedgwood's heads of Illustrious Moderns*, catalogue of a loan exhibition at the Chicago Art Institute, 1958.

Stoke-on-Trent, *Commemorative exhibition of ceramics, paintings, drawings, documents and maps, held at the City Museum and Art Gallery, Stoke-on-Trent, 1930*.

Tattersall, Bruce, *Stubbs & Wedgwood*, catalogue of an exhibition held at the Tate Gallery, London, 1974; *Wedgwood Portraits and the American Revolution*, National Portrait Gallery Washington, 1976.

Victoria and Albert Museum, *Wedgwood Bicentenary Exhibition, 1759-1959*.

Wedgwood Institute, *Catalogue of the Wedgwood Institute, Burslem*, 1869.

Wedgwood, Josiah & Sons Ltd., *Early Wedgwood Pottery* (catalogue of the Eustace Calland Collection), 1951.

3. Sale Catalogues

Agnew, Thomas, *The Collection of Wedgwood ware of Messrs. Thomas Agnew & Sons, Manchester*, nd.

Barlow, Thomas Oldham, *Catalogue of the very choice collection of Wedgwood ware*, Christie's 1869.

Braxton-Hicks, J., *Catalogue of the collection of J. Braxton-Hicks*, Christie's 1887.

Crowley, T.F., *Illustrated catalogue of the . . . collection formed by T.F. Crowley*, American Art Galleries, New York 1915.

De la Rue, Thomas, *Catalogue of Old Wedgwood Ware*, Christie's 1866.

Milestone, Milton, *The Milton Milestone Collection of Early Wedgwood Pottery*, 2 parts, Sotheby Parke Bernet 1975-76.

Oster, Catherine G., and Samuel B., *Catalogue of the well-known Collection of Wedgwood Pottery*, 2 parts, 1971-72.

Rathbone, Frederick, *Catalogue of Wedgwood ware and Old English Pottery, the property of J.F. Rathbone*, Christie's 1919.

Sibson, Francis, *Catalogue of the collection of Old Wedgwood . . . the property of Francis Sibson*, Christie's 1877.

Walker, T. Shadford, *Catalogue of the collection of Old Wedgwood . . . the property of T. Shadford Walker*, Christie's 1885.

Wedgwood & Bentley, *A Catalogue of cameos, intaglios, bas-reliefs, medallions, busts, vases, statues . . . now in joint property of Mr. Wedgwood & Mrs. Bentley*, Christie & Ansell 1781.